# The Earth and Its Peoples

## A Global History

# The Earth and Its Peoples

## A Global History

BRIEF THIRD EDITION

## Volume II: Since 1500

**Richard W. Bulliet**
*Columbia University*

**Pamela Kyle Crossley**
*Dartmouth College*

**Daniel R. Headrick**
*Roosevelt University*

**Steven W. Hirsch**
*Tufts University*

**Lyman L. Johnson**
*University of North Carolina–Charlotte*

**David Northrup**
*Boston College*

Houghton Mifflin Company      Boston   New York

Publisher: Charles Hartford
Senior Sponsoring Editor: Nancy Blaine
Assistant Editor: Christina Lembo
Senior Project Editor: Carol Newman
Editorial Assistant: Robert Woo
Senior Art and Design Coordinator: Jill Haber
Senior Composition Buyer: Sarah Ambrose
Senior Photo Editor: Jennifer Meyer Dare
Senior Designer: Henry Rachlin
Manufacturing Coordinator: Renee Ostrowski
Senior Marketing Manager: Sandra McGuire

Cover illustration: Siqueiros, David Alfaro (1896–1974). Detail from the mural, For the Complete Safety of All Mexicans at Work (1952–1954). Hospital de la Raze, Mexico City, D. F., Mexico. Schalkwijk/Art Resource, NY © VAGA.

Printed in U.S.A.

Library of Congress Catalog Card Number: 2004114277

ISBN-13: 978-0-618-47116-4
ISBN-10: 0-618-47116-2

5 6 7 8 9—VH—11 10 09  08  07

# Brief Contents

Introduction: The World Before
1500  xxiv

14 The Maritime Revolution,
to 1550  337

**PART FIVE**
**The Globe Encompassed,**
**1500–1800  361**

15 Transformations in Europe,
1500–1750  364

16 The Americas, the Atlantic, and
Africa, 1530–1770  387

17 Southwest Asia and the Indian
Ocean, 1500–1750  411

18 Northern Eurasia, 1500–1800  432

**PART SIX**
**Revolutions Reshape the World,**
**1750–1870  457**

19 Revolutionary Changes in the Atlantic
World, 1750–1850  460

20 The Early Industrial Revolution,
1760–1851  480

21 Africa, India, and the New British
Empire, 1750–1870  498

22 Land Empires in the Age of
Imperialism, 1800–1870  518

**PART SEVEN**
**Global Dominance and Diversity,**
**1850–1949  545**

23 The New Power Balance,
1850–1900  548

24 The New Imperialism,
1869–1914  569

25 The Crisis of the Imperial Order,
1900–1929  596

26 The Collapse of the Old Order,
1929–1949  619

27 Striving for Independence: Africa,
India, and Latin America,
1900–1949  641

**PART EIGHT**
**The Perils and Promises of a Global**
**Community, 1945 to the Present  665**

28 The Cold War and Decolonization,
1945–1975  668

29 Crisis, Realignment, and the Dawn of
the Post–Cold War World,
1975–1991  689

30 Globalization at the Turn of the
Millennium  712

# Contents

Maps xiii
Environment and Technology xiv
Diversity and Dominance xiv
Issues in World History xiv
Preface xv
About the Authors xxi
Note on Spelling and Usage xxiii

## Introduction: The World Before 1500 xxiv

## 14 The Maritime Revolution, to 1550 337

**Global Maritime Expansion Before 1450** 338
The Pacific Ocean 338 • The Indian Ocean 340 • The Atlantic Ocean 341

**Iberian Expansion, 1400–1550** 342
Background to Iberian Expansion 342 • Portuguese Voyages 343 • Spanish Voyages 345

**Encounters with Europe, 1450–1550** 348
Western Africa 348 • Eastern Africa 352 • Indian Ocean States 353 • The Americas 354 • Patterns of Dominance 356

Conclusion 357 / Key Terms 357 / Suggested Reading 357 / Notes 358

Diversity and Dominance: Kongo's Christian King 350

Issues in World History: Climate and Population, to 1500 359

## PART FIVE
## The Globe Encompassed, 1500–1800
361

## 15 Transformations in Europe, 1500–1750 364

**Culture and Ideas** 365
Religious Reformation 365 • Traditional Thinking and Witch-Hunts 369 • The Scientific Revolution 370 • The Early Enlightenment 372

**Social and Economic Life** 372
The Bourgeoisie 373 • Peasants and Laborers 375 • Women and the Family 377

**Political Innovations** 378
State Development 379 • Religious Policies 379 • Monarchies in England and France 380 • Warfare and Diplomacy 382 • Paying the Piper 383

Conclusion 385 / Key Terms 385 / Suggested Reading 386 / Notes 386

Environment and Technology: Mapping the World 376

## 16 The Americas, The Atlantic, and Africa, 1530–1770 387

**Spanish America and Brazil** 388
State and Church 388 • Colonial Economies 391 • Society in Colonial Latin America 392

**English and French Colonies in North America** 396
The South 396 • New England 397 • Middle Atlantic Region 398 • French America 398

**Plantations in the West Indies** 399
Sugar and Slaves 399 • Technology and Environment 401

**Creating the Atlantic Economy** 403
Capitalism and Mercantilism 403 • The Great Circuit and the Middle Passage 404

**Africa and the Atlantic** 405
The Gold Coast and the Slave Coast 406 • The Bight
of Biafra and Angola 406

**The Columbian Exchange** 407
Transfers to the Americas 407 • Transfers from the
Americas 408

CONCLUSION 409 / KEY TERMS 410 /
SUGGESTED READING 410 / NOTES 410

  ■ DIVERSITY AND DOMINANCE: Race and Ethnicity in
    the Spanish Colonies: Negotiating
    Hierarchies 394

---

**17**    Southwest Asia and the
      Indian Ocean, 1500-1750 411

**The Ottoman Empire** 412
Expansion and Frontiers 412 • Central
Institutions 415 • Crisis of the Military State, 1585–
1650 416 • Economic Change and Growing
Weakness 417

**The Safavid Empire** 420
Safavid Society and Religion 421 • Isfahan and
Istanbul 421 • Economic Crisis and Political
Collapse 424

**The Mughal Empire** 424
Political Foundations 425 • Hindus and
Muslims 425 • Central Decay and Regional
Challenges 426

**Trade Empires in the Indian Ocean** 427
Muslims in the East Indies 427 • Muslims in East
Africa 429 • The Coming of the Dutch 430

CONCLUSION 430 / KEY TERMS 431 /
SUGGESTED READING 431 / NOTES 431

  ■ DIVERSITY AND DOMINANCE: Islamic Law and
    Ottoman Rule 418

---

**18**    Northern Eurasia,
      1500-1800 432

**Japanese Reunification** 433
Civil War and the Invasion of Korea, 1500–1603
433 • The Tokugawa Shogunate, to 1800 434 •
Japan and the Europeans 434 • Elite Decline and
Social Crisis 437

**The Later Ming and Early Qing Empires** 438
The Ming Empire, 1500–1644 438 • Ming Collapse
and the Rise of the Qing 439 • Trading Companies
and Missionaries 440 • Emperor Kangxi 440 •
Chinese Influences on Europe 443 • Tea and
Diplomacy 444 • Population and Social Stress 445

**The Russian Empire** 445
The Drive Across Northern Asia 445 • Russian
Society and Politics to 1725 446 • Peter the
Great 449 • Consolidation of the Empire 450

**Comparative Perspectives** 451
Political Comparisons 451 • Cultural, Social, and
Economic Comparisons 451

CONCLUSION 452 / KEY TERMS 452 /
SUGGESTED READING 453 / NOTES 454

  ■ ENVIRONMENT AND TECHNOLOGY:
    East Asian Porcelain 436

  ISSUES IN WORLD HISTORY: The Little Ice Age 455

---

**PART SIX
Revolutions Reshape the World,
1750–1870**
457

---

**19**    Revolutionary Changes in the
      Atlantic World, 1750-1850 460

**Prelude to Revolution: War and the
Enlightenment** 461

**The American Revolution** 462
Frontiers and Taxes 462 • The Course of
Revolution 464 • New Republican Institutions 464

**The French Revolution** 465
French Society and Fiscal Crisis 465 • Protest
Turns to Revolution 466 • Reaction and
Dictatorship 468 • Retrenchment, Reform, and
Revolution 469

**Revolution in Haiti and Latin America** 469
The Haitian Revolution 469 • Latin American
Revolutions 471 • Mexico 473

**Economic and Social Liberation
Movements** 475

The Abolition of Slavery  475  •  Equal Rights for Women and Blacks  477

CONCLUSION  478 / KEY TERMS  478 / SUGGESTED READING  478

▪ ENVIRONMENT AND TECHNOLOGY: Constructing the Port of Buenos Aires, Argentina  476


**20  The Early Industrial Revolution,** 1760–1851  480

**Causes of the Industrial Revolution**  481
Preconditions for Industrialization  481  •  Britain's Advantages  482

**The Technological Revolution**  484
Mass Production and Mechanization  484  •  The Iron Industry  486  •  The Steam Engine  487  •  Railroads  488  •  Communication over Wires  489

**The Impact of the Industrial Revolution**  489
The New Industrial Cities  490  •  Rural Environments  490  •  Working Conditions  491  •  Changes in Society  492

**New Economic and Political Ideas**  493
Laissez Faire  493  •  Positivism and Utopian Socialism  493  •  Protests and Reforms  494  •  Emigration  494

**Industrialization and the Nonindustrial World**  495

CONCLUSION  496 / KEY TERMS  497 / SUGGESTED READING  497 / NOTES  497

▪ ENVIRONMENT AND TECHNOLOGY: The Origin of Graphs  484


**21  Africa, India, and the New British Empire,** 1750–1870  498

**Changes and Exchanges in Africa**  499
New African States  499  •  Modernization in Egypt and Ethiopia  500  •  European Penetration  500  •  Secondary Empires in Eastern Africa  504

**India Under British Rule**  504
Company Men  504  •  Raj and Rebellion, 1818–1857  506  •  Political Reform and Industrial Impact  507  •  Rising Indian Nationalism  509

**Britain's Eastern Empire**  510
Colonies and Commerce  510  •  Imperial Policies and Shipping  511  •  Colonization of Australia and New Zealand  512  •  New Labor Migrations  513

CONCLUSION  516 / KEY TERMS  517 / SUGGESTED READING  517 / NOTES  517

▪ ENVIRONMENT AND TECHNOLOGY: Whaling  514


**22  Land Empires in the Age of Imperialism,** 1800–1870  518

**The Ottoman Empire**  519
Egypt and the Napoleonic Example, 1798–1840  519  •  Ottoman Reform and the European Model, 1807–1853  520  •  The Crimean War and Its Aftermath, 1853–1877  527

**The Russian Empire**  529
Russia and Europe  529  •  Russia and Asia  531  •  Cultural Trends  531

**The Qing Empire**  532
Economic and Social Disorder, 1800–1839  533  •  The Opium War and Its Aftermath, 1839–1850  533  •  The Taiping Rebellion, 1850–1864  536  •  Decentralization at the End of the Qing Empire, 1864–1875  539

CONCLUSION  540 / KEY TERMS  541 / SUGGESTED READING  541

▪ DIVERSITY AND DOMINANCE: The French Occupation of Egypt  522

▪ ISSUES IN WORLD HISTORY: State Power, the Census, and the Question of Identity  542


**PART SEVEN**
**Global Dominance and Diversity, 1850–1949**
545


**23  The New Power Balance,** 1850–1900  548

**New Technologies and the World Economy**  549
The Steel and Chemical Industries  549  •  Electricity  549  •  Shipping and Telegraph Cables  550  •  Railroads  550  •  World Trade and Finance  550

**Social Transformations** 550
Population and Migrations 552 • Urbanization and
Social Structures 552 • Labor Movements and
Socialist Politics 552 • Working-Class Women and
Men 553 • The Victorian Age and Women's
"Separate Sphere" 553

**Nationalism and the Unification of
Germany** 557
National Identity Before 1871 557 • The Unification
of Germany 558 • Nationalism After 1871 558

**The Great Powers of Europe, 1871–1900** 560
Germany at the Center of Europe 560 • The Liberal
Powers: France and Great Britain 560 • The
Conservative Powers: Russia and Austria-
Hungary 560

**New Great Powers: The United States and
Japan** 562
The United States, 1865–1900 562 • The Crisis of
the Tokugawa Shogunate 563 • The Meiji
Restoration and the Modernization of Japan,
1868–1894 564 • The Birth of Japanese Imperialism,
1894–1905 565

CONCLUSION 567 / KEY TERMS 567 /
SUGGESTED READING 567

■ DIVERSITY AND DOMINANCE: Marx and Engels on
Global Trade and the Bourgeoisie 554

**24    The New Imperialism,**
1869–1914 569

**The New Imperialism: Motives and
Methods** 570
Political Motives 570 • Cultural Motives 572 •
Economic Motives 574 • The Tools of the
Imperialists 574 • Colonial Agents and
Administration 575

**The Scramble for Africa** 577
Egypt 577 • Western and Equatorial Africa 579 •
Southern Africa 580 • Political and Social
Consequences 581 • Cultural Responses 582

**Asia and Western Dominance** 583
Central Asia 583 • Southeast Asia and
Indonesia 583 • Hawaii and the Philippines,
1878–1902 587

**Imperialism in Latin America** 589
Railroads and the Imperialism of Free Trade 590 •
American Expansionism and the Spanish-American

War, 1898 591 • American Intervention in the
Caribbean and Central America, 1907–1914 591

**The World Economy and the Global
Environment** 592
Expansion of the World Economy 592 •
Transformation of the Global Environment 593

CONCLUSION 594 / KEY TERMS 594 /
SUGGESTED READING 594 / NOTES 595

■ DIVERSITY AND DOMINANCE: Two Africans Recall the
Arrival of the Europeans 584

**25    The Crisis of the Imperial
Order,** 1900–1929 596

**Origins of the Crisis in Europe and the Middle
East** 597
The Ottoman Empire and the Balkans 597 •
Nationalism, Alliances, and Military Strategy 597

**The "Great War" and the Russian
Revolutions** 601
Stalemate, 1914–1917 601 • The Home Front and
the War Economy 603 • The Ottoman Empire
at War 603 • Double Revolution in Russia, 1917
604 • The End of the War in Western Europe,
1917–1918 605

**Peace and Dislocation in Europe** 605
The Impact of the War 605 • The Peace
Treaties 606 • Russian Civil War and the New
Economic Policy 606 • An Ephemeral Peace 607

**China and Japan: Contrasting Destinies** 608
Revolution in China 608 • Japan and World
War I 609 • China in the 1920s 609

**The New Middle East** 610
The Rise of Modern Turkey 610 • Arab Lands and
the Question of Palestine 612

**Society, Culture, and Technology in the
Industrialized World** 612
Class and Gender 613 • Revolution in the
Sciences 614 • The New Technologies of
Modernity 614 • Technology and the
Environment 615

CONCLUSION 617 / KEY TERMS 617 /
SUGGESTED READING 617

■ ENVIRONMENT AND TECHNOLOGY:
Cities Old and New 598

# 26 The Collapse of the Old Order, 1929-1949 619

**Stalin's Revolution** 620
Five-Year Plans 620 • Collectivization of Agriculture 620 • Terror and Opportunities 622

**The Depression** 623
Economic Crisis 623 • Depression in Industrial Nations 623 • Depression in Nonindustrial Regions 623

**The Rise of Fascism** 626
Mussolini's Italy 626 • Hitler's Germany 627 • The Road to War, 1933-1939 628

**East Asia, 1931-1945** 629
The Manchurian Incident of 1931 629 • The Chinese Communists and the Long March 629 • The Sino-Japanese War, 1937-1945 630

**The Second World War** 631
The War of Movement 631 • War in Europe and North Africa 631 • War in Asia and the Pacific 632 • The End of the War 634 • Chinese Civil War and Communist Victory 634

**The Character of Warfare** 635
The War of Science 635 • Bombing Raids 637 • The Holocaust 637 • The Home Front 638 • War and the Environment 638

CONCLUSION 639 / KEY TERMS 639 / SUGGESTED READING 639

▪ DIVERSITY AND DOMINANCE: Women, Family Values, and the Russian Revolution 624

# 27 Striving for Independence: Africa, India, and Latin America, 1900-1949 641

**Sub-Saharan Africa, 1900-1945** 642
Colonial Africa: Economic and Social Changes 642 • Religious and Political Changes 644

**The Indian Independence Movement, 1905-1947** 646
The Land and the People 646 • British Rule and Indian Nationalism 647 • Mahatma Gandhi and Militant Nonviolence 648 • India Moves Toward Independence 649 • Partition and Independence 651

**The Mexican Revolution, 1910-1940** 652
Mexico in 1910 652 • Revolution and Civil War, 1911-1920 654 • The Revolution Institutionalized, 1920-1940 654

**Argentina and Brazil, 1900-1949** 656
The Transformation of Argentina 657 • Brazil and Argentina, to 1929 657 • The Depression and the Vargas Regime in Brazil 658 • Argentina After 1930 659 • Mexico, Argentina, and Brazil: A Comparison 660

CONCLUSION 660 / KEY TERMS 661 / SUGGESTED READING 661 / NOTES 661

▪ ENVIRONMENT AND TECHNOLOGY: Gandhi and Technology 650

▪ ISSUES IN WORLD HISTORY: Famines and Politics 662

## PART EIGHT
# The Perils and Promises of a Global Community, 1945 to the Present
665

# 28 The Cold War and Decolonization, 1945-1975 668

**The Cold War** 669
The United Nations 669 • Capitalism and Communism 670 • West Versus East in Europe and Korea 672 • U.S. Defeat in Vietnam 673 • The Race for Nuclear Supremacy 674

**Decolonization and Nation Building** 675
New Nations in Southern Asia 675 • The Struggle for Independence in Africa 675 • The Quest for Economic Freedom in Latin America 678 • Challenges of Nation Building 679

**Beyond a Bipolar World** 679
The Third World 679 • Japan and China 683 • The Middle East 684 • The Emergence of Environmental Concerns 687

CONCLUSION 687 / KEY TERMS 687 / SUGGESTED READING 687

▪ DIVERSITY AND DOMINANCE: Race and the Struggle for Justice in South Africa 680

# 29 Crisis, Realignment, and the Dawn of the Post–Cold War World, 1975–1991  689

**Postcolonial Crises and Asian Economic Expansion, 1975–1991**  690
Revolutions, Repression, and Democratic Reform in Latin America  690 • Islamic Revolutions in Iran and Afghanistan  693 • Asian Transformation  696

**The End of the Bipolar World, 1989–1991**  699
Crisis in the Soviet Union  699 • The Collapse of the Socialist Bloc  700 • The Persian Gulf War, 1990–1991  702

**The Challenge of Population Growth**  703
Demographic Transition  703 • The Industrialized Nations  704 • The Developing Nations  705

**Unequal Development and the Movement of Peoples**  706
The Problem of Growing Inequality  706 • Internal Migration: The Growth of Cities  706 • Global Migration  707

**Technological and Environmental Change**  708
New Technologies and the World Economy 708 • Conserving and Sharing Resources  709 • Responding to Environmental Threats  709

CONCLUSION  710  /  KEY TERMS  710  /
SUGGESTED READING  711  /  NOTES  711

◼ DIVERSITY AND DOMINANCE: The Struggle for Women's Rights in an Era of Global Political and Economic Change  694

# 30 Globalization at the Turn of the Millennium  712

**Global Political Economies**  714
The Spread of Democracy  714 • Global Politics  716 • Arms Control and Terrorism  717 • The Global Economy  718 • Managing the Global Economy  720

**Trends and Visions**  722
A New Age?  722 • Militant Islam  722 • Universal Rights and Values  723 • Women's Rights  725

**Global Culture**  726
The Media and the Message  727 • The Spread of Pop Culture  729 • The Emerging Global Elite Culture  730 • Enduring Cultural Diversity  731

CONCLUSION  732  /  KEY TERMS  732  /
SUGGESTED READING  733  /  NOTES  733

◼ ENVIRONMENT AND TECHNOLOGY:
   Global Warming  726

GLOSSARY  G-1
INDEX  I-1

# Maps

**14.1** Exploration and Settlement in the Indian and Pacific Oceans Before 1500   340
**14.2** European Exploration, 1420–1542   346

**15.1** Religious Reformation in Europe   368
**15.2** Europe in 1740   384

**16.1** Colonial Latin America in the Eighteenth Century   390

**17.1** Muslim Empires in the Sixteenth and Seventeenth Centuries   414
**17.2** European Colonization in the Indian Ocean to 1750   428

**18.1** The Qing Empire, 1644–1783   441
**18.2** The Expansion of Russia, 1500–1800   448

**19.1** Napoleon's Europe, 1810   470
**19.2** Latin America by 1830   474

**20.1** The Industrial Revolution in Britain, ca. 1850   482

**21.1** Africa in the Nineteenth Century   502
**21.2** India, 1707–1805   505

**22.1** The Ottoman and Russian Empires, 1829–1914   525
**22.2** Conflicts in the Qing Empire, 1839–1870   535

**23.1** The Unification of Germany, 1866–1871   559
**23.2** Expansion and Modernization of Japan, 1868–1918   566

**24.1** Africa in 1878 and 1914   578
**24.2** Asia in 1914   588

**25.1** The First World War in Europe   600
**25.2** Territorial Changes in the Middle East After World War I   611

**26.1** World War II in Europe and North Africa   633
**26.2** World War II in Asia and the Pacific   636

**27.1** The Mexican Revolution   655

**28.1** Decolonization, 1947–1999   676
**28.2** Middle East Oil and the Arab-Israeli Conflict, 1947–1973   685

**29.1** The End of Soviet Domination in Eastern Europe   701
**29.2** The End of the Soviet Union   702

**30.1** Regional Trade Associations, 2004   721

# Environment And Technology

Mapping the World   376
East Asian Porcelain   436
Constructing the Port of Buenos Aires,
   Argentina   476
The Origin of Graphs   484

Whaling   514
Cities Old and New   598
Gandhi and Technology   650
Global Warming   726

# Diversity and Dominance

Kongo's Christian King   350
Race and Ethnicity in the Spanish Colonies:
   Negotiating Hierarchy   394
Islamic Law and Ottoman Rule   418
The French Occupation of Egypt   522
Marx and Engels on Global Trade and the
   Bourgeoisie   554
Two Africans Recall the Arrival of the
   Europeans   584

Women, Family Values, and the Russian
   Revolution   624
Race and the Struggle for Justice in South
   Africa   680
The Struggle for Women's Rights in an Era of
   Global Political and Economic Change   694

# Issues in World History

Climate and Population, to 1500   359
The Little Ice Age   455

State Power, the Census, and the Question of
   Identity   542
Famines and Politics   662

# Preface

Reaching the point of preparing the third edition of a textbook is particularly gratifying for its authors. The sustained appeal of their writing tells them that they have done something good and useful. But that in turn prompts them to ponder what they can do to make their book still better. Fortunately, feedback from teachers and students provides a regular stream of helpful suggestions. We have tried to respond to the most frequent and constructive of these suggestions in preparing the third edition.

Varying rationales prompt different teachers to prefer the Brief Edition of *The Earth and Its Peoples*. Some feel that a shorter text makes room for more supplementary reading. Some find it more suitable to the students in their particular classrooms. Some find that a reduced number of chapters better fits their academic schedule. Thus the job of revising the Brief Edition to accommodate the changes introduced in the third edition of the comprehensive text is one of balancing change with adherence to the continuing goal of providing a significantly shorter text for those users who prefer this option.

The Brief Edition is produced in two formats: A complete edition covers the entire chronology from prehistory to the present, and a two-volume edition can be used for the two-semester survey. Volume I covers the period from prehistory to 1550 and Volume II covers 1500 to the present. There is a brief introduction to Volume II that orients students to the general political and social climate of the world at 1500.

Our overall goal of *The Earth and Its Peoples* remains unchanged: to produce a textbook that not only speaks for the past, but speaks to today's student and today's teacher. Students and instructors alike should take away from this text a broad vision of human societies beginning as sparse and disconnected communities reacting creatively to local circumstances; experiencing ever more intensive stages of contact, interpenetration, and cultural expansion and amalgamation; and arriving at a twenty-first century world situation in which people increasingly visualize a single global community.

Process, not progress, is the keynote of this book: a steady process of change over time, at first differently experienced in various regions, but eventually interconnecting peoples and traditions from all parts of the globe. Students should come away from this book with a sense that the problems and promises of their world are rooted in a past in which people of every sort, in every part of the world, confronted problems of a similar character and coped with them as best they could. We believe our efforts will help students see where their world has come from and learn thereby something useful for their own lives.

## Central Themes

We have subtitled *The Earth and Its Peoples* "A Global History" because the book explores the common challenges and experiences that unite the human past. Although the dispersal of early humans to every liveable environment resulted in a myriad different economic, social, political, and cultural systems, all societies displayed analogous patterns in meeting their needs and exploiting their environments. Our challenge was to select the particular data and episodes that would best illuminate these global patterns of human experience.

To meet this challenge, we adopted two themes to serve as the spinal cord of our history: "technology and the environment," and "diversity and dominance." The former represents the commonplace material bases of all human societies at all times. It grants no special favor to any cultural group even as it embraces subjects of the broadest topical, chronological, and geographical range. The latter expresses the reality that every human society has constructed or inherited structures of domination, whether political, religious, or cultural, but simultaneously recognizes that alternative lifestyles and visions of societal organization continually manifest themselves both within and in dialogue with every structure of domination.

With respect to "technology and the environment," it is vital for students to understand that technology, in the broad sense of experience-based knowledge of the physical world, underlies all human activity. Writing is a technology, but so is oral transmission from generation to generation of lore about medicinal or poisonous plants. The magnetic compass is a navigational technology, but so is a Polynesian mariner's hard-won knowledge of winds, currents, and tides that made possible the settlement of the Pacific islands.

All technological development, moreover, has come about in interaction with environments, both physical and human, and has, in turn, affected those environments. The story of how humanity has changed the face of the globe is an integral part of this central theme.

Yet technology and the environment do not by themselves explain or underlie all important episodes of human change and experience. In keeping with the theme of "diversity and dominance," discussions of politics, culture, and society interweave with our presentation of the material base of human society to reveal additional historical patterns. Thus when narrating the histories of empires, we describe a range of human experiences within and beyond the imperial frontiers without assuming that the imperial institutions are a more fit topic for discussion than the economic and social organization of pastoral nomads or the life patterns of peasant women. And when religious and cultural traditions occupy our narrative, our primary concern is to complement descriptive presentation with commentary on cultural alternatives within the societies in question.

# Changes in the Third Edition

This third Brief Edition retains the main structural features of its predecessors, but also incorporates the most important of the changes made in the comprehensive text:

A new primary source feature, "Diversity and Dominance," has replaced the brief "Society and Culture" excerpts of the previous edition. The fea-

ture gives students extended documentary selections on which to hone their analytical skills, encouraging them to consider the many forms of dominance that have developed over time and the many ways in which human diversity has continued to express itself regardless of these forms of dominance. The topics covered range from "Hierarchy and Conduct in the Analects of Confucius" (Chapter 2) to "Two Africans Recall the Arrival of the Europeans" (Chapter 24).

"Issues in World History" is a new feature comprised of original essays that appear at the end of Parts One through Seven. As we surveyed the burgeoning field of global history, we became aware of issues of such broad significance that they could not easily be discussed in a chapter concentrating on a specific time and place. We therefore highlight seven of these issues in part-ending essays, addressing topics that range from "Animal Domestication," to "Famines and Politics."

Chapters 2 and 3 have been rethought and reorganized: Chapter 2 now deals with several civilizations that emerged independently in different parts of the world in the second and first millennia B.C.E., while Chapter 3 focuses on the same time period in Western Asia and the Mediterranean, giving greater stress to continuity and interaction in that region.

Chapter 8, on early medieval Europe, has been reorganized so that it opens with Byzantium and then proceeds to western Europe.

We have greatly increased the coverage of Russian history, including an expanded discussion in Chapter 18 and a section in the new Chapter 22, "Land Empires in the Age of Imperialism, 1800–1870."

The history and impact of the Mongols are now covered in a single chapter, Chapter 11, "Mongol Eurasia and Its Aftermath, 1200–1500." This combination allowed us to make more evident the parallels and contrasts between the impact of the Mongols in the west and in the east.

The discussion in Chapter 23 of the modernization of late nineteenth century Japan has been expanded into three sections.

The final chapter, Chapter 30, "Globalization at the Turn of the Millennium," has been entirely rewritten to reflect current developments in global politics, the global economy, and global culture.

The terrorist attacks of September 11 and the responses to them receive special attention.

# Organization

*The Earth and Its Peoples,* Brief Edition uses eight broad chronological divisions to define its conceptual scheme of global historical development. In **Part One: The Emergence of Human Communities, to 500 B.C.E.,** we examine important patterns of human communal organization. Small, dispersed human communities living by foraging spread to most parts of the world over tens of thousands of years. They responded to enormously diverse environmental conditions, at different times and in different ways discovering how to cultivate plants and utilize the products of domestic animals. On the basis of these new modes of sustenance, population grows, permanent towns appear, and political and religious authority, based on collection and control of agricultural surpluses, spreads over extensive areas.

**Part Two: The Formation of New Cultural Communities, 1000 B.C.E.–600 C.E.,** introduces the concept of a "cultural community," in the sense of a coherent pattern of activities and symbols pertaining to a specific human community. While all human communities develop distinctive cultures, including those discussed in Part One, historical development in this stage of global history prolonged and magnified the impact of some cultures more than others. In the geographically contiguous African-Eurasian land mass, the cultures that proved to have the most enduring influence traced their roots to the second and first millennia B.C.E.

**Part Three: Growth and Interaction of Cultural Communities, 600–1200,** deals with early episodes of technological, social, and cultural exchange and interaction on a continental scale both within and beyond the framework of imperial expansion. These are so different from earlier interactions arising from more limited conquests or extensions of political boundaries that they constitute a distinct era in world history, an era that set the world on the path of increasing global interaction and interdependence that it has been following ever since.

**In Part Four: Interregional Patterns of Culture and Contact, 1200–1550,** we take a look at the world during three centuries that saw both intensified cultural and commercial contact and increasingly confident self-definition of cultural communities in Europe, Asia, and Africa. The Mongol conquest of a vast empire extending from the Pacific Ocean to eastern Europe greatly stimulated trade and interaction. In the West, strengthened European kingdoms began maritime expansion in the Atlantic, forging direct ties with sub-Saharan Africa and laying the base for expanded global contacts after 1500.

**Part Five: The Globe Encompassed, 1500–1800,** treats a period dominated by the global effects of European expansion and continued economic growth. European ships took over, expanded, and extended the maritime trade of the Indian Ocean, coastal Africa, and the Asian rim of the Pacific Ocean. This maritime commercial enterprise had its counterpart in European colonial empires in the Americas and a new Atlantic trading system. The contrasting capacities and fortunes of traditional land empires and new maritime empires, along with the exchange of domestic plants and animals between the hemispheres, underline the technological and environmental dimensions of this first era of complete global interaction.

**In Part Six: Revolutions Reshape the World, 1750–1870,** the word revolution is used in several senses: in the political sense of governmental overthrow, as in France and the Americas; in the metaphorical sense of radical transformative change, as in the Industrial Revolution; and in the broadest sense of a perception of a profound change in circumstances and worldview. Technology and environment lie at the core of these developments. With the rapid ascendancy of the Western belief that science and technology could overcome all challenges, technology became not only an instrument of transformation but also an instrument of domination, to the point of threatening the integrity and autonomy of cultural traditions in nonindustrial lands.

**Part Seven: Global Dominance and Diversity, 1850–1949,** examines the development of a world arena in which people conceived of events on a global scale. Imperialism, world war, international economic connections, and world-encompassing ideological tendencies, like nationalism and socialism, present the picture of a globe becoming increasingly interconnected. European dominance took on a worldwide dimension, seeming at times to threaten the diversity of human cultural experience with permanent subordination to European values and philosophies, while at other times triggering strong political or cultural resistance. The accelerating pace of technological change deepened other sorts of cleavages as well.

**For Part Eight: The Perils and Promises of a Global Community, 1945 to the Present,** we decided to divide the last half of the twentieth century into three time periods: 1945 to 1975, 1975 to 1991, and 1991 to the present. Nevertheless, there is a good deal of continuity from chapter to chapter. The challenges of the Cold War and postcolonial nation building dominate the period and involve global economic, technological, and political forces that become increasingly important factors in all aspects of human life. Technology plays a central role in this part both because of its integral role in the growth of a global community and because its many benefits in improving the quality of life seem clouded by real and potential negative impacts on the environment.

## Supplements

In keeping with Houghton Mifflin's goal of being your primary source for history, we are proud to announce the History Companion, your new primary source for history technology solutions. The History Companion has three components:

The *Instructor Companion* is an easily searchable CD-ROM that makes hundreds of historical images and maps instantly accessible in PowerPoint format. Each image is accompanied by notes that place it in its proper historical context and tips for ways it can be presented in the classroom. This CD is free to instructors with the adoption of this or any Houghton Mifflin history textbook. It also includes our HM Testing program, a computerized version of the Test Items to enable instructors to alter, replace, or add questions, and the Instructor's Resource Manual, both of which have been thoroughly revised by John Reisbord (Ph.D. Northwestern University). You can also access all of these resources, with the exception of the testing material, on the text's Instructor Companion Website. To reach the site, logon to history.college.hmco.com/instructors and select this book.

The *Student Research Companion* is a free Internet-based tool with 100 interactive maps and 500 primary sources. The primary sources include headnotes that provide pertinent background information and questions that students can answer and email to their instructors. To access the site, logon to history.college.hmco.com/students and select this book.

The *Student Study Companion* is a free online study guide that contains ACE self-tests, which feature multiple-choice questions with feedback, an audio pronunciation guide, web-based flashcards, internet exercises, and web links. These study tools will help your students succeed in the classroom. To access the site, logon to history.college.hmco.com/students and select this book.

*The Earth and Its Peoples, Brief, 3/e* has robust *Blackboard and Web CT* cartridges with all of our instructional and study assets for easy use at institutions using these platforms.

## Acknowledgments

As always we are grateful to the following colleagues who took the time to review and comment upon *The Earth and Its Peoples:* Henry Abramson, Florida Atlantic University; Joseph Adams, Walton High School, Cobb County, Georgia; Paul V. Adams, Shippensburg University/University of San Carlos; Siamak Adhami, Saddleback College; William H. Alexander, Norfolk State University; Maria S. Arbelaez, University of Nebraska at Omaha; Monty Armstrong, Cerritos High School, Cerritos, California; William J. Astore, United States Air Force Academy; David G. Atwill, Pennsylvania State University; Lawrence Backlund, Montgomery County Community College; Fritz Blackwell, Washington State University; Corinne Blake, Rowan University; Olwyn M. Blouet, Virginia State University; Eric Bobo, Hinds Community College; Thomas Borstelmann, Cornell University; James Boyden, Tulane University; Byron Cannon, University of Utah; Bruce Castleman, San Diego State University; Craige B. Champion, Syracuse University; David A. Chappell, University of Hawaii; Nancy Clark, California Polytechnic State University at San Luis Obispo; Aaron Cohen, California State University, Sacramento; Eleanor A. Congdon, Youngstown State University; Lee Congdon, James Madison University; James Coolsen, Shippensburg University; Ransom P. Cross, University of Texas at El Paso; Bruce Cruikshank, Hastings College; Philip Daileader, The College of William and Mary; Linda T. Darling, University of Arizona; Susan Deans-Smith, University of Texas at Austin; Gregory C. Ference, Salisbury State University; Alan Fisher, Michigan State University; Donald M. Fisher, Niagara County Community College; Nancy Fitch, California State University, Fullerton; Cathy A. Frierson, University of New Hampshire; Jeffrey S. Gaab, SUNY College at Farmingdale; Rosanna Gatens, Belmont University; Lorne E. Glaim, Pacific Union College; Matthew S. Gordon, Miami University; Steve Gosch, University of Wisconsin at Eau Claire; Kolleen M. Guy, University of Texas at San Antonio; James R. Hansen, Auburn University; Jay Harmon, Catholic High School, Baton Rouge, Louisiana; Randolph C. Head, University of California at Riverside; David Hertzel, Southwestern Oklahoma State University; Catherine Higgs, University of Tennessee; Richard J. Hoffman, San Francisco State University; Amy J. Johnson, Berry College; Catherine M. Jones, North Georgia College and State University; Joy Kammerling, Eastern Illinois University; Carol A. Keller, San Antonio College; Hal Langfur, University of North Carolina, Wilmington; Jonathan Lee, San Antonio College; Miriam R. Levin, Case Western Reserve University; Richard Lewis, St. Cloud State University; James E. Lindsay, Colorado State University; Susan Maneck, Jackson State University; Laurie S. Mannino, Magruder High School, North Potomac, Maryland; Margaret Malamud, New Mexico State University; Dorothea A.L. Martin, Appalachian State University; Charles W. McClellan, Radford University; Andrea McElderry, University of Louisville; Stephen L. McFarland, Auburn University; Randall McGowen, University of Oregon; Margaret McKee, Castilleja School, Palo Alto, California; Mark McLeod, University of Delaware; Gregory McMahon, University of New Hampshire; Stephen S. Michot, Mississippi County Community College; Shawn W. Miller, Brigham Young University; Stephen Morillo, Wabash College; Kalala Joseph Ngalamulume, Central Washington University; Peter A. Ngwafu, Albany State University; Patricia O'Neill, Central Oregon Community College; Chandrika Paul, Shippensburg University; John R. Pavia, Ithaca College; Thomas Earl Porter, North Carolina A&T State University; Diethelm Prowe, Carleton College; Jean H. Quataert, SUNY at Binghamton; Stephen Rapp, Georgia State University; William Reddy, Duke University; Thomas Reeves, Roxbury Community College; Dennis Reinhartz, University of Texas at Arlington; Richard Rice, University of Tennessee at Chattanooga; Michael D. Richards, Sweet Briar College; Jane Scimeca, Brookdale Community College; William Schell, Murray State University; Alyssa Goldstein Sepinwall, California State University at San Marcos; Deborah Shackleton, United States Air Force Academy; Anita Shelton, Eastern Illinois University; Jeffrey M. Shumway, Brigham Young University; Jonathan Skaff, Shippensburg University of Pennsylvania; David R. Smith, California State Polytechnic University at Pomona; Linda Smith, Samford University; Mary Frances Smith, Ohio University; George E. Snow, Shippensburg University; Charlotte D. Staelin, Washington College; Tracy L. Steele, Sam Houston State University; Paul D. Steeves, Stetson University; Robert Shannon Sumner, State University of West Georgia; Yi Sun, University of San Diego; Willard Sunderland, University of Cincinnati; Karen Sundwick, Southern Oregon University; Thaddeus Sunseri, Colorado State University; Sara W. Tucker, Washburn University; David J. Ulbrich, Temple University; John M. VanderLippe, SUNY at New Paltz; Mary A. Watrous-Schlesinger, Washington State University; James A. Wood, North Carolina A&T State University; Eric Van Young, University of California at San Diego; Peter von Sivers, University of Utah; and Alex Zukas, National University, San Diego.

We also want to extend our thanks to Lynda Schaffer for her early conceptual contributions and to the history departments of Shippensburg University, the United States Air Force Academy, and the State University of New York at New Paltz for arranging reviewer conferences that provided crucial feedback for our revisions.

We thank also the many students whose questions and concerns, expressed directly or through their instructors, shaped much of this revision. We continue to welcome all our readers' suggestions, queries, and criticisms. Please contact us at our respective institutions or at this e-mail address: college_history@hmco.com.

# About the Authors

**Richard W. Bulliet** Professor of Middle Eastern History at Columbia University, Richard W. Bulliet received his Ph.D. from Harvard University. He has written scholarly works on a number of topics: the social history of medieval Iran (*The Patricians of Nishapur*), the historical competition between pack camels and wheeled transport (*The Camel and the Wheel*), the process of conversion to Islam (*Conversion to Islam in the Medieval Period*), and the overall course of Islamic social history (*Islam: The View from the Edge*). He is the editor of the *Columbia History of the Twentieth Century*. He has published four novels, co-edited *The Encyclopedia of the Modern Middle East*, and hosted an educational television series on the Middle East. He was awarded a fellowship by the John Simon Guggenheim Memorial Foundation.

**Pamela Kyle Crossley** Pamela Kyle Crossley received her Ph.D. in Modern Chinese History from Yale University. She is Professor of History and Rosenwald Research Professor in the Arts and Sciences at Dartmouth College. Her books include *A Translucent Mirror: History and Identity in Qing Imperial Ideology; The Manchus; Orphan Warriors: Three Manchu Generations and the End of the Qing World;* and (with Lynn Hollen Lees and John W. Servos) *Global Society: The World Since 1900*. Her research, which concentrates on the cultural history of China, Inner Asia, and Central Asia, has been supported by the John Simon Guggenheim Memorial Foundation and the National Endowment for the Humanities.

**Daniel R. Headrick** Daniel R. Headrick received his Ph.D. in History from Princeton University. Professor of History and Social Science at Roosevelt University in Chicago, he is the author of several books on the history of technology, imperialism, and international relations, including *The Tools of Empire: Technology and European Imperialism in the Nineteenth Century; The Tentacles of Progress: Technology Transfer in the Age of Imperialism; The Invisible Weapon: Telecommunications and International Politics;* and *When Information Came of Age: Technologies of Knowledge in the Age of Reason and Revolution, 1700–1850*. His articles have appeared in the *Journal of World History* and the *Journal of Modern History,* and he has been awarded fellowships by the National Endowment for the Humanities, the John Simon Guggenheim Memorial Foundation, and the Alfred P. Sloan Foundation.

**Steven W. Hirsch** Steven W. Hirsch holds a Ph.D. in Classics from Stanford University and is currently Associate Professor Classics and History at Tufts University. He has received grants from the National Endowment for the Humanities and the Massachusetts Foundation for Humanities and Public Policy. His research and publications include *The Friendship of the Barbarians: Xenophon and the Persian Empire,* as well as articles and reviews in the *Classical Journal,* the *American Journal of Philology,* and the *Journal of Interdisciplinary History.* He is currently working on a comparative study of ancient Mediterranean and Chinese civilizations.

**Lyman L. Johnson** Professor of History at the University of North Carolina at Charlotte, Lyman L. Johnson earned his Ph.D. in Latin American History from the University of Connecticut. A two-time Senior Fulbright-Hays Lecturer, he also has received fellowships from the Tinker Foundation, the Social Science Research Council, the National Endowment for the Humanities, and the American Philosophical Society. His recent books include *Death, Dismemberment, and Memory; The Faces of Honor* (with Sonya Lipsett-Rivera); *The Problem of Order in Changing Societies; Essays on the Price History of Eighteenth-Century Latin America* (with Enrique Tandeter); and *Colonial Latin America* (with Mark A. Burkholder). He also has published in journals, including the *Hispanic American Historical Review,* the *Journal of Latin American Studies,* the *International Review of Social History, Social History,* and *Desarrollo Económico.* He recently served as president of the Conference on Latin American History.

**David Northrup** Professor of History at Boston College, David Northrup earned his Ph.D. in African and European History from the University of California at Los Angeles. He earlier taught in Nigeria with the Peace Corps and at Tuskegee Institute. Research supported by the Fulbright-Hays Commission, the National Endowment for the Humanities, and the Social Science Research Council led to publications concerning pre-colonial Nigeria, the Congo (1870–1940), the Atlantic slave trade, and Asian, African, and Pacific Islander indentured labor in the nineteenth century. A contributor to the *Oxford History of the British Empire* and *Blacks in the British Empire,* his latest book is *Africa's Discovery of Europe, 1450–1850.* For 2004 and 2005 he serves as president of the World History Association.

# Note on Spelling and Usage

Where necessary for clarity, dates are followed by the letters C.E. or B.C.E. The abbreviation C.E. stands for "Common Era" and is equivalent to A.D. (*anno Domini*, Latin for "in the year of the Lord"). The abbreviation B.C.E stands for "before the Common Era" and means the same as B.C. ("before Christ"). In keeping with our goal of approaching world history without special concentration on one culture or another, we chose these neutral abbreviations as appropriate to our enterprise. Because many readers will be more familiar with English than with metric measurements, however, units of measure are generally given in the English system, with metric equivalents following in parentheses.

In general, Chinese has been romanized according to the *pinyin* method. Exceptions include proper names well established in English (e.g., Canton, Chiang Kai-shek) and a few English words borrowed from Chinese (e.g., kowtow). Spellings of Arabic, Ottoman Turkish, Persian, Mongolian, Manchu, Japanese, and Korean names and terms avoid special diacritical marks for letters that are pronounced only slightly differently in English. An apostrophe is used to indicate when two Chinese syllables are pronounced separately (e.g., Chang'an).

For words transliterated from languages that use the Arabic script—Arabic, Ottoman Turkish, Perisan, Urdu—the apostrophe indicating separately pronounced syllables may represent either of two special consonants, the *hamza* or the *ain*. Because most English-speakers do not hear the distinction between these two, they have not been distinguished in transliteration and are not indicated when they occur at the beginning or end of a word. As with Chinese, some words and commonly used place-names from these languages are given familiar English spellings (e.g., Quran instead of Qur'an, Cairo instead of al-Qahira). Arabic romanization has normally been used for terms relating to Islam, even where the context justifies slightly different Turkish or Persian forms, again for ease of comprehension.

Before 1492 the inhabitants of the Western Hemisphere had no single name for themselves. They had neither a racial consciousness nor a racial identity. Identity was derived from kin groups, language, cultural practices, and political structures. There was no sense that physical similarities created a shared identity. America's original inhabitants had racial consciousness and racial identity imposed on them by conquest and the occupation of their lands by Europeans after 1492. All of the collective terms for these first American peoples are tainted by this history. *Indians, Native Americans, Amerindians, First Peoples, and Indigenous Peoples* are among the terms in common usage. In this book the names of individual cultures and states are used wherever possible. *Amerindian* and other terms that suggest transcultural identity and experience are used most commonly for the period after 1492.

There is an ongoing debate about how best to render Amerindian words in English. It has been common for authors writing in English to follow Mexican usage for Nahuatl and Yucatec Maya words and place-names. In this style, for example, the capital of the Aztec state is spelled Tenochtitlán, and the important late Maya city-state is spelled Chichén Itzá. Although these forms are still common even in the specialist literature, we have chosen to follow the scholarship that sees these accents as unnecessary. The exceptions are modern place-names, such as Mérida and Yucatán, which are accented. A similar problem exists for the spelling of Quechua and Aymara words from the Andean region of South America. Although there is significant disagreement among scholars, we follow the emerging consensus and use the spellings khipu (not quipu), Tiwanaku (not Tiahuanaco), and Wari (not Huari). However, we keep Inca (not Inka) and Cuzco (not Cusco), since these spellings are expected by most of our potential readers and we hope to avoid confusion.

# Introduction
# The World
# Before 1500

**The World, 1200–1500**

Antiquity: Humans, Cultures, and Conquests, to 400 C.E.

Growth and Interaction, 400–1200

Interregional Conquests and Exchanges, 1200–1500

History occurs in a continuous stream. Because new events are the products of their past, each historical period is intimately linked to what preceded it. As a Roman historian put it, "History doesn't make leaps." Nevertheless, modern historians find it useful to divide the past into eras or ages to make sense of the sweep of history. The longest historical eras are antiquity, the Middle Ages, and modern times. Volume II of *The Earth and Its Peoples* is devoted to the third of these—modern world history, the five centuries since about 1500.

In order to explain how the modern era came into being, the first chapter of Volume II of *The Earth and Its Peoples* (Chapter 14) begins in about 1450. To help the reader understand the broader sweep of history, this Introduction provides an overview of earlier eras. The Introduction reviews three periods of decreasing temporal length. The first is the very long period from the beginnings of agriculture and animal breeding until the end of ancient history in about 400 C.E. Next comes the early medieval period down to about 1200; and, finally, the three hundred years immediately preceding 1500. Because the centuries after 1200 were most important for shaping the transition to the modern era, they receive the most detailed treatment.

# ANTIQUITY: HUMANS, CULTURES, AND CONQUESTS, TO 400 C.E.

All historical periods were shaped by natural environment and human technology (whether simple tools, techniques, or complex machines). Our ancestors used their minds to devise technologies for transforming nature to suit their needs. By the standards of today, these early technologies may seem crude—stone tools for cutting and chopping, clothing made from plants and animal skins, shelters in caves and huts—but they were sufficient to enable humans to survive environmental changes in their homelands. They also enabled bands of humans to migrate to new environments in every part of the world. Through trial and error Stone Age people learned what could safely be eaten in new environments. Other primates acted primarily by instinct; humans acted according to the dictates of culture. The capacity to create and change material and intellectual culture marked the beginning of human history.

## Agricultural Civilizations

Beginning about 10,000 years ago, the transition from food gathering to food production marked a major turning point in history. Human communities in many different parts of the world learned to alter the natural food supply. Some people promoted the growth of foods they liked by scattering seeds on good soils and restricting the growth of competing plants. In time some people became full-time farmers. Other communities tamed wild animals whose meat, milk, fur, and hides they desired, and they controlled their breeding to produce animals with the most desired characteristics. Promoted by a warmer world climate, these agricultural revolutions slowly spread from the Middle East around the Mediterranean. People in South and East Asia, Africa, and the Americas domesticated other wild plants and animals for their use. Just as humans had ceased to rely on evolution to enable them to adjust to new surroundings, so too they had bypassed evolution in bringing new species of plants and animals into existence.

The agricultural revolutions greatly enhanced people's chances for survival in two ways. One was a rapid increase in population fostered by the ability to grow and store more food. A second change was taking place in the composition of human communities. The earliest communities consisted of small bands of biologically related people and their spouses from other bands. However, more complex societies made their first appearances as more and more unrelated people concentrated in lush river valleys, whose soils, temperatures, and rainfall suited them for farming.

In the Fertile Crescent of the Middle East, Egypt, India, and China the existence of a regular food surplus enabled a few people to develop highly specialized talents and tools that were not tied to food production. Some specialized in fighting—to defend crops from raiders and to expand their lands. Some talented warriors became rulers of large areas and headed government with specialized administrators. Specialists constructed elaborate irrigation systems, monumental palaces, and temples. Others made special metal tools and weapons, first of bronze, then of iron. Because of the value of their talents these specialists acquired privileges. It was grandest to be a king, queen, or head priest. For the average person, life was harder in complex societies than in parts of the world where such specialization had not yet occurred.

## Culture and Civilization

Complex and populous agricultural societies developed specialists who dealt with abstract and unseen forces. This development was not entirely new. For tens of thousands of years before the first settled societies, humans had used their minds to think about the meaning of life. The remains of elaborate burials and sites of worship suggest that some early societies had clear beliefs in an afterlife and in spiritual forces that controlled their lives. Many cultures believed the sun, moon, and nature had supernatural powers.

Another form of intellectual activity was the collection of technical knowledge about the environment. Cultural communities learned what plants were best for food, clothing, or building materials and passed this knowledge along to later generations. Most specialized was the knowledge of how to make medicines and poisons. Assigning names for all these facilitated the transmission of this knowledge. In the absence of written records, very little specific information about these early treasuries of knowledge exists, but the elaborate and beautiful paintings in caves dating to tens of thousands of years before the emergence of early agricultural societies provide the clearest evidence of the cultural sophistication of early humans.

Cultural change surged as settled agricultural communities became more specialized. Temple priests devised elaborate rituals and texts for state religions and studied the heavens for signs of the progress of the seasons or for more mystical meanings. In Mesopotamia, Egypt, and elsewhere a new class of scribes wrote down laws, bodies of knowledge, and records in special codes. Writing gave rise to recorded literature and records that might be sent unchanged over long distances or even lost for millennia only to be discovered and deciphered in recent times, giving future generations specific records of what went before. Thoughtful people recorded the myths and legends passed down orally from earlier days, systematizing them and often adapting them to new social conditions.

## Empires and Regional Cultures

In time governments weakened or fell victim to conquest. Egypt, for example, fell to the Assyrians from Mesopotamia, then to Nubians from up the Nile. Some conquerors created vast new empires. Late in the fourth century B.C.E., Alexander the Great brought everything from the eastern Mediterranean to India and Egypt under his sway, spreading Greek culture and language. After the collapse of Alexander's empire in the third century B.C.E., the first of a series of Indian empires arose. In the second and first centuries B.C.E., Latin-speakers spread their rule, language, and culture throughout the Roman Empire, which encompassed the Mediterranean and reached across the Alps into Gaul (France) and Britain. At much the same time, the Han consolidated control over the densely populated lands of China, and successive rulers extended the sway of imperial China over much of East Asia. In the isolated continents of the Americas, advanced agricultural societies were also building larger states in late antiquity.

Essential to empire formation was the significant enhancement of old technologies and the development of new ones. In many parts of the world iron replaced bronze as the preferred metal for tools and weapons. In the Middle East and China soldiers on horseback played important military roles. In most places there were advances in the fighting techniques and in defensive strategies and fortifications.

Empires encouraged the growth of cities to serve as administrative, economic, and cultural centers. Temples, palaces, monuments, markets, and public amenities advertised the glory of these imperial centers. Large states regularly mobilized large pools of labor for massive construction projects. By late antiquity, a few cities had populations in the hundreds of thousands—Alexandria in Egypt, Rome in Italy, Chang'an in China, Palaliputra in India—though such large numbers strained cities' capacities to supply food and water and dispose of waste. Such architectural monuments established "classical" styles that affected wide areas even after the empires were gone.

Other imperial building projects were more practical. The Roman and Chinese governments built thousands of miles of paved roads for moving troops and communication; long barrier walls and strings of forts defended frontier areas from invasion. Trade often flourished on these political frontiers, and good roads further encouraged trade. Improvements in shipping also encouraged the movement of goods over long distances. Much long-distance trade in antiquity was in luxury goods for the privileged classes in urban civilizations. The search for exotic items tied remote parts of the world together and gave rise to new specialists both within the urban civilizations and in less stratified parts of the world. Gold, animal pelts, and exotic feathers from inner Africa reached Egypt. Phoenician mariners marketed lumber, papyrus (for paper), wine, and fish around the Mediterranean Sea. Other merchants carried silk from China across arid Central Asia to the Middle East and lands to the west. The advent of coinage in the first millennium B.C.E. stimulated local and regional economies.

The routes that carried goods also helped spread religions, inventions, and ideas. The Zoroastrian religion of the Persians became one of the great ethical creeds of antiquity. The diaspora of Jews from Palestine after their northern kingdom was destroyed by the Assyrian Empire in the eighth century B.C.E. and the activities of Jewish traders also helped spread monotheistic beliefs. The beliefs and culture of the Greeks and Romans spread throughout their empires. Similarly, Indian traders introduced Hinduism to Southeast Asia.

# GROWTH AND INTERACTION, 400-1200

During the Early Middle Ages expanding political and commercial links drew regions closer together. In addition, the growth of interregional trade and the spread of new world religions helped unite and redefine the boundaries of cultural regions, though divisions within religions undercut some of this cultural unity. All of these factors were interrelated, but let's begin with the one that left the most enduring impression on the course of history: the spread of world religions.

## World Religions

The first religious tradition to experience widespread growth in this period was Buddhism, which spread from the Indian homeland where it had arisen around 500 B.C.E. One direction of growth was eastward into Southeast Asia. By 400 C.E. there were particular strongholds of the faith on the large islands of Ceylon and Java, whose kings supported the growth of schools and monasteries and constructed temple complexes. Traders also carried Buddhism to China and from there to Korea, Japan, and Tibet. In some places Buddhism's growing strength led to political reactions. In China the Tang emperors reduced the influence of the monasteries in 840 by taking away their tax exemption and by promoting traditional Confucian values. A similar effort by the Tibetan royal family to curtail Buddhism failed, and Buddhist monks established their political dominance in mountainous Tibet. In India, however, Buddhism gradually lost support during this period and by 1200 had practically disappeared from the land of its origin.

Meanwhile, people in western Eurasia were embracing two newer religious systems. In the fourth century, Christianity became the official religion of the Roman Empire, adding new followers all around the Mediterranean to this once persecuted faith. But when the western half of the empire collapsed under the onslaught of "barbarian" invasions in the late fifth century, the Latin Church had to shoulder alone the tasks of converting these peoples to Christianity and preserving the intellectual, political, and cultural heritage of Roman antiquity. In its religious mission the Latin Church was quite successful. One by one Frankish, German, English, Irish, Hungarian, and other leaders were converted, and their subjects gradually followed suit. Preserving other Roman achievements was more difficult. The church continued to use the Latin language and Roman law, and Christian monasteries preserved manuscripts of many ancient works. But the trading economy and urban life that had been the heart blood of ancient Rome became only a memory in most of the Latin West.

In the eastern Mediterranean, Byzantine Roman emperors continued to rule, and the Greek-speaking Christian church continued to enjoy political protection. Greek monks were also active Christian missionaries among the Slavic peoples of eastern Europe. The conversion of the Russian rulers in the tenth century was a notable achievement. However, by the middle of the next century, cultural, linguistic, and theological differences led to a deep rift between Greek and Russian Christians in the east and Latin Christians in the west.

Meanwhile, prophetic religion founded by Muhammad in the seventh century was spreading like a whirlwind out of its Arabian homeland. With great fervor Arab armies introduced Islam and an accompanying state system into the Middle East, across North Africa, and into the Iberian Peninsula. Over time most Middle Eastern and African Christians and members of other religions chose to adopt the new faith. Muslim merchants helped spread the faith along trade routes into sub-Saharan Africa and across southern Asia. Like Christianity, Islam eventually split along cultural, theological, and political lines as it expanded. Beginning in 1095, Latin Christians launched military Crusades against Muslim dominance of Christian holy places in Palestine. In later Crusades, political and commercial ends became more important than religious goals, and the boundaries between Christianity and Islam changed little.

## Commercial and Political Contacts

In many other parts of the world empires played a fundamental role in defining and unifying cultural areas. Under the Tang and Song dynasties (618–1279) China continued to have stability and exhibited periods of remarkable economic growth and technological creativity. Ghana, the first notable empire in sub-Saharan Africa, emerged to control one end of the trans-Saharan trade. In the isolated continents of the Americas a series of cultural complexes formed in the Andes, among the Maya of the Yucatán, along the Mississippi, and in the arid North American southwest. But despite efforts by Christian northern Europeans to create a loosely centralized "Holy Roman Empire," a very decentralized political system prevailed in most of western Europe. In Japan development was moving in a similar direction.

Political and religious expansion helped stimulate regional and long-distance trade. The challenge of moving growing quantities of goods over long distances produced some important innovations in land and sea travel. Two of the most important land-based, long-distance routes in this period depended on pack animals, especially the camel. One was the Silk Road, a caravan route across Central Asia. On the other trade route, between sub-Saharan Africa and North Africa, camels carried goods across the Sahara, the world's largest desert.

The Silk Road took its name from the silk textiles that were carried from eastern China to the Mediterranean Sea. In return, the Chinese received horses and other goods from the West. In existence since about 250 B.C.E., this series of roads nearly 6,000 miles (9,000 kilometers) in length passed through arid lands whose pastoral populations provided guides, food, and fresh camels (specially bred for caravan work).

After 900 C.E. the Silk Road declined for a time. By coincidence, the trans-Saharan caravan routes were growing more important during the period from 700 to 1200. Here, too, horses were an important trade purchased by African rulers to the south in return for gold, slaves, and other goods. The pastoralists who controlled the Saharan oases became essential guides for the camel caravans.

Since ancient times sea travel had been important in moving goods over relatively short distances, usually within sight of land, as around the Mediterranean Sea, the Red Sea, the Persian Gulf, and among the islands of the East Indies. During this period the water links around and through the Indian Ocean were increasing enough to make it an alternative to moving goods from China to the Middle East. Shipments went from port to port and were exchanged many times. Special ships known as dhows made use of the seasonal shifts in the winds across the Indian Ocean to plan their voyages in each direction. These centuries also saw remarkable maritime voyages in the Pacific (see Chapter 15).

# INTERREGIONAL CONQUESTS AND EXCHANGES, 1200–1500

Between 1200 and 1500, cultural and commercial contacts grew rapidly across wide expanses of Eurasia, Africa, the Americas, and the Indian Ocean. In part, the increased contacts were the product of an unprecedented era of empire building around the world. The Mongols conquered a vast empire spanning Eurasia from the Pacific to eastern Europe. Muslim peoples created new empires in India, the Middle East, and sub-Saharan Africa. Amerindian empires united extensive regions of the Americas. Most of Europe continued to lack political unity, but unusually powerful European kingdoms were expanding their frontiers.

Empires stimulated commercial exchanges. The Mongol conquests revived the Silk Road across Central Asia, while a complex maritime network centered on the Indian Ocean stretched around southern Eurasia from the South China Sea to the North Atlantic, with overland connections in all directions. Trade in the Americas and Africa also expanded. In the fifteenth century, Portuguese and Spanish explorers began an expansion southward along the Atlantic coast of Africa that by 1500 had opened a new all-water route to the riches of the Indian Ocean and set the stage for transoceanic routes that for the first time were to span the globe.

Mongol, Muslim, and European expansion promoted the spread of technologies. Printing, compasses, crossbows, gunpowder, and firearms—all East Asian inventions found broader applications

and new uses in western Eurasia. Both the Ottomans and the kingdoms of western Europe made extensive use of gunpowder technologies. However, the highly competitive and increasingly literate peoples of the Latin West surpassed all others of this period in their use of technologies that they borrowed from elsewhere or devised themselves. Europeans mined and refined more metals, produced more books, built more kinds of ships, and made more weapons than did people in any other comparable place on earth.

Why was so much change taking place all at once? Historians attribute many of the changes in South and Central Asia directly or indirectly to the empire building of the Mongols. But other changes took place far from that area. The role of simple coincidence, of course, should never be overlooked in history. And some historians believe that larger environmental factors were also at work—changes in climate that promoted population growth, trade, and empire building.

## Mongols and Turks

The earliest and largest of the new empires was the work of the Mongols of northeastern Asia. Using their extraordinary command of horses and refinements in traditional forms of military and social organization, Mongols and allied groups united under Genghis Khan overran northern China in the early thirteenth century and spread their control westward across Central Asia to eastern Europe. By the later part of the century, the Mongol Empire stretched from Korea to Poland. It was ruled initially in four separate khanates: one in Russia, one in Iran, one in Central Asia, and one in China.

By ensuring traders protection from robbers and excessive tolls, the Mongol Empire revitalized the Silk Road. Never before had there been such a volume of commercial exchanges between eastern and western Eurasia. Easier travel also helped Islam and Buddhism spread to new parts of Central Asia.

The strains of holding such vast territories together caused the Mongol Empire to disintegrate over the course of the fourteenth and early fifteenth centuries. The Ming rulers of China overthrew

Mongol rule in 1368 and began an expansionist foreign policy to reestablish China's predominance and prestige. Their armies repeatedly invaded Mongolia, reestablished dominion over Korea, and occupied northern Vietnam (Annam). One by one the other khanates collapsed.

The Mongols left a formidable legacy, but it was not Mongolian. Instead, Mongol rulers tended to adopt and promote the political systems, agricultural practices, and local customs of the peoples they ruled. Their encouragement of local languages helped later literary movements to flower. The political influence of the administrations the Mongols established in China, Iran, and Russia lingered even after locals had overthrown their rule, creating the basis for new national regimes.

At about the same time as the early Mongol expansion, Turkic war leaders from what is now Afghanistan were surging through the Khyber Pass and established a Muslim empire centered at Delhi. In short order, they overwhelmed the several Hindu states of north and central India and established a large empire ruled from the city of Delhi. The subsequent migration of large numbers of Muslims into India and the prestige and power of the Muslim ruling class brought India into the Islamic world. After their conquests in the Middle East, Mongols had recruited other Turkic-speaking Muslims from Central Asia to serve as their agents. In the decades after 1250, a large Turkic community in Anatolia (now Turkey) known as Ottomans took advantage of the weakness of the Byzantine Empire to extend their base in Anatolia. They then crossed into the Balkan Peninsula of southeastern Europe.

In the late 1300s, the Central Asian conqueror Timur (Tamerlane) shattered the Delhi Sultanate and stopped the expansion of the Ottoman Empire. The conquest and pillage of Timur's armies left the Delhi Sultanate a shadow of its former self, but the Ottoman Turks were able to reconstitute their empire in the fifteenth century. Ottoman conquerors swept deep into southeastern Europe (taking Constantinople, the last surviving remnant of the Byzantine Empire, in 1453) and southward into the Middle East, establishing a stable presence that was to endure into the twentieth century.

## Indian Ocean Exchanges

In the wake of the Mongol Empire's collapse, the Indian Ocean assumed greater importance in the movement of goods across Eurasia. Alliances among Muslim merchants of many nationalities made these routes the world's richest trading area. Merchant dhows sailed among the trading ports, carrying cotton textiles, leather goods, grains, pepper, jewelry, carpets, horses, ivory, and many other goods. Chinese silk and porcelain and Indonesian spices entered from the east, meeting Middle Eastern and European goods from the west. It is important to note that Muslim merchant networks were almost completely independent of the giant Muslim land empires.

As a consequence of the Islamic world's political and commercial expansion, the number of adherents to the Muslim faith also grew. By 1500 Islam had replaced Buddhism as the second most important faith in India and was on its way to displacing Hinduism and Buddhism in Southeast Asia. The faith was also spreading in the Balkans. Meanwhile, raids by Arab pastoralists undermined ancient Christian states along Africa's upper Nile, leaving Ethiopia as the only Christian-ruled state in Africa. In the trading cities below the Sahara and along the Indian Ocean coast where Islam had established itself well before 1200, the strength and sophistication of Islamic religious practice was growing.

## Mediterranean Exchanges

The Mediterranean Sea, which since antiquity had been a focus of commerce and cultural exchange for the peoples of Europe, the Middle East, and Africa, saw increased activity in the later Middle Ages. Part of the Mediterranean's importance derived from its trading links to the Indian Ocean by land and water routes. Another area that contributed to expanded trade was northern Africa. Camel caravans brought great quantities of gold and large numbers of slaves to the Mediterranean from the lands below the Sahara. This trade facilitated the growth of the powerful empire of Mali, which controlled some of the main gold-producing regions of West Africa. The rulers of Mali became rich and Muslim. Their wars and those of other states produced the captives that were sold north. In the fourteenth century the disruption of supplies of slaves from the eastern Mediterranean led to more slaves being purchased in southern Europe.

Another part of the expansion of Mediterranean trade was tied to the revival of western Europe. In 1204 the Italian city-state of Venice had shown its determination to be a dominant player in the eastern Mediterranean by attacking the Greek city of Constantinople and ensuring access to the Black Sea. Trade routes from the Mediterranean spread northward to the Netherlands and connected by sea to the British Isles, the Baltic Sea, and the Atlantic. The growth of trade in Europe accompanied a revival of urban life and culture. Both the cities and the countryside saw increased use of energy, minerals, and technologies from printing to gunpowder. Despite a high level of warfare among European states and devastating population losses in the fourteenth century, much of Europe was exhibiting cultural and economic vitality that was to have great consequences for the entire world in the centuries that followed.

## The Aztecs and Inca

In the continents of the Western Hemisphere, American peoples were also creating important empires in the period from 1200 to 1500, although they had more limited resources with which to do so. For thousands of years their cultures had developed in isolation from the rest of humanity and thus had been unable to borrow any plants, animals, or technologies. Amerindian conquests were made without the aid of riding animals like the Mongols' horses, without the iron weapons all Old World empire builders had been using for many centuries, and without the new gunpowder weaponry that some Eurasians were employing in their conquests in this period.

In the wake of the collapse of the Toltec Empire, a martial people known as the Aztecs pushed southward into the rich agricultural lands of central Mexico. At first the Aztecs placed themselves at the service of strong indigenous residents, but after 1300 they began to build their own empire. Relying on their military skills, members of the Aztec warrior elite were able to conquer territories and reduce peasants to their service. The growth of a servile class at the bottom of society was paralleled by the growth of a powerful ruling class housed in well-constructed two-story dwellings in the Aztec capital cities. The servile laborers supplied the food needs of the growing cities and were impressed into building elaborate canals and land reclamation projects. Underpinning the power of the Aztec rulers were religious rituals that emphasized human sacrifice, mostly captives of the armies. By 1500 the Aztecs ruled a densely populated empire of subject and allied peoples.

Meanwhile, in the Andean highlands of western South America another powerful Amerindian empire was forming. Like central Mexico this region already had a rich agricultural base and a dense population when, in the fifteenth century, the Inca began using military skills to expand from a chiefdom into an empire. The Inca rulers, like the Aztecs, built impressive cities, promoted irrigation projects, and relied on religious rituals to bolster their authority. Tribute in goods and labor from their subject peoples supported their projects, and a network of mountain roads tied together the pieces of an empire that stretched for more than 3,000 miles (nearly 5,000 kilometers) north to south.

Both empires were cultural and commercial centers as well as political ones. In the Aztec Empire, well-armed private merchants controlled a long-distance trade in luxuries for the elites, including gold, jewels, feathered garments, and animal skins. There was also a network of local markets, large and small, that supplied the needs of more ordinary folks. State direction featured more prominently in Inca-ruled areas and promoted a vast exchange of specialized goods and a huge variety of foodstuffs grown at different altitudes.

# The Maritime Revolution, to 1550

# 14

CHAPTER OUTLINE

**Global Maritime Expansion Before 1450**

**Iberian Expansion, 1400–1550**

**Encounters with Europe, 1450–1550**

DIVERSITY AND DOMINANCE: **Kongo's Christian King**

In 1511, the young Ferdinand Magellan sailed from Europe around the southern tip of Africa and eastward across the Indian Ocean as a member of the first Portuguese expedition to explore the East Indies (maritime Southeast Asia). Eight years later, in the service of Spain, he headed an expedition that sought to reach the East Indies by sailing westward from Europe. By the middle of 1521, Magellan's expedition had sailed across the Atlantic, rounded the southern tip of South America, and crossed the Pacific Ocean—but at a high price.

One of the five ships wrecked on a reef; the captain of another deserted and sailed back to Spain. The passage across the Pacific took much longer than anticipated. Dozens of sailors died of starvation and disease. In the Philippines, Magellan himself was killed on April 27, 1521, while aiding a local king who had prom-

ised to become a Christian. Magellan's successor met the same fate a few days later.

The expedition's survivors consolidated their resources by burning the least seaworthy of their remaining three ships and transferring the men and supplies to the smaller *Victoria*, which continued westward across the Indian Ocean, around Africa, and back to Europe. Magellan's flagship, the *Trinidad*, tried unsuccessfully to recross the Pacific to Central America. However, the *Victoria*'s return to Spain on September 8, 1522, confirmed Europe's ability and determination to master the oceans. The Portuguese crown had backed a century of daring and dangerous voyages to open routes to Africa, Brazil, and the Indian Ocean. Since 1492, Spain had opened contacts with the American continents. Now the broad Pacific Ocean had been crossed.

**337**

Before 1500, powerful states and the rich trading networks of Asia had led the way in overland and maritime expansion. The Iberians set out on their voyages of exploration to reach Eastern markets, and their success began a new era in which the West gradually became the world's center of power, wealth, and innovation.

As you read this chapter, ask yourself the following questions:

- Why did Portugal and Spain undertake voyages of exploration?

- Why do the voyages of Magellan and other Iberians mark a turning point in world history?

- What were the consequences for the different peoples of the world of the contacts resulting from these voyages?

# GLOBAL MARITIME EXPANSION BEFORE 1450

B y 1450, mariners had discovered and settled most of the islands of the Pacific, the Atlantic, and the Indian Oceans, and a great trading system united the peoples around the Indian Ocean. But we know of no individual crossing the Pacific in either direction. Even the narrower Atlantic formed a barrier that kept the peoples of the Americas, Europe, and Africa in ignorance of each other's existence. The inhabitants of Australia were also completely cut off from contact with the rest of humanity. All this was about to change.

## The Pacific Ocean

The vast distances that Polynesian peoples voyaged out of sight of land across the Pacific Ocean are one of the most impressive feats in maritime history before 1450 (see Map 14.1). Though they left no written records, over several thousand years mariners from the Malay° Peninsula of Southeast Asia explored and settled the island

Malay (May-LAY)

chains of the East Indies and continued on to New Guinea and the smaller islands of Melanesia°. Beginning sometime before the Common Era (C.E.), a wave of expansion from the area of Fiji brought the first humans to the islands of the central Pacific known as Polynesia. Their sailing canoes reached the easternmost Marquesas° Islands about 400 C.E.; Easter Island, 2,200 miles (3,540 kilometers) off the coast of South America, a century later; and the Hawaiian Islands by 500 C.E. Settlement in New Zealand began about 1200. Between 1100 and 1300, new voyages northward from Tahiti brought more Polynesian settlers to Hawaii.

Historians have puzzled over how the Polynesians reached the eastern Pacific islands without compasses to plot their way, particularly in view of the difficulties Magellan's flagship encountered sailing eastward across the Pacific. In 1947, explorer Thor Heyerdahl° argued that Easter Island and Hawaii were settled from the Americas and sought to prove his theory by sailing his balsawood raft *Kon Tiki* westward from Peru.

Although some Amerindian voyagers did use ocean currents to travel northward from Peru to Mexico between 300 and 900 C.E., there is now considerable evidence that planned expansion by Polynesian mariners accomplished the settlement of the islands of the eastern Pacific. The languages of the islanders relate closely to the languages of the western Pacific and ultimately to those of Malaya. In addition, accidental voyages could not have brought sufficient numbers of men and women for founding a new colony along with all the plants and domesticated animals common to other Polynesian islands.

In 1976, a Polynesian crew led by anthropologist Ben Finney used traditional navigational methods to sail the *Hokulea*, a 62-foot-long (19-meter-long) double canoe, from Hawaii south to Tahiti. Patterned after old oceangoing canoes, some of which measured 120 feet (35 meters) long, it used inverted triangular sails and was steered by paddles (not by a rudder). The *Hokulea*'s crew navigated using only their observation of the currents, stars, and evidence of land.

Melanesia (mel-uh-NEE-zhuh)   Marquesas (mar-KAY-suhs)   Heyerdahl (HIGH-uhr-dahl)

# C H R O N O L O G Y

| | Pacific Ocean | Atlantic Ocean | Indian Ocean |
|---|---|---|---|
| **Pre-1400** | **400–1300** Polynesian settlement of Pacific Islands | **700–1200** Viking voyages<br>**1300s** Settlement of Madeira, Azores, Canaries<br>**Early 1300s** Mali voyages | |
| **1400 to 1500** | | **1418–1460** Voyages of Henry the Navigator<br>**1440s** Slaves from West Africa<br>**1482** Portuguese at Gold Coast and Kongo<br>**1486** Portuguese at Benin<br>**1492** Columbus reaches Caribbean<br>**1493** Columbus returns to Caribbean (second voyage)<br>**1493–1502** Spanish conquer Hispaniola<br>**1498** Columbus reaches mainland of South America (third voyage)<br>**1500** Cabral reaches Brazil | **1405–1433** Voyages of Zheng He<br><br>**1498** Vasco da Gama reaches India |
| **1500 to 1550** | **1519–1522** Magellan expedition | **1513** Ponce de Léon explores Florida<br>**1519–1520** Cortés conquers Aztec Empire<br>**1532–1533** Pizarro conquers Inca Empire | **1505** Portuguese bombard Swahili Coast cities<br>**1510** Portuguese take Goa<br>**1511** Portuguese take Malacca<br>**1515** Portuguese take Hormuz<br>**1535** Portuguese take Diu<br>**1538** Portuguese defeat Ottoman fleet<br>**1539** Portuguese aid Ethiopia |

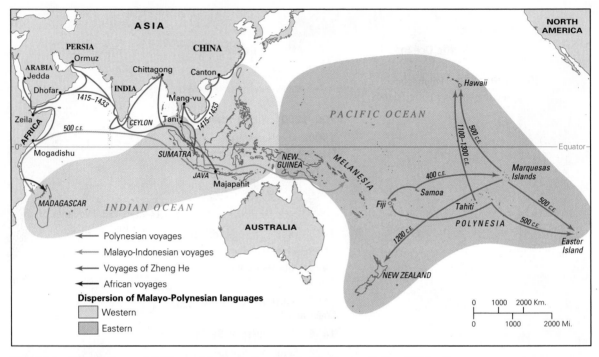

**Map 14.1   Exploration and Settlement in the Indian and Pacific Oceans Before 1500**   Over many centuries, mariners originating in Southeast Asia gradually colonized the islands of the Pacific and Indian Oceans. The Chinese voyages led by Zheng He in the fifteenth century were lavish official expeditions.

## The Indian Ocean

While Polynesian mariners settled the Pacific islands, other Malayo-Indonesians sailed westward across the Indian Ocean and colonized the large island of Madagascar off the southeastern coast of Africa. These voyages continued through the fifteenth century. To this day, the inhabitants of Madagascar speak Malayo-Polynesian languages. However, part of the island's population is descended from Africans who crossed the 600 miles (1,000 kilometers) from the mainland to Madagascar, most likely in the centuries just before 1500.

The rise of Islam gave Indian Ocean trade an important boost. The great Muslim cities of the Middle East provided a demand for valuable commodities, and networks of Muslim traders tied the region together. The Indian Ocean traders operated largely independent of the empires and states that they served, but in East Asia, China's early Ming emperors took an active interest in these

wealthy ports of trade, sending Admiral **Zheng He**° on a series of expeditions.

The first Ming fleet in 1405 consisted of sixty-two specially built "treasure ships," large Chinese junks each about 300 feet long by 150 feet wide (90 by 45 meters). Most of the one hundred smaller accompanying vessels exceeded in size the flagship in which Columbus later sailed across the Atlantic. Each treasure ship had nine masts, twelve sails, many decks, and a carrying capacity of 3,000 tons (six times the capacity of Columbus's entire fleet). One expedition carried over 27,000 individuals, including infantry and cavalry troops. Although the ships carried small cannon, highly accurate crossbows dominated most Chinese sea battles.

One Chinese-Arabic interpreter kept a journal recording the customs, dress, and beliefs of the people visited, along with the trade, towns, and ani-

**Zheng He** (jung huh)

**Polynesian Canoes**    Pacific Ocean mariners sailing canoes such as these, shown in an eighteenth-century painting, made epic voyages of exploration and settlement. A large platform connects two canoes at the left, providing more room for the members of the expedition, and a sail supplements the paddlers.    ("Tereoboo, King of Owyhee, bringing presents to Captain Cook," D. L. Ref. p. xx 2f. 35. Courtesy, The Dixson Library, State Library of New South Wales)

mals of their countries. Among his observations were these: exotic animals such as the black panther of Malaya and the tapir of Sumatra; beliefs in legendary "corpse-headed barbarians" whose heads left their bodies at night and caused infants to die; the division of coastal Indians into five classes, which correspond to the four Hindu varnas and a separate Muslim class; and the fact that traders in the Indian port of Calicut° could perform error-free calculations by counting on their fingers and toes rather than using the Chinese abacus. After his return, the interpreter went on tour in China, telling of these exotic places and "how far the majestic virtue of [China's] imperial dynasty extended."[1]

Interest in new contacts was not confined to the Chinese side. In 1415–1416, at least three trading cities on the Swahili° Coast of East Africa sent delegations to China. Although no record of African and Chinese reactions to one another survives, China's lavish gifts to local rulers stimulated the Swahili market for silk and porcelain.

## The Atlantic Ocean

The Vikings, northern European raiders and pirates, used their small, open ships to attack coastal European settlements for several centuries. They also discovered and settled one island after another in the North Atlantic. Like the Polynesians, the Vikings had neither maps nor navigational devices. They found their way using their knowledge of the heavens and the seas.

**Calicut** (KAL-ih-kut)

**Swahili** (swah-HEE-lee)

The Vikings first settled Iceland in 770. From there, some moved on to Greenland in 982, and one group sighted North America in 986. Fifteen years later, Leif Ericsson established a short-lived Viking settlement on the island of Newfoundland, which he called Vinland. When the climate turned colder after 1200, the northern settlements in Greenland went into decline. Vinland became a mysterious place mentioned in Norse sagas.

Some southern Europeans also explored the Atlantic. In 1291, two Vivaldo brothers from Genoa set out to sail around Africa to India. They were never heard of again. Other Genoese and Portuguese expeditions into the Atlantic in the fourteenth century discovered (and settled) the islands of Madeira°, the Azores°, and the Canaries.

Mention also occurs of African voyages of exploration in the Atlantic. The Syrian geographer al-Umari (1301–1349) relates that when Mansa Kankan Musa°, the ruler of the West African empire of Mali, passed through Egypt on his lavish pilgrimage to Mecca in 1324, he told of voyages to cross the Atlantic undertaken by his predecessor, Mansa Muhammad. Muhammad had sent out four hundred vessels with men and supplies, telling them, "Do not return until you have reached the other side of the ocean or if you have exhausted your food or water." After a long time, one canoe returned, reporting the others had been swept away by a "violent current in the middle of the sea." Muhammad himself then set out at the head of a second, even larger, expedition, from which no one returned.

On the other side of the Atlantic, Amerindian voyagers from South America colonized the West Indies. By the year 1000, Amerindians known as the **Arawak°** had moved from the small islands of the Lesser Antilles (Barbados, Martinique, Guadaloupe) into the Greater Antilles (Cuba, Hispaniola, Jamaica, and Puerto Rico), as well as into the Bahamas. Another people, the Carib, followed their route. By the late fifteenth century, they had overrun most Arawak settlements in the Lesser Antilles and were raiding parts of the Greater Antilles. From the West Indies, Arawak and Carib also undertook voyages to the North American mainland.

---

Madeira (muh-DEER-uh)  **Azores** (A-zorz)  **Mansa Kankan Musa** (MAHN-suh KAHN-kahn MOO-suh) **Arawak** (AR-uh-wahk)

# IBERIAN EXPANSION, 1400–1550

The preceding survey shows that maritime exploration occurred in many parts of the world before 1450. The sea voyages sponsored by the Iberian kingdoms of Portugal and Spain attract special interest because they began a maritime revolution that profoundly altered the course of world history. The Portuguese and Spanish expeditions ended the isolation of the Americas and increased global interaction. The influence in world affairs of the Iberians and other Europeans who followed them overseas rose steadily after 1500.

Iberian overseas expansion arose from two related phenomena. First, Iberian rulers had strong economic, religious, and political motives to expand their contacts and increase their dominance. Second, improvements in maritime and military technologies gave them the means to master treacherous and unfamiliar ocean environments, seize control of existing maritime trade routes, and conquer new lands.

## Background to Iberian Expansion

In many ways, these voyages continued four trends evident in the Latin West from about the year 1000: (1) the revival of urban life and trade, (2) a struggle with Islamic powers for dominance of the Mediterranean that mixed religious motives with the desire for trade with distant lands, (3) growing intellectual curiosity about the outside world, and (4) a peculiarly European alliance between merchants and rulers.

The city-states of northern Italy took the lead in all of these developments. By 1450, they had well-established trade links to northern Europe, the Indian Ocean, and the Black Sea, and their merchant princes had sponsored an intellectual and artistic Renaissance. But the Italian states did not take the lead in exploring the Atlantic, even after the expansion of the Ottoman Empire in the fourteenth and fifteenth centuries disrupted their trade to the East, because Venice and Genoa preferred to continue the lucrative alliances with Muslims that had given their merchants privileged positions and because Mediterranean ships were ill suited to the more violent weather of the Atlantic. However, many individual Italians played leading roles in Atlantic exploration.

By contrast, the Iberian kingdoms had engaged in anti-Muslim warfare since the eighth century, when Muslim forces overran most of the peninsula. By about 1250, the Iberian kingdoms of Portugal, Castile, and Aragon had conquered all the Muslim lands in Iberia except the southern kingdom of Granada, which finally fell to the united kingdom of Castile and Aragon in 1492. These territories gradually amalgamated to form Spain, sixteenth-century Europe's most powerful state.

Christian militancy continued to drive Portugal and Spain in their overseas ventures. But the Iberian rulers and their adventurous subjects also sought material returns. Their small share of the Mediterranean trade made them more willing than the Italians to take risks to find new routes to Africa and Asia through the Atlantic. Moreover, both kingdoms participated in the shipbuilding changes and the gunpowder revolution under way in Atlantic Europe. Though not centers of Renaissance learning, both states had exceptional rulers who appreciated new geographical knowledge.

## Portuguese Voyages

When the Muslim government of Morocco in northwestern Africa weakened in the fifteenth century, the Portuguese went on the attack, beginning with the city of Ceuta° in 1415. This assault combined aspects of a religious crusade, a plundering expedition, and a military tournament in which young Portuguese knights displayed their bravery. Despite the capture of several more ports along Morocco's Atlantic coast, the Portuguese could not push inland and gain access to the gold trade they learned about, so they sought more direct contact with the gold producers by sailing down the African coast.

Young Prince Henry (1394–1460), third son of the king of Portugal, led the attack on Ceuta. Because he devoted the rest of his life to promoting exploration, he is known as **Henry the Navigator.** His official biographer emphasized his desire to

convert Africans to Christianity, make contact with Christian rulers believed to exist in Africa, and launch joint crusades with them against the Ottomans. Profit also figured in his dreams. His initial explorations focused on Africa. His ships established permanent contact with the islands of Madeira in 1418 and the Azores in 1439. Only later did reaching India become a goal.

"The Navigator" himself never ventured farther from home than North Africa. Instead, he founded a sort of research institute at Sagres° for studying navigation and collecting information about new lands. His staff drew on the pioneering efforts of Italian merchants, especially the Genoese, who had learned some of the secrets of the trans-Saharan trade, and of fourteenth-century Jewish cartographers who used information from Arab and European sources to produce remarkably accurate sea charts and maps of distant places. They also studied and improved navigational instruments that had come into Europe from China and the Islamic world: the magnetic compass, first developed in China, and the astrolabe, an instrument of Arab or Greek invention that enabled mariners to determine their latitude by measuring the position of the sun or the stars.

The Portuguese developed a new type of long-distance sailing vessel, the **caravel°.** The many-oared galleys of the Mediterranean could not carry enough food and water for long ocean voyages. The three-masted ships of the North Atlantic, powered by square sails, could not sail at much of an angle against the wind. The caravel, which was only one-fifth the size of the largest European ships and the large Chinese junks, could enter shallow coastal waters and explore upriver, yet it had the strength to weather ocean storms. When equipped with lateen sails, caravels had great maneuverability and could sail deeply into the wind; when sporting square Atlantic sails, they had great speed. The addition of small cannon made them good fighting ships as well. The caravels' economy, speed, agility, and power justified a contemporary's claim that they were "the best ships that sailed the seas."[2]

Pioneering captains had to overcome crews' fears that the South Atlantic waters were boiling hot and contained ocean currents that would prevent

---

**Chinese Junk**   This modern drawing shows how much larger one of Zheng He's ships was than one of Vasco da Gama's vessels. Watertight interior bulkheads made junks the most seaworthy large ships of the fifteenth century. Sails made of pleated bamboo matting hung from the junk's masts, and a stern rudder provided steering. European ships of exploration, though smaller, were faster and more maneuverable.   (Dugald Stermer)

their ever returning home. It took Prince Henry from 1420 to 1434 to coax an expedition to venture beyond southern Morocco in northwest Africa (see Map 14.2). The next stretch of coast, 800 miles (1,300 kilometers) of desert, offered little of interest to the explorers. Finally in 1444, the mariners reached the Senegal River and the populous, well-watered lands below the Sahara beginning at what they named Cape Verde (Green Cape) because of its vegetation.

In the years that followed, Henry's explorers learned how to return speedily to Portugal. Instead of battling the prevailing northeast trade winds and currents back up the coast, they discovered that by sailing northwest into the Atlantic to the latitude of the Azores, ships could pick up prevailing westerly winds that would blow them back to Portugal. The knowledge that ocean winds tend to form large circular patterns helped explorers discover many other ocean routes.

To pay for the research, ships, and expeditions,

Prince Henry drew partly on the income of the Order of Christ, a military religious order of which he was the governor. The Order of Christ had been founded to inherit the Portuguese properties and the crusading tradition of the Order of Knights Templar, which had disbanded in 1314. The Order of Christ received the exclusive right to promote Christianity in all the lands that were discovered, and the Portuguese emblazoned their ships' sails with the crusaders' red cross.

The first financial returns came from selling into slavery Africans captured in raids on the northwest coast of Africa and the Canary Islands during the 1440s. The Portuguese had captured or purchased eighty thousand Africans by the end of the century. However, gold quickly became more important than slavery. By 1457, enough African gold was coming back to Portugal for the kingdom to issue a new gold coin called the *cruzado* (crusade), another reminder of how deeply the Portuguese entwined religious and secular motives.

By the time Prince Henry died in 1460, his explorers had established a base of operations in the uninhabited Cape Verde Islands and explored 600 miles (950 kilometers) of coast beyond Cape Verde, as far as what they named Sierra Leone° (Lion Mountain). From there, they knew the coast of Africa curved sharply toward the east. After spending four decades covering the 1,500 miles (2,400 kilometers) from Lisbon to Sierra Leone, Portuguese explorers traveled the remaining 4,000 miles (6,400 kilometers) to the continent's southern tip in only three decades.

Royal sponsorship continued, but private commercial participation sped the progress. In 1469, a Lisbon merchant named Fernão Gomes purchased from the Crown the privilege of exploring 350 miles (550 kilometers) of new coast a year for five years and a monopoly on any resulting trade. Gomes discovered the uninhabited island of São Tomé° on the equator; in the next century, it became a major source of sugar produced with African slave labor. He also explored what later Europeans called the **Gold Coast,** which became the headquarters of Portugal's West African trade.

The expectation of finding a passage around Africa to the Indian Ocean spurred the final thrust down the African coast. **Bartolomeu Dias** rounded the southern tip of Africa (in 1488) and entered the Indian Ocean. In 1497–1498, **Vasco da Gama** led a Portuguese expedition around Africa to India. In 1500, ships in an expedition under Pedro Alvares Cabral°, while swinging wide to the west in the South Atlantic to catch the winds that would sweep them around southern Africa and on to India, came on the eastern coast of South America, laying the basis for Portugal's later claim to Brazil.

## Spanish Voyages

Spain's early discoveries owed more to haste and blind luck than to careful planning. Only in the last decade of the fifteenth century did the Spanish monarchs turn their attention from reconquest and organization of previously Muslim territories to overseas exploration. By this time, the Portuguese had already found their route to the Indian Ocean.

Sierra Leone (see-ER-uh lee-OWN)   São Tomé (sow toh-MAY)   Cabral (kah-BRAHL)

The leader of their overseas mission would be **Christopher Columbus** (1451–1506), a Genoese mariner. His three voyages between 1492 and 1498 would reveal the existence of vast and unexpected lands across the Atlantic. But this momentous discovery fell disappointingly short of Columbus's intention of finding a new route to the Indian Ocean even shorter than that of the Portuguese.

As a younger man, Columbus had gained considerable experience while participating in Portuguese explorations along the African coast, but he dreamed of a shorter way to the riches of the East. By his reckoning (based on a serious misreading of a ninth-century Arab authority), a mere 2,400 nautical miles (4,450 kilometers) separated the Canary Islands from Japan. The actual distance was five times greater.

Portuguese authorities twice rejected his plan to reach the East by sailing west, first in 1485 following a careful study and again in 1488 after Dias had established the feasibility of the African route. Columbus received more sympathy, but initially no support, from Queen Isabella of Castile. A Castilian commission appointed by Isabella studied the proposal for four years and concluded that a westward sea route to the Indies rested on questionable geographical assumptions. Nevertheless, Columbus's persistence finally won over the queen and her husband, King Ferdinand of Aragon. In 1492, elated perhaps by finally expelling the Muslims from Granada, they agreed to fund a modest expedition.

Columbus recorded in his log that the *Santa María*, the *Santa Clara* (nicknamed the *Niña*), and a vessel now known only by its nickname, the *Pinta*, with a mostly Spanish crew of ninety men "departed Friday the third day of August of the year 1492," toward "the regions of India." Their mission, the royal contract stated, was "to discover and acquire certain islands and mainland in the Ocean Sea." Columbus carried letters of introduction from the Spanish sovereigns to Eastern rulers, including one to the "Grand Khan" (meaning the Chinese emperor). An Arabic-speaking Jewish convert to Christianity had the job of communicating with the peoples of eastern Asia.

Unfavorable headwinds had discouraged other attempts to explore the Atlantic west of the Azores. But on earlier voyages along the African coast,

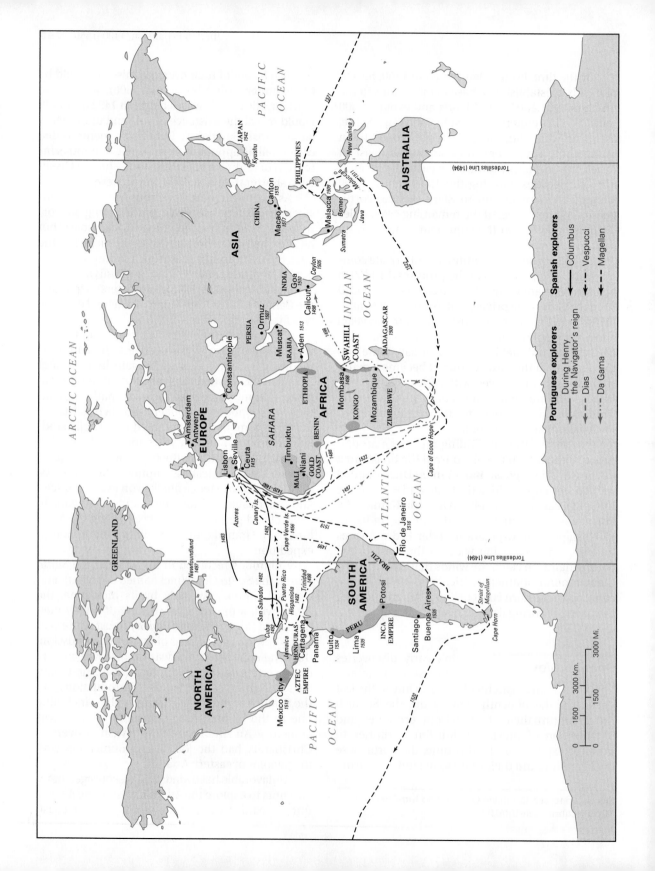

PACIFIC OCEAN

ARCTIC OCEAN

ASIA

JAPAN
1542
Kyushu

CHINA
Canton 1513
Macao 1517

PHILIPPINES

New Guinea

AUSTRALIA

1521

Tordesillas Line (1494)

Malacca 1509
Borneo
Moluccas
1511

Java

Sumatra

Ceylon 1505

INDIA
Goa 1510
Calicut 1498

SWAHILI COAST
INDIAN OCEAN

MADAGASCAR 1500

Ormuz 1507

PERSIA

Muscat
ARABIA
Aden 1513

1498

ETHIOPIA

Mombasa 1498
KONGO
Mozambique

AFRICA

ZIMBABWE

EUROPE
Amsterdam
Antwerp

Constantinople

Lisbon
Seville
Ceuta 1415

SAHARA

Timbuktu
Niani
MALI
GOLD COAST
BENIN

1498

1522

Cape of Good Hope

1497

1420–1460

Azores

Canary Is.
1492

Cape Verde Is. 1456

ATLANTIC OCEAN

1519

Rio de Janeiro 1516

1499

1483

GREENLAND

Newfoundland 1497

NORTH AMERICA

Cuba 1492
Jamaica
HONDURAS
Mexico City 1519
AZTEC EMPIRE

San Salvador 1492
Puerto Rico
Hispaniola 1492
Trinidad 1498
Cartagena
Panama

Quito 1534
Lima 1535
PERU
INCA EMPIRE

SOUTH AMERICA

BRAZIL

Potosí

Santiago
Buenos Aires 1535

Strait of Magellan

Cape Horn

1520

PACIFIC OCEAN

Tordesillas Line (1494)

Portuguese explorers

→ During Henry the Navigator's reign
–·–· Dias
–··–·· Da Gama

Spanish explorers

Columbus
Vespucci
Magellan

0   1500   3000 Km.
0   1500   3000 Mi.

**Columbus Prepares to Cross the Atlantic, 1492**   This later representation shows Columbus with the ships, soldiers, priests, and seamen that were part of Spain's enterprise.   (G. Dagli Orti/The Art Archive)

Columbus had learned about winds blowing westward at the latitude of the Canaries. After reaching the Canaries, he replaced the *Niña*'s lateen sails with square sails, for he knew that from then on, speed would be more important than maneuverability since his supplies would last for only a fixed number of days.

In October, the expedition encountered the islands of the Caribbean. Columbus called the in-

**Map 14.2   European Exploration, 1420–1542**   Portuguese and Spanish explorers showed the possibility and practicality of intercontinental maritime trade. Before 1540 European trade with Africa and Asia was much more important than that with the Americas, but after the Spanish conquest of the Aztec and Inca Empires transatlantic trade began to increase. Notice the Tordesillas line, which in theory separated the Spanish and Portuguese spheres of activity.

habitants "Indians" because he believed he had reached the East Indies. A second voyage in 1493 did nothing to change his mind. On a third voyage in 1498, two months after Vasco da Gama reached India, Columbus sighted the mainland of South America, which he insisted was part of Asia. But by then, other Europeans had become convinced that his discoveries were of lands previously unknown to the Old World (Europe, Asia, and Africa). Amerigo Vespucci's explorations, first on behalf of Spain and then for Portugal, led mapmakers to name the new continents "America," after him.

To prevent disputes about exploiting these new lands and spreading Christianity among their peoples, Spain and Portugal agreed to split the world between them. Modifying an earlier papal proposal, the Treaty of Tordesillas°, negotiated

---

**Tordesillas** (tor-duh-SEE-yuhs)

by the pope in 1494, drew an imaginary north-south line down the middle of the Atlantic Ocean. Lands east of the line in Africa and southern Asia could be claimed by Portugal; lands to the west in the Americas belonged to Spain. Cabral's discovery of Brazil, however, gave Portugal a valid claim to the part of South America that bulged east of the line.

But if the Tordesillas line were extended around the earth, where would Spain's and Portugal's spheres of influence divide in the East? Given European ignorance of the earth's true size in 1494, no one knew whether the Moluccas°, the source of the valuable spices of the East Indies, belonged to Portugal or Spain. The missing information concerned the size of the Pacific Ocean, which a Spanish adventurer named Vasco Núñez de Balboa° had spotted in 1513 when he crossed the isthmus (a narrow neck of land) of Panama from the east. The 1519 expedition of **Ferdinand Magellan** (ca. 1480–1521) sought to complete Columbus's interrupted westward voyage by sailing around the Americas and across the Pacific. The Moluccas turned out to lie well within Portugal's sphere, as Spain formally acknowledged in 1529.

Magellan's voyage laid the basis for Spanish colonization of the Philippine Islands after 1564. It also gave Magellan credit, despite his death, for being the first person to encircle the globe, for a decade earlier, he had sailed from Europe to the East Indies on an expedition sponsored by his native Portugal.

Columbus and those who followed in his path laid the basis for the colonial empires of Spain and other European nations. In turn, these empires promoted, among the four Atlantic continents, a new trading network whose importance rivaled and eventually surpassed that of the Indian Ocean. Of more immediate importance, Portugal's entry into the Indian Ocean led quickly to a major European presence and profit. Both the eastward and the westward voyages of exploration marked a tremendous expansion of Europe's role in world history.

---

Moluccas (muh-LOO-kuhz)   Balboa (bal-BOH-uh)

# ENCOUNTERS WITH EUROPE, 1450–1550

The ways in which Africans, Asians, and Amerindians perceived their European visitors and interacted with them influenced their future relations. Some welcomed the Europeans as potential allies; others viewed them as rivals or enemies. In general, Africans and Asians readily recognized the benefits and dangers of European contact. However, the long isolation of the Amerindians added to the strangeness of their encounter with the Spanish and made them more vulnerable to the unfamiliar diseases the Spanish inadvertently introduced.

## Western Africa

Many Africans welcomed trade with the Portuguese, which gave them new markets for their exports and access to imports cheaper than those coming by caravan across the Sahara. Miners in the hinterland of the Gold Coast, which the Portuguese first visited in 1471, had long sold their gold to merchants from trading cities along the southern edge of the Sahara for transshipment to North Africa. Recognizing the possibility of more favorable trading terms, coastal Africans negotiated with the royal representative of Portugal, who arrived in 1482 seeking permission to erect a trading fort.

The Portuguese noble in charge and his officers (likely including the young Christopher Columbus, who had entered Portuguese service in 1476) strove to make a proper impression. They dressed in their best clothes, erected a fancy reception platform, celebrated a Catholic Mass, and signaled the start of negotiations with trumpets, tambourines, and drums. The African king, Caramansa, staged his entrance with equal ceremony, arriving with a large retinue of attendants and musicians. Through an African interpreter, the two leaders exchanged flowery speeches pledging goodwill and mutual benefit. Caramansa then gave permission for a small trading fort, assured, he said, by the appearance of these royal delegates that they were honorable persons, unlike the "few, foul, and vile" Portuguese visitors of the previous decade.

Neither side made a show of force, but Caramansa warned that if the Portuguese failed to be peaceful and honest traders, he and his people would move away and deprive their post of food and trade. Trade at the post of Saint George of the Mine (later called Elmina) enriched both sides. The Portuguese crown was soon purchasing gold amounting to one-tenth of the world's production at the time. In return, Africans received shiploads of goods brought by the Portuguese from Asia, Europe, and other parts of Africa.

Early contacts involved a mixture of commercial, military, and religious interests. Some African rulers quickly saw the value of European firearms. Coastal rulers also proved willing to test the value of Christian practices, which the Portuguese eagerly promoted. The rulers of Benin and Kongo, the largest coastal kingdoms, invited Portuguese missionaries and soldiers to accompany them into battle to test the Christians' religion along with their muskets (see Diversity and Dominance: Kongo's Christian King).

The kingdom of Benin in the Niger Delta, near the peak of its power after a century of aggressive expansion, had a large capital city, also known as Benin. Its *oba* (king) responded to a Portuguese visit in 1486 by sending an ambassador to Portugal to learn more about their homeland. Then he established a royal monopoly on Portuguese trade, selling pepper and ivory tusks (to be taken back to Portugal) as well as stone beads, textiles, and prisoners of war (to be resold at Elmina). In return, Portuguese merchants provided Benin with copper and brass, fine textiles, glass beads, and a horse for the king's royal procession. In the early sixteenth century, as the demand for slaves for the Portuguese sugar plantations on the nearby island of São Tomé grew, the oba first raised the price of slaves and then imposed restrictions on their sale.

Efforts to spread Catholicism ultimately failed. Early kings showed some interest, but after 1538, the rulers declined to receive further missionaries. They also closed the market in male slaves for the rest of the sixteenth century. Both steps illustrate their power to control how much interaction they wanted.

Farther south, on the lower Congo River, the *manikongo°* (king) of Kongo also sent delegates to

---

*manikongo* (mah-NEE-KONG-goh)

**Afro-Portuguese Ivory** A skilled ivory carver from the kingdom of Benin probably made this saltcellar. Intended for a European market, it depicts a Portuguese ship on the cover and Portuguese nobles around the base. However European the subject, the craftsmanship is typical of Benin. (Courtesy of the Trustees of the British Museum)

Portugal, established a royal monopoly on trade, and expressed interest in missionary teachings. But here the royal family made Catholicism the kingdom's official faith. Lacking ivory and pepper, Kongo sold more and more slaves to acquire the goods brought by the Portuguese and to pay missionary expenses.

Soon the royal trade monopoly broke down. In 1526, the Christian manikongo, Afonso I (r. 1506–ca. 1540), wrote to his royal "brother," the king of Portugal, begging for his help in stopping the slave trade

# DIVERSITY AND DOMINANCE

## KONGO'S CHRISTIAN KING

*T*he new overseas voyages brought conquest to some and opportunities for fruitful borrowings and exchanges to others. The decision of the ruler of the kingdom of Kongo to adopt Christianity in 1491 added cultural diversity to Kongolese society and in some ways strengthened the hand of the king. From then on Kongolese rulers sought to introduce Christian beliefs and rituals while at the same time Africanizing Christianity to make it more intelligible to their subjects. In addition, the kings of Kongo sought a variety of more secular aid from Portugal, including schools and medicine. Trade with the Portuguese introduced new social and political tensions, especially in the case of the export trade in slaves for the Portuguese sugar plantations on the island of São Tomé to the north.

Two letters sent to King João (zhwao) III of Portugal in 1526 illustrate how King Afonso of Kongo saw his kingdom's new relationship with Portugal and the problems that resulted from it. (Afonso adopted that name when he was baptized as a young prince.) After the death of his father in 1506, Afonso successfully claimed the throne and ruled until 1542. His son Henrique became the first Catholic bishop of the Kongo in 1521.

These letters were written in Portuguese and penned by the king's secretary João Teixera (tay-SHER-uh), a Kongo Christian, who, like Afonso, had been educated by Portuguese missionaries.

6 July 1526

To the very powerful and excellent prince Dom João, our brother:

On the 20th of June just past, we received word that a trading ship from your highness had just come to our port of Sonyo. We were greatly pleased by that arrival for it had been many days since a ship had come to our kingdom, for by it we would get news of your highness, which many times we had desired to know, . . . and likewise as there was a great and dire need for wine and flour for the holy sacrament; and of this we had had no great hope for we have the same need frequently. And that, sir, arises from the great negligence of your highness's officials toward us and toward shipping us those things. . . .

Sir, your highness should know how our kingdom is being lost in so many ways that we will need to provide the needed cure, since this is caused by the excessive license given by your agents and officials to the men and merchants who come to this kingdom to set up shops with goods and many things which have been prohibited by us, and which they spread throughout our kingdoms and domains in such abundance that many of our vassals, whose submission we could once rely on, now act independently so as to get the things in greater abundance than we ourselves; whom we had formerly held content and submissive and under our vassalage and jurisdiction, so it is doing a great harm not only to the service of God, but also to the security and peace of our kingdoms and state.

And we cannot reckon how great the damage is, since every day the mentioned merchants are taking our people, sons of the land and the sons of our noblemen and vassals and our relatives, because the thieves and men of bad conscience grab them so as to have the things and wares of this kingdom that they crave; they grab them and bring them to be sold. In such a manner, sir, has been the corruption and deprivation that our land is becoming completely depopulated, and your highness should not deem this good nor in your service. And to avoid this we need from these kingdoms [of yours] no more than priests and a few people to teach in schools, and no other goods except wine and flour for the holy sacrament, which is why we beg of your highness to help and assist us in this matter. Order your agents to send here neither merchants nor wares, because it is our will that in these kingdoms there should not be any dealing in slaves nor outlet for them, for the reasons stated above. Again we beg your highness's agreement, since otherwise we cannot cure such manifest harm. May Our Lord in His mercy have your highness always under His protection and may you always do the things of His holy service. I kiss your hands many times.

From our city of Kongo. . . .

The King, Dom Afonso


18 October 1526

Very high and very powerful prince King of Portugal, our brother,

Sir, your highness has been so good as to promise us that anything we need we should ask for in our letters, and that everything will be provided. And so that there may be peace and health of our kingdoms, by God's will, in our lifetime. And as there are among us old folks and people who have lived for many days, many and different diseases happen so often that we are pushed to the ultimate extremes. And the same happens to our children, relatives, and people, because this country lacks physicians and surgeons who might know the proper cures for such diseases, as well as pharmacies and drugs to make them better. And for this reason many of those who had been already confirmed and instructed in the things of the holy faith of Our Lord Jesus Christ perish and die. And the rest of the people for the most part cure themselves with herbs and sticks and other ancient methods, so that they live putting all their faith in these herbs and ceremonies, and die believing that they are saved; and this serves God poorly.

And to avoid such a great error, I think, and inconvenience, since it is from God and from your highness that all the good and the drugs and medicines have come to us for our salvation, we ask your merciful highness to send us two physicians and two pharmacists and one surgeon, so that they may come with their pharmacies and neces-

sary things to be in our kingdoms, for we have extreme need of each and every one of them. We will be very good and merciful to them, since sent by your highness, their work and coming should be for good. We ask your highness as a great favor to do this for us, because besides being good in itself it is in the service of God as we have said above.

Moreover, sir, in our kingdoms there is another great inconvenience which is of little service to God, and this is that many of our people, out of great desire for the wares and things of your kingdoms, which are brought here by your people, and in order to satisfy their disordered appetite, seize many of our people, freed and exempt men. And many times noblemen and the sons of noblemen, and our relatives are stolen, and they take them to be sold to the white men who are in our kingdoms and take them hidden or by night, so that they are not recognized. And as soon as they are taken by the white men, they are immediately ironed and branded with fire. And when they are carried off to be embarked, if they are caught by our guards, the whites allege that they have bought them and cannot say from whom, so that it is our duty to do justice and to restore to the free their freedom. And so they went away offended.

And to avoid such a great evil we passed a law so that every white man living in our kingdoms and wanting to purchase slaves by whatever means should first inform three of our noblemen and officials of our court on whom we rely in this matter, namely Dom Pedro Manipunzo and Dom Manuel Manissaba, our head bailiff, and Gonçalo Pires, our chief supplier, who should investigate if the said slaves are captives or free men, and, if cleared with them, there will be no further doubt nor embargo and they can be taken and embarked. And if they reach the opposite conclusion, they will lose the aforementioned slaves. Whatever favor and license we give them [the white men] for the sake of your highness in this case is because we know that it is in your service too that these slaves are taken from our kingdom; otherwise we should not consent to this for the reasons stated above that we make known completely to your highness so that no one could say the contrary, as they said in many other cases to your highness, so that the care and remembrance that we and this kingdom have should not be withdrawn. . . .

We kiss your hands of your highness many times.

From our city of Kongo, the 18th day of October,

The King, Dom Afonso

## QUESTIONS FOR ANALYSIS

1. What sorts of things does King Afonso desire from the Portuguese?
2. What is he willing and unwilling to do in return?

3. What problem with his own people has the slave trade created, and what has King Afonso done about it?
4. Does King Afonso see himself as an equal to King João or his subordinate? Do you agree with that analysis?

Source: From António Brásio, ed., *Monumenta Missionaria Africana: Africa Ocidental (1471–1531)* (Lisbon: Agência Geral do Ultramar, 1952), I:468, 470–471, 488–491. Translated by David Northrup.

because unauthorized Kongolese were kidnapping and selling people, even members of good families. Afonso's appeal that contacts be limited to "some priests and a few people to teach in the schools, and no other goods except wine and flour for the holy sacrament" received no reply. After 1540, the major part of the slave trade from this part of Africa moved farther south.

### Eastern Africa

As Vasco da Gama sailed up the eastern coast of Africa in 1498, most rulers of the coastal trading states received him coolly. Visitors who painted crusader crosses on their sails raised their suspicions. The ruler of Malindi, however, saw in the Portuguese an ally who could help him expand Malindi's trade, and he provided da Gama with a pilot to guide him to India. The suspicions of most rulers came to fruition seven years later when a Portuguese war fleet bombarded and looted most of the coastal cities in the name of Christ and commerce. It spared Malindi.

Christian Ethiopia also saw benefits in allying with the Portuguese. In the fourteenth and fifteenth centuries, Ethiopian conflicts with Muslim states along the Red Sea increased. After the Ottoman Turks conquered Egypt and launched a fleet in the Indian Ocean to counter the Portuguese in 1517, the warlord of the Muslim state of Adal attacked Ethiopia. A decisive victory in 1529 put the Christian kingdom in jeopardy, making Portuguese support a crucial matter.

For decades, delegations from Portugal and Ethiopia had talked of a Christian alliance. Queen Helena of Ethiopia, who acted as regent for her young sons after her husband's death in 1478, sent a letter in 1509 to "our very dear and well-beloved brother," the king of Portugal, along with a gift of two tiny crucifixes said to be made of wood from the cross on which Christ was crucified. She proposed to combine her land army and Portugal's fleet against the Turks. At her death in 1522, no alliance had come into being, but the worsening situation brought renewed Ethiopian appeals.

Finally, a small Portuguese force commanded by Vasco da Gama's son Christopher reached Ethiopia in 1539. With Portuguese help, another queen rallied the desperate Ethiopians. Muslim foes captured Christopher da Gama and tortured him to death but lost heart when their leader fell in battle. Portuguese aid helped save the Ethiopian kingdom from extinction, but Ethiopia's refusal to transfer their Christian affiliation from the patriarch of Alexandria to the pope prevented a permanent alliance.

As these examples illustrate, African encounters with the Portuguese before 1550 varied considerably. Africans and Portuguese might become royal brothers, bitter opponents, or partners in a mutually profitable trade, but Europeans were still a minor presence in most of Africa in 1550. The

Indian Ocean trade by then was occupying most of their attention.

## Indian Ocean States

Vasco da Gama's arrival on the Malabar Coast of India in May 1498 did not impress the citizens of Calicut. The Chinese fleets of gigantic junks that had called at Calicut sixty-five years earlier dwarfed his four small ships, which were no larger than many of the dhows° already filling the harbor. The *samorin* (ruler) of Calicut and his Muslim officials showed mild interest, but the gifts da Gama brought evoked derisive laughter: twelve pieces of striped cloth, four scarlet hoods, six hats, and six wash basins. When da Gama defended his gifts as those of an explorer, not a merchant, the samorin cut him short, asking whether he had come to discover men or stones: "If he had come to discover men, as he said, why had he brought nothing?"

Coastal rulers soon discovered that the Portuguese had no intention of remaining poor competitors in the Indian Ocean trade. Upon da Gama's return to Portugal in 1499, the jubilant King Manuel styled himself "Lord of the Conquest, Navigation, and Commerce of Ethiopia, Arabia, Persia, and India." Previously, the Indian Ocean had been an open sea, used by merchants (and pirates) of all the surrounding coasts. Now the Portuguese crown intended to make it Portugal's sea, which others might use only on Portuguese terms.

Portugal's hope of controlling the Indian Ocean stemmed from the superiority of its ships and weapons over the smaller and lightly armed merchant dhows. In 1505, the Portuguese fleet of 81 ships and some 7,000 men bombarded Swahili Coast cities. Goa, on the west coast of India, fell to a well-armed fleet in 1510, becoming the base from which the Portuguese menaced the trading cities of Gujarat° to the north and Calicut and other Malabar Coast cities to the south. The port of Hormuz, controlling the entry to the Persian Gulf, fell in 1515. Aden, at the entrance to the Red Sea, preserved its independence, but the capture of the Gujarati port of Diu in 1535 consolidated Portuguese dominance of the western Indian Ocean.

Farther east, the independent city of Malacca° on the strait separating the Malay Peninsula and Sumatra became the focus of their attention. During the fifteenth century, Malacca had become the main entrepôt° (a place where goods are stored or deposited and from which they are distributed) for the trade from China, Japan, India, the Southeast Asian mainland, and the Moluccas. The city's 100,000 residents spoke eighty-four different languages, according to a Portuguese source, and included merchants from Cairo, Ethiopia, and the Swahili Coast. Many non-Muslim residents supported letting the Portuguese join this cosmopolitan trading community, perhaps to offset the growing solidarity of Muslim traders. In 1511, however, the Portuguese seized Malacca with a force of a thousand fighting men, including three hundred recruited in southern India.

On the China coast, local officials and merchants persuaded the imperial government to allow the Portuguese to establish a trading post at Macao° in 1557. Subsequently, Portuguese ships nearly monopolized trade between China and Japan.

Control of the major port cities enabled the Portuguese to enforce their demands that all spices be carried in Portuguese ships, as well as all goods on the major ocean routes such as between Goa and Macao. The Portuguese also tried to control and tax other Indian Ocean trade. Merchant ships entering and leaving their ports had to carry a Portuguese passport and pay customs duties. Portuguese patrols seized vessels that did not comply, confiscated their cargoes, and either killed the captain and crew or sentenced them to forced labor.

Reactions to this power grab varied. Like the emperors of China, the Mughal° emperors of India largely ignored Portugal's maritime intrusions. The Ottomans confronted the Christian intruders more aggressively. They supported Egypt's defensive efforts from 1501 to 1509 and then sent their own fleet into the Indian Ocean in 1538. However, Ottoman galleys proved no match for the faster, better-armed Portuguese vessels in the open ocean. They retained their advantage only in the Red Sea and Persian Gulf, where they controlled many ports.

---

**dhow** (dow)   **Gujarat** (goo-juh-RAHT)

**Malacca** (muh-LAH-kuh)   **entrepôt** (ON-truh-poh)
**Macao** (muh-COW)   **Mughal** (MOO-gahl)

Smaller trading states could not challenge the Portuguese. Mutual rivalry kept them from forming a common front. Some cooperated with the Portuguese to safeguard their prosperity and security. Others engaged in evasion and resistance.

When the merchants of Calicut put up sustained resistance, the Portuguese embargoed all trade with Aden, Calicut's principal trading partner, and centered their trade on the port of Cochin, which had once been a dependency of Calicut. Some Calicut merchants evaded their patrols, but Calicut's importance shrank as Cochin gradually became the major pepper-exporting port on the Malabar Coast.

Farther north, Gujarat initially resisted Portuguese attempts at monopoly and in 1509 joined Egypt's futile effort to sweep the Portuguese from the Arabian Sea. But in 1535, with his state weakened by Mughal attacks, the ruler allowed the Portuguese to build a fort at Diu in return for their support. Once established, the Portuguese gradually extended their control. By midcentury, they were licensing and taxing all Gujarati ships. Even after the Mughals took control of Gujarat in 1572, the Mughal emperor, Akbar, permitted the Portuguese to continue their maritime monopoly in return for allowing one pilgrim ship a year to sail to Mecca without paying a fee.

The Portuguese never gained complete control of the Indian Ocean trade, but their domination of key ports and trade routes brought them considerable profit in the form of spices and other luxury goods. The Portuguese broke the trading monopoly of Venice and Genoa by selling pepper for less than what they charged for shipments obtained through Egyptian middlemen.

## The Americas

In the Americas, the Spanish established a vast territorial empire, in contrast to the trading empire of the Portuguese. The Spanish kingdoms drew on somewhat greater resources, but the Spanish and Portuguese monarchies had similar motives for expansion and used identical ships and weapons. The isolation of the Amerindian peoples provided a key difference. The first European settlers in the Caribbean resorted to conquest and plunder rather than trade. They later extended this practice to the more powerful Amerindian kingdoms on the American mainland. After 1518, deadly epidemics among the Amerindians weakened their ability to resist.

The Arawak whom Columbus first encountered on Hispaniola (modern Haiti and the Dominican Republic) in the Greater Antilles and the Bahamas to the north cultivated maize (corn), cassava (a tuber), sweet potatoes, and hot peppers, as well as cotton and tobacco. They mined and worked gold, but they did not trade gold, nor did they have iron. They extended a cautious welcome to Columbus but told him exaggerated stories about gold in other places to persuade him to move on.

Columbus brought with him several hundred settlers from southern Iberia, as well as missionaries, on his second trip to Hispaniola in 1493. The settlers stole gold ornaments, confiscated food, and raped women, provoking the Hispaniola Arawak to war in 1495. With the advantage of horses and body armor, the Spaniards slaughtered tens of thousands of Arawak and forced the survivors to pay a heavy tax in gold, spun cotton, and food. Whoever failed to meet the quotas faced forced labor. Meanwhile, the cattle, pigs, and goats introduced by the settlers devoured the Arawak's food crops, causing deaths from famine and disease. A governor appointed by the Spanish crown in 1502 forced the Arawak on Hispaniola to become laborers under the control of Spanish settlers.

The actions of the Spanish in the Antilles reflected Spanish behavior during the wars against the Muslims in the previous centuries. They sought to serve God by defeating, controlling, and converting nonbelievers and to become rich in the process. Individual **conquistadors°** (conquerors) extended that pattern around the Caribbean. Some raided the Bahamas for gold and labor as both grew scarce on Hispaniola. Arawak from the Bahamas served as slaves on Hispaniola. Juan Ponce de León (1460–1521), a veteran of the conquest of Muslim Spain and the seizure of Hispaniola, conquered the island of Borinquen (Puerto Rico) in 1508 and in 1513 explored southeastern Florida.

An ambitious and ruthless nobleman, **Hernán Cortés°** (1485–1547), led the most audacious expedition to the mainland. Cortés left Cuba in 1519 with six hundred fighting men and most of the is-

conquistador (kon-KEY-stuh-dor)   Cortés (kor-TEZ)

land's weapons to assault the Mexican mainland in search of slaves and trade. Learning of the rich Aztec Empire in central Mexico, Cortés expanded on the American mainland the exploitation and conquest carried out in the Greater Antilles.

Many of the Amerindians whom the Aztecs had subjugated during the previous century resented the tribute, forced labor, and the large-scale human sacrifices to Aztec gods their rulers imposed on them. Consequently, some gave the Spanish their support as allies against the Aztecs. Like the Caribbean people, the mainland Amerindians had no precedent by which to judge these strangers. Later accounts suggest that some believed Cortés to be the legendary ruler Quetzalcoatl°, whose return to earth had been prophesied, and treated him with great deference.

Another consequence of millennia of isolation proved even more fatal: the lack of acquired immunity to Old World diseases. Smallpox, the most deadly of the early epidemics, appeared for the first time on the island of Hispaniola late in 1518. An infected member of the Cortés expedition then transmitted smallpox to Mexico in 1519, where it spread with deadly efficiency.

The Aztec emperor **Moctezuma**° II (r. 1502–1520) sent messengers to greet Cortés and determine whether he was god or man, friend or foe. Cortés advanced steadily toward the capital, Tenochtitlan°, overcoming Aztec opposition with cavalry charges and steel swords and gaining the support of discontented tributary peoples. When the Spaniards drew near, the emperor went out in a great procession, dressed in all his finery, to welcome Cortés with gifts and flower garlands.

Despite Cortés's initial promise of friendship, Moctezuma quickly found himself a prisoner in his own palace. The Spaniards looted his treasury, melting down its gold. Soon full-scale battle broke out. The Aztecs and their supporters briefly gained the upper hand. They destroyed half the Spanish force and four thousand of their Amerindian allies, sacrificing fifty-three Spanish prisoners and four horses to their gods and displaying their severed heads in rows on pikes. Reinforcements from Cuba enabled Cortés to regain the advantage. Smallpox,

**Death from Smallpox**   This Aztec drawing shows a healer attending smallpox victims. The little puffs coming from their mouths represent speech.   (Biblioteca Medicea Laurenziana. Photo: MicroFoto, Florence)

which weakened and killed more of the city's defenders than died in the fighting, also assisted his capture of Tenochtitlan in 1520. One source remembered that the disease "spread over the people as a great destruction."

After the capital fell, the conquistadors took over other parts of Mexico. Then some Spaniards began eyeing the Inca Empire, stretching nearly 3,000 miles (5,000 kilometers) south from the equator and containing half of the population in South America. The Inca had conquered the inhabitants of the Andes Mountains and the Pacific coast of South America during the previous century, and their rule was not fully accepted by the subjugated peoples.

The Inca rulers administered a well-organized empire with highly productive agriculture, exquisite stone cities (such as the capital, Cuzco), and rich gold and silver mines. The power of the Inca emperor rested on the belief that he was descended from the Sun God and on an efficient system of roads and messengers that kept him informed about major events. Yet at the end of the 1520s, before the Spanish had even been heard of, smallpox claimed countless lives, perhaps including the Inca emperor in 1530.

An even more devastating threat loomed: **Francisco Pizarro**° (ca. 1478–1541) and his motley band

---

Quetzalcoatl (ket-zahl-COH-ah-tal)   **Moctezuma** (mock-teh-ZOO-ma)   **Tenochtitlan** (teh-noch-TIT-lan)

**Pizarro** (pih-ZAHR-oh)

of 180 men, 37 horses, and 2 cannon. With limited education and some military experience, Pizarro had come to the Americas in 1502 at the age of twenty-five to seek his fortune. He had participated in the conquest of Hispaniola and in Balboa's expedition across the isthmus of Panama. By 1520 a wealthy landowner and official in Panama, he nevertheless gambled his fortune on exploring the Pacific coast to a point south of the equator, where he learned of the riches of the Inca. With a license from the king of Spain, he set out from Panama in 1531 to conquer them.

In November 1532, Pizarro arranged to meet the new Inca emperor, **Atahualpa°** (r. 1531–1533), near the Andean city of Cajamarca°. With supreme boldness and brutality, Pizarro's small band grabbed Atahualpa from a rich litter borne by eighty nobles as it passed through an enclosed courtyard. Though surrounded by an Inca army of at least 40,000, the Spaniards used their cannon to create confusion while their swords sliced the emperor's lightly armed retainers and servants to pieces.

Noting the glee with which the Spaniards seized gold, silver, and emeralds, the captive Atahualpa offered them what he thought would satisfy even the greediest among them in exchange for his freedom: a roomful of gold and silver. But after receiving 13,400 pounds (6,000 kilograms) of gold and 26,000 pounds (12,000 kilograms) of silver, the Spaniards gave Atahualpa a choice: being burned at the stake as a heathen or being strangled after a Christian baptism. He chose the latter. His death and the Spanish occupation broke the unity of the Inca Empire.

In 1533, the Spaniards took Cuzco and from there set out to conquer and loot the rest of the empire. The defeat of a final rebellion in 1536 spelled the end of Inca rule. Five years later, Pizarro himself met a violent death at the hands of Spanish rivals, but the conquest of the mainland continued. Incited by the fabulous wealth of the Aztecs and Inca, conquistadors extended Spanish conquest and exploration in South and North America, dreaming of new treasuries to loot.

---

Atahualpa (ah-tuh-WAHL-puh)  Cajamarca (kah-hah-MAHR-kah)

## Patterns of Dominance

Within fifty years of Columbus's first landing, the Spanish had located and occupied the major population centers of the Americas and penetrated many of the more thinly populated areas. Why did the peoples of the Americas suffer a fate so different from that of peoples in Africa and Asia? Why were the Spanish able to erect a vast land empire in the Americas so quickly?

First, unfamiliar illnesses devastated the Caribbean islands and then the mainland. Contemporaries estimated that between 25 and 50 percent of those infected with smallpox died. Repeated epidemics inhibited the Amerindians' ability to regain control. Estimates of the size of the population before Columbus's arrival, based on sparse evidence, vary widely. Yet historians agree that the Amerindian population fell sharply during the sixteenth century. The Americas became a "widowed land," open to resettlement from across the Atlantic.

A second factor was Spain's superior military technology. Steel swords, protective armor, and horses gave the Spaniards an advantage over their Amerindian opponents. Though few in number, muskets and cannon provided a psychological edge. However, the Spanish conquests depended heavily on large numbers of Amerindian allies armed with indigenous weapons. The most decisive military advantage may have been the no-holds-barred fighting techniques the Spaniards had developed during their wars at home.

The third factor in Spain's conquest was the precedent established by the reconquest of Granada in 1492: forced labor, forced conversion, and the incorporation of conquered lands into a new empire.

The same three factors help explain the different outcomes elsewhere. Centuries of contacts before 1500 meant that Europeans, Africans, and Asians shared the same Old World diseases. Only very isolated peoples in Africa and Asia suffered a demographic calamity. The Iberians enjoyed a military advantage at sea, but on land they had no decisive advantage against more numerous indigenous armies. Everywhere, Iberian religious zeal went hand in hand with a desire for riches. In Iberia and America, conquest itself brought wealth. But in

Africa and Asia, existing trading networks made wealth dependent on commercial domination rather than conquest.

## CONCLUSION

Historians consider the century between 1450 and 1550 a turning point in world history. Some assign names: the "Vasco da Gama epoch," the "Columbian era," the "age of Magellan," or simply the "modern period." During those years, European explorers opened new long-distance trade routes across the world's oceans, for the first time establishing regular contact among all the continents. By 1550, those who followed them had broadened trading contacts with sub-Saharan Africa, gained mastery of the Indian Ocean trade routes, and conquered a land empire in the Americas.

What gave this maritime revolution unprecedented importance had more to do with what happened after 1550 than with what happened earlier. European overseas empires would endure longer than the Mongols' and would continue to expand for three and a half centuries. Unlike the Chinese, the Europeans did not turn their backs on the world after an initial burst of exploration. Not content with dominating the Indian Ocean, Europeans opened in the Atlantic a maritime network of comparable wealth. They also established regular trade across the Pacific. The maritime expansion begun between 1450 and 1550 marked the beginning of an age of growing global interaction.

## ■ Key Terms

| | |
|---|---|
| Zheng He | Christopher Columbus |
| Arawak | Ferdinand Magellan |
| Henry the Navigator | conquistadors |
| caravel | Hernán Cortés |
| Gold Goast | Moctezuma |
| Bartolomeu Dias | Francisco Pizarro |
| Vasco da Gama | Atahualpa |

## ■ Suggested Reading

The selections edited by Joseph R. Levenson, *European Expansion and the Counter Example of Asia, 1300–1600*

(1967), describe Chinese expansion and Western impressions of China. Janet Abu-Lughod, *Before European Hegemony: The World System, A.D. 1250–1350* (1989), affords a speculative reassessment of the Mongols and the Indian Ocean trade in creating the modern world system; she summarizes her thesis in the American Historical Association (AHA) booklet *The World System in the Thirteenth Century: Dead-End or Precursor?* (1993).

The Chinese account of Zheng He's voyages is Ma Huan, *Ying-yai Sheng-lan: "The Overall Survey of the Ocean's Shores"* [1433], edited and translated by J. V. G. Mills (1970). On Polynesian expansion, see Jesse D. Jennings, ed., *The Prehistory of Polynesia* (1979). In it, the chapter "Voyaging," by Ben R. Finney, encapsulates his *Voyage of Rediscovery: A Cultural Odyssey Through Polynesia* (1994). Felipe Fernandez-Armesto, *Before Columbus: Exploration and Colonization from the Mediterranean to the Atlantic, 1229–1492* (1987), summarizes the medieval background to European intercontinental voyages. Tim Severin, *The Brendan Voyage* (2000), vividly recounts a modern retracing of even earlier Irish voyages.

For the technologies of European expansion, see Carlo M. Cipolla, *Guns, Sails, and Empires: Technological Innovation and the Early Phases of European Expansion, 1400–1700* (1965; reprint, 1985), or the more advanced study by Roger C. Smith, *Vanguard of Empire: Ships of Exploration in the Age of Columbus* (1993).

Surveys of European explorations based on contemporary records include Boies Penrose, *Travel and Discovery in the Age of the Renaissance, 1420–1620* (1952); J. H. Parry, *The Age of Reconnaissance: Discovery, Exploration, and Settlement, 1450–1650* (1963); and G. V. Scammell, *The World Encompassed: The First European Maritime Empires, c. 800–1650* (1981).

C. R. Boxer, *The Portuguese Seaborne Empire, 1415–1825* (1969), gives a general account, with more detail to be found in Bailey W. Diffie and George D. Winius, *Foundations of the Portuguese Empire, 1415–1580* (1977); A. J. R. Russell-Wood, *The Portuguese Empire: A World on the Move* (1998); and Luc Cuyvers, *Into the Rising Sun: The Journey of Vasco da Gama and the Discovery of the Modern World* (1998). John William Blake, ed., *Europeans in West Africa, 1450–1560* (1942), excerpts contemporary Portuguese, Castilian, and English sources. Elaine Sanceau, *The Life of Prester John: A Chronicle of Portuguese Exploration* (1941), covers Portuguese relations with Ethiopia. *The Summa Oriental of Tomé Pires: An Account of the East, from the Red Sea to Japan, Written in Malacca and India in 1512–1515*, translated by Armando Cortesão (1944), provides a firsthand account of the Portuguese in the Indian Ocean.

For Spanish expansion, see J. H. Parry, *The Spanish Seaborne Empire* (1967). Samuel Eliot Morison's excellent *Admiral of the Ocean Sea: A Life of Christopher Columbus* (1942) is available in an abridged version as *Christopher Columbus, Mariner* (1955). Tzvetan Todorov, *The Conquest of America,* translated by Richard Howard (1985), focuses on Spanish shortcomings. Marvin Lunenfeld, ed., *1492: Discovery, Invasion, Encounter* (1991), critically examines contemporary sources and interpretations. William D. Phillips and Carla Rhan Phillips, *The Worlds of Christopher Columbus* (1992), looks at the subject in terms of modern concerns. Peggy K. Liss, *Isabel the Queen: Life and Times* (1992), affords a sympathetic account. James Lockhart's *Men of Cajamarca: A Social and Biographical Study of the First Conquerors of Peru* (1972) contains biographies of Pizarro's men. A firsthand account of Magellan's expedition is Antonio Pigafetta, *Magellan's Voyage: A Narrative Account of the First Circumnavigation,* available in a two-volume edition (1969) that includes a facsimile reprint of the manuscript.

J. H. Elliott, *The Old World and the New, 1492–1650* (1970), describes the transatlantic encounters of Europe and the Americas. Alfred W. Crosby, *The Columbian Voyages, the Columbian Exchange, and Their Historians* (1987), available as an American Historical Association booklet, surveys the first encounters and their long-term consequences. Mark A. Burkholder and Lyman L. Johnson, *Colonial Latin America,* 2d ed. (1994), give a balanced account of the Spanish conquest.

David Northrup, *Africa's Discovery of Europe, 1450–1850* (2002), and John Thornton, *Africa and Africans in the Making of the Atlantic World, 1400–1800,* 2d ed. (1998), examine encounters with Europeans, Africa in the Atlantic economy, and African impact in the New World. *The Broken Spears: The Aztec Account of the Conquest of Mexico,* edited by Miguel Leon-Portilla (1962), presents Amerindian chronicles, as does Nathan Wachtel, *The Vision of the Vanquished: The Spanish Conquest of Peru Through Indian Eyes* (1977). Anthony Reid, *Southeast Asia in the Age of Commerce, 1450–1680,* 2 vols. (1988, 1993), deals with that region.

# ■ Notes

1. Ma Huan, *Ying-yai Sheng-lan: "The Overall Survey of the Ocean's Shores,"* ed. Feng Ch'eng-Chün, trans. J. V. G. Mills (Cambridge, England: Cambridge University Press, 1970), 180.
2. Alvise da Cadamosto in *The Voyages of Cadamosto and Other Documents,* ed. and trans. G. R. Crone (London: Hakluyt Society, 1937), 2.

# Climate and Population, to 1500

During the millennia before 1500 human populations expanded in three momentous surges. The first occurred after 50,000 B.C.E. when humans emigrated from their African homeland to all of the inhabitable continents. After that, the global population remained steady for several millennia. During the second expansion, between about 5000 and 500 B.C.E., population rose from about 5 million to 100 million as agricultural societies spread around the world (see Figure 1). Again population growth then slowed for several centuries before a third surge took world population to over 350 million by 1200 C.E. (see Figure 2).

For a long time historians tended to attribute these population surges to cultural and technological advances. Indeed, a great many changes in culture and technology are associated with adaptation to different climates and food supplies in the first surge and with the domestication of plants and animals in the second. However, historians have not found a cultural or technological change to explain the third surge, nor can they explain why creativity would have stagnated for long periods between the surges. Something else must have been at work.

Recently historians have begun to pay more attention to the impact of long-term variations in global climate. By examining ice cores drilled out of glaciers, scientists have been able to compile records of thousands of years of climate change. The comparative width of tree rings from ancient forests has provided additional data on periods of favorable and unfavorable growth. Such evidence shows that cycles of population growth and stagnation followed changes in global climate.

Historians now believe that global temperatures were above normal for extended periods from the late 1100s to the late 1200s C.E. In the temperate lands where most of the world's people lived, above-normal temperatures meant a longer growing season, more bountiful harvests, and thus a more adequate and reliable food supply. The ways in which societies responded to the medieval warm period are as important as the climate change, but it is unlikely that human agency alone would have produced the medieval surge. One notable response was that of the Vikings, who increased the size and range of their settlements in the North Atlantic, although their raids also caused death and destruction.

Some of the complexities involved in the interaction of human agency, climate, and other natural factors are also evident in the demographic changes that followed the medieval warm period. During the 1200s the Mongol invasions caused death and disruption of agriculture across Eurasia. China's population, which had been over 100 million in 1200, declined by a third or more by 1300. The Mongol invasions did not cause harm west of Russia, but climate changes in the 1300s resulted in population losses in Europe. Unusually heavy rains caused crop failures and a prolonged famine in northern Europe from 1315 to 1319.

The freer movement of merchants within the Mongol empire also facilitated the spread of disease across Eurasia, culminating in the great pandemic known as the Black Death in Europe. The demographic recovery underway in China was reversed. The even larger population losses in Europe may have been affected by the decrease in global temperatures to their lowest point in many millennia between 1350 and 1375. Improving economic conditions enabled population to recover more rapidly in Europe after 1400 than in China, where the conditions of rural life remained harsh.

Because many other historical circumstances interact with changing weather patterns, historians have a long way to go in deciphering the role of climate in history. Nevertheless, it is a factor that can no longer be ignored.

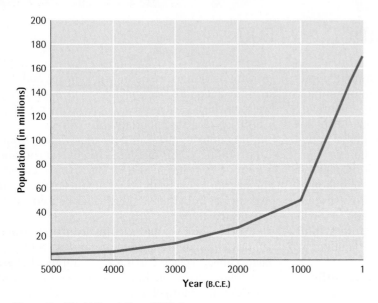

**Figure 1** World Population, 5000–1 B.C.E.

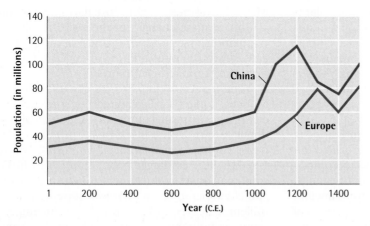

**Figure 2** Population in China and Europe, 1–1500 C.E.

## PART FIVE

# The Globe Encompassed, 1500–1800

CHAPTER 15
Transformations in Europe, 1500–1750

CHAPTER 16
The Americas, the Atlantic, and Africa, 1530–1770

CHAPTER 17
Southwest Asia and the Indian Ocean, 1500–1750

CHAPTER 18
Northern Eurasia, 1500–1800

The decades between 1500 and 1800 witnessed a tremendous expansion of commercial, cultural, and biological exchanges around the world. New long-distance sea routes linked Europe with sub-Saharan Africa and the existing maritime networks of the Indian Ocean and East Asia. Spanish and Portuguese voyages ended the isolation of the Americas and created new webs of exchange in the Atlantic and Pacific. Overland expansion of Muslim, Russian, and Chinese empires also increased global interaction.

These expanding contacts had major demographic and cultural consequences. In the Americas, European diseases devastated the Amerindian population, facilitating the establishment of large Spanish, Portuguese, French, and British empires. Europeans introduced enslaved Africans to relieve the labor shortage. Immigrant Africans and Europeans brought new languages, religious practices, music, and forms of personal adornment.

In Asia and Africa, by contrast, the most important changes owed more to internal forces than to European actions. The Portuguese seized control of some important trading ports and networks in the Indian Ocean and pioneered new contacts with China and Japan. In time, the Dutch, French, and English expanded these profitable connections, but in 1750 Europeans were still primarily a maritime force. Asians and Africans generally retained control of their lands and participated freely in overseas trade.

The Islamic world saw the expansion of the Ottoman Empire in the Middle East and the establishment of the Safavid Empire in Iran and the Mughal Empire in South Asia. In northern Eurasia, Russia and China acquired vast new territories and populations, while a new national government in Japan promoted economic development and stemmed foreign influence.

Ecological change was rapid in areas of rising population and economic activity. Forests were cut down to meet the increasing need for farmland, timber, and fuel. Population growth in parts of Eurasia placed great strain on the environment. On a more positive note, domesticated animals and crops from the Old World transformed agriculture in the Americas, while Amerindian foods such as the potato became staples of the diet of the Old World.

New goods, new wealth, and new tastes from overseas transformed Europe in this period. Global and regional trade promoted urban growth, but conflict was also rife. States spent heavily on warfare in Europe and abroad. The printing press spread new religious and scientific ideas, and challenges to established values and institutions.

By 1750 the balance of power in the world had begun to shift from the East to the West. The Ottoman, Mughal, and Chinese empires had declined in relative strength compared to the much smaller but technologically more sophisticated states of northwestern Europe.

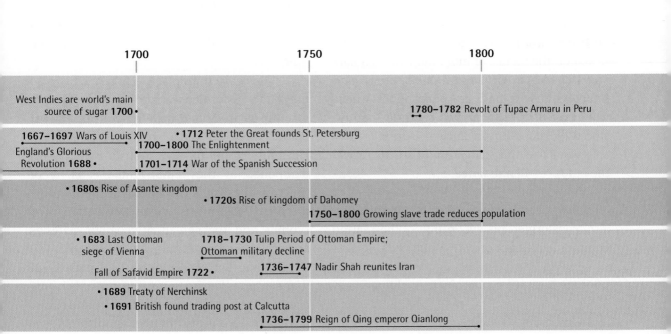

| 1700 | 1750 | 1800 |
|---|---|---|

West Indies are world's main source of sugar **1700** •

**1780–1782** Revolt of Tupac Armaru in Peru

**1667–1697** Wars of Louis XIV • **1712** Peter the Great founds St. Petersburg

England's Glorious Revolution **1688** • **1700–1800** The Enlightenment

**1701–1714** War of the Spanish Succession

• **1680s** Rise of Asante kingdom

• **1720s** Rise of kingdom of Dahomey

**1750–1800** Growing slave trade reduces population

• **1683** Last Ottoman siege of Vienna

**1718–1730** Tulip Period of Ottoman Empire; Ottoman military decline

Fall of Safavid Empire **1722** •

**1736–1747** Nadir Shah reunites Iran

• **1689** Treaty of Nerchinsk

• **1691** British found trading post at Calcutta

**1736–1799** Reign of Qing emperor Qianlong

# 15 Transformations in Europe, 1500–1750

**CHAPTER OUTLINE**
**Culture and Ideas**
**Social and Economic Life**
**Political Innovations**
ENVIRONMENT AND TECHNOLOGY: Mapping the World

As he neared the end of his life in 1575, the French scholar and humanist Loys Le Roy° reflected on the times in which he lived. It was, he believed, a golden age for Europe, and he ticked off the names of more than 130 scholars and translators, writers and poets, artists and sculptors, and explorers and philosophers whose work over the preceding two centuries had restored the standards of ancient learning. Later ages would call this scholarly and artistic revival the European **Renaissance**.

In addition, Le Roy enumerated a series of technological innovations that he believed had also transformed his age: printing, the marine compass, and cannonry. He put printing first because its rapid spread across Europe had done so much to communicate the literary and scholarly revival. The marine compass had made possible the sea voyages that now connected Europe directly to Africa and Asia and had led to the discovery and conquest of the Americas.

Le Roy gave third place to firearms because they had transformed warfare. Cannon and more recently devised hand-held weapons had swept before them all older military instruments. His enthusiasm for this transformation was dampened by the demonstrated capacity of firearms to cause devastation and ruin. Among the other evils of his age Le Roy enumerated syphilis and the spread of religious heresies and sects.

Reading Loys Le Roy's analysis more than four centuries later, one is struck not only by the acuity of his judgment and the beauty and clarity of his prose, but also by the astonishing geo-

**Loys Le Roy** (lwa-EES le-RWAH)

graphical and historical range of his understanding. He credits both ancient and modern Greeks and Italians for their cultural contributions, the Germans for their role in perfecting printing and cannonry, and the Spanish for their overseas voyages. But his frame of reference is not confined to Europe. He cites the mathematical skills of ancient Egyptians; the military conquests of Mongols, Turks, and Persians (Iranians); Arabs' contributions to science and medicine; and China's contributions to the development of printing.

The global framework of Le Roy's analysis led him to conclude that he was living at a turning point in world history. For long centuries, he argued, the military might of the Mongols and Turks had threatened the peoples of Europe, and Safavid Iran and Mamluk Egypt had surpassed any European land in riches. Now the West was in the ascendancy. Europeans' military might equaled that of their Middle Eastern neighbors. They were amassing new wealth from Asian trade and American silver. Most of all, the explosion of learning and knowledge had given Europe intellectual equality and perhaps superiority. Le Roy noted perceptively that while printing presses were in use all across Europe, the Islamic world had closed itself off from the benefits of this new technology, refusing to allow presses to be set up and even forbidding the printing of Arabic works about their lands in Europe.

As you read this chapter, ask yourself these questions:

- How perceptive was Loys Le Roy about his own age and its place in world history?

- How much did learning, printing, and firearms define early modern Europe?

- Would someone from a lower social station in Europe share Le Roy's optimism about this era?

# CULTURE AND IDEAS

One place to observe the conflict and continuity of early modern Europe is in the world of ideas. Theological controversies broke the religious unity of the Latin Church and contributed to violent wars. A huge witch scare showed the power of Christian beliefs about the Devil and of traditional folklore about malevolent powers. The influence of classical ideas from Greco-Roman antiquity increased among better-educated people, but some thinkers challenged the authority of the ancients. Their new models of the motion of the planets encouraged others to challenge traditional social and political systems, with important implications for the period after 1750. Each of these events had its own causes, but the technology of the printing press enhanced the impact of all.

## Religious Reformation

In 1500 the **papacy,** the central government of Latin Christianity, was simultaneously gaining stature and suffering from corruption and dissent. Larger donations and tax receipts let popes fund ambitious construction projects in Rome, their capital city. During the sixteenth century Rome gained fifty-four new churches and other buildings, which showcased the artistic Renaissance then under way. However, the church's wealth and power also attracted ambitious men, including some whose personal lives became the source of scandal.

The jewel of the building projects was the new Saint Peter's Basilica in Rome. The unprecedented size and splendor of this church were intended to glorify God and enhance the standing of the papacy. Such a project required refined tastes and vast sums of money.

The skillful overseer of the design and financing of the new Saint Peter's was Pope Leo X (r. 1513–1521), a member of the wealthy Medici° family of Florence, famous for its patronage of the arts. Pope Leo's artistic taste was superb and his personal life free from scandal, but he was more a man of action than a spiritual leader. One

**Medici** (MED-ih-chee)

technique that he used to raise funds for the basilica was to authorize an **indulgence**—a forgiveness of the punishment due for past sins, granted by church authorities as a reward for a pious act such as making a pilgrimage, saying a particular prayer, or making a donation to a religious cause.

A young professor of sacred scripture, Martin Luther (1483–1546), objected to the way the new indulgence was preached. As the result of a powerful religious experience, Luther had forsaken money and marriage for a monastic life of prayer, self-denial, and study. He found personal consolation in a passage in Saint Paul's Epistle to the Romans stating that salvation came not from "doing certain things" but from religious faith. That passage also led Luther to object to the way the indulgence preachers appeared to emphasize giving money more than the faith behind the act. He wrote to Pope Leo, asking him to stop this abuse, and challenged the preachers to a debate on the theology of indulgences.

This theological dispute escalated into a contest between two strong-minded men. Largely ignoring Luther's theological objections, Pope Leo regarded his letter as a challenge to papal power and moved to silence him. During a debate in 1519, a papal representative led Luther into open disagreement with some church doctrines, for which the papacy condemned him. Unable to reform the church from within, Luther burned the papal bull (document) of condemnation, rejecting the pope's authority and beginning the movement known as the **Protestant Reformation.**

Accusing those whom he called "Romanists" (Roman Catholics) of relying on "good works," Luther insisted that the only way to salvation was through faith in Jesus Christ. He further declared that Christian belief must be based on the word of God in the Bible and on Christian tradition, not on the authority of the pope, as Catholics held. Eventually his conclusions led him to abandon his monastic prayers and penances and to marry a former nun.

Today Roman Catholics and Lutherans have resolved many of their theological differences, but in the sixteenth century stubbornness on both sides made reconciliation impossible. Moreover, Luther's use of the printing press to promote his ideas won him the support of powerful Germans, who responded to his nationalist portrayal of the dispute as an effort of an Italian pope to beautify his city with German funds.

Inspired by Luther's denunciation of church corruption, leaders elsewhere called for a return to authentic Christian practices and beliefs. John Calvin (1509–1564), a Frenchman who turned from the study of law to theology after experiencing a religious conversion, became a highly influential Protestant leader. As a young man, Calvin published *The Institutes of the Christian Religion,* a masterful synthesis of Christian teachings, in 1535. Calvin's teaching differed from that of Roman Catholics and Lutherans in two respects. First, while agreeing with Luther's emphasis on faith over works, Calvin denied that even human faith could merit salvation. Salvation, said Calvin, was a gift God gave to those He "predestined" for salvation. Second, Calvin went farther than Luther in curtailing the power of a clerical hierarchy and in simplifying religious rituals. Calvinist congregations elected their own governing committees and in time created regional and national synods (councils) to regulate doctrinal issues. Calvinists also displayed simplicity in dress, life, and worship. In an age of ornate garments, they wore simple black clothes, avoided ostentatious living, and worshiped in churches devoid of statues, most musical instruments, stained-glass windows, incense, and vestments.

The Reformers appealed to genuine religious sentiments, but political circumstances (discussed below) and the social agendas that motivated people to join them contributed to their successes and failures. Lutheranism appealed most strongly to German speakers and linguistically related Scandinavians. Peasants and urban laborers sometimes defied their masters by adopting a different faith. Protestants were no more inclined than Roman Catholics to question male dominance in the church and the family, but most Protestants rejected the tradition of celibate priests and nuns and advocated Christian marriage for all adults.

Shaken by the Protestant Reformers' appeal, the Catholic Church undertook its own reforms. A council that met at the city of Trent, in northern Italy, in three sessions between 1545 and 1563 painstakingly distinguished proper Catholic doctrines from Protestant "errors." The council also

# C H R O N O L O G Y

|  | Politics and Culture | Environment and Technology | Warfare |
|---|---|---|---|
| **1500** | **1500s**  Spain's golden century | **Mid-1500s**  Increasing land drainage in Holland | **1526–1571**  Ottoman wars |
|  | **1519**  Protestant Reformation begins |  | **1546–1555**  German Wars of Religion |
|  | **1540s**  Scientific Revolution begins |  | **1562–1589**  French Wars of Religion |
|  | **1545**  Catholic Reformation begins |  | **1566–1648**  Netherlands Revolt |
|  | **Late 1500s**  Witch-hunts increase | **1590s**  Dutch develop flyboats; Little Ice Age begins |  |
| **1600** | **1600s**  Holland's golden century | **1600s**  Depletion of forests growing |  |
|  |  | **1609**  Galileo's astronomical telescope |  |
|  |  |  | **1618–1648**  Thirty Years War |
|  |  |  | **1642–1648**  English Civil War |
|  |  |  | **1652–1678**  Anglo-Dutch Wars |
|  |  |  | **1667–1697**  Wars of Louis XIV |
|  |  | **1682**  Canal du Midi completed | **1683–1697**  Ottoman wars |
| **1700** | **1700s**  The Enlightenment begins |  | **1700–1721**  Great Northern War |
|  |  |  | **1701–1714**  War of the Spanish Succession |
|  |  | **1750**  English mine nearly 5 million tons of coal a year |  |
|  |  | **1755**  Lisbon earthquake |  |

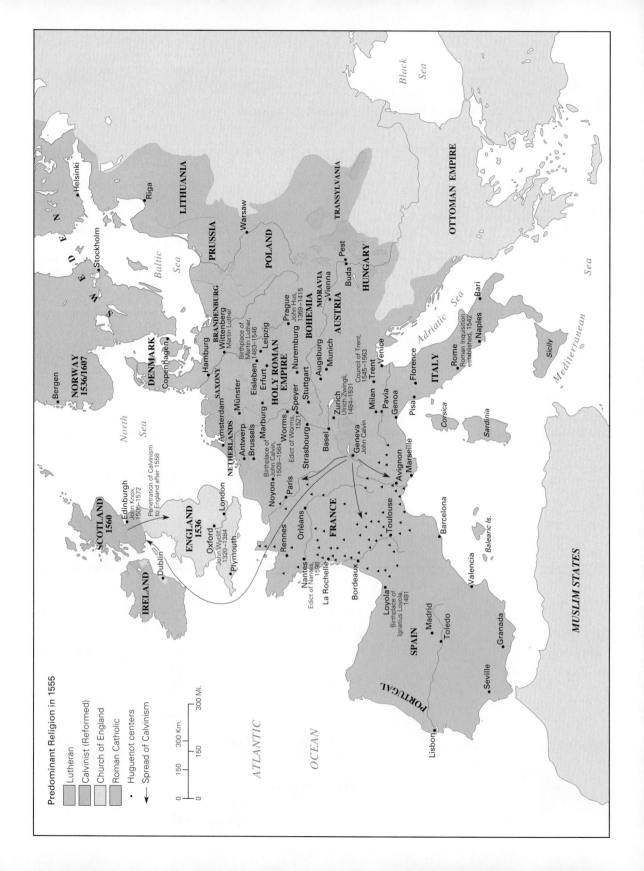

**Predominant Religion in 1555**

- Lutheran
- Calvinist (Reformed)
- Church of England
- Roman Catholic
- ▲ Huguenot centers
- → Spread of Calvinism

*Black Sea*

OTTOMAN EMPIRE

Helsinki

Riga

LITHUANIA

*Baltic Sea*

Warsaw

Stockholm

PRUSSIA

POLAND

Bergen

NORWAY
1536/1607

DENMARK

Copenhagen

BRANDENBURG

Hamburg

Wittenberg
Birthplace of
Martin Luther,
1483–1546

Prague
John Hus,
1369–1415

TRANSYLVANIA

Pest
Buda

HUNGARY

MORAVIA

Vienna

AUSTRIA

BOHEMIA

Nuremberg

Leipzig

Erfurt

Eisleben
Birthplace of
Martin Luther

SAXONY

Münster

Amsterdam

Antwerp

Brussels

NETHERLANDS

Marburg

Birthplace of
John Calvin,
1509–1564

Edict of Worms,
1521

Worms

Speyer

Stuttgart

HOLY ROMAN
EMPIRE

Augsburg

Munich

Council of Trent,
1545–1563

Trent

Zurich
Ulrich Zwingli,
1484–1531

Basel

Geneva
John Calvin

Milan

Pavia

Venice

Genoa

*Adriatic Sea*

Bari

Naples

*Mediterranean Sea*

Rome
Roman Inquisition
established, 1542

Florence

Pisa

ITALY

*Sicily*

*Corsica*

*Sardinia*

*North Sea*

Edinburgh
John Knox,
1505–1572

Penetration of Calvinism
to England after 1558

SCOTLAND
1560

ENGLAND
1536

Oxford
John Wyclif,
1320–1384

London

Plymouth

IRELAND

Dublin

Rennes

Orléans

Paris

Noyon

Strasbourg

Avignon

Marseille

FRANCE

Toulouse

Barcelona

Nantes
Edict of Nantes,
1598

La Rochelle

Bordeaux

Valencia

*Balearic Is.*

Loyola
Birthplace of
Ignatius Loyola,
1491

SPAIN

Madrid

Toledo

Granada

Seville

PORTUGAL

Lisbon

MUSLIM STATES

*ATLANTIC OCEAN*

300 Mi.

300 Km.

150

150

0

0

reaffirmed the supremacy of the pope and called for a number of reforms, including requiring each bishop to reside in his diocese and each diocese to have a theological seminary to train priests. Also important to this **Catholic Reformation** were the activities of a new religious order—the Society of Jesus, or "Jesuits," that Ignatius of Loyola (1491–1556), a Spanish nobleman, founded in 1540. Well-educated Jesuits helped win back some adherents by their teaching and preaching (see Map 15.1). Other Jesuits became missionaries overseas (see Chapters 16 and 18).

Given the complexity of the issues and the intensity of the emotions that the Protestant Reformation stirred, it is not surprising that violence often flared up. Both sides persecuted and sometimes executed those of differing views. Bitter "wars of religion," fought over a mixture of religious and secular issues, continued in parts of western Europe until 1648.

## Traditional Thinking and Witch-Hunts

Religious differences among Protestants and between them and Catholics continued to generate animosity long after the first generation of reformers, but from a global perspective European Christians still had much in common both in their theology and in the local folk customs and pre-Christian beliefs that remained powerful everywhere in Europe. The widespread **witch-hunts** that Protestants and Catholics undertook in early modern Europe are a dramatic illustration of those common beliefs.

Prevailing European ideas about the natural world blended two distinct traditions: the folklore about magic and forest spirits passed down orally from pre-Christian times, and the teachings of the Bible heard by all in church and read by growing numbers in vernacular translations. In the minds

**Map 15.1   Religious Reformation in Europe**   The Reformation brought greater religious freedom but also led to religious conflict and persecution. In many places the Reformation accelerated the trend toward state control of religion and added religious differences to the motives for wars among Europeans.

of most people, Christian teachings about miracles, saints, and devils mixed with folklore.

Like people in other parts of the world, most early modern Europeans believed that natural events could have supernatural causes. When crops failed or domestic animals died unexpectedly, many people blamed unseen spirits. People also attributed human triumphs and tragedies to supernatural causes. When an earthquake destroyed much of Lisbon, Portugal's capital city, in November 1755, for example, both educated and uneducated people saw the event as a punishment sent by God. A Jesuit charged it "scandalous to pretend that the earthquake was just a natural event." An English Protestant leader agreed, comparing Lisbon's fate with that of Sodom, the biblical city that God destroyed because of the sinfulness of its citizens.

The extraordinary fear of the power of witches that swept across northern Europe in the late sixteenth and seventeenth centuries grew out of these beliefs. It is estimated that secular and church authorities tried over a hundred thousand people—some three-fourths of them women—for practicing witchcraft. Some were acquitted; some recanted; but more than half were executed—most in Protestant lands. Torture and badgering questions persuaded many accused witches to confess to casting spells and to describe in vivid detail their encounters with the Devil and their attendance at nighttime assemblies of witches.

The trial records make it clear that both the accusers and the accused believed that it was possible for angry and jealous individuals to use evil magic and the power of the Devil to attack people and domestic animals or to cause crops to wither in the fields. Researchers think that at least some of those accused may really have tried to use witchcraft to harm their enemies. However, it was the Reformation's focus on the Devil—the enemy of God—as the source of evil that made such malevolence so serious a crime and that helped revive older fears of witchcraft.

Modern historians also argue that many accusations against widows and independent-minded women drew on the widespread distrust of women not directly under the control of fathers or husbands. The fact that such women had important roles in tending animals and the sick and in childbirth also made them suspects if death occurred.

**Death to Witches**   This woodcut from 1574 depicts three women convicted of witchcraft being burned alive in Baden, Switzerland. The well-dressed townsmen look on stolidly.   (Zentralbibliothek Zurich)

In parts of the world where belief in witchcraft is still strong, witch-hunts arise at times of social stress, and people who are marginalized by poverty and by the suspicions of others often relish the celebrity that public confession brings. "Confessing" may even bring release from the guilt the accused feel for wishing evil on their neighbors.

No single reason can explain the witchcraft hysteria in early modern Europe, but, for both the accusers and the accused, there are plausible connections between the witch-hunts and rising social tensions, rural poverty, and environmental strains. Far from being a bizarre aberration, witch-hunts reflected the larger social climate of early modern Europe.

## The Scientific Revolution

Among the educated, the Bible and the writings of Greco-Roman antiquity, many of them newly discovered by Renaissance scholars, were more trusted guides to the natural world than was folklore. The greatest authority on physics was Aristotle, a Greek philosopher who taught that everything on earth was reducible to four elements. The surface of the earth was composed of the two heavy elements, earth and water. The atmosphere was made up of two lighter elements, air and fire, which floated above the ground. Higher still were the sun, moon, planets, and stars, which, according to Aristotelian physics, were so light and pure that they floated in crystalline spheres. This theory accorded perfectly with the commonsense perception that all heavenly bodies revolved around the earth.

The ideas of the ancient Greek mathematician Pythagoras supported this view. Pythagoreans attributed to mystical properties the ability of simple mathematical equations to describe physical objects. They attached special significance to the simplest (to them perfect) geometrical shapes: the circle (a point rotated around another point) and the sphere (a circle rotated on its axis). They believed that celestial objects were perfect spheres orbiting the earth in perfectly circular orbits.

In the sixteenth century, however, careful observations and mathematical calculations, many of them made by astronomers in the Muslim world and translated into Latin, led some imaginative European investigators to challenge these traditional views. These pioneers of the **Scientific Revolution** took issue with the efforts of earlier astronomers and mathematicians to fit their observations of the heavens into the prevailing theories of circular orbits. Rejecting the accumulation of ingenious theories and eighty hypothetical spheres used to explain some seemingly irregular movements, a Polish monk and mathematician named Nicholas Copernicus (1473–1543), possibly building on the theories of Muslim astronomers, came up with a mathematically simpler solution: switching the center of the different orbits from the earth to the sun, which would reduce the number of spheres that were needed.

Copernicus did not challenge the idea that the sun, moon, and planets were light, perfect spheres or that they moved in circular orbits. But his placement of the sun, not the earth, at the center of things began a revolution in understanding the structure of the heavens and the place of humans in the universe. To escape the anticipated controversies, Copernicus delayed the publication of his heliocentric (sun-centered) theory until the end of his life.

Other astronomers, including the Danish Tycho Brahe (1546–1601) and his German assistant Johannes Kepler (1571–1630), strengthened and improved on Copernicus's model, showing that planets actually move in elliptical, not circular orbits. The most brilliant of the Copernicans was the Italian Galileo Galilei° (1564–1642). In 1609 Galileo built a telescope through which he took a closer look at the heavens. Able to magnify distant objects thirty times beyond the power of the naked eye, Galileo saw that heavenly bodies were not the perfectly smooth spheres of the Aristotelians. The moon, he reported in *The Starry Messenger* (1610), had mountains and valleys; the sun had spots; other planets had their own moons. In other words, the earth was not alone in being heavy and changeable.

At first, the Copernican universe found more critics than supporters because it so directly challenged not just popular ideas but also the intellectual synthesis of classical and biblical authorities. How, demanded Aristotle's defenders, could the heavy earth move without producing vibrations that would shake the planet apart? Is the Bible wrong, asked the theologians, when the Book of Joshua says that, by God's command, "the sun [not the earth] stood still . . . for about a whole day" to give the ancient Israelites victory in their conquest of Palestine? If Aristotle's physics was wrong, worried other traditionalists, would not the theological synthesis built on other parts of his philosophy be open to question?

Intellectual and religious leaders encouraged political authorities to suppress the new ideas. Most Protestant leaders, following the lead of Martin Luther, condemned the heliocentric universe as contrary to the Bible. Catholic authorities waited longer to act. After all, both Copernicus and Galileo were Roman Catholics. Copernicus had dedicated his book to the pope, and in 1582 another pope, Gregory XIII, had used the latest astronomical findings to issue a new and more accurate calendar (still used today). Galileo ingeniously argued that the conflict between scripture and sci-

ence was only apparent: the word of God revealed in the Bible was expressed in the imperfect language of ordinary people, but in nature God's truth was revealed more perfectly in a language that could be learned by careful observation and scientific reasoning.

Unfortunately, Galileo also ridiculed those who were slow to accept his findings, charging that Copernican ideas were "mocked and hooted at by an infinite multitude . . . of fools." Smarting under Galileo's stinging sarcasm, some Jesuits and other critics got his ideas condemned by the Roman Inquisition in 1616, which put *The Starry Messenger* on the Index of Forbidden Books and prohibited Galileo from publishing further on the subject. (In 1992 the Catholic Church officially retracted its condemnation of Galileo.)

Despite official opposition, printed books spread the new scientific ideas among scholars across Europe. In England, Robert Boyle (1627–1691) used experimental methods and a trial-and-error approach to examine the inner workings of chemistry. Through the Royal Society, chartered in London in 1662 to promote knowledge of the natural world, Boyle and others became enthusiastic missionaries of mechanical science and fierce opponents of the Aristotelians.

Meanwhile, English mathematician Isaac Newton (1642–1727) was carrying Galileo's demonstration that the heavens and earth share a common physics to its logical conclusion. Newton formulated a set of mathematical laws that all physical objects obeyed. It was the force of gravity—not angels—that governed the elliptical orbits of heavenly bodies. It was gravitation (and the resistance of air) that caused cannonballs to fall back to earth. From 1703 until his death Newton served as president of the Royal Society, using his prestige to promote the new science that came to bear his name.

As the condemnation of Galileo demonstrates, in 1700 most religious and intellectual leaders viewed the new science with suspicion or outright hostility because of the challenge it posed to established ways of thought. Yet the principal pioneers of the Scientific Revolution were convinced that scientific discoveries and revealed religion were not in conflict. At the peak of his fame Newton promoted a series of lectures devoted to proving the validity of Christianity. However, by showing that

**Galileo Galilei** (gal-uh-LAY-oh gal-uh-LAY-ee)

the Aristotelians and biblical writers held ideas about the natural world that were naive and unfactual, these pioneers opened the door to others who used reason to challenge a broader range of unquestioned traditions and superstitions. The world of ideas was forever changed.

## The Early Enlightenment

The advances in scientific thought inspired a few brave souls to question the reasonableness of everything from agricultural methods to laws, religion, and social hierarchies. The belief that human reason could discover scientific laws governing social behavior, parallel to those governing physical properties, energized a movement known as the **Enlightenment.** Like the Scientific Revolution, this movement was the work of a few "enlightened" individuals, who often faced bitter opposition from the political, intellectual, and religious establishment. Leading Enlightenment thinkers became accustomed to having their books burned or banned and spent long periods in exile to escape being imprisoned.

Influences besides the Scientific Revolution affected the Enlightenment. The partisan bickering and bloodshed of the Reformation had led some people to doubt the superiority of any theological position and to recommend toleration of all religions. The killing of suspected witches also shocked many thoughtful people. The leading French thinker Voltaire (1694–1778) declared: "No opinion is worth burning your neighbor for."

Accounts of cultures in other parts of the world also raised questions about the presumed superiority of European political institutions, moral standards, and religious beliefs. Reports of Amerindian life, though romanticized, led some to conclude that those whom they had called savages were in many ways nobler than European Christians. Matteo Ricci, a Jesuit missionary to China whose journals made a strong impression in Europe, contrasted the lack of territorial ambition of the Chinese with the constant warfare in the West and attributed the difference to the fact that China was wisely ruled by educated men whom he called "Philosophers."

Although many circumstances shaped "enlightened" thinking, the new scientific methods and discoveries provided the clearest model for changing European society. Voltaire posed the issues in these terms: "it would be very peculiar that all nature, all the planets, should obey eternal laws" but a human being, "in contempt of these laws, could act as he pleased solely according to his caprice." The English poet Alexander Pope (1688–1774) made a similar point in verse: "Nature and Nature's laws lay hidden in night;/God said, 'Let Newton be' and all was light."

The Enlightenment was more a frame of mind than a coherent movement. By 1750 its proponents were clearer about what they disliked than about what new institutions should be created. Some thought society could be made to function with the mechanical orderliness of planets spinning in their orbits. Nearly all were optimistic that—at least in the long run—human beliefs and institutions could be improved. This belief in progress would help foster political and social revolutions after 1750, as Chapter 19 recounts.

Despite the enthusiasm the Enlightenment aroused in some circles, it was decidedly unpopular with many absolutist rulers and with most clergymen. Europe in 1750 was neither enlightened nor scientific. It was a place where political and religious divisions, growing literacy, and the printing press made possible the survival of the new ideas that profoundly changed life in future centuries.

# SOCIAL AND ECONOMIC LIFE

From a distance European society seemed quite rigid. At the top of the social pyramid a small number of noble families monopolized high offices in the church, government, and military and enjoyed many special privileges, including exemption from taxation. Merchants and professionals, who had acquired wealth but no legal privileges, ranked well below them. At the base of the pyramid, the masses, mostly rural peasants and landless laborers, served everyone above them. The subordination of women to men seemed equally rigid.

However, even contemporaries knew that this model was too simple. A study of English society in 1688, for example, distinguished twenty-five different social categories and pointed up the shocking inequality among them. It argued that less than half the population contributed to increasing the wealth of the kingdom, while the rest—the majority—were too poor and unskilled to make any substantial contribution.

Some social mobility did occur, particularly in the middle. The principal engine of social change was the economy, and the places where social change occurred most readily were the cities. A secondary means of change was education—for those who could get it.

## The Bourgeoisie

Europe's growing cities were the products of a changing economy. In 1500 Paris was the only northern European city with over 100,000 inhabitants. By 1700 both Paris and London had populations over 500,000, and twenty other European cities contained over 60,000 people.

The wealth of the cities came from manufacturing and finance, but especially from trade, both within Europe and overseas. The French called the urban class that dominated these activities the **bourgeoisie°** (burghers, town dwellers). Members of the bourgeoisie poured much of their profit back into their businesses or into new ventures. Even so, they had enough money to live comfortably in large houses with many servants. In the seventeenth and eighteenth centuries wealthier urban classes could buy exotic luxuries imported from the far corners of the earth—Caribbean and Brazilian sugar and rum, Mexican chocolate, Virginia tobacco, North American furs, East Indian cotton textiles and spices, and Chinese tea.

The Netherlands showed great bourgeois enterprise in the seventeenth century. A wide variety of goods flowed from factories and workshops of the many Dutch cities and towns. The highly successful textile industry concentrated on weaving and printing of cloth, leaving the spinning of thread to low-paid workers elsewhere. Along with fine woolens and linens the Dutch made cheaper textiles for mass markets. Other factories in Holland refined West Indian sugar, brewed beer from Baltic grain, processed Virginia tobacco, and made imitations of Chinese ceramics (see Environment

and Technology: East Asian Porcelain in Chapter 18). Free from the censorship imposed in neighboring countries, Holland's printers published books in many languages, including manuals with the latest advances in machinery, metallurgy, agriculture, and other technical areas. For a small province barely above sea level, lacking timber and other natural resources, this was a remarkable achievement.

Burgeoning from a fishing village to a metropolis of some 200,000 by 1700, Amsterdam was Holland's largest city and Europe's major port. The bourgeoisie there and in other cities developed huge commercial fleets that dominated sea trade in Europe and overseas. Dutch ships carried over 80 percent of the trade between Spain and northern Europe, even while Spain and the Netherlands were at war. By one estimate, the Dutch conducted more than half of all the oceangoing commercial shipping in the world in the seventeenth century (for details see Chapters 17 and 18).

Amsterdam also served as Europe's financial center. Seventeenth-century Dutch banks had such a reputation for security that wealthy individuals and governments from all over western Europe entrusted them with their money. The banks in turn invested these funds in real estate, loaned money to factory owners and governments, and provided capital for business operations overseas.

Maritime expansion led to new designs for merchant ships. In this, too, the Dutch played a dominant role, using timber imported from northern Europe to build their own vast fleets as well as ships for export. Especially successful was the fluit, or "flyboat," a large-capacity cargo ship developed in the 1590s. It was inexpensive to build and required only a small crew. Another successful type of merchant ship, the heavily armed "East Indiaman," helped the Dutch establish their supremacy in the Indian Ocean. The Dutch also excelled at mapmaking (see Environment and Technology: Mapping the World).

Like merchants in the Islamic world, Europe's merchants relied on family and ethnic networks. Many northern European cities contained merchant colonies from Venice, Florence, Genoa, and other Italian cities. In Amsterdam and Hamburg lived Jewish merchants who had fled religious persecution in Iberia. Other Jewish communities

**bourgeoisie** (boor-zwah-ZEE)

**Port of Amsterdam**    Ships, barges, and boats of all types are visible in this busy seventeenth-century scene. The large building in the center is the Admiralty House, the headquarters of the Dutch East India Company.    (Mansell TimeLife Pictures/Getty Images)

expanded out of eastern Europe into the German states, especially after the Thirty Years War. Armenian merchants from Iran were moving into the Mediterranean and became important in Russia in the seventeenth century.

The bourgeoisie sought mutually beneficial alliances with European monarchs, who welcomed economic growth as a means of increasing state revenues. The Dutch government pioneered chartering **joint-stock companies.** The Dutch East India Company received a monopoly over trade to the East Indies, as did the Dutch West India Company for the New World. France and England chartered companies of their own. The companies sold shares to individuals to fund their overseas enterprises, thus spreading the risks (and profits) among many investors (see Chapter 16). Investors bought and sold shares in specialized markets called **stock exchanges,** an Italian innovation transferred to the cities of northwestern Europe in the sixteenth century. The greatest stock market in the seventeenth and eighteenth centuries was the Amsterdam Exchange, founded in 1530. Large insurance companies also emerged in this period, and insuring long voyages against loss became a standard practice after 1700.

Governments also undertook large projects to improve water transport. The Dutch built numerous canals for transport and to drain the lowlands for agriculture. Other governments also financed canals, which included elaborate systems of locks to raise barges up over hills. One of the most important was the 150-mile (240-kilometer) Canal du Midi in France, built by the French government between 1661 and 1682 to link the Atlantic and the Mediterranean. By the seventeenth century rulers sought the talents of successful businessmen as administrators. Jean Baptiste Colbert° (1619–1683), Louis XIV's able minister of finance, was a notable example.

Some members of the bourgeoisie in England and France used their wealth to raise their social status. By retiring from their businesses and buying country estates, they could become members of the **gentry.** These landowners affected the lifestyle of the old aristocracy. The gentry loaned money to impoverished peasants and to members of the nobility and in time increased their ownership of land. Some families sought aristocratic husbands for their daughters. The old nobility found such

---

**Colbert** (kohl-BEAR)

alliances attractive because of the large dowries that the bourgeoisie provided. In France a family could gain the exemption from taxation by living in gentility for three generations or, more quickly, by purchasing a title from the king.

## Peasants and Laborers

At the other end of society things were bad, but they had been worse. Serfdom, which bound men and women to land owned by a local lord, had been in deep decline since the great plague of the mid-fourteenth century. In western Europe the institution did not return even though competition for work exerted a downward pressure on wages as the population recovered. In eastern Europe, however, the development of large estates raising grain for the cities led to the rise of serfdom for the first time. Slavery, which had briefly expanded in southern Europe around 1500 as the result of the Atlantic slave trade from sub-Saharan Africa, declined. After 1600, Europeans shipped nearly all African slaves to the Americas.

There is much truth in the argument that western Europe continued to depend on unfree labor but kept it at a distance rather than at home. In any event, legal freedom did little to make a peasant's life safer and more secure. The techniques and efficiency of European agriculture had improved little since 1300. As a result, bad years brought famine; good ones provided only small surpluses. Indeed, the condition of the average person in western Europe may have worsened between 1500 and 1750 as the result of prolonged warfare, environmental problems, and varying economic conditions. In addition, Europeans felt the adverse effects of a century of relatively cool weather that began in the 1590s. During this **Little Ice Age** average temperatures fell only a few degrees, but the effects were startling (see Issues in World History: The Little Ice Age).

By 1700 high-yielding new crops from the Americas were helping the rural poor avoid starvation. Once grown only as hedges against famine, potatoes and maize (corn) became staples for the rural poor in the eighteenth century. Potatoes sustained life in northeastern and central Europe and in Ireland, and poor peasants in Italy subsisted on maize. Ironically, all of these lands were major exporters of wheat, which the agricultural laborers could not afford to eat. Instead, the grain was put on carts, barges, and ships and carried to the cities of western Europe. Other fleets brought wine from southern to northern Europe. Parisians downed 100,000 barrels of wine a year at the end of the seventeenth century. Some of the grain was made into beer, which the poor drank because it was cheaper than wine. In 1750 Parisian breweries brewed 23 million quarts (22 million liters) of beer for local consumption.

Some rural men worked as miners, lumberjacks, and charcoal makers. The expanding iron industry in England provided work for all three, but the high consumption of wood fuel for this and other purposes caused serious **deforestation.** One early-seventeenth-century observer lamented: "within man's memory, it was held impossible to have any want of wood in England. But . . . at present, through the great consuming of wood . . . and the neglect of planting of woods, there is a great scarcity of wood throughout the whole kingdom."[1] The managers of the hundreds of ironworks in England tried to meet the shortages by importing timber and charcoal from more heavily forested Scandinavian countries and Russia. Eventually, the high price of wood and charcoal encouraged smelters to use coal as an alternative fuel. England's coal mining increased twelvefold, from 210,000 tons in 1550 to 2,500,000 tons in 1700. Starting in 1709, coke—coal refined to remove impurities—gradually replaced charcoal in the smelting of iron. These new demands drove English coal production to nearly 5 million tons a year by 1750.

France was much more forested than England, but increasing deforestation there prompted Colbert to predict that "France will perish for lack of wood." By the late eighteenth century deforestation had become an issue even in Sweden and Russia, where iron production had become a major industry. New laws in France and England designed to protect the forests were largely inspired by fears of shortages for naval vessels, whose keels required high-quality timbers of exceptional size and particular curvature. Although wood consumption remained high, rising prices encouraged some individuals to plant trees for future harvest. Everywhere in Europe the rural poor felt the depletion of the forests most strongly, since for centuries they

# ENVIRONMENT + TECHNOLOGY

## Mapping the World

In 1602 in China the Jesuit missionary Matteo Ricci printed an elaborate map of the world. Working from maps produced in Europe and incorporating the latest knowledge gathered by European maritime explorers, Ricci introduced two changes to make the map more appealing to his Chinese hosts. He labeled it in Chinese characters, and he split his map down the middle of the Atlantic so that China lay in the center. This version pleased Chinese elite, who considered China the "Middle Kingdom" surrounded by lesser states. A copy of Ricci's map in six large panels adorned the emperor's Beijing palace.

The stunningly beautiful maps and globes of sixteenth-century Europe were the most complete, detailed, and useful representations of the earth that any society had ever produced. The best mapmaker of the century was Gerhard Kremer, who is remembered as Mercator (the merchant) because his maps were so useful to European ocean traders. By incorporating the latest discoveries and scientific measurements, Merca-

tor could depict the outlines of the major continents in painstaking detail, even if their interiors were still largely unknown to outsiders.

To represent the spherical globe on a flat map, Mercator drew the lines of longitude as parallel lines. Because such lines actually meet at the poles, Mercator's projection greatly exaggerated the size of every landmass and body of water distant from the equator. However, Mercator's rendering offered a very practical advantage: sailors could plot their course by drawing a straight line between their point of departure and their destination. Because of this useful feature, the Mercator projection of the world remained in common use until quite recently. To some extent, its popularity came from the exaggerated size this projection gave to Europe. Like the Chinese, Europeans liked to think of themselves as at the center of things. Europeans also understood their true geographical position better than people in any other part of the world.

had depended on woodlands for wild nuts and berries, free firewood and building materials, and wild game.

Modest improvements in food production in some places were overwhelmed by population growth. Rural women had long supplemented household incomes by spinning yarn. From the mid-1600s rising wages in towns led textile manufacturers to farm more and more weaving out to rural areas with high underemployment. This provided men and women with enough to survive on, but the piecework paid very little for long hours of tedious labor.

Throughout this period, many rural poor migrated to the towns and cities in hopes of better jobs, but only some were successful. Even in the prosperous Dutch towns, half of the population lived in acute poverty. Authorities estimated that

those permanent city residents who were too poor to tax, the "deserving poor," made up 10 to 20 percent of the population. That calculation did not include the large numbers of "unworthy poor"— recent migrants from impoverished rural areas, peddlers traveling from place to place, and beggars (many with horrible deformities and sores) who tried to survive on charity. Desperation forced many young women into prostitution. There were also many criminals, usually organized in gangs, ranging from youthful pickpockets to highway robbers.

The pervasive poverty of rural and urban Europe shocked those who were not hardened to it. In about 1580 the mayor of the French city of Bordeaux° asked a group of visiting Amerindian chiefs what impressed them most about European cities.

---

**Bordeaux** (bor-DOH)

**Dutch World Map, 1641**   It is easy to see why the Chinese would not have liked to see their empire at the far right edge of this widely printed map. Besides the distortions caused by the Mercator projection, geographical ignorance exaggerates the size of North America and Antarctica. (Courtesy of the Trustees of the British Museum)

The chiefs are said to have expressed astonishment at the disparity between the fat, well-fed people and the poor, half-starved men and women in rags. Why, the visitors wondered, did the poor not grab the rich by the throat or set fire to their homes?[2]

In fact, misery provoked many rebellions in early modern Europe. For example, in 1525 peasant rebels in the Alps attacked both nobles and clergy as representatives of the privileged and landowning classes. They had no love for merchants either, whom they denounced for lending at interest and charging high prices. Rebellions multiplied as rural conditions worsened. In southwestern France alone some 450 uprisings occurred between 1590 and 1715, many of them set off by food shortages and tax increases. The exemption of the wealthy from taxation was a frequent source of complaint. A rebellion in southern France in 1670 began when a mob of townswomen attacked the tax collector. It quickly spread to the country, where peasant leaders cried, "Death to the people's oppressors!" Authorities dealt severely with such revolts and executed or maimed their leaders.

## Women and the Family

Women's status and work were closely tied to those of their husbands and families. In rare instances, a woman in a royal family might inherit a throne (see Table 15.1 for examples) in the absence of a male heir, but such exceptions do not negate the rule that women everywhere ranked below men. Nevertheless, class and wealth defined a woman's position in life more than gender. A wife or daughter in a rich family, for example, had a much better life than any poor man.

Occasionally, a single woman might be secure and respected, as in the case of women from good families heading convents of nuns in Catholic countries. But unmarried women and widows fared poorly compared to their married sisters.

Men and women in early modern Europe most often chose their own spouses. Ironically, privileged families were more inclined to control marriage plans than poor ones. Royal and noble families carefully plotted their children's marriages to further the family's status. Bourgeois parents were less likely to force their children into arranged marriages. Nevertheless, nearly all found spouses within their social class, sometimes to buttress business connections.

Europeans also married late. The children of craftspeople and the poor had to delay marriage until they could afford to live on their own. Young men served long apprenticeships to learn trades. Young women worked helping their parents, or as domestic servants, or in some other capacity to save money for their dowry: the money and household goods—the amount varied by social class—that enabled a young couple to begin marriage independent of their parents. The typical groom in western and central Europe could not hope to marry before his late twenties. His bride would be a few years younger. Marriage also came late in bourgeois families, in part to allow young men to complete their education.

The late age of marriage held down the birthrate and thus limited family size. Even so, about one in ten urban babies was born to an unmarried woman, often a servant. Such newborns were generally left on the doorsteps of churches, convents, or rich homes. Many perished. Public brothels also went with delayed marriage. They provided a place for young men to satisfy their desires at the expense of unfortunate young women, often newly arrived from impoverished villages. Nevertheless, rape was a common occurrence, especially assaults by gangs of young men. Some historians believe these crimes reflect the envy poor young men had of older men's easier access to women.

Bourgeois parents focused on giving their children the education and training necessary for success. They promoted the establishment of municipal schools where they could learn Latin and perhaps Greek. Then they sent their sons abroad to learn modern languages or to a university to earn a law degree. Legal training helped them conduct business and was necessary for obtaining a judgeship or treasury position. Daughters were less likely to be groomed for business careers, but wives often helped their husbands as bookkeepers and sometimes inherited businesses.

The fact that most schools, like most guilds and professions, barred females explains why women were not prominent in the cultural movements of the period. Yet from a global perspective, women in early modern Europe were more prominent in the creation of high culture than were women in most other parts of the world. Recent research has identified successful women who were painters, musicians, and writers. Indeed, the spread of learning, the stress on religious reading, and the growth of business may have made Europe the leading area of the world in female literacy. Nevertheless, illiteracy was widespread for both sexes, and only women in wealthier families might have a good education. From the late 1600s some wealthy French women ran intellectual gatherings in their homes. Others were prominent letter writers. Galileo's daughter, Maria Celeste Galilei, carried on a detailed correspondence with her father from behind the walls of her convent, which she had vowed never to leave.

## POLITICAL INNOVATIONS

The monarchs of early modern Europe occupied the apex of the social order, arbitrated intellectual and religious conflicts, and greatly influenced economic life. Thus an overview of political life incorporates all the developments so far described in this chapter. In addition, royal political agendas introduced new elements of conflict and change.

Though no unified European empire emerged, a higher degree of political centralization was achieved in separate kingdoms. The frequent civil and international conflicts of this era sometimes promoted cooperation and often encouraged innovation. Leadership and success passed from Spain to the Netherlands and then to England and France.

## State Development

Political diversity characterized Europe. City-states and principalities abounded, either independently or bound into loose federations, of which the **Holy Roman Empire** of the German heartland was the most notable example. In western Europe the strong monarchies that had emerged earlier were acquiring national identities, but some rulers dreamed of a European empire comparable to that of Rome or some Asian realm.

In 1519 electors of the Holy Roman Empire chose Charles V (r. 1519–1556) as emperor. Like his predecessors for three generations, Charles belonged to the powerful **Habsburg°** family of Austria, but he had recently inherited the Spanish thrones of Castile and Aragon. With the vast resources of these lands behind him, Charles hoped to centralize his imperial power and lead a Christian coalition to halt the advance into southeastern Europe of the Ottoman Empire, which already controlled most of the Middle East and North Africa.

Stout defense and bad weather eventually halted the Ottomans at the gates of Vienna in 1529, but Charles's efforts to forge his several possessions into Europe's strongest state failed as Ottoman attacks continued on and off until 1697. King Francis I of France, who had lost to Charles in the election for Holy Roman Emperor, openly supported the Muslim Turks to weaken his rival. In addition, some of the Holy Roman Empire's many member states used Luther's religious Reformation to frustrate Charles's efforts to curb their autonomy. Swayed partly by Luther's appeals to German national sentiment, many German princes opposed Charles's defense of Catholic doctrine in the imperial Diet (assembly).

After decades of bitter squabbles turned to open warfare in 1546 (the German Wars of Religion), Charles V finally gave up his efforts at unification, abdicated control of his various possessions to different heirs, and retired to a monastery. By the Peace of Augsburg (1555), he recognized the princes' right to choose either Catholicism or Lutheranism as their state religion, and he allowed them to keep the church lands they had seized before 1552. The triumph of religious diversity that derailed Charles's plan for centralizing authority in central Europe postponed German political unification for three centuries.

Meanwhile, the rulers of Spain, France, and England were building more effective programs of political centralization and religious unity. The most successful rulers reduced the autonomy of the church and the nobility, while making them part of a unified national structure headed by the monarch. Getting control of the church in the sixteenth century was a stormy process, but the outcome was clear. Bringing the nobles and other powerful interests into a centralized political system took longer and led to more diverse outcomes.

## Religious Policies

The rulers of Spain and France successfully defended the Catholic tradition against Protestant challenges. Adopting the techniques of his predecessors for suppressing Jews and Muslims, King Philip II of Spain used an ecclesiastical court, the Spanish Inquisition, to bring into line those who resisted his authority. Suspected Protestants, as well as critics of the king, found themselves accused of heresy, an offense punishable by death. Even those who were acquitted of the charge learned not to oppose the king again.

In France the Calvinist opponents of the Valois rulers gained the military advantage in the French Wars of Religion (1562–1598), but in the interest of forging lasting unity, their leader Prince Henry of Navarre then embraced the Catholic faith of the majority of his subjects. The Bourbon king who followed him, Henry IV, his son King Louis XIII, and his grandson King Louis XIV were as supportive of the Catholic Church as their counterparts in Spain. In 1685 Louis XIV even revoked the Edict of Nantes°, by which his grandfather had granted the Protestants religious freedom in 1598.

In England King Henry VIII initially defended the papacy against Lutheran criticism. But when the pope refused to annul his marriage to Catherine of Aragon, who had not produced a male heir, Henry challenged the papacy's authority by ordering the English archbishop of Canterbury to annul the marriage in 1533. The breach with Rome was sealed

---

**Habsburg** (HABZ-berg)

**Nantes** (nahnt)

**Table 15.1**  **Rulers in Early Modern Western Europe**

| Spain | France | England/Great Britain |
|---|---|---|
| **Habsburg Dynasty** | **Valois Dynasty** | **Tudor Dynasty** |
| Charles I (1516–1556) (Holy Roman Emperor Charles V) | Francis I (1515–1547) | Henry VIII (1509–1547) |
|  | Henry II (1547–1559) | Edward VI (1547–1553) |
| Philip II (1556–1598) | Francis II (1559–1560) | Mary I (1553–1558) |
|  | Charles IX (1560–1574) | Elizabeth I (1558–1603) |
|  | Henry III (1574–1589) |  |
|  | **Bourbon Dynasty** | **Stuart Dynasty** |
| Philip III (1598–1621) | Henry IV (1589–1610)[a] | James I (1603–1625) |
| Philip IV (1621–1665) | Louis XIII (1610–1643) | Charles I (1625–1649)[a, b] |
| Charles II (1665–1700) | Louis XIV (1643–1715) | (Puritan Republic, 1649–1660) |
|  |  | Charles II (1660–1685) |
|  |  | James II (1685–1688)[b] |
|  |  | William III (1689–1702) |
| **Bourbon Dynasty** |  | and Mary II (1689–1694) |
| Philip V (1700–1746) |  | Anne (1702–1714) |
|  |  | **Hanoverian Dynasty** |
|  | Louis XV (1715–1774) | George I (1714–1727) |
| Ferdinand VI (1746–1759) |  | George II (1727–1760) |

[a]Died a violent death.   [b]Was overthrown.

the next year when Parliament made the English monarch head of the Church of England.

Like many Protestant rulers, Henry disbanded monasteries and convents and seized their lands. He gave some lands to his powerful allies and sold others to pay for his new navy. Yet the attitudes toward ritual and theology of the new Anglican Church remained too close to those of Roman Catholicism to satisfy English Puritans (Calvinists who wanted to "purify" the Anglican Church of Catholic practices and beliefs). In 1603 the first Stuart king, James I, dismissed a Puritan petition to eliminate bishops with the statement "No bishops, no king"—a reminder of the essential role of the church in supporting royal power.

## Monarchies in England and France

Over the course of the seventeenth century, the rulers of England and France contested with their leading subjects over the limits of royal authority. Religion was never absent in these struggles, but the different constitutional outcomes they produced were more significant in the long run.

To evade any check on his power, King Charles I of England (see Table 15.1) ruled for eleven years without summoning Parliament, his kingdom's representative body. Lacking Parliament's consent to new taxes, he raised funds by coercing "loans" from wealthy subjects and applying existing tax laws more broadly. Then in 1640 a rebellion in Scotland forced him to summon a Parliament to approve new taxes to pay for an army. Noblemen and churchmen sat in the House of Lords. Representatives from the towns and counties sat in the House of Commons. Before it would authorize new taxes, Parliament insisted on strict guarantees that the king would never again ignore the body's traditional rights. These King Charles refused to grant. When he ordered the arrest of his leading critics in the House of Commons in 1642, he plunged the kingdom into the **English Civil War.**

**Versailles, 1722**    This painting by P.-D. Martin shows the east expanse of buildings and court-yards that make up the palace complex built by King Louis XIV.    (Giraudon/Art Resource, NY)

Even after defeat on the battlefield, Charles refused to compromise. In 1649 a "Rump" Parliament (one purged of his supporters) ordered him executed and replaced the monarchy with a republic under Oliver Cromwell, a Puritan general. Cromwell expanded England's presence overseas and imposed firm control over Ireland and Scotland, but he was as unwilling as the Stuart kings to share power with Parliament. After his death Parliament restored the Stuart line, making it unclear, for a time, which side had won the war.

King James II clarified matters when he refused to respect Parliament's rights and had his heir baptized a Roman Catholic. Parliament responded by forcing James into exile in the bloodless coup known as "the Glorious Revolution of 1688." The Bill of Rights of 1689 specified that Par-liament had to be called frequently and had to consent to changes in laws and to the raising of an army in peacetime. Another law reaffirmed the official status of the Church of England but extended religious toleration to the Puritans.

A similar struggle in France produced a different outcome. There the Estates General represented the traditional rights of the clergy, the nobility, and the towns (that is, the bourgeoisie). The Estates General was able to assert its rights during the sixteenth-century French Wars of Religion, when the monarchy was weak. But thereafter the Bourbon monarchs generally ruled without having to call it into session. They avoided financial crises by more efficient tax collection and by selling appointments to high government offices. In justification they claimed that the monarch had absolute authority to rule in God's name.

Louis XIV's gigantic new palace at **Versailles**° symbolized the monarch's triumph over the nobility, clergy, and towns. Capable of housing ten thousand people and surrounded by elaborately landscaped grounds and parks, the palace was a sort of theme park of royal absolutism. Elaborate ceremonies and banquets centered on the king deterred the nobles who lived at Versailles from plotting rebellion. According to one of them, the duke of Saint-Simon°, "no one was so clever in devising petty distractions" as the king.

Though the balance of powers in the English model would be widely admired in later times, most European rulers admired and imitated the centralized powers and absolutist claims of the French until well after 1750. Some even built imitations of Versailles. The English model exerted its influence more slowly. In his *Second Treatise of Civil Government* (1690), the English political philosopher John Locke (1632–1704) disputed monarchial claims to absolute authority by divine right. Rather, he argued, rulers derived their authority from the consent of the governed and, like everyone else, were subject to the law. If monarchs overstepped the law, citizens had not only the right but also the duty to rebel. The later consequences of this idea are considered in Chapter 19.

## Warfare and Diplomacy

In addition to the bitter civil wars that pounded the Holy Roman Empire, France, and England, European states engaged in numerous international conflicts. Warfare was almost constant in early modern Europe (see the Chronology at the beginning of the chapter). The worst of the international conflicts, the Thirty Years War (1618–1648), caused long-lasting depopulation and economic decline in much of the Holy Roman Empire.

The wars also produced dramatic improvements in weaponry and war-making skills, causing European armed forces to become the most powerful in the world. The numbers of men in arms increased steadily. French forces, for example, grew from about 150,000 in 1630 to 400,000 by the early eighteenth century. Even smaller European states

built up impressive armies. Sweden, with under a million people, had one of the best-armed military forces in seventeenth-century Europe. Prussia, a country with fewer than 2 million inhabitants in 1700, had a strong army that made it one of Europe's major powers.

Larger armies required more effective command structures. In the words of a modern historian, European armies "evolved . . . the equivalent of a central nervous system, capable of activating technologically differentiated claws and teeth."[3] New signaling techniques improved control of battlefield maneuvers. Frequent marching drills trained troops to obey orders instantly and gave them a close sense of comradeship. Since battles between evenly matched armies often ended in stalemates that prolonged the wars, victory increasingly depended on naval superiority.

England alone did without a peacetime standing army, but England's rise as a sea power had begun under King Henry VIII, who spent heavily on ships and promoted a domestic iron-smelting industry to supply cannon. The Royal Navy also copied innovative ship designs from the Dutch in the second half of the seventeenth century. By the early eighteenth century the Royal Navy surpassed the rival French fleet in numbers. By then, England had merged with Scotland to become Great Britain, annexed Ireland, and built a North American empire.

Although France was Europe's most powerful state, Louis XIV's efforts to expand were increasingly frustrated by coalitions of the other great powers. In a series of eighteenth-century wars beginning with the War of the Spanish Succession (1701–1714), the combination of Britain's naval strength and the land armies of its Austrian and Prussian allies blocked French ambitions and prevented the Bourbons from uniting the thrones of France and Spain.

This defeat of the French monarchy's empire-building efforts illustrated the principle of **balance of power** in international relations: the major European states formed temporary alliances to prevent any one state from becoming too powerful. Russia emerged as a major power in Europe after its modernized armies defeated Sweden in the Great Northern War (1700–1721). During the next two centuries, though adhering to four differ-

Versailles (vuhr-SIGH)    Saint-Simon (san see-MON)

ent branches of Christianity, the great powers of Europe—Catholic France, Anglican Britain, Catholic Austria, Lutheran Prussia, and Orthodox Russia (see Map 15.2)—maintained an effective balance of power by shifting their alliances for geopolitical rather than religious reasons. These pragmatic alliances were the first successful efforts at international peacekeeping.

## Paying the Piper

To pay the heavy military costs of their wars, European rulers had to increase their revenues. The most successful of them after 1600 promoted mutually beneficial alliances with the rising commercial elite. Both sides understood that trade thrived where government taxation and regulation were not excessive, where courts enforced contracts and collected debts, and where military power stood ready to protect overseas expansion.

Spain, sixteenth-century Europe's mightiest state, illustrates how the financial drains of an aggressive military policy and the failure to promote economic development could lead to decline. Expensive wars against the Ottomans, northern European Protestants, and rebellious Dutch subjects caused the treasury to default on its debts four times during the reign of King Philip II. Moreover, the Spanish rulers' concerns for religious uniformity and traditional aristocratic privilege further undermined the country's economy. In the name of religious uniformity they expelled Jewish merchants, persecuted Protestant dissenters, and forced tens of thousands of farmers and artisans into exile because of their Muslim ancestry. In the name of aristocratic privilege the 3 percent of the population that controlled 97 percent of the land in 1600 was exempt from taxation, while high sales taxes discouraged manufacturing.

For a time, vast imports of silver and gold bullion from Spain's American colonies filled the government treasury. These bullion shipments also contributed to severe inflation (rising prices), not just in Spain but also to a lesser degree throughout the rest of Europe. A Spanish saying captured the problem: American silver was like rain on the roof—it poured down and washed away. Huge debts for foreign wars drained bullion from Spain to its creditors. More

wealth flowed out to purchase manufactured goods and even food in the seventeenth century.

The rise of the Netherlands as an economic power stemmed from opposite policies. The Spanish crown had acquired these resource-poor but commercially successful provinces as part of Charles V's inheritance. But King Philip II's decision to impose Spain's ruinously heavy sales tax and enforce Catholic orthodoxy drove the Dutch to revolt in 1566 and again in 1572. If successful, those measures would have discouraged business and driven away the Calvinists, Jews, and other key contributors to Dutch prosperity. The Dutch fought with skill and ingenuity, raising and training an army and a navy that were among the most effective in Europe. By 1609 Spain was forced to agree to a truce that recognized the autonomy of the northern part of the Netherlands. In 1648, after eight decades of warfare, the independence of these seven United Provinces of the Free Netherlands (their full name) became final.

Rather than being ruined by the long war, the United Netherlands emerged as the dominant commercial power in Europe and the world's greatest trading nation. This economic success owed much to a decentralized government. During the long struggle against Spain, the provinces united around the prince of Orange, their sovereign, who served as commander-in-chief of the armed forces. But in economic matters each province was free to pursue its own interests. The maritime province of Holland grew rich by favoring commercial interests.

After 1650 the Dutch faced growing competition from the English, who were developing their own close association of business with government. In a series of wars (1652–1678) England used its naval might to break Dutch dominance in overseas trade and to extend its own colonial empire. With government support, the English merchant fleet doubled between 1660 and 1700, and foreign trade rose by 50 percent. As a result, state revenue from customs duties tripled. During the eighteenth century Britain's trading position strengthened still more.

The debts run up by the Anglo-Dutch Wars helped persuade the English monarchy to greatly enlarge the government's role in managing the economy. The outcome has been called a "financial revolution." The government increased revenues

RUSSIAN EMPIRE

OTTOMAN EMPIRE

*Caspian Sea*

*Tigris*

*Volga*

*Don*

*Red Sea*

*Nile*

*Euphrates*

*Black Sea*

CRIMEA

• Moscow

St. Petersburg •

KINGDOM OF SWEDEN

ESTONIA

LIVONIA
Riga •

LITHUANIA

Stockholm •

*Baltic Sea*

Königsberg •

EAST PRUSSIA

POLAND

Warsaw •

MOLDAVIA

BESSARABIA

*Dniepr*

*Danube*

BULGARIA

Constantinople •

PRUSSIA

SILESIA

HUNGARY

BOSNIA

SERBIA

BOHEMIA

AUSTRIA

Buda • Pest

BRANDENBURG

Berlin •

SAXONY

Vienna •

*Mediterranean Sea*

Christiania •

KINGDOM OF DENMARK AND NORWAY

HANOVER

BAVARIA

TYROL

REPUBLIC OF VENICE

*Adriatic Sea*

KINGDOM OF THE TWO SICILIES

Cologne •

*Danube*

SWITZERLAND

MILAN

Rome •

PAPAL STATES

UNITED NETHERLANDS

Amsterdam •

Utrecht •

*Rhine*

SAVOY

GENOA

TUSCANY

North Sea

Antwerp •

AUSTRIAN NETHERLANDS

LORRAINE

Paris •

CORSICA

SARDINIA

GREAT BRITAIN

SCOTLAND

ENGLAND

WALES

London •

Versailles •

FRANCE

*Rhône*

Avignon •

MINORCA (Br.)

IRELAND

ATLANTIC OCEAN

*Ebro*

SPAIN

Madrid •

Gibraltar (to Britian 1713)

PORTUGAL

Lisbon •

Ruled by Bourbons

Ruled by Habsburgs

Boundary of Holy Roman Empire

400 Mi.

400 Km.

200

200

0

0

**Map 15.2   Europe in 1740**   By the middle of the eighteenth century the great powers of Europe were France, the Austrian Empire, Great Britain, Prussia, and Russia. Spain, the Holy Roman Empire, and the Ottoman Empire were far weaker in 1740 than they had been two centuries earlier.

by taxing the formerly exempt landed estates of the aristocrats and by collecting taxes directly. Previously, private individuals known as tax farmers had advanced the government a fixed sum of money; in return they could keep whatever money they were able to collect from taxpayers. England also followed the Dutch lead in creating a central bank, from which the government was able to obtain long-term loans at low rates.

Under the leadership of Colbert, the French too experienced economic development. He streamlined tax collection, promoted French manufacturing and shipping by imposing taxes on foreign goods, and improved inland transportation. Yet the power of the wealthy aristocrats kept the French government from following England's lead in taxing wealthy landowners, collecting taxes directly, and securing low-cost loans. Nor did France succeed in managing its debt as efficiently as England. (The role of governments in promoting overseas trade is further discussed in Chapter 16.)

## CONCLUSION

European historians have used the word *revolution* to describe many different changes taking place in Europe between 1500 and 1750. The expansion of trade has been called a commercial revolution, the reform of state spending a financial revolution, and the changes in weapons and warfare a military revolution. We have also encountered a scientific revolution and the religious revolution of the Reformation.

These important changes in government, economy, society, and thought were parts of a dynamic process that began in the Late Middle Ages and led to even bigger industrial and political revolutions before the eighteenth century was over. Yet the years from 1500 to 1750 were not simply—perhaps

not even primarily—an age of progress for Europe. For many, the ferocious competition of European armies, merchants, and ideas was a wrenching experience. The growth of powerful states exacted a terrible price in death, destruction, and misery. The Reformation brought greater individual choice in religion but widespread religious persecution as well. The expanding economy benefited members of the emerging merchant elite and their political allies, but most Europeans became worse off as prices rose faster than wages. New scientific and enlightened ideas ignited controversies long before they yielded any tangible benefits.

The historical significance of this period of European history is clearer when viewed in a global context. What stands out are the powerful and efficient European armies, economies, and governments, which larger states elsewhere in the world feared, envied, and sometimes imitated. From a global perspective, the balance of political and economic power was shifting slowly, but inexorably, in the Europeans' favor. In 1500 the Ottomans threatened Europe. By 1750, as the remaining chapters of Part Five detail, Europeans had brought the world's seas and a growing portion of its lands and peoples under their control. No single group of Europeans accomplished this. The Dutch eclipsed the pioneering Portuguese and Spanish; then the English and French bested the Dutch. Competition, too, was a factor in European success.

Other changes in Europe during this period had no great overseas significance at the time. The new ideas of the Scientific Revolution and the Enlightenment were still of minor importance. Their full effects in furthering global European dominion were felt after 1750, as Parts Six and Seven explore.

## ■ Key Terms

Renaissance (European)
papacy
indulgence
Protestant Reformation
Catholic Reformation
witch-hunt
Scientific Revolution
Enlightenment
bourgeoisie
joint-stock company
stock exchange
gentry
Little Ice Age
deforestation
Holy Roman Empire
Habsburg
English Civil War
Versailles
balance of power

# ■ Suggested Reading

Overviews of this period include Euan Cameron, ed., *Early Modern Europe* (1999); H. G. Koenigsberger, *Early Modern Europe: Fifteen Hundred to Seventeen Eighty-Nine* (1987); and Joseph Bergin, *The Short Oxford History of Europe: The Seventeenth Century* (2001). Global perspectives can be found in Fernand Braudel, *Civilization and Capitalism, 15th–18th Century,* trans. Siân Reynolds, 3 vols. (1979), and Immanuel Wallerstein, *The Modern World-System,* vol. 2, *Mercantilism and the Consolidation of the European World-Economy, 1600–1750* (1980).

Technological and environmental changes are the focus of Geoffrey Parker, *Military Revolution: Military Innovation and the Rise of the West, 1500–1800,* 2d ed. (1996); William H. McNeill, *The Pursuit of Power: Technology, Armed Force, and Society Since A.D. 1000* (1982); Robert Greenhalgh Albion, *Forests and Sea Power: The Timber Problem of the Royal Navy, 1652–1862* (1965); Emmanuel Le Roy Ladurie, *Times of Feast, Times of Famine: A History of Climate Since the Year 1000,* trans. Barbara Bray (1971); and Brian Fagan, *The Little Ice Age: How Climate Made History, 1300–1850* (1988). Robert C. Allen, *Enclosure and the Yeoman: The Agricultural Development of the South Midlands, 1450–1850* (1992), focuses on England.

Steven Stapin, *The Scientific Revolution* (1998), and Hugh Kearney, *Science and Change, 1500–1700* (1971), are accessible introductions. Thomas S. Kuhn, *The Structure of Scientific Revolution,* 3d ed. (1996), and A. R. Hall, *The Scientific Revolution, 1500–1800: The Formation of the Modern Scientific Attitude,* 2d ed. (1962), are classic studies. Carolyn Merchant, *The Death of Nature: Women, Ecology and the Scientific Revolution* (1980), tries to combine several broad perspectives. *The Sciences in Enlightened Europe,* ed. W. Clark, J. Golinski, and S. Schaffer (1999), examines particular topics in a sophisticated way. Dorinda Outram, *The Enlightenment* (1995), provides a recent summary of research.

Excellent introductions to social and economic life are George Huppert, *After the Black Death: A Social History of Early Modern Europe* (1986), and Carlo M. Cipolla, *Before the Industrial Revolution: European Society and Economy, 1000–1700,* 2d ed. (1980). Peter Burke, *Pop-*ular Culture in Early Modern Europe* (1978), offers a broad treatment of nonelite perspectives, as does Robert Jütte, *Poverty and Deviance in Early Modern Europe* (1994). For more economic detail, see Robert S. DuPlessis, *Transitions to Capitalism in Early Modern Europe* (1997); Myron P. Gutmann, *Toward the Modern Economy: Early Industry in Europe, 1500–1800* (1988); and Carlo M. Cipolla, ed., *The Fontana Economic History of Europe,* vol. 2, *The Sixteenth and Seventeenth Centuries* (1974).

Topics of women's history are examined by Merry Wiesner, *Women and Gender in Early Modern Europe,* 2d ed. (2000); Bonie S. Anderson and Judith Zinsser, *A History of Their Own: Women in Europe,* vol. 2, rev. ed. (2000); and Monica Chojnacka and Merry E. Wiesner-Hanks, *Ages of Woman, Ages of Man* (2002). An excellent place to begin examining the complex subject of witchcraft is Brian Levack, *The Witch-Hunt in Early Modern Europe,* 2d ed. (1995); other up-to-date perspectives can be found in J. Barry, M. Hester, and G. Roberts, eds., *Witchcraft in Early Modern Europe: Studies in Culture and Belief* (1998), and Carlo Ginzburg, *The Night Battles: Witchcraft and Agrarian Cults in the Sixteenth and Seventeenth Centuries,* trans. John and Anne Tedechi (1983).

Good single-country surveys are J. A. Sharpe, *Early Modern England: A Social History,* 2d ed. (1997); Emmanuel Le Roy Ladurie, *The Royal French State, 1460–1610* (1994) and *The Ancien Régime: A History of France, 1610–1774* (1998); Jonathan Israel, *The Dutch Republic: Its Rise, Greatness and Fall, 1477–1806* (1995); and James Casey, *Early Modern Spain: A Social History* (1999).

# ■ Notes

1. Quoted by Carlo M. Cipolla, "Introduction," *The Fontana Economic History of Europe,* vol. 2, *The Sixteenth and Seventeenth Centuries* (Glasgow: Collins/Fontana Books, 1974), 11–12.

2. Michel de Montaigne, *Essais* (1588), ch. 31, "Des Cannibales."

3. William H. McNeill, *The Pursuit of Power: Technology, Armed Force, and Society Since A.D. 1000* (Chicago: University of Chicago Press, 1982), 124.

# The Americas, the Atlantic, and Africa, 1530–1770

## 16

**CHAPTER OUTLINE**

Spanish America and Brazil

English and French Colonies in North America

Plantations in the West Indies

Creating the Atlantic Economy

Africa and the Atlantic

The Columbian Exchange

DIVERSITY AND DOMINANCE: Race and Ethnicity in the Spanish Colonies: Negotiating Hierarchy

---

Because of their long isolation from other continents, the peoples of the New World lacked immunity to diseases introduced from the Old World. Smallpox arrived in the Caribbean in 1518, killing most of the native peoples there. In short order, smallpox killed 50 percent or more of the Amerindian population of Mexico and Central America. The disease then spread to North and South America with equally devastating effects. Other diseases added to the toll: measles in the 1530s, followed by diphtheria, typhus, influenza, and perhaps pulmonary plague. Between 1520 and 1521, influenza in combination with other ailments attacked the Cakchiquel of Guatemala. Their chronicle recalls:

Great was the stench of the dead. After our fathers and grandfathers succumbed, half the people fled to the fields. The dogs and vultures devoured the bodies. . . . So it was that we became orphans, oh my sons! . . . We were born to die![1]

By the mid-seventeenth century, malaria and yellow fever were also present in tropical regions.

The development of English and French colonies in North America in the seventeenth century led to similar patterns of contagion and mortality. In 1616 and 1617, epidemics nearly exterminated many of New England's indigenous groups. French fur traders transmitted measles, smallpox, and other diseases as far as Hudson Bay and the Great Lakes.

Although there is very little evidence that Europeans consciously used disease as a tool of empire, the deadly results of contact clearly undermined the ability of native peoples to resist European settlement. Europeans and their African slaves occupied these depopulated lands. The Americas were transformed biologically and culturally. They were subjected to Europeans' political and economic demands.

The colonies of the Americas were crucial pieces of a new **Atlantic system.** This network of trading links moved people and cultures as well as goods and wealth around the Atlantic. The Atlantic system also affected Africa, but less severely than the Americas. Despite the loss of millions of people to the slave trade, Africa did not suffer such severe population loss as the Americas. Most important, Africans remained in control of their lands.

Amerindians, Europeans, and Africans all contributed to the creation of new cultures in the Americas. The societies that arose reflected each colony's mix of native peoples, its connections to the slave trade, and the policies of its European rulers.

As you read this chapter, ask yourself the following questions:

- How different and how similar were the colonial societies and economies of the Americas?

- Why did forced labor and slavery become so important in many New World colonies?

- How did participation in the Atlantic system affect Europe, Africa, and the Americas?

# SPANISH AMERICA AND BRAZIL

The frontiers of conquest and settlement expanded rapidly. Within one hundred years of Columbus's first voyage to the Western Hemisphere, the Spanish Empire in America included most of the islands of the Caribbean, Mexico, the American Southwest, Central America, the Caribbean and Pacific coasts of South America, the Andean highlands, and the vast plains of the Río de la Plata region (a region that includes the modern nations of Argentina, Uruguay, and Paraguay). Portuguese settlement in the New World developed more slowly. But before the end of the sixteenth century, Portugal occupied most of the Brazilian coast.

Early settlers from Spain and Portugal sought to create colonial societies based on the institutions and customs of their homelands. They viewed society as a vertical arrangement of estates (classes of society), as uniformly Catholic, and as an arrangement of patriarchal extended-family networks. Despite the imposition of foreign institutions and the massive loss of life caused by epidemics, indigenous peoples still exercised a powerful influence on the development of colonial societies. Aztec and Inca elite families sought to protect their traditional privileges and rights through marriage or less formal alliances with the Spanish settlers. They also often used colonial courts to defend their claims to land. Nearly everywhere, Amerindian religious beliefs and practices survived beneath the surface of an imposed Christianity. Amerindian languages, cuisine, medical practices, and agricultural techniques also survived the conquest and influenced the development of Latin American culture.

The African slave trade added a third cultural stream to colonial Latin American society. By the end of the colonial era, Africans and their descendants were living throughout Latin America, enriching colonial societies with their traditional agricultural practices, music, religious beliefs, cuisine, and social customs.

**State and Church** The Spanish crown moved quickly to curb the independent power of the conquistadors and establish royal authority over both the defeated native populations and the rising tide of European settlers. Created in 1524, the **Council of the Indies** in Spain supervised all government, ecclesiastical, and commercial activity in the Spanish colonies. Political and economic power was concentrated in Mexico City, capital of the Viceroyalty of New Spain

# C H R O N O L O G Y

| | Latin America | North America | West Indies | Atlantic |
|---|---|---|---|---|
| **1500** | **1518**  Smallpox arrives in Caribbean | | **ca. 1500**  Spanish settlers introduce sugar-cane cultivation | |
| | | **1524–1554** French explore New-foundland and Gulf of St. Lawrence | | **1530**  Amsterdam Exchange opens |
| | **1535**  Creation of Viceroyalty of New Spain | | | |
| | **1540s**  Creation of Viceroyalty of Peru | | | |
| | **1542**  New Laws outlaw Amerindian enslavement | | | |
| | **1545**  Silver dis-covered at Potosí, Bolivia | | | |
| **1600** | | **1607**  Jamestown founded | | |
| | | **1608**  Quebec founded | | |
| | **By 1620**  African slaves the majority of Brazilian planta-tion workers | **1620**  Plymouth founded | **1620s and 1630s** English and French colonies in Caribbean | **1621**  Dutch West India Company chartered |
| | | | **1640s**  Dutch bring sugar plantation system from Brazil | |
| | | | **1655**  English take Jamaica | |
| | | **1660**  Slavery in Virginia begins to grow rapidly | | **1660s**  English Navigation Acts |
| | | **1664**  English take New York from Dutch | | |
| | | | **1670s**  French occupy western half of Hispaniola | **1672**  Royal African Company chartered |
| | | **1699**  Louisiana founded | | **1698**  French *Exclusif* |
| **1700** | | | **1700**  West Indies surpass Brazil in sugar production | **1700–1830**  Slave trade at its peak |
| | | **1756–1763**  French and Indian War | | |

NEW
FRANCE

*Mississippi*

*Colorado*

Effective frontier
of Spanish settlement

ENGLISH COLONIES
(Independence declared, 1776)

ATLANTIC
OCEAN

Silver

Silver

COAHUILA

*Rio Grande*

FLORIDA
(Ceded to England, 1763–1783)

*Gulf of Mexico*

VICEROYALTY OF NEW SPAIN
(1535)

Silver

Sugar cane
Beef
Tobacco

Havana

Guadalajara

BAJIO LEÓN   Silver

Silver

Mexico City

Veracruz

HAITI [SAINT DOMINGUE]
(Ceded to France, 1697)

Silver

Sugar cane
Indigo

Beef

Sugar cane

Cacao

PUERTO RICO

BRITISH
HONDURAS

Sugar cane

SANTO DOMINGO

Sugar
cane
Cochineal

Guatemala

JAMAICA
(Conquered by England, 1655)

Sugar cane

Silver

Cochineal
Cacao
Indigo

*Caribbean
Sea*

Pearls

Sugar cane

Caracas

Cacao

Gold

*Magdalena*

*Suarez*

Bogotá

GUIANA

VICEROYALTY OF
NEW GRANADA
(Separated from
Viceroyalty of Peru,
1717, 1739)

*Amazon*

Quito

ANDES

Forest
products

PACIFIC
OCEAN

VICEROYALTY
OF PERU
(1590s)

Sugar cane

VICEROYALTY
OF BRAZIL
(1720)

Pernambuco

Sugar
cane

Lima

Cuzco

Salvador

Sugar
cane

La Paz

Cacao

Chuquisaca
(La Plata; Sucre)

Silver

Potosí

Diamonds
Gold

*Paraná*

São Paulo

Yerba
Tobacco

Rio de Janeiro
(Capital, 1763)

ANDES

**Spanish colonies**

Viceroyalty of New Spain

Viceroyalty of New Granada

Viceroyalty of Peru and Audiencia of Chile

Viceroyalty of Río de la Plata

**Portuguese colonies**

Viceroyalty of Brazil

VICEROYALTY OF
LA PLATA
(Separated from
Viceroyalty of Peru,
1776)

Wheat

Beef and
hides

Santiago

Buenos Aires

Montevideo

Beef and
hides

AUDIENCIA
OF CHILE
(Retained by
Viceroyalty of Peru,
1776)

Claimed but
not settled by Spain

0   500   1000 Km.

0   500   1000 Mi.

*Islas Malvinas
(Falkland Islands)*

Cape Horn

(created in 1535), and in Lima, capital of the Viceroyalty of Peru (created in the 1540s). Each viceroyalty was divided into a number of judicial and administrative districts. Until the seventeenth century, almost all of the officials appointed to high positions in Spain's colonial bureaucracy were born in Spain. Later, local-born members of the colonial elite gained many offices.

In the sixteenth century, Portugal concentrated its resources and energies on Asia and Africa, because early settlers found neither mineral wealth nor rich native empires in Brazil. Finally, the king appointed a governor-general in 1549 and designated Salvador, in the northern province of Bahia, Brazil's capital. In 1720, the first viceroy of Brazil was named (see Map 16.1).

Just as these colonial bureaucracies imposed Iberian economic and political institutions, the Catholic Church became the primary agent for the introduction and transmission of Christian belief and European culture in South America. Spain and Portugal justified their American conquests by assuming an obligation to convert native populations to Christianity. In Mexico alone, hundreds of thousands of conversions and baptisms were achieved within a few years of the conquest.

The Catholic clergy sought to win over the Amerindians by first converting native elites. But these efforts were abandoned when church authorities discovered that many converts were secretly observing old beliefs and rituals. In the 1560s, Spanish clergy resorted to torture, executions, and the destruction of native manuscripts to eradicate traditional beliefs and rituals among the Maya. Repelled by these events, the church hierarchy ended both the violent repression of native religious practice and efforts to recruit an Amerindian clergy.

Despite its failures, the Catholic clergy did provide native peoples with some protections against

**Map 16.1  Colonial Latin America in the Eighteenth Century**  Spain and Portugal controlled most of the Western Hemisphere in the eighteenth century. In the sixteenth century they had created new administrative jurisdictions—viceroyalties—to defend their respective colonies against European rivals. Taxes assessed on colonial products helped pay for this extension of governmental authority.

the abuse and exploitation of Spanish settlers. The priest **Bartolomé de Las Casas** (1474–1566), who served as the most important advocate for native peoples, wrote a number of books that detailed their mistreatment by the Spanish. His most important achievement was the enactment of the New Laws of 1542, which outlawed the enslavement of Amerindians and limited other forms of forced labor.

Despite the disapproval of most European clergy and settlers, Amerindians blended Catholic Christian beliefs with important elements of traditional native cosmology and ritual. Most commonly, indigenous beliefs and rituals came to be embedded in the celebration of saints' days or Catholic rituals associated with the Virgin Mary, illustrating the cultural borrowing and innovation that contributed to a distinct and original Latin American culture.

After 1600, the Catholic Church redirected most of its resources from the countryside to growing colonial cities and towns with large European populations. One important outcome of this altered mission was the founding of universities and secondary schools, which stimulated urban intellectual life.

## Colonial Economies

The silver mines of Peru and Mexico and the sugar plantations of Brazil dominated the colonial economy and fueled the early development of European capitalism. Profits produced in these economic centers also promoted the growth of colonial cities, concentrated scarce investment capital and labor resources, and stimulated the development of livestock raising and agriculture in neighboring rural areas. Dependence on mineral and agricultural exports was an enduring theme in Latin America.

Although millions of pesos of gold were mined in Latin America, silver mines generated more wealth and exercised greater economic influence. In 1545, the single richest silver deposit in the Americas was discovered at **Potosí°**, in what is now Bolivia, and until 1680 the silver production of Bolivia and Peru dominated the Spanish colonial economy.

Silver mining also greatly altered the environment. Within a short time, wasteful use of forest

**Potosí** (poh-toh-SEE)

resources for fuel destroyed forests near the mining centers. Faced with rising fuel costs, miners developed an efficient method of chemical extraction that relied on mixing mercury with the silver ore. But mercury is a poison, and its use contaminated the environment and sickened the Amerindian work force.

From the time of Columbus, indigenous populations had been compelled to provide labor for European settlers in the Americas. Until the 1540s in Spanish colonies, Amerindian peoples were divided among the settlers and were forced to provide them with labor or with textiles, food, or other goods. This form of forced labor was called the **encomienda°**. The discovery of silver in Peru led to a new form of compulsory labor called the mita°. Under this system, one-seventh of the adult male Amerindians were compelled to work for six months each year in mines or on farms or in textile factories. The most dangerous working conditions existed in the silver mines.

In the Spanish mita, few Amerindian workers could survive on their wages. Wives and children were commonly forced to join the work force to help meet expenses. Even those who remained behind in the village were forced to send food and cash to support mita workers.

The Portuguese, who had developed sugar plantations that depended on slave labor on the Atlantic islands of Madeira, the Azores, the Cape Verdes, and São Tomé, transferred this profitable form of agriculture to Brazil. By the seventeenth century, sugar dominated the Brazilian economy. At first, the Portuguese enslaved Amerindian men as field hands, but sugar planters eventually came to rely more on African slaves, who were more resistant to disease. Imports of African slaves rose from an average of 2,000 per year in the late sixteenth century to approximately 7,000 per year a century later, far outstripping the immigration of free Portuguese settlers.

The mining centers of Latin America exercised global economic influence. American silver increased the European money supply, promoting commercial expansion. Large amounts of silver also flowed across the Pacific, where it was exchanged for Asian spices, silks, and pottery. In the Americas, the rich mines stimulated urban population growth, as well as commercial links with agricultural and textile producers.

The sugar plantations of Brazil played a similar role in integrating the economy of the South Atlantic region. At the end of the seventeenth century, the discovery of gold in Brazil helped overcome this large region's currency shortage and promoted further economic integration.

Both Spain and Portugal attempted to control the trade of their American colonies, but the combination of monopoly commerce and convoy shipping slowed the flow of European goods to the colonies and kept prices high. Frustrated by these restraints, colonial populations established illegal commercial relations with the English, French, and Dutch. By the middle of the seventeenth century, a majority of European imports were arriving in Latin America illegally.

## Society in Colonial Latin America

With the exception of a few early viceroys, few members of Spain's great noble families came to the New World. *Hidalgos°*—lesser nobles—were well represented, as were Spanish merchants, artisans, miners, priests, and lawyers. Small numbers of criminals, beggars, and prostitutes also found their way to the colonies. Spanish settlers, however, were always a tiny minority in a colonial society numerically dominated by Amerindians and rapidly growing populations of Africans, **creoles** (whites born in America to European parents), and people of mixed ancestry (see Diversity and Dominance: Race and Ethnicity in the Spanish Colonies).

Conquistadors and early settlers who received from the Crown grants of labor and tribute goods (encomienda) from Amerindian communities as rewards for service to Spain dominated colonial society in early Spanish America. These *encomenderos* sought to create a hereditary social and political class comparable to the nobles of Europe. But their systematic abuse of Amerindian communities and the catastrophic loss of Amerindian life during the epidemics of the sixteenth century undermined their position, as did the growing power

*encomienda* (in-co-mee-EN-dah)  *mita* (MEE-tah)

**hidalgos** (ee-DAHL-goes)

of colonial viceroys, judges, and bishops appointed by the king.

By the end of the sixteenth century, the elite of Spanish America included both European immigrants and creoles. Europeans dominated the highest levels of the church and government, as well as commerce. Creoles commonly controlled colonial agriculture and mining. Although tensions between Spaniards and creoles were inevitable, most elite families had members from both groups.

Before the Europeans arrived in the Americas, the native peoples were members of a large number of distinct cultural and linguistic groups. Cultural diversity and class distinctions were present even in the highly centralized Aztec and Inca Empires. The loss of life provoked by the European conquest undermined this rich social and cultural complexity, and the imposition of Catholic Christianity further eroded ethnic boundaries among native peoples. Colonial administrators and settlers broadly applied the racial label *Indian,* which facilitated the imposition of special taxes and labor obligations while erasing long-standing class and ethnic differences.

Indigenous Amerindian elites survived only briefly in the Spanish colonies and Brazil. Some of the conquistadors and early settlers married or established less formal relations with elite Amerindian women, but fewer of these alliances occurred after European women began to arrive. Some descendants of the powerful Amerindian families prospered in the colonial period as ranchers, muleteers, and merchants; many others lived in the same materially deprived conditions as Amerindian commoners.

Thousands of blacks participated in the conquest and settlement of Spanish America, and the opening of a direct slave trade with Africa added millions more. Settlers' views of African slaves' cultural differences as signs of inferiority ultimately served as a justification for slavery. By 1600, anyone with black ancestry was barred from positions in church, government, and many skilled crafts. Even so, African languages, religious beliefs, and marriage customs mixed with European (and in some cases Amerindian) languages and beliefs to forge distinct local cultures. The rapid growth of an American-born slave population accelerated this process of cultural change.

**Painting of Castas**    This is an example of a common genre of colonial Spanish American painting. In the eighteenth century there was increased interest in ethnic mixing, and wealthy colonials as well as some Europeans commissioned sets of paintings that showed mixed families. The paintings commonly also indicated what the artist believed was an appropriate class setting. In this painting a richly dressed Spaniard is depicted with his Amerindian wife dressed in European clothing. Notice that the painter has the mestiza daughter look to her European father for guidance.    (Private Collection. Photographer: Camilo Garza/Fotocam, Monterrey, Mexico)

African slaves became skilled artisans, musicians, servants, artists, cowboys, and even soldiers. However, the vast majority worked in agriculture. To escape harsh discipline, brutal punishments, and backbreaking labor, many slaves rebelled or ran away. Communities of runaways (called *quilombos°* in Brazil and *palenques°* in Spanish colonies) were common. The largest quilombo was Palmares, where thousands of slaves defended

---

*quilombos* (ley-LOM-bos)    *palenques* (pah-LEN-kays)

# DIVERSITY AND DOMINANCE

## RACE AND ETHNICITY IN THE SPANISH COLONIES: NEGOTIATING HIERARCHY

*M*any European visitors to colonial Latin America were interested in the mixing of Europeans, Amerindians, and Africans in the colonies. Many also commented on the treatment of slaves. The passages that follow allow us to examine two colonial societies.

The first selection was written by two young Spanish naval officers and scientists, Jorge Juan and Antonio de Ulloa, who arrived in the colonies in 1735 as members of a scientific expedition. They visited the major cities of the Pacific coast of South America and traveled across some of the most difficult terrain in the hemisphere. In addition to their scientific chores, they described architecture, local customs, and the social order. In this section they describe the ethnic mix in Quito, now the capital of Ecuador.

The second selection was published in Lima under the pseudonym Concolorcorvo around 1776. We now know that the author was Alonso Carrío de la Vandera. Born in Spain, he traveled to the colonies as a young man. He served in many minor bureaucratic positions, one of which was the inspection of the postal route between Buenos Aires and Lima. Carrío turned his long and often uncomfortable trip into an insightful, and sometimes highly critical, examination of colonial society. The selection that follows describes Córdoba, Argentina.

Juan and Ulloa and Carrío seem perplexed by colonial efforts to create and enforce a racial taxonomy that stipulated and named every possible mixture of European, Amerindian, and African, noting the vanity and social presumptions of the dominant white population. We are fortunate to have these contemporary descriptions of the diversity of colonial society, but it is important to remember that these authors were clearly rooted in their time and confident in the superiority of Europe. Although they noted many of the abuses of Amerindian, mixed, and African populations while puncturing the pretensions of the colonial elites, they were also quick to assume the inferiority of the nonwhite population.

### Quito

This city is very populous, and has, among its inhabitants, some families of high rank and distinction; though their number is but small considering its extent, the poorer class bearing here too great a proportion. The former are the descendants either of the original conquerors, or of presidents, auditors, or other persons of character [high rank], who at different times came over from Spain invested with some lucrative post, and have still preserved their luster, both of wealth and descent, by intermarriages, without intermixing with meaner families though famous for their riches. The commonalty may be divided into four classes; Spaniards or Whites, Mestizos, Indians or Natives, and Negroes, with their progeny. These last are not proportionally so numerous as in the other parts of the Indies; occasioned by it being something inconvenient to bring Negroes to Quito, and the different kinds of agriculture being generally performed by Indians.

The name of Spaniard here has a different meaning from that of Chapitone [sic] or European, as properly signifying a person descended from a Spaniard without a mixture of blood. Many Mestizos, from the advantage of a fresh complexion, appear to be Spaniards more than those who are so in reality; and from only this fortuitous advantage are accounted as such. The Whites, according to this construction of the word, may be considered as one sixth part of the inhabitants.

The Mestizos are the descendants of Spaniards and Indians, and are to be considered here in the same different degrees between the Negroes and Whites, as before at Carthagena [sic]; but with this difference, that at Quito the degrees of Mestizos are not carried so far back; for, even in the second or third generations, when they acquire the European color, they are considered as Spaniards. The complexion of the Mestizos is swarthy and reddish, but not of that red common in the fair Mulattos. This is the first degree, or the immediate issue of a Spaniard and Indian. Some are, however, equally tawny with the Indians themselves, though they are distinguished from them by their beards: while others, on the contrary, have so fine a complexion that they might pass for Whites, were it not for some signs which betray them, when viewed attentively. Among these, the most remarkable is the lowness of the forehead, which often leaves but a small space between their hair and eye-brows; at the same time the hair grows remarkably forward on the temples, extending to the lower part of the ear. Besides, the hair itself is harsh, lank, coarse, and very black; their nose very small, thin, and has a little rising on the middle, from whence it forms a small curve, terminating in a point, bending towards the upper lip. These marks, besides some dark spots on the body, are so constant and invariable, as to make it very difficult to conceal the fallacy of their complexion. The Mestizos may be reckoned a third part of the inhabitants.

The next class is the Indians, who form about another third; and the others, who are about one sixth, are the Castes [mixed]. These four classes, according to the most authentic accounts taken from the parish register, amount to between 50 and 60,000 persons, of all ages, sexes, and ranks. If among these classes the Spaniards, as is natural to think, are the most eminent for riches, rank, and power, it must at the same time be owned, however melancholy the truth may appear, they are in proportion the most poor, miserable and distressed; for they refuse to apply themselves to any mechanic business, considering it as a disgrace to that quality they so highly value themselves upon, which consists in not being black, brown, or of a copper color. The Mestizos, whose pride is regulated by prudence, readily apply themselves to arts and trades, but chose those of the greatest repute, as painting, sculpture, and the like, leaving the meaner sort to the Indians.

## Córdoba

There was not a person who would give me even an estimate of the number of residents comprising this city, because neither the secular nor the ecclesiastical council has a register, and I know not how these colonists prove the ancient and distinguished nobility of which they boast; it may be that each family has its genealogical history in reserve. In my computation, there must be within the city and its limited common lands around 500 to 600 residents, but in the principal houses there are a very large number of slaves, most of them Creoles [native born] of all conceivable classes, because in this city and in all of Tucumán there is no leniency about granting freedom to any of them. They are easily supported since the principal aliment, meat, is of such moderate price, and there is a custom of dressing them only in ordinary cloth which is made at home by the slaves themselves, shoes being very rare. They aid their masters in many profitable ways and under this system do not think of freedom, thus exposing themselves to a sorrowful end, as is happening in Lima.

As I was passing through Córdoba, they were selling 2,000 Negroes, all Creoles from Temporalidades [property confiscated from the Jesuit order in 1767], from just the two farms of the [Jesuit] colleges of this city. I have seen the lists, for each one has its own, and they proceed by families numbering from two to eleven, all pure Negroes and Creoles back to the fourth generation, because the priests used to sell all of those born with a mixture of Spanish, mulatto, or Indian blood. Among this multitude of Negroes were many musicians and many of other crafts; they proceeded with the sale by families. I was assured that the nuns of Santa Teresa alone had a group of 300 slaves of both sexes, to whom they give their just ration of meat and dress in the coarse cloth which they make, while these good nuns content themselves with what is left from other ministrations. The number attached to other religious establishments is much smaller, but there is a private home which has 30 or 40, the majority of whom are engaged in various gainful activities. The result is a large number of excellent washerwomen whose accomplishments are valued so highly that they never mend their outer skirts in order that the whiteness of their undergarments may be seen. They do the laundry in the river, in water up to the waist, saying vaingloriously that she who is not soaked cannot wash well. They make ponchos [hand-woven capes], rugs, sashes,

*(continued)*

and sundries, and especially decorated leather cases which the men sell for 8 reales each, because the hides have no outlet due to the great distance to the port; the same thing happens on the banks of the Tercero and Cuarto rivers, where they are sold at 2 reales and frequently for less.

The principal men of the city wear very expensive clothes, but this is not true of the women, who are an exception in both Americas and even in the entire world, because they dress decorously in clothing of little cost. They are very tenacious in preserving the customs of their ancestors. They do not permit slaves, or even freedmen who have a mixture of Negro blood, to wear any cloth other than that made in this country, which is quite coarse. I was told recently that a certain bedecked mulatto [woman] who appeared in Córdoba was sent word by the ladies of the city that she should dress according to her station, but since she paid no attention to this reproach, they endured her negligence until one of the ladies, summoning her to her home under some other pretext, had the servants undress her, whip her, burn her finery before her eyes, and dress her in the clothes befitting her class; despite the fact that the [victim] was not lacking in persons to defend her, she disappeared lest the tragedy be repeated.

## QUESTIONS FOR ANALYSIS

1. What do the authors of these selections seem to think about the white elites of the colonies? Are there similarities in the ways that Juan and Ulloa and Carrió describe the mixed population of Quito and the slave population of Córdoba?

2. Are there differences in the way that the authors characterize the relationship between color and class?

3. What does the humiliation of the mixed-race woman in Córdoba tell us about ideas of race and class in the Spanish colony?

*Sources:* Jorge Juan and Antonio de Ulloa, *A Voyage to South America,* The John Adams translation (abridged), Introduction by Irving A. Leonard (New York: Alfred A. Knopf, 1964), 135–137, copyright © 1964 by Alfred A. Knopf, Inc. Used by permission of Alfred A. Knopf, a division of Random House, Inc.; Concolorcorvo, *El Lazarillo, A Guide for Inexperienced Travelers between Buenos Aires and Lima,* 1773, translated by Walter D. Kline (Bloomington: Indiana University Press, 1965), 78–80. Used with permission of Indiana University Press.

themselves against Brazilian authorities for sixty years until they were finally overrun in 1694.

# ENGLISH AND FRENCH COLONIES IN NORTH AMERICA

The North American colonial empires of England and France and the colonies of Spain and Portugal had many characteristics in common. The governments of England and France hoped to find easily extracted forms of wealth or great indigenous empires like those of the Aztecs or Inca. Like the Spanish and Portuguese, English and French settlers responded to native peoples with a mixture of diplomacy and violence. African slaves proved crucial to the development of all four colonial economies.

There were also important differences. The English and French colonies were founded nearly a century after Cortés's conquest of Mexico and initial Portuguese settlement in Brazil. Distracted by ventures elsewhere, neither England nor France imitated the large and expensive colonial bureaucracies that Spain and Portugal established. Instead, private companies and individual proprietors pioneered the development of English and French colonies. This practice led to greater regional variety in economic activity, political institutions and culture, and social structure than was evident in Latin American colonies.

## The South

London investors, organized as the privately funded Virginia Company, got off to a rocky start. Nearly 80 percent of the settlers at Jamestown in 1607 and 1608 soon died of disease or Amerindian attacks. After the English crown dissolved the Virginia Company in 1624 because of its mismanagement, colonists pushed deeper into the interior, developing a sustainable economy based on furs, timber, and, increasingly, tobacco. The profits from tobacco soon attracted new immigrants and new capital. Along the shoreline of Chesapeake Bay and the rivers that fed it, settlers spread out, developing plantations and farms.

**Indentured servants** eventually accounted for approximately 80 percent of all English immigrants to the Chesapeake Bay region. Young men and women unable to pay for their transportation to the New World accepted indentures (contracts) that bound them to a term ranging from four to seven years of labor in return for passage, a small parcel of land, and some tools and clothes. During the seventeenth century, approximately fifteen hundred indentured servants, mostly male, arrived each year. As life expectancy in the colony improved, planters began to purchase more slaves. They calculated that greater profits could be secured by paying the higher initial cost of slaves owned for life than by purchasing the contracts of indentured servants bound for short periods of time. As a result, Virginia's slave population grew rapidly, from 950 in 1660 to 120,000 by 1756.

Ironically, this dramatic increase in the colony's slave population occurred along with the expansion in colonial liberties and political rights. At first, colonial government had been administered by a Crown-appointed governor and his council, as well as by representatives of towns meeting together as the **House of Burgesses.** When these representatives began to meet alone as a deliberative body, they initiated a form of democratic representation that distinguished the English colonies of North America from the colonies of other European powers. The intertwined evolution of freedom and slavery gave England's southern colonies a unique and conflicted political character.

Colonial South Carolina was the most hierarchical society in British North America. Planters controlled the economy and political life. The richest maintained households in both the countryside and Charleston, the largest city in the southern colonies. Small farmers, cattlemen, artisans, merchants, and fur traders held an intermediate but clearly subordinate social position. African slaves were present from the founding of Charleston. They were instrumental in introducing irrigated rice agriculture and in developing indigo (a plant that produced a blue dye) plantations. Native peoples remained influential participants in colonial society through commercial contacts and alliances, but they were increasingly marginalized.

## New England

New England was colonized by two separate groups of Protestant dissenters. The **Pilgrims** established the colony of Plymouth on the coast of present-day Massachusetts in 1620. Although nearly half of the settlers died during the first winter, the colony survived. In 1691, Plymouth was absorbed into the larger Massachusetts Bay Colony of the **Puritans.** The Puritan leaders had received a royal charter to finance the Massachusetts Bay Colony. By 1643, more than 20,000 Puritans had settled in the Bay Colony.

Unlike in the southern colonies, most newcomers to Massachusetts arrived with their families. A normal gender balance and a healthy climate resulted in a rapid natural increase in population. Massachusetts also was more homogeneous and less hierarchical than the southern colonies.

Political institutions evolved out of the terms of the royal charter. A governor was elected, along with a council of magistrates drawn from the board of directors of the Massachusetts Bay Company. Disagreements between this council and elected representatives of the towns led, by 1650, to the creation of a lower legislative house that selected its own speaker and began to develop procedures and rules similar to those of the House of Commons in England.

Economically, Massachusetts differed dramatically from the southern colonies. Agriculture met basic needs, but poor soils and harsh climate offered no opportunity to develop cash crops like tobacco or rice. To pay for imported tools, textiles, and other essentials, the colonists began to provide commercial and shipping services to the southern colonies, the smaller Caribbean islands, Africa, and Europe.

In contrast to Latin America's heavily capitalized monopolies, New England merchants' success rested on market intelligence, flexibility, and streamlined organization. With 16,000 inhabitants in 1740, Boston was the largest city in British North America.

## Middle Atlantic Region

The rapid economic development and remarkable cultural diversity of the Middle Atlantic colonies added to the success of English-speaking North America. The **Iroquois Confederacy,** an alliance of several native peoples, established treaties and trading relationships with the Dutch. When confronted by an English military expedition in 1664, the Dutch surrendered their colony of New Netherland without a fight. Renamed New York, the colony's success was guaranteed in large measure by the development of New York City as a commercial and shipping center. Located at the mouth of the Hudson River, the city played an essential role in connecting the region's grain farmers to the booming markets of the Caribbean and southern Europe. By the early eighteenth century, New York Colony had a diverse population that included (in addition to English colonists) Dutch, German, and Swedish settlers, as well as a large slave community.

Pennsylvania began as a proprietary colony in 1682 and as a refuge for Quakers, a persecuted religious minority. The founder, William Penn, quickly lost control of the colony's political life, but the colony enjoyed remarkable success. By 1700, Pennsylvania had a population of more than 21,000, and Philadelphia, its capital, soon passed Boston to become the largest city in the British colonies. Healthy climate, excellent land, and relatively peaceful relations with native peoples attracted free workers, including a large number of German families. As a result, Pennsylvania's economic expansion in the late seventeenth century occurred without reproducing South Carolina's hierarchical and repressive social order. By the early eighteenth century, however, the prosperous city of Philadelphia included a large population of black slaves, servants, and skilled tradesmen.

## French America

French settlement patterns more closely resembled those of Spain and Portugal than of England. The French were committed to missionary activity among Amerindian peoples and emphasized extracting resources—in this case, furs.

Coming to Canada after spending years in the West Indies, Samuel de Champlain founded the

**Canadian Fur Trader**    The fur trade provided the economic foundation of early Canadian settlement. The trade depended on a mix of native and European skills and resources. Fur traders were cultural intermediaries. They transmitted European technologies and products like firearms and machine-made textiles to native peoples and native technologies and products like canoes and furs to European settlements. Many were the sons of native women, and nearly all were fluent in native languages. (National Archives of Canada)

colony of **New France** at Quebec°, on the banks of the St. Lawrence River, in 1608. The European market for fur, especially beaver, fueled French settlement. Young Frenchmen were sent to live among native peoples to master their languages and customs. These men and their children by native women organized the fur trade and led French expansion to the west and south. Amerindians ac-

---

**Quebec** (kwuh-BEC)

tively participated in this trade because they came to depend on the goods they received in exchange for furs: firearms, metal tools and utensils, textiles, and alcohol.

The Iroquois Confederacy responded to the increased military strength of France's Algonkian allies by forging commercial and military links with Dutch and later English settlements in the Hudson River Valley. Well armed by the Dutch and English, the Iroquois Confederacy nearly eradicated the Huron in 1649 and inflicted a series of humiliating defeats on the French. At the high point of their power in the early 1680s, Iroquois hunters and military forces gained control of much of the Great Lakes region and the Ohio River Valley. A large French military expedition and a relentless attack focused on Iroquois villages and agriculture finally checked Iroquois power in 1701.

Use of firearms in hunting and warfare moved west and south, reaching indigenous plains cultures that previously had adopted the horse introduced by the Spanish. This intersection of horse and gun frontiers in the early eighteenth century dramatically increased the military power and hunting efficiency of the Sioux, Comanche, Cheyenne, and other indigenous peoples and slowed the pace of European settlement in North America.

In French Canada, the Jesuits led the effort to convert native peoples to Christianity. Building on earlier evangelical efforts in Brazil and Paraguay, French Catholic missionaries mastered native languages, created boarding schools for young boys and girls, and set up model agricultural communities for converted Amerindians. The Jesuits' greatest successes coincided with a destructive wave of epidemics and renewed warfare among native peoples in the 1630s. Nevertheless, local cultures persisted.

Although the fur trade flourished, settlers were few. Founded at about the same time, Virginia had twenty times as many European residents as Canada by 1627. Canada's small settler population and the fur trade's dependence on Amerindians allowed indigenous peoples to retain greater independence and more control over their encounters with new religious, technological, and market realities.

The French aggressively expanded. Louisiana, founded in 1699, depended on the fur trade with Amerindians. France's North American colonies were threatened by a series of wars with England and the neighboring English colonies. The "French and Indian War" (also known as the Seven Years War, 1756–1763) proved to be the final contest for the North American empire. England committed a larger military force to the struggle and, despite early defeats, took the French capital of Quebec in 1759. The peace agreement forced France to yield Canada to the English and cede Louisiana to Spain. The French then concentrated their efforts on their sugar-producing colonies in the Caribbean.

# PLANTATIONS IN THE WEST INDIES

The West Indies was the first place in the Americas that Columbus reached and the first part of the Americas where native populations collapsed. It took a long time to repopulate these islands from abroad and forge new economic links between them and other parts of the Atlantic. But after 1650, sugar plantations, African slaves, and European capital made these islands a major center of the Atlantic economy.

Spanish settlers had introduced sugar-cane cultivation into the West Indies shortly after 1500, but these colonies soon fell into neglect as attention shifted to colonizing the American mainland. In the 1620s and 1630s, the West Indies revived as a focus of colonization, this time by English and French settlers interested in growing tobacco and other crops. The islands' value mushroomed after the Dutch reintroduced sugar cultivation from Brazil in the 1640s and supplied the African slaves and European capital necessary to create a new economy.

**Sugar and Slaves**  The English colony of Barbados illustrates the dramatic transformation that sugar brought to the seventeenth-century Caribbean. In 1640, Barbados's economy depended largely on tobacco, mostly grown by European settlers, both free and indentured. By the 1680s, sugar had become the colony's principal crop, and enslaved Africans were three

**Market in Rio de Janeiro**   In many of the cities of colonial Latin America female slaves and black free women dominated retail markets. In this scene from late colonial Brazil, Afro-Brazilian women sell a variety of foods and crafts.   (Sir Henry Chamberlain, Views and Costumes of the City and Neighborhoods of Rio de Janeiro, London, 1822)

times as numerous as Europeans. Exporting up to 15,000 tons of sugar a year, Barbados had become the wealthiest and most populous of England's American colonies. By 1700, the West Indies had surpassed Brazil as the world's principal source of sugar.

The expansion of sugar plantations in the West Indies required a sharp increase in the volume of the slave trade from Africa. During the first half of the seventeenth century, about 10,000 slaves a year had arrived from Africa, most destined for Brazil and the mainland Spanish colonies. In the second half of the century, the trade averaged 20,000 slaves a year. More than half were intended for the English, French, and Dutch West Indies and most of the rest for Brazil. A century later, the volume of the Atlantic slave trade was three times larger.

What produced this shift in favor of African slaves? Recent scholarship has cast doubt on the once-common assertion that Africans were more suited than Europeans to field labor; in fact, both died in large numbers in the American tropics. The West Indian historian Eric Williams has also refuted the idea that the rise of African slave labor was primarily motivated by prejudice. Citing the West Indian colonies' prior use of enslaved Amerindians and indentured Europeans, along with European convicts and prisoners of war, he argued, "Slavery was not born of racism: rather, racism was the consequence of slavery."[2] Williams suggested the shift was due to the lower cost of African labor.

Yet slaves were far from cheap. Cash-short tobacco planters in the seventeenth century preferred indentured Europeans because they cost half as much as African slaves. Poor European men and women were willing to work for little to get to the Americas, where they could acquire their own land cheaply at the end of their term of service. However, as the cultivation of sugar spread after 1750, rich speculators drove the price of land in the West Indies up so high that end-of-term indentured servants could not afford to buy it. As a result, poor Europeans chose to indenture themselves in the mainland North American colonies, where cheap land was still available. Rather than raise wages to attract European laborers, Caribbean sugar planters switched to slaves.

Rising sugar prices helped the West Indian sugar planters afford the higher cost of African slaves. The planters could rely on the Dutch and other traders to supply them with enough new slaves to meet the demands of the expanding plantations. Rising demand drove slave prices up steadily during the eighteenth century. These high labor costs were one more factor favoring large plantations over smaller operations.

To find more land for sugar plantations, France and England founded new Caribbean colonies. In 1655, the English had wrested the island of Jamaica from the Spanish (see Map 16.1). The French seized the western half of the large Spanish island of Hispaniola in the 1670s. During the eighteenth century, this new French colony of Saint Domingue° (present-day Haiti) became the greatest producer of sugar in the Atlantic world, while Jamaica surpassed Barbados as England's most important sugar colony.

## Technology and Environment

What made the sugar plantation a complex investment was that it had to be a factory as well as a farm. Freshly cut canes needed to be crushed within a few hours to extract the sugary sap. Thus, for maximum efficiency, each plantation needed its own expensive crushing and processing equipment.

At the heart of the sugar works was the mill where canes were crushed between sets of heavy rollers. From the mill, lead-lined wooden troughs carried the cane juice to a series of large copper kettles in the boiling shed, where the excess water boiled off, leaving a thick syrup. Workers poured the syrup into conical molds in the drying shed.

**Saint Domingue** (san doh-MANGH)

The sugar crystals that formed in the molds were packed in wooden barrels for shipment to Europe.

To make their operation more efficient and profitable, investors gradually increased the size of the typical West Indian plantation from around 100 acres (40 hectares) in the seventeenth century to at least twice that size in the eighteenth century. A plantation became a huge investment. One source estimated that a planter had to invest nearly £20,000 ($100,000) to acquire a Jamaican plantation of 600 acres (240 hectares) in 1774: a third for land, a quarter for equipment, and £8,000 for 200 slaves. Jamaica specialized so heavily in sugar production that the island had to import most of its food. Saint Domingue was more diverse in its economy.

In some ways, the mature sugar plantation was environmentally responsible. The crushing mill was powered by water, wind, or animal power, not fossil fuels. The boilers were largely fueled by burning the crushed canes, and the fields were fertilized by cattle manure. In two respects, however, the plantation was very damaging to the environment: soil exhaustion and deforestation.

Instead of rotating sugar with other crops to restore the nutrients naturally, planters found it more profitable to clear new lands when yields declined too much in the old fields. When land close to the sea was exhausted, planters moved on to new islands. Many of the English who first settled Jamaica were from Barbados, and the pioneer planters on Saint Domingue came from older French sugar colonies. In the second half of the eighteenth century, Jamaican sugar production began to fall behind that of Saint Domingue, which still had access to virgin land. Thus, the plantations of this period were not a stable form of agriculture but one that gradually laid waste to the landscape.

Deforestation, the second form of environmental damage, continued a trend begun in the sixteenth century. By the end of the eighteenth century, only land in the interior of the islands retained dense forests.

The most tragic and dramatic transformation in the West Indies occurred in the human population. During the eighteenth century, West Indian plantation colonies were the world's most polarized societies. On most islands, 90 percent or more of the inhabitants became slaves. A small number of very rich men owned most of the slaves and most of the land as well. Between the slaves and the masters might be found only a few others: a few estate managers and government officials and, in the French islands, some small farmers, both white and black. The profitability of a Caribbean plantation depended on extracting as much work as possible from the slaves through the use of force and the threat of force.

On a typical Jamaican plantation, about 80 percent of the slaves actively engaged in productive tasks; the only exceptions were infants, the seriously ill, and the very old. Slave labor was organized by age, sex, and ability. About 70 percent of the able-bodied slaves worked in the fields, generally in one of three labor gangs. Women formed the majority of the field laborers, even in the great gang. A little over half of the adult males were employed in nongang work, tending the livestock or serving as blacksmiths and carpenters. The most important artisan slave was the head boiler, who oversaw the delicate process of reducing the cane sap to crystallized sugar and molasses.

Skilled slaves received rewards of food and clothing or time off for good work, but the most common reason for working hard was to escape punishment. A slave gang was headed by a privileged male slave, appropriately called the **driver,** whose job was to ensure that the gang completed its work. Production quotas were high, and slaves toiled in the fields from sunup to sunset, except for meal breaks. Those who fell behind because of fatigue or illness soon felt the sting of the whip. Openly rebellious slaves who refused to work, disobeyed orders, or tried to escape were punished with flogging, confinement in irons, or mutilation.

The harsh conditions of plantation life played a major role in shortening slaves' lives, but the greatest killer was disease. The very young were carried off by dysentery caused by contaminated food and water. Slaves newly arrived from Africa went through a period of adjustment to the new environment known as **seasoning,** during which one-third on average died of unfamiliar diseases. Slaves also suffered from diseases they brought with them, including malaria. On one plantation, for example, more than half of the slaves incapacitated by illness had yaws, a painful and debilitating skin disease common in Africa.

Such high mortality greatly added to the volume of the Atlantic slave trade, since plantations had to purchase new slaves every year or two to replace those who had died. The additional imports of slaves to permit the expansion of the sugar plantations meant that the majority of slaves on most West Indian plantations were African-born. As a result, African religious beliefs, patterns of speech, styles of dress and adornment, and music were prominent parts of West Indian life.

Given the harsh conditions of their lives, it is not surprising that slaves in the West Indies often sought to regain the freedom into which most had been born. Individual slaves often ran away, hoping to elude the men and dogs who would track them. Sometimes large groups of plantation slaves rose in rebellion against their bondage and abuse. For example, a large rebellion in Jamaica in 1760 was led by a slave named Tacky, who had been a chief on the Gold Coast of Africa. One night, his followers broke into a fort and armed themselves. Joined by slaves from nearby plantations, they stormed several plantations, setting them on fire and killing the planter families. Tacky died in the fighting that followed, and three other rebel leaders stoically endured cruel deaths by torture that were meant to deter others from rebellion.

Because they believed rebellions were usually led by slaves with the strongest African heritage, European planters tried to curtail African cultural traditions. They required slaves to learn the colonial language and discouraged the use of African languages by deliberately mixing slaves from different parts of Africa. In French and Portuguese colonies, slaves were encouraged to adopt Catholic religious practices, though African deities and beliefs also survived. In the British West Indies, where only Quaker slave owners encouraged Christianity among their slaves before 1800, African herbal medicine remained strong, as did African beliefs concerning nature spirits and witchcraft.

As in Latin America, slavery also provoked flight. In the Caribbean, runaways were known as **maroons.** Maroon communities were especially numerous in the mountainous interiors of Jamaica and Hispaniola, as well as in the island parts of the Guianas°. The Jamaican maroons, after withstand-

---

**Guianas** (guy-AHN-uhs)

ing several attacks by the colony's militia, signed a treaty in 1739 that recognized their independence in return for their cooperation in stopping new runaways and suppressing slave revolts. Similar treaties with the large maroon population in the Dutch colony of Surinam (Dutch Guiana) recognized their possession of large inland regions.

# CREATING THE
# ATLANTIC ECONOMY

The West Indian plantation colonies were at once archaic in their cruel system of slavery and oddly modern in their specialization in a single product. Besides the plantation system itself, three other elements went into the creation of the new Atlantic economy: new economic institutions, new partnerships between private investors and governments in Europe, and new working relationships between European and African merchants. The new trading system is a prime example of how European capitalist relationships were reshaping the world.

## Capitalism and Mercantilism

The Spanish and Portuguese voyages of exploration in the fifteenth and sixteenth centuries were government ventures, and both countries tried to keep their overseas trade and colonies royal monopolies. Monopoly control, however, proved both expensive and inefficient. The success of the Atlantic economy in the seventeenth and eighteenth centuries owed much to private enterprise, which made trading venues more efficient and profitable.

Two European innovations, capitalism and mercantilism, enabled private investors to fund the rapid growth of the Atlantic economy. **Capitalism** was a system of large financial institutions—banks, stock exchanges, and chartered trading companies—that enabled wealthy investors to reduce risks and increase profits. Early capitalism was buttressed by **mercantilism,** policies adopted by European states to promote their citizens' overseas trade and defend it, by armed force when necessary.

**Chartered companies** were one of the first examples of mercantilist capitalism. A charter issued by the government of the Netherlands in 1602 gave the Dutch East India Company a legal monopoly over all Dutch trade in the Indian Ocean. This privilege encouraged private investors to buy shares in the company. They were amply rewarded when the Dutch East India Company captured control of the long-distance trade routes in the Indian Ocean from the Portuguese (see Chapter 17). A sister firm, the **Dutch West India Company,** was chartered in 1621 to engage in the Atlantic trade and to seize sugar-producing areas in Brazil and African slaving ports from the Portuguese.

Such successes inspired other governments to set up their own chartered companies. In 1672, a royal charter placed all English trade with West Africa in the hands of the new **Royal African Company,** which established its headquarters at Cape Coast Castle, just east of Elmina on the Gold Coast. The French government chartered East India and West India companies to reduce French colonies' dependence on Dutch and English traders.

French and English governments also used military force in pursuit of commercial dominance, especially to break the trading advantage of the Dutch in the Americas. Restrictions on Dutch access to French and English colonies provoked a series of wars with the Netherlands between 1652 and 1678, during which the larger English and French navies defeated the Dutch and drove the Dutch West India Company into bankruptcy.

With Dutch competition in the Atlantic reduced, the French and English governments moved to revoke the monopoly privileges of their chartered companies. England opened trade in Africa to any English subject in 1698 on the grounds that ending monopolies would be "highly beneficial and advantageous to this kingdom." It was hoped that such competition would also cut the cost of slaves to West Indian planters, though the demand for slaves soon drove the prices up again.

Such new mercantilist policies fostered competition among a nation's own citizens, while using high tariffs and restrictions to exclude foreigners. In the 1660s, England had passed a series of Navigation Acts that confined trade with its colonies to English ships and cargoes. The French called their mercantilist legislation, first codified in 1698, the

*Exclusif°*, highlighting its exclusionary intentions. Other mercantilist laws defended manufacturing and processing interests in Europe against competition from colonies, imposing prohibitively high taxes on any manufactured goods and refined sugar imported from the colonies.

As a result of such mercantilist measures, the Atlantic became Britain, France, and Portugal's most important overseas trading area in the eighteenth century. Britain's imports from its West Indian colonies in this period accounted for over one-fifth of the value of total British imports. The French West Indian colonies played an even larger role in France's overseas trade. Only the Dutch, closed out of much of the American trade, found Asian trade of greater value. Profits from the Atlantic economy, in turn, promoted further economic expansion and increased the revenues of European governments.

## The Great Circuit and the Middle Passage

At the heart of the Atlantic system was a great clockwise network of trade routes known as the **Great Circuit.** It began in Europe, ran south to Africa, turned west across the Atlantic Ocean to the Americas, and then swept back to Europe. Like Asian sailors in the Indian Ocean, Atlantic mariners depended on the prevailing winds and currents to propel their ships. What drove the ships as much as the winds and currents was the desire for the profits that each leg of the circuit was expected to produce.

The first leg, from Europe to Africa, carried European manufactures—notably metal bars, hardware, and guns—as well as great quantities of cotton textiles brought from India. Some of these goods were traded for West African gold, timber, and other products, which were taken back to Europe. More goods went to purchase slaves, who were transported across the Atlantic to the plantation colonies in the part of the Great Circuit known as the **Middle Passage.** On the third leg, plantation goods from the colonies returned to Europe. Each leg of the circuit carried goods from where they were abundant and relatively cheap to where they were scarce and therefore more valuable. Thus, in theory, each leg of the Great Circuit could earn

much more than its costs, and a ship that completed all three legs could return a handsome profit to its owners. In practice, shipwrecks, deaths, piracy, and other risks could turn profit into loss.

The three-sided Great Circuit is only the simplest model of Atlantic trade. Many other trading voyages supplemented the basic circuit. Cargo ships made long voyages from Europe to the Indian Ocean, passed southward through the Atlantic with quantities of African gold and American silver, and returned with the cotton textiles necessary to the African trade. Other sea routes brought to the West Indies manufactured goods from Europe or foodstuffs and lumber from New England.

European interests dominated the Atlantic system. The manufacturers who supplied the trade goods and the investors who provided the capital were all based in Europe, as were the principal consumers of the plantation products. Before the seventeenth century, sugar had been rare and fairly expensive in western Europe. By 1700, annual consumption of sugar in England had risen to about 4 pounds (nearly 2 kilograms) per person. Rising western European prosperity and declining sugar prices promoted additional consumption, starting with the upper classes and working its way down the social ladder. People spooned sugar into popular new beverages imported from overseas—tea, coffee, and chocolate—to overcome the beverages' natural bitterness. By 1750, annual sugar consumption in Britain had doubled, and it doubled again to about 18 pounds (8 kilograms) per person by the early nineteenth century.

The flow of sugar to Europe depended on another key component of the Atlantic trading system: the flow of slaves from Africa. The rising volume of the Middle Passage also measures the Atlantic system's expansion. During the first 150 years after the European discovery of the Americas, some 800,000 Africans had begun the journey across the Atlantic. During the boom in sugar production between 1650 and 1800, the slave trade amounted to nearly 7.5 million. Of the survivors, over half landed in the West Indies and nearly a third in Brazil. Plantations in North America imported another 5 percent, and the rest went to other parts of Spanish America.

In these peak decades, the transportation of slaves from Africa was a highly specialized trade.

---

*Exclusif* (ek-skloo-SEEF)

Most slaves were carried in ships that had been specially built or modified for the slave trade by the construction between the ships' decks of additional platforms on which the human cargo was packed as tightly as possible.

Seventeenth-century mercantilist policies placed much of the Atlantic slave trade in the hands of chartered companies. During their existence, the Dutch West India Company and the English Royal African Company each carried about 100,000 slaves across the Atlantic. In the eighteenth century, private English traders from Liverpool and Bristol controlled about 40 percent of the slave trade. The French, operating out of Nantes and Bordeaux, handled about half as much, and the Dutch hung on to only 6 percent. The Portuguese, supplying Brazil and other places, had nearly 30 percent of the Atlantic slave trade, in contrast to the 3 percent carried in North American ships.

To make a profit, European slave traders had to buy slaves in Africa for less than the cost of the goods they traded in return. Then they had to deliver as many healthy slaves as possible across the Atlantic for resale in the plantation colonies. The treacherous voyage to the Americas lasted from six to ten weeks. Some ships completed it with all of their slaves alive, but large, even catastrophic losses of life were common. On average between 1650 and 1800, about one slave in every six perished during the Middle Passage.

Some deaths resulted from the efforts of the captives to escape. To inhibit such attempts, African men were confined below deck during most of the voyage, and special netting was installed around the outside of the ship. Some slaves fell into deep psychological depression, known to contemporaries as "fixed melancholy," from which many perished. Others refused to eat, so forced feeding was used to keep slaves alive. When opportunities presented themselves (nearness to land, illness among the crew), some cargoes of enslaved Africans tried to overpower their captors. Such "mutinies" were rarely successful and were put down with brutality that occasioned further losses of life.

Other deaths during the Middle Passage were due to the ill treatment slaves received. Although it was in the interests of the captain and crew to deliver their slave cargo in good condition, whippings, beatings, and even executions were used to maintain order and force the captives to take nourishment. Moreover, the dangers and brutalities of the slave trade were so notorious that many ordinary seamen shunned such work. As a consequence, cruel and brutal characters abounded among the officers and crews on slave ships.

Although examples of unspeakable cruelties are common in the records, most deaths in the Middle Passage were the result of disease rather than abuse, just as on plantations. Dysentery spread by contaminated food and water caused many deaths. Others died of contagious diseases such as smallpox, carried by persons whose infections were not detected during the medical examinations of slaves prior to boarding. Such maladies spread quickly in the crowded and unsanitary confines of the ships, claiming the lives of many slaves already physically weakened and mentally traumatized by their ordeals.

Crew members who were in close contact with the slaves were equally exposed to the epidemics and regularly suffered heavy losses. Moreover, sailors often fell victim to tropical diseases, such as malaria, to which Africans had acquired resistance. It is a measure of the callousness of the age, as well as the cheapness of European labor, that over the course of a Great Circuit voyage the proportion of crew deaths could be as high as the slave deaths on the Middle Passage.

## AFRICA AND THE ATLANTIC

The Atlantic system took a terrible toll in African lives both during the Middle Passage and under the harsh conditions of plantation slavery. Many other Africans died while being marched to African coastal ports for sale overseas. The overall effects on Africa of these losses and of other aspects of the slave trade have been the subject of considerable historical debate. It is clear that the trade's impact depended on the intensity and terms of different African regions' involvement.

Any assessment of the Atlantic system's effects in Africa must also take into consideration the fact that some Africans profited from the trade by capturing and selling slaves. They chained the slaves together or bound them to forked sticks for the march to the coast, then bartered them to the European slavers for trade goods. The effects on the enslaver were different from the effects on the enslaved.

## The Gold Coast and the Slave Coast

The transition to slave trading was not sudden. Even as slaves were becoming Atlantic Africa's most valuable export, nonslave goods remained a significant part of the total trade. For example, during its eight decades of operation from 1672 to 1752, the English Royal African Company made 40 percent of its profits from dealings in gold, ivory, and forest products. In some parts of West Africa, such nonslave exports remained predominant even at the peak of the trade.

African merchants were very discriminating about what merchandise they received in return for slaves or other goods. A European ship that arrived with goods of low quality or unsuited to local tastes found it hard to purchase a cargo at a profitable price. Africans' greatest demands were for textiles, hardware, and guns. Of the goods the Royal African Company traded in West Africa in the 1680s, over 60 percent were Indian and European textiles and 30 percent hardware and weaponry. Beads and other jewelry formed 3 percent. The rest consisted of cowrie shells, which were used as money. In the eighteenth century, tobacco and rum from the Americas became welcome imports.

Both Europeans and Africans naturally attempted to drive the best bargain for themselves and sometimes engaged in deceitful practices. The strength of the African bargaining position, however, may be inferred from the fact that as the demand for slaves rose, so too did their price in Africa. In the course of the eighteenth century, the goods needed to purchase a slave on the Gold Coast doubled and in some places tripled or quadrupled.

African governments on the Gold Coast and the Slave Coast just east of it made Europeans observe African trading customs and prevented them from taking control of African territory. Rivalry among European nations, each of which established its own trading "castles" along the Gold Coast, also reduced Europeans' bargaining strength.

How did African kings and merchants obtain slaves for sale? Most accounts agree that prisoners taken in war were the greatest source of slaves for the Atlantic trade, but it is difficult to say how often capturing slaves for export was the main cause of warfare. An early-nineteenth-century king of Asante stated, "I cannot make war to catch slaves in the bush, like a thief. My ancestors never did so. But if I fight a king, and kill him when he is insolent, then certainly I must have his gold, and his slaves, and his people are mine too. Do not the white kings act like this?"[3] English rulers had indeed sentenced seventeenth-century Scottish and Irish prisoners to forced labor in the West Indies.

## The Bight of Biafra and Angola

In the eighteenth century, the slave trade expanded eastward to the Bight (bay) of Biafra. In contrast to the Gold and Slave Coasts, where strong kingdoms predominated, the densely populated interior of the Bight of Biafra contained no large states. Even so, the powerful merchant princes of the coastal ports made European traders give them rich presents. Because of the absence of sizeable states, there were no large-scale wars and consequently few prisoners of war. Instead, kidnapping was the major means of getting slaves.

As the volume of the Atlantic trade along the Bight of Biafra expanded in the late eighteenth century, some inland markets evolved into giant fairs, with different sections specializing in slaves and imported goods. An English ship's doctor reported that in the 1780s slaves were "bought by the black traders at fairs, which are held for that purpose, at a distance of upwards of two hundred miles from the sea coast." He reported seeing from twelve hundred to fifteen hundred enslaved men and women arriving at the coast from a single fair.[4]

Angola, south of the Congo estuary, was the greatest source of slaves for the Atlantic trade. This was also the one place along the Atlantic coast where a single European nation, Portugal, controlled a significant amount of territory. Portuguese residents of the main coastal ports served as middlemen between caravans that arrived from the far interior and ships from Brazil.

Many of the slaves sold at Angolan markets were prisoners of war captured by expanding African states. As elsewhere in Africa, such prisoners seem to have been a byproduct of African wars rather than the purpose for which the wars were fought.

Recent research has linked other enslavement with environmental crises in the hinterland of Angola. During the eighteenth century, these southern grasslands periodically suffered severe droughts, which drove famished refugees to areas with more plentiful water. In return for food and water, powerful African leaders gained control of many refugees and sold into the Atlantic trade the men, who were more likely than the women and children to escape or challenge the ruler's authority. The most successful of these inland Angolan leaders became heads of powerful new states that stabilized areas devastated by war and drought and repopulated them with the refugees and prisoners they retained. The slave frontier then moved farther inland. This cruel system worked to the benefit of a few African rulers and merchants at the expense of the many thousands of Africans who were sent to death or perpetual bondage in the Americas.

It is impossible to assess with precision the complex effects of the goods received in sub-Saharan Africa from these trades. Africans were very particular about what they received, so it is unlikely that they could have been consistently cheated. Some researchers have suggested that imports of textiles and metals undermined African weavers and metalworkers, but most economic historians calculate that, on a per capita basis, the volume of these imports was too small to have idled many African artisans. Imports supplemented rather than replaced local production. The goods received in sub-Saharan Africa were intended for consumption and thus did not develop the economy. Likewise, the sugar, tea, and chocolate Europeans consumed did little to promote economic development in Europe. However, both African and European merchants profited from trading these consumer goods. Because they directed the whole Atlantic system, Europeans gained far more wealth than Africans did.

Historians disagree in their assessment of how deeply European capitalism dominated Africa before 1800, but Europeans clearly had much less political and economic impact in Africa than in the West Indies or in other parts of the Americas. Still, it is significant that Western capitalism was expanding rapidly in the seventeenth century, while the Ottoman Empire, the dominant state of the Middle East, was entering a period of economic and political decline (see Chapter 17). The tide of influence in Africa was thus running in the Europeans' direction.

# THE COLUMBIAN EXCHANGE

The term **Columbian Exchange** refers to the transfer of peoples, animals, plants, diseases, and technology between the New and Old Worlds that European trade in the Atlantic opened up. We have already seen how Old World diseases devastated Amerindian peoples and led to the resettlement of the Americas by Europeans and Africans. In addition, the domesticated livestock and major agricultural crops of the Old World spread over much of the Americas, and Amerindians' staple crops enriched the agricultures of Europe and Africa. This vast exchange of plants and animals radically altered diets and lifestyles around the Atlantic.

## Transfers to the Americas

Within a century of Columbus's first voyage, new settlers in the Americas were growing all the staples of southern European agriculture—wheat, olives, grapes, and garden vegetables—along with African and Asian crops such as rice, bananas, coconuts, breadfruit, and sugar cane. Native peoples remained loyal to their traditional staples but added many Old World plants to their diet. Citrus fruits, melons, figs, and sugar, as well as onions, radishes, and salad greens, all found a place in Amerindian cuisine.

By the eighteenth century, nearly all of the domesticated animals and cultivated plants in the Caribbean were ones that Europeans had introduced. The Spanish had brought cattle, pigs, and horses, all of which multiplied rapidly. They had also introduced new plants. Of these, bananas and plantain from the Canary Islands were a valuable addition to the food supply, and sugar and rice formed the basis of plantation agriculture, along with native tobacco. Other food crops arrived with the slaves from Africa, including okra, black-eyed peas, yams, grains such as millet and sorghum, and mangoes. Many of these new animals and plants were useful additions to the islands, but they crowded out indigenous species. The central importance of sugar cane in transforming Brazil and the Caribbean has already been noted.

The introduction of European livestock to the mainland had a dramatic impact. Faced with few natural predators, cattle, pigs, horses, and sheep, as well as pests like rats and rabbits, multiplied rapidly in the open spaces of the Americas. On the vast plains of present-day southern Brazil, Uruguay, and Argentina, herds of wild cattle and horses exceeded 50 million by 1700. Large herds of both animals also appeared in northern Mexico and what became the Southwest of the United States.

Where Old World livestock spread most rapidly, environmental changes were most dramatic. Marauding livestock often had a destructive impact on Amerindian agriculturists. But on the plains of South America, northern Mexico, and Texas, cattle provided indigenous peoples with abundant supplies of meat and hides. In the present-day south-

western United States, the Navajo became sheepherders and expert weavers of woolen cloth. Individual Amerindians became muleteers, cowboys, and sheepherders.

No animal had a more striking effect on the cultures of native peoples than the horse, which increased the efficiency of hunters and the military capacity of warriors on the plains. The horse permitted the Apache, Sioux, Blackfoot, Comanche, Assiniboine, and others to hunt the vast herds of buffalo in North America more efficiently.

## Transfers from the Americas

In return, the Americas offered the Old World an abundance of useful plants. The New World staples of maize and potatoes revolutionized agriculture and diet in parts of Europe, because they provided more calories per acre than any of the Old World staples except rice. Beans, squash, tomatoes, sweet potatoes, peanuts,

**Tobacco Factory Machinery in Colonial Mexico City**    The tobacco factory in eighteenth-century Mexico City used a horse-driven mechanical shredder to produce snuff and cigarette tobacco. (Archivo General de la Nacion, Buenos Aires)

chilis, and chocolate also gained widespread acceptance in Europe and other parts of the Old World. The New World also provided the Old with plants that provided dyes, medicines, and tobacco.

Maize and cassava (a Brazilian plant cultivated for its edible roots) moved across the Atlantic to Africa. Cassava became the most important New World food in Africa. Truly a marvel, cassava had the highest yield of calories per acre of any staple food and thrived even in poor soils and during droughts. Both the leaves and the root could be eaten. Ground into meal, the root could be made into a bread that would keep for up to six months, or it could be fermented into a beverage.

Cassava and maize were probably introduced accidentally into Africa by Portuguese ships from Brazil that discarded leftover supplies after reaching Angola. It did not take long for local Africans to recognize the food value of these new crops, especially in drought-prone areas. By the eighteenth century, Central African rulers hundreds of miles from the Angolan coast were actively promoting the cultivation of maize and cassava on their royal estates in order to provide a more secure food supply. Some historians believe that in the inland areas these Amerindian food crops provided the nutritional base for a population increase that partially offset losses due to the Atlantic slave trade.

## CONCLUSION

The New World colonial empires of Spain, Portugal, France, and England had many characteristics in common. All subjugated Amerindian peoples and introduced large numbers of enslaved Africans. Within all four empires, forests were cut down, virgin soils were turned with the plow, and Old World animals and plants were introduced. Colonists in all four applied the technologies of the Old World to the resources of the New, producing wealth and exploiting the commercial possibilities of the emerging Atlantic market. Yet each of the New World empires also reflected the distinctive cultural and institutional heritages of its colonizing power.

Mineral wealth allowed Spain to develop the most centralized empire. Political and economic power was concentrated in the great capital cities of Mexico City and Lima. Portugal and France pursued similar objectives in their colonies. However, neither Brazil's agricultural economy nor France's Canadian fur trade produced the financial resources that made possible the centralized control achieved by Spain. Nevertheless, all three of these Catholic powers were able to impose and enforce significant levels of religious and cultural uniformity.

Greater cultural and religious diversity characterized British North America. Thus, colonists there were better able to respond to changing economic and political circumstances. Most important, the British colonies attracted many more European immigrants than did the other New World colonies.

The new Atlantic trading system had great importance and momentous implications for world history. In the first phase of their expansion, Europeans had conquered and colonized the Americas and captured major Indian Ocean trade routes. The development of the Atlantic system showed Europeans' ability to move beyond the conquest and capture of existing systems to create a major new trading system that could transform a region almost beyond recognition.

The West Indies felt the transforming power of capitalism more profoundly than did any other place outside Europe in this period. The establishment of sugar plantation societies was not just a matter of replacing native vegetation with alien plants and native peoples with Europeans and Africans. More fundamentally, it made these once-isolated islands part of a dynamic trading system controlled from Europe. To be sure, the Caribbean was not the only place affected. Parts of northern Brazil were touched as deeply by the sugar revolution, and other parts of the Americas were yielding to the power of European colonization and capitalism.

Historians have seen the Atlantic system as a model of the kind of highly interactive economy that became global in later centuries. For that reason, the Atlantic system was a milestone in a much larger historical process, but not a monument to be admired. Its transformations were destructive as well as creative, producing victims as well as victors. Yet one cannot ignore that the system's awesome power came from its ability to create wealth. As the next chapter describes, southern Asia and the Indian Ocean Basin were also beginning to feel the effects of Europeans' rising power.

## ■ Key Terms

| | |
|---|---|
| Atlantic system | driver |
| Council of the Indies | seasoning |
| Bartolomé de Las Casas | maroon |
| Potosí | capitalism |
| encomienda | mercantilism |
| creole | chartered companies |
| indentured servants | Dutch West India Company |
| House of Burgesses | Royal African Company |
| Pilgrims | Great Circuit |
| Puritans | Middle Passage |
| Iroquois Confederacy | Columbian Exchange |
| New France | |

## ■ Suggested Reading

Alfred W. Crosby, Jr., is justifiably the best-known student of the Columbian Exchange. See his *The Columbian Exchange: Biological and Cultural Consequences of 1492* (1972) and *Ecological Imperialism* (1986). William H. McNeill, *Plagues and People* (1976), puts the discussion of the American exchange in a world history context. Elinor G. K. Melville, *A Plague of Sheep: Environmental Consequences of the Spanish Conquest of Mexico* (1994), is the most important recent contribution to this field.

*Colonial Latin America*, 4th ed. (2001), by Mark A. Burkholder and Lyman L. Johnson, provides a good introduction to colonial Latin American history. *Early Latin America* (1983) by James Lockhart and Stuart B. Schwartz and *Spain and Portugal in the New World, 1492–1700* (1984) by Lyle N. McAlister are both useful introductions as well.

Among the useful general studies of the British colonies are Charles M. Andrews, *The Colonial Period of American History: The Settlements*, 3 vols. (1934–1937); David Hackett Fischer, *Albion's Seed: Four British Folkways in America* (1989); and Gary B. Nash, *Red, White, and Black: The Peoples of Early America*, 2d ed. (1982). For slavery,

see David Brion Davis, *The Problem of Slavery in Western Culture* (1966).

On French North America, William J. Eccles, *France in America*, rev. ed. (1990), is an excellent overview; see also his *The Canadian Frontier, 1534–1760* (1969).

The global context of early modern capitalism is examined by Immanuel Wallerstein, *The Modern World-System*, 3 vols. (1974–1989), and by Fernand Braudel, *Civilization and Capitalism, 15th–18th Century*, 3 vols. (1982–1984). The best general introductions to the Atlantic system are Philip D. Curtin, *The Rise and Fall of the Plantation Complex* (1990), Herbert S. Klein, *The Atlantic Slave Trade* (1999), and David Ellis, *The Rise of African Slavery in the Americas* (2000). A useful collection of primary and secondary sources is David Northrup, ed., *The Atlantic Slave Trade*, 2d ed. (2001).

The cultural connections among African communities on both sides of the Atlantic are explored by John Thornton, *Africa and Africans in the Making of the Atlantic World, 1400–1800*, 2d ed. (1998). Herbert S. Klein's *African Slavery in Latin America and the Caribbean* (1986) is an exceptionally fine synthesis of research on New World slavery, including North American slave systems. For recent research on slavery and the African, Atlantic, and Muslim slave trades with Africa, see Paul Lovejoy, *Transformations in Slavery: A History of Slavery in Africa*, 2d ed. (2000).

## ■ Notes

1. Quoted in Alfred W. Crosby, Jr., *The Columbian Exchange: Biological and Cultural Consequences of 1492* (Westport, CT: Greenwood, 1972), 58.
2. Eric Williams, *Capitalism and Slavery* (Charlotte: University of North Carolina Press, 1944), 7.
3. King Osei Bonsu, quoted in David Northrup, ed., *The Atlantic Slave Trade*, 2d ed. (Boston: Houghton Mifflin, 2001), 176.
4. Alexander Falconbridge, *Account of the Slave Trade on the Coast of Africa* (London: J. Phillips, 1788), 12.

# Southwest Asia and the Indian Ocean, 1500–1750

# 17

## CHAPTER OUTLINE

**The Ottoman Empire**
**The Safavid Empire**
**The Mughal Empire**
**Trade Empires in the Indian Ocean**
DIVERSITY AND DOMINANCE: **Islamic Law and Ottoman Rule**

Anthony Jenkinson, merchant-adventurer for the Muscovy Company, founded in 1555 to develop trade with Russia, was the first Englishman to set foot in Iran. Eight years after the first English ship dropped anchor at Archangel on the White Sea in Russia's frigid north, Jenkinson made his way through Russia, down the Volga River, and across the Caspian Sea. The local ruler he met when he disembarked in 1561 in northwestern Iran was an object of wonder:

> richly appareled with long garments of silk, and cloth of gold, embroidered with pearls of stone; upon his head was a *tolipane* [headdress shaped like a tulip] with a sharp end pointing upwards half a yard long, of rich cloth of gold, wrapped about with a piece of India silk of twenty yards long, wrought in gold richly enameled, and set

with precious stones; his earrings had pendants of gold a handful long, with two rubies of great value, set in the ends thereof.

Moving on to Qazvin°, Iran's capital, Jenkinson met the shah. After presenting a letter from Queen Elizabeth in Latin, English, Hebrew, and Italian but finding no one capable of reading it, he managed nevertheless to propose trade between England and Iran. The shah rejected the idea, since diverting Iranian silk from the markets of the Ottoman sultans, with whom he was negotiating a truce after a half-century of intermittent war, would have been undiplomatic.

---

**Qazvin** (kaz-VEEN)

Though Central Asia's bazaars were only meagerly supplied with goods, as Jenkinson and later merchants discovered, the idea of bypassing the Ottomans in the eastern Mediterranean and trading directly with Iran through Russia remained tempting. By the same token, the Ottomans were tempted by the idea of outflanking Safavid Iran. In 1569, an Ottoman army tried unsuccessfully to dig a 40-mile (64-kilometer) canal between the Don River, which opened into the Black Sea, and the Volga, which flowed into the Caspian. Their objective was to enable Ottoman ships to reach the Caspian and attack Iran from the north.

The Ottomans' foe was Russia, then ruled by Tsar Ivan IV (r. 1533–1584), known as Ivan the Terrible or Awesome. Ivan transformed his principality from a second-rate power into the sultan's primary competitor in Central Asia. In the river-crossed steppe, where Turkic nomads had long enjoyed uncontested sway, Slavic Christian Cossacks from the region of the Don and Dnieper Rivers used armed wagon trains and river craft fitted with small cannon to push southward and establish a Russian presence.

A contest for trade with or control of Central Asia was natural after the centrality conferred on the region by three centuries of Mongol and Turkic conquest, highlighted by the campaigns of Genghis Khan and Timur. But, as we shall see, changes in the organization of trade were sapping the vitality of the Silk Road. Wealth and power were shifting to European seaborne empires linking the Atlantic with the Indian Ocean. Though the Ottomans were a formidable naval power in the Mediterranean, neither they nor the Safavid shahs in Iran nor the Mughal emperors of India deployed more than a token navy in the southern seas.

As you read this chapter, ask yourself the following questions:

- What were the advantages and disadvantages of a land as opposed to a maritime empire?
- What role did religion play in political alliances and rivalries and in the formation of states?
- How did trading patterns change between 1500 and 1750?

## THE OTTOMAN EMPIRE

The most long-lived of the post-Mongol Muslim empires was the **Ottoman Empire,** founded around 1300 (see Map 17.1). By extending Islamic conquests into eastern Europe, starting in the late fourteenth century, and by taking Syria and Egypt from the Mamluk rulers in the early sixteenth, the Ottomans seemed to recreate the might of the original Islamic caliphate, the empire established by the Muslim Arab conquests in the seventh century. However, the empire was actually more like the new centralized monarchies of France and Spain (see Chapter 15) than any medieval model.

Enduring more than five centuries, until 1922, the Ottoman Empire survived several periods of wrenching change, some caused by internal problems, others by the growing power of European adversaries. These periods of change reveal the problems faced by huge land-based empires around the world.

### Expansion and Frontiers

Established around 1300, the Ottoman Empire grew from a tiny state in northwestern Anatolia because of three factors: (1) the shrewdness of its founder, Osman (from which the name *Ottoman* comes), and his descendants, (2) control of a strategic link between Europe and Asia on the Dardanelles strait, and (3) the creation of an army that took advantage of the traditional skills of the Turkish cavalryman and the new military possibilities presented by gunpowder.

At first, Ottoman armies concentrated on Christian enemies in Greece and the Balkans, in 1389 conquering a strong Serbian kingdom at the Battle of

## CHRONOLOGY

| | Ottoman Empire | Safavid Empire | Mughal Empire |
|---|---|---|---|
| **1500** | **1516–1517**  Selim I conquers Egypt and Syria | **1502–1524**  Shah Ismail establishes Safavid rule in Iran | |
| | **1520–1566**  Reign of Suleiman the Magnificent; peak of Ottoman Empire | | **1526**  Babur defeats last sultan of Delhi |
| | **1529**  First Ottoman siege of Vienna | | **1556–1605**  Akbar rules in Agra; peak of Mughal Empire |
| | **1571**  Ottoman naval defeat at Lepanto | **1587–1629**  Reign of Shah Abbas the Great; peak of Safavid Empire | |
| **1600** | **1610**  End of Anatolian revolts | | |
| | | | **1658–1707**  Aurangzeb imposes conservative Islamic regime |
| **1700** | | **1722**  Afghan invaders topple last Safavid shah | |
| | **1730**  Janissary revolt | | |
| | **1730**  Janissary revolt begins period of Ottoman conservatism | **1736–1747**  Nadir Shah temporarily reunites Iran; invades India (1739) | |
| | | | **1739**  Iranians under Nadir Shah sack Delhi |

Kosovo°. Much of southeastern Europe and Anatolia was under the control of the sultans by 1402. In 1453, Sultan Mehmed II, "the Conqueror," laid siege to Constantinople. His forces used enormous cannon to bash in the city's walls, dragged warships over a high hill from the Bosporus strait to the city's inner harbor to get around its sea defenses, and finally penetrated the city's land walls through a series of direct infantry assaults. The fall of Constantinople—henceforth commonly known as Istanbul—brought to an end over eleven hundred years of Byzantine rule and made the Ottomans seem invincible.

**Kosovo** (KO-so-vo)

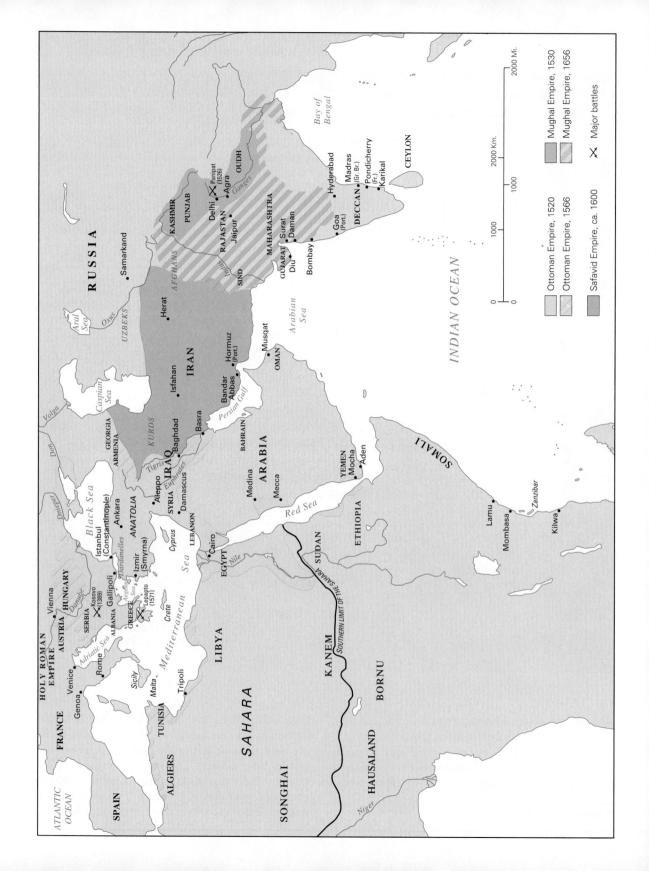

2000 Mi.

2000 Km.

1000

1000

Mughal Empire, 1530
Mughal Empire, 1656
Major battles

Ottoman Empire, 1520
Ottoman Empire, 1566

Safavid Empire, ca. 1600

*Bay of Bengal*

CEYLON

Hyderabad
Madras (Gr. Br.)
Pondicherry (Fr.)
Karikal

DECCAN

Goa (Port.)

MAHARASHTRA

*INDIAN OCEAN*

KASHMIR
PUNJAB
Delhi
Agra
Panipat (1526)
*Ganges*
OUDH

RAJASTAN
Jaipur

AFGHANS

SIND

GUJARAT
Surat
Daman
Diu
Bombay

RUSSIA

Samarkand

*Arabian Sea*

*Aral Sea*
*Oxus*

UZBEKS

Herat

IRAN

Isfahan

Bandar Abbas
Hormuz (Port.)

Musqat

OMAN

*Persian Gulf*

Baghdad
Basra

*Caspian Sea*

*Volga*

KURDS

*Tigris*
*Euphrates*

IRAQ
SYRIA
Damascus
Aleppo

GEORGIA
ARMENIA

BAHRAIN

ARABIA

Medina
Mecca

YEMEN
Mocha
Aden

*Red Sea*

SOMALI

Zanzibar

Lamu
Mombasa

Kilwa

*Don*
*Dnieper*

*Black Sea*

Istanbul (Constantinople)
Ankara

ANATOLIA

Izmir (Smyrna)

Cyprus

LEBANON

*Dardanelles*

Gallipoli

*Aegean Sea*

GREECE
ALBANIA
SERBIA
Kosovo (1389)

Lepanto (1571)

Crete

Cairo
EGYPT
*Nile*

SUDAN

ETHIOPIA

HOLY ROMAN EMPIRE
Vienna
AUSTRIA
HUNGARY
*Danube*

FRANCE

Venice
Genoa
Rome
Sicily
Malta
Tripoli

*Adriatic Sea*

*Mediterranean Sea*

LIBYA

KANEM

*SOUTHERN LIMIT OF THE SAHARA*

BORNU

SPAIN

*ATLANTIC OCEAN*

ALGIERS
TUNISIA

SAHARA

SONGHAI

HAUSALAND

*Niger*

**Map 17.1   Muslim Empires in the Sixteenth and Seventeenth Centuries**   Iran, a Shi'ite state flanked by Sunni Ottomans on the west and Sunni Mughals on the east, had the least exposure to European influences. Ottoman expansion across the southern Mediterranean Sea intensified European fears of Islam. The areas of strongest Mughal control dictated that Islam's spread into Southeast Asia would be heavily influenced by merchants and religious figures from Gujarat instead of from eastern India.

Selim° I, "the Inexorable," conquered Egypt and Syria in 1516 and 1517, making the Red Sea the Ottomans' southern frontier. His son, **Suleiman° the Magnificent** (r. 1520–1566), presided over the greatest Ottoman assault on Christian Europe. Suleiman seemed unstoppable: he conquered Belgrade in 1521, expelled the Knights of the Hospital of St. John from the island of Rhodes the following year, and laid siege to Vienna in 1529. Vienna was saved by the need to retreat before the onset of winter more than by military action. In later centuries, Ottoman historians looked back on the reign of Suleiman as the period when the imperial system worked to perfection, and they spoke of it as the golden age of Ottoman greatness.

While Ottoman armies pressed deeper and deeper into eastern Europe, the sultans also sought to control the Mediterranean. Between 1453 and 1502, the Ottomans fought the opening rounds of a two-century war with Venice, the most powerful of Italy's commercial city-states. The initial fighting left Venice in control of its lucrative islands for another century. But it also left Venice a reduced military power compelled to pay tribute to the Ottomans.

It never occurred to the Ottomans that a sea empire held together by flimsy ships could truly rival a great land empire fielding an army of a hundred thousand men. In the early sixteenth century, merchants from southern India and Sumatra sent emissaries to Istanbul requesting naval support against the Portuguese. The Ottomans responded vigorously to Portuguese threats close to their territories, such as at Aden at the southern entrance to the Red Sea, but their efforts farther afield were insufficient to stifle growing Portuguese domination.

Eastern luxury products still flowed to Ottoman markets. Portuguese power was territorially limited to fortified coastal points, such as Hormuz at the entrance to the Persian Gulf, Goa in western India, and Malacca in Malaya. Why commit major resources to subduing an enemy whose main threat was a demand that merchant vessels, mostly belonging to non-Ottoman Muslims, buy protection from Portuguese attack? The Ottomans did send a small naval force to Indonesia, but they never formulated a consistent or aggressive policy with regard to political and economic developments in the Indian Ocean.

## Central Institutions

By the 1520s, the Ottoman Empire was the most powerful and best-organized state in either Europe or the Islamic world. Its military was balanced between cavalry archers, primarily Turks, and **Janissaries°**, Christian prisoners of war induced to serve as military slaves.

Slave soldiery had a long history in Islamic lands, but the conquest of Christian territories in the Balkans in the late fourteenth century gave the Ottomans access to a new military resource. Converted to Islam, these "new troops," called *yeni cheri* in Turkish and *Janissaries* in English, gave the Ottomans unusual military flexibility. Since horseback riding and bowmanship were not part of their cultural backgrounds, they readily accepted the idea of fighting on foot and learning to use guns, which at that time were still too heavy and awkward for a horseman to load and fire. The Janissaries lived in barracks and trained all year round.

The process of selection for Janissary training changed early in the fifteenth century. The new system imposed a regular levy of male children on Christian villages in the Balkans and occasionally elsewhere. Recruited children were placed with Turkish families to learn their language and then were sent to the sultan's palace in Istanbul for an education that included instruction in Islam, military training, and, for the most talented, what we might call liberal arts. This regime, sophisticated for its time, produced not only the Janissary soldiers

Selim (seh-LEEM)   Suleiman (SOO-lay-man)         Janissaries (JAN-nih-say-rees)

but also, from among the chosen few who received special training, senior military commanders and heads of government departments up to the rank of grand vizier.

The cavalrymen were supported by land grants and administered most rural areas in Anatolia and the Balkans. They maintained order, collected taxes, and reported for each summer's campaign with their horses, retainers, and supplies, all paid for from the taxes they collected. When not campaigning, they stayed at home.

A galley-equipped navy was manned by Greek, Turkish, Algerian, and Tunisian sailors, usually under the command of an admiral from one of the North African ports. The balance of the Ottoman land forces brought success to Ottoman arms in recurrent wars with the Safavids, who were much slower to adopt firearms, and in the inexorable conquest of the Balkans. Expansion by sea was less dramatic. A major expedition against Malta in the western Mediterranean failed in 1565. Combined Christian forces also achieved a massive naval victory at the Battle of Lepanto, off Greece, in 1571. But the Ottomans' resources were so extensive that in a year's time they had replaced all of the galleys sunk in that battle.

The Ottoman Empire became cosmopolitan in character. The sophisticated court language, Osmanli° (the Turkish form of *Ottoman*), shared basic grammar and vocabulary with Turkish, but Arabic and Persian elements made it distinct from the language spoken by Anatolia's nomads and villagers. Everyone who served in the military or the bureaucracy and conversed in Osmanli was considered to belong to the *askeri*°, or "military," class. Members of this class were exempt from taxes and owed their well-being to the sultan.

The Ottomans saw the sultan as providing justice for his "flock of sheep" (*raya*°) and the military protecting them. In return, the raya paid the taxes that supported both the sultan and the military. In reality, the sultan's government remained comparatively isolated from the lives of most subjects. As Islam gradually became the majority religion in Balkan regions, Islamic law (the Shari'a°) conditioned urban institutions and social life. Local cus-

Osmanli (os-MAHN-lee)    *askeri* (AS-keh-ree)
*raya* (RAH-yah)    Shari'a (sha-REE-ah)

**Ottoman Glassmakers on Parade**    Celebrations of the circumcisions of the sultan's sons featured parades organized by the craft guilds of Istanbul. This float features glassmaking, a common craft in Islamic realms. The most elaborate glasswork included oil lamps for mosques and colored glass for the small stained-glass windows below mosque domes.    (Topkapi Saray Museum)

toms prevailed among non-Muslims and in many rural areas; and non-Muslims looked to their own religious leaders for guidance in family and spiritual matters (see Diversity and Dominance: Islamic Law and Ottoman Rule).

### Crisis of the Military State, 1585–1650

As military technology evolved, cannon and lighter-weight firearms played an ever-larger role on the battlefield. Accordingly, the size of the Janissary corps—and its cost to the government—grew steadily, and the role of the Turkish cavalry diminished. To pay the Janissaries, the sultan started reducing the number of landholding cavalrymen. Revenues previously spent on their living expenses and military equipment went directly into the imperial treasury. Inflation caused by a flood of cheap silver from the New World bankrupted many of the remaining landholders restricted by law to collecting a fixed amount of taxes. Their land was returned to the state. Displaced cavalrymen, armed and un-happy, became a restive element in rural Anatolia.

This complicated situation resulted in revolts that devastated Anatolia between 1590 and 1610. Former landholding cavalrymen, short-term sol-diers released at the end of the campaign season, peasants overburdened by emergency taxes, and even impoverished students of religion formed bands of marauders. Anatolia experienced the worst of the rebellions and suffered greatly from emigration and the loss of agricultural production. But an increase in banditry, made worse by the government's inability to stem the spread of mus-kets among the general public, beset other parts of the empire as well.

In the meantime, the Janissaries took advan-tage of their growing influence to gain relief from prohibitions on their marrying and engaging in business. Janissaries who involved themselves in commerce lessened the burden on the state bud-get, and married Janissaries who enrolled sons or relatives in the corps made it possible in the sev-enteenth century for the government to save state funds by abolishing forced recruitment. These sav-ings, however, were more than offset by the in-crease in the total number of Janissaries and in their steady deterioration as a military force, which necessitated the hiring of more and more supple-mental troops.

## Economic Change and Growing Weakness

A very different Ottoman Empire emerged from this crisis. The sultan once had led armies. Now he mostly resided in his palace and had little experience of the real world, and the affairs of government were overseen more and more by the chief administra-tors—the grand viziers.

The Janissaries took advantage of their in-creased power to make membership in their corps hereditary. Their involvement in crafts and trading took a toll on their military skills, but they contin-ued to be a powerful faction in urban politics. Land grants in return for military service also disap-peared. Tax farming arose in their place. Tax farm-ers paid specific taxes, such as customs duties, in advance in return for the privilege of collecting a greater amount from the actual taxpayers.

Rural administration, already disrupted by the rebellions, suffered from the transition to tax farms. The former military landholders had kept order on their lands in order to maintain their incomes. Tax farmers were less likely to live on the land. The imperial government therefore faced greater ad-ministrative burdens and came to rely heavily on powerful provincial governors or on wealthy men who purchased lifelong tax collection rights and behaved more or less like private landowners.

Rural disorder and decline in administrative control sometimes opened the way for new eco-nomic opportunities. The Aegean port of Izmir° (an-cient Smyrna) was able to transform itself between 1580 and 1650 from a small Muslim Turkish town into a multiethnic, multireligious, multilinguistic en-trepôt because of the Ottoman government's inability to control trade and the slowly growing dominance of European traders in the Indian Ocean. Local farm-ers who previously had grown grain for subsistence shifted their plantings more and more to cotton and other cash crops sought by European traders at Izmir. After its introduction in the 1590s, tobacco quickly became popular in the Ottoman Empire de-spite government prohibitions. In this way, the agri-cultural economy of western Anatolia, the Balkans, and the Mediterranean coast—the Ottoman lands most accessible to Europe—became enmeshed in the seventeenth century in a growing European commercial network.

The Ottoman Empire lacked both the wealth and the inclination to match European economic advances. Overland trade from the east dwindled as political disorder in Safavid Iran cut deeply into Iranian silk production. Coffee, an Arabian prod-uct that rose from obscurity in the fifteenth cen-tury to become the rage first in the Ottoman Empire and then in Europe, was grown in the high-lands of Yemen and exported by way of Egypt. By 1770, however, Muslim merchants trading in the Yemeni port of Mocha° (literally "the coffee place") were charged 15 percent in duties and fees. But Eu-ropean traders, benefiting from long-standing trade agreements with the Ottoman Empire, paid little more than 3 percent. Such trade agreements led to European domination of Ottoman import and export trade by sea.

**Izmir** (IZ-meer)    **Mocha** (MOH-kuh)

# DIVERSITY AND DOMINANCE

## ISLAMIC LAW AND OTTOMAN RULE

*Ebu's-Su'ud was the mufti of Istanbul from 1545 to 1574, serving under the sultans Suleiman the Magnificent (1520–1566) and his son Selim II (1566–1574). Originally one of many city-based religious scholars giving opinions on matters of law, the mufti of Istanbul by Ebu's-Su'ud's time had become the top religious official in the empire and the personal adviser to the sultan on religious and legal matters. The position would later acquire the title Shaikh al-Islam.*

*Historians debate the degree of independence these muftis had. Since the ruler, as a Muslim, was subject to the Shari'a, the mufti could theoretically veto his policies. On important matters, however, the mufti more often seemed to come up with the answer that best suited the sultan who appointed him. This bias is not apparent in more mundane areas of the law.*

*The collection of Ebu's-Su'ud's fatwas, or legal opinions, from which the examples below are drawn shows the range of matters that came to his attention. They are also an excellent source for understanding the problems of his time, the relationship between Islamic law and imperial governance, and the means by which the state asserted its dominance over the common people. Some opinions respond directly to questions posed by the sultan. Others are hypothetical, using the names Zeyd, 'Amr, and Hind the way police today use John Doe and Jane Doe. While qadis, or Islamic judges, made findings of fact in specific cases on trial, muftis issued only opinions on matters of law. A qadi as well as a plaintiff or defendant might ask a question of a mufti. Later jurists consulted collections of fatwas for precedents, but the fatwas had no permanent binding power.*

### On the Plan of Selim II to Attack the Venetians in Crete in 1570

A land was previously in the realm of Islam. After a while, the abject infidels overran it, destroyed the colleges and mosques, and left them vacant. They filled the pulpits and the galleries with the tokens of infidelity and error, intending to insult the religion of Islam with all kinds of vile deeds, and by spreading their ugly acts to all corners of the earth.

His Excellency the Sultan, the Refuge of Religion, has, as zeal for Islam requires, determined to take the aforementioned land from the possession of the shameful infidels and to annex it to the realm of Islam.

When peace was previously concluded with the other lands in the possession of the said infidels, the aforenamed land was included. An explanation is sought as to whether, in accordance with the Pure shari'a, this is an impediment to the Sultan's determining to break the treaty.

Answer: There is no possibility that it could ever be an impediment. For the Sultan of the People of Islam (may God glorify his victories) to make peace with the infidels is legal only when there is a benefit to all Muslims. When there is no benefit, peace is never legal. When a benefit has been seen, and it is then observed to be more beneficial to break it, then to break it becomes absolutely obligatory and binding.

His Excellency [Muhammad] the Apostle of God (may God bless him and give him peace) made a ten-year truce with the Meccan infidels in the sixth year of the Hegira. His Excellency 'Ali (may God ennoble his face) wrote a document that was corroborated and confirmed. Then, in the following year, it was considered more beneficial to break it and, in the eighth year

**418**

of the Hegira, [the Prophet] attacked [the Meccans], and conquered Mecca the Mighty.

## On War Against the Shi'ite Muslim Safavids of Iran

Is it licit according to the shari'a to fight the followers of the Safavids? Is the person who kills them a holy warrior, and the person who dies at their hands a martyr?

Answer: Yes, it is a great holy war and a glorious martyrdom.

Assuming that it is licit to fight them, is this simply because of their rebellion and enmity against the [Ottoman] Sultan of the People of Islam, because they drew the sword against the troops of Islam, or what?

Answer: They are both rebels and, from many points of view, infidels.

Can the children of Safavid subjects captured in the Nakhichevan campaign be enslaved?

Answer: No.

The followers of the Safavids are killed by order of the Sultan. If it turns out that some of the prisoners, young and old, are [Christian] Armenian[s], are they set free?

Answer: Yes. So long as the Armenians have not joined the Safavid troops in attacking and fighting against the troops of Islam, it is illegal to take them prisoner.

## On the Holy Land

Are all the Arab realms Holy Land, or does it have specific boundaries, and what is the difference between the Holy Land and other lands?

Answer: Syria is certainly called the Holy Land. Jerusalem, Aleppo and its surroundings, and Damascus belong to it.

## On Land Grants

What lands are private property, and what lands are held by feudal tenure [i.e., assignment in exchange for military service]?

Answer: Plots of land within towns are private property. Their owners may sell them, donate them or convert them to trust. When [the owner] dies, [the land] passes to all the heirs. Lands held by feudal tenure are cultivated lands around villages, whose occupants bear the burden of their services and pay a portion of their [produce in tax]. They cannot sell the land,

donate it or convert it to trust. When they die, if they have sons, these have the use [of the land]. Otherwise, the cavalryman gives [it to someone else] by tapu [title deed].

## On the Consumption of Coffee

Zeyd drinks coffee to aid concentration or digestion. Is this licit?

Answer: How can anyone consume this reprehensible [substance], which dissolute men drink when engaged in games and debauchery?

The Sultan, the Refuge of Religion, has on many occasions banned coffee-houses. However, a group of ruffians take no notice, but keep coffee-houses for a living. In order to draw the crowds, they take on unbearded apprentices, and have ready instruments of entertainment and play, such as chess and backgammon. The city's rakes, rogues and vagabond boys gather there to consume opium and hashish. On top of this, they drink coffee and, when they are high, engage in games and false sciences, and neglect the prescribed prayers. In law, what should happen to a judge who is able to prevent the said coffee-sellers and drinkers, but does not do so?

Answer: Those who perpetrate these ugly deeds should be prevented and deterred by severe chastisement and long imprisonment. Judges who neglect to deter them should be dismissed.

## On Matters of Theft

How are thieves to be "carefully examined"?

Answer: His Excellency 'Ali (may God ennoble his face) appointed Imam Shuraih as judge. It so happened that, at that time, several people took a Muslim's son to another district. The boy disappeared and, when the people came back, the missing boy's father brought them before Judge Shuraih. [When he brought] a claim [against them on account of the loss of his son], they denied it, saying: "No harm came to him from us." Judge Shuraih thought deeply and was perplexed.

When the man told his tale to His Excellency 'Ali, [the latter] summoned Judge Shuraih and questioned him. When Shuraih said; "Nothing came to light by the shari'a," ['Ali] summoned all the people who had taken the man's son, separated them from one another, and questioned them separately. For each of their stopping

*(continued)*

places, he asked: "What was the boy wearing in that place? What did you eat? And where did he disappear?" In short, he made each of them give a detailed account, and when their words contradicted each other, each of their statements was written down separately. Then he brought them all together, and when the contradictions became apparent, they were no longer able to deny [their guilt] and confessed to what had happened.

This kind of ingenuity is a requirement of the case.

[This fatwa appears to justify investigation of crimes by the state instead of by the qadi. Judging from court records, which contain very few criminal cases, it seems likely that in practice, many criminal cases were dealt with outside the jurisdiction of the qadi's court.]

Zeyd takes 'Amr's donkey without his knowledge and sells it. Is he a thief?

Answer: His hand is not cut off.

Zeyd mounts 'Amr's horse as a courier and loses it. Is compensation necessary?

Answer: Yes.

In which case: What if Zeyd has a Sultanic decree [authorising him] to take horses for courier service?

Answer: Compensation is required in any case. He was not commanded to lose [the horse]. Even if he were commanded, it is the person who loses it who is liable.

## On Homicides

Zeyd enters Hind's house and tries to have intercourse forcibly. Since Hind can repel him by no other means, she strikes and wounds him with an axe. If Zeyd dies of the wound, is Hind liable for anything?

Answer: She has performed an act of Holy War.

### QUESTIONS FOR ANALYSIS

1. What do these fatwas indicate with regard to the balance between practical legal reasoning and religious dictates?

2. How much was the Ottoman government constrained by the Shari'a?

3. What can be learned about day-to-day life from materials of this sort?

*Source:* Excerpts from Colin Imber, *Ebu's-Su'ud: The Islamic Legal Tradition* (Stanford, CA: University Press, 1997), 84–88, 93–94, 223–226, 250, 257. Copyright © 1997 Colin Imber, originating publisher Edinburg University Press. Used with permission of Stanford University Press, www.sup.org.

To most people, the downward course of imperial power was not evident, much less the reasons behind it. Far from seeing Europe as the enemy that eventually would dismantle the weakening Ottoman Empire, the Istanbul elite experimented with European clothing and furniture styles and purchased printed books from the empire's first (and short-lived) press.

In 1730, however, a conservative Janissary revolt with strong religious overtones toppled Sultan Ahmed III. The rebellion confirmed the perceptions of a few that the Ottoman Empire was facing severe difficulties. But decay at the center spelled benefit elsewhere. In the provinces, ambitious and competent governors, wealthy landholders, urban notables, and nomad chieftains were well placed to take advantage of the central government's weakness.

By the middle of the eighteenth century, groups of Mamluks had regained a dominant position in Egypt, and Janissary commanders had become virtually independent rulers in Baghdad. Although no region declared full independence, the sultan's power was slipping away to the advantage of a broad array of lower officials and upstart chieftains in all parts of the empire, and the Ottoman economy was reorienting itself toward Europe.

## THE SAFAVID EMPIRE

The **Safavid Empire** of Iran (see Map 17.1) resembled its long-time Ottoman foe in many ways: it initially relied militarily on cavalry paid through land grants; its population spoke several different languages; and it was oriented inward away from the sea. It also had distinct qualities that to this day set Iran off from its neighbors: it derived part of its legitimacy from the pre-Islamic dynasties of ancient Iran, and it adopted the Shi'ite form of Islam.

## Safavid Society and Religion

The ultimate victor in a complicated struggle for power among Turkish chieftains west of the Ottoman Empire was Ismail°, a boy of Kurdish, Iranian, and Greek ancestry. In 1502, at the age of sixteen, Ismail proclaimed himself shah of Iran and declared that from that time forward his realm would be devoted to **Shi'ite** Islam, which revered the family of Muhammad's son-in-law Ali. Although Ismail's reasons for compelling Iran's conversion to Shi'ism are unknown, the effect of this radical act was to create a deep chasm between Iran and its neighbors, all of which were Sunni. Iran became a truly separate country for the first time since its incorporation into the Islamic caliphate in the seventh century.

The imposition of Shi'ite belief made the split permanent, but differences between Iran and its neighbors had long been in the making. Persian, written in the Arabic script from the tenth century onward, had emerged as the second language of Islam. Iranian scholars and writers normally read Arabic as well as Persian and sprinkled their writings with Arabic phrases, but their Arab counterparts were much less inclined to learn Persian. After the Mongols destroyed Baghdad, the capital of the Islamic caliphate, in 1258, Iran developed largely on its own, having more extensive contacts with India—where Muslim rulers favored the Persian language—than with the Arabs.

In the post-Mongol period, artistic styles in the East also went their own way. Painted and molded tiles and tile mosaics, often in vivid turquoise blue, became the standard exterior decoration of mosques in Iran but never were used in Syria and Egypt. Persian poets raised verse to peaks of perfection that had no reflection in Arabic poetry, generally considered to be in a state of decline.

To be sure, Islam itself provided a tradition of belief, learning, and law that crossed ethnic and linguistic borders, but Shah Ismail's imposition of Shi'ism set Iran significantly apart. Shi'ite doctrine says that all temporal rulers, regardless of title, are temporary stand-ins for the **"Hidden Imam"**: the twelfth descendant of Ali, the prophet Muhammad's cousin and son-in-law who disappeared as a child in the ninth century. Some Shi'ite scholars concluded that the faithful should calmly accept the world as it was and wait quietly for the Hidden Imam's return. Others maintained that they themselves should play a stronger role in political affairs because they were best qualified to know the Hidden Imam's wishes. These two positions, which still play a role in Iranian Shi'ism, tended to enhance the self-image of religious scholars as independent of imperial authority and stood in the way of their becoming subordinate government functionaries, as happened in the Ottoman Empire.

Shi'ism also affected the psychological life of the people. Annual commemoration of the martyrdom of Imam Husayn (d. 680), Ali's son and the third Imam, regularized an emotional outpouring with no parallel in Sunni lands. Day after day for two weeks, preachers recited the woeful tale to crowds of weeping believers, and elaborate street processions, often organized by craft guilds, paraded chanting and self-flagellating men past crowds of reverent onlookers. Of course, Shi'ites elsewhere observed rites of mourning for Imam Husayn, but the impact of these rites was especially great in Iran, where 90 percent of the population was Shi'ite. Over time, the subjects of the Safavid shahs came to feel more than ever a people apart.

## Isfahan and Istanbul

Outwardly, the Ottoman capital of Istanbul looked quite different from Isfahan°, which became Iran's capital in 1598 by decree of **Shah Abbas I** (r. 1587–1629). Built on seven hills on the south side of the narrow Golden Horn inlet, Istanbul boasted a skyline punctuated by the gray stone domes and thin, pointed minarets of the great imperial mosques. The mosques surrounding the royal plaza in Isfahan, in contrast, had unobtrusive minarets and brightly tiled domes that rose to gentle peaks. High walls surrounded the sultan's palace in Istanbul. Shah Abbas in Isfahan focused his capital on the giant royal plaza, which

**Ismail** (IS-ma-eel)

**Isfahan** (is-fah-HAHN)

**Safavid Shah with Attendants and Musicians**   This painting by Ali-Quli Jubbadar, a European convert to Islam working for the Safavid armory, reflects Western influences. Notice the use of light and shadow to model faces and the costume of the attendant to the shah's right. The shah's water-pipe indicates the spread of tobacco, a New World crop, to the Middle East.   (Courtesy of Oriental Institute, Academy of Sciences, Leningrad. Reproduced from Album of Persian and Indian Miniatures [Moscow, 1962], ill. no. 98)

was large enough for his army to play polo, and he used an airy palace overlooking the plaza to receive dignitaries and review his troops.

The harbor of Istanbul, the primary Ottoman seaport, teemed with sailing ships and smaller craft, many of them belonging to a colony of European merchants perched on a hilltop on the north side of the Golden Horn. Isfahan, far from the sea, was only occasionally visited by Europeans. Most of its trade was in the hands of Jews, Hindus, and especially a colony of Armenian Christians brought in by Shah Abbas.

Beneath these superficial differences, the two capitals had much in common. Wheeled vehicles were scarce in hilly Istanbul and nonexistent in Isfahan. Both cities were built for walking and, aside from the royal plaza in Isfahan, lacked the open spaces common in contemporary European cities. Streets were narrow and irregular. Houses crowded against each other in dead-end lanes. Residents enjoyed their privacy in interior courtyards. Arti-

sans and merchants organized themselves into guilds that had strong social and religious as well as economic bonds. The shops of each guild adjoined each other in the markets.

Women were seldom seen in public, even in Istanbul's mazelike covered market or in Isfahan's long, serpentine bazaar. At home, the women's quarters—called *anderun*°, or "interior," in Iran and *harem*, or "forbidden area," in Istanbul—were separate from the public rooms where the men of the family received visitors. In both areas, low cushions, charcoal braziers for warmth, carpets, and small tables constituted most of the furnishings.

The private side of family life has left few traces, but it is apparent that women's society—consisting of wives, children, female servants, and sometimes one or more eunuchs—was not entirely cut off from the outside world. Ottoman court records reveal that women, using male agents,

*anderun* (an-deh-ROON)

**Aya Sofya Mosque in Istanbul**   Originally a Byzantine cathedral, Aya Sofya (in Greek, Hagia Sophia) was transformed into a mosque after 1453, and four minarets were added. It then became a model for subsequent Ottoman mosques. To the right behind it is the Bosporus strait dividing Europe and Asia, to the left the Golden Horn inlet separating the old city of Istanbul from the newer parts. The gate to the Ottoman sultan's palace is to the right of the mosque. The pointed tower to the left of the dome is part of the palace.   (Robert Frerck/Woodfin Camp & Associates)

were very active in the urban real estate market. Often they were selling inherited shares of their father's estate, but some both bought and sold real estate on a regular basis and even established religious endowments for pious purposes. The fact that Islamic law, unlike some European codes, permitted a wife to retain her property after marriage gave some women a stake in the general economy and a degree of independence from their spouses. Women also appeared in other types of court cases, where they often testified for themselves, for Islamic courts did not recognize the role of attorney. Although comparable Safavid court records do not survive, historians assume that a parallel situation prevailed in Iran.

European travelers commented on the veiling of women outside the home, but the norm for both sexes was complete coverage of arms, legs, and hair. Miniature paintings indicate that ordinary female garb consisted of a long, ample dress with a scarf or long shawl pulled tight over the forehead to conceal the hair. Lightweight trousers, either close-fitting or baggy, were often worn under the dress. This mode of dress was not far different from that of men. Poor men wore light trousers, a long shirt, a jacket, and a hat or turban. Wealthier men wore over their trousers ankle-length caftans, often closely fitted around the chest. Public life was almost entirely the domain of men. Poetry and art, both somewhat more elegantly developed in Isfahan than in Istanbul, were as likely to extol the charms of beardless boys as pretty women. Despite religious disapproval of homosexuality, attachments to adolescent boys were neither unusual nor hidden. Women who appeared in public—aside from non-Muslims, the aged, and the very poor—were likely to be slaves. Miniature paintings frequently depict female dancers, musicians, and even acrobats in attitudes and costumes that range from decorous to decidedly erotic.

Despite social similarities, the overall flavors of Isfahan and Istanbul were not the same. Isfahan had its prosperous Armenian quarter across the river from the city's center, but it was not a truly cosmopolitan capital, just as the peoples of the Safavid realm were not remarkably diverse. Like other rulers of extensive land empires, Shah Abbas located his capital toward the center of his domain within comparatively easy reach of any threatened frontier. Istanbul, in contrast, was a great seaport and a crossroads located on the straits separating the sultan's European and Asian possessions. People of all sorts lived or spent time in Istanbul: Venetians, Genoese, Arabs, Turks, Greeks, Armenians, Albanians, Serbs, Jews, Bulgarians, and more. In this respect, Istanbul conveyed the cosmopolitan character of major seaports from London to Canton (Guangzhou) and belied the fact that its prosperity rested on the vast reach of the sultan's territories rather than on the voyages of its merchants.

## Economic Crisis and Political Collapse

The silk fabrics of northern Iran were the mainstay of the Safavid Empire's foreign trade. However, the manufacture that eventually became most powerfully associated with Iran was the deep-pile carpet made by knotting colored yarns around stretched warp threads. Different cities produced distinctive carpet designs. Women and girls did much of the actual knotting work.

Overall, Iran's manufacturing sector was neither large nor notably productive. Most of the shah's subjects, whether Iranians, Turks, Kurds, or Arabs, lived by subsistence farming or herding. Neither area of activity recorded significant technological advances during the Safavid period.

The Safavids, like the Ottomans, had difficulty finding the money to pay troops armed with firearms. This crisis occurred somewhat later in Iran because of its greater distance from Europe. By the end of the sixteenth century, it was evident that a more systematic adoption of cannon and firearms in the Safavid Empire would be needed to hold off the Ottomans and the Uzbeks° (Turkish rulers who had succeeded the Timurids on Iran's Central Asian frontier; see Map 17.1). Like

the Ottoman cavalry a century earlier, the warriors furnished by the nomad leaders were not inclined to trade in their bows for firearms. Shah Abbas responded by establishing a slave corps of year-round soldiers and arming them with guns. The Christian converts to Islam who initially provided the manpower for the new corps were mostly captives taken in raids on Georgia in the Caucasus°.

In the late sixteenth century, the inflation caused by cheap silver spread into Iran; then overland trade through Safavid territory declined because of mismanagement of the silk monopoly after Shah Abbas's death in 1629. As a result, the country faced the unsolvable problem of finding money to pay the army and bureaucracy. Trying to unseat the nomads from their lands to regain control of taxes was more difficult and more disruptive militarily than the piecemeal dismantlement of the land-grant system in the Ottoman Empire. The nomads were still a cohesive military force, and pressure from the center simply caused them to withdraw to their mountain pastures until the pressure subsided. By 1722, the government had become so weak and commanded so little support from the nomadic groups that an army of marauding Afghans was able to capture Isfahan and effectively end Safavid rule.

## THE MUGHAL EMPIRE

What distinguished the Indian empire of the Mughal° sultans from the empires of the Ottomans and Safavids was the fact that India was a land of Hindus ruled by a Muslim minority. Muslim dominion in India was the result of repeated military campaigns from the early eleventh century onward, and the Mughals had to contend with the Hindus' long-standing resentment of the destruction of their culture by Muslims. Thus, the challenge facing the Mughals was not just conquering and organizing a large territorial state but also finding a formula for Hindu-Muslim coexistence.

---

**Uzbeks** (UHZ-bex)

**Caucasus** (CAW-kuh-suhs)   **Mughal** (MOH-guhl)

## Political Foundations

Babur° (1483–1530), the founder of the **Mughal Empire,** was a Muslim descendant of both Timur and Genghis Khan (*Mughal* is Persian for "Mongol"). Invading from Central Asia, Babur defeated the last Muslim sultan of Delhi° in 1526. Babur's grandson **Akbar** (r. 1556–1605), a brilliant but mercurial man, established the central administration of the expanding state. Under him and his three successors—the last of whom died in 1707—all but the southern tip of India fell under Mughal rule, administered first from Agra and then from Delhi.

Akbar granted land revenues to military officers and government officials in return for their service. Ranks, called *mansabs°,* some high and some low, entitled their holders to revenue assignments. As in the other Islamic empires, revenue grants were not considered hereditary, and the central government kept careful track of their issuance.

With a population of 100 million, a thriving trading economy based on cotton cloth, and a generally efficient administration, India under Akbar was probably the most prosperous empire of the sixteenth century. He and his successors faced few external threats and experienced generally peaceful conditions in their northern Indian heartland.

Foreign trade boomed at the port of Surat in the northwest, which also served as an embarkation point for pilgrims on their way to Mecca. Like the Safavids, the Mughals had no navy or merchant ships. The government saw the Europeans—after Akbar's time, primarily Dutch and English, the Portuguese having lost most of their Indian ports—less as enemies than as shipmasters whose naval support could be procured as needed in return for trading privileges.

**Elephants Breaking Bridge of Boats** This illustration of an incident in the life of Akbar illustrates the ability of Mughal miniature painters to depict unconventional action scenes. Because the flow of rivers in India and the Middle East varied greatly from dry season to wet season, boat bridges were much more common than permanent constructions. (Victoria and Albert Museum, London/Bridgeman Art Library)

## Hindus and Muslims

The Mughal state inherited traditions of unified imperial rule from both the Islamic caliphate and the more recent examples of Genghis Khan and Timur. Those traditions did not necessarily mean religious intolerance. Seventy percent of the *mansabdars°* (officials holding land revenues) appointed under Akbar were Muslim soldiers born outside India, but 15 percent were Hindus. Most of the Hindu appointees were warriors from the north called **Rajputs°,** one of whom rose to be a powerful revenue minister.

---

**Babur** (BAH-bur)  **Delhi** (DEL-ee)  *mansabs* (MAN-sabz)

*mansabdars* (man-sab-DAHRZ)  **Rajputs** (RAHJ-putz)

Akbar, the most illustrious ruler of his dynasty, differed from his Ottoman and Safavid counterparts—Suleiman the Magnificent and Shah Abbas the Great—in his striving for social harmony and not just for more territory and revenue. His marriage to a Rajput princess signaled his desire for reconciliation and even intermarriage between Muslims and Hindus. The birth of a son in 1569 ensured that future rulers would have both Muslim and Hindu ancestry.

Akbar ruled that in legal disputes between two Hindus, decisions would be made according to village custom or Hindu law as interpreted by local Hindu scholars. Shari'a law was in force for Muslims. Akbar made himself the legal court of last resort, creating an appeals process not usually present in Islamic jurisprudence.

Akbar also made himself the center of a new "Divine Faith" incorporating Muslim, Hindu, Zoroastrian, Sikh°, and Christian beliefs. He was strongly attracted by Sufi ideas, which permeated the religious rituals he instituted at his court. To promote serious consideration of his religious principles, he oversaw, from a catwalk high above the audience, debates among scholars of all religions assembled in his octagonal private audience chamber. When courtiers uttered the Muslim exclamation "Allahu Akbar"—"God is great"—they also understood it in its second grammatical meaning: "God is Akbar."

Akbar's religious views did not survive him, but the court culture he fostered, reflecting a mixture of Muslim and Hindu traditions, flourished until his zealous great-grandson Aurangzeb° (r. 1658–1707) reinstituted many restrictions on Hindus. Mughal and Rajput miniature paintings reveled in precise portraits of political figures and depictions of scantily clad women, even though they brought frowns to the faces of pious Muslims, who deplored the representation of human beings. Most of the leading painters were Hindus. In addition to the florid style of Persian verse favored at court, a new taste developed for poetry and prose in the popular language of the Delhi region. The modern descendant of this language is called *Urdu* in Pakistan and *Hindi* in India.

## Central Decay and Regional Challenges

Mughal power did not long survive Aurangzeb's death in 1707. Some historians consider the land-grant system a central element in the rapid decline of imperial authority, but other factors were at play as well. Aurangzeb's additions to Mughal territory in southern India were not all well integrated into the imperial structure, and strong regional powers arose to challenge Mughal military supremacy. A climax came in 1739 when Nadir Shah, a warlord who had seized power in Iran after the fall of the Safavids, invaded the Mughal capital and carried off to Iran the "peacock throne," the priceless jewel-encrusted symbol of Mughal grandeur. Another throne was found for the later Mughals to sit on; but their empire, which survived in name to 1857, was finished.

In 1723, Nizam al-Mulk°, the powerful vizier of the Mughal sultan, gave up on the central government and established his own nearly independent state at Hyderabad in the eastern Deccan. Other officials bearing the title *nawab*° became similarly independent in Bengal and Oudh° in the northeast, as did the Marathas in the center. In the northwest, simultaneous Iranian and Mughal weakness allowed the Afghans to establish an independent kingdom.

Some of these regional powers, and the smaller princely states that arose on former Mughal territory, were prosperous and benefited from the removal of the sultan's heavy hand. Linguistic and religious communities, freed from the religious intolerance instituted during the reign of Aurangzeb, similarly enjoyed greater opportunity for political expression. However, this disintegration of central power favored the intrusion of European adventurers.

Joseph François Dupleix° took over the presidency of the French stronghold of Pondicherry° in 1741 and began a new phase of European involvement in India. He captured the English trading center of Madras and used his small contingent of European and European-trained Indian troops to

---

Sikh (sick)   Aurangzeb (ow-rang-ZEB)

**Nizam al-Mulk** (nee-ZAHM al-MULK)   *nawab* (NAH-wab)
**Oudh** (OW-ad)   **Dupleix** (doo-PLAY)   **Pondicherry** (pon-dih-CHER-ree)

become a power broker in southern India. Though offered the title *nawab,* Dupleix preferred to operate behind the scenes, using Indian princes as puppets. His career ended in 1754 when he was called home. Deeply involved in wars in Europe, the French government was unwilling to pursue further adventures in India. Dupleix's departure opened the way for the British, whose ventures in India are described in Chapter 21.

# TRADE EMPIRES IN
# THE INDIAN OCEAN

Although the Ottomans, Safavids, and Mughals did not seriously contest the growth of Portuguese and then Dutch, English, and French maritime power, the majority of non-European shipbuilders, captains, sailors, and traders were Muslim. Groups of Armenian, Jewish, and Hindu traders were also active, but they remained almost as aloof from the Europeans as the Muslims did. The presence in every port of Muslims following the same legal traditions and practicing their faith in similar ways cemented the Muslims' trading network. Islam, from its very outset in the life and preachings of Muhammad (570–632), was always congenial to trade and traders. Unlike Hinduism, it was a proselytizing religion, a factor that encouraged the growth of coastal Muslim communities as local non-Muslims were drawn into Muslim commercial activities, were converted, and intermarried with Muslims from abroad.

Although European missionaries, particularly the Jesuits, tried to extend Christianity into Asia and Africa (see Chapters 14 and 18), most Europeans, the Portuguese excepted, were less inclined than the Muslims were to treat local converts or the offspring of mixed marriages as full members of their communities. As a consequence, Islam spread extensively into East Africa and Southeast Asia during precisely the time of rapid European commercial expansion. Even without the support of the Muslim land empires, Islam became a source of resistance to growing European domination.

## Muslims in the East Indies

Historians disagree about the chronology and manner of Islam's spread in Southeast Asia. Arab traders were well known in southern China as early as the eighth century, so Muslims probably reached the East Indies at a similarly early date. Nevertheless, the dominance of Indian cultural influences in the area for several centuries thereafter indicates that early Muslim visitors had little impact on local beliefs. Clearer indications of conversion and the formation of Muslim communities date from roughly the fourteenth century. The strongest overseas linkage is to the port of Cambay in India (see Map 17.2) rather than to the Arab world. Islam took root first in port cities and in some royal courts and spread inland slowly, possibly transmitted by itinerant Sufis.

Although appeals to the Ottoman sultan for support against the Europeans ultimately proved of little use, Islam as a political ideology strengthened resistance to Portuguese, Spanish, and Dutch intruders. When the Spaniards conquered the Philippines during the decades following the establishment of their first fort in 1565, they encountered Muslims on the southern island of Mindanao° and the nearby Sulu archipelago. They called them "Moros," the Spanish term for their old enemies, the Muslims of North Africa. In the ensuing Moro wars, the Spaniards portrayed the Moros as greedy pirates who raided non-Muslim territories for slaves. In fact, they were political, religious, and commercial competitors whose perseverance enabled them to establish the Sulu Empire based in the southern Philippines, one of the strongest states in Southeast Asia from 1768 to 1848.

Other local kingdoms that looked on Islam as a force to counter the aggressive Christianity of the Europeans included the actively proselytizing Brunei° Sultanate in northern Borneo and the **Acheh° Sultanate** in northern Sumatra. At its peak in the early seventeenth century, Acheh succeeded Malacca as the main center of Islamic expansion in Southeast Asia. It prospered from trade in pepper and cotton cloth from Gujarat in India. Acheh declined after the Dutch seized Malacca from Portugal in 1641.

---

**Mindanao** (min-duh-NOW)    **Brunei** (BROO-nie)    **Acheh** (AH-cheh)

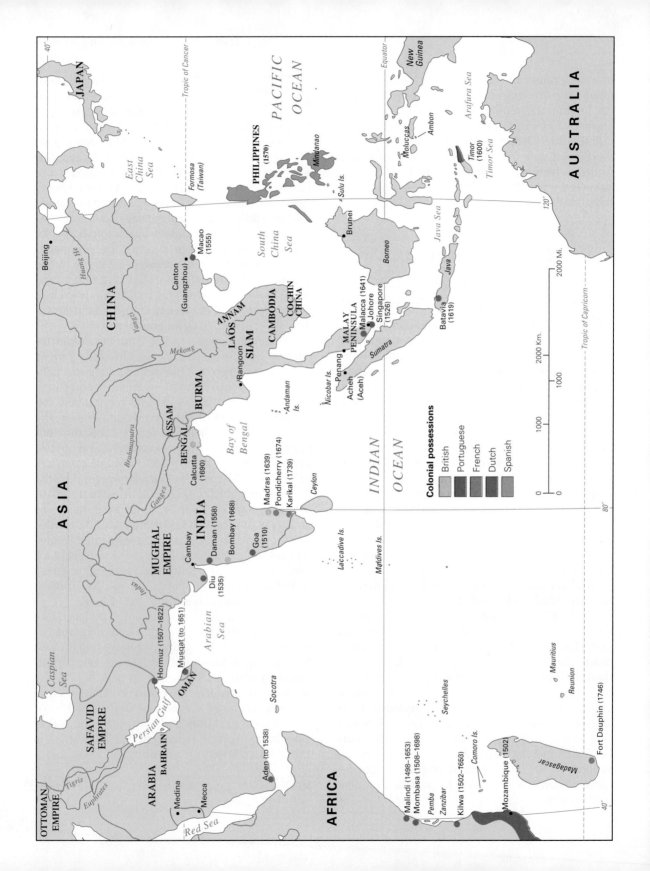

JAPAN

PACIFIC OCEAN

New Guinea

Equator

AUSTRALIA

*East China Sea*

*Formosa (Taiwan)*

PHILIPPINES (1570)

*Mindanao*

*Moluccas*

*Ambon*

*Timor (1600)*

*Arafura Sea*

*Timor Sea*

*Sulu Is.*

120°

*Beijing* •

*Huang He*

*Macao (1555)*

*Canton (Guangzhou)* •

CHINA

*South China Sea*

*Brunei* •

*Borneo*

*Java Sea*

*Yangzi*

ANNAM

LAOS

SIAM

CAMBODIA

COCHIN CHINA

*Mekong*

MALAY PENINSULA

Malacca (1641)

Johore

Singapore (1526)

*Java*

Batavia (1619)

2000 Mi.

BURMA

*Rangoon* •

*Sumatra*

ASSAM

BENGAL

Calcutta (1690)

*Brahmaputra*

Madras (1639)

Pondicherry (1674)

Karikal (1739)

Penang

Acheh (Aceh)

*Nicobar Is.*

*Andaman Is.*

2000 Km.

1000

*Ganges*

*Ceylon*

INDIAN OCEAN

Tropic of Capricorn

MUGHAL EMPIRE

INDIA

Cambay •

Daman (1558)

Bombay (1668)

Goa (1510)

1000

80°

ASIA

*Indus*

Diu (1535)

*Laccadive Is.*

*Maldives Is.*

0

0

**Colonial possessions**

British

Portuguese

French

Dutch

Spanish

*Caspian Sea*

SAFAVID EMPIRE

Hormuz (1507–1622)

Musqat (to 1651)

OMAN

*Arabian Sea*

*Socotra*

*Mauritius*

*Reunion*

*Seychelles*

*Persian Gulf*

BAHRAIN

Fort Dauphin (1746)

OTTOMAN EMPIRE

ARABIA

*Tigris*

*Euphrates*

Medina •

Mecca •

Aden (to 1538)

Malindi (1498–1653)

Mombasa (1508–1698)

*Pemba*

*Zanzibar*

Kilwa (1502–1663)

*Comoro Is.*

Mozambique 1502

*Madagascar*

AFRICA

*Red Sea*

40°

**Map 17.2   European Colonization in the Indian Ocean to 1750**   Since Portuguese explorers were the first Europeans to reach India by rounding Africa, Portugal gained a strong foothold in both areas. Rival Spain was barred from colonizing the region by the Treaty of Tordesillas in 1494, which limited Spanish efforts to lands west of a line drawn through the mid-Atlantic Ocean. The line carried around the globe provided justification of Spanish colonization in the Philippines. French, British, and Dutch colonies date from after 1600, when joint-stock companies provided a new stimulus for overseas commerce.

How well Islam was understood in these Muslim kingdoms is open to question. In Acheh, for example, a series of women ruled between 1641 and 1699. This practice came to an end when local Muslim scholars obtained a ruling from scholars in Mecca and Medina that Islam did not approve of female rulers. This ruling became a turning point after which scholarly understandings of Islam gained greater prominence in the East Indies.

Historians have theorized that the first propagators of Islam in Southeast Asia were merchants, Sufi preachers, or both. The scholarly vision of Islam, however, took root in the sixteenth century by way of pilgrims returning from years of study in Mecca and Medina. Islam was the primary force in the dissemination of writing in the region. Some of the returning pilgrims wrote in Arabic, others in Malay or Javanese. As Islam continued to spread, *adat,* a form of Islam rooted in pre-Muslim religious and social practices, retained its preeminence in rural areas over practices centered on the Shari'a, the religious law. But the royal courts in the port cities began to heed the views of the pilgrim teachers, as in their condemnation of female rulers. Though different in many ways, both varieties of Islam provided believers with a firm basis of identification in the face of the growing European presence. Christian missionaries gained most of their converts in regions that had not yet converted to Islam, such as the northern Philippines.

## Muslims in East Africa

The East African ports that the Portuguese began to visit in the fifteenth century were governed by Muslim rulers but were not linked politically (see Map 17.2). People living in

the millet and rice lands of the Swahili Coast—from the Arabic *sawahil*° meaning "coasts"—had little contact with those in the dry hinterlands. Throughout this period, the East African lakes region and the highlands of Kenya witnessed unprecedented migration and relocation of peoples because of drought conditions that persisted from the late sixteenth through most of the seventeenth century.

Cooperation among the trading ports of Kilwa, Mombasa, and Malindi was hindered by the thick bush country that separated the cultivated tracts of coastal land and by the fact that the ports competed with one another in the export of ivory; ambergris° (a whale byproduct used in perfumes); and forest products such as beeswax, copal tree resin, and wood (Kilwa also exported gold). In the eighteenth century, slave trading, primarily to Arabian ports but also to India, increased in importance. Because Europeans—the only peoples who kept consistent records of slave-trading activities—played a minor role in this slave trade, few records have survived to indicate its extent. Perhaps the best estimate is that 2.1 million slaves were exported between 1500 and 1890, a little over 12.5 percent of the total traffic in African slaves during that period (see Chapter 16).

The Portuguese conquered all of the coastal ports from Mozambique northward except Malindi, with whose ruler Portugal cooperated. A Portuguese description of the ruler indicates some of the cloth and metal goods that Malindi imported, as well as some local manufactures:

> The King wore a robe of damask trimmed with green satin and a rich [cap]. He was seated on two cushioned chairs of bronze, beneath a rough sunshade of crimson satin attached to a pole. An old man, who attended him as a page, carried a short sword in a silver sheath. There were many players on [horns], and two trumpets of ivory richly carved and of the size of a man, which were blown through a hole in the side, and made sweet harmony with the [horns].[1]

Initially, the Portuguese favored the port of Malindi, which caused the decline of Kilwa and Mombasa. Repeatedly plagued by local rebellion, Portuguese power suffered severe blows when the Arabs of **Oman** in southeastern Arabia captured

---

*sawahil* (suh-WAH-hil)   **ambergris** (AM-ber-grees)

their south Arabian stronghold at Musqat (1650) and then went on in support of African resistance to seize Mombasa (1698), which had become the Portuguese capital in East Africa. The Portuguese briefly retook Mombasa but lost control permanently in 1729. From then on, the Portuguese had to content themselves with Mozambique in Africa and a few remaining ports in India (Goa) and farther east (Macao and Timor).

The Omanis created a maritime empire of their own, but one that worked in greater cooperation with the African populations. The Bantu language of the coast, broadened by the absorption of Arabic, Persian, and Portuguese loan words, developed into **Swahili°,** which was spoken throughout the region. Arabs and other Muslims who settled in the region intermarried with local families, giving rise to a mixed population that played an important role in developing a distinctive Swahili culture.

Islam also spread in the southern Sudan in this period, particularly in the dry areas away from the Nile River. This growth coincided with a waning of Ethiopian power as a result of Portugal's stifling of trade in the Red Sea. Yet no significant contact developed between the emerging Muslim Swahili culture and that of the Muslims in the Sudan, to the north.

## The Coming of the Dutch

The Dutch played a major role in driving the Portuguese from their possessions in the East Indies. They were better organized than the Portuguese through the Dutch East India Company (see Chapter 16). Just as the Portuguese had tried to dominate the trade in spices, so the Dutch concentrated at first on the spice-producing islands of Southeast Asia. The Portuguese had seized Malacca, a strategic town on the narrow strait at the end of the Malay Peninsula, from a local Malay ruler in 1511. The Dutch took it away from them in 1641, leaving Portugal little foothold in the East Indies except the islands of Ambon° and Timor (see Map 17.2).

Although the United Netherlands was one of the least autocratic countries of Europe, the governors-general appointed by the Dutch East India Company deployed almost unlimited powers in their efforts to maintain their trade monopoly. They could even order the execution of their own employees for "smuggling"—that is, trading on their own. Under strong governors-general, the Dutch fought a series of wars against Acheh and other local kingdoms on Sumatra and Java. In 1628 and 1629, their new capital at **Batavia,** now the city of Jakarta on Java, was besieged by a fleet of fifty ships belonging to the sultan of Mataram°, a Javanese kingdom. The Dutch held out with difficulty and eventually prevailed when the sultan was unable to get effective help from the English.

Suppressing local rulers, however, was not enough to control the spice trade once other European countries adopted Dutch methods, became more knowledgeable about where goods might be acquired, and started to send more ships to Southeast Asia. In the course of the eighteenth century, therefore, the Dutch gradually turned from being a middleman for Southeast Asian producers and European buyers to being a producer of crops in areas they controlled, notably in Java. Javanese teak forests yielded high-quality lumber, and coffee, transplanted from Yemen, grew well in the hilly regions of western Java. In this new phase of colonial export production, Batavia developed from being the headquarters town of a far-flung enterprise to being the administrative capital of a conquered land.

Beyond the East Indies, the Dutch utilized their discovery of a band of powerful eastward-blowing winds (called the "Roaring Forties" because they blow throughout the year between 40 and 50 degrees south latitude) to reach Australia in 1606. In 1642 and 1643, Abel Tasman became the first European to set foot on Tasmania and New Zealand and to sail around Australia, signaling European involvement in that region.

## CONCLUSION

It is no coincidence that the Mughal, Safavid, and Ottoman Empires declined simultaneously in the seventeenth and eighteenth centuries. The complex changes in military technology and in the world economy that were under way in smaller Eu-

---

**Swahili** (swah-HEE-lee)  **Ambon** (am-BOHN)          **Mataram** (MAH-ah-ram) ropean countries either passed them by or affected them adversely. Despite their efforts on conquering more and more land, these land-based empires faced increasing difficulty in maintaining traditional military forces paid through land grants.

The opposite was true for seafaring countries intent on turning trade networks into maritime empires. Improvements in ship design, navigation accuracy, and the use of cannon gave an ever-increasing edge to European powers competing with local seafaring peoples. In contrast to the age-old Asian tradition that imperial wealth came from control of broad expanses of agricultural land, European countries promoted joint-stock companies and luxuriated in the prosperity gained from their ever-increasing control of Indian Ocean commerce.

That a major shift in world economic and political alignments was well under way by the late seventeenth century was scarcely perceivable in those parts of Asia and Africa ruled by the Ottoman and Mughal sultans and the Safavid shahs. They relied mostly on land taxes, usually indirectly collected via holders of land grants or tax farmers, rather than on customs duties or control of markets to fill the government coffers. With ever-increasing military expenditures, these taxes fell short of the rulers' needs. Oblivious to the fundamental problem of the entire economic system, imperial courtiers pursued their luxurious ways, poetry and the arts continued to flourish, and the quality of manufacturing and craft production remained generally high. Eighteenth-century European observers marveled no less at the riches and industry of these eastern lands than at the fundamental weakness of their political and military systems.

## ■ Key Terms

| | |
|---|---|
| Ottoman Empire | Akbar |
| Suleiman the Magnificent | *mansabs* |
| Janissaries | Rajputs |
| Safavid Empire | Acheh Sultanate |
| Shi'ite | Oman |
| Hidden Imam | Swahili |
| Shah Abbas I | Batavia |
| Mughal Empire | |

## ■ Suggested Reading

The best comprehensive and comparative account of the post-Mongol Islamic land empires, with an emphasis on social history, is Ira Lapidus, *A History of Islamic Societies* (1988). For a brief, general introduction to the relations between the Muslim land empires and the development of Indian Ocean trade, see Patricia Risso, *Merchants and Faith: Muslim Commerce and Culture in the Indian Ocean* (1995).

On the Ottoman Empire in its prime, see Colin Imber, *The Ottoman Empire, 1300–1650* (2002). Daniel Goffman, *The Ottoman Empire and the Early Modern Europe* (2002), compares the Ottomans with contemporary European kingdoms. Jason Goodwin, *Lords of the Horizons: A History of the Ottoman Empire* (1999), offers a more readable and journalistic account.

The most comprehensive treatment of the history of Safavid Iran is in the articles in Peter Jackson and Laurence Lockhart, eds., *The Cambridge History of Iran*, vol. 6, *The Timurid and Safavid Periods* (1986). For the artistic side of Safavid history, abundantly illustrated, see Anthony Welch, *Shah Abbas and the Arts of Isfahan* (1973).

A highly readable work that situates the Mughal Empire within the overall history of the subcontinent is Stanley Wolpert, *A New History of India*, 6th ed. (1999). For a broad treatment of the entire development of Islamic society in India with emphasis on the Mughal period, see S. M. Ikram, *History of Muslim Civilization in India and Pakistan* (1989). Wheeler Thackston has made a lively translation of Babur's autobiography in *The Baburnama: Memoirs of Babur, Prince and Emperor* (1996). For a comprehensive history of the Mughals, see John F. Richards, *The Mughal Empire* (1993).

For a brief introduction to the relations between the Muslim land empires and the development of Indian Ocean trade, see Patricis Risso, *Merchants and Faith: Muslim Commerce in the Indian Ocean* (1995).

## ■ Notes

1. Esmond Bradley Martin and Chrysse Perry Martin, *Cargoes of the East: The Ports, Trade and Culture of the Arabian Seas and Western Indian Ocean* (London: Elm Tree Books, 1978), 17.

# 18 Northern Eurasia, 1500–1800

CHAPTER OUTLINE

**Japanese Reunification**

**The Later Ming and Early Qing Empires**

**The Russian Empire**

**Comparative Perspectives**

ENVIRONMENT AND TECHNOLOGY: East Asian Porcelain

Li Zicheng° was an apprentice ironworker in a barren northern Chinese province. His dreams for the future were dashed when, in a desperate effort to save money, the Hanli emperor ordered the elimination of Li's job and those of many other government employees. The savings went to fund more troops to defend the capital city of Beijing° against attacks by **Manchu** armies from Manchuria in the northeast. By 1630 Li Zicheng had found work as a soldier, but he and his fellow soldiers mutinied when the government failed to provide them with needed supplies. A natural leader, Li soon headed a group of several thousand Chinese rebels. In 1635 he and other rebel leaders were strong enough to control much of north central China.

Wedged between the armies of the Manchu pressing from the north and the rebels to the southwest, the Ming government grew ever weaker. Taking advantage of the weakness, Li Zicheng's forces began to move toward Beijing. Along the way they captured towns and conscripted young men into their army. The rebels also won popular support with promises to end the abuses of the Ming and restore peace and prosperity. In April 1644 Li's armies were able to take over Beijing without a fight. The last Ming emperor hanged himself in the palace garden, bringing to an end the dynasty that had ruled China since 1368.

The rebels' success was short-lived. Believing there was more to fear from uneducated, violent men like Li, the Ming general Wu Sangui joined forces with the Manchu. Wu may have been influenced by the fact that Li had captured

---

**Li Zicheng** (lee ZUH-cheng)   **Beijing** (bay-JING))

one of the general's favorite concubines and taken her for himself. Together Wu and the Manchu retook Beijing in June. Li's forces scattered, and a year later he was dead, either a suicide or beaten to death by peasants whose food he tried to steal.[1]

Meanwhile, the Manchu were making it clear that they intended to be the new masters of China. They installed their young sovereign as the new emperor and over the next two decades hunted down the last of the Ming loyalists and heirs to the throne.

China was not the only state in northern Eurasia facing uprisings from within and foreign threats. In the period from 1500 to 1800 Japan and Russia experienced turbulence as they underwent massive political change and economic growth. Besides challenges from nearby neighbors, the three also faced new contacts and challenges from the commercially and militarily powerful European states.

As you read this chapter, ask yourself the following questions:

- How did Japan, China, and Russia respond to internal social, economic, and political pressures?

- How did China and Russia deal with military challenges from their immediate neighbors?

- How did Japan, China, and Russia differ in the ways they reacted to western European commercial and cultural contacts?

# JAPANESE REUNIFICATION

Like China and Russia in the centuries between 1500 and 1800, Japan experienced three major changes: internal and external military conflicts, political growth and strengthening, and expanded commercial and cultural contacts. Along with its culturally homogenous population and natural boundaries, Japan's smaller size made the process of political unification shorter than in the great empires of China and Russia. Japan also differed in its responses to new contacts with western Europeans.

## Civil War and the Invasion of Korea, 1500–1603

In the twelfth century different parts of Japan had fallen under the rule of warlords known as *daimyo*° (see Chapter 11). Each daimyo had a castle town, a small bureaucracy, and a band of warriors, the *samurai*°. Daimyo pledged a loose allegiance to the Japanese emperor residing in the capital city of Kyoto° and to the shogun, the hereditary chief of the emperor's government and armies. But neither figure held significant political power.

Warfare among the different daimyo was common, and in the late 1500s it culminated in a prolonged civil war. The warlord to emerge from the war was Hideyoshi°. In 1592, buoyed with his success in Japan, the supremely confident Hideyoshi invaded the Asian mainland with 160,000 men. His apparent intention was not just to conquer the Korean peninsula but also to make himself emperor of China.

The Korean and Japanese languages are closely related, but the dominant influence on Korean culture had long been China, to which Korean rulers generally paid tribute. In many ways the Yi dynasty that ruled Korea from 1392 to 1910 was a model Confucian state. Although Korea had developed its own system of writing in 1443 and made extensive use of printing with movable type from the fifteenth century on, most printing continued to use Chinese characters.

Against Hideyoshi's invaders the Koreans employed all the technological and military skill for which the Yi period was renowned. Ingenious covered warships, or "turtle boats," intercepted a portion of the Japanese fleet. The mentally unstable Hideyoshi countered with brutal punitive measures as his armies advanced through the Korean peninsula and into the Chinese province of Manchuria. However, after Hideyoshi's death in 1598, the other Japanese military leaders withdrew their

---

*daimyo* (DIE-mee-oh)   *samurai* (SAH-moo-rye)   **Kyoto** (KYOH-toh)   **Hideyoshi** (HEE-duh-YOH-shee) forces, and the Japanese government made peace in 1606.

The invasion devastated Korea. In the turmoil after the Japanese withdrawal, the Korean *yangban* (nobility) were able to lay claim to so much tax-paying land that royal revenues may have fallen by two-thirds. China, however, suffered even more dire consequences. The battles in Manchuria weakened Chinese garrisons there, permitting Manchu opposition to consolidate. Manchu forces invaded Korea in the 1620s and eventually compelled the Yi to become a tributary state. As already related, the Manchus would be in possession of Beijing, China's capital, by 1644.

## The Tokugawa Shogunate, to 1800

After Hideyoshi's demise, Tokugawa Ieyasu° (1543–1616) asserted his domination over other daimyo and in 1603 established a new military government known as the **Tokugawa Shogunate.** The shoguns created a new administrative capital at Edo° (now Tokyo). Trade along the well-maintained road between Edo and the imperial capital of Kyoto promoted the development of the Japanese economy and the formation of other trading centers (see Map 18.1).

Although the Tokugawa Shogunate gave Japan more political unity than the islands had seen in centuries, the regionally based daimyo still had a great deal of power and autonomy. Ieyasu and his successors worked hard to keep the political system from disintegrating; nevertheless, economic integration was more a feature of Tokugawa Japan than political centralization. Because shoguns required the daimyo to visit Edo frequently, good roads and maritime transport linked the city to the castle towns on three of Japan's four main islands. Commercial traffic developed along these routes. The shogun paid the lords in rice, and the lords paid their followers in rice. Recipients converted much of this rice into cash, a practice that led to the development of rice exchanges at Edo and at Osaka°, where merchants speculated in rice prices. By the late seventeenth century Edo was one of the largest cities in the world, with nearly a million inhabitants.

The domestic peace of the Tokugawa era forced the warrior class to adapt itself to the growing bureaucratic needs of the state. As the samurai became better educated and more attuned to the tastes of the civil elite, they became important customers for merchants dealing in silks, *sake*° (rice wine), fans, porcelain, lacquer ware, books, and money-lending. The state attempted—unsuccessfully—to curb the independence of the merchants when the economic well-being of the samurai was threatened by low rice prices or high interest rates.

The 1600s and 1700s were centuries of high achievement in artisanship, and Japanese skills in steel making, pottery, and lacquer ware were joined by excellence in the production and decoration of porcelain (see Environment and Technology: East Asian Porcelain), thanks in no small part to Korean experts brought back to Japan after the invasion of 1592. In the early 1600s manufacturers and merchants amassed enormous family fortunes. Several of the most important industrial and financial enterprises—for instance, the Mitsui° companies—had their origins in sake breweries of the early Tokugawa period and then branched out into manufacturing, finance, and transport.

Wealthy merchants weakened the Tokugawa policy of controlling commerce by cultivating close alliances with their regional daimyo and, if possible, with the shogun himself. By the end of the 1700s the merchant families of Tokugawa Japan held the key to future modernization and the development of heavy industry.

## Japan and the Europeans

Direct contacts with Europeans presented Japan with new opportunities and problems. Within thirty years of the arrival of the first Portuguese in 1543, the daimyo were fighting with Western-style firearms, copied and improved upon by Japanese armorers.

The Japanese welcomed but closely regulated traders from Portugal, Spain, the Netherlands, and England. Aside from the brief boom in porcelain exports in the seventeenth century, few Japanese

---

**Tokugawa Ieyasu** (TOH-koo-GAH-wah ee-ay-YAH-soo)
**Edo** (ED-oh)  **Osaka** (OH-sah-kah)

*sake* (SAH-kay)  **Mitsui** (MIT-soo-ee)

# C H R O N O L O G Y

| | Korea and Japan | China and Central Asia | Russia |
|---|---|---|---|
| **1500** | **1543**   First Portuguese contacts | **1517**   Portuguese embassy to China | **1547**   Ivan IV adopts title of tsar |
| | **1592**   Japanese invasion of Korea | | **1582**   Russians conquer Khanate of Sibir |
| **1600** | | **1601**   Matteo Ricci allowed to reside in Beijing | |
| | **1603**   Tokugawa Shogunate formed | | **1613–1645**   Rule of Mikhail, the first Romanov tsar |
| | **1633–1639**   Edicts close down trade with Europe | | |
| | | **1644**   Qing conquest of Beijing | **1649**   Subordination of serfs complete |
| | | **1662–1722**   Rule of Emperor Kangxi | |
| | | **1689**   Treaty of Nerchinsk with Russia | **1689–1725**   Rule of Peter the Great |
| | | **1691**   Qing control of Inner Mongolia | |
| **1700** | **1702**   Trial of the Forty-Seven Ronin | | |
| | | | **1712**   St. Petersburg becomes Russia's capital |
| | | **1736–1796**   Rule of Emperor Qianlong | |
| | | | **1762–1796**   Rule of Catherine the Great |
| | **1792**   Russian ships first spotted off the coast of Japan | | **1799**   Alaska becomes a Russian colony |

## East Asian Porcelain

By the 1400s artisans in China, Korea, and Japan were all producing high-quality pottery with lustrous surface glazes. The best quality, intended for the homes of the wealthy and powerful, was made of pure white clay and covered with a hard translucent glaze. Artisans often added intricate decorations in cobalt blue and other colors. Cheaper pottery found a huge market in East Asia.

Such pottery was also exported to Southeast Asia, the Indian Ocean, and the Middle East. Little found its way to Europe before 1600, but imports soared once the Dutch established trading bases in East Asia. Europeans called the high-quality ware "porcelain." Blue and white designs were especially popular.

One of the great centers of Chinese production was at the large artisan factory at Jingdezhen (JING-deh-JUHN). No sooner had the Dutch tapped into this source than the civil wars and Manchu conquests disrupted production in the middle 1600s. Desperate for a substitute source, the Dutch turned to porcelain from Japanese producers at Arita and Imari, near Nagasaki. Despite Japan's restriction of European trade, the Dutch East India Company transported some 190,000 pieces of Japanese ceramic ware to the Netherlands between 1653 and 1682.

In addition to a wide range of Asian designs, Chinese and Japanese artisans made all sorts of porcelain for the European market. These included purely decorative pottery birds, vases, and pots as well as utilitarian vessels and dishes intended for table use. The serving dish illustrated here came from dinnerware sets the Japanese made especially for the Dutch East India Company. The VOC logo at the center represents the first letters of the company's name in Dutch. It is surrounded by Asian design motifs.

After the return of peace in China, the VOC imported tens of thousands of Chinese porcelain pieces a year. The Chinese artisans sometimes produced imitations of Japanese designs that had become popular in Europe. Meanwhile, the Dutch were experimenting with making their own imitations of East Asian porcelain, right down to the Asian motifs and colors that had become so fashionable in Europe.

**Japanese Export Porcelain**  Part of a larger set made for the Dutch East India Company.  (Photograph courtesy Peabody Essex Museum, #83830)

goods went to Europe, and not much from Europe found a market in Japan. The Japanese sold the Dutch copper and silver, which the Dutch exchanged in China for silks that they then resold in Japan. The Japanese, of course, had their own trade with China.

Portuguese and Spanish merchant ships also brought Catholic missionaries. One of the first, Francis Xavier, went to India in the mid-sixteenth century looking for converts and later traveled throughout Southeast and East Asia. He spent two years in Japan and died in 1552, hoping to gain entry to China.

Japanese responses to Xavier and other Jesuits (members of the Catholic religious order the Society of Jesus) were decidedly mixed. Many ordinary Japanese found the new faith deeply meaningful, but the Japanese elite more often opposed it as disruptive and foreign. By 1580 more than 100,000 Japanese had become Christians, and one daimyo gave Jesuit missionaries the port city of Nagasaki°. In 1613 Date Masamune°, the fierce and independent daimyo of northern Honshu°, sent his own embassy to the Vatican, by way of the Philippines (where there were significant communities of Japanese merchants and pirates) and Mexico City. Some daimyo converts ordered their subjects to become Christians as well.

By the early seventeenth century there were some 300,000 Japanese Christians and even some Japanese priests. However, suspicions about the intentions of the Europeans and their well-armed ships turned the new shogunate in Edo into a center of hostility toward Christianity. A decree issued in 1614 banned Christianity and charged its adherents with seeking to overthrow true doctrine, change the government, and seize the country. Some missionaries left Japan; others worked underground. The government began persecutions in earnest in 1617, and the beheadings, crucifixions, and forced recantations over the next several decades destroyed almost the entire Christian community.

To keep Christianity from resurfacing, a series of decrees issued between 1633 and 1639 sharply curtailed trade with Europe. Europeans who entered illegally faced the death penalty. Japanese subjects were required to produce certificates from Buddhist temples attesting to their religious orthodoxy and loyalty to the regime.

The exclusion of Europe was not total. A few Dutch were permitted to reside on a small artificial island in Nagasaki's harbor, and a few Japanese were licensed to supply their needs. What these intermediaries learned about European weapons technology, shipbuilding, mathematics and astronomy, anatomy and medicine, and geography was termed "Dutch studies."

Tokugawa restrictions on the number of Chinese ships that could trade in Japan were harder to enforce. Regional lords in northern and southern Japan not only pursued overseas trade and piracy but also claimed dominion over islands between Japan and Korea and southward toward Taiwan, including present-day Okinawa. Despite such evasions, the new shogunate unquestionably achieved substantial success in exercising its authority.

## Elite Decline and Social Crisis

During the 1700s population growth put a great strain on the well-developed lands of central Japan. In more remote provinces, where the lords promoted new settlements and agricultural expansion, the rate of economic growth was significantly greater.

Also troubling the Tokugawa government in the 1700s was the shogunate's inability to stabilize rice prices and halt the economic decline of the samurai. The Tokugawa government realized that the rice brokers could manipulate rice prices and interest rates to enrich themselves at the expense of the samurai, who had to convert their rice allotments into cash. Early Tokugawa laws designed to regulate interest and prices were later supplemented by laws requiring moneylenders to forgive samurai debts. But these laws were not always enforced. By the early 1700s many lords and samurai were dependent on the willingness of merchants to provide credit.

The legitimacy of the Tokugawa shoguns rested on their ability to reward and protect the interests of the lords and samurai who had supported their rise to power. Moreover, the Tokugawa government, like the governments of China, Korea, and Vietnam, accepted the Confucian idea that agriculture should be the basis of state wealth and that merchants, who were considered morally weak, should occupy lowly positions in society. Tokugawa decentralization, however, not only failed to hinder but actually stimulated the growth of commercial activities. From the founding of the Tokugawa Shogunate in 1603 until 1800, the economy grew faster than the population. Household amenities and cultural resources that in China appeared only in the cities were common in the Japanese countryside. Despite official disapproval, merchants enjoyed relative freedom and influence in eighteenth-century Japan. They produced a vivid

---

**Nagasaki** (NAH-guh-SAHK-kee)    **Date Masamune** (DAH-tay mah-suh-MOO-nay)    **Honshu** (HOHN-shoo)

**Woodblock Print of the "Forty-Seven Ronin" Story**
The saga of the forty-seven ronin and the avenging of their fallen leader has fascinated the Japanese public since the event occurred in 1702. This watercolor from the Tokugawa period shows the leaders of the group pausing on the snowy banks of the Sumida River in Edo (Tokyo) before storming their enemy's residence.    (Private Collection)

culture of their own, fostering the development of *kabuki* theater, colorful woodblock prints and silk-screened fabrics, and restaurants.

The "Forty-Seven Ronin°" incident of 1701–1703 exemplified the ideological and social crisis of Japan's transformation from a military to a civil society. A senior minister provoked a young daimyo into drawing his sword at the shogun's court. For this offense the young lord was sentenced to commit *seppuku*°, the ritual suicide of the samurai. His own followers then became *ronin*, "masterless samurai," obliged by the traditional code of the warrior to avenge their deceased master. They broke into the house of the senior minister and

killed him and others in his household. Then they withdrew to a temple in Edo and notified the shogun of what they had done out of loyalty to their lord and to avenge his death.

A legal debate ensued. To deny the righteousness of the ronin would be to deny samurai values. But to approve their actions would create social chaos, undermine laws against murder, and deny the shogunal government the right to try cases of samurai violence. The shogun ruled that the ronin had to die but would be permitted to die honorably by committing seppuku. Traditional samurai values had to surrender to the supremacy of law. The purity of purpose of the ronin is still celebrated in Japan, but since then Japanese writers, historians, and teachers have recognized that the self-sacrifice of the ronin for the sake of upholding civil law was necessary.

# THE LATER MING AND EARLY QING EMPIRES

Like Japan, China after 1500 experienced civil and foreign wars, an important change in government, and new trading and cultural relations with Europe and its neighbors. The internal and external forces at work in China were different and operated on a much larger scale, but they led in similar directions. By 1800 China had a greatly enhanced empire, an expanding economy, and growing doubts about the importance of European trade and Christianity.

**The Ming Empire, 1500–1644**

The economic and cultural achievements of the early **Ming Empire** (see Chapter 11) continued during the 1500s. But this productive period was followed by many decades of political weakness, warfare, and rural woes until a new dynasty, the Qing° from Manchuria, guided China back to peace and prosperity.

The Europeans whose ships began to seek out new contacts with China in the early sixteenth cen-

---

**ronin** (ROH-neen)    *seppuku* (SEP-poo-koo)

**Qing** (ching)

tury left many accounts of their impressions. They were astonished at Ming China's imperial power, exquisite manufactures, and vast population. European merchants bought such large quantities of the high-grade blue-on-white porcelain commonly used by China's upper classes that in English all fine dishes became known simply as "china."

The growing integration of China into the world economy stimulated rapid growth in the silk, cotton, and porcelain industries. Agricultural regions that supplied raw materials to these industries and food for the expanding urban populations also prospered. In exchange for Chinese exports, tens of thousands of tons of silver from Japan and Latin America flooded into China in the century before 1640. The influx of silver led many Chinese to substitute payments in silver for land taxes, labor obligations, and other kinds of dues.

Ming cities had long been culturally and commercially vibrant. Many large landowners and absentee landlords lived in town, as did officials, artists, and rich merchants who had purchased ranks or prepared their sons for the examinations. The elite classes had created a brilliant culture in which novels, operas, poetry, porcelain, and painting were all closely interwoven. Small businesses catering to the urban elites prospered through printing, tailoring, running restaurants, or selling paper, ink, ink-stones, and writing brushes. The imperial government operated factories for the production of ceramics and silks. Enormous government complexes at Jingdezhen and elsewhere invented assembly-line techniques and produced large quantities of high-quality ceramics for sale in China and abroad.

Despite these achievements, serious problems developed that left the Ming Empire economically and politically exhausted. There is evidence that the climate changes known as the Little Ice Age in seventeenth-century Europe affected the climate in China as well (see Issues in World History: The Little Ice Age). Annual temperatures dropped, reached a low point about 1645, and remained low until the early 1700s. The resulting agricultural distress and famine fueled large uprisings that speeded the end of the Ming Empire. The devastation caused by these uprisings and the spread of epidemic disease resulted in steep declines in local populations.

The rapid urban growth and business speculation that were part of the burgeoning of the trading economy also produced problems. Some provinces suffered from price inflation caused by the flood of silver. In contrast to the growing involvement of European governments in promoting economic growth, the Ming government pursued some policies that hindered growth. Despite the fact that experiments with paper currency had failed as far back as the 1350s, Ming governments persisted in issuing new paper money and copper coinage, even after abundant supplies of silver had won the approval of the markets. Corruption was also a serious government problem. By the end of the Ming period the imperial factories were plagued by disorder and inefficiency. The situation became so bad during the late sixteenth and seventeenth centuries that workers held strikes with increasing frequency. During a labor protest at Jingdezhen in 1601, workers threw themselves into the kilns to protest working conditions.

Yet the urban and industrial sectors of later Ming society fared much better than the agricultural sector, which failed to maintain the strong growth of early Ming times. Despite knowledge of new African and American crops gained from European traders, farmers were slow to change their ways. Neither the rice-growing regions in southern China nor the wheat-growing regions in northern China experienced a meaningful increase in productivity under the later Ming. After 1500 economic depression in the countryside, combined with recurring epidemics in central and southern China, kept rural population growth in check.

## Ming Collapse and the Rise of the Qing

Although these environmental, economic, and administrative problems existed, the primary reasons for the fall of the Ming Empire were internal rebellion and rising Manchu power on the frontier. Insecure boundaries had been a recurrent peril. The Ming had long been under pressure from the powerful Mongol federations of the north and west. In the late 1500s large numbers of Mongols were unified by their devotion to the Dalai Lama°,

**Dalai Lama** (DAH-lie LAH-mah)

or universal teacher, of Tibetan Buddhism, whom they regarded as their spiritual leader. Building on this spiritual unity, a brilliant leader named Galdan restored Mongolia as a regional military power around 1600. The Manchus, an agricultural people who controlled the region north of Korea, grew stronger in the northeast.

In the southwest, native peoples repeatedly resisted the immigration of Chinese farmers. Pirates based in Okinawa and Taiwan, many of them Japanese, frequently looted the southeast coast. Ming military resources, concentrated against the Mongols and the Manchus in the north, could not be deployed to defend the coasts. As a result, many southern Chinese migrated to Southeast Asia to profit from the sea-trading networks of the Indian Ocean.

The Japanese invasion of 1592 to 1598 (see section on Japan) prompted the Ming to seek the assistance of Manchu troops that they were then unable to restrain. With the rebel leader Li Zicheng in possession of Beijing (see the beginning of this chapter) and the emperor dead by his own hand, a Ming general joined forces with the Manchu leaders in the summer of 1644. Instead of restoring the Ming, however, the Manchus claimed China for their own and began a forty-year conquest of the rest of the Ming territories, as well as Taiwan and parts of Mongolia and Central Asia (see Map 18.1).

A Manchu family headed the new **Qing Empire,** and Manchu generals commanded the military forces. But Manchus made up a very small portion of the population. The overwhelming majority of Qing officials, soldiers, merchants, and farmers were ethnic Chinese. Like other successful invaders of China, the Qing soon adopted Chinese institutions and policies.

**Trading Companies and Missionaries**

For European merchants, the China trade was second in importance only to the spice trade of southern Asia. China's vast population and manufacturing skills drew a steady stream of ships from western Europe, but enthusiasm for the trade developed only slowly at the imperial court.

A Portuguese ship reached China at the end of 1513 but was not permitted to trade. A formal Portuguese embassy in 1517 got bogged down in Chi-

nese protocol and procrastination, and China expelled the Portuguese in 1522. Finally, in 1557 the Portuguese gained the right to trade from a base in Macao° on the southern coast. Spain's Asian trade was conducted from Manila in the Philippines, which also linked with South America across the Pacific. For a time, the Spanish and the Dutch both maintained trading outposts on the island of Taiwan, but in 1662 they were forced to concede control to the Qing, who for the first time incorporated Taiwan into China.

By then, the Dutch East India Company (VOC) had displaced the Portuguese as the major European trader in the Indian Ocean and was establishing itself as the main European trader in East Asia. VOC representatives courted official favor in China by acknowledging the moral superiority of the emperor. They performed the ritual kowtow (in which the visitor knocked his head on the floor while crawling toward the throne) to the Ming emperor.

Catholic missionaries accompanied the Portuguese and Spanish merchants to China, just as they did to Japan. While the Franciscans and Dominicans pursued the conversion efforts at the bottom of society that had worked so well in Japan, the Jesuits focused on China's intellectual and political elite. In this they were far more successful than they had been in Japan—at least until the eighteenth century.

The outstanding Jesuit of late Ming China, Matteo Ricci° (1552–1610), became expert in the Chinese language and an accomplished scholar of the Confucian classics. Under Ricci's leadership, the Jesuits sought to adapt Catholic Christianity to Chinese cultural traditions while enhancing their status by introducing the Chinese to the latest science and technology from Europe. From 1601 Ricci was allowed to reside in Beijing on an imperial stipend as a Western scholar. Later Jesuits headed the office of astronomy that issued the official calendar.

**Emperor Kangxi**

The seventeenth and eighteenth centuries—particularly the reigns of the **Kangxi**° (r. 1662–1722) and Qianlong° (r. 1736–1796) emperors—were a pe-

**Macao** (muh-KOW)   **Matteo Ricci** (mah-TAY-oh REE-chee)
**Kangxi** (KAHNG-shee)   **Qianlong** (chee-YEN-loong)

**Map 18.1    The Qing Empire, 1644–1783**    The Qing Empire began in Manchuria and captured north China in 1644. Between 1644 and 1783 the Qing conquered all the former Ming territories and added Taiwan, the lower Amur River Basin, Inner Mongolia, eastern Turkestan, and Tibet. The resulting state was more than twice the size of the Ming Empire.

riod of great economic, military, and cultural achievement in China. To foster economic and demographic recovery, the early Qing emperors repaired the roads and waterworks, lowered transit taxes, mandated comparatively low rents and interest rates, and established economic incentives for resettling areas devastated by peasant rebellions. Foreign trade was encouraged. Vietnam, Burma, and Nepal sent regular embassies to the Qing tribute court and carried the latest Chinese fashions back home. Overland routes of communication from Korea to Central Asia revived, and through its conquests the Qing Empire gained access to the superior horses of Afghanistan.

The Manchu aristocrats who led the conquest of Beijing and north China dominated the first Qing emperor and served as regents for his young son, who was declared emperor in 1662. This child-emperor, Kangxi, sparred politically with the regents until 1669, when he executed the chief regent and thereby gained real control of the government. He was then sixteen and an intellectual prodigy who had mastered classical Chinese, Manchu, and Mongolian at an early age and memorized the Chinese classics. His reign, lasting until his death in 1722, was marked not only by imperial expansion but also by great stability.

In the north, the Qing rulers especially feared

**Emperor Kangxi** In a portrait from about 1690, the young Manchu ruler is portrayed as a refined scholar in the Confucian tradition. He was a scholar and had great intellectual curiosity, but this portrait would not suggest that he was also capable of leading troops in battle. (The Palace Museum, Beijing)

an alliance between Galdan's Mongol state and the expanding Russian presence along the **Amur°** **River.** In the 1680s Qing forces attacked the wooden forts built by hardy Russian scouts on the river's northern bank. Neither empire sent large forces into the Amur territories, so the contest was partly a struggle for the goodwill of the local Evenk and Dagur peoples. The Qing emperor emphasized the importance of treading lightly in the struggle and well understood the principles of espionage:

Amur (AH-moor)

Upon reaching the lands of the Evenks and the Dagurs you will send to announce that you have come to hunt deer. Meanwhile, keep a careful record of the distance and go, while hunting, along the northern bank of the Amur until you come by the shortest route to the town of Russian settlement at Albazin. Thoroughly reconnoiter its location and situation. I don't think the Russians will take a chance on attacking you. If they offer you food, accept it and show your gratitude. If they do attack you, don't fight back. In that case, lead your people and withdraw into our own territories. For I have a plan of my own.[2]

That delicacy gives a false impression of the intensity of the struggle between these two great empires. Qing forces twice attacked Albazin. The Qing were worried about Russian alliances with other frontier peoples, while Russia wished to protect its access to the furs, timber, and metals concentrated in Siberia, Manchuria, and Yakutsk. The Qing and Russians were also rivals for control of northern Asia's Pacific coast. Continued conflict would benefit neither side. In 1689 the Qing and Russian Empires negotiated the Treaty of Nerchinsk, using Jesuit missionaries as interpreters. The treaty fixed the border along the Amur River and regulated trade across it. Although this was a thinly settled area, the treaty proved important since the frontier it demarcated has long endured.

The next step was to settle the Mongolian frontier. Kangxi personally led troops in the great campaigns that defeated Galdan and brought Inner Mongolia under Qing control by 1691.

Kangxi was distinguished by his openness to new ideas and technologies from different regions. Unlike the rulers of Japan, who drove Christian missionaries out, he welcomed Jesuit advisers, discussed scientific and philosophical issues with them, and put them in important offices. Jesuits helped create maps in the European style as practical guides to newly conquered regions and as symbols of Qing dominance. Kangxi considered introducing the European calendar, but protests from the Confucian elite caused him to drop the plan. When he fell ill with malaria in the 1690s, Jesuit medical expertise (in this case, the use of quinine) aided his recovery. Kangxi also ordered the creation of illustrated books in Manchu detailing European anatomical and pharmaceutical knowledge.

**From the Jesuit Library at Beijing**    Jesuits such as Matteo Ricci were willing to share books on technology and science with Chinese scholars. But without firsthand experience it was impossible for Chinese translators to convey how the devices actually worked. Here, a man walking in a wheel drives a shaft that changes the pressure inside two pumps. In the Chinese translation of the drawing, the mechanisms were all lost.    (Left: From Zonca, *Trombe da Rota per Cavar Aqua* [1607]. Right: "Diagram Number Eight" from *Qi tushuo* [*Illustrations on Energy*] [1627]. Both courtesy of Joseph Needham, *Science and Civilization in China*, vol. 4)

To gain converts among the Chinese elite, the Jesuits made important compromises in their religious teaching. The most important was their toleration of Confucian ancestor worship. The matter caused great controversy between the Jesuits and their Catholic rivals in China, the Franciscans and Dominicans, and also between the Jesuits and the pope. In 1690 the disagreement reached a high pitch. Kangxi wrote to Rome supporting the Jesuit position. Further disagreement with a papal legate to China led Kangxi to order the expulsion of all missionaries who refused to sign a certificate accepting his position. Most of the Jesuits signed, but relations with the imperial court were irreparably harmed. The Jesuit presence in China declined in the eighteenth century, and later Qing emperors persecuted Christians rather than naming them to high offices.

## Chinese Influences on Europe

The exchange of information between the Qing and the Europeans that Kangxi had fostered was never one-way. When the Jesuits informed the Qing court on matters of anatomy, for instance, the Qing were able to demonstrate an early form of inoculation, called "variolation," that had been used to stem the spread of smallpox after the Qing conquest of Beijing. The technique helped inspire the development of other vaccines later in Europe.

Similarly, Jesuit writings about the intellectual and cultural achievements of China excited admiration in Europe. The wealthy and the aspiring middle classes of Europe demanded Chinese things—or things that looked to Europeans as if they could be Chinese. Silk, porcelain, and tea were avidly sought, along with cloisonné jewelry, lacquered and jeweled room dividers, painted fans, and carved jade and ivory (which originated in Africa and was finished in China). One of the most striking Chinese influences was wallpaper—an adaptation of the Chinese practice of covering walls with enormous loose-hanging watercolors or calligraphy scrolls. By the mid-1700s special workshops throughout China were producing wallpaper and other consumer items according to the specifications of European merchants. The items were shipped to Canton for export to Europe.

In political philosophy, too, the Europeans felt they had something to learn. In the late 1770s poems supposedly written by Emperor Qianlong were translated into French and disseminated in European intellectual circles. These works depicted the Qing emperors as benevolent despots who campaigned against superstition and ignorance, curbed the excesses of the aristocracy, and patronized science and the arts. European intellectuals who were questioning their own political systems found the image of a practical, secular, compassionate ruler intriguing. The French thinker Voltaire proclaimed the Qing emperors model philosopher-kings and advocated such rulership as a protection against the growth of aristocratic privilege.

## Tea and Diplomacy

To maintain strict control over trade, facilitate tax collection, and suppress piracy, the Qing permitted only one market point for each foreign sector. Thus Europeans were permitted to trade only at Canton.

This system worked well enough for European traders until the late 1700s, when Britain became worried about its massive trade deficit with China. From bases in India and Singapore, British traders moved eastward to China and eventually displaced the Dutch as China's leading European trading partner. The directors of the East India Company (EIC) believed that China's technological achievements and gigantic potential markets could produce limitless profit. By the early 1700s the EIC dominated European trading in Canton.

Tea from China had spread overland on Eurasian routes in medieval and early modern times to become a prized import in Russia, Central Asia, and the Middle East, all of which know it by its northern Chinese name, *cha*—as do the Portuguese. Other western Europeans acquired tea from the sea routes and thus know it by its name in the Fujian province of coastal China and Taiwan: *te*. In much of Europe, tea competed with chocolate and coffee as a fashionable drink by the mid-1600s.

Great fortunes were being made in the tea trade, but the English had not found a comparable product to sell to China. They believed that China was a vast unexploited market, with hundreds of millions of potential consumers of lamp oil made from whale blubber, cotton grown in India or the American South, or guns manufactured in London or Connecticut. Particularly after the loss of the thirteen American colonies, Britain feared that its markets would diminish, and the EIC and other British merchants concluded that the Qing trade system—the "Canton system," as the British called it—stood in the way of opening new commercial paths.

A massive trade deficit constituted another British worry. Because the Qing Empire rarely bought anything from Britain, British silver poured into China to pay for tea and other imports. The Qing government, whose revenues were declining in the later 1700s while its expenses rose, needed the silver and was not inclined to loosen restrictions on imported foreign goods. To make matters worse, the East India Company had managed its worldwide holdings badly, and as it teetered on bankruptcy, its attempts to manipulate Parliament became increasingly intrusive. In 1792 the British government dispatched Lord George Macartney, a well-connected peer with practical experience in Russia and India, to China. Including scientists, artists, and translators as well as guards and diplomats, the **Macartney mission** showed Britain's great interest in the Qing Empire as well as the EIC's desire to revise the trade system.

China was not familiar with the European system of ambassadors, and Macartney struggled to portray himself in Chinese terms as a "tribute emissary" come to salute the Qianlong emperor's eightieth birthday. However, he steadfastly refused to perform the kowtow, though he did agree to bow on one knee as he would to his own monarch, King George III. The Qianlong emperor received

Macartney courteously in September 1793 but refused to alter the Canton trading system, open new ports of trade, or allow the British to establish a permanent mission in Beijing. Qianlong sent a letter to King George explaining that China had no need to increase its foreign trade, had no use for Britain's ingenious devices and manufacturers, and set no value on closer diplomatic ties.

Dutch, French, and Russian embassies soon attempted to achieve what Macartney had failed to do. When they also failed, European frustration with the Qing mounted. The great European admiration for China faded. Political solutions seemed impossible because the Qing court would not communicate with foreign envoys or observe the simplest rules of the diplomatic system familiar to Europeans. In Macartney's view, China was like a venerable old warship, well maintained and splendid to look at, but obsolete and no longer up to the task.

## Population and Social Stress

The Chinese who escorted Macartney and his entourage in 1792–1793 took them through China's prosperous cities and productive farmland. The visitors did not see evidence of the economic and environmental decline that had set in during the last decades of the 1700s. Population growth had intensified demand for rice and wheat, as well as for growing new crops like corn and sweet potatoes, and for more thorough exploitation of land already in use.

In the peaceful decades of Qing rule, China grew to three times its size in 1500. If one accepts an estimate of some 350 million in the late 1700s, China had twice the population of all of Europe. Despite the efficiency of Chinese agriculture and the gradual adoption of New World crops, population growth led to social and environmental problems. More people meant less farmland per person. Increased demand for building materials and firewood reduced woodlands. Deforestation, in turn, accelerated wind and water erosion and increased flooding. Dams and dikes were not maintained, and silted-up river channels were not dredged. By the end of the eighteenth century parts of the thousand-year-old Grand Canal linking the rivers of north and south

China were nearly unusable, and the towns that bordered it were starved for commerce.

The result was misery in many parts of interior China. Some districts responded by increasing production of tea, cotton, and silk, crops that were tied to the export market. Some peasants sought seasonal jobs in better-off agricultural areas or worked in low-status jobs as barge pullers, charcoal burners, or night soil carriers. Many drifted to the cities to make their way by begging, prostitution, or theft. In central and southwestern China, where floods had impoverished many farmers, rebellions became endemic. Indigenous peoples concentrated in the less fertile lands in the south and in the northern and western borderlands of the empire often joined in revolts.

The Qing government was not up to controlling its vast empire. It was twice the size of the Ming geographically, but it employed about the same number of officials. The government's dependence on working alliances with local elites had led to widespread corruption and shrinking government revenues. As was the case with other empires, the Qing's spectacular rise had ended, and decline had set in.

# THE RUSSIAN EMPIRE

From modest beginnings in 1500, Russia expanded rapidly during the next three centuries to create an empire that stretched from eastern Europe across northern Asia and into North America. Russia also became one of the major powers of Europe by 1750, with armies capable of mounting challenges to its Asian and European neighbors.

## The Drive Across Northern Asia

During the centuries just before 1500, the history of the Russians had been dominated by steppe nomads (see Chapter 11). The Mongol Khanate of the Golden Horde ruled the Russians and their neighbors from the 1240s until 1480.

Under the Golden Horde Moscow became the most important Russian city and the center of political power. Moscow lay in the forest zone that stretched across Eurasia north of the treeless steppe (plains) favored by Mongol horsemen. The princes of **Muscovy°**, the territory surrounding the city of Moscow, led the movement against the Golden Horde and ruthlessly annexed the territories of the neighboring Russian state of Novgorod in 1478.

Once free from Mongol domination, the princes of Muscovy set out on conquests that in time made them masters of all the Golden Horde territories and then of a far greater empire. Prince Ivan IV (r. 1533–1584) pushed the conquests south and east at the expense of the Khanates of Kazan and Astrakhan (see Map 18.2).

At the end of the sixteenth century, Russians ruled the largest state in Europe and large territories on the Asian side of the **Ural Mountains** as well. Since 1547 the Russian ruler used the title **tsar°** (from the Roman imperial title *caesar*), the term Russians had used for the rulers of the Mongol Empire. The Russian church promoted the idea of Moscow as the "third Rome," successor to the Roman Empire's second capital, Constantinople, which had fallen to the Ottoman Turks in 1453. But such foreign titles did not disguise a very Russian pattern of expansion.

Russian claims to greatness were also exaggerated: in 1600 the empire was poor, backward, and landlocked. Only the northern city of Arkhangelsk was connected by water to the rest of the world— when its harbor was not frozen. The Turkic-speaking Crimean peoples to the south were powerful enough to sack Moscow in 1571. Beyond them, the still vigorous Ottoman Empire controlled the shores of the Black Sea, while the Safavid rulers of Iran dominated the trade routes of southern Central Asia. The powerful kingdoms of Sweden and Poland-Lithuania to the west turned back Russian forces seeking access to ports on the Baltic Sea.

A path of less resistance lay to the east across **Siberia,** and it had much to recommend it. Many Russians felt more at home in the forested north than on the open steppes; and the thinly inhabited region abounded in valuable resources, most notably the soft, dense fur that forest animals grew to survive the long winter cold. Like their counter-

parts in Canada (see Chapter 16), hardy Russian pioneers in Siberia made a living from animal pelts. The merchants from western Europe and other lands who came to buy these furs in Moscow provided the tsars with revenue and access to European technology.

Early Russian exploration of Siberia was not the work of the state but of the Strogonovs, a wealthy Russian trading family. The small bands of hunting and fishing peoples who inhabited this cold and desolate region had no way of resisting the armed adventurers the Strogonovs hired. Using rifles, their troops attacked and destroyed the only political power in the region, the Khanate of Sibir, in 1582. Rivers provided the best routes for moving through the dense forests and enabled Russian fur trappers to reach the Pacific during the seventeenth century. Soon they crossed over into Alaska. Russian political control followed at a much slower pace. In the seventeenth century Siberia was a frontier zone with widely scattered forts, not a province under full control. The Russians had to placate rebellious leaders of the native Siberian peoples with gifts and acknowledge their rights and authority. Beginning in the early seventeenth century the tsar also used Siberia as a penal colony for criminals and political prisoners.

In the 1640s Russian settlers began to move into the valley of the Amur River east of Mongolia in order to grow grain. As seen already, by the time the Qing were in a position to confront the Russian presence, the worrisome threat of Galdan's Mongol military power had arisen. The Russians, who shared a concern about the Mongols, were pleased to work out a frontier agreement with China. The 1689 Treaty of Nerchinsk recognized Russian claims west of Mongolia but required the Russians to withdraw their settlements farther east. Moreover, the negotiations signaled China's recognition of Russia as an important and powerful neighbor.

## Russian Society and Politics to 1725

Russian expansion involved demographic changes as well as new relations between the tsar and the elite classes. A third transformation affected the freedom and mobility of the Russian peasantry.

---

**Muscovy** (MUSS-koe-vee)    **tsar** (zahr)

As the empire expanded, it incorporated people with different languages, religious beliefs, and ethnic identities. Language differences were not hard to overcome, but religious and other cultural differences often caused tensions, especially when differences were manipulated for political purposes. Orthodox missionaries made great efforts to Christianize the peoples of Siberia in much the same way that Catholic missionaries did in Canada. But among the relatively more populous steppe peoples, Islam won out over Christianity as the dominant religion. More fundamental than language, ethnicity, or religion were the differences in how people made their living. Russians tended to live as farmers, hunters, builders, scribes, or merchants, while those newly incorporated into the empire were mostly herders, caravan workers, and soldiers.

As people mixed, individual and group identities became complex. Even among Russian speakers who were members of the Russian Orthodox Church there was wide diversity of identity. The **Cossacks** are a revealing example. The name probably came from a Turkic word for a warrior or mercenary soldier and referred to bands of people living on the steppes between Moscovy and the Caspian and Black Seas. In practice, Cossacks became highly diverse in their origins and beliefs. What mattered was that they belonged to close-knit bands, were superb riders and fighters, and were feared by both the villagers and the legal authorities. Cossacks made temporary allegiances with many rulers but were most loyal to their bands and to whoever was currently paying for their military services.

Cossacks constituted the majority of the soldiers and early settlers employed by the Strogonovs to penetrate Siberia. Most historians believe that Cossacks founded all the major towns of Russian Siberia. They also manned the Russian camps on the Amur River. The Cossacks west of the Urals performed distinctive service for Russia in defending against Swedish and Ottoman incursions, but they also resisted any efforts to undermine their own political autonomy. Those in the rich and populous lands of the Ukraine, for example, rebelled when the tsar agreed to a division of their lands with Poland-Lithuania in 1667.

In the early seventeenth century Swedish and Polish forces briefly occupied Moscow on separate occasions. In the midst of this "Time of Troubles" the old line of Muscovite rulers was finally deposed, and the Russian aristocracy—the boyars°— allowed one of their own, Mikhail Romanov°, to become tsar (r. 1613–1645). The early Romanov rulers saw a close connection between the consolidation of their own authority and successful competition with neighboring powers. They tended to represent conflicts between Slavic Russians and Turkic peoples of Central Asia as being between Christians and "infidels" or between the civilized and the "barbaric." Despite this rhetoric, it is important to understand that these cultural groups were defined less by blood ties than by the way in which they lived.

The political and economic transformations of the Russian Empire had serious repercussions for the peasants who tilled the land in European Russia. As centralized power rose, the freedom of the peasants fell. The process was longer and more complex than the rise of slavery in the Americas. The Moscovy rulers and early tsars rewarded their loyal nobles with grants of land that included obligations of the local peasants to work for these lords. Law and custom permitted peasants to change masters during a two-week period each year, which encouraged lords to treat their peasants well; but the rising commercialization of agriculture also raised the value of these labor obligations.

Long periods of civil and foreign warfare in the late sixteenth and early seventeenth centuries caused such disruption that many peasants fled to the Cossacks or across the Urals. Some who couldn't flee sold themselves into slavery to ensure a steady supply of food. When peace returned, landlords sought to recover these runaway peasants and bind them more firmly to their land. A law change in 1649 completed the transformation of peasants into **serfs** by eliminating the period when they could change masters and decreeing that runaways could be forced to return to their masters no matter how many years had elapsed.

Like slavery, serfdom was a hereditary status. In theory the serf was tied to a piece of land, not owned by a master. In practice, the difference

**boyar** (BOY-ar)    **Romanov** (ROH-man-off or roh-MAN-off)

**The Russian Empire**

- Russia in 1533
- Added by 1598
- Added by 1721
- Added by 1796
- ■ Fort

PACIFIC OCEAN

BRITISH NORTH AMERICA (CANADA)

Novo Arkhangelsk (Sitka)

TLINGIT

Border set in 1826

RUSSIAN AMERICA (ALASKA)

ALEUTS

INUIT

INUIT

INUIT

Bering Strait

Bering Sea

CHUKCHI

KORYAKS

Kolyma

Petropavlovsk

ALEUTS

Kamchatka Peninsula

Zashiversk

Okhotsk

Sea of Okhotsk

Yana

Sakalin

ARCTIC OCEAN

GREENLAND

Novaya Zemliya

Kara Sea

Barents Sea

Arctic Circle

SWEDEN

Obdorsk

SAMOYEDS

URAL MOUNTAINS

Arkhangelsk

FINLAND

Baltic Sea

St. Petersburg

Novgorod

Riga

PRUSSIA

Moscow

Smolensk

POLAND

Kiev

UKRAINIANS

Dniester

Dnieper

AUSTRIA

Saratov

COSSACKS

Nizhni Novgorod

Samara

Kama

Ural

COSSACKS

Volga

Verkhoturye

Tura

Tobol

Ishim

TARTARS

OSTYAKS

Ob

Surgut

Tobol

Irtysh

KAZAKS

Omsk

Tom

Yenisey

Kem

Biysk

Khatanga

Lower Tunguska

TUNGUSY

OSTYAKS

Bratsk

Krasnoyarsk

Irkutsk

MONGOLIA

SIBERIA

Olenek

Lena

Zhigansk

EVENKI

Vilyuy

YAKUTS

Yakutsk

LAMUTS

EVENKI

Nerchinsk

Amur

MANCHURIA

QING EMPIRE

Aral Sea

OTTOMAN EMPIRE

Black Sea

GEORGIA

Caspian Sea

IRAN

AFGHANISTAN

TIBET

NEPAL

BHUTAN

BURMA

INDIA

50°

60°

70°

80°

100° 120° 140°

180°

160°

140°

120°

100°

80°

60°

40°

20°

0°

20°

40° 60° 80°

70°

80°

**Map 18.2    The Expansion of Russia, 1500–1800**
Sweden and Poland initially blocked Russian expansion in
Europe, while the Ottoman Empire blocked the southwest.
In the sixteenth century, Russia began to expand east,
toward Siberia and the Pacific Ocean. By the end of the rule
of Catherine the Great in 1796, Russia encompassed all of
northern and northeastern Eurasia.

between serfdom and slavery narrowed as the laws
regulating selfdom became stricter. By 1723 all Russian slaves were transformed into serfs. In the Russian census of 1795, serfs made up over half the
population and were under the control of landowners, who made up only 2 percent, similar to the size
of the slave-owning class in the Caribbean.

## Peter the Great

The greatest of the Ro-
manovs was Tsar **Peter
the Great** (r. 1689–1725), who reduced Russia's isolation and increased the empire's size and power.
Tsar Peter is remembered for his efforts to turn Russia away from its Asian cultural connections and
toward what he deemed the advanced civilization
of the West. In fact, he accelerated trends under way
for some time. When he ascended the throne, there
were already hundreds of foreign merchants in
Moscow. Military officers from western Europe had
already trained a major part of the army in new
weapons and techniques, and Italian builders had
already influenced church and palace architecture.
It was on this substantial base that Peter erected a
more rapid transformation of Russia.

Peter matured quickly both physically and
mentally. In his youth the government was in the
hands of his half-sister Sophia, who was regent on
behalf of him and her sickly brother Ivan. Living
on an estate near the foreigners' quarter outside
Moscow, Peter learned what he could of life outside
Russia and busied himself gaining practical skills
in blacksmithing, carpentry, shipbuilding, and the
arts of war. He organized his own military drill unit
among other young men. When Princess Sophia
tried to take complete control of the government in
1689, Peter rallied enough support to send her to a
monastery, secure the abdication of Ivan, and take
charge of Russia. He was still in his teens.

Peter concerned himself with Russia's expansion and modernization. To secure a warm-water

**Peter the Great**   This portrait from his time as a student
in Holland in 1697 shows Peter as ruggedly masculine and
practical, quite unlike most royal portraits of the day that
posed rulers in foppish elegance and haughty majesty. Peter
was a popular military leader as well as an autocratic ruler.
(Collection, Countess Bobrinskoy/Michael Holford)

port on the Black Sea, he constructed a small but
formidable navy that could blockade Ottoman
ports. Describing his wars with the Ottoman Empire as a new crusade to liberate Constantinople
from the Muslim sultans, Peter also saw himself as
the legal protector of Orthodox Christians living
under Ottoman rule. Peter's forces seized the port
of Azov in 1696, but the fortress was lost again
in 1713, and Russian expansion southward was
blocked for the rest of Peter's reign.

In the winter of 1697–1698, after his Black Sea
campaign, Peter traveled in disguise across Europe
to discover how western European societies were

becoming so powerful and wealthy. The young tsar paid special attention to ships and weapons, even working for a time as a ship's carpenter in the Netherlands. With great insight, he perceived that western European success owed as much to trade and toleration as to technology. Trade generated the money to spend on weapons, while toleration attracted talented persons fleeing persecution. Upon his return to Russia, Peter resolved to expand and reform his vast and backward empire.

In the long and costly Great Northern War (1700–1721), his modernized armies broke Swedish control of the Baltic Sea, making possible more direct contacts between Russia and Europe. Peter's victory forced the European powers to recognize Russia as a major power for the first time.

On land captured from Sweden at the eastern end of the Baltic, Peter built St. Petersburg, a new city that was to be his window on the West. In 1712 the city became Russia's capital. To demonstrate Russia's new sophistication, Peter ordered architects to build St. Petersburg's houses and public buildings in the baroque style then fashionable in France.

Peter also pushed the Russian elite to imitate western European fashions. He personally shaved off his noblemen's long beards to conform to Western styles and ordered them to wear Western clothing. To end the traditional seclusion of upper-class Russian women, Peter required officials, military officers, and merchants to bring their wives to the social gatherings he organized in the capital. He also directed the nobles to educate their children.

Another of Peter's strategies was to reorganize Russian government along the lines of the powerful German state of Prussia. To break the power of the boyars he sharply reduced their traditional roles in government and the army. The old boyar council of Moscow was replaced by a group of advisers in St. Petersburg whom the tsar appointed. Members of the traditional nobility continued to serve as generals and admirals, but officers in Peter's modern, professional army and navy were promoted according to merit, not birth.

The goal of Peter's westernization strategy was to strengthen the Russian state and increase the power of the tsar. A decree of 1716 proclaimed that the tsar "is not obliged to answer to anyone in the world for his doings, but possesses power and authority over his kingdom and land, to rule them at his will and pleasure as a Christian ruler." Under this expansive definition of his role, Peter brought the Russian Orthodox Church more firmly under state control, built factories and iron and copper foundries to provide munitions and supplies for the military, and increased the burdens of taxes and forced labor on the serfs. Peter was an absolutist ruler of the sort then common in western Europe, and he had no more intention of improving the conditions of the serfs, on whose labors the production of basic foodstuffs depended, than did the European slave owners of the Americas.

## Consolidation of the Empire

Russia's eastward expansion also continued under Peter the Great and his successors. The frontier settlement with China and Qianlong's quashing of Inner Mongolia in 1689 freed Russians to concentrate on the northern Pacific. The Pacific northeast was colonized, and in 1741 an expedition led by Captain Vitus Bering crossed the strait (later named for him) into North America. In 1799 a Russian company of merchants received a monopoly over the Alaskan fur trade, and its agents were soon active along the entire northwestern coast of North America.

Far more important than these immense territories in the cold and thinly populated north were the populous agricultural lands to the west acquired during the reign of Catherine the Great (r. 1762–1796). A successful war with the Ottoman Empire gave Russia control of the north shore of the Black Sea by 1783. As a result of three successive partitions of the once powerful kingdom of Poland between 1772 and 1795, Russia's frontiers advanced 600 miles (nearly 1,000 kilometers) to the west (see Map 18.2). When Catherine died, the Russian Empire extended from Poland in the west to Alaska in the east, from the Barents Sea in the north to the Black Sea in the south.

Catherine also made important additions to Peter's policies of promoting industry and building a canal system to improve trade. Besides furs, the Russians had also become major exporters of gold, iron, and timber. Catherine implemented administrative reforms and showed a special talent for diplomacy. Through her promotion of the ideas of the Enlightenment, she expanded Peter's policies of westernizing the Russian elite.

# COMPARATIVE PERSPECTIVES

Considered separately, the histories of Japan, China, and Russia overlap very little. Contacts with each other were far less important than forces within each state. However, when examined comparatively, these separate histories reveal similarities and differences that help explain the global dynamics and larger historical patterns of this period.

## Political Comparisons

China and Russia exemplify the phenomenal flourishing of Eurasian empires between 1500 and 1800. Already a vast empire under the Ming, China doubled in size under the Qing, mostly through westward expansion into less densely populated areas. As for Russia, the addition of rich and well-populated lands to the west and south and far larger but less populous lands to the east transformed a modestly sized principality into the world's largest land empire. Russia and China were land based, just like the Ottoman, Safavid, and Mughal Empires (see Chapter 17), with the strengths and problems of administrative control and tax collection that size entailed.

Although western Europe is often seen as particularly imperialist in the centuries after 1500, only Spain's empire merits comparison with Russia's. By contrast, the new seaborne trading empires of the Portuguese, Dutch, French, and English had much less territory, far tighter administration, and a much more global sweep.

Japan was different. Though nominally headed by an emperor, Japan's size and ethnic homogeneity do not support calling it an empire in the same breath with China and Russia. Tokugawa Japan was similar in size and population to France, the most powerful state of western Europe, but its political system was much more decentralized. Japan's efforts to add colonies on the East Asian mainland had failed.

China had once led the world in military innovation (including the first uses of gunpowder), but the modern "gunpowder revolution" of the fifteenth and sixteenth centuries was centered in the Ottoman Empire and western European states. Although the centuries after 1500 were full of successful military operations, Chinese armies continued to depend on superior numbers and tactics for their success, rather than on new technology.

The military forces of Japan and Russia underwent more innovative changes than those of China, in part through Western contacts. In the course of its sixteenth-century wars of unification, Japan produced its own gunpowder revolution but thereafter lacked the motivation and the means to stay abreast of the world's most advanced military technology. By the eighteenth century Russia had made greater progress in catching up with its European neighbors, but its armies still relied more on their size than on the sophistication of their weapons.

Naval power provides the greatest military contrast among the three. Eighteenth-century Russia constructed modern fleets of warships in the Baltic and the Black Seas, but neither China nor Japan developed navies commensurate with their size and coastlines. China's defenses against pirates and other sea invaders were left to its maritime provinces, whose small war junks were armed with only a half-dozen cannon. Japan's naval capacity was similarly decentralized. In 1792, when Russian ships exploring the North Pacific turned toward the Japanese coast, the local daimyo used his own forces to chase them away. All Japanese daimyo understood that they would be on their own if foreign incursions increased.

## Cultural, Social, and Economic Comparisons

The expansion of China and Russia incorporated not just new lands but also diverse new peoples. Both empires pursued policies that tolerated diversity along with policies to promote cultural assimilation. In contrast, Japan remained more culturally homogeneous, and the government reacted with great intolerance to the growing influence of converts to Christianity.

Chinese society had long been diverse, and its geographical, occupational, linguistic, and religious differences grew as the Qing expanded. China had also long used Confucian models, imperial customs, and a common system of writing to transcend such differences. These techniques were most effective in assimilating elites. It is striking how quickly and thoroughly the Manchu conquerors adopted Chinese imperial ways of thinking and acting as well as of dressing, speaking, and writing.

Kangxi's reign is a notable example of how receptive the Chinese elite could be to new ideas. Yet the Jesuits' success owed much to their portraying themselves as supporters of Confucian values and learning. Although Chinese converts to Catholicism were instrumental in introducing European techniques of crop production and engineering, influential members of China's government were highly suspicious of the loyalties of these converts, persecuted them, and eventually moved to prohibit or severely limit missionary activity.

Russia likewise approached its new peoples with a mixture of pragmatic tolerance and a propensity for seeing Russian ways and beliefs as superior. Religion was a particular sore point. With the support of the tsars, Russian Orthodox missionaries encouraged conversion of Siberian peoples. In the new lands of eastern Europe, Orthodoxy was a common bond for some new subjects, but the Roman Catholic Poles, incorporated in the late 1700s, would soon suffer greatly for their divergent beliefs and practices. The Russian language was strongly promoted. Russia was also notable for its absorption of new ideas and styles from western Europe, especially under the leadership of its eighteenth-century rulers. Even among the elite, however, these influences often overlay Russian cultural traditions in a very superficial way.

Forced labor remained common in the Russian and Chinese Empires. Serfdom grew more brutal and widespread in Russia in the seventeenth and eighteenth centuries, although the expansion of the frontier eastward across Siberia also opened an escape route for many peasants and serfs. Some Chinese peasants also improved their lot by moving to new territories, but population growth increased overall misery in the eighteenth century. China was also notable for the size of its popular insurrections, especially the one that toppled the Ming.

In striking contrast to the rising importance of elite merchants in the West, private merchants in China and Japan occupied precarious positions. Confucian thought ranked merchants below peasants in their contributions to society. In Japan maritime traders were also sometimes pirates, though Chinese and even European sea trade was not much different. Governments conducted diplomatic and strategic missions but had no interest in encouraging overseas voyages or colonies. Instead both Japan and China moved to restrict overseas trade. In the end, commercial contacts were far more important to Europe than to East Asia.

## CONCLUSION

As the world has grown more interconnected, it has become increasingly difficult to sort out the degree to which major historical changes were due to forces within a society or to outside forces acting upon it. The histories of Japan, China, and Russia between 1500 and 1800 reveal how internal forces operated separately from external ones and the degree to which they were intertwined.

The formation of the Tokugawa Shogunate in Japan is a clear example of a society changing from within. The decisions of government to suppress Christianity and sharply curtail commercial and intellectual contacts with distant Europe illustrate how easily even the most decentralized of the three states could control its dealings with outsiders.

China's history illustrates a more complex interplay of internal and external forces, notably in the details of the final days of the Ming dynasty, which involved a Japanese invasion through Korea, a rebellion from within, and a conquering army from Manchuria.. The Qing's settlement of the Amur frontier with Russia illustrates how diplomacy and compromise could serve mutual interests. Finally, the Chinese added new European customers to already extensive internal and external markets and developed both positive and problematic cultural relations with the Jesuits and some other Europeans. From a Chinese perspective, European contacts could be useful but were neither essential nor of great importance.

The internal and external factors in Russia's history are the hardest to sort out. Especially problematic is assessing the rising importance of the West in light of Russia's growing trade in that direction, Russia's emergence as a European Great Power, and the stated policies of both Peter the Great and Catherine the Great to westernize their people. Clearly, Western influences were very important, but just as clearly their importance can easily be exaggerated. The impetus for Muscovy's expansion came out of its own history and domination by the Mongols. Trade with western Europe was not the center of the Russian economy. Tsar Peter was more interested in Western technology than in the full range of Western culture. The Russian church was quite hostile to the Catholics and Protestants to their west, whom it regarded as heretics. Peter the Great banned the Jesuits from Russia, considering them a subversive and backward influence.

Looking at each country separately and from within, the influence of western Europeans seems clearly inferior to a host of internal and regional influences. Yet when one looks at what happened in Japan, China, and Russia in the decades after 1800, it is hard to avoid the conclusion that their relationship with the West was a common factor that, when combined with unresolved internal problems, would have a tremendous impact on the course of their history. Qianlong might tell Macartney and the British that he had no use for expanded contacts, but the sentiment was not mutual. As the next part details, after the increasingly powerful Western societies got over dealing with their own internal problems, they would be back, and they would be impossible to dismiss or resist.

## ■ Key Terms

| | |
|---|---|
| Manchu | Macartney mission |
| *daimyo* | Muscovy |
| *samurai* | Ural Mountains |
| Tokugawa Shogunate | tsar |
| Ming Empire | Siberia |
| Qing Empire | Cossacks |
| Kangxi | serfs |
| Amur River | Peter the Great |

## ■ Suggested Reading

A fascinating place to begin is with John E. Wills, Jr., *1688: A Global History* (2001), Part III, "Three Worlds Apart: Russia, China, and Japan."

On Japan in this period, see Andrew Gordon, *A Modern History of Japan: From Tokugawa Times to the Present* (2003); *The Cambridge History of Japan,* vol. 4, *Early Modern Japan,* ed. John Whitney Hall (1991); Chie Nakane and Shinzaburo Oishi, *Tokugawa Japan: The Social and Economic Antecedents of Modern Japan,* trans. Conrad Totman (1990); and Tessa Morris-Suzuki, *The Technological Transformation of Japan from the Seventeenth to the Twenty-First Century* (1994). Mary Elizabeth Berry, *Hideyoshi* (1982), is an account of the reunification of Japan at the end of the sixteenth century and the invasion of Korea. See also Michael Cooper, ed., *They Came to Japan: An Anthology of European Reports on Japan, 1543–1640* (1965).

For China during the transition from the Ming to Qing periods, see Jonathan D. Spence, *The Search for Modern China* (1990); James W. Tong, *Disorder Under Heaven: Collective Violence in the Ming Dynasty* (1991); Frederic Wakeman, *The Great Enterprise* (1985); and Lynn Struve, *Voices from the Ming-Qing Cataclysm: In Tiger's Jaws* (1993). The latest work on the late Ming is summarized in *The Cambridge History of China,* vol. 8, *The Ming Dynasty, 1368–1644,* Part 2 (1998). On the history of the Manchu and of the Qing Empire, see Evelyn Sakakida Rawski, *The Last Emperors* (1999), and Pamela Kyle Crossley, *The Manchus* (1997).

On Chinese society generally in this period, see two classic (though slightly dated) works by Ping-ti Ho, *The Ladder of Success in Imperial China: Aspects of Social Mobility, 1368–1911* (1962), and *Studies in the Population of China 1368–1953* (1959); and see the general study by Susan Naquin and Evelyn S. Rawski, *Chinese Society in the Eighteenth Century* (1987). On the two greatest of the Qing emperors and their times, see Jonathan D. Spence, *Emperor of China; Self Portrait of K'ang Hsi, 1654–1722* (1974). For a more scholarly treatment, see Lawrence D. Kessler, *K'ang-hsi and the Consolidation of Ch'ing Rule, 1661–1684* (1976); Jonathan D. Spence, *Ts'ao Yin and the K'ang-hsi Emperor: Bondservant and Master* (1966); and Harold Kahn, *Monarchy in the Emperor's Eyes: Image and Reality in the Ch'ien-lung Reign* (1971).

On the Qing trade systems, see John E. Wills, *Embassies and Illusions: Dutch and Portuguese Envoys to K'ang-hsi, 1666–1687* (1984), and Craig Clunas, *Chinese Export Art and Design* (1987). There is a great deal published on the Macartney mission, much of it originating in the diaries and memoirs of the participants. See the exhaustively detailed Alain Peyrefitte, *The Immobile Empire,* trans. Jon Rothschild (1992). For a more theoretical discussion, see James L. Hevia, *Cherishing Men from Afar: Qing Guest Ritual and the Macartney Embassy of 1793* (1995).

On early modern Russian history, see Robert O. Crummey, *Aristocrats and Servitors: The Boyar Elite in Russia, 1613–1689* (1983), and Andreas Kappeler, *The Russian Empire: A Multiethnic History* (2001). Western perceptions of Russia are examined in Marshall T. Poe, *"A People Born to Slavery": Russia in Early Modern European Ethnography* (2000), and Lloyd E. Berry and Robert O. Crummey, ed., *Rude and Barbarous Kingdom: Russia in the Accounts of Sixteenth-Century English Voyagers* (1968). Among the best-known recent books on Tsar Peter are Matthew Smith Anderson, *Peter the Great,* 2d ed. (1995); Robert K. Massie, *Peter the Great: His Life and World* (1980); and Lindsey Hughes, *Russia in the Age of Peter the Great: 1682–1725* (1998). For Russian naval development and Russian influence in the Pacific and in America, see Glynn Barratt, *Russia in Pacific Waters, 1715–1825: A Survey of the Origins of Russia's Naval Presence in the North and South Pacific* (1981), and Howard I. Kushner, *Conflict on the Northwest Coast: American-Russian Rivalry in the Pacific Northwest, 1790–1867* (1975).

For Jesuits in East Asia in the sixteenth and seventeenth centuries, see Michael Cooper, S. J., *Rodrigues the Interpreter: An Early Jesuit in Japan and China* (1974); David E. Mungello, *Curious Land: Jesuit Accommodation and the Origins of Sinology* (1985); and Jonathan D. Spence, *The Memory Palace of Matteo Ricci* (1984). Still useful are C. R. Boxer, *The Christian Century in Japan, 1549–1650* (1951), and Cornelius Wessels, *Early Jesuit Travellers in Central Asia, 1603–1721* (1924). On European images of and interactions with China connected to the Jesuits, see the relevant portions of Jonathan D. Spence, *The Chan's Great Continent: China in Western Minds* (1998); Joanna Waley-Cohen, *The Sextants of Beijing: Global Currents in Chinese History* (1999); and David E. Mungello, *The Great Encounter of China and the West, 1500–1800* (1999).

On the East India companies, see John E. Wills, *Pepper, Guns, and Parleys: The Dutch East India Company and China, 1662–1681* (1974); Dianne Lewis, *Jan Compagnie in the Straits of Malacca, 1641–1795* (1995); and John Keay, *The Honourable Company: A History of the English East India Company* (1991). On the development of global commerce in tea, coffee, and cocoa, see the relevant chapters in Roy Porter and Mikulás Teich, *Drugs and Narcotics in History* (1995).

## ■ Notes

1. Adapted from Jonathan D. Spence, *The Search for Modern China* (New York: W. W. Norton, 1990), 21–25.
2. Adapted from G. V. Melikhov, "Manzhou Penetration into the Basin of the Upper Amur in the 1680s," in S. L. Tikhvinshii, ed., *Manzhou Rule in China* (Moscow: Progress Publishers, 1983).

# The Little Ice Age

A giant volcanic eruption in the Peruvian Andes in 1600 affected the weather in many parts of the world for several years. When volcanic ash from the eruption of Mount Huanyaputina (hoo-AHN-yah-poo-TEE-nuh) shot into the upper atmosphere and spread around the world, it screened out sunlight. As a result, the summer of 1601 was the coldest in two hundred years in the northern hemisphere.

Archaeologist Brian Fagan has pointed out that Mount Huanyaputina's chilling effects were a spectacular event in a much longer pattern of climate change that has been called the Little Ice Age.[1] Although global climate had been cooling since the late 1200s, in the northern temperate regions the 1590s had been exceptionally cold. Temperatures remained cooler than normal throughout the seventeenth century.

The most detailed information on the Little Ice Age comes from Europe. Glaciers in the Alps grew much larger. Trade became difficult when rivers and canals that had once been navigable in winter froze solid from bank to bank. In the coldest years, the growing season in some places was as much as two months shorter than normal. Unexpectedly late frosts withered the tender shoots of newly planted crops in spring. Wheat and barley ripened more slowly during cooler summers and were often damaged by early fall frosts.

People could survive a smaller-than-average harvest in one year by drawing on food reserves, but when cold weather damaged crops in two or more successive years, the consequences were devastating. Deaths due to malnutrition and cold increased sharply when summer temperatures in northern Europe registered 2.7°F (1.5°C) lower than average in 1674 and 1675 and again in 1694 and 1695. The cold spell of 1694 and 1695 caused a famine in Finland that carried off a quarter to a third of the population.

At the time people had no idea what was causing the unusual cold of the Little Ice Age. Advances in climate history make it clear that the cause was not a single terrestrial event such as the eruption of Mount Huanyaputina. Nor was the Little Ice Age the product of human actions, unlike some climate changes such as today's global warming.

Ultimately, the earth's weather is governed by the sun. In the seventeenth century astronomers in Europe reported seeing fewer sunspots, dark spots on the sun's surface that are indicative of solar activity and thus the sun's warming power. Diminished activity in the sun was primarily responsible for the Little Ice Age.

If the sun was the root cause, the effects of global cooling should not have been confined to northern Europe. Although contemporary accounts are much scarcer in other parts of the world, there is evidence of climate changes around the world in this period. Observations of sunspots in China, Korea, and Japan drop to zero between 1639 and 1700. China experienced unusually cool weather in the seventeenth century, but the warfare and disruption accompanying the fall of the Ming and the rise of the Qing probably were much more to blame for the famines and rural distress of that period.

By itself, a relatively slight decrease in average annual temperature would not have a serious effect on human life outside the northern temperate areas. However, evidence suggests that there was also a significant rise in humidity in this period in other parts of the world. Ice cores drilled into ancient glaciers in the Arctic and Antarctic show increased snowfall. Information compiled by historian James L. A. Webb, Jr., shows that lands south of the Sahara received more rainfall between 1550 and 1750 than they had during the previous era.[2] Increased rainfall would have been favorable for pastoral people, whose herds found new pasture in what had once been desert, and for the farmers farther south whose crops got more rain.

In the eighteenth century the sun's activity began to return to normal. Rising temperatures led to milder winters and better harvests in northern Eurasia. Falling rainfall allowed the Sahara to advance southward, forcing the agricultural frontier to retreat.

## ■ Notes

1. Brian Fagan, *The Littlest Ice Age: How Climate Made History, 1300–1850* (New York: Basic Books, 2000).
2. James L. A. Webb, Jr., *Desert Frontier: Ecological Change Along the Western Sahel, 1600–1850* (Madison: University of Wisconsin Press, 1995).

## PART SIX

# Revolutions Reshape the World, 1750–1870

CHAPTER 19
Revolutionary Changes in the Atlantic World, 1750–1850

CHAPTER 20
The Early Industrial Revolution, 1760–1851

CHAPTER 21
Africa, India, and the New British Empire, 1750–1870

CHAPTER 22
Land Empires in the Age of Imperialism, 1800–1870

Between 1750 and 1870, nearly every part of the world experienced dramatic political, economic, and social change. The beginnings of industrialization, the American and French Revolutions, and the revolutions for independence in Latin America transformed political and economic life in Europe and the Americas. European nations expanded into Africa, Asia, and the Middle East while Russia and the United States acquired vast new territories.

The American, French, and Latin American revolutions unleashed the forces of nationalism and social reform. The Industrial Revolution introduced new technologies and work patterns making industrial societies wealthier, mightier, and more fluid socially. The practical benefits of science and technology pushed Western intellectual life to become more secular. Reformers led efforts to abolish the Atlantic slave trade and, later, slavery itself in the Western Hemisphere. Expanded voting rights and improvement in the status of women gained support in Europe and the Americas.

European empires in the Western Hemisphere were largely dismantled by 1825. But the Industrial Revolution led to a new wave of imperialist expansion. France conquered Algeria, while Great Britain expanded its colonial rule in India and established new colonies in Australia and New Zealand.

European economic influence expanded throughout Africa, cementing the region's connection to the Atlantic economy. Some African states were invigorated by this era of intensified cultural exchange, creating new institutions and developing new products for export. The Ottoman Empire and the Qing Empire also responded to Western expansionism. Both empires met this challenge by implementing reform programs while adopting elements of Western technology and organization. The Qing Empire survived the period of European expansion, but a series of military defeats and a prolonged civil war severely weakened the authority of the central government. Russia lagged behind Western Europe in transforming its economy and political institutions, but military failures and internal reform pressures spurred modernization efforts, including the abolition of serfdom.

Some of the nations of Asia, Africa, and Latin America resisted foreign intrusions by reforming and strengthening their own institutions, forms of production, and military technologies. Others pushed for more radical change, adopting Western commercial policies, industrial technologies, and government institutions. But after 1870, all these states would face even more aggressive Western imperialism, which few of them would be able to resist.

| | 1750 | 1775 | 1800 |
|---|---|---|---|
| **Americas** | 1754–1763 French and Indian War | U.S. Declaration of Independence 1776 • | • 1789 U.S. Constitution implemented / • 1791 Slaves revolt in Haiti / 1809–1825 Wars for independence in Spanish America |
| **Europe** | • ca. 1750 Industrial Revolution begins in Britain / 1756–1763 Seven Years War | | 1789–1799 French Revolution / 1814–1815 Congress of Vienna / 1799–1815 Rule of Napoleon in Franc |
| **Africa** | 1750–1800 Growing slave trade reduces population | Britain takes Cape Colony 1795 • | Sokoto Caliphate founded 1809 • / Shaka founds Zulu kingdom 1818 • |
| **Middle East** | 1769–1772 High point of restored Mamluk influence in Egypt | | 1789–1807 Reign of Ottoman sultan Selim III / • 1798 Napoleon invades Egypt / Muhammad Ali founds dynasty in Egypt 1805 • |
| **Asia and Oceania** | • 1755 Qing conquest of Turkestan / East India Company rule of Bengal begins 1765 • | 1769–1778 Captain Cook's exploration of Australia, New Zealand | White Lotus Rebellion in China 1796–1804 / East India Company creates Bombay presidency 1818 • |

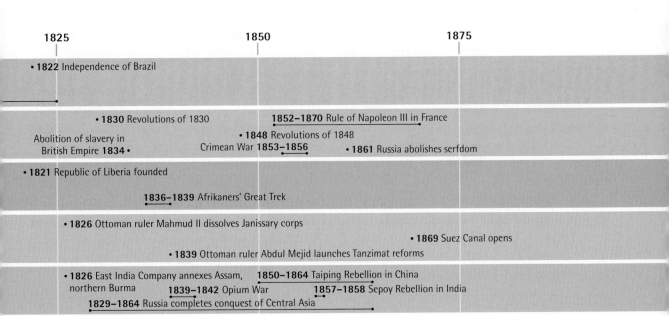

| 1825 | 1850 | 1875 |
|---|---|---|

• **1822** Independence of Brazil

• **1830** Revolutions of 1830     **1852–1870** Rule of Napoleon III in France

Abolition of slavery in     • **1848** Revolutions of 1848
British Empire **1834** •     Crimean War **1853–1856**     • **1861** Russia abolishes serfdom

• **1821** Republic of Liberia founded

**1836–1839** Afrikaners' Great Trek

• **1826** Ottoman ruler Mahmud II dissolves Janissary corps

    • **1869** Suez Canal opens

• **1839** Ottoman ruler Abdul Mejid launches Tanzimat reforms

• **1826** East India Company annexes Assam,     **1850–1864** Taiping Rebellion in China
northern Burma     **1839–1842** Opium War     **1857–1858** Sepoy Rebellion in India
**1829–1864** Russia completes conquest of Central Asia

# 19 Revolutionary Changes in the Atlantic World, 1750–1850

## CHAPTER OUTLINE

Prelude to Revolution: War and the Enlightenment

The American Revolution

The French Revolution

Revolution in Haiti and Latin America

Economic and Social Liberation Movements

ENVIRONMENT AND TECHNOLOGY: Constructing the Port of Buenos Aires, Argentina

On the evening of August 14, 1791, more than two hundred slaves and black freedmen met in secret in the plantation district of northern Saint Domingue° (present-day Haiti) to set the date for an armed uprising against local slave owners. Although the delegates agreed to delay the attack for a week, violence began almost immediately. During the following decade, the Haitian rebels abolished slavery, defeated military forces from Britain and France, and gained independence.

News and rumors about revolutionary events in France that had spread through the island incited the slave community and divided the island's white population between royalists (supporters of France's King Louis XVI) and re-publicans (supporters of democracy). The free mixed-race population initially gained some political rights from the French Assembly but was then forced to rebel when the slave-owning elite reacted violently.

Among those planning the insurrection was Toussaint L'Ouverture°, a black freedman. This remarkable revolutionary organized the rebels into a potent military force, negotiated with the island's royalist and republican factions, and, with representatives of Great Britain and France, wrote his nation's first constitution. Throughout the Western Hemisphere, Toussaint became a towering symbol of resistance to oppression for slaves and a fiend in the eyes of slave owners.

---

Saint Domingue (san doe-MANG)

Toussaint L'Ouverture (too-SAN loo-ver-CHORE)

The Haitian slave rebellion was an important episode in the long and painful political and cultural transformation of the modern Western world. Economic expansion and the growth of trade were creating unprecedented wealth. Intellectuals were questioning the traditional place of monarchy and slavery in society. An emerging class of merchants, professionals, and manufacturers began to press for a larger political role, and economies were increasingly opened to competition.

Imperial powers resisted the loss of colonies, and monarchs and nobles struggled to retain their ancient privileges. Revolutionary steps forward were often matched by reactionary steps backward. The liberal and nationalist ideals of the eighteenth-century revolutionary movements were only imperfectly realized in Europe and the Americas in the nineteenth century.

As you read this chapter, ask yourself the following questions:

- How did imperial wars among European powers provoke revolution?

- How did revolution in one country help to incite revolution elsewhere?

- Why were the revolutions in France and Haiti more violent than the American Revolution?

- How were political revolts linked to the abolition of slavery?

# PRELUDE TO REVOLUTION: WAR AND THE ENLIGHTENMENT

In large measure, the cost of wars fought among Europe's major powers over colonies and trade precipitated the revolutionary era that began in 1775 with the American Revolution. The struggle of Britain, France, and Spain for political preeminence in western Europe and overseas produced many violent conflicts during the eighteenth century. In the Seven Years War (1756–1763), known as the French and Indian War in America, Britain gained dominance in North America and in India. All parties suffered from the enormous costs of these conflicts.

However, new Western ideas and political environments now made people much more critical of any effort to extend the power of a monarch or impose new taxes, and they also raised questions about the rights of individuals. As Chapter 15 recounted, the **Enlightenment** applied the methods and questions of the Scientific Revolution to the study of human society. Some thinkers challenged long-established religious and political institutions. They argued that if scientists could understand the laws of nature, then surely similar forms of disciplined investigation might reveal laws of human nature. Others wondered whether society and government might be better regulated and more productive if guided by reason rather than by hereditary rulers and the church.

These new perspectives and the intellectual optimism that fed them were to help guide the English political philosopher John Locke (1632–1704). Locke argued in 1690 that governments were created to protect life, liberty, and property and that the people had a right to rebel when a monarch violated these natural rights. In *The Social Contract*, published in 1762, the French-Swiss intellectual Jean-Jacques Rousseau° (1712–1778) asserted that the will of the people was sacred and that the legitimacy of the monarch depended on the consent of the people. Although both men believed that government rested on the will of the people rather than divine will, Locke emphasized the importance of individual rights, and Rousseau envisioned the people acting collectively because of their shared historical experience.

The Enlightenment is commonly associated with hostility toward monarchy, but Voltaire, one of the Enlightenment's most critical intellects, believed that Europe's monarchs were likely agents

---

**Jean-Jacques Rousseau** (zhahn-zhock roo-SOE)

of political and economic reform, and he wrote favorably of China's Qing° emperors. Indeed, some sympathetic members of the nobility and reforming monarchs in Spain, Russia, Austria, and Prussia actively sponsored and promoted the dissemination of new ideas, providing patronage for many intellectuals. They recognized that elements of the Enlightenment critique of the *ancien régime*° buttressed their own efforts to expand royal authority at the expense of religious institutions, the nobility, and regional autonomy. Monarchs also understood that the era's passion for science and technology held the potential of fattening national treasuries and improving economic performance.

The Western Hemisphere shared in the debates of Europe. In colonial societies where political rights were even more limited than in Europe, the idea that government authority ultimately rested on the consent of the governed was potentially explosive. The efforts of ordinary men and women to resist the growth of government power and the imposition of new cultural forms provide an important political undercurrent to much of the revolutionary agitation and conflict from 1750 to 1850. But spontaneous popular uprisings gained revolutionary potential only when they coincided with ideological divisions and conflicts within the governing class itself.

# THE AMERICAN REVOLUTION

After defeating the French in the French and Indian War, the British government faced two related problems in its North American colonies. One was the likelihood of armed conflict with Amerindian peoples as settlers quickly pushed west of the Appalachian Mountains and across the Ohio River. Already burdened with war debts, Britain desperately wanted to avoid additional expenditures for frontier defense. The other problem was how to get the colonists to shoulder more of the costs of imperial defense and colonial administration. Every effort to impose new taxes or prevent the settlement of the trans-Appalachian frontier provoked angry protests in the colonies. The con-

frontational and impolitic way in which a succession of weak British governments responded made the situation politically explosive.

## Frontiers and Taxes

The British Proclamation of 1763, which sought to establish an effective western limit for settlement, threw into question the claims of thousands of already established farmers without effectively protecting Amerindian land. The Quebec Act of 1774 annexed disputed lands to the province of Quebec, thus denying eastern colonies the authority to distribute lands claimed as a result of original charters. Colonists saw the Quebec Act as punitive and tyrannical, and Amerindian peoples received no relief from the continuous assault on their land.

New commercial regulations that increased the cost of foreign molasses and endangered New England's profitable trade with Spanish and French Caribbean sugar colonies provoked widespread boycotts of British goods. The Stamp Act of 1765, which imposed a tax on all legal documents, newspapers, pamphlets, and other types of printed material, led to violent protest and more effective boycotts. Parliament imposed new taxes and duties soon after repealing the Stamp Act in 1766, even sending British troops to quell urban riots. Unable to control the streets of Boston, British authorities reacted by threatening traditional liberties, dissolving the colonial legislature of Massachusetts, and dispatching a warship and two regiments of soldiers to reestablish control. Support for a complete break with Britain grew when a British force fired on an angry Boston crowd on March 5, 1770, killing five civilians. This "Boston Massacre," which seemed to expose the naked force on which colonial rule rested, radicalized public opinion throughout the colonies.

Parliament attempted to calm public opinion by repealing some of the taxes and duties, then stumbled into another crisis by granting the British East India Company a monopoly for importing tea to the colonies, which raised anew the constitutional issue of Parliament's right to tax the colonies. It also offended wealthy colonial merchants, who were excluded from this profitable commerce. The crisis came to a head in the already politically overheated port of Boston when tea worth £10,000 was

---

**Qing** (ching)　*ancien régime* (ahn-see-EN ray-ZHEEM)

## C H R O N O L O G Y

| The Americas | Europe |
|---|---|
| **1756–1763**  French and Indian War | **1756–1763**  Seven Years War |
| **1770**  Boston Massacre | |
| **1776**  American Declaration of Independence | |
| **1783**  Treaty of Paris ends American Revolution | |
| | **1789**  Storming of Bastille begins French Revolution |
| **1791**  Slaves revolt in Saint Domingue (Haiti) | |
| | **1793–1794**  Reign of Terror in France |
| | **1795–1799**  The Directory rules France |
| **1798**  Toussaint L'Ouverture defeats British in Haiti | **1799**  Napoleon overthrows the Directory |
| **1804**  Haitians defeat French invasion and declare independence | **1804**  Napoleon crowns himself emperor |
| **1808**  Portuguese royal family arrives in Brazil | |
| **1808–1809**  Revolutions for independence begin in Spanish South America | |
| | **1814**  Napoleon abdicates; Congress of Vienna opens |
| **1822**  Brazil gains independence | **1830**  Greece gains independence; revolution in France |
| **1848**  Women's Rights Convention in Seneca Falls, New York | **1848**  Revolutions in France, Austria, Germany, Hungary, and Italy |
| **1861–1865**  American Civil War | |
| **1865**  End of slavery in United States | |
| **1886**  End of slavery in Cuba | |
| **1888**  End of slavery in Brazil | |

Left margin timeline: 1750, 1775, 1800, 1825, 1850, 1875

**The Tarring and Feathering of a British Official, 1774**
This illustration from a British periodical shows the unfortunate John Malcomb, commissioner of customs at Boston. By the mid-1770s British periodicals were focusing public opinion on mob violence and the breakdown of public order in the colonies. British critics of colonial political protests viewed the demand for liberty as little more than an excuse for mob violence.   (The Granger Collection, New York)

dumped into the harbor by protesters disguised as Amerindians.

### The Course of the Revolution

As the crisis mounted, patriots created new governing bodies, effectively deposed many British governors and other officials, passed laws, appointed judges, and even took control of colonial militias. Simultaneously, radical leaders organized crowds to intimidate loyalists— people who were pro-British—and to enforce the boycott of British goods.

Events were propelling the colonies toward revolution. Elected representatives, meeting in Philadelphia as the Continental Congress in 1775, assumed the powers of government, creating a currency and organizing an army. **George Washington** (1732–1799), a Virginia planter who had served in the French and Indian War, was named commander. On July 4, 1776, Congress approved the Declaration of Independence, the document that proved to be the most enduring statement of the revolutionary era's ideology:

> We hold these truths to be self evident: That all men are created equal; that they are endowed by their creator with certain unalienable rights; that among these are life, liberty and the pursuit of happiness; that, to secure these rights, governments are instituted among men, deriving their just powers from the consent of the governed.

This affirmation of popular sovereignty and individual rights influenced the language of revolution and popular protest around the world.

To shore up British authority, Great Britain sent more than 400 ships, 50,000 soldiers, and 30,000 German mercenaries. But this military commitment proved futile. Although British forces won most of the battles, Washington slowly built a competent Continental army and civilian support networks that provided supplies and financial resources. In the final decisive battle, fought at Yorktown, Virginia, an American army, supported by French soldiers, besieged a British army led by General Charles Cornwallis. With escape cut off by a French fleet, Cornwallis surrendered to Washington as the British military band played "The World Turned Upside-Down."

### New Republican Institutions

Ignoring the British example of an unwritten constitution, representatives in each of the newly independent states drafted formal charters and submitted the results to voters for ratification. Europeans were fascinated by these written constitutions and by their formal ratification by the people. Here was the social contract of Locke and Rousseau made manifest. The state constitutions also placed severe limits on executive authority but granted legislatures greater powers than in colonial times. Many states also inserted in their constitutions a bill of rights to provide further protection against government tyranny.

An effective constitution for the new national government was developed more slowly and hesitantly. The Articles of Confederation—the first constitution of the United States—were not accepted by all the states until 1781. With the coming of peace in 1783, there was an effort to fashion a new constitution.

Debate at the **Constitutional Convention,** which began meeting in May 1787, focused on several issues: representation, electoral procedures, executive powers, and the relationship between the federal government and the states. The final compromise provided for a two-house legislature: the lower house (the House of Representatives) to be elected directly by voters and the upper house (the Senate) to be elected by state legislatures. The chief executive—the president—was to be elected indirectly by "electors" selected by ballot in the states (each state had a number of electors equal to the number of its representatives and senators).

Although the U.S. Constitution created the most democratic government of the era, only a minority of the adult population was given full rights. Southern leaders were able to protect the institution of slavery by counting three-fifths of the slave population in the calculations that determined their states' congressional representatives. Although women had led prewar boycotts and had organized relief and charitable organizations during the war, they were denied political rights in the new republic.

# THE FRENCH REVOLUTION

The French Revolution confronted the entrenched privileges of an established church, monarchy, and aristocracy more directly than the American Revolution did. It also expanded mass participation in political life and radicalized the democratic tradition. But in the end, the passions unleashed in France by revolutionary events could not be sustained.

## French Society and Fiscal Crisis

French society was divided into three groups. The clergy, the First Estate, numbered about 130,000 in a nation of 28 million. The Catholic Church owned about 10 percent of the nation's land and extracted substantial amounts of wealth from the economy in the form of tithes and ecclesiastical fees. Despite its substantial wealth, the church was exempted from nearly all taxes.

The 300,000 members of the nobility, the Second Estate, controlled about 30 percent of the land and retained ancient rights on much of the rest. Nobles held the vast majority of high administrative, judicial, military, and church positions. Though traditionally barred from some types of commercial activity, nobles were important participants in wholesale trade, banking, manufacturing, and mining.

The Third Estate included everyone else. There were three times as many members of the bourgeoisie° in 1774, when Louis XVI took the throne, as there had been in 1715, at the end of Louis XIV's reign. Peasants accounted for 80 percent of the French population. They owned some property and lived decently when crops were good and prices stable. By 1780, poor harvests had decreased their incomes.

The nation's poor were a large, growing, and troublesome sector. Urban streets swarmed with beggars and prostitutes. Unable to afford decent housing, obtain steady employment, or protect their children, the poor periodically erupted in violent protest and rage. In the countryside, violence was often the reaction to increased dues and fees. In towns and cities, an increase in the price of bread often provided the spark.

These explosive episodes, however, were not revolutionary in character. The remedies sought were conventional and immediate rather than structural and long term. That was to change when the Crown tried to solve its fiscal crisis by imposing new taxes on the nobility and on other groups that in the past had enjoyed exemptions. But this effort failed in the face of widespread protest and the refusal of the Parlement of Paris, a court of appeal that heard appeals from local courts throughout France, to register the new tax. In 1768, frustrated authorities exiled the members of that Parlement and pushed through a series of unpopular fiscal measures. Despite the worsening fiscal crisis, the

**bourgeoisie** (boor-zwah-ZEE)

French took on the heavy burden of supporting the American Revolution, delaying collapse by borrowing enormous sums. By the end of the war with Britain, more than half of France's national budget was required to service the debt alone. In 1787, the desperate king called an Assembly of Notables to approve a radical and comprehensive reform of the economy and fiscal policy. Although the members of this assembly were selected by the king's advisers from the high nobility, the judiciary, and the clergy, they proved unwilling to act as a rubber stamp for the proposed reforms or new taxes. Instead, these representatives of France's most privileged classes sought to protect their interests by questioning the competence of the king and his ministers to supervise the nation's affairs, thus creating the conditions for political revolution.

## Protest Turns to Revolution

Unable to extract needed tax concessions from the notables, King Louis XVI was forced to call the **Estates General,** the French national legislature, which had not met since 1614. Traditionally, the three estates met separately, and a positive vote by two of the three was required for action. Tradition, however, was quickly overturned when the Third Estate refused to conduct business until the king ordered the other two estates to sit with it in a single body. During a six-week period of stalemate, many parish priests deserted the First Estate to meet with them.

When this expanded Third Estate declared itself the **National Assembly,** the king and his advisers recognized that the reformers intended to force them to accept a constitutional monarchy. Louis's agenda for fiscal reform was being displaced by the central ideas of the era: the people were sovereign, and the legitimacy of political institutions and individual rulers ultimately depended on their carrying out the people's will. Louis prepared for a confrontation with the National Assembly by moving military forces to Versailles. But before he could act, the people of Paris intervened.

A succession of bad harvests beginning in 1785 had propelled bread prices upward throughout France and provoked an economic depression. By the time the Estates General met, nearly a third of the Parisian work force was unemployed. Hunger and anger marched hand in hand through working-class neighborhoods.

When the people of Paris heard that the king was massing troops to arrest their representatives, crowds of common people began to seize arms and mobilize. On July 14, 1789, a crowd searching for military supplies attacked the Bastille°, a medieval fortress used as a prison. The futile defense of the Bastille cost ninety-eight lives before its garrison surrendered. Enraged, the attackers hacked the commander to death and then paraded through the city with his head and that of Paris's chief magistrate stuck on pikes.

These events coincided with uprisings in the country. Peasants sacked manor houses and destroyed documents that recorded their traditional obligations. They refused to pay taxes and dues to landowners and seized common lands. Forced to recognize the fury raging through rural areas, the National Assembly voted to end traditional obligations and to reform the tax system. Having forced acceptance of their narrow agenda, the peasants ceased their revolt.

These popular uprisings strengthened the hand of the National Assembly in its dealings with the king. One manifestation of this altered relationship was passage of the **Declaration of the Rights of Man.** The French declaration, however, was more sweeping in its language than the American Declaration of Independence. Among the enumerated natural rights were "liberty, property, security, and resistance to oppression." The Declaration of the Rights of Man also guaranteed free expression of ideas, equality before the law, and representative government.

While delegates debated political issues in Versailles, the economic crisis worsened in Paris. Because the working women of Paris faced high food prices every day as they struggled to feed their families, their anger had a hard edge. On October 5, market women organized a crowd of thousands to march the 12 miles (19 kilometers) to Versailles°. Once there, they forced their way into the National Assembly to demand action from the frightened representatives: "The point is that we want bread." The crowd then entered the royal apartments, killed some of the king's guards, and searched for Queen

**Bastille** (bass-TEEL) **Versailles** (vuhr-SIGH)

**Parisians Storm the Bastille**  This depiction of the storming of the Bastille on July 14, 1789, was painted by an artist who witnessed the epochal event, still celebrated by the French as a national holiday.  (Photos12.com-ARJ)

Marie Antoinette°, whom they loathed as a symbol of extravagance. Eventually, the crowd demanded that the royal family return to Paris. Preceded by the heads of two aristocrats carried on pikes and hauling away the palace's supply of flour, the triumphant crowd escorted the royal family to Paris.

The National Assembly achieved a radically re-structured French society in the next two years. It passed a new constitution that dramatically limited monarchical power and abolished the nobility as a hereditary class. Economic reforms swept away monopolies and trade barriers within France. The Legislative Assembly created by the new constitution seized church lands to use as collateral for a new paper currency, and priests, who were to be

Antoinette (ann-twah-NET)

elected, were put on the state payroll. When the government tried to force priests to take a loyalty oath, however, many Catholics joined a growing counterrevolutionary movement.

At first, many European monarchs had welcomed the weakening of the French king, but by 1791 Austria and Prussia threatened to intervene in support of the monarchy. The Legislative Assembly responded by declaring war. Although the war went badly at first for French forces, people across France responded patriotically to foreign invasions, forming huge new volunteer armies and mobilizing national resources to meet the challenge. By the end of 1792, French armies had gained the upper hand everywhere.

In this period of national crisis and foreign threat, the French Revolution entered its most radical phase. A failed effort by the king and queen to escape from Paris and find foreign allies cost the king any remaining popular support. As foreign armies crossed into France, his behavior was increasingly viewed as treasonous. In August 1792, the Legislative Assembly suspended the king, ordered his imprisonment, and called for the formation of a new National Convention to be elected by the vote of all men. Swept along by popular passion, the newly elected National Convention convicted Louis XVI of treason, sentencing him to death and proclaiming France a republic.

The guillotine ended the king's life in January 1793. Invented in the spirit of the era as a more humane way to execute the condemned, this machine was to become the bloody symbol of the revolution. During the period of repression called the Reign of Terror (1793–1794), approximately 40,000 people were executed or died in prison. This radical phase ended in July 1794 when the Terror's leaders were executed by guillotine.

## Reaction and Dictatorship

Purged of the radicals, the National Convention—the new legislative assembly of the French republic—began to undo the radical reforms. It removed many of the emergency economic controls that had been holding down prices and protecting the working class. When the Paris working class rose in protest in 1795, the Convention approved the use of overwhelming military force. The Convention also permitted the Catholic Church to regain much of its former influence, but it would not return the church's confiscated wealth. Finally, it ratified a more conservative constitution, which protected property, established a voting process that reduced the power of the masses, and created a new executive authority, the Directory. Once installed in power, however, the Directory proved unable to end the foreign wars or solve domestic economic problems.

After losing the election of 1797, the Directory suspended the results. The republican phase of the Revolution was clearly dead. Legitimacy was now based on coercive power rather than on elections. Two years later, **Napoleon Bonaparte** (1769–1821), a brilliant young general in the French army, seized

power. Just as the American and French Revolutions had been the start of the modern democratic tradition, the military intervention that brought Napoleon to power in 1799 marked the advent of another modern form of government: popular authoritarianism.

In contrast to the National Convention, Napoleon proved capable of realizing France's dream of dominating Europe and providing effective protection for persons and property at home. Negotiations with the Catholic Church led to the Concordat of 1801, which gave French Catholics the right to practice their religion freely. Napoleon's Civil Code of 1804 asserted two basic principles inherited from the moderate first stage of the French Revolution: equality in law and protection of property. Even some members of the nobility became supporters after Napoleon declared himself emperor and France an empire in 1804.

While providing personal security, the Napoleonic system denied or restricted many individual rights. Women were denied basic political rights. Free speech and free expression were limited. Criticism of the government, viewed as subversive, was proscribed, and most opposition newspapers disappeared.

Ultimately, the Napoleonic system depended on the success of French arms and French diplomacy (see Map 19.1). From Napoleon's assumption of power until his fall, no single European state could defeat the French military. Austria and Prussia were forced to become allies of France. Only Britain, protected by its powerful navy, remained able to thwart Napoleon's plans to dominate Europe. In June 1812, Napoleon made the fateful decision to invade Russia with the largest army ever assembled in Europe, approximately 600,000 men. Five weeks after occupying Moscow, he was forced to retreat. The brutal Russian winter and attacks by Russian forces destroyed his army. A broken and battered fragment of 30,000 men returned home to France.

After the debacle in Russia, Austria and Prussia deserted Napoleon and entered an alliance with Britain and Russia. Unable to defend Paris, Napoleon was forced to abdicate the French throne in April 1814. The allies exiled Napoleon to the island of Elba off the coast of Italy and restored the French monarchy.

## Retrenchment, Reform, and Revolution

The French Revolution and Napoleon's imperial ambitions had threatened the survival of the European old order. Ancient monarchies had been overturned and long-established political institutions tossed aside. The very existence of the nobility and church had been put at risk. Under the leadership of the Austrian foreign minister, Prince Klemens von Metternich° (1773–1859), Britain, Russia, Austria, and Prussia, along with representatives of other nations, worked together in Vienna to create a comprehensive peace settlement that they hoped would safeguard the conservative order. Because the participants in the **Congress of Vienna** believed that a strong and stable France was the best guarantee of future peace, the French monarchy was reestablished. Metternich sought to offset French strength with a balance of power.

Despite the power of the conservative monarchs, popular support for national self-determination and democratic reform grew throughout Europe. In 1821, Greek patriots launched a movement for independence from Ottoman control. In 1830, Russia, France, and Great Britain forced the Ottoman Empire to recognize Greek independence. That same year, the people of Paris rose up and forced King Charles X to abdicate. His successor, Louis Philippe° (r. 1830–1848), reestablished the constitution and extended voting privileges.

Despite limited political reform, conservatives continued to hold the upper hand in Europe. Finally, in 1848, the desire for democratic reform and national self-determination and the frustrations of urban workers led to upheavals across Europe. The **Revolutions of 1848** began in Paris, where members of the middle class and workers united to overthrow the regime of Louis Philippe and create the Second French Republic. Adult men were given voting rights, slavery was abolished in French colonies, the death penalty was ended, and a ten-hour workday was legislated for Paris. But Parisian workers' demand for programs to reduce unemployment and lower prices provoked conflicts with the middle class, which wanted to protect property rights. Desiring the reestablishment of order, the French elected Louis Napoleon, nephew of the former emperor, president in December 1848. Three years later, he overturned the constitution as a result of popular plebiscite and, after ruling briefly as dictator, became Emperor Napoleon III. He remained in power until 1871.

Despite their heroism on the barricades of Vienna, Rome, and Berlin, the revolutionaries of 1848 also failed to gain either their nationalist or their republican objectives. Metternich, the symbol of reaction, fled Vienna in disguise, but little lasting change occurred. Monarchs retained the support not only of aristocrats but also of professional militaries, largely recruited from among peasants who had little sympathy for urban workers.

# REVOLUTION IN HAITI AND LATIN AMERICA

In the Americas, the revolutionary ideology of the American and French Revolutions was spreading and taking hold. On the island of Hispaniola, a revolution ended slavery and French rule in Saint Domingue. The same economic and political forces that had undermined British rule in the colonies that became the United States were present in Spanish America and Brazil.

## The Haitian Revolution

The French colony of Saint Domingue produced two-thirds of France's tropical imports and generated nearly one-third of all French foreign trade. This impressive wealth depended on a brutal slave regime. Saint Domingue's harsh punishments and high mortality were notorious throughout the Caribbean.

In 1789, when news of the calling of France's Estates General arrived on the island, wealthy white planters sent a delegation to Paris charged with seeking more home rule and greater economic freedom. The *gens de couleur*° also sent representatives. Mostly small planters or urban merchants, these free mixed-race delegates focused on ending

---

**Metternich** (MET-uhr-nik)   **Louis Philippe** (loo-EE fee-LEEP)

*gens de couleur* (zhahn deh koo-LUHR)

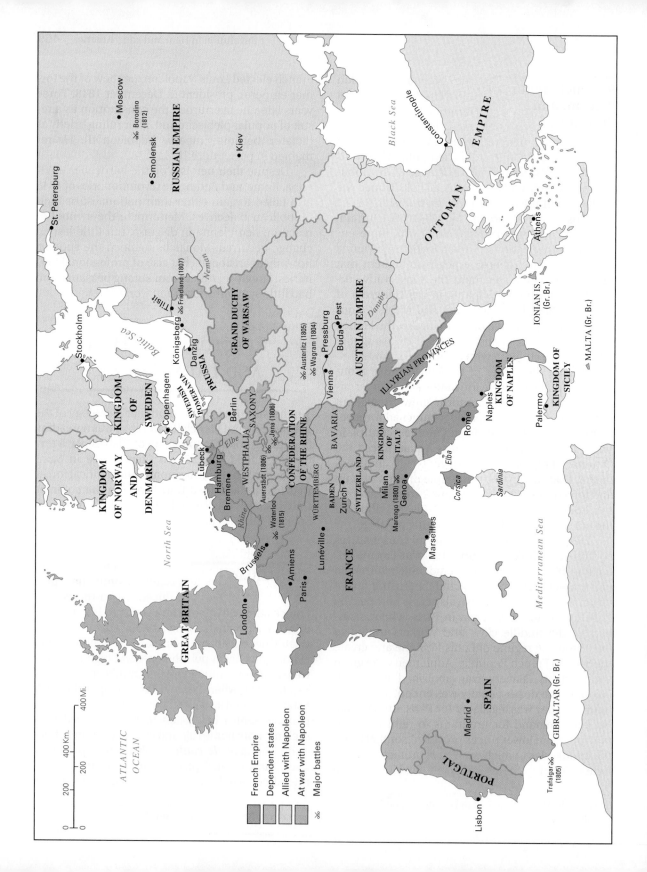

Moscow
• Borodino (1812)

Smolensk

RUSSIAN EMPIRE

Kiev

St. Petersburg

Black Sea

Constantinople

OTTOMAN EMPIRE

Stockholm

Baltic Sea

KINGDOM OF SWEDEN

Neman

Tilsit
Friedland (1807)
Königsberg
Danzig

PRUSSIA

GRAND DUCHY OF WARSAW

SWEDISH POMERANIA

Copenhagen

KINGDOM OF NORWAY AND DENMARK

Lübeck
Hamburg
Bremen

Elbe

Berlin

SAXONY
Jena (1806)

WESTPHALIA

Auerstädt (1806)

Rhine

CONFEDERATION OF THE RHINE

WÜRTTEMBERG

BADEN

Zurich

SWITZERLAND

BAVARIA

Pressburg
Buda • Pest
Wagram (1804)
Vienna
Austerlitz (1805)

Danube

AUSTRIAN EMPIRE

ILLYRIAN PROVINCES

IONIAN IS. (Gr. Br.)

MALTA (Gr. Br.)

KINGDOM OF ITALY

Milan
Marengo (1800)
Genoa

Elba

Corsica

Sardinia

Naples

KINGDOM OF NAPLES

Rome

Palermo

KINGDOM OF SICILY

North Sea

Waterloo (1815)

Brussels

Amiens

Lunéville

Paris

FRANCE

Marseilles

Mediterranean Sea

GREAT BRITAIN

London

ATLANTIC OCEAN

Madrid

SPAIN

GIBRALTAR (Gr. Br.)

Trafalgar (1805)

PORTUGAL

Lisbon

400 Mi.

400 Km.

200

200

0

0

French Empire
Dependent states
Allied with Napoleon
At war with Napoleon
Major battles

**Map 19.1    Napoleon's Europe, 1810**    By 1810 Great Britain was the only remaining European power at war with Napoleon. Because of the loss of the French fleet at the Battle of Trafalgar in 1805, Napoleon was unable to threaten Britain with invasion, and Britain was able to actively assist the resistance movements in Spain and Portugal, thereby helping weaken French power.

race discrimination and political inequality. They did not seek freedom for slaves, because the most prosperous gens de couleur were slave owners themselves.

The political turmoil in France weakened colonial authority, permitting rich planters, poor whites, gens de couleur, and slaves to pursue their narrow interests, in an increasingly bitter and confrontational struggle. By 1791, whites and the gens de couleur were engaged in open warfare. This breach between the two groups of slave owners gave the slaves an opening. Their rebellion began on the plantations of the north and spread throughout the colony. Plantations were destroyed, masters and overseers killed, and crops burned.

The rebellious slaves eventually gained the upper hand under the military leadership of **Toussaint L'Ouverture,** a former domestic slave. Politically strengthened in 1794 when the radical National Convention in Paris abolished slavery in all French possessions, Toussaint overcame his rivals in Saint Domingue, defeated a British expeditionary force in 1798, and then led an invasion of neighboring Santo Domingo, freeing the slaves there. Toussaint continued to assert his loyalty to France but gave the French government no effective role in local affairs.

In 1802, Napoleon sent a large military force to Saint Domingue to reestablish both French authority and slavery. At first, the French forces were successful. Toussaint was captured and sent to France, where he died in prison. Eventually, however, French losses to yellow fever and the resistance of the revolutionaries turned the tide. Few slave women had taken up arms during the early stages of the Haitian Revolution, but now they joined the armed resistance. In 1804, the free republic of Haiti joined the United States as the second independent nation in the Western Hemisphere. But independence and emancipation were achieved at a terrible price. Tens of thousands had died, and the economy was destroyed.

## Latin American Revolutions

The great works of the Enlightenment as well as revolutionary documents like the Declaration of Independence and the Declaration of the Rights of Man circulated widely in Latin America. But it was Napoleon's decision to invade Portugal (1807) and Spain (1808), not revolutionary ideas, that ignited Latin America's struggle for independence.

In 1808, the royal family of Portugal fled to Brazil and maintained court there for over a decade. In Spain, in contrast, Napoleon forced King Ferdinand VII to abdicate and placed his own brother, Joseph Bonaparte, on the throne. When Spanish patriots fighting against the French created a new political body, the Junta° Central, and claimed the right to exercise the king's powers over Spain's colonies, a vocal minority of powerful colonists objected. In late 1808 and 1809, popular movements overthrew Spanish colonial officials in Venezuela, Mexico, and Bolivia and created local juntas. In each case, Spanish officials' harsh repression gave rise to a greater sense of a separate American nationality. By 1810, Spanish colonial authorities were facing a new round of revolutions more clearly focused on the achievement of independence.

In Caracas (the capital city of modern Venezuela), a revolutionary junta led by creoles (colonial-born whites) declared independence in 1811. Its leaders were large landowners who espoused popular sovereignty and representative democracy, defended slavery, and opposed full citizenship for the black and mixed-race majority. The junta's narrow agenda spurred loyalists in the colonial administration and church hierarchy to rally thousands of free blacks and slaves to defend the Spanish Empire. **Simón Bolívar°** (1783–1830) became the preeminent leader of the independence movement in Spanish South America.

Between 1813 and 1817, military advantage

**Junta** (HUN-tah)    **Simón Bolívar** (see-MOAN bow-LEE-varh)

**Haiti's Former Slaves Defend Their Freedom** In this representation, a veteran army sent by Napoleon to reassert French control in Haiti battles with Haitian forces in a tropical forest. The combination of Haitian resistance and yellow fever defeated the French invasion. (Bettmann/Corbis)

shifted back and forth between the patriots and loyalists, but by 1820, momentum swung irreversibly to the patriots. After liberating present-day Venezuela, Colombia, Ecuador, Peru, and Bolivia, Bolívar's army defeated the last Spanish armies in 1824. But Bolívar's attempt to draw the former Spanish colonies into a formal confederation failed (see Map 19.2).

Buenos Aires (the capital city of modern Argentina) was the second important center of revolutionary activity in Spanish South America (see Environment and Technology: Constructing the Port of Buenos Aires, Argentina). In the south, a coalition of militia commanders, merchants, and ranchers declared independence as the United Provinces of the Río de la Plata in 1816. Patriot leaders in Buenos Aires at first sought to retain control over the old Viceroyalty of Río de la Plata, but a separatist movement defeated these ambitions. A mixed force of Chileans and Argentines, led by José de San Martín° (1778–1850), liberated Chile in 1820. Simón Bolívar overcame final Spanish resistance in Peru in 1824.

The arrival of the Portuguese royal family in Brazil in 1808 had helped to maintain the loyalty of the colonial elite and to stimulate the local economy. But when King John VI returned to Portugal in 1821, Brazilians began to reevaluate Brazil's relationship with Portugal and to talk openly of independence.

Unwilling to return to Portugal and committed to maintaining his family's hold on Brazil, King John's son Pedro aligned himself with the rising tide of independence sentiment. In 1822, he declared Brazilian independence. Unlike its neighbors, which became constitutional republics, Brazil gained independence as a constitutional monarchy with Pedro I, heir to the throne of Portugal, as

**José de San Martín** (hoe-SAY deh san mar-TEEN)

**The Revolutionary Tradition in Mexico**    This 1948 mural by José Clemente Orozco commemorates the Mexican struggle to restore its republican tradition after France intervened—using collection of overdue debts as a pretext—and enthroned the Austrian archduke Maximilian as emperor of Mexico. Maximilian reigned from 1864 to 1867, when he was overthrown and executed by a popular movement led by Benito Juarez, shown in the center of the painting. Orozco depicts Maximilian's bandage-swathed body being borne by the Catholic clergy, military commanders, and foreign interlopers who constituted the conservative opposition to Juarez's republicanism.    (Muséo Nacional de Historia/CENIDIAP-INBA)

emperor. The monarchy lasted until 1889, when it was overthrown by republicans.

## Mexico

In 1810, Mexico was Spain's richest and most populous colony. But the sharp distinctions among its creole, native, and Spanish populations made it ripe for revolution. The first stage of the revolution against Spain occurred in central Mexico, where wealthy ranchers and farmers had aggressively forced many Amerindian communities from their traditional agricultural lands. By the time news of Napoleon's invasion of Spain reached the region,

crop failures and epidemics had further afflicted the poor.

On September 16, 1810, **Miguel Hidalgo y Costilla°,** parish priest of the small town of Dolores, rang the church bells, attracting thousands. In a fiery speech, he urged the crowd to rise up against the oppression of Spanish officials. Tens of thousands of the rural and urban poor joined his movement. They lacked military discipline and adequate weapons but knew who their oppressors were. At first sympathetic to Hidalgo's objectives, wealthy

---

**Miguel Hidalgo y Costilla** (mee-GEHL ee-DAHL-go ee cos-TEA-ah)

OREGON
COUNTRY
(Joint U.S.-British
occupation)

BRITISH NORTH AMERICA
(Gr. Br.)

UNITED STATES

*Mississippi*

*Colorado*

MEXICO
1821

*Rio Grande*

• San
Antonio

ATLANTIC
OCEAN

*Gulf of Mexico*

• Mexico City

• Veracruz

• Havana

BAHAMA IS.
(Gr. Br.)

CUBA
(Spain)

HAITI 1804

PUERTO RICO (Spain)

BRITISH
HONDURAS (Gr. Br.)

GUATEMALA
• Guatemala City

JAMAICA (Gr. Br.)

*Caribbean
Sea*

UNITED PROVINCES OF
CENTRAL AMERICA
1823—1839

• Panama

• Caracas

TRINIDAD (Gr. Br.)

VENEZUELA
• Socorro
• Bogotá

BR. GUIANA (Gr. Br.)

DUTCH GUIANA (Neth.)

FRENCH GUIANA (France)

*Magdalena*

GRAN COLOMBIA
1819—1830

*Galápagos
Islands*

• Quito
ECUADOR

*Amazon*

EMPIRE OF BRAZIL
1822

PACIFIC
OCEAN

PERU
1824

• Lima

BOLIVIA
1825
• La Paz
• Sucre

• Salvador

*Paraná*

PARAGUAY
1811

• São Paulo
• Rio de Janeiro

CHILE
1817

UNITED
PROVINCES OF
THE RÍO DE
LA PLATA
1816

• Valparaíso
• Santiago

ARGENTINA
• Buenos Aires
• Bahía
Blanca

URUGUAY
1828

• Montevideo

1811 Year independence gained

Colony

0      500    1000 Km.

0      500    1000 Mi.

*PATAGONIA*
(Disputed between
Argentina and Chile)

*Islas Malvinas*
(Falkland Islands)

Map 19.2   **Latin America by 1830**   By 1830 patriot forces had overturned the Spanish and Portuguese Empires of the Western Hemisphere. Regional conflicts, local wars, and foreign interventions challenged the survival of many of these new nations following independence.

Mexicans eventually turned against Hidalgo, who was captured, tried, and executed in 1811.

Although insurgents continued to wage war against Spanish forces, colonial rule seemed secure in 1820. However, news of the military revolt in Spain unsettled the conservative groups and church officials who had defended Spanish rule against Hidalgo and José Morelos, who continued the revolution after Hidalgo's execution. In 1821, Colonel Agustín de Iturbide° and other loyalist commanders forged an alliance with remaining insurgents and declared Mexico's independence. The conservative origins of Mexico's transition to independence were highlighted by the decision to create a monarchial form of government and crown Iturbide as emperor. In early 1823, however, the army overthrew Iturbide and Mexico became a republic.

# ECONOMIC AND SOCIAL LIBERATION MOVEMENTS

During the nineteenth century, the newly independent nations of the Western Hemisphere struggled to realize the Enlightenment ideals of freedom and individual liberty. The persistence of slavery and women's inequality raised troubling questions about these ideals. By century's end, reform movements in many of the hemisphere's nations had made significant progress, but much remained to be done.

## The Abolition of Slavery

In both the United States and Latin America, strong antislavery sentiments were expressed during the struggles for independence. In nearly all the new nations of the Western Hemisphere, revolutionary leaders asserted universal ideals of freedom and citizenship that contrasted sharply with the reality of slavery. Men and women who wanted to outlaw slavery were called **abolitionists.** Despite their efforts, slavery survived in much of the hemisphere until the 1850s. In regions where the export of plantation products was most important—such as the United States, Brazil, and Cuba—the abolition of slavery was achieved with great difficulty.

In the United States, some northern states had abolished slavery after the Revolution, and Congress banned the importation of new slaves in 1808. But this progress was stalled by the profitable expansion of cotton agriculture after the War of 1812. In Spanish America, tens of thousands of slaves gained freedom by joining revolutionary armies during the wars for independence. After independence, most Spanish American republics prohibited the slave trade. Counteracting that trend was the growing international demand for sugar and coffee, products traditionally produced on plantations by slaves. As prices rose for plantation products in the first half of the nineteenth century, Brazil and Cuba (a Spanish colony until 1899) increased their imports of slaves.

During the long struggle to end slavery in the United States, American abolitionists argued that slavery offended both morality and the universal rights asserted in the Declaration of Independence. Two groups denied full rights of citizenship under the Constitution, women and free African-Americans, played important roles in the abolition of slavery. Women served on the executive committee of the American Anti-Slavery Society and produced some of the most effective propaganda against slavery. Many women abolitionists advocated female suffrage as well. Frederick Douglass, a former slave, became one of the most effective abolitionist speakers and writers. More radical black leaders saw civil war or slave insurrection as necessary for ending slavery.

During the Civil War, pressure for emancipation rose as tens of thousands of black freemen and escaped slaves joined the Union army. Hundreds of thousands of other slaves fled their masters' plantations and farms for the protection of advancing northern armies. In 1863, in the midst of

**Agustín de Iturbide** (ah-goos-TEEN deh ee-tur-BEE-deh)

## Constructing the Port of Buenos Aires, Argentina

Located on the banks of the Río de la Plata, Buenos Aires had been a major commercial center and port since the late eighteenth century. But Buenos Aires was not a natural harbor. Because of the shallowness of the river, the largest oceangoing ships were forced to anchor hundreds of yards offshore while goods and passengers were unloaded by small boats or by specially built ox carts with huge wheels. Smaller vessels docked at a river port to the city's south.

By the 1880s the Argentine economy was being transformed by the growing demands of European consumers for meat and grain. As exports surged and land values exploded, the wages of Argentines rose, and the nation became a favored destination for European immigrants. Argentina was becoming the wealthiest nation in Latin America.

The nation's political and economic elites decided that future growth required the modernization and expansion of port facilities. Two competing plans were debated. The first emphasized the incremental expansion and dredging of the river port. This plan was supported by local engineers and political groups suspicious of foreign economic interests. The second, and ultimately successful, plan involved dredging a port and deep-water channel from the low mud flats near the city center. This plan was more expensive and relied on British engineering firms, British banks, and British technology. It was supported by Argentine economic interests most closely tied to the European export trade and by national political leaders who believed progress and prosperity required the imitation of European models. Already the British were the nation's primary creditors as well as leaders in the development of the nation's railroads, streetcar lines, and gas works in Buenos Aires.

The photograph shows the construction of Puerto Madero, the new port of Buenos Aires, in the 1890s. The work force was almost entirely recruited from recent immigrants. The engineering staff was dominated by British experts. Most of the profits were culled by the local elite through real estate deals and commissions associated with construction. Puerto Madero, named after its local promoter, was opened in stages beginning in 1890. Cost overruns and corruption

---

the Civil War, President Lincoln began the abolition of slavery by issuing the Emancipation Proclamation, which ended slavery in rebel states not occupied by the Union army. Final abolition was accomplished in 1865, by the Thirteenth Amendment to the Constitution.

After Britain ended its participation in the slave trade in 1807, it negotiated treaties with Spain, Brazil, and other importers of slaves to eliminate the slave trade to the Americas. But enforcement proved difficult. For example, Brazil, despite its treaty of 1830, illegally imported over a half-million more African slaves before the British navy finally forced compliance in the 1850s. The Brazilian parliament passed legislation abolishing slavery in 1888.

Slavery lasted longest in Cuba. Despite strong British pressure, the Spanish colony continued to import large numbers of African slaves until the 1860s. More important, however, was the growth of support for abolition in these colonies. Both Cuba and Puerto Rico had larger white and free colored populations than did the Caribbean colonies of Britain and France. As a result, there was less fear in Cuba and Puerto Rico that abolition would lead to the political ascendancy of former slaves (as had occurred in Haiti). In Puerto Rico, where slaves numbered approximately thirty thousand, local reformers sought and gained the abolition of slavery in 1873. Eventually, during a decade-long war to defeat forces seeking the independence of Cuba, the Spanish government moved

**Excavation of Port of Buenos Aires, Argentina** Relying on foreign capital and engineering, the government of Argentina improved the port to facilitate the nation's rapidly expanding export economy. (Courtesy, Hack Hoffenburg, South American Resources)

lion tons. But the project was poorly designed, and "improvements" were still being made in the 1920s.

Why had the government of Argentina chosen the costliest and most difficult design? Argentine politicians were seduced by the idea of modernity; they chose the most complex and technologically sophisticated solution to the port problem. And they believed that British engineering and British capital were guarantees of modernity. The new port facilities did facilitate a boom in exports and imports, and the huge public works budget did provide incomes for thousands of laborers. However, debts, design flaws, and the increased influence of foreign capital in Argentina left a legacy of problems that Argentina would be forced to

stretched out completion to 1898. By 1910 arrivals and departures reached thirty thousand ships and 18 million tons. deal with in the future. (See the discussion of Juan Perón in Chapter 27.)

## Equal Rights for Women and Blacks

The abolition of slavery in the Western Hemisphere did not end racial discrimination or provide full political rights for every citizen. Not only blacks but also women suffered political and economic discrimination during the nineteenth century.

In 1848, a group of women angered by their exclusion from an international antislavery meeting issued a call for a meeting to discuss women's rights. The **Women's Rights Convention** at Seneca Falls, New York, issued a statement that said in part, "We hold these truths to be self-evident: that all men and women are equal." While moderates focused on the issues of greater economic independence and full legal rights, increasing numbers of women demanded the right to vote. Others lobbied to provide better conditions for women working outside the home, especially in textile factories.

Progress toward equality between men and women was equally slow in Canada and Latin America. Canada's first women doctors received their training in the United States because no woman was able to receive a medical degree in Canada until 1895. Argentina and Uruguay were among the first Latin American nations to provide public education for women. Both nations introduced coeducation in the 1870s. Chilean women

toward gradual abolition. Finally, in 1886, slavery was abolished.

gained access to some careers in medicine and law in the 1870s. In Brazil, where many women were active in the abolitionist movement, four women graduated in medicine by 1882. Throughout the hemisphere, more rapid progress was achieved in lower-status careers that threatened male economic power less directly, and by the end of the century, women dominated elementary school teaching throughout the Western Hemisphere.

From Canada to Argentina and Chile, the majority of working-class women had no direct involvement in these reform movements, but in their daily lives, they succeeded in transforming gender relations. By the end of the nineteenth century, large numbers of poor women worked outside the home on farms, in markets, and, increasingly, in factories.

Throughout the hemisphere, there was little progress toward eliminating racial discrimination. Blacks were denied the vote throughout the southern United States and subjected to the indignity of segregation. Racial discrimination against men and women of African descent was also common in Latin America, though seldom spelled out in legal codes. Latin Americans tended to view racial identity across a continuum of physical characteristics rather than in the narrow terms of black and white that defined race relations in the United States.

# CONCLUSION

The revolutions of the late eighteenth century hastened the transformation of Western society. Royal governments attempting to impose new taxes to pay war debts collided with ideas of elections and representative institutions. French officers who took part in the American Revolution helped ignite the French Revolution. Black freemen from Haiti traveled to France to seek their rights and returned to spread revolutionary passions. Napoleon's invasion of Portugal and Spain then helped initiate the movement toward independence in Latin America. The promises of universal citizenship were only partially achieved.

Each revolution had its own character. The revolutions in France and Haiti were more violent and destructive than the mainland American revo-

lutions. In many places, monarchy, multinational empires, and the established church contested with liberal and nationalist sentiments well into the nineteenth century. Only a minority gained full political rights. Democratic institutions often failed, and slavery endured in the Americas past the mid-1800s.

## ■ Key Terms

Enlightenment

George Washington

Constitutional Convention

Estates General

National Assembly

Declaration of the Rights of Man

Napoleon Bonaparte

Congress of Vienna

Revolutions of 1848

*gens de couleur*

Toussaint L'Ouverture

Simón Bolívar

Miguel Hidalgo y Costilla

abolitionists

Women's Rights Convention

## ■ Suggested Reading

Eric Hobsbawm's *The Age of Revolution* (1962) provides a clear analysis of the class issues that appeared during this era. The American Revolution has received a great amount of attention from scholars. Colin Bonwick, *The American Revolution* (1991), and Edward Countryman, *The American Revolution* (1985), provide excellent introductions.

François Furet, *Interpreting the French Revolution* (1981), breaks with interpretations that emphasize class and ideological interpretations. Georges Lefebve, *The Coming of the French Revolution*, trans. R. R. Palmer (1947), presents the classic class-based analysis. George Rudé, *The Crowd in History: Popular Disturbances in France and England* (1981), remains the best introduction to the role of mass protest in the period. The recently published *The Women of Paris and Their French Revolution* (1998) by Dominique Godineau; Felix Markham, *Napoleon* (1963); and Robert B. Holtman, *The Napoleonic Revolution* (1967), provide reliable summaries of the period. For a brief survey of the revolutions of 1830 and 1848, see Arthur J. May, *The Age of Metternich, 1814–48*, rev. ed. (1963).

The classic study of the Haitian Revolution is C. L. R. James, *The Black Jacobins*, 2d ed. (1963). For the independence era in Latin America, see John Lynch, *The Spanish American Revolutions, 1808–1826*, 2d ed. (1986); Jay Kinsbruner, *Independence in Spanish America* (1994); and A. J. R. Russell-Wood, ed., *From Colony to Nation: Essays on the Independence of Brazil* (1976).

On the issue of slavery, see David Brion Davis, *Slavery and Human Progress* (1984); George M. Frederickson, *The Black Image in the White Mind: The Debate on Afro-American Character and Destiny, 1817–1914* (1971); and Benjamin Quarles, *Black Abolitionists* (1969). For abolition in Latin America and the Caribbean, see Rebecca Scott, *Slave Emancipation in Cuba: The Transition to Free Labor, 1860–1899* (1985); Robert Conrad, *The Destruction of Brazilian Slavery, 1850–1888* (1973); and William A. Green, *British Slave Emancipation: The Sugar Colonies and the Great Experiment, 1830–1865* (1976).

For the women's rights movement, see Ellen Carol DuBois, *Feminism and Suffrage: The Emergence of an Independent Women's Movement in America, 1848–1869* (1999).

# 20 The Early Industrial Revolution, 1760–1851

CHAPTER OUTLINE

Causes of the Industrial Revolution
The Technological Revolution
The Impact of the Industrial Revolution
New Economic and Political Ideas
Industrialization and the Nonindustrial World
ENVIRONMENT AND TECHNOLOGY: The Origin of Graphs

From 1765 until the 1790s a small group of men calling themselves the Lunar Society met once a month in Birmingham, England. They gathered on nights when the moon was full so they could find their way home in the dark. Among them were the pottery manufacturer Josiah Wedgwood, the engine designer James Watt, the chemist Joseph Priestley, the iron manufacturer Matthew Boulton, and the naturalist Erasmus Darwin. They did not leave a record of what they discussed, but the fact that businessmen, craftsmen, and scientists had interests in common was something new in the history of the world. Though members of very different professions, they were willing to exchange ideas and discoveries in an atmosphere of experimentation and innovation. They invited experts in industry, science, and engineering to speak at their meetings so that they could obtain the latest information in their fields.

By focusing on the practical application of knowledge, groups like the Lunar Society laid the groundwork for the economic and social transformations that historians call the **Industrial Revolution.** This revolution involved dramatic innovations in manufacturing, mining, transportation, and communications and equally rapid changes in society and commerce. New relationships between social groups created an environment that was conducive to technical innovation and economic growth. New technologies and new social and economic arrangements allowed the industrializing countries— first Britain, then western Europe and the United

States—to unleash massive increases in production and productivity, exploit the world's natural resources as never before, and transform the environment and human life in unprecedented ways.

The distribution of power and wealth generated by the Industrial Revolution was very uneven, for industrialization widened the gap between rich and poor. The people who owned and controlled the innovations amassed wealth and power over nature and over other people. Some of them lived lives of spectacular luxury. Workers, including children, worked long hours in dangerous factories and lived crowded together in unsanitary tenements.

The effect of the Industrial Revolution around the world was also very uneven. The first countries to industrialize grew rich and powerful. In Egypt and India, the economic and military power of the European countries stifled the tentative beginnings of industrialization. Regions that had little or no industry were easily taken advantage of. The disparity between the industrial and the developing countries that exists today has its origins in the early nineteenth century.

As you read this chapter, ask yourself the following questions:

- What caused the Industrial Revolution?

- What were the key innovations that increased productivity and drove industrialization?

- What was the impact of these changes on the society and environment of the industrializing countries?

- How did the Industrial Revolution affect the relations between the industrialized and the nonindustrialized parts of the world?

# CAUSES OF THE INDUSTRIAL REVOLUTION

What caused the Industrial Revolution, and why did it begin in England in the late eighteenth century? The basic preconditions of this momentous event seem to have been population growth, an agricultural revolution, the expansion of trade, and an openness to innovation.

## Preconditions for Industrialization

The population of Europe rose in the eighteenth century—slowly at first, faster after 1780, then even faster in the early nineteenth century. The population of England and Wales rose unusually fast—from 5.5 million in 1688 to 18 million by 1851. Industrialization and the population boom reinforced each other. A high birthrate meant a large percentage of children, which explains both the vitality of the British people in that period and the widespread use of child labor.

This population explosion and urbanization could only have taken place alongside an **agricultural revolution** that provided food for city dwellers and forced poorer peasants off the land. Long before the eighteenth century, the introduction and acceptance of the potato and maize from the Americas had increased food supplies in Europe. In the cool and humid regions of Europe, from Ireland to Russia, potatoes yielded two or three times more food per acre than grain. Maize (American corn) was grown across Europe from southwestern France to the Balkans.

During the seventeenth century, rich English landowners began draining marshes, improving the soil, and introducing crop rotation using turnips, legumes, and clover that did not deplete the soil and could be fed to cattle. Additional manure from improved breeds of livestock fertilized the soil for other crops. Some also "enclosed" land—that is, consolidated their holdings, including commons that in the past had been open to all. This "enclosure movement" also turned tenants and sharecroppers into landless farm laborers.

Many moved to the cities to seek work; others became homeless migrants and vagrants; still others emigrated.

The growth of the population and food supply was accompanied by the growth of trade. Most of it was local, but a growing share consisted of imports from other parts of the world like tea and sugar and simple goods that even middle-class people could afford, such as cotton textiles, iron hardware, and pottery.

Trade was accompanied by a growing interest in technology and innovation among educated people throughout Europe and eastern North America. They read descriptions of new techniques and inventions in many publications, and some experimented on their own.

## Britain's Advantages

These changes were widespread, but Britain in the eighteenth century had the fastest-growing population, food supply, and overseas trade. The British also put inventions into practice more quickly than other people. (see Environment and Technology: The Origin of Graphs). In the eighteenth century, Britain became the world's leading exporter of tools, guns, hardware, and other craft goods. Its mining and metal industries employed engineers willing to experiment with new ideas. It had the largest merchant marine and produced more ships, naval supplies, and navigation instruments than other countries.

Moreover, Britain had a more fluid society than the rest of Europe. Political power was not as centralized as on the European continent, and the government employed fewer bureaucrats and officials. Class lines eased as members of the gentry, and even some aristocrats, married into merchant families. Intermarriage among the families of petty merchants, yeoman farmers, and town craftsmen was common.

At a time when transportation by land was very costly, Great Britain had good water transportation, thanks to its indented coastline, navigable rivers, and growing network of canals (see Map 20.1). It had a unified internal market, with none of the duties and tolls that goods had to pay every few miles in France. This encouraged specialization and trade. More people there were involved in pro-

**Map 20.1 The Industrial Revolution in Britain, ca. 1850** The first industries arose in northern and western England. These regions had abundant coal and iron-ore deposits for the iron industry and moist climate and fast-flowing rivers for the cotton textile industry.

duction for export and in trade and finance than in any other major country. It had financial and insurance institutions able to support growing business enterprises and a patent system that offered inventors the hope of rich rewards.

By 1830, the political climate in western Europe was as favorable to business as Britain's had been a half-century earlier. Industrialization first took hold in Belgium and northern France, as their businessmen visited Britain to observe the changes and to spy out industrial secrets. In spite of British laws forbidding the emigration of skilled workers and

| C H R O N O L O G Y | | |
|---|---|---|
| | **Technology** | **Economy, Society, and Politics** |
| **1750** | | |
| | **1759** Josiah Wedgwood opens pottery factory | |
| | **1764** Spinning jenny | |
| | **1769** Richard Arkwright's water frame; James Watt patents steam engine | |
| | | **1776** Adam Smith's *Wealth of Nations* |
| | | **1776–1783** American Revolution |
| | **1779** First iron bridge | |
| | **1785** Boulton and Watt sell steam engines; Samuel Crompton's mule | |
| | | **1789–1799** French Revolution |
| | **1793** Eli Whitney's cotton gin | |
| **1800** | **1800** Alessandro Volta's battery | |
| | | **1804–1815** Napoleonic Wars |
| | **1807** Robert Fulton's *North River* | |
| | **1820s** Construction of Erie Canal | **1820s** U.S. cotton industry begins |
| | | **1833** Factory Act in Britain |
| | | **1834** Robert Owen's Grand National Consolidated Trade Union |
| | **1837** Wheatstone and Cooke's telegraph | |
| | **1838** First ships steam across the Atlantic | |
| | **1840** *Nemesis* sails to China | |
| | **1843** Samuel Morse's Baltimore-to-Washington telegraph | |
| | | **1847–1848** Irish famine |
| | | **1848** Collapse of chartist movement; revolutions in Europe |
| **1850** | **1851** Crystal palace opens in London | |

the export of textile machinery, many slipped through, setting up machines, training workers in the new methods, and even starting their own businesses. European governments created technical schools; eliminated internal tariff barriers, tolls, and other hindrances to trade; and encouraged the formation of joint-stock companies and banks to channel private savings into industrial investments.

# ENVIRONMENT + TECHNOLOGY

## The Origin of Graphs

Not all technologies involve hardware. There are also information technologies, such as graphs, the visual representation of numerical tables. We see graphs so often in textbooks, magazines, and newspapers that we take them for granted. But they too have a history.

Scientists in France and England created the first graphs in the seventeenth century to illustrate natural phenomena. Some represented tables of data, such as the movements of stars and atmospheric pressure. Until the late eighteenth century few people outside of scientific circles knew or cared about such graphs. This changed with the growing public interest in economic data, population statistics, and other secular subjects that were so much a part of the Enlightenment.

The first person to publish graphs of interest to the general public was William Playfair (1729–1823), an Englishman who started his career as a draftsman for

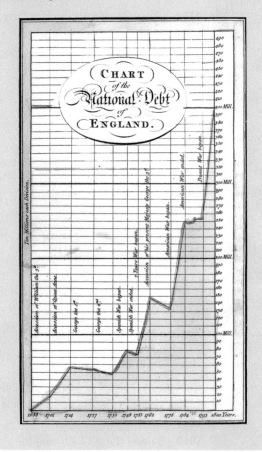

**Line Graph of National Debt of England, 1803** This graph by William Playfair is designed to shock the viewer by showing the national debt of Britain skyrocketing out of control, especially during the country's many wars. (British Library)

---

On the European continent, as in Britain, cotton was the first industry to industrialize.

## THE TECHNOLOGICAL REVOLUTION

Five revolutionary innovations spurred industrialization: (1) mass production through the division of labor, (2) new machines and mechanization, (3) a great increase in the supply of iron, (4) the steam engine and the changes it made possible in industry and transportation, and (5) the electric telegraph.

**Mass Production and Mechanization**

The pottery industry offers a good example of **mass production,** the making of many identical items by breaking the process into simple repetitive tasks. **Josiah Wedgwood** opened a pottery

484

the engine-manufacturing firm of Boulton and Watt. In 1786 he published *The Commercial and Political Atlas*, a book that was widely read and went though several editions. All but one of the forty-four graphs in it were line graphs with the vertical axis showing economic data and the horizontal axis representing time. Playfair explained to skeptical readers how a line could represent money:

> This method has struck several persons as being fallacious, because geometrical measurement has not any relation to money or to time; yet here it is made to represent both. The most familiar and simple answer to this objection is by giving an example. Suppose the money received by a man in trade were all in guineas, and that every evening he made a single pile of all the guineas received during the day, each pile would represent a day, and its height would be proportioned to the receipts of that day; so that by this plain operation, time, proportion, and amount would all be physically combined.
>
> Lineal arithmetic then, it may be averred, is nothing more than those piles of guineas represented on paper, and on a small scale, in which an inch (suppose) represents the thickness of five millions of guineas, as in geography it does the breadth of a river, or any other extent of country.

As for why it was necessary to show economic data in the form of a graph, Playfair explained:

> Men of high rank, or active business, can only pay attention to general outlines; nor is attention to particulars of use, any further than they give a general information; it is hoped that, with the Assistance of these Charts, such information will be got, without the fatigue and trouble of studying the particulars of which it is composed.

Today, graphs are an indispensable means of conveying information in business and finance, in the sciences, and in government. We need graphs because they give us information quickly and efficiently, "without the fatigue and trouble of studying the particulars."

Source: William Playfair, *The Commercial and Political Atlas*, 3rd ed. (London: J. Wallis, 1801), ix, xiv–xv.

business in 1759 that was able to produce porcelain cheaply, by means of the **division of labor.** He subdivided the work into highly specialized and repetitive tasks, such as unloading the clay, mixing it, pressing flat pieces, dipping the pieces in glaze, putting handles on cups, packing kilns, and carrying things from one part of his plant to another. He substituted the use of molds for the potter's wheel wherever possible, a change that not only saved labor but also created identical plates and bowls that could be stacked. These radical departures from the age-old methods of craftsmanship allowed Wedgwood to lower the cost of his products while improving their quality. As a result, his factory grew far larger than his competitors' factories and employed several hundred workers. His own salesmen traveled throughout England touting his goods.

Wedgwood was also interested in new technologies. He invested in toll roads and canals so that clay could be shipped economically from southwestern England to his factories in the Midlands. In 1782, to mix clay and grind flint, he purchased one of the first steam engines to be used in industry. Wedgwood's interest in applying technology to manufacturing was connected with his membership in the Birmingham Lunar Society, a group of manufacturers, scientists, and inventors who met to exchange ideas and discoveries. They were part of the atmosphere of experimentation and innovation that characterized late-eighteenth-century England. Similar societies throughout Britain were creating a vogue for science and giving the word *progress* a new meaning: "change for the better."

The cotton industry, the largest industry in this period, illustrates the role of **mechanization,** the use of machines to do work previously done by hand. The cotton plant did not grow in Europe, but the cloth was so much cooler, softer, and cleaner than wool that wealthy Europeans developed a liking for this costly import. When the powerful English woolen industry persuaded Parliament to forbid the import of cotton cloth into England, it stimulated attempts to import cotton fiber and make the cloth locally. Here was an opportunity for enterprising inventors to reduce costs with labor-saving machinery.

Beginning in the 1760s, a series of inventions—the spinning jenny, the water frame, and the mule—revolutionized the spinning of cotton thread and allowed British industry to undersell high-quality handmade cotton cloth from India. British cotton output increased tenfold between 1770 and 1790.

When the boom in thread production and the soaring demand for cloth created bottlenecks in weaving, inventors in England rose to the challenge with power looms, carding machines, chlorine bleach, and cylindrical printing presses. By the 1830s, large English textile mills powered by steam engines were turning raw cotton into printed cloth. This was a far cry from the cottage industries of the previous century.

Mechanization offered two advantages: (1) productivity for the manufacturer and (2) price for the consumer. Whereas in India it took 500 hours to spin a pound of cotton, the improved mule of 1830 required only 80 minutes. Cotton mills needed very few skilled workers, and managers often hired children to tend the spinning machines. Mechanization and cheap labor allowed the price of cloth to fall by 90 percent from 1782 to 1812, and it kept on dropping.

The industrialization of Britain made cotton into America's most valuable crop. In 1793, the American Eli Whitney patented his cotton gin, a simple device that separated the bolls from the fiber and made the growing of short-staple cotton economical. This invention permitted the spread of cotton farming into Georgia, then into Alabama, Mississippi, and Louisiana, and finally as far west as Texas. By the late 1850s, the southern states were producing a million tons of cotton a year, five-sixths of the world's total.

With the help of British craftsmen who introduced jennies, mules, and power looms, Americans developed a cotton industry in the 1820s. By 1840, the United States had 1,200 cotton mills, two-thirds of them in New England, powered by water rather than steam.

## The Iron Industry

Iron making also was transformed during the Industrial Revolution. Iron had been in use for thousands of years for tools, swords and other weapons, and household items such as knives, pots, hinges, and locks. Wherever it was produced, however, deforestation eventually drove up the cost of charcoal (used for smelting) and restricted output. Furthermore, iron had to be repeatedly heated and hammered to drive out impurities, a difficult and costly process. Then in 1709, Abraham Darby discovered that coke (coal from which the impurities have been cooked out) could be used in place of charcoal. The resulting metal was of lower quality than charcoal iron but much cheaper to produce, for coal was plentiful. Just as importantly, in 1784 Henry Cort found a way to remove some of the impurities in coke-iron by puddling—stirring the molten iron with long rods. Cort's process made it possible to turn high-sulfur English coal into coke to produce wrought iron (a soft and malleable form of iron) very cheaply. By 1790 four-fifths of Britain's iron was made with coke, while other countries were still using charcoal. Coke-iron was cheaper and less destructive of forests, and it allowed a great expansion in the size of individual blast furnaces, substantially reducing the cost of iron. There seemed almost no limit to the quantity of iron that could be produced with coke. Britain's iron production began rising fast, from 17,000 tons in 1740 to 3 million tons in 1844, as much as in the rest of the world put together.

In turn, there seemed no limit to the amount of iron that an industrializing society would purchase or to the novel applications for this cheap and useful material. In 1779 the iron manufacturer Abraham Darby III (grandson of the first Abraham Darby) built a bridge of iron across the Severn River. In 1851 Londoners marveled at the **Crystal Palace,** a huge greenhouse made entirely of iron and glass and large enough to enclose the tallest trees.

The availability of cheap iron made the mass production of objects such as guns, hardware, and tools appealing. However, fitting together the parts of these products required a great deal of labor. To reduce labor costs, manufacturers turned to the idea of interchangeable parts. This idea originated in the eighteenth century when French army officers attempted, without success, to persuade gun makers to produce precisely identical parts. Craftsmen continued to use traditional methods to make parts that had to be filed to fit together with other parts. By the mid-nineteenth century, however, interchangeable-parts procedures had been adopted in the manufacture of firearms, farm equipment, and sewing machines. At the Crystal Palace exhibition of 1851, Europeans called it the "American system of manufactures." In the next hundred years the use of machinery to mass-produce consumer items was to become the hallmark of American industry.

## The Steam Engine

The first machine to transform fossil fuel into mechanical energy was the **steam engine.** Although the mechanization of manufacturing was very important, the steam engine was what set the Industrial Revolution apart from all previous periods of growth and innovation.

Before the eighteenth century, many activities had been limited by the lack of energy. For example, deep mines filled with water faster than horses could pump it out. Scientists understood the concept of atmospheric pressure and had created experimental devices to turn heat into motion, but they had not found a way to put those devices to practical use. Then, between 1702 and 1712 Thomas Newcomen developed the first practical steam engine, a crude but effective device. One engine could pump water out of a mine as fast as four horses and could run day and night without getting tired.

The Newcomen engine's voracious appetite for fuel mattered little in coal mines, where fuel was cheap, but it made the engine too costly for other uses. In 1764 **James Watt,** an instrument maker at Glasgow University in Scotland, was asked to repair the university's model Newcomen engine. Watt realized that the engine wasted fuel because the cylinder had to be alternately heated and cooled. He developed a separate condenser—a vessel into which the steam was allowed to escape after it had done work, leaving the cylinder always hot and the condenser always cold. Watt patented his idea in 1769. He enlisted the help of the iron manufacturer Matthew Boulton to turn his invention into a commercial product. Their first engines were sold to pump water out of copper and tin mines, where fuel was too costly for Newcomen engines. In 1781 Watt invented the sun-and-planet gear, which turned the back-and-forth action of the piston into rotary motion. This allowed steam engines to power machinery in flour and cotton mills, pottery factories, and other industries.

Watt's steam engine was the most celebrated invention of the eighteenth century. Because there seemed almost no limit to the amount of coal in the ground, steam-generated energy seemed an inexhaustible source of power, and steam engines could be used where animal, wind, and water power were lacking.

Inspired by the success of Watt's engine, inventors in France in 1783, in the United States in 1787, and in England in 1788 put steam engines on boats. The need to travel great distances explains why the first commercially successful steamboat was Robert Fulton's *North River,* which steamed between New York City and Albany in 1807. Soon steamboats were launched on other American rivers. In the 1820s the Erie Canal linked the Atlantic seaboard with the Great Lakes and opened Ohio, Indiana, and Illinois to European settlement. Steamboats proliferated west of the Appalachian Mountains; by 1830 some three hundred plied the Mississippi and its tributaries. To counter the competition from New York State, Pennsylvania built a thousand miles of canals by 1840. The United States was fast becoming a nation that moved by water.

**Pit Head of a Coal Mine** This is a small coal mine. In the center of this picture stands a New-comen engine used to pump water. The work of hauling coal out of the mine was still done by horses and mules. The smoke coming out of the smokestack is a trademark of the early industrial era. (National Museums and Galleries on Merseyside, Walker Art Gallery [WAG 659])

Oceangoing steam-powered ships were much more difficult to build than riverboats, for the first steam engines used so much coal that no ship could carry more than a few days' supply. The *Savannah*, which crossed the Atlantic in 1819, was a sailing ship with an auxiliary steam engine that was used for only ninety hours of its twenty-nine-day trip. However, engineers soon developed more efficient engines, and in 1838 two steamers, the *Great Western* and the *Sirius*, crossed the Atlantic on steam power alone.

## Railroads

On land as on water, the problem was not imagining uses for steam-powered vehicles but building ones that worked, for steam engines were too heavy and weak to pull any weight. After Watt's patent expired in 1800, inventors experimented with lighter, more powerful high-pressure engines and in the early 1800s built several steam-powered vehicles able to travel on roads or rails. Between 1830 and 1850, a railroad-building mania swept Britain. The first lines linked towns and mines with the nearest harbor or waterway. As passenger traffic soared, entrepreneurs built lines between the major cities and then to small towns as well. Railroads were far cheaper, faster, and more comfortable than stagecoaches, and millions of people got in the habit of traveling.

In the United States, entrepreneurs built railroads as fast and cheaply as possible. By the 1840s, 6,000 miles (10,000 kilometers) of track radiated westward from Boston, New York, Philadelphia, and Baltimore. The boom of the 1840s was dwarfed by the mania of the 1850s, when 21,000 miles (34,000 kilometers) of new track were laid, much of it westward across the Appalachians to Memphis, St. Louis, and Chicago. The trip from New York to Chicago, which once took three weeks by boat and on horseback, could be made in forty-eight hours. The railroads opened up the Midwest, turning the vast prairie into wheat fields and pasture for cattle to feed the industrial cities of the eastern United States.

Railways triggered the industrialization of Europe. Belgium, independent since 1830, quickly copied the British. State-planned and -supervised

**Transatlantic Steamship Race**    In 1838, two ships equipped with steam engines, the *Sirius* and the *Great Western*, steamed from England to New York. Although the *Sirius* left a few days earlier, the *Great Western*—shown here arriving in New York harbor—almost caught up with it, arriving just four hours after the *Sirius*. This race inaugurated regular transatlantic steamship service.    (Courtesy of the Mariners' Museum, Newport News, VA)

railroad construction in the mid-1840s in France and Prussia not only satisfied the long-standing need for transportation, but also stimulated the iron, machinery, and construction industries. In the 1850s and 1860s, the states of Germany also experienced an industrial boom.

### Communication over Wires

The advent of railroads coincided with the development of the **electric telegraph.** After the Italian scientist Alessandro Volta invented the battery in 1800, making it possible to produce an electric current, many inventors tried to apply electricity to communication. The first practical telegraphy systems were developed almost simultaneously in England and America. In England, Wheatstone and Cooke introduced a five-needle telegraph in 1837; it remained in use until the early twentieth century. That same year, the American Samuel Morse introduced a code of dots and dashes that could be transmitted with a single wire; in 1843, he erected a line between Washington and Baltimore.

By the late 1840s, telegraph wires were being strung throughout the eastern United States and western Europe. In 1851, the first submarine telegraph cable was laid across the English Channel from England to France; it was the beginning of a network that eventually enclosed the entire globe. The world was rapidly shrinking, to the applause of Europeans and Americans, for whom speed was a clear measure of progress. No longer were communications limited to the speed by which a ship could sail or a horse could gallop.

## THE IMPACT OF THE INDUSTRIAL REVOLUTION

Although inventions were the most visible aspect of the Industrial Revolution, many other changes in society, politics, and the economy took place. Early changes—smoky cities, slum neighborhoods, polluted water, child labor in mines and textile mills—were being alleviated by the mid-nineteenth century. But by then national or even international problems were replacing these local ones: business cycles, labor conflicts, and the transformation of entire regions into industrial landscapes.

## New Industrial Cities

The most dramatic environmental changes brought about by industrialization occurred in the towns. Never before had towns grown so fast. London, one of the largest cities in Europe in 1700 with 500,000 inhabitants, grew to 959,000 by 1800 and to 2,363,000 by 1850, by then the largest city in the world. Smaller towns grew even faster. Manchester's population increased eightfold in a century. Liverpool grew sixfold in the first sixty years of the nineteenth century. New York City, already 100,000 strong in 1815, reached 600,000 (including Brooklyn) in 1850. In some areas, towns merged and formed megalopolises, such as Greater London, the English Midlands, central Belgium, and the Ruhr district of Germany.

People who prospered greatly from industrialization poured their new wealth into fine new homes, churches, museums, and theaters. Yet by all accounts, the industrial cities grew much too fast. As poor migrants streamed in from the countryside, developers built cheap, shoddy row houses for them to rent. These tenements were dangerously overcrowded. Often, several families had to live in one small room. Town dwellers recently arrived from the country brought country ways with them. People threw their sewage and trash out the windows to be washed down the gutters in the streets. The poor kept pigs and chickens, the rich kept horses, and pedestrians stepped into the street at their own risk. Air pollution from burning coal got steadily worse. People drank water drawn from wells and rivers contaminated by sewage and industrial runoff. The River Irwell, which ran through Manchester, was, in the words of one visitor, "considerably less a river than a flood of liquid manure."[1] To the long list of preindustrial urban diseases such as smallpox, dysentery, and tuberculosis, industrialization added new ailments. Rickets, a bone disease caused by lack of sunshine, became endemic in dark and smoky industrial

cities. Steamships brought cholera from India, causing great epidemics that struck the poor neighborhoods especially hard. In the 1850s, when the average life expectancy in England was forty years, it was only twenty-four years in Manchester, and around seventeen years in Manchester's poorest neighborhoods, because of the high infant mortality. Shocking reports of slum life led to municipal reforms, such as garbage removal, water and sewage systems, and parks and schools. These measures began to alleviate the ills of urban life after the mid-nineteenth century.

## Rural Environments

Long before the Industrial Revolution began, practically no wilderness areas were left in Britain and very few in western Europe. Human activity had turned almost every exploitable piece of land into fields, pastures, or towns. The most serious problem was deforestation. People cut timber to build ships and houses, to heat homes, and to manufacture bricks, iron, glass, beer, bread, and many other items.

Americans transformed their environment even faster than Europeans did. Settlers viewed forests not as a valuable resource but as a hindrance to development. In their haste to "open up the West," pioneers felled trees and burned them, built houses and abandoned them when they moved on. The cultivation of cotton was especially harmful. Planters cut down forests, grew cotton for a few years until it depleted the soil, and then moved west, abandoning the land to scrub pines. The American idea of nature as an obstacle to be overcome and dominated persisted long after the entire continent was occupied.

To contemporaries, the new transportation systems brought the most obvious changes in rural life. Governments and private trusts built numerous roads. Canal building boomed in Britain, France, and the Low Countries in the late eighteenth century. Canals were marvels of construction, with deep cuts, tunnels, and even aqueducts that carried barges over rivers. They also were a sort of school where engineers learned skills they were able to apply to the next great transportation system: the railroads. They laid track across rolling country by

**Overcrowded London**    The French artist Gustave Doré depicted the tenements of industrial London where workers and their families lived. This drawing shows crowded and unsanitary row houses, each one room wide with tiny back yards, and a train steaming across a viaduct overhead.    (New York Public Library/Art Resource, NY)

cutting deeply into hillsides and erecting daringly long bridges of stone and iron across valleys. Soon, clanking trains pulled by puffing, smoke-belching locomotives were invading long-isolated districts.

Thus, in the century after industrialization began, the landscape of industrializing countries was transformed more rapidly than ever before. But the ecological changes, like the technological and economic changes that caused them, were only beginning.

## Working Conditions

Most industrial jobs were unskilled, repetitive, and boring. Factory work did not vary with the seasons or the time of day but began and ended by the clock. Workdays were long, there were few breaks, and foremen watched constantly. Workers who performed one simple task over and over had little sense of achievement or connection to the final product. Industrial accidents were common and could ruin a family.

Unlike even the poorest preindustrial farmer or artisan, factory workers had no control over their tools, jobs, or working hours.

Women workers were concentrated in textile mills, partly because of ancient traditions, partly because textile work required less strength than metalworking, construction, or hauling. On average, women earned one-third to one-half as much as men. Young unmarried women worked to support themselves or to save for marriage. Married women took factory jobs when their husbands were unable to support the family. Mothers of infants faced a hard choice: whether to leave their babies with wet nurses at great expense and danger or to bring them to the factory and keep them quiet with opiates. Rather than working together as family units, husbands and wives increasingly worked in different places.

Factory work was never the main occupation of working women. Most young women who sought paid employment in the early years of industrialization became domestic servants in spite of the low pay, drudgery, and risk of sexual abuse. Other women with small children tried hard to find work they could do at home, such as laundry, sewing, embroidery, millinery, or taking in lodgers.

Even with both parents working, poor families found it hard to make ends meet. As in preindustrial societies, parents thought children should contribute to their upkeep as soon as they were able to. The first generation of workers brought their children with them to the factories and mines as early as age five or six; they had little choice, since there were no public schools or day-care centers. Employers encouraged the practice and even hired orphans. They preferred children because they were cheaper and more docile than adults and were better able to tie broken threads or crawl under machines to sweep the dust. Mine operators used children to pull coal carts along the low passageways from the coal face to the mine shaft. In the mid-nineteenth century, when the British government began restricting child labor, mill owners increasingly recruited Irish immigrants.

American industry began on a somewhat different note than the British. When Francis Cabot Lowell built a cotton mill in Massachusetts, he deliberately hired the unmarried daughters of New England farmers, promising decent wages and housing in dormitories under careful moral supervision. Other manufacturers eager to combine profits with morality followed his example. But soon the profit motive won out, and manufacturers imposed longer hours, harsher working conditions, and lower wages. When the young women went on strike, the factory owners replaced them with Irish immigrant women willing to accept lower pay and worse conditions.

The rising demand for cotton and the abolition of the African slave trade in the United States in 1808 caused an increase in the price of slaves. As the "Cotton Kingdom" expanded, the number of slaves rose through natural increase, from 700,000 in the 1790s to 3,200,000 slaves by 1850. Similarly, Europe and North America's surging demand for tea and coffee prolonged slavery on sugar plantations in the West Indies and caused it to spread to the coffee-growing regions of southern Brazil. Slavery was part and parcel of the Industrial Revolution, just as much as child labor in Britain, the clothes that people wore, and the beverages they drank.

## Changes in Society

Industrialization accentuated the polarization of society and disparities of income. In Britain, the worst-off were those who clung to an obsolete skill or craft, such as handloom weavers in a time of power looms. Even by working more hours, they could not escape destitution.

The wages and standard of living of factory workers did not decline steadily like those of handloom weavers; they fluctuated wildly with the cycles of economic growth and contraction. During the war years 1792 to 1815, the poor suffered hardship when the price of food rose faster than wages. Then, in the 1820s, real wages and public health began to improve, as industrial production grew at over 3 percent a year, pulling the rest of the economy along. Prices fell so that even the poor could afford comfortable, washable cotton clothes.

Overall, the benefits of industrialization—cheaper food, clothing, and utensils—did not improve workers' standard of living until the 1850s. The real beneficiaries of the early Industrial Revolution were the entrepreneurs whose money came from manufacturing. Most were the sons of middling shopkeepers, craftsmen, or farmers who had a little capital to start a cotton-spinning or machine-building business. Many tried and some succeeded, largely by plowing their profits back into the business. A generation later, in the nineteenth century, some newly rich industrialists bought their way into high society. With industrialization also came a "cult of domesticity" that removed middle-class women from contact with the business world and left them responsible for the home, the servants, the education of children, and the family's social life.

# NEW ECONOMIC AND POLITICAL IDEAS

Changes as profound as the Industrial Revolution could not occur without political ferment and ideological conflict. So many other momentous events took place during those years—the American Revolution (1776–1783), the French Revolution (1789–1799), the Napoleonic Wars (1804–1815), the reactions and revolts that periodically swept over Europe after 1815—that we cannot neatly separate out the consequences of industrialization from the rest. But it is clear that the Industrial Revolution strengthened the ideas of laissez faire° and socialism and sparked workers' protests.

## Laissez Faire

The most celebrated exponent of **laissez faire** ("let them do") was Adam Smith (1723–1790), a Scottish economist. In *The Wealth of Nations* (1776), Smith argued that if individuals were allowed to seek their personal gain, the effect, as though guided by an "invisible hand," would be to increase the general welfare. Except to protect private property, the government should refrain from interfering in business; it should even allow duty-free trade with foreign countries.

Although it was true that governments at the

time were incompetent at regulating their national economies, it was becoming obvious that industrialization was not improving the general welfare but was for some causing great misery. Other thinkers blamed the workers' plight on the population boom, which outstripped the food supply and led to falling wages. The workers' poverty, they claimed, was as much a result of "natural law" as the wealth of successful businessmen, and the only way the working class could avoid mass famine was to delay marriage and practice self-restraint and sexual abstinence.

Laissez faire provided an ideological justification for a special kind of capitalism: banks, stock markets, and chartered companies allowed investors to obtain profits with reasonable risks but with much less government control and interference than in the past. But not everyone accepted the grim conclusions of the "dismal science," as economics was then known. Jeremy Bentham (1748–1832) believed that it was possible to maximize "the greatest happiness of the greatest number," if only a Parliament of enlightened reformers would study the social problems of the day and pass appropriate legislation; his philosophy became known as utilitarianism.

## Positivism and Utopian Socialism

Some French social thinkers, moved by sincere concern for the poor, offered a more radically new vision of a just civilization. Espousing a philosophy called **positivism,** the count of Saint-Simon (1760–1825) argued that the scientific method could solve social as well as technical problems. He recommended that the poor, guided by scientists and artists, form workers' communities under the protection of benevolent business leaders. These ideas found no following among workers, but they attracted the enthusiastic support of bankers and entrepreneurs, who were inspired by visions of railroads, canals, and other symbols of progress and invested their money accordingly.

Meanwhile, the **utopian° socialism** of Charles Fourier (1768–1837), who loathed capitalists, imagined an ideal society in which groups of sixteen

laissez faire (lay-say fair)

utopian (you-TOE-pee-uhn)

hundred workers would live in dormitories and work together on the land and in workshops where music, wine, and pastries would soften the hardships of labor. For this idea, critics called him "utopian"—a dreamer.

The person who came closest to creating a utopian community was the Englishman Robert Owen (1771–1858), a successful cotton manufacturer who believed that industry could provide prosperity for all. Conscience-stricken by the appalling plight of the workers, Owen took over the management of New Lanark, a mill town south of Glasgow. He improved the housing and added schools, a church, and other amenities. He also testified before Parliament against child labor and for government inspection of working conditions, thereby angering his fellow industrialists.

## Protests and Reforms

Workers benefited little from the ideas of these middle-class philosophers. Instead, they resisted the harsh working conditions in their own ways. They changed jobs frequently and were often absent, especially on Mondays. Periodically, workers rioted or went on strike. Such acts of resistance did nothing, however, to change the nature of industrial work. Not until workers learned to act together could they hope to have much influence.

Gradually, they formed benevolent societies and organizations to demand universal male suffrage and shorter workdays. In 1834, Robert Owen organized the Grand National Consolidated Trade Union to lobby for an eight-hour workday; it gained half a million members but failed a few months later in the face of government prosecution of trade union activities. The Chartist movement had more success, gathering petitions by the thousands to present to Parliament. Although Chartism collapsed in 1848, it left a legacy of labor organizing. Eventually, mass movements persuaded political leaders to look into the abuses of industrial life, despite the prevailing laissez-faire philosophy.

In the 1820s and 1830s, the British Parliament began investigating conditions in the factories and mines. The Factory Act of 1833 prohibited the employment of children under age nine in textile mills and limited the working hours of children between the ages of nine and eighteen. The Mines Act of 1842 prohibited the employment of all women and of boys under age ten underground. Several decades passed before the government appointed enough inspectors to enforce the new laws.

The British learned to seek reform through accommodation. On the European continent, in contrast, the revolutions of 1848 (see Chapter 19) revealed widespread discontent with repressive governments but failed to soften the hardships of industrialization.

## Emigration

Another response to growing population, rural crises, and business cycles was emigration. Many poor Irish emigrated to England in search of work in construction and factories. After the potato crop failed in Ireland in 1847–1848, one-quarter of the Irish population died in the resulting famine, and another quarter emigrated to England and America. On the European continent, the negative effects of economic downturns were tempered by the existence of small family farms to which urban workers could return when they were laid off, but vast numbers still left Europe in search of better opportunities in the Western Hemisphere.

The United States received approximately 600,000 European immigrants in the 1830s, 1.5 million in the 1840s, and then 2.5 million per decade until 1880. In the 1890s, an astonishing total of 5.2 million immigrants arrived. European immigration to Latin America also increased dramatically after 1880. Immigrants from Europe faced prejudice and discrimination from those who believed they threatened the well-being of native-born workers by accepting low wages, and they threatened national culture by resisting assimilation.

Asian immigration to the Western Hemisphere also increased after 1850. Between 1849 and 1875, approximately 570,000 Chinese immigrants arrived in the Americas, half in the United States. India also contributed more than a half-million immigrants to the Caribbean region. Asians faced more obstacles to immigration than did Europeans and were often victims of violence and more extreme forms of discrimination in the New World.

Despite discrimination, most immigrants were also motivated to assimilate. Many intellectuals and political leaders wondered if the evolving mix of culturally diverse populations could sustain a common citizenship. As a result, efforts were directed toward compelling immigrants to assimilate. They learned the language spoken in their adopted countries as fast as possible in order to improve their earning capacity.

Union movements and electoral politics in the hemisphere also felt the influence of new arrivals who aggressively sought to influence government and improve working conditions. Immigrants also introduced new languages, foods, and customs. Mutual benevolent societies and less formal ethnic associations pooled resources to help immigrants open businesses, aid the immigration of their relatives, or bury their family members, sometimes worsening the fears of the native-born that immigration posed a threat to national culture. They also established links with political movements, sometimes exchanging votes for favors.

# INDUSTRIALIZATION AND THE NONINDUSTRIAL WORLD

The spread of the Industrial Revolution in the early nineteenth century transformed the relations of western Europe and North America with the rest of the world. For most of the world, trade with the industrial countries meant exporting raw materials, not locally made handicraft products. However, new machines helped England defeat and humiliate China, and in Egypt and India cheap industrial imports, backed by the power of Great Britain, delayed industrialization for a century or more. In these three cases, we can discern the outlines of the Western domination that has characterized the history of the world since the late nineteenth century.

In January 1840 a shipyard in Britain launched a radically new ship. The *Nemesis* had an iron hull, a flat bottom that allowed it to navigate in shallow waters, and a steam engine to power it upriver and against the wind. The ship was heavily armed. In November it arrived off the coast of China. Though ships from Europe had been sailing to China for three hundred years, the *Nemesis* was the first

steam-powered iron gunboat seen in Asian waters. A Chinese observer noted: "Iron is employed to make it strong. The hull is painted black, weaver's shuttle fashion. On each side is a wheel, which by the use of coal fire is made to revolve as fast as a running horse. . . . At the vessel's head is a Marine God, and at the head, stern, and sides are cannon, which give it a terrific appearance. Steam vessels are a wonderful invention of foreigners, and are calculated to offer delight to many."[2]

Instead of offering delight, the *Nemesis* and other steam-powered warships that soon joined it steamed up the Chinese rivers, bombarded forts and cities, and transported troops and supplies from place to place along the coast and up rivers far more quickly than Chinese soldiers could move on foot. With this new weapon, Britain, a small island nation half a world away, was able to defeat the largest and most populated country in the world (see Chapter 22).

Egypt, strongly influenced by European ideas since the French invasion of 1798, began to industrialize in the early nineteenth century. The driving force was its ruler, Muhammad Ali (1769–1849), a man who was to play a major role in the history of not only Egypt but also the Middle East and East Africa (see Chapter 21). He wanted to build up the Egyptian economy and military in order to become less dependent on the Ottoman sultan, his nominal overlord. To do so, he imported advisers and technicians from Europe and built cotton mills, foundries, shipyards, weapons factories, and other industrial enterprises. To pay for all this, he made the peasants grow wheat and cotton, which the government bought at a low price and exported at a profit. He also imposed high tariffs on imported goods to force the pace of industrialization.

Muhammad Ali's efforts fell afoul of the British, who did not want a powerful country threatening to interrupt the flow of travelers and mail across Egypt, the shortest route between Europe and India. When Egypt went to war against the Ottoman Empire in 1839, Britain intervened and forced Muhammad Ali to eliminate all import duties in the name of free trade. Unprotected, Egypt's fledgling industries could not compete with the flood of cheap British products. Thereafter, Egypt exported raw cotton, imported manufactured goods, and became, in effect, an economic dependency of Britain.

**Steam Tractor in India**    Power machinery was introduced into India because of the abundance of skilled low-cost labor. In this scene, a steam tractor fords a shallow stream to the delight of onlookers. The towerlike construction on the right is probably a pier for a railroad bridge.    (Billie Love Historical Society)

Until the late eighteenth century, India had been the world's largest producer and exporter of cotton textiles, handmade by skilled spinners and weavers. The British East India Company took over large parts of India just as the Industrial Revolution was beginning in Britain (see Chapter 21). It allowed cheap British factory-made yarn and cloth to flood the Indian market duty-free, putting spinners and later handloom weavers out of work. Unlike Britain, India had no factories to which displaced handicraft workers could turn for work. Most of them became landless peasants, eking out a precarious living.

Like other tropical regions, India became an exporter of raw materials and an importer of British industrial goods. To hasten the process, British entrepreneurs and colonial officials introduced railroads into the subcontinent. The construction of India's railroad network began in the mid-1850s, along with coal mining to fuel the locomotives and the installation of telegraph lines to connect the major cities.

Some Indian entrepreneurs saw opportunities in the atmosphere of change that the British created. In 1854 the Bombay merchant Cowasjee Nanabhoy Davar imported an engineer, four skilled workers, and several textile machines from Britain and started India's first textile mill. This was the beginning of India's mechanized cotton industry. But despite many gifted entrepreneurs, India's industrialization proceeded at a snail's pace, for the government was in British hands and the British did nothing to encourage Indian industry.

The cases of Egypt, India, and China show how the demands of Western nations and the military advantage that industrialization gave them led them to interfere in the internal affairs of nonindustrial societies. As we shall see in Chapter 21, this was the start of a new age of Western dominance.

## CONCLUSION

The great change we call the Industrial Revolution began in Great Britain, a society that was open to innovation, commercial enterprise, and the cross-fertilization of science, technology, and business. New machines and processes in the cotton and iron industries were instrumental in launching the Industrial Revolution, but what made industrialization an ongoing phenomenon was a new source of energy, the steam engine.

In the period from 1760 to 1851 the new technologies of the Industrial Revolution greatly increased humans' power over nature. Goods could be manufactured in vast quantities at low cost. People and messages could travel at unprecedented speeds. Most important, humans gained access to the energy stored in coal and used it to power machinery and propel ships and trains faster than vehicles had ever traveled before. With their newfound power, humans turned woodland into farmland, dug canals and laid tracks, bridged rivers and cut through mountains, and covered the countryside with towns and cities.

The ability to command nature, far from benefiting everyone, increased the disparities between individuals and societies. Industrialization brought forth entrepreneurs—whether in the mills of England or on plantations in the American South—

with enormous power over their employees or slaves, a power that they found easy and profitable to abuse. Some people acquired great wealth; others lived in poverty and squalor. While middle-class women were restricted to caring for their homes and children, many working-class women had to leave home to earn wages in factories or as domestic servants. These changes in work and family life provoked intense debates among intellectuals. Some defended the disparities in the name of laissez faire; others criticized the injustices the industrialization brought. Society was slow to bring these abuses under control.

By the 1850s the Industrial Revolution had spread from Britain to western Europe and the United States, and its impact was being felt around the world. To make a product that was sold on every continent, the British cotton industry used African slaves, American land, British machines, and Irish workers. As we shall see in Chapter 24, this was the start of a new age of Western dominance.

## ■ Key Terms

| | |
|---|---|
| Industrial Revolution | Crystal Palace |
| agricultural revolution (eighteenth century) | steam engine |
| | James Watt |
| mass production | electric telegraph |
| Josiah Wedgwood | laissez faire |
| division of labor | positivism |
| mechanization | utopian socialism |

## ■ Suggested Reading

General works on the history of technology give pride of place to industrialization. For an optimistic overview, see Joel Mokyr, *The Lever of Riches: Technological Creativity and Economic Progress* (1990). Other important recent works include James McClellan III and Harold Dorn, *Science and Technology in World History* (1999); David Landes, *The Wealth and Poverty of Nations* (1998); and Ian Inkster, *Technology and Industrialization: Historical Case Studies and International Perspectives* (1998).

There is a rich literature on the British industrial revolution, beginning with T. S. Ashton's classic *The Industrial Revolution, 1760–1830,* published in 1948 and often reprinted.

The impact of industrialization on workers is the theme of E. P. Thompson's classic work, *The Making of the English Working Class* (1963), but see also E. R. Pike, *"Hard Times": Human Documents of the Industrial Revolution* (1966). The role of women is most ably revealed in Lynn Y. Weiner, *From Working Girl to Working Mother: The Female Labor Force in the United States, 1820–1980* (1985), and in Louise Tilly and Joan Scott, *Women, Work, and Family* (1978).

European industrialization is the subject of J. Goodman and K. Honeyman, *Gainful Pursuits: The Making of Industrial Europe: 1600–1914* (1988); John Harris, *Industrial Espionage and Technology Transfer: Britain and France in the Eighteenth Century* (1998); and David Landes, *The Unbound Prometheus: Technological Change and Industrial Development in Western Europe from 1750 to the Present* (1972). On the beginnings of American industrialization, see David Jeremy, *Artisans, Entrepreneurs and Machines: Essays on the Early Anglo-American Textile Industry, 1770–1840* (1998).

An excellent history of immigration is Walter Nagent, *Crossings: The Great Transatlantic Migrations, 1870–1914* (1992).

On the environmental impact of industrialization, see Richard Wilkinson, *Poverty and Progress: An Ecological Perspective on Economic Development* (1973), and Richard Tucker and John Richards, *Global Deforestation in the Nineteenth-Century World Economy* (1983).

The first book to treat industrialization as a global phenomenon is Peter Stearns, *The Industrial Revolution in World History* (1993); see also Louise Tilly's important article "Connections," *American Historical Review* (February 1994).

## ■ Notes

1. Quoted in Lewis Mumford, *The City in History* (New York: Harcourt Brace, 1961), 460.
2. *Nautilus Magazine* 12 (1843): 346.

# 21

# Africa, India, and the New British Empire, 1750–1870

CHAPTER OUTLINE

**Changes and Exchanges in Africa**
**India Under British Rule**
**Britain's Eastern Empire**
ENVIRONMENT AND TECHNOLOGY: Whaling

In 1782, Tipu Sultan inherited the throne of Mysore°, which his father had made the most powerful state in south India. The ambitious and talented new ruler also inherited a healthy distrust of the British East India Company's territorial ambitions. Before the company could invade Mysore, Tipu Sultan launched his own attack in 1785. He then sent an embassy to France in 1788 seeking an alliance against Britain. Neither of these ventures was immediately successful.

Not until a decade later did the French agree to a loose alliance with Tipu Sultan to challenge Britain's colonial and commercial supremacy in the Indian Ocean. General Napoleon Bonaparte invaded Egypt in 1798 to threaten British trade routes to India and hoped to use the alliance

---

**Mysore** (MY-sore)

with Tipu Sultan to drive the British out of India. The French invasion of Egypt went well enough at first, but a British naval blockade and the ravages of disease crippled the French force. When the French withdrew, another military adventurer, Muhammad Ali, commander of the Ottoman army in Egypt, took advantage of the situation to revitalize Egypt and expand its rule.

Meanwhile, Tipu's alliance with France did not protect him from the East India Company, whose military victory in 1792 deprived him of most of his seacoast. Tipu lost his life in 1799 while defending his capital against another British assault. Mysore was divided between the British and their Indian allies.

As these events illustrate, talented local leaders and European powers were both vying to expand their influence in South Asia and Africa between 1750 and 1870. Midway through that period, it was by no means clear who would gain the upper hand. Britain and France were as likely to fight each other as they were to fight any Asian or African state. In 1800, the two nations were engaged in their third major war for overseas supremacy since 1750. By 1870, however, Britain had gained a decisive advantage over France and had established commercial dominance in trade in Africa, the Indian Ocean, and East Asia. Moreover, Britain created a new colonial empire in the East.

As you read this chapter, ask yourself the following questions:

- Why were the British able to gain decisive advantages in distant lands?

- Why were Asians and Africans so divided, some choosing to cooperate with the Europeans while others resisted their advances?

- How important an advantage were Britain's weapons, ships, and economic motives?

- How much of the outcome was the result of advance planning, and how much was due to particular individuals or to chance?

# CHANGES AND EXCHANGES IN AFRICA

D uring the century before 1870, Africa underwent dynamic political changes and a great expansion of foreign trade. Indigenous African leaders as well as Middle Eastern and European imperialists built powerful new states or expanded old ones. As the continent's external slave trades to the Americas and to Islamic lands died slowly under British pressure, trade in goods such as palm oil, ivory, timber, and gold grew sharply. In return, Africans imported large quantities of machine-made textiles and firearms. These complex changes are best understood by looking at African regions separately.

## New African States

Internal forces produced clusters of new states in two parts of sub-Saharan Africa in the early nineteenth century (see Map 21.1). In the fertile coastlands of southeastern Africa (in modern South Africa), a serious drought at the beginning of the nineteenth century led to conflict for grazing and farming lands among the small, independent chiefdoms of the region. An upstart named Shaka emerged in 1818 as head of a new **Zulu** kingdom, whose military discipline and courage soon made them the most powerful and most feared fighters in southern Africa. Shaka's regiments raided his African neighbors, seized their

**Zulu in Battle Dress, 1838**   Elaborate costumes helped impress opponents with the Zulu's strength. Shown here are long-handled spears and thick leather shields. The stabbing spear is not shown.   (Killie Campbell Africana Library. Photo: Jane Taylor/Sonia Halliday Photographs)

cattle, and captured their women and children. To protect themselves from the Zulu, some neighboring Africans created their own states.

Although Shaka ruled for little more than a decade, he successfully instilled a new national identity into his newly conquered subjects. He grouped all the young people into regiments that lived together and were taught Zulu customs and fighting methods. At public festivals, regiments of young men and women paraded, danced, and pledged their loyalty to Shaka.

Meanwhile, Islamic reform movements were creating another powerful state in the savannas of West Africa. The reformers followed a classic Muslim pattern: a *jihad* (holy war) added new lands, spreading Islamic beliefs and laws among conquered people. The largest reform movement was led by Usuman dan Fodio° (1745–1817), whose armed supporters conquered and combined the older Hausa states into a new empire ruled by a caliph (sultan) in the city of Sokoto. The **Sokoto Caliphate** (1809–1906) was the largest state in West Africa since the fall of Songhai in the sixteenth century (see Chapter 12).

In addition to being a center of Islamic learning and reform, the Sokoto Caliphate became a center of slavery. Many captured in the wars were enslaved and put to work in the empire or sold away across the Sahara or the Atlantic.

## Modernization in Egypt and Ethiopia

In northeastern Africa, the ancient African states of Egypt and Ethiopia were undergoing a period of growth and **modernization.** Napoleon's invasion of Egypt ended in 1801, but the shock of this display of European strength and Egyptian weakness prompted **Muhammad Ali,** who eliminated his rivals and ruled Egypt from 1805 to 1848, to begin political, social, and economic reforms in that country.

As we saw in the last chapter, Muhammad Ali's central aim was to strengthen Egypt militarily by making use of European experts and technology. Despite the shattering of his imperial dreams by the British after 1839, by the end of Muhammad Ali's

reign in 1848, modernization was well rooted in Egypt. The trade with Europe had expanded by almost 600 percent, and a new class of educated Egyptians had begun to replace the old ruling aristocracy.

Ali's grandson Ismail° (r. 1863–1879) placed even more emphasis on Westernizing Egypt. "My country is no longer in Africa," Ismail declared, "it is in Europe."[1] A huge increase in cotton exports during the American Civil War helped finance a network of new irrigation canals, 800 miles (1,300 kilometers) of railroads, a modern postal service, and dazzling changes in the capital city of Cairo.

State building and reform also were under way in the ancient Christian kingdom of Ethiopia. Beginning in the 1840s, Ethiopian rulers purchased modern weapons from European sources and created strong armies loyal to the ruler. Emperor Téwodros° II (r. 1833–1868) and his successor, Yohannes° IV (r. 1872–1889), brought back under imperial rule large areas of ancient Ethiopia. When King Menelik of Shoa succeeded Yohannes as emperor in 1889, the merger of their separate realms created the modern boundaries of Ethiopia.

## European Penetration

France's long and difficult war to conquer the North African country of Algeria from 1830 to 1847 was a rare example of European use of force in Africa before 1870. More typical was the peaceful penetration of European explorers, missionaries, and traders.

Small expeditions of adventurous explorers, using their own funds or financed by private geographical societies, were seeking to uncover the mysteries of inner Africa that had eluded earlier Europeans. Many of the explorers sought to map the course of Africa's great rivers: the Niger, the Nile, and the Congo.

In contrast to these heavily financed expeditions with hundreds of African porters, the Scottish missionary David Livingstone (1813–1873) organized modest treks through southern and Central Africa to scout out locations for Christian missions. His several expeditions in southern and equatorial Africa

---

**Usuman dan Fodio** (OO-soo-mahn dahn FOH-dee-oh)

**Ismail** (is-MAH-eel)   **Téwodros** (tay-WOH-druhs)
**Yohannes** (yoh-HAHN-nehs)

## C H R O N O L O G Y

| | Africa | India | Empire |
|---|---|---|---|
| **1750** | | **1756** Black Hole of Calcutta | **1763** End of Seven Years War |
| | | **1765** East India Company (EIC) rule of Bengal begins | **1769–1778** Captain James Cook explores New Zealand and eastern Australia |
| | **1795** Britain seizes Cape Colony from Dutch | **1795** Britain seizes Ceylon from the Dutch | **1795** End of Dutch East India Company |
| **1800** | **1798** Napoleon invades Egypt | **1799** EIC defeats Mysore | |
| | **1805** Muhammad Ali seizes Egypt | | |
| | **1807–1808** Britain outlaws slave trade and takes over Sierra Leone | | **1808** Britain outlaws slave trade |
| | **1809** Sokoto Caliphate founded | | |
| | **1818** Shaka founds Zulu kingdom | **1818** EIC creates Bombay Presidency | |
| | **1821** Foundation of Republic of Liberia; Egypt takes control of Sudan | **1826** EIC annexes Assam and northern Burma | |
| | | **1828** Brahmo Samaj founded | |
| | **1830–1847** Algerians resist French takeover | | **1834** Britain abolishes slavery |
| | **1834** Britain abolishes slavery | | |
| | **1840** Omani sultan moves capital to Zanzibar | | |
| **1850** | | **1857–1858** Sepoy Rebellion leads to end of EIC rule and Mughal rule | |
| | **1867** End of Atlantic slave trade | | **1867** End of Atlantic slave trade |
| | | **1877** Queen Victoria becomes empress of India | **1877** Victoria becomes Empress of India |
| | | **1885** First Indian National Congress | |
| | **1889** Menelik unites modern Ethiopia | | |

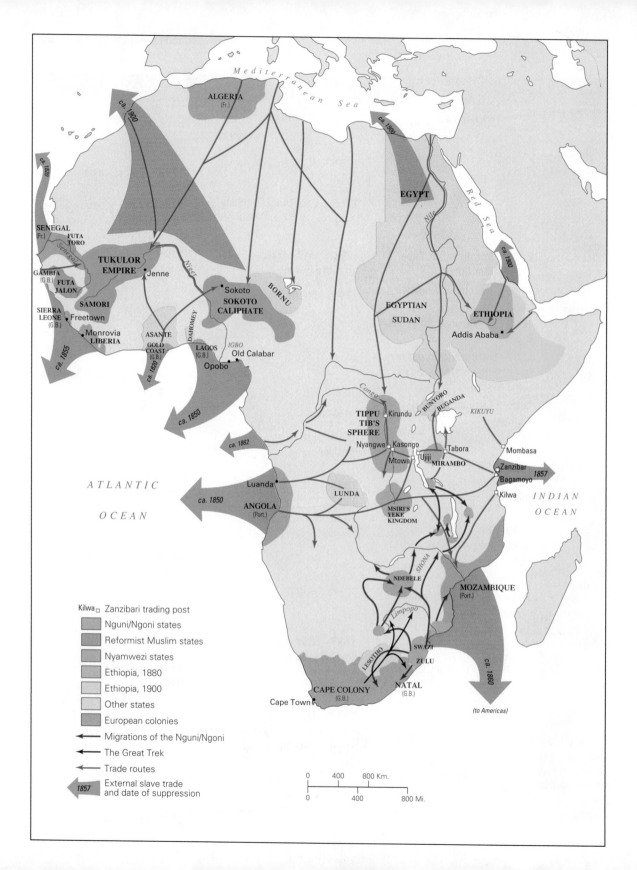

*Mediterranean Sea*

ALGERIA
(Fr.)

ca. 1900

EGYPT

*Red Sea*

ca. 1900

ca. 1820

SENEGAL
(Fr.)

FUTA
TORO

*Senegal*

TUKULOR
EMPIRE

Jenne

*Niger*

Sokoto

SOKOTO
CALIPHATE

BORNU

EGYPTIAN

SUDAN

*Nile*

ETHIOPIA

Addis Ababa

GAMBIA
(G.B.)

FUTA
JALON

SAMORI

SIERRA
LEONE
(G.B.)

Freetown

Monrovia
LIBERIA

ca. 1855

ASANTE

GOLD
COAST
(G.B.)

DAHOMEY

LAGOS
(G.B.)

*IGBO*

Old Calabar

Opobo

ca. 1820

ca. 1850

ca. 1862

*Congo*

TIPPU
TIB'S
SPHERE

Kirundu

BUNYORO

BUGANDA

*KIKUYU*

Nyangwe

Kasongo

Tabora

Mombasa

Mtowa

Ujiji

MIRAMBO

Zanzibar

Bagamoyo

*1857*

Kilwa

*INDIAN*

*OCEAN*

*ATLANTIC*

*OCEAN*

ca. 1850

Luanda

LUNDA

ANGOLA
(Port.)

MSIRI'S
YEKE
KINGDOM

*SHONA*

NDEBELE

MOZAMBIQUE
(Port.)

*Limpopo*

ca. 1860

LESOTHO

SWAZI

ZULU

CAPE COLONY
(G.B.)

NATAL
(G.B.)

Cape Town

*(to Americas)*

Kilwa ☐ Zanzibari trading post

Nguni/Ngoni states

Reformist Muslim states

Nyamwezi states

Ethiopia, 1880

Ethiopia, 1900

Other states

European colonies

← Migrations of the Nguni/Ngoni

← The Great Trek

← Trade routes

← *1857* External slave trade
and date of suppression

0    400    800 Km.

0    400    800 Mi.

made him a celebrity. In 1871, he was met by the Welsh-American journalist Henry Morton Stanley (1841–1904) on a publicity-motivated search for the "lost" missionary doctor. On an expedition from 1874 to 1877, Stanley descended the Congo River to its mouth.

The most significant European influence in Africa between 1750 and 1870 was commercial. No sooner was the mouth of the Niger River discovered in 1830 than eager entrepreneurs began to send expeditions up the river to scout out its potential for trade. The value of trade between Africa and the other Atlantic continents more than doubled between the 1730s and the 1780s, then doubled again by 1870.[2] Before about 1825, the slave trade accounted for most of that increase, but thereafter African exports of vegetable oils, gold, ivory, and other goods drove overseas trade to new heights.

As Chapter 19 recounted, the successful revolutions in the United States, France, Saint Domingue, and Latin America helped turn Western opinion against the slave trade and slavery. Once the world's greatest slave traders, the British became the most aggressive abolitionists. During the half-century after 1815, Britain spent some $60 million (£12 million) in its efforts to end the slave trade through naval patrols, a sum equal to the profits British slave traders had made in the fifty years before the trade was banned in 1807. Although British patrols captured 1,635 slave ships and liberated over 160,000 enslaved Africans, continued demand for slaves in Cuba and Brazil kept the trade going until 1867.

The demand for slaves in the Americas claimed the lives and endangered the safety of untold numbers of Africans, but the exchanges satisfied other Africans' desires for cloth, metals, and other goods. To continue their access to those imports after slavery was outlawed, Africans expanded their **"legitimate" trade** (exports other than slaves). The most successful of the new exports from West Africa was palm oil, a vegetable oil used by British manufacturers for soap, candles, and lubricants. From the mid-1830s, the trading states of the Niger Delta emerged as the premier exporters of palm oil. Coastal Africans there grew rich and used their wealth to buy large numbers of male slaves to paddle the giant dugout canoes that transported palm oil from inland markets along the narrow delta creeks to the trading ports.

Another effect of the suppression of the slave trade was the spread of Western cultural influences in West Africa. To serve as a base for their anti–slave trade naval squadron, in 1808 the British had taken over the small colony of Sierra Leone°. Over the next several years, 130,000 men, women, and children taken from "captured" vessels were liberated in Sierra Leone. Christian missionaries helped settle these impoverished and dispirited **recaptives** in and around Freetown, the capital. In time, the mission churches and schools made many willing converts among such men and women.

Sierra Leone's schools also produced a number of distinguished graduates. For example, Samuel Adjai Crowther (1808–1891), freed as a youth from a slave ship in 1821 by the British squadron, became the first Anglican bishop in West Africa in 1864, administering a pioneering diocese along the lower Niger River. James Africanus Horton (1835–1882), the son of a slave liberated in Sierra Leone, became a doctor and the author of many studies of West Africa.

Other Western cultural influences came from people of African birth or descent returning to their ancestral homeland in this era. In 1821, to the south of Sierra Leone, free black Americans began a settlement that grew into the Republic of Liberia, a place of liberty at a time when slavery was legal and flourishing in the United States. Free blacks from Brazil and Cuba chartered ships to return to their West African homelands, bringing with them Roman Catholicism, architectural motifs, and clothing fashions from the New World. Although the number of Africans exposed to Western culture in 1870 was still small, this influence grew rapidly.

**Map 21.1 Africa in the Nineteenth Century** Expanding internal and overseas trade drew much of Africa into global networks, but foreign colonies in 1870 were largely confined to Algeria and southern Africa. Growing trade, Islamic reform movements, and other internal forces created important new states throughout the continent.

**Sierra Leone** (see-ER-uh lee-OWN)

## Secondary Empires in Eastern Africa

When British patrols hampered the slave trade in West Africa, slavers moved southward and then around the tip of southern Africa to eastern Africa. There the Atlantic slave trade joined an existing trade in slaves to the Islamic world that also was expanding. Two-thirds of the 1.2 million slaves exported from eastern Africa in the nineteenth century went to markets in North Africa and the Middle East; the other third went to European plantations in the Americas and the Indian Ocean.

Slavery within eastern Africa also grew between 1800 and 1873, as Arab and Swahili owners purchased some 700,000 slaves from inland eastern Africa to do the labor-intensive work of harvesting cloves on plantations on Zanzibar Island and the neighboring coast. These territories belonged to the sultan of Oman, an Arabian kingdom on the Persian Gulf. The sultan moved his court to Zanzibar in 1840. Zanzibar also was an important market for ivory, most of which was shipped to India, where much of it was carved into decorative objects for middle-class Europeans.

Caravans led by African and Arab merchants brought ivory from hundreds of miles inland. Some of these merchants created large personal empires by using capital they had borrowed from Indian bankers and modern firearms they had bought from Europeans and Americans. These modern rifles felled countless elephants for their ivory tusks and inflicted widespread devastation and misery on the inland people.

One can blame the Zanzibari traders for the pillage and havoc in the once-peaceful center of Africa. However, the circle of responsibility was still broader. Europeans supplied the weapons used by the invaders and were major consumers of ivory and cloves. For this reason, histories have referred to the states carved out of eastern Africa as "secondary empires," in contrast to the empire that Britain was establishing directly. At the same time, Britain was working to bring the Indian Ocean slave trade to an end in eastern Africa. British officials pressured the sultan of Oman into halting the Indian Ocean slave trade from Zanzibar in 1857 and ending the import of slaves into Zanzibar in 1873.

# INDIA UNDER BRITISH RULE

The people of South Asia felt the impact of European commercial, cultural, and colonial expansion more immediately and profoundly than did the people of Africa. While Europeans were laying claim to only small parts of Africa between 1750 and 1870, nearly all of India (with three times the population of all of Africa) came under Britain's direct or indirect rule. After the founding of the East India Company in 1600, it took British interests 250 years to commandeer the colonies and trade of the Dutch, fight off French and Indian challenges, and pick up the pieces of the decaying Mughal° Empire. By 1763 the French were stymied, in 1795 the Dutch company was dissolved, and in 1858 the last Mughal emperor was dethroned, leaving the vast subcontinent in British hands.

## Company Men

As Mughal power weakened in the eighteenth century, British, Dutch, and French companies expanded into India (see Map 21.2). Such far-flung European trading companies were speculative and risky ventures. Their success depended on hard-drinking and ambitious young "Company Men," who used hard bargaining, and hard fighting when necessary, to persuade Indian rulers to allow them to establish trading posts at strategic points along the coast. To protect their fortified warehouses from attack by other Europeans or by native states, the companies hired and trained Indian troops known as **sepoys**°. In divided India, these private armies came to hold the balance of power.

In 1691, the East India Company (EIC) had convinced the **nawab**° (the term used for Mughal governors) of the large state of Bengal in northeast India to let the company establish a fortified outpost at the fishing port of Calcutta. A new nawab, pressing claims for additional tribute from the prospering port, overran the fort in 1756 and imprisoned a group of EIC men in a cell so small that many died of suffocation. To avenge their deaths in this "Black Hole of Calcutta," a large EIC force from Madras overthrew the nawab. The weak Mughal

---

**Mughal** (MOO-guhl)   **sepoy** (SEE-poy)   **nawab** (NAH-wab)

**Map 21.2   India, 1707–1805**   As Mughal power weakened during the eighteenth century, other Indian states and the British East India Company expanded their territories.

emperor was persuaded to acknowledge the EIC's right to rule Bengal in 1765. Fed by the tax revenues of Bengal as well as by profits from trade, the EIC was on its way. Calcutta grew into a city of 250,000 by 1788.

In southern India, EIC forces secured victory for the British Indian candidate for nawab of Arcot during the Seven Years War, thereby gaining an advantage over French traders who had supported the loser. The defeat of Tipu Sultan of Mysore at the end of the century (described at the start of the chapter) secured south India for the company and prevented a French resurgence.

Along with Calcutta and Madras, the third major center of British power in India was Bombay, on the western coast. There, after a long conflict with Indian rulers, the EIC gained a decisive advantage in 1818, annexing large territories to form the core of what was called the "Bombay Presidency." Some states were taken over completely, as Bengal had been, but very many others remained in the hands of local princes who accepted the political control of the company.

## Raj and Rebellion, 1818–1857

In 1818, the EIC controlled an empire with more people than in all of western Europe and fifty times the population of the colonies the British had lost in North America. One thrust of **British raj** (reign) was to remake India on a British model through administrative and social reform, economic development, and the introduction of new technology. But at the same time, the Company Men—like the Mughals before them—had to temper their interference with Indian social and religious customs lest they provoke rebellion or lose the support of their Indian princely allies. For this reason and because of the complexity of the task of ruling such a vast empire, there were many inconsistencies in Britain's policies toward India.

The main policy was to create a powerful and efficient system of government. British rule before 1850 relied heavily on military power—170 sepoy regiments and 16 European regiments. Another policy was to disarm approximately 2 million warriors who had served India's many states and turn them to civilian tasks, mostly cultivation. A third policy gave freer rein to Christian missionaries eager to convert and uplift India's masses. Few converts were made, but the missionaries kept up steady pressure for social reforms.

Another key British policy was to turn India's complex and overlapping patterns of landholding into private property. In Bengal, this reform worked to the advantage of large landowners, but

in Mysore, the peasantry gained. Private ownership made it easier for the state to collect the taxes that were needed to pay for the costs of administration, the army, and economic reform.

Such policies of "Westernization, Anglicization, and modernization," as they have been called, were only one side of British rule. The other side was the bolstering of "traditions"—both real and newly invented. In the name of tradition, the Indian princes who ruled nearly half of British India were permitted by their British overlords to expand their power, splendor, and tenure well beyond what their predecessors had ever had. The British rulers themselves invented many "traditions"—including elaborate parades and displays—half borrowed from European royal pomp, half freely improvised from Mughal ceremonies.

The British and Indian elites danced sometimes in close partnership, sometimes in apparent opposition. But the ordinary people of India—women of every status, members of subordinate Hindu castes, the "untouchables" and "tribals" outside the caste system, and the poor generally—found less benefit in the British reforms and much new oppression in the new taxes and "traditions."

The transformation of British India's economy was also doubled-edged. On the one hand, British raj created many new jobs as a result of the growth of internal and external trade and the expansion of agricultural production, such as in opium in Bengal (largely for export to China), coffee in Ceylon (an island off the tip of India), and tea in Assam (a state in northeastern India). On the other hand, competition from cheap cotton goods produced in Britain's industrial mills drove many Indians out of the handicraft textile industry. In the eighteenth century, India had been the world's greatest exporter of cotton textiles; in the nineteenth century, India increasingly shipped raw cotton fiber to Britain.

Even the beneficial economic changes introduced under British rule were disruptive, and there were no safety nets for the needy. Thus, local rebellions by displaced ruling elites, disgruntled religious traditionalists, and the economically dispossessed were almost constant during the first half of the nineteenth century. The greatest concern was over the continuing loyalty of Indian sepoys in the EIC's army.

Discontent was growing among Indian soldiers. In the early decades of EIC rule, most sepoys came from Bengal, one of the first states the company had annexed. The Bengali sepoys resented the active recruitment of other ethnic groups into the army after 1848, such as Sikhs° from Punjab and Gurkhas from Nepal. Many high-caste Hindus objected to a new law in 1856 requiring new recruits to be available for service overseas in the growing Indian Ocean empire, for their religion prohibited ocean travel. The replacement of the standard military musket by the far more accurate Enfield rifle in 1857 also caused problems. Soldiers were ordered to use their teeth to tear open the ammunition cartridges, which were greased with animal fat. Hindus were offended by this order if the fat came from cattle, which they considered sacred. Muslims were offended if the fat came from pigs, which they considered unclean.

Although the cartridge-opening procedure was quickly changed, the initial discontent grew into rebellion by Hindu sepoys in May 1857. British troubles mushroomed when Muslim sepoys, peasants, and discontented elites joined in. The rebels asserted old traditions to challenge British authority: sepoy officers in Delhi proclaimed their loyalty to the Mughal emperor; others rallied behind the Maratha leader Nana Sahib. The rebellion was put down by March 1858, but it shook this piecemeal empire to its core.

Historians have attached different names and meanings to the events of 1857 and 1858. Concentrating on the technical fact that the uprising was an unlawful action by soldiers, nineteenth-century British historians labeled it the **"Sepoy Rebellion"** or the "Mutiny," and these names are still commonly used. Seeing in these events the beginnings of the later movement for independence, some modern Indian historians have termed it the "Revolution of 1857." In reality, it was much more than a simple mutiny, because it involved more than soldiers, but it was not yet a nationalist revolution, for the rebels' sense of a common Indian national identity was weak.

**Sikh** (seek)

## Political Reform and Industrial Impact

Whatever it is called, the rebellion of 1857–1858 was a turning point in the history of modern India. In its wake, Indians gained a new centralized government, entered a period of rapid economic growth, and began to develop a new national consciousness.

The changes in government were immediate. In 1858, Britain eliminated the last traces of Mughal and EIC rule. In their place, a new secretary of state for India in London oversaw Indian policy, and a new governor-general in Delhi acted as the British monarch's viceroy on the spot. A proclamation by Queen Victoria in November 1858 guaranteed all Indians equal protection of the law and the freedom to practice their religions and social customs; it also assured Indian princes that so long as they were loyal to the queen, British India would respect their control of territories and "their rights, dignity and honour."[3]

A powerful and efficient bureaucracy controlled the Indian masses. Members of the elite **Indian Civil Service** (ICS), mostly graduates of Oxford and Cambridge Universities, held the senior administrative and judicial posts. Only a thousand men at the end of the nineteenth century, they visited the villages in their districts, heard lawsuits and complaints, and passed judgments. Beneath them were a far greater number of Indian officials and employees. Recruitment into the ICS was by open examination given only in England and thus inaccessible to most Indians. In 1870, only one Indian was a member of the ICS. Subsequent reforms led to fifty-seven Indian appointments by 1887, but there the process stalled.

A second transformation of India after 1857 resulted from involvement with industrial Britain. The government invested millions of pounds sterling in harbors, cities, irrigation canals, and other public works. British interests felled forests to make way for tea plantations, persuaded Indian farmers to grow cotton and jute for export, and created great irrigation systems to alleviate the famines that periodically decimated whole provinces. As a result, India's trade expanded rapidly.

Most of the exports were agricultural commodities for processing elsewhere: cotton fiber, opium,

**Delhi Durbar, January 1, 1903**    The parade of Indian princes on ornately decorated elephants and accompanied by retainers fostered their sense of belonging to the vast empire of India that British rule had created. The durbar was meant to evoke the glories of India's earlier empires, but many of the details and ceremonies were nineteenth-century creations.    (British Empire and Commonwealth Museum, Bristol, UK/The Bridgeman Art Library)

tea, silk, and sugar. In return, India imported manufactured goods from Britain, including the flood of machine-made cotton textiles that severely undercut Indian handloom weavers. The effects on individual Indians varied enormously. Some women found new jobs, though at very low pay, on plantations or in the growing cities, where prostitution flourished. Others struggled to hold families together or ran away from abusive husbands. Everywhere in India, poverty remained the norm.

The Indian government also promoted the introduction of new technologies into India not long after their appearance in Britain. Earlier in the century, there were steamboats on the rivers and a massive program of canal building for irrigation. Beginning in the 1840s, a railroad boom (paid for out of government revenues) gave India its first na-

tional transportation network, followed shortly by telegraph lines. Indeed, in 1870, India had the greatest rail network in Asia and the fourth largest in the world.

The freer movement of Indians and rapid urban growth promoted the spread of cholera°, a disease transmitted through water contaminated by human feces. In 1867, officials demonstrated the close connection between cholera and pilgrims who bathed in and drank from sacred pools and rivers. The installation of a new sewerage system (1865) and a filtered water supply (1869) in Calcutta dramatically reduced cholera deaths there. Similar measures in Bombay and Madras also led to great reductions, but most Indians lived in small

**cholera** (KAHL-uhr-uh)

**Indian Railroad Station, 1866**   British India built the largest network of railroads in Asia. People of every social class traveled by train.   (Eyre and Hobbs House Art Gallery)

villages, where famine and lack of sanitation kept cholera deaths high. Only after 1900 did sanitary improvements lower the death rate from cholera.

## Rising Indian Nationalism

Both the successes and the failures of British rule stimulated the development of Indian nationalism. The failure of the rebellion of 1857 led some thoughtful Indians to argue that the only way to regain control of their destiny was to reduce their country's social and ethnic divisions.

Individuals such as Rammohun Roy (1772–1833) had promoted pan-Indian nationalism a generation earlier. A Western-educated Bengali from a Brahmin family, Roy was a successful ad-ministrator for the EIC and a thoughtful student of comparative religion. His Brahmo Samaj° (Divine Society), founded in 1828, attracted Indians who sought to reconcile the values they found in the West with the ancient religious traditions of India. They backed the British outlawing of widow burning (*sati*°) in 1829 and of slavery in 1843 and sought to correct other abuses of women and female infanticide. Roy and his followers advocated reforming the caste system and urged a return to the founding principles set out in the Upanishads, ancient sacred writings of Hinduism.

Although Brahmo Samaj remained an influential movement, a growing number of Indian intellectuals based their nationalism on the secular

**Brahmo Samaj** (BRAH-moh suh-MAHJ    *sati* (suh-TEE)

values they absorbed in Western schools. European and American missionaries played a prominent role in the spread of Western education. In 1870, there were 790,000 Indians in over 24,000 elementary and secondary schools, and India's three universities (established in 1857) awarded 345 degrees.

Many of the new nationalists came from the Indian middle class. Hoping to increase their influence and improve their employment opportunities in the Indian government, they convened the first **Indian National Congress** in 1885. The members sought a larger role for Indians in the civil service and called for more money to be spent on alleviating the poverty of the Indian masses. The Indian National Congress effectively voiced the opinions of elite, Western-educated Indians, but it would need the support of the masses to challenge British rule.

# BRITAIN'S EASTERN EMPIRE

In 1750 Britain's empire was centered on slave-based plantation and settler colonies in the Americas. A century later its main focus was on commercial networks and colonies in the East. In 1750 the French and Dutch were also serious contenders for global dominion. A century later they had been eclipsed by the British colossus that was straddling the world.

Several distinct changes facilitated the expansion and transformation of Britain's overseas empire. A string of military victories pushed aside other rivals for overseas trade and colonies; new policies favored free trade over mercantilism; and changes in shipbuilding techniques increased the speed and volume of maritime commerce. Linked to these changes were new European settlements in southern Africa, Australia, and New Zealand and the growth of a new long-distance trade in indentured labor.

**Colonies and Commerce**

As the story of Tipu Sultan told at the beginning of this chapter illustrates, France was still a serious rival for dominion in the Indian Ocean at the end of the eighteenth century. However, defeats in the wars of the French Revolu-

tion (see Chapter 19) ended Napoleon's dream of restoring French dominance overseas. The wars also dismantled much of the Netherlands' Indian Ocean empire. When French armies occupied the Netherlands, the Dutch ruler, who had fled to Britain in January 1795, authorized the British to take over Dutch possessions overseas in order to keep them out of French hands. During 1795 and 1796 British forces quickly occupied the Cape Colony at the tip of southern Africa, the strategic Dutch port of Malacca on the strait between the Indian Ocean and the South China Sea, and the island of Ceylon (modern Sri Lanka).

Then the British occupied Dutch Guiana and Trinidad in the southern Caribbean. In 1811 they even seized the island of Java, the center of the Netherlands' East Indian empire. British forces had also attacked French possessions, gaining control of the islands of Mauritius and Réunion in the southwestern Indian Ocean. At the end of the Napoleonic Wars in 1814, Britain returned Java to the Dutch and Réunion to the French but kept the Cape Colony, British Guiana (once part of Dutch Guiana), Trinidad, Ceylon, Malacca, and Mauritius.

The Cape Colony was valuable because of Cape Town's strategic importance as a supply station for ships making the long voyages between Britain and India. With the port city came some twenty thousand descendants of earlier Dutch and French settlers who occupied far-flung farms and ranches in its hinterland. Despite their European origins, these people thought of themselves as permanent residents of Africa and were beginning to refer to themselves as "Afrikaners" ("Africans" in their dialect of Dutch). British governors prohibited any expansion of the white settler frontier because such expansion invariably led to wars with indigenous Africans. This decision, along with the imposition of laws protecting African rights within Cape Colony (including the emancipation of slaves in 1834), alienated many Afrikaners.

Between 1836 and 1839 parties of Afrikaners embarked on a "Great Trek," leaving British-ruled Cape Colony for the fertile high *veld* (plateau) to the north that two decades of Zulu wars had depopulated. The Great Trek led to the foundation of three new settler colonies in southern Africa by 1850: the Afrikaners' Orange Free State and Transvaal on the high veld and the British colony of Na-

**Great Trek Aided by African Servants**  The ox-drawn wagons of the Afrikaners struggled over the Drakensberg Mountains to the high plains in an effort to escape British control.  (Liaison/Getty Images)

tal on the Indian Ocean coast. Although firearms enabled the settlers to win some important battles against the Zulu and other Africans, they were still a tiny minority surrounded by the populous and powerful independent African kingdoms that had grown up at the beginning of the century. A few thousand British settlers came to Natal and the Cape Colony by midcentury, but these colonies were important to Britain only as stopovers between Britain and British India.

Meanwhile, another strategic British outpost was being established in Southeast Asia. One prong of the advance was led by Thomas Stamford Raffles, who had governed Java during the period of British occupation from 1811 to 1814. After Java's return to the Dutch, Raffles helped the British East India Company establish a new free port at Singapore in 1824, on the site of a small Malay fishing village with a superb harbor. By attracting British

merchants and Chinese businessmen and laborers, Singapore soon became the center of trade and shipping between the Indian Ocean and China. Along with Malacca and other possessions on the strait, Singapore formed the "Straits Settlements," which British India administered until 1867.

Further British expansion in Malaya (now Malaysia) did not occur until after 1874, but it came more quickly in neighboring Burma. Burma had emerged as a powerful kingdom by 1750, with plans for expansion. In 1785 Burma tried to annex neighboring territories of Siam (now Thailand) to the east, but a coalition of Thai leaders thwarted Burmese advances by 1802. Burma next attacked Assam to the west, but this action led to war with British India, which was concerned for the security of its own frontier with Assam. After a two-year war, India annexed Assam in 1826 and occupied two coastal provinces of northern Burma. As rice and timber trade from these provinces grew important, the occupation became permanent, and in 1852 British India annexed the port of Rangoon and the rest of coastal Burma.

## Imperial Policies and Shipping

Through such piecemeal acquisitions, by 1870 Britain had added several dozen colonies to the twenty-six colonies it had in 1792, after the loss of the thirteen in North America (see Chapter 19). Nevertheless, historians usually portray Britain in this period as a reluctant empire builder, its leaders unwilling to acquire new outposts that could prove difficult and expensive to administer. This apparent contradiction is resolved by the recognition that the underlying goal of most British imperial expansion during these decades was trade rather than territory. Most of the new colonies were meant to serve as ports in the growing network of shipping that encircled the globe or as centers of production and distribution for those networks.

This new commercial expansion was closely tied to the needs of Britain's growing industrial economy and reflected a new philosophy of overseas trade. Rather than rebuilding the closed, mercantilist network of trade with its colonies, Britain sought to trade freely with all parts of the world. Free trade was also a wise policy in light of the independence of so many former colonies in the Americas (see Chapter 19).

Whether colonized or not, more and more African, Asian, and Pacific lands were being drawn into the commercial networks created by British expansion and industrialization. As was pointed out earlier, uncolonized parts of West Africa became major exporters to Britain of vegetable oils for industrial and domestic use and of forest products for dyes and construction, while areas of eastern Africa free of European control exported ivory that ended up as piano keys and decorations in the elegant homes of the industrial middle class. From the far corners of the world came coffee, cocoa, and tea (along with sugar to sweeten them) for the tables of the new industrial classes in Britain and other parts of Europe, and indigo dyes and cotton fibers for their expanding textile factories.

In return, the factories of the industrialized nations supplied manufactured goods at very attractive prices. By the mid-nineteenth century a major part of their textile production was destined for overseas markets. Sales of cotton cloth to Africa increased 950 percent from the 1820s to the 1860s. British trade to India grew 350 percent between 1841 and 1870, while India's exports increased 400 percent. Trade with other regions also expanded rapidly. In most cases such trade benefited both sides, but there is no question that the industrial nations were the dominant partners.

A second impetus to global commercial expansion was the technological revolution in the construction of oceangoing ships under way in the nineteenth century. The middle decades of the century were the golden age of the sailing ship. Using iron to fasten timbers together permitted shipbuilders to construct much larger vessels. Merchant ships in the eighteenth century rarely exceeded 300 tons, but after 1850 swift American-built **clipper ships** of 2,000 tons were commonplace in the British merchant fleet. Huge canvas sails hung from tall masts made the streamlined clippers faster than earlier vessels. Ships from the East Indies or India had taken six months to reach Europe in the seventeenth century; after 1850 the new ships could complete the voyage in half that time.

This increase in size and speed lowered shipping costs and further stimulated maritime trade. The growth in size and numbers of ships increased the tonnage of British merchant shipping by 400 percent between 1778 and 1860. To extend the life of such ships in tropical lands, clippers intended for Eastern service generally were built of teak and other tropical hardwoods from new British colonies in South and Southeast Asia. Although tropical forests began to be cleared for rice and sugar plantations as well as for timbers, the effects on the environment and people of Southeast Asia came primarily after 1870.

## Colonization of Australia and New Zealand

The development of new ships and shipping contributed to a third form of British rule in the once-remote South Pacific. Rather than rule indigenous populations, as they did in India, or set up commercial outposts, as they did in Singapore and Cape Town, British settlers displaced indigenous populations in the new colonies of Australia and New Zealand, just as they had done in North America.

Portuguese mariners had sighted the continent of Australia in the early seventeenth century, but it was too remote to be of much interest to Europeans. However, after the English adventurer Captain James Cook systematically explored New Zealand and the fertile eastern coast of Australia between 1769 and 1778, expanding shipping networks brought in growing numbers of visitors and settlers.

At the time of Cook's visits Australia was the home of about 650,000 hunting-and-gathering people, whose Melanesian° ancestors had settled there some forty thousand years earlier. The two islands of New Zealand, lying 1,000 miles (1,600 kilometers) southeast of Australia, were inhabited by about 250,000 Maori°, who practiced hunting, fishing, and simple forms of agriculture, which their Polynesian ancestors had introduced around 1200 C.E. Because of their long isolation from the rest of humanity, the populations of Australia and New Zealand were as vulnerable as the Amerindians had been to unfamiliar diseases introduced by new overseas contacts. In the 1890s only 93,000 aboriginal Australians and 42,000 Maori had survived the

---

**Melanesian** (mel-uh-NEE-zhuhn)   **Maori** (MOW-ree [*ow* as in *cow*])

exposure to Europeans. By then, British settler populations had come to outnumber and dominate the indigenous peoples.

The first permanent British settlers in Australia were 736 convicts, of whom 188 were women, sent into exile from British prisons in 1788. Over the next few decades, Australian penal colonies grew slowly and had only slight contact with the indigenous population, whom the British called "Aborigines." However, the discovery of gold in 1851 brought a flood of free European settlers (and some Chinese) and hastened the end of the penal colonies. When the gold rush subsided, government subsidies enabled tens of thousands of British settlers to settle "down under." Improved sailing ships made possible a voyage halfway around the world, although it still took more than three months to reach Australia from Britain. By 1860 Australia had a million immigrants, and the settler population doubled during the next fifteen years.

British settlers were drawn more slowly to New Zealand. Some of the first were temporary residents along the coast who slaughtered seals and exported seal pelts to Western countries to be made into men's felt hats. A single ship in 1806 took away sixty thousand sealskins. By the early 1820s overhunting had nearly exterminated the seal population. Special ships also hunted sperm whales extensively near New Zealand for their oil, used for lubrication, soap, and lamps; ambergris°, an ingredient in perfume; and bone, used in women's corsets (see Environment and Technology: Whaling). Military action that overcame Maori resistance, a brief gold rush, and the availability of faster ships and subsidized passages attracted more British immigrants after 1860. The colony especially courted women immigrants to offset the preponderance of single men. By the early 1880s the fertile agricultural lands of this most distant frontier of the British Empire had a settler population of 500,000.

Britain encouraged the settlers in Australia and New Zealand to become self-governing, following the 1867 model that had formed the giant Dominion of Canada out of the very diverse and thinly settled colonies of British North America. In

**ambergris** (AM-ber-grees)

1901 a unified Australia emerged from the federation of six separate colonies. New Zealand became a self-governing dominion in 1907.

Britain's policies toward its settler colonies in Canada and the South Pacific reflected a desire to avoid the conflicts that had led to the American Revolution in the eighteenth century. By gradually turning over governing power to the colonies' inhabitants, Britain accomplished three things. It satisfied the settlers' desire for greater control over their own territories; it muted demands for independence; and it made the colonial governments responsible for most of their own expenses. Indigenous peoples were outvoted by the settlers or even excluded from voting.

North American patterns also shaped the indigenous peoples' fate. An 1897 Australian law segregated the remaining Aborigines onto reservations, where they lacked the rights of Australian citizenship. The requirement that voters had to be able to read and write English kept Maori from voting in early New Zealand elections, but four seats in the lower house of the legislature were reserved for Maori from 1867 on.

In other ways the new settler colonies were more progressive. Australia developed very powerful trade unions, which improved the welfare of skilled and semiskilled urban white male workers, promoted democratic values, and exercised considerable political clout. In New Zealand, where sheep raising was the main occupation, populist and progressive sentiments promoted the availability of land for the common person. Australia and New Zealand were also among the first states in the world to grant women the right to vote, beginning in 1894.

## New Labor Migrations

Europeans were not the only people to transplant themselves overseas in the mid-nineteenth century. Between 1834 and 1870 many thousands of Indians, Chinese, and Africans responded to labor recruiters, especially to work overseas on sugar plantations. In the half-century after 1870 tens of thousands of Asians and Pacific Islanders made similar voyages.

In part these migrations were linked to the end of slavery. After their emancipation in British

# ENVIRONMENT + TECHNOLOGY

## Whaling

The rapid expansion of whaling aptly illustrates the growing power of technology over nature in this period. Many contemporaries, like many people today, were sickened by the killing of the planet's largest living mammals. American novelist Herman Melville captured the conflicting sentiments in his epic whaling story, *Moby Dick* (1851). One of his characters enthusiastically explains why the grisly and dangerous business existed:

> But, though the world scorns us as whale hunters, yet does it unwittingly pay us the profoundest homage; yea, an all abounding adoration! for almost all the tapers, lamps, and candles that burn around the globe, burn, as before so many shrines, to our glory!

Melville's character overstates the degree to which whale oil dominated illumination and does not mention its many other industrial uses. Neither does he describe the commercial importance of whalebone (baleen). For a time its use in corsets allowed fashionable women to achieve the hourglass shape that fashion dictated. Whalebone's use for umbrella stays, carriage springs, fishing rods, suitcase frames, combs, brushes, and many other items made it the plastic of its day.

New manufacturing technologies went hand in hand with new hunting technologies. The revolution in ship design enabled whalers from Europe and North America to extend the hunt into the southern oceans off New Zealand. By the nineteenth century whaling ships were armed with guns that shot a steel harpoon armed with vicious barbs deep into the whale. In the 1840s explosive charges on harpoon heads ensured the whale's immediate death. Yet, as this engraving of an expedition off New Zealand shows, flinging small harpoons from rowboats in the open sea continued to be part of the dangerous work.

Another century of extensive hunting devastated many whale species before international agreements finally limited the killing of these giant sea creatures.

---

colonies in 1834, the freed men and women were no longer willing to put in the long hours they had been forced to work as slaves. When given full freedom of movement, many left the plantations. To compete successfully with sugar plantations in Cuba, Brazil, and the French Caribbean that were still using slave labor, British colonies had to recruit new laborers.

India's impoverished people seemed one obvious alternative. After planters on Mauritius successfully introduced Indian laborers, the Indian labor trade moved to the British Caribbean in 1838. In 1841 the British government also allowed Caribbean planters to recruit Africans whom British patrols had rescued from slave ships and liberated in Sierra Leone and elsewhere. By 1870 nearly 40,000 Africans had settled in British colonies, along with over 500,000 Indians and over 18,000 Chinese. Af-

ter the French and Dutch abolished slavery in 1848, their colonies also recruited over 150,000 new laborers from Asia and Africa.

Slavery was not abolished in Cuba until 1886, but the rising cost of slaves led the burgeoning sugar plantations to recruit 138,000 new laborers from China between 1847 and 1873. Indentured labor recruits also became the mainstay of new sugar plantations in places that had never known slave labor. After 1850 American planters in Hawaii recruited labor from China and Japan; British planters in Natal recruited from India; and those in Queensland (in northeastern Australia) relied on laborers from neighboring South Pacific islands.

Larger, faster ships made transporting laborers halfway around the world affordable, though voyages from Asia to the Caribbean still took an average of three months. Despite close regulation and

**South Pacific Whaling**   One boat was swamped, but the hunters killed the huge whale.
(The Granger Collection, New York)

supervision of shipboard conditions, the crowded accommodations encouraged the spread of cholera and other contagious diseases that took many migrants' lives.

All of these laborers served under **contracts of indenture,** which bound them to work for a specified period (usually from five to seven years) in return for free passage to their overseas destination. They were paid a small salary and were provided with housing, clothing, and medical care. Indian indentured laborers also received the right to a free passage home if they worked a second five-year contract. British Caribbean colonies required forty women to be recruited for every hundred men as a way to promote family life. So many Indians chose to stay in Mauritius, Trinidad, British Guiana, and Fiji that they constituted a third or more of the total population of these colonies by the early twentieth century.

Although many early recruits from China and the Pacific Islands were kidnapped or otherwise coerced into leaving their homes, in most cases the new indentured migrants had much in common with contemporary emigrants from Europe (described in Chapter 20). Both groups chose to leave their homelands in hopes of improving their economic and social conditions. Both earned modest salaries. Many saved to bring money back when they returned home, or they used their earnings to buy land or to start a business in their new countries, where large numbers chose to remain. One major difference was that people recruited as indentured laborers were generally so much poorer than emigrants from Europe that they had to accept lower-paying jobs in less desirable areas because they could not pay their own way. However, it is also true that many European immigrants into distant places like Australia and New Zealand had their passages subsidized but did not have to sign a contract of indenture. This shows that racial and cultural preferences, not just economics, shaped the flow of labor into European colonies.

A person's decision to accept an indentured labor contract could also be shaped by political circumstances. In India disruption brought by British colonial policies and the suppression of the 1857 rebellion contributed significantly to people's desire to emigrate. Poverty, famine, and warfare had not been strangers in precolonial India. Nor were these causes of emigration absent in China and Japan.

The indentured labor trade reflected the unequal commercial and industrial power of the West, but it was not an entirely one-sided creation. The men and women who signed indentured contracts were trying to improve their lives by emigrating, and many succeeded. Whether for good or ill, more and more of the world's peoples saw their lives being influenced by the existence of Western colonies, Western ships, and Western markets.

# CONCLUSION

What is the global significance of these complex political and economic changes in southern Asia, Africa, and the South Pacific? One perspective stresses the continuing exploitation of the weak by the strong, of African, Asian, and Pacific peoples by aggressive Europeans. In this view, the emergence of Britain as a dominant power in the Indian Ocean basin and South Pacific continued the European expansion that the Portuguese and the Spanish pioneered and the Dutch took over. Likewise, Britain's control over the densely populated lands of South and Southeast Asia and over the less populated lands of Australia and New Zealand can be seen as a continuation of the conquest and colonization of the Americas.

From another perspective what was most important about this period was not the political and military strength of the Europeans but their growing domination of the world's commerce, especially through long-distance ocean shipping. In this view, the British, like other Europeans, were drawn to Africa and southern Asia by a desire to obtain new materials.

However, Britain's commercial expansion in the nineteenth century was also the product of Easterners' demand for industrial manufactures. The growing exchanges could be mutually beneficial. African and Asian consumers found industrially produced goods far cheaper and sometimes better than the handicrafts they replaced or supplemented. Industrialization created new markets for African and Asian goods, as in the case of the vegetable-oil trade in West Africa or of cotton in Egypt and India. There were also negative impacts, as in the case of the weavers of India and the damage to species of seals and whales.

Europeans' military and commercial strength did not reduce Africa, Asia, and the Pacific to mere appendages of Europe. While the balance of power shifted in the Europeans' favor between 1750 and 1870, other cultures were still vibrant and local initiatives often dominant. Islamic reform movements and the rise of the Zulu nation had greater significance for their respective regions of Africa than did Western forces. Despite some ominous concessions to European power, Southeast Asians were still largely in control of their own destinies. Even in India, most people's lives and beliefs showed more continuity with the past than with the changes caused by British rule.

Finally, it must not be imagined that Asians and Africans were powerless in dealing with European expansion. The Indian princes who extracted concessions from the British in return for their cooperation and the Indians who rebelled against the raj both forced the system to accommodate their needs. Moreover, some Asians and Africans were beginning to use European education, technology, and methods to transform their own societies. Leaders in Egypt, India, and other lands, like those in Russia, the Ottoman Empire, and China—the subject of Chapter 22—were learning to challenge the power of the West on its own terms. In 1870 no one could say how long and how difficult that learning process would be, but Africans and Asians would continue to shape their own futures.

## ■ Key Terms

| | |
|---|---|
| Zulu | nawab |
| Sokoto Caliphate | British raj |
| modernization | Sepoy Rebellion |
| Muhammad Ali | Indian Civil Service |
| "legitimate" trade | Indian National Congress |
| recaptives | clipper ship |
| sepoys | contract of indenture |

## ■ Suggested Reading

Volumes 2 and 3 of *The Oxford History of the British Empire,* edited by William Roger Louis, (1998, 1999), are the most up-to-date global surveys of this period. Less Anglo-centric in its interpretation is Immanuel Wallerstein's *The Modern World-System III: The Second Era of Great Expansion of the Capitalist World-Economy, 1730–1840s* (1989).

For more on African topics, see Roland Oliver and Anthony Atmore, *Africa Since 1800,* 4th ed. (1994); J. D. Omer-Cooper, *The Zulu Aftermath* (1966); Murray Last, *The Sokoto Caliphate* (1967); A. G. Hopkins, *An Economic History of West Africa* (1973); and Norman R. Bennett, *Arab Versus European: War and Diplomacy in Nineteenth Century East Central Africa* (1985).

Very readable introductions to India in this period are Sugata Bose and Ayeshia Jalal, *Modern South India* (1998); Burton Stein, *A History of India* (1998); and Stanley Wolpert, *A New History of India,* 6th ed. (1999). See also Daniel Headrick, *The Tentacles of Progress: Technology Transfer in the Age of Imperialism, 1850–1940* (1988).

A good introduction to the complexities of Southeast Asian history is D. R. SarDesai, *Southeast Asia: Past and Present,* 2nd ed. (1989). More detail can be found in the appropriate chapters of Nicholas Tarling, ed., *The Cambridge History of South East Asia,* 2 vols. (1992). The second and third volumes of *The Oxford History of Australia,* ed. Geoffrey Bolton (1992, 1988), deal with the period covered by this chapter. A very readable multicultural and gendered perspective is provided by *Images of Australia,* ed. Gillian Whitlock and David Carter (1992). *The Oxford Illustrated History of New Zealand,* ed. Keith Sinclair (1990), provides a wide-ranging introduction to that nation.

For summaries of recent scholarship on the indentured labor trade see David Northrup, *Indentured Labor in the Age of Imperialism, 1834-1922* (1995), and Robin Cohen, ed., *The Cambridge Survey of World Migration,* part 3, "Asian Indentured and Colonial Migration" (1995).

An outstanding analysis of British whaling is Gordon Jackson's *The British Whaling Trade* (1978). Edouard A. Stackpole's *Whales & Destiny: The Rivalry Between America, France, and Britain for Control of the Southern Whale Fishery, 1785-1825* (1972) is more anecdotal.

## ■ Notes

1. Quoted in P. J. Vatikiotis, *The History of Modern Egypt: From Muhammad Ali to Mubarak,* 4th ed. (Baltimore: Johns Hopkins University Press, 1991), 74.
2. David Eltis, "Precolonial Western Africa and the Atlantic Economy," in *Slavery and the Rise of the Atlantic Economy,* ed. Barbara Solow (New York: Cambridge University Press, 1991), table 1.
3. Quoted by Bernard S. Cohn, "Representing Authority in Victorian England," in *The Invention of Tradition,* ed. Eric Hobsbawm and Terence Ranger (Cambridge: Cambridge University Press, 1983), 165.

# 22 Land Empires in the Age of Imperialism, 1800–1870

## CHAPTER OUTLINE

The Ottoman Empire

The Russian Empire

The Qing Empire

DIVERSITY AND DOMINANCE: The French Occupation of Egypt

When the emperor of the Qing° (the last empire to rule China) died in 1799, the imperial court received a shock. For decades officials had known that the emperor was indulging his handsome young favorite, Heshen°, allowing him extraordinary privileges and power. Senior bureaucrats hated Heshen, suspecting him of overseeing a widespread network of corruption. They believed he had been scheming to prolong the inconclusive wars against the native Miao° peoples of southwest China in the late 1700s. Glowing reports of successes against the rebels had poured into the capital, and enormous sums of government money had flowed to the battlefields. But there was no adequate accounting for the funds, and the war persisted.

After the emperor's death, Heshen's enemies ordered his arrest. When they searched his mansion, they discovered a magnificent hoard of silk, furs, porcelain, furniture, and gold and silver. His personal cash alone exceeded what remained in the imperial treasury. The new emperor ordered Heshen to commit suicide with a rope of gold silk. The government seized Heshen's fortune, but the financial damage could not be undone. The declining agricultural base could not replenish the state coffers, and much of the income that did flow in was squandered by an increasingly corrupt bureaucracy. In the 1800s the Qing Empire faced increasing challenges from Europe and the United States with an empty treasury, a stagnant economy, and a troubled society.

The Qing Empire's problems were not unique. They were common to all the land-based empires

---

**Qing** (ching)   **Heshen** (huh-shun)   **Miao** (mee-ow)

518

of Eurasia, where old and inefficient ways of governing put states at risk. The international climate was increasingly dominated by industrializing European economies drawing on the wealth of their overseas colonies. During the early 1800s rapid population growth and slow agricultural growth affected much of Eurasia. Earlier military expansion had stretched the resources of imperial treasuries (see Chapter 18), leaving the land-based empires vulnerable to European military pressure. Responses to this pressure varied, with reform and adaptation gaining headway in some lands and tradition being reasserted in others. In the long run, attempts to meet western Europe's economic and political demands produced financial indebtedness to France, Britain, and other Western powers.

This chapter contrasts the experiences of the Qing Empire with those of the Russian and Ottoman Empires. Whereas the Qing opted for resistance, the others made varying attempts to adapt and reform. Russia eventually became part of Europe and shared in many aspects of European culture, while the Ottomans and the Qing became subject to ever-greater imperialist pressure. These different responses raise the question of the role of culture in shaping western Europe's relations with the rest of the world in the nineteenth century.

As you read this chapter, ask yourself the following questions:

- Why did the Ottoman and Qing Empires find themselves on the defensive in their encounters with Europeans in the 1800s?

- By what strategies did the land-based empires try to adapt to nineteenth-century economic and political conditions?

- How did the Russian Empire maintain its status as both a European power and a great Asian land empire?

# THE OTTOMAN EMPIRE

During the eighteenth century the central government of the Ottoman Empire lost much of its power to provincial governors, military commanders, ethnic leaders, and bandit chiefs. In several parts of the empire local officials and large landholders tried to increase their independence and divert imperial funds into their own coffers.

A kingdom in Arabia led by the Saud family, following the puritanical and fundamentalist religious views of an eighteenth-century leader named Muhammad ibn Abd al-Wahhab°, took control of the holy cities of Mecca and Medina and deprived the sultan of the honor of organizing the annual pilgrimage. In Egypt factions of mamluk slave-soldiers reemerged as political forces for the first time since the Ottoman conquest in 1517.

For the sultans, the outlook was bleak. The inefficient Janissary corps used the political power it enjoyed in Istanbul to force Sultan Selim III to abandon efforts to train a modern, European-style army at the end of the eighteenth century. This situation unexpectedly changed when France invaded Egypt.

## Egypt and the Napoleonic Example, 1798–1840

Napoleon Bonaparte and an invasion force of 36,000 men and four hundred ships invaded Egypt in May 1798 (see Diversity and Dominance: The French Occupation of Egypt). The French quickly defeated the mamluk forces that for several decades had dominated the country under the loose jurisdiction of the Ottoman sultan in Istanbul. Fifteen months later, after being stopped by Ottoman land and British naval forces in an attempted invasion of Syria, Napoleon secretly left Cairo and returned to France. Three months later he seized power and made himself emperor.

Back in Egypt, his generals tried to administer a country that they only poorly understood. Cut off from France by British ships in the Mediterranean, they had little hope of remaining in power and

**Muhammad ibn Abd al-Wahhab** (Moo-HAH-muhd ib-uhn ab-dahl-wa HAHB)

agreed to withdraw in 1801. For the second time in three years, a collapse of military power produced a power vacuum in Egypt. The winner of the ensuing contest was **Muhammad Ali°,** the commander of a contingent of Albanian soldiers sent by the sultan to restore imperial control. By 1805 he had taken the place of the official Ottoman governor, and by 1811 he had dispossessed the mamluks of their lands and privileges.

Muhammad Ali's rise to power coincided with the meteoric career of Emperor Napoleon I. It is not surprising, therefore, that he adopted many French practices in rebuilding the Egyptian state. Militarily, he established special schools for training artillery and cavalry officers, army surgeons, military bandmasters, and others. The curricula of these schools featured European skills and sciences, and Muhammad Ali began to send promising officer trainees to France for education. In 1824 he started a gazette devoted to official affairs, the first newspaper in the Islamic world.

As discussed in Chapter 20, Muhammad Ali built all sorts of factories to outfit his new army. These did not prove efficient enough to survive, but they showed a determination to achieve independence and parity with the European powers.

In the 1830s Muhammad Ali's son Ibrahim invaded Syria and instituted some of the changes already under way in Egypt. The improved quality of the new Egyptian army had been proven during the Greek war of independence (see below), when Ibrahim had commanded an expeditionary force to help the sultan. In response, the sultan embarked on building his own new army in 1826. The two armies met when Ibrahim attacked northward into Anatolia in 1839 and defeated the army of his suzerain, the Ottoman sultan. The road to Istanbul seemed open until the European powers intervened and forced a withdrawal to the present-day border between Egypt and Israel.

Muhammad Ali remained Egypt's ruler, under the suzerainty of the sultan, until his death in 1849; and his family continued to rule the country until 1952. But his dream of making Egypt a mighty country capable of standing up to Europe faded. What survived was the example he had set for the sultans in Istanbul.

## Ottoman Reform and the European Model, 1807–1853

At the end of the eighteenth century Sultan Selim° III (r. 1789–1807), a forward-looking ruler who stayed abreast of events in Europe, introduced reforms to create European-style military units, bring provincial governors under central government control, and standardize taxation. These reforms failed for political, more than economic, reasons.

The most violent and persistent opposition came from the **Janissary°** military corps (see Chapter 17). In the eighteenth century the Janissaries became a significant political force in Istanbul and in provincial capitals like Baghdad. At times, Janissary power produced military uprisings. In the Ottoman territory of **Serbia,** local residents intensely resented the control exercised by Janissary governors. The Orthodox Christians claimed that the Janissaries abused them. In response, Selim threatened to reassign the Janissaries to Istanbul. Suspecting that the sultan wanted to curb their political power, in 1805 the Janissaries revolted and massacred Christians in Serbia. Unable to reestablish central Ottoman rule over Serbia, the sultan had to rely on the ruler of Bosnia, another Balkan province, who joined his troops with the peasants of Serbia to suppress the Janissary uprising. The threat of Russian intervention prevented the Ottomans from disarming the victorious Serbians, so Serbia became effectively independent.

In the face of widespread rejection of his reforms, Selim suspended his program in 1806. Nevertheless, a massive military uprising occurred at Istanbul, and the sultan was deposed and imprisoned. Reform forces recaptured the capital, but not before Selim had been executed. Selim's cousin, Sultan Mahmud° II (r. 1808–1839), cautiously revived Selim's program, but he realized that reforms needed to be more systematic and imposed more forcefully. The effectiveness of radical reform in Muhammad Ali's Egypt drove this lesson home, as did the insurrection in Greece, during which the Egyptian military performed much better than the main Ottoman army.

---

**Muhammad Ali** (moo-HAM-mad AH-lee)

**Selim** (seh-LEEM)    **Janissary** (JAN-nih-say-ree)
**Mahmud** (MAH-mood)

| C H R O N O L O G Y | | |
|---|---|---|
| **Ottoman Empire** | **Russian Empire** | **Qing Empire** |

**1800**

|  |  | **1794–1804**  White Lotus Rebellion |
|---|---|---|
|  | **1801–1825**  Reign of Alexander I |  |
| **1805–1849**  Muhammad Ali governs Egypt |  |  |
| **1808–1839**  Rule of Mahmud II |  |  |
|  | **1812**  Napoleon's retreat from Moscow |  |
|  | **1825**  Decembrist revolt |  |
|  | **1825–1855**  Reign of Nicholas I |  |
| **1826**  Janissary corps dissolved |  |  |
| **1829**  Greek independence |  |  |
| **1839**  Abdul Mejid begins Tanzimat reforms |  | **1839–1842**  Opium War |

**1850**

| **1853–1856**  Crimean War | **1853–1856**  Crimean War | **1850–1864**  Taiping Rebellion |
|---|---|---|
|  | **1855–1881**  Reign of Alexander II | **1856–1860**  Arrow War |
|  | **1861**  Emancipation of the serfs |  |
| **1876**  First constitution by an Islamic government |  |  |

파운드폭탄 4발 투하… 두 아들과 함께 사망

...실진지 구축… 이틀째 시가戰

령이 대중 앞에 나타나거나 애국심  라크 전
을 고취하는 노래만을 내보내던 방  외에서는
송마저 중단됐다.  영국 주

# DIVERSITY AND DOMINANCE

## THE FRENCH OCCUPATION OF EGYPT

*Napoleon's invasion of Egypt in 1798 strikingly illustrates the techniques of dominance employed by the French imperial power and the means of resistance available to noncombatant Egyptian intellectuals in reasserting their cultural diversity and independence. Abd al-Rahman al-Jabarti (1753–1826), from whose writings the first four passages are drawn, came from a family of ulama, or Muslim religious scholars. His three works concerning the French occupation, which lasted until 1801, provide the best Egyptian account of that period. The selections below start with the first half of Napoleon's first proclamation to the Egyptian people, which was published in Arabic at the time of the invasion and is quoted here from al-Jabarti's text.*

In the Name of God the Compassionate the Merciful: There is no god but God. He has not begotten a son, and does not share in His Kingship.

On behalf of the French Republic, which is founded upon the principles of liberty and equality, the Commander-in-Chief of the French armies, the great head-general Bonaparte, hereby declares to all inhabitants of Egyptian lands that the Sanjaqid rulers of Egypt [i.e., the Mamluk commanders] have persisted far too long in their maltreatment and humiliation of the French nation and have unjustly subjected French merchants to all manner of abuse and extortion. The hour of their punishment has now come.

It is a great pity that this group of slave fighters [mamluks], caught in the mountains of Abkhazia and Georgia, have for such a long time perpetrated so much corruption in the fairest of all lands on the face of the globe. Now, the omnipotent Lord of the Universe has ordained their demise.

O people of Egypt, should they say to you that I have only come hither to defile your religion, this is but an utter lie that you must not believe. Say to my accusers that I have only come to rescue your rights from the hands of tyrants, and that I am a better servant of God—may He be praised and exalted—and that I revere His Prophet Muhammad and the grand Koran more than the group of slave fighters do.

Tell them also that all people stand equally before God and that reason, virtue, and knowledge comprise the only distinguishing qualities among them. Now, what do the group of slave fighters possess of reason, virtue, and knowledge that would distinguish them from the rest of the people and qualify them exclusively to benefit from everything that is desirable in this worldly life?

The most fertile of all agricultural lands, the prettiest concubines, the best horses, and most attractive residences, all are appropriated exclusively by them. If the land of Egypt was ever conferred upon this group of slave fighters exclusively, let them show us the document that God has written for them: of course, the Lord of the Universe acts with compassion and equity toward mankind. With His help—may He be Exalted—from this day on no Egyptian shall be excluded from high positions nor barred from acquiring high ranks, and men of reason, virtue and learning from among them will administer the affairs, and as a result the welfare of the entire Muslim community (*umma*) shall improve.

*The following passages provide examples of al-Jabarti's line-by-line commentary on the proclamation and two examples of his more general comments on the French and on French rule.*

Explanation of the wretched proclamation composed of incoherent words and vulgar phrases:

By saying, "in the Name of God the Compassionate the Merciful: There is no god but God. He has not begotten a son, and does not share in His Kingship" [the French] implicitly claim in three propositions that they concur with the three religions [Islam, Christianity, and Judaism] whereas in truth they falsify all three and indeed any other [viable] doctrine. They concur with the Muslims in opening [the statement] with the name of God and in rejecting His begetting a son or sharing in His Kingship. They differ from them in not professing the two essential Articles of Faith: refusing to recognize Prophet Muhammad, and rebuffing the essential teachings of Islam in word and deed. They concur with the Christians in most of what they say and do, but diverge over the question of Trinity, in their rejection of the vocation [of Christ], and furthermore in rebuffing their beliefs and rituals, killing the priests, and desecrating places of worship. They concur with the Jews in believing in one God, as the Jews also do not believe in the Trinity but hold on to anthropomorphism. [The French Republicans] do not share in the religious beliefs and practices of the Jews either. Apparently they do not follow any particular religion and do not adhere to a set of specific rituals: each of them fathoms a religion as it suits his own reason. The rest of the [people of France] are Christians but keep it hidden, and there are some real Jews among them as well. However, even those who may follow a religion, when they come to Egypt, they concur with the agents of the Republic in their insistence upon leading the Egyptians astray.

Their saying "On behalf of the French Republic, etc." implies that the proclamation comes from the Republic or their people directly, because unlike other nations they have no overlord or sovereign whom they unanimously appoint, and who has exclusive authority to speak on their behalf. It is now six years since they revolted against their sovereign and murdered him. Subsequently, the people agreed not to have a single ruler but rather to put the affairs of the government, provincial issues, legislation and administration, into the hands of men of discretion and reason among themselves. They chose and appointed men in a hierarchy: a head of the entire army followed in rank by generals and military commanders each in charge of groups of a thousand, two hundred, or ten men. They similarly appointed administrators and advisers by observing their essential equality and nonsupremacy of one over the others, in the same way that people are created equally in essence. This constitutes the foundation and touchstone of their system, and this is what "founded upon the principles of liberty and equality" means. The reference to "liberty" implies that unlike

the slaves and [the slave fighters ruling over Egypt] they are not anybody's slaves; the meaning of "equality" has already been explained.

[On that day the French] started to operate a new court bureau, which they named the Ad hoc Court (*mahkamat al-qadaya*). On this occasion they drafted a decree that included clauses framed in most unacceptable terms that sounded rather repellant to the ear. Six Copts and six Muslim merchants were appointed to the bureau, and the presiding judge and chief of the bureau was the Copt from Malta who used to work as secretary to Ayyub Bey, the notary (*daftardar*). Ad hoc cases involving commercial, civil, inheritance disputes, and other suits were referred to this bureau. [The French] formulated corrupt principles for this institution that were based on heresy, founded in tyranny, and rooted in all sorts of abominable unprecedented rulings (*bid'a al-sayyi'a*).

[The French] devastated the palace of Yusuf Salah al-Din including the cities where sovereigns and sultans held audiences, and they tore down strong foundations and demolished towering columns. They also destroyed mosques, meditation spots (*zawaya*), and shrines of martyrs (*mashahid*). They defaced the Grand Congregational Mosque, built by the venerable Muhammad b. Qalawan al-Malik al-Nasir: wrecked the pulpit, spoiled the mosque's courtyard, looted its lumber, undermined its columns, and razed the well-wrought iron enclosure inside of which the sultan used to pray.

*The final passage, which is not in any of al-Jabarti's chronicles, is the full text of an announcement distributed to Napoleon's thirty-six thousand troops on board ship as they headed for Egypt.*

Soldiers,—You are about to undertake a conquest the effects of which on civilization and commerce are incalculable. The blow you are about to give to England will be the best aimed, and the most sensibly felt, she can receive until the time arrive when you can give her her death-blow.

We must make some fatiguing marches; we must fight several battles; we shall succeed in all we undertake. The destinies are with us. The Mameluke Beys, who favour exclusively English commerce, whose extortions oppress our merchants, and who tyrannise over the unfortunate inhabitants of the Nile, a few days after our arrival will no longer exist.

The people amongst whom we are going to live are Mahometans. The first article of their faith is this: "there is no God but God, and Mahomet is His prophet." Do not contradict them. Behave to them as you have behaved to the Jews—to the Italians. Pay respect to their muftis [jurists], and their Imaums [sic], as you did to the rabbis and the bishops. Extend to the ceremonies prescribed by the Koran and to the mosques the same toleration which you showed to the synagogues, to the religion of Moses and of Jesus Christ.

The Roman legions protected all religions. You will find here customs different from those of Europe. You must accommodate yourselves to them. The people amongst whom we are to mix differ from us in the treatment of women; but in all countries he who violates is a monster. Pillage enriches only a small number of men; it dishonours us; it destroys our resources; it converts into enemies the people whom it is our interest to have for friends.

The first town we shall come to was built by Alexander. At every step we shall meet with grand recollections, worthy of exciting the emulations of Frenchmen. Bonaparte

## QUESTIONS FOR ANALYSIS

1. Why are the reasons for invading Egypt given to the French soldiers different from those announced to the Egyptians?

2. How do Napoleon and al-Jabarti use religious feeling as a political tool?

3. What do texts like these suggest about the role culture plays in confrontations between imperial powers and imperialized peoples?

*Source*: First selection from *Abd al-Rahman al-Jabarti's History of Egypt*, ed. Thomas Phillipp and Moshe Perlmann (Stuttgart, 1994), translated by Hossein Kamaly. Second selection from Louis Antoine Fauvelet de Bourrienne, *Memoirs of Napoleon Bonaparte* (1843).

Greek independence in 1829 had dramatic international significance. A combination of Greek nationalist organizations and interlopers from Albania formed the independence movement. Europe's interest in the classical age of Greece and Rome led many Europeans to consider the Greeks' struggle for independence a campaign to recapture their classical glory from Muslim oppression. Some—including the "mad, bad and dangerous to know" English poet Lord Byron, who lost his life in the war—went to Greece to fight as volunteers. When the combined squadrons of the British, French, and Russian fleets, under orders to observe but not intervene in the war, made an unauthorized attack that sank the Ottoman fleet at the Battle of Navarino, Greek victory was assured (see Map 22.1).

Mahmud II concurred with the pro-Greek Europeans in viewing Ottoman military reversals in Greece as a sign of profound weakness. With popular outrage over the military setbacks strong, the sultan made his move in 1826. First he announced the creation of a new artillery unit, which he had

secretly been training. When the Janissaries rose in revolt, he ordered the new unit to bombard the Janissary barracks. The Janissary corps was officially dissolved.

Like Muhammad Ali, Mahmud felt he could not implement major changes without reducing the political power of the religious elite. He visualized restructuring the bureaucracy and the educational and legal systems, where ulama power was strongest. Before such strong measures could be undertaken, however, Ibrahim attacked from Syria in 1839. Battlefield defeat, the decision of the rebuilt Ottoman navy to switch sides and support Egypt, and the death of Mahmud, all in the same year, left the empire completely dependent on the European powers for survival.

Mahmud's reforming ideas received their widest expression in the **Tanzimat**° ("reorganization"), a series of reforms announced by his sixteen-year-old son and successor, Abdul Mejid°, in 1839 and

**Tanzimat** (TAHNZ-ee-MAT)    **Abdul Mejid** (ab-dul meh-JEED)

**Map 22.1   The Ottoman and Russian Empires, 1829–1914**   At its height the Ottoman Empire controlled most of the perimeter of the Mediterranean Sea. But in the 1800s Ottoman territory shrank as many countries gained their independence. The Black Sea, where the Turkish coast was vulnerable to assault, became a weak spot as Russian naval power grew. Russian challenges to the Ottomans at the eastern end of the Black Sea and to the Persians east and west of the Caspian aroused fears in Europe that Russia was trying to reach the Indian Ocean.

strongly endorsed by the European ambassadors. One proclamation called for public trials and equal protection under the law for all, whether Muslim, Christian, or Jew. It also guaranteed some rights of privacy, equalized the eligibility of men for conscription into the army (a practice copied from Egypt), and provided for a new, formalized method of tax collection that legally ended tax farming in the Ottoman Empire. It took many years and strenuous efforts by reforming bureaucrats, known as the "men of the Tanzimat," to give substance to these reforms.

European observers praised the reforms for their noble principles and rejection of religious influence. Ottoman citizens were more divided; the Christians and Jews, for whom the Europeans showed the greatest concern, were generally more enthusiastic than the Muslims. Many historians see the Tanzimat as the dawn of modern thought and enlightened government in the

Middle East. Others point out that removing the religious elite from influence in government also removed the one remaining check on authoritarian rule.

Over time, one legal code after another—commercial, criminal, civil procedure—was introduced to take the place of the corresponding areas of religious legal jurisdiction. All the codes were modeled closely on those of Europe. The Shari'a, or Islamic law, gradually became restricted to matters of family law such as marriage and inheritance. As the Shari'a was displaced, job opportunities for the ulama shrank.

Like Muhammad Ali, Sultan Mahmud sent military cadets to France and the German states for training. In the 1830s an Ottoman imperial school of military sciences, later to become Istanbul University, was established. Instructors from western Europe taught chemistry, engineering, mathematics, and physics in addition to military history. Military education became the model for more general educational reforms. In 1838 the first medical school was established to train army doctors and surgeons. Later, a national system of preparatory schools was created to feed graduates into the military schools. The subjects that were taught and many of the teachers were foreign, raising the issue of whether Turkish should be a language of instruction. Because it was easier to import and use foreign textbooks than to write new ones in Turkish, French became the preferred language in all advanced professional and scientific training. In numerical terms, however, the great majority of students still learned to read and write in Quran schools down to the twentieth century.

In the capital city of Istanbul, the reforms stimulated the growth of a small but cosmopolitan milieu embracing European language and culture. The first Turkish newspaper, a government gazette modeled on that of Muhammad Ali, appeared in 1831. Other newspapers followed, many written in French. Travel to Europe—particularly to England and France—became popular among wealthy Turks. Interest in importing European military, industrial, and communications technology remained strong through the 1800s.

Changes in military practice had unforeseen cultural and social effects. Accepting the European notion that modern weapons and drill required modern military dress, beards were deemed unhygienic and, in artillery units, a fire hazard. Military headgear also became controversial. European military caps, which had leather bills on the front to protect against the glare of the sun, were not acceptable because they interfered with Muslim soldiers' touching their foreheads to the ground in prayer. The compromise was the brimless cap now called the *fez*, which was adopted by the military and then by Ottoman civil officials in the early years of Mahmud II's reign.

The empire's new orientation spread beyond the military. Government ministries that normally recruited from traditional bureaucratic families and relied on on-the-job training were gradually transformed into formal civil services hiring men educated in the new schools. Among self-consciously progressive men, particularly those in government service, European dress became the fashion in the Ottoman cities of the later 1800s. Traditional dress became a symbol of the religious, the rural, and the parochial.

Secularization of the legal code particularly affected non-Muslim Ottoman subjects. Islamic law had required non-Muslims to pay a special head tax that was sometimes explained as a substitute for military service. Under the Tanzimat, the tax was abolished and non-Muslims became liable for military service—unless they bought their way out by paying a new military exemption tax. The new law codes gave all male subjects equal access to the civil courts, while the operations of the Islamic law courts shrank. What enhanced the status of non-Muslims most, however, was the strong concern for their welfare consistently expressed by the European powers. The Ottoman Empire became a rich field of operation for Christian missionaries and European supporters of Jewish community life in the Muslim world.

The public rights and political participation granted during the Tanzimat applied specifically to men. Private life, including everything connected to marriage and divorce, remained within the sphere of religious law, and at no time was there a question of political participation or reformed education for women. Indeed, the reforms may have decreased the influence of women. The political changes ran parallel to economic changes that also narrowed women's opportunities.

After silver from the Americas began to flood the empire in the 1600s, workers were increasingly paid in cash rather than in goods, and businesses associated with banking and finance developed. But women were barred from the early industrial labor and the professions, and traditional "woman's work" such as weaving was increasingly mechanized and done by men.

Nevertheless, in the early 1800s women retained considerable power in the management and disposal of their own property, gained mostly through fixed shares of inheritance. After marriage a woman was often pressured to convert her landholdings to cash in order to transfer her personal wealth to her husband's family, with whom she and her husband would reside. However, this was not a requirement, since men were legally obligated to support their families single-handedly. Until the 1820s many wealthy women retained their say in the distribution of property through the creation of charitable trusts for their sons. Because these trusts were set up in the religious courts, they could be designed to conform to the wishes of family members. Then, in the 1820s and 1830s the secularizing reforms of Mahmud II, which did not always produce happy results, transferred jurisdiction over the charitable trusts from religious courts to the state and ended women's control over this form of property.

## The Crimean War and Its Aftermath, 1853–1877

Since the reign of Peter the Great (r. 1689–1725) the Russian Empire had been attempting to expand southward at the Ottomans' expense (see "Russia and Asia," below). By 1815 Russia had pried the Georgian region of the Caucasus away from the Ottomans, and the threat of Russian intervention had prevented the Ottomans from crushing Serbian independence. When Muhammad Ali's Egyptian army invaded Syria in 1833, Russia signed a treaty in support of the Ottomans. In return, the sultan recognized Russia's claim to being the protector of all of the empire's Orthodox subjects. This set the stage for an obscure dispute that resulted in war.

Bowing to British and French pressure, the sultan named France Protector of the Holy Sepulchre in Jerusalem in 1852. Russia protested, but the sultan held firm. So Russia invaded Ottoman territories in what is today Romania, and Britain and France went to war as allies of the sultan. The real causes of the war went beyond church quarrels in Jerusalem and involved diplomatic maneuvering among European powers over whether the Ottoman Empire should continue to exist and, if not, who should take over its territory. The Eastern Question was the simple name given to this complex issue. Though the powers, including Russia, had agreed to save the empire in 1839, Britain subsequently became suspicious of Russian ambitions. Prominent anti-Russian politicians in Britain feared that Russia would threaten the British hold on India.

Between 1853 and 1856 the **Crimean° War** raged in Romania, on the Black Sea, and on the Crimean peninsula. Britain, France, and the Italian kingdom of Sardinia-Piedmont sided with the Ottomans. Austria mediated the outcome. Britain and France trapped the Russian fleet in the Black Sea, where its commanders decided to sink the ships to protect the approaches to Sevastopol, their main base in Crimea. An army largely made up of British and French troops landed and laid siege to the city. Official corruption and lack of railways hampered the Russians' attempts to supply their forces. On the Romanian front, the Ottomans resisted effectively. At Sevastopol, the Russians were outmatched militarily and suffered badly from disease. Tsar Nicholas died as defeat loomed, leaving his successor, Alexander II (r. 1855–1881), to sue for peace when Sevastopol finally fell three months later.

The Crimean War brought significant changes to all the combatants. The tsar and his government, already beset by demands for the reform of serfdom, education, and the military (discussed later), were further discredited. In Britain and France, the conflict was accompanied by massive propaganda campaigns. For the first time newspapers effectively mobilized public support for a war. British press accounts so glamorized British participation that the false impression has lingered that Ottoman troops played a negligible role in the conflict. At the time, however, British and French commanders noted the massive losses among Turkish troops in particular. The French press, dominant in Istanbul, promoted a sense of unity between Turkish and

**Crimean** (cry-ME-uhn)

**Interior of the Ottoman Financial Bureau**   This engraving from the eighteenth century depicts
the governing style of the Ottoman Empire before the era of westernizing reforms. By the end of
the Tanzimat period in 1876, government offices and the costumes of officials looked much more
like those in contemporary European capitals.   (From Ignatius Mouradgea d'Ohsson, *Tableau General de
l'Empire Ottoman,* large folio edition, Paris, 1787–1820, pl. 178, following p. 340)

French society that continued to influence many
aspects of Turkish urban culture.

The larger significance of the Crimean War was
that it marked the transition from traditional to
modern warfare. All the combatants had previously prided themselves on the use of highly
trained cavalry to smash through the front lines of
infantry. Cavalry coexisted with firearms until the
early 1800s, primarily because early rifles were
awkward to load and not very accurate. Cavalry
could attack during the intervals between volleys.
Then in the 1830s and 1840s percussion caps that
did away with pouring gunpowder into the barrel
of a musket came into use. In Crimean War battles
many cavalry units were destroyed by the rapid fire
of rifles that loaded at the breech rather than down
the barrel. That was the fate of the famed British

Light Brigade, which was sent to relieve an Ottoman unit surrounded by Russian troops.

After the Crimean War, the Ottoman Empire
increased its involvement with European commerce. The Ottoman imperial bank was founded in
1840, and a few years later currency reform pegged
the value of Ottoman gold coins to the British
pound. Sweeping changes in the 1850s expedited
the creation of banks, insurance companies, and
legal firms throughout the empire. Bustling trade
also encouraged a migration from country to city
between about 1850 and 1880. Many of the major
cities of the empire—Istanbul, Damascus, Beirut,
Alexandria, Cairo—expanded. A small but influential urban professional class emerged, as did a
considerable class of wage laborers. Other demographic shifts involved refugees from Poland and

Hungary, where rivalry between the European powers and the Russian Empire caused political tension and sporadic warfare, and from Georgia and other parts of the Caucasus, where Russian expansion forced many Muslims to emigrate (discussed later).

However, commercial vigor and urbanization could not make up for declining revenues and the chronic insolvency and corruption of the imperial government. From the conclusion of the Crimean War in 1856 on, the Ottoman government became heavily dependent on foreign loans. In return it lowered tariffs to favor European imports and allowed European banks to open in Ottoman cities. Europeans living in Istanbul and other commercial centers enjoyed **extraterritoriality,** the right to be subject to their own laws and exempt from Ottoman jurisdiction.

As the result of these measures, imported goods multiplied, but—apart from tobacco and the Turkish opium that American traders took to China to compete against British opium from India—Anatolia produced few exports. As foreign debt grew, so did inflationary trends that left urban populations in a precarious position. By contrast, Egyptian cotton exports soared during the American Civil War, when American cotton exports plummeted; but the profits benefited Muhammad Ali's descendants, who had become the hereditary governors of Egypt, rather than the Ottoman government. The Suez Canal, which was partly financed by cotton profits, opened in 1869, and Cairo was redesigned and beautified. Eventually overexpenditure on such projects plunged Egypt into the same debt crisis that plagued the empire as a whole.

The decline of Ottoman power and prosperity had a strong impact on a group of well-educated young urban men who aspired to wealth and influence. They doubted that the empire's rulers and the Tanzimat officials who worked for them would ever stand up to European domination. Though lacking a sophisticated organization, these **Young Ottomans** (sometimes called Young Turks, though that term properly applies to a later movement) promoted a mixture of liberal ideas derived from Europe, national pride in Ottoman independence, and modernist views of Islam. Prominent Young Ottomans helped draft a constitution that was promulgated in 1876 by a new and as yet untried sultan, Abdul Hamid II. This apparent triumph of liberal reform

was short-lived. With war against Russia again threatening in the Balkans in 1877, Abdul Hamid suspended the constitution and the parliament that had been elected that year. Though he ruthlessly opposed further political reforms, the Tanzimat programs of extending modern schooling, utilizing European military practices and advisers, and making the government bureaucracy more orderly continued during his reign.

# THE RUSSIAN EMPIRE

In 1812, when Napoleon's march on Moscow ended in a disastrous retreat brought on more by what a later tsar called "Generals January and February" than by Russian military action, the European image of Russia changed. Just as Napoleon's withdrawal from Egypt led to Muhammad Ali briefly becoming a political power, so his withdrawal from Russia conferred status on Tsar Alexander I (r. 1801–1825). Conservative Europeans still saw Russia as alien, backward, and oppressive, but they acknowledged its immensity and potential and included the tsar in efforts to suppress revolutionary tendencies throughout Europe.

In several important respects Russia resembled the Ottoman Empire more than the conservative kingdoms of Europe whose autocratic practices it so staunchly supported. Socially dominated by nobles whose country estates were worked by unfree serfs, Russia had almost no middle class. Industry was still at the threshold of development by the standards of the rapidly industrializing European powers, though it was somewhat more dynamic than Ottoman industry. Like Egypt and the Ottoman Empire, Russia engaged in reforms from the top down under Alexander I, but when his conservative brother Nicholas I (r. 1825–1855) succeeded to the throne, iron discipline and suspicion of modern ideas took priority over reform.

**Russia and Europe**

In 1700 only three Russians out of a hundred lived in cities, two-thirds of them in Moscow alone. By the mid-1800s the town population had grown tenfold, though it still

**Raising of the Alexander Monument in St. Petersburg**   The death of Alexander I in 1825 brought to power his conservative brother Nicholas I. Yet Alexander remained a heroic figure for his resistance to Napoleon. This monument in Winter Palace Square was erected in 1829. (Novosti Photo Library)

accounted for only 6 percent of the total because the territories of the tsars had grown greatly through wars and colonization (see Chapter 18). These figures demonstrate that, like the Ottoman Empire, Russia was an overwhelmingly agricultural land. However, it had poorer transportation than the Ottoman Empire, since many Ottoman cities were seaports. Both empires encompassed peoples speaking many different languages.

Well-engineered roads did not begin to appear until 1817, and steam navigation commenced on the Volga in 1843. Tsar Nicholas I built the first railroad from St. Petersburg, the Russian capital, to his summer palace in 1837. A few years later his commitment to strict discipline led him to insist that the trunk line from St. Petersburg to Moscow run in a perfectly straight line. American engineers, among them the father of the painter James McNeill Whistler, who learned to paint in St. Petersburg, oversaw the laying of track and built locomotive workshops. Industrialization projects depended heavily on foreign expertise. British engineers set up

the textile mills that gave woolens and cottons a prominent place among Russia's industries.

Until the late nineteenth century the Russian government's interest in industry was limited. An industrial revolution required educated and independent-minded artisans and entrepreneurs, but Nicholas feared the spread of literacy and modern education—especially anything smacking of liberalism, socialism, or revolution—beyond the minimum needed to train the officer corps and the bureaucracy. He preferred serfs to factory workers, and he paid for imported industrial goods with exports of grain and timber.

Like Egypt and the Ottoman Empire, Russia aspired to Western-style economic development. But when France and Britain entered the Crimean War, they faced a Russian army equipped with obsolete weapons and bogged down by lack of transportation. At a time when European engineers were making major breakthroughs in loading cannon through an opening at the breech end, muzzle-loading artillery remained the Russian standard.

Yet in some ways Russia bore a closer resemblance to other European countries than the Ottoman Empire did. From the point of view of the French and the British, the Cyrillic alphabet and the Russian Orthodox form of Christianity seemed foreign, but they were not nearly as foreign as the Arabic alphabet and the Muslim faith. Britain and France feared Russia as a rival for power in the east, but they increasingly accepted Tsar Nicholas's view of the Ottoman Empire as "the sick man of Europe," capable of surviving only so long as the European powers permitted.

From the Russian point of view, kinship with western Europe was of questionable value. Westernizers, like the men of the Tanzimat in the Ottoman Empire, put their trust in technical advances and governmental reform. Opposing them were intellectuals known as **Slavophiles,** who in some respects resembled the Young Ottomans and considered the Orthodox faith, the solidity of peasant life, and the tsar's absolute rule to be the proper bases of Russian civilization. After Russia's humiliation in the Crimea, the Slavophile tendency gave rise to **Pan-Slavism,** a militant political doctrine advocating unity of all the Slavic peoples, including those living under Austrian and Ottoman rule.

On the diplomatic front, the tsar's inclusion as a major European ruler contrasted sharply with the sultan's exclusion. However, this did not prevent a powerful sense of Russophobia from developing in the West. Britain in particular saw Russia as a threat to India and despised the subjection of the serfs, who gained their freedom from Tsar Alexander II only in 1861, twenty-seven years after the British had abolished slavery. The passions generated by the Crimean War and its outcome affected the relations of Russia, Europe, and the Ottoman Empire for the remainder of the nineteenth century.

### Russia and Asia

The Russian drive to the east in the eighteenth century brought the tsar's empire to the Pacific Ocean and the frontiers of China (see Map 18.1) by century's end. In the nineteenth century Russian expansionism focused on the south. There the backwardness of the Russian military did not matter since the peoples they faced were even less industrialized and technologically advanced. In 1860 Russia established a military outpost on the Pacific coast that would eventually grow into the great naval port of Vladivostok, today Russia's most southerly city. In Central Asia the steppe lands of the Kazakh nomads came under Russian control early in the century, setting the stage for a confrontation with three Uzbek states farther south. They succumbed one by one, beginning in 1865, giving rise to the new province of Turkestan, with its capital at Tashkent in present-day Uzbekistan. In the region of the Caucasus Mountains, the third area of southward expansion, Russia first took over Christian Georgia (1786), Muslim Azerbaijan° (1801), and Christian Armenia (1813) before gobbling up the many small principalities in the heart of the mountains. Between 1829 and 1864 Dagestan, Chechnya°, Abkhazia°, and other regions that would one day gain political prominence after the breakup of the Soviet Union became parts of the Russian Empire.

The drive to the south intensified political friction with Russia's new neighbors: Qing China and Japan in the east, Iran on the Central Asian and Caucasus frontiers, and the Ottoman Empire at the eastern end of the Black Sea. In the latter two instances, Muslim refugees from the territories newly absorbed by Russia spread anti-Russian feelings, though some of them brought with them modern skills and ideas gained from exposure to Russian administration and education.

The Russian drive to the south added a new element to the Eastern Question. Many British statesmen and strategists reckoned that a warlike Russia would press on until it had conquered all the lands separating it from British India, a prospect that made them shudder, given India's enormous contribution to Britain's prosperity. The competition that ensued over which power would control southern Central Asia resulted in a standoff in Afghanistan, which became a buffer zone under the control of neither. In Iran, the standoff between the powers helped preserve the weak Qajar dynasty of shahs.

### Cultural Trends

Unlike Egypt and the Ottoman Empire, which

---

**Azerbaijan** (ah-zer-by-JAHN)   **Chechnya** (CHECH-nee-yah)   **Abkhazia** (ab-KAH-zee-yah) began to send students to Europe for training only in the nineteenth century, Russia had been in cultural contact with western Europe since the time of Peter the Great (r. 1689–1725). Members of the Russian court knew Western languages, and the tsars employed officials and advisers from western countries. Peter had also enlisted the well-educated Ukrainian clerics who headed the Russian Orthodox Church to help spread a Western spirit of education. As a result, Alexander I's reforms met a more positive reception than those of Muhammad Ali and Mahmud II. However, his reforms promised more on paper than they brought about in practice. It took many years to develop a sufficient pool of trained bureaucrats to make the reforms effective.

Ironically, much of the opposition to Alexander's reforms came from well-established families that were not at all unfriendly to Western ideas. Their fear was that the new government bureaucrats, who often came from humbler social origins, would act as agents of imperial tyranny. This fear was realized during the conservative reign of Nicholas I in the same way that the Tanzimat-inspired bureaucracy of the Ottoman Empire served the despotic purposes of Sultan Abdul Hamid II after 1877. Individuals favoring more liberal reforms, including military officers who had served in western Europe, intellectuals who read Western political tracts, and members of Masonic lodges who exchanged views with Freemasons in the West, formed secret societies of opposition. Some placed their highest priority on freeing the serfs; others advocated a constitution and a republican form of government. When Alexander I died in December 1825, confusion over who was to succeed him encouraged a group of reform-minded army officers to try to take over the government and provoke an uprising. The so-called **Decembrist revolt** failed, and many of the participants were severely punished. These events ensured that the new tsar, Nicholas I, would pay little heed to calls for reform over the next thirty years.

The great powers meeting in Paris to settle the Crimean War in 1856 forced Russia to return land to the Ottomans in both Europe and Asia. This humiliation spurred Nicholas's son and successor, Alexander II (r. 1855–1881), to institute major new reforms to reinvigorate the country. The greatest of

his reforms was the emancipation of the serfs in 1861. He also authorized new joint-stock companies, projected a railroad network to tie the country together, and modernized the legal and administrative arms of government.

Earlier intellectual and cultural trends flourished under Alexander II. More and more people became involved in intellectual, artistic, and professional life. Most prominent intellectuals received some amount of instruction at Moscow University or some German university. Universities also appeared in provincial cities like Kharkov and Kazan. Student clubs, along with Masonic lodges, became places for discussing new ideas. As Russian scholars and scientists began to achieve recognition for their contributions to European thought, scholarly careers attracted young men from clerical families, who in turn helped stimulate reforms in religious education.

Just as the Tanzimat reforms of the Ottoman Empire preceded the emergence of the Young Ottomans as a new and assertive political and intellectual force in the second half of the nineteenth century, so the initially ineffective reforms of Alexander I set in motion cultural currents that would make Russia a dynamic center of intellectual, artistic, and political life under his nephew Alexander II. Thus Russia belonged to two different spheres of development. It entered the nineteenth century a recognized force in European politics, but in other ways it resembled the Ottoman Empire. Rulers in both empires instituted reforms, overcame opposition, and increased the power of their governments. These activities stimulated intellectual and political trends that would ultimately work against the absolute rule of tsar and sultan. Yet Russia would eventually develop much closer relations with western Europe and become an arena for every sort of European intellectual, artistic, and political tendency, while the Ottoman Empire would ultimately succumb to European imperialism.

# THE QING EMPIRE

In 1800 the Qing Empire faced many problems, but no reform movement of the kind initiated by

Sultan Selim III emerged in China. The reasons are not difficult to understand. The Qing emperors had skillfully countered Russian strategic and diplomatic moves in the 1600s. Instead of having a Napoleon threatening them with invasion, they enjoyed the admiration of Jesuit priests, who likened them to enlightened philosopher-kings. In 1793, however, a British attempt to establish diplomatic and trade relations—the Macartney mission—turned European opinion against China (see Chapter 18).

China's most serious crises were domestic, not foreign: rebellions by displaced indigenous peoples and the poor, and protests against the injustice of the local magistrates. The Qing dealt with these problems in the usual way, by suppressing rebels and dismissing incompetent or untrustworthy officials. They paid little attention to the far-off Europeans and brushed aside the complaints from European merchants who chafed against the restrictions of the "Canton system" by which the Qing limited and controlled foreign trade.

## Economic and Social Disorder, 1800–1839

Early Qing successes and territorial expansion sowed the seeds of the domestic and political chaos of the later period. The early emperors encouraged the recovery of farmland, the opening of previously uncultivated areas, and the restoration and expansion of the road and canal systems. These measures expanded the agricultural base and supported a doubling of the population between about 1650 and 1800. Enormous numbers of farmers, merchants, and day laborers migrated in search of less crowded conditions, and a permanent floating population of the unemployed and homeless emerged. By 1800 population strain had caused serious environmental damage in some parts of central and western China.

While farmers tried to cope with agricultural deterioration, other groups vented grievances against the government: minority peoples in central and southwestern China complained about being driven off their lands during the boom of the 1700s; Mongols resented appropriation of their grazing lands and the displacement of their traditional elites. In some regions, village vigilante or-

ganizations took over policing and governing functions from Qing officials who had lost control. Growing numbers of people mistrusted the government, suspecting that all officials were corrupt. The growing presence of foreign merchants and missionaries in Canton and in the Portuguese colony of Macao aggravated discontent in neighboring districts.

In some parts of China the Qing were hated as foreign conquerors and were suspected of sympathy with the Europeans. In 1794 the White Lotus Rebellion—partly inspired by a messianic ideology that predicted the restoration of the Chinese Ming dynasty and the coming of the Buddha—raged across central China and was not suppressed until 1804. It initiated a series of internal conflicts that continued through the 1800s. Ignited by deepening social instabilities, these movements were sometimes intensified by local ethnic conflicts and by unapproved religions. The ability of some village militias to defend themselves and attack others intensified the conflicts, though the same techniques proved useful to southern coastal populations attempting to fend off British invasion.

## The Opium War and Its Aftermath, 1839–1850

Unlike the Ottomans, the Qing knew little about the enormous fortunes being made in the early 1800s by European and American merchants smuggling opium into China. They did not know that silver gained in this illegal trade was helping finance the industrial transformation of England and the United States. Only slowly did Qing officials become aware of British colonies in India that grew and exported opium, and of the major naval base at Singapore through which British opium reached East Asia.

In 1729 the first Qing law banning opium imports was promulgated. By 1800, however, opium smuggling had swelled the annual import level to as many as four thousand chests. Though British merchants had pioneered this profitable trade, Chinese merchants likewise profited from distributing the drugs. A price war in the early 1820s stemming from competition between British and American importers raised demand so sharply that as many as thirty thousand chests were being imported by the 1830s. Addiction spread to people at all levels of Qing society, including high-ranking officials. The Qing emperor and his officials debated whether to legalize and tax opium or to enforce the existing ban more strictly. Having decided to root out the use and importation of opium, in 1839 they sent a high official to Canton to deal with the matter.

Britain considered the ban on opium importation an intolerable limitation on trade, a direct threat to Britain's economic health, and a cause for war. British naval and marine forces arrived on the south China coast in late 1839. The **Opium War** (1839–1842) broke out when negotiations between the Qing official and British representatives reached a stalemate. The war exposed the fact that the traditional, hereditary soldiers of the Qing Empire—the **Bannermen**—were, like the Janissaries of the Ottoman Empire, hopelessly obsolete. As in the Crimean War, the British excelled at sea, where they deployed superior technology. British ships landed marines who pillaged coastal cities and then sailed to new destinations (see Map 22.2). The Qing had no imperial navy. Thus until they were able to engage the British in prolonged fighting on land, they were unable to defend themselves against British attacks. Even in the land engagements, Qing resources proved woefully inadequate. The British could quickly transport their forces by sea along the coast; Qing troops moved primarily on foot. Moving Qing reinforcements from central to eastern China took more than three months; and when the defense forces arrived, they were exhausted and basically without weapons.

The Bannermen used the few muskets the Qing had imported during the 1700s. The weapons were matchlocks, which required the soldiers to ignite the load of gunpowder in them by hand. Firing the weapons was dangerous, and the canisters of gunpowder that each musketeer carried on his belt were likely to explode if a fire broke out nearby—a frequent occurrence in encounters with British artillery. Most of the Bannermen, however, had no guns at all and fought with swords, knives, spears, and clubs. Soldiers under British command—many of them Indians—carried percussion-cap rifles, which were far quicker, safer, and more accurate than the matchlocks. In addition, the long-range

British artillery could be moved from place to place and proved deadly in the cities and villages of eastern China.

Qing commanders thought that British gunboats rode so low in the water that they could not sail up the Chinese rivers. So they evacuated the coastal areas to counter the British threat. But the British deployed new gunboats for shallow waters and moved without difficulty up the Yangzi River (see Chapter 20).

When the invaders approached Nanjing, the former Ming capital, the Qing decided to negotiate. In 1842 the terms of the **Treaty of Nanking** (the British name for Nanjing) dismantled the old Canton system. The number of **treaty ports**—cities opened to foreign residents—increased from one (Canton) to five (Canton, Xiamen, Fuzhou, Ningbo, and Shanghai°). The island of Hong Kong became a British colony, and British residents in China gained extraterritorial rights. The Qing government agreed to set a low tariff of 5 percent on imports and to pay Britain an indemnity of 21 million ounces of silver as a penalty for having started the war. A supplementary treaty the following year guaranteed **most-favored-nation status** to Britain: any privileges that China granted to another country would be automatically extended to Britain as well. This provision effectively prevented the colonization of China, because giving land to one country would have necessitated giving it to all.

With each round of treaties came a new round of privileges for foreigners. In 1860 a new treaty legalized their right to import opium. Later, French treaties established the rights of foreign missionaries to travel in the Chinese countryside and preach their religion. The number of treaty ports grew, too; by 1900 they numbered more than ninety.

The treaty system and the principle of extraterritoriality resulted in the colonization of small pockets of Qing territory, where foreign merchants lived at ease. Greater territorial losses resulted when outlying regions gained independence or were ceded to neighboring countries. Districts north and south of the Amur River in the northeast fell to Russia by treaty in 1858 and 1860; parts of

**Shanghai** (shahng-hie)

**Map 22.2    Conflicts in the Qing Empire, 1839–1870**    In both the Opium War of 1839–1842 and the Arrow War of 1856–1860, the seacoasts saw most of the action. Since the Qing had no imperial navy, the well-armed British ships encountered little resistance as they shelled the southern coasts. In inland conflicts, such as the Taiping Rebellion, the opposing armies were massive and slow moving. Battles on land were often prolonged attempts by one side to starve out the other side before making a major assault.

modern Kazakhstan and Kirgizstan in the northwest met the same fate in 1864. From 1865 onward the British gradually gained control of territories on China's Indian frontier. In the late 1800s France forced the court of Vietnam to end its tribute rela-

tionship to the Qing, while Britain encouraged Tibetan independence.

In Canton, Shanghai, and other coastal cities, Europeans and Americans maintained offices and factories that employed local Chinese as menial laborers. The foreigners built comfortable housing in zones where Chinese were not permitted to live, and they entertained themselves in exclusive restaurants and bars. Around the foreign establishments, gambling and prostitution offered employment to part of the local urban population.

Whether in town or in the countryside, Christian missionaries whose congregations sponsored hospitals, shelters, and soup kitchens or gave stipends to Chinese who attended church enjoyed a good reputation. But just as often the missionaries themselves were regarded as another evil. They seemed to subvert Confucian beliefs by condemning ancestor worship, pressuring poor families to put their children into orphanages, or fulminating against footbinding. The growing numbers of foreigners, and their growing privileges, became targets of resentment for a deeply dissatisfied, daily more impoverished, and increasingly militarized society.

## The Taiping Rebellion, 1850–1864

The inflammatory mixture of social unhappiness and foreign intrusion exploded in the great civil war usually called the **Taiping° Rebellion.** In Guangxi, where the Taiping movement originated, entrenched social problems had been generating disorders for half a century. Agriculture in the region was unstable, and many people made their living from arduous and despised trades such as disposing of human waste, making charcoal, and mining. Ethnic divisions complicated economic distress. The lowliest trades frequently involved a minority group, the Hakkas, and tensions between them and the majority were rising. Problems may have been intensified by sharp fluctuations in the opium trade and reactions to the cultural and economic impact of the Europeans and Americans in Canton.

Hong Xiuquan°, the founder of the Taiping movement, experienced all of these influences. Hong came from a humble Hakka background. After years of study, he competed in the provincial Confucian examinations, hoping for a post in government. He failed the examinations repeatedly, and it appears that he suffered a nervous breakdown in his late thirties. Afterward he spent some time in Canton, where he met both Chinese and American Protestant missionaries, who inspired him with their teachings. Hong had his own interpretation of the Christian message. He saw himself as the younger brother of Jesus, commissioned by God to found a new kingdom on earth and drive the Manchu conquerors, the Qing, out of China. The result would be universal peace. Hong called his new religious movement the "Heavenly Kingdom of Great Peace."

Hong quickly attracted a community of believers, primarily Hakkas like himself. They believed in the prophecy of dreams and claimed they could walk on air. Hong and his rivals for leadership in the movement went in and out of ecstatic trances. They denounced the Manchus as creatures of Satan. News of the sect reached the government, and Qing troops arrived to arrest the Taiping leaders. But the Taipings soundly repelled the imperial troops. Local loyalty to the Taipings spread quickly; their numbers multiplied; and they began to enlarge their domain.

The Taipings relied at first on Hakka sympathy and the charismatic appeal of their religious doctrine to attract followers. But as their numbers and power grew, they altered their methods of preaching and governing. They replaced the anti-Chinese appeals used to enlist Hakkas with anti-Manchu rhetoric designed to enlist Chinese. They forced captured villages to join their movement. Once people were absorbed, the Taipings strictly monitored their activities. They segregated men and women and organized them into work and military teams. Women were forbidden to bind their feet (the Hakkas had never practiced footbinding) and participated fully in farming and labor. Brigades of women soldiers took to the field against Qing forces.

As the movement grew, it began to move toward eastern and northern China (see Map 22.2). Panic preceded the Taipings. Villagers feared being forced into Taiping units, and Confucian elites recoiled in horror from the bizarre ideology of foreign gods, totalitarian rule, and walking, working,

---

**Taiping** (tie-PING)   **Hong Xiuquan** (hoong shee-OH-chew-an)

**Nanjing Encircled**　For a decade the Taipings held the city of Nanjing as their capital. For years Qing and international troops attempted to break the Taiping hold. By the summer of 1864, Qing forces had built tunnels leading to the foundations of Nanjing's city walls and had planted explosives. The detonation of the explosives signaled the final Qing assault on the rebel capital. As shown here, the common people of the city, along with their starving livestock, were caught in the cross-fire. Many of the Taiping leaders escaped the debacle at Nanjing, but nearly all were hunted down and executed.　(Roger-Viollet/Getty Images)

warring women. But the huge numbers the Taipings were able to muster overwhelmed attempts at local defense. The tremendous growth in the number of Taiping followers required the movement to establish a permanent base. When the rebel army conquered Nanjing in 1853, the Taiping leaders decided to settle there and make it the capital of the new "Heavenly Kingdom of Great Peace."

Qing forces attempting to defend north China became more successful as problems of organization and growing numbers slowed Taiping momentum. Increasing Qing military success resulted mainly from the flexibility of the imperial military commanders in the face of an unprecedented challenge. In addition, the military commanders received strong backing from a group of civilian provincial governors who had studied the techniques developed by local militia forces for self-defense. Certain provincial governors combined their knowledge of civilian self-defense and local terrain with more efficient organization and the use of modern weaponry. The result was the formation of new military units, in which many of the Bannermen voluntarily served under civilian governors. The Qing court agreed to special taxes to fund the new armies and acknowledged the new combined leadership.

When the Taipings settled into Nanjing, the new Qing armies surrounded the city, hoping to starve out the rebels. The Taipings, however, had provisioned and fortified themselves well. They also had the services of several brilliant young military commanders, who mobilized enormous campaigns in nearby parts of eastern China, scavenging supplies and attempting to break the encirclement of Nanjing. For more than a decade the Taiping leadership remained ensconced at Nanjing, and the "Heavenly Kingdom" endured.

In 1856 Britain and France, freed from their preoccupation with the Crimean War, turned their attention to China. European and American missionaries had visited Nanjing, curious to see what their fellow Christians were up to. Their reports were discouraging. Hong Xiuquan and the other leaders appeared to lead lives of indulgence and abandon, and more than one missionary accused them of homosexual practices. Relieved of the possible accusation of quashing a pious Christian movement, the British and French surveyed the situation. Though the Taipings were not going to topple the Qing, rebellious Nian ("Bands") in northern China added a new threat in the 1850s. A series of simultaneous large insurrections might indeed destroy the empire. Moreover, since the Qing had not observed all the provisions of the treaties signed after the Opium War, Britain and France were now considering renewing war on the Qing themselves.

In 1856 the British and French launched a series of swift, brutal coastal attacks—a second opium war, called the Arrow War (1856–1860)—which culminated in a British and French invasion of Beijing and the sacking of the Summer Palace in 1860. A new round of treaties punished the Qing for not enacting all the provisions of the Treaty of Nanking. Having secured their principal objective,

the British and French forces then joined the Qing campaign against the Taipings. Attempts to coordinate the international forces were sometimes riotous and sometimes tragic, but the injection of European weaponry and money helped quell both the Taiping and the Nian rebellions during the 1860s.

The Taiping Rebellion ranks as the world's bloodiest civil war and the greatest armed conflict before the twentieth century. Estimates of deaths range from 20 million to 30 million. The loss of life came primarily from starvation and disease, for most engagements consisted of surrounding fortified cities and waiting until the enemy forces died, surrendered, or were so weakened that they could be easily defeated. Many sieges continued for months. Reports of people eating grass, leather, hemp, and human flesh were widespread. The dead were rarely buried properly, and epidemic disease was common.

The area of early Taiping fighting was close to the regions of southwest China in which bubonic plague had been lingering for centuries. When the rebellion was suppressed, many Taiping followers sought safety in the highlands of Laos and Vietnam, which soon showed infestation by plague. Within a few years the disease reached Hong Kong. From there it spread to Singapore, San Francisco, Calcutta, and London. In the late 1800s there was intense apprehension over the possibility of a worldwide outbreak, and Chinese immigrants were regarded as likely carriers. This fear became a contributing factor in the passage of discriminatory immigration bans on Chinese in the United States in 1882.

The Taiping Rebellion devastated the agricultural centers of China. Many of the most intensely cultivated regions of central and eastern China were depopulated. Some were still uninhabited decades later, and major portions of the country did not recover until the twentieth century.

Cities, too, were hard hit. Shanghai, a treaty port of modest size before the rebellion, saw its population multiplied many times by the arrival of refugees from war-blasted neighboring provinces. The city then endured months of siege by the Taipings. Major cultural centers in eastern China lost masterpieces of art and architecture; imperial libraries were burned or their collections exposed to the weather; and the printing blocks used to make books were destroyed. While the empire faced the mountainous challenge of dealing with the material and cultural destruction of the war, it also was burdened by a major ecological disaster in the north. The Yellow River changed course in 1855, destroying the southern part of impoverished Shandong province with flood and initiating decades of drought along the former riverbed in northern Shandong.

## Decentralization at the End of the Qing Empire, 1864–1875

The Qing government emerged from the 1850s with no hope of achieving solvency. The corruption of the 1700s, attempts in the very early 1800s to restore waterworks and roads, and declining yields from land taxes had bankrupted the treasury. By 1850, before the Taiping Rebellion, Qing government expenditures were ten times revenues. The indemnities demanded by Europeans after the Opium and Arrow Wars compounded the problem. Vast stretches of formerly productive rice land were devastated, and the population was dispersed. Refugees pleaded for relief, and the imperial, volunteer, foreign, and mercenary troops that had suppressed the Taipings demanded unpaid wages.

Britain and France became active participants in the period of recovery that followed the rebellion. To ensure repayment of the debt to Britain, Robert Hart was installed as inspector-general of a newly created Imperial Maritime Customs Service. Britain and the Qing split the revenues he collected. Britons and Americans worked for the Qing government as advisers and ambassadors, attempting to smooth communications between the Qing, Europe, and the United States.

The real work of the recovery, however, was managed by provincial governors who had come to the forefront in the struggle against the Taipings. To prosecute the war, they had won the right to levy their own taxes, raise their own troops, and run their own bureaucracies. These special powers were not entirely canceled when the war ended. Chief among these governors was Zeng Guofan°, who oversaw programs to restore agriculture, commu-

nications, education, and publishing, as well as efforts to reform the military and industrialize armaments manufacture.

Like many provincial governors, Zeng preferred to look to the United States rather than to Britain for models and aid. He hired American advisers to run his weapons factories, shipyards, and military academies. He sponsored a daring program in which promising Chinese boys were sent to Hartford, Connecticut, a center of missionary activity, to learn English, science, mathematics, engineering, and history. They returned to China to assume some of the positions previously held by foreign advisers. Though Zeng was never an advocate of participation in public life by women, his Confucian convictions taught him that educated mothers were more than ever a necessity. He not only encouraged but also partly oversaw the advanced classical education of his own daughters. Zeng's death in 1872 deprived the empire of a major force for reform.

The period of recovery marked a fundamental structural change in the Qing Empire. Although the emperors after 1850 were ineffective rulers, a coalition of aristocrats supported the reform and recovery programs. Without their legitimization of the new powers of provincial governors like Zeng Guofan, the empire might have evaporated within a generation. A crucial member of this alliance was Cixi°, who was known as the "Empress Dowager" after the 1880s. Later observers, both Chinese and foreign, reviled her as a monster of corruption and arrogance. But in the 1860s and 1870s Cixi supported the provincial governors, some of whom became so powerful that they were managing Qing foreign policy as well as domestic affairs.

No longer a conquest regime dominated by a Manchu military caste and its Chinese civilian appointees, the empire came under the control of a group of reformist aristocrats and military men, independently powerful civilian governors, and a small number of foreign advisers. The Qing lacked strong, central, unified leadership and could not recover their powers of taxation, legislation, and military command once these had been granted to the provincial governors. From the 1860s forward, the Qing Empire disintegrated into a number of large

---

**Zeng Guofan** (zung gwoh-FAN)

**Cixi** (TSUH-shee)

**Cixi's Allies**   In the 1860s and 1870s, Cixi was a supporter of reform. In later years she was widely regarded as corrupt and self-centered and as an obstacle to reform. Her greatest allies were the court eunuchs. Introduced to palace life in early China as managers of the imperial harems, eunuchs became powerful political parties at court. The first Qing emperors refused to allow the eunuchs any political influence, but by Cixi's time the eunuchs once again were a political factor.   (Freer Gallery of Art and Arthur M. Sackler Gallery Archives. Smithsonian Institution, Washington, D.C. Photographer: Xunling, negative #SC-GR-261)

power zones in which provincial governors handed over leadership to their protégés in a pattern that the Qing court eventually could only ritually legitimate.

## CONCLUSION

M ost of the subjects of the Ottoman, Russian, and Qing rulers did not think of European pressure or competition as determining factors in their lives during the first half of the nineteenth century. They continued to live according to the social and economic institutions they inherited from previous generations. By the 1870s, however, the challenge of Europe had become widely recog-

nized. The Crimean War, where European allies achieved a hollow victory for the Ottomans and then pressured the sultan for more reforms, confirmed both Ottoman and Russian military weakness. The Opium War did the same for China. Though all three empires faced similar problems of reform and military rebuilding, Russia enjoyed a comparative advantage in being less appealing to rapacious European merchants and strategists concerned with protecting overseas empires.

The policies adopted by the three imperial governments responded both to traditional concerns and to European demands. The sultans gave first priority to strengthening the central government to prevent territorial losses that began when Serbia, Egypt, and Greece became fully or partially independent. The Qing emperors confronted population growth and agricultural decline that resulted in massive rebellions. The tsars focused on continued territorial expansion. However, each faced different European pressures. In China, the Europeans and Americans wanted trade rights. In the Ottoman Empire, Britain, France, and Russia wanted equality for Christians and freedom from naval and commercial competition in the eastern Mediterranean. In Russia, moral demands for the abolition of serfdom accompanied British determination to stop territorial advances in Asia that might threaten India.

Repeated crises in all three empires would eventually result in the fall of the Qing, Romanov, and Ottoman dynasties in the first two decades of the twentieth century, but in 1870 it was still unclear whether the traditional land empires of Asia would be capable of weathering the storm. One thing that had become clear, however, at least to European eyes, was that Russia was part of Europe, while the other two empires were fundamentally alien. This judgment was based partly on religion, partly on the enthusiasm of westernizing Russian artists and intellectuals for European cultural trends, and partly on the role Russia had played in defeating Napoleon at the beginning of the century, a role that brought the tsars into the highest councils of royal decision making in Europe.

## ■ Key Terms

| | |
|---|---|
| Muhammad Ali | Pan-Slavism |
| Janissaries | Decembrist revolt |
| Serbia | Opium War |
| Tanzimat | Bannermen |
| Crimean War | Treaty of Nanking |
| extraterritoriality | treaty ports |
| Young Ottomans | most-favored-nation status |
| Slavophiles | Taiping Rebellion |

## ■ Suggested Reading

For widely available general histories of the Ottoman Empire, see Stanford Shaw, *History of the Ottoman Empire and Modern Turkey* (1976–1977), and J. P. D. B. Kinross, *The Ottoman Centuries: The Rise and Fall of the Turkish Empire* (1977).

On the economy and society of the nineteenth-century Ottoman Empire, see Huri Islamoglu-Inan, ed., *The Ot-*

*toman Empire and the World-Economy* (1987); Resat Kasaba, *The Ottoman Empire and the World Economy: The Nineteenth Century* (1988); Sevket Pamuk, *The Ottoman Empire and European Capitalism, 1820–1913: Trade, Investment, and Production* (1987); Kemal H. Karpat, *Ottoman Population, 1830–1914: Demographic and Social Characteristics* (1985); and Carter V. Findley, *Bureaucratic Reform in the Ottoman Empire: The Sublime Porte, 1789–1922* (1980). On the reform program and the emergence of national concepts, see also Selim Deringil, *The Well-Protected Domains: Ideology and the Legitimation of Power in the Ottoman Empire, 1876–1909* (1998).

Marc Raeff, *Understanding Imperial Russia* (1984), sets nineteenth-century Russian developments in a broad context and challenges many standard ideas. Andreas Kappeler, *The Russian Multi-Ethnic Empire* (2001), and Mark Bassin, *Imperial Visions: Nationalist Imagination and Geographical Expansion in the Russian Far East, 1840–1865* (1999), address Russian expansion and the problems inherent in diversity of population. On economic matters see W. L. Blackwell, *The Beginnings of Russian Industrialization, 1800–1860* (1968). Daniel Field, *The End of Serfdom: Nobility and Bureaucracy in Russia, 1855–1861* (1976), addresses the primary problem besetting Russian society during this period. On the intellectual debates see M. Malia, *Alexander Herzen and the Birth of Russian Socialism* (1961), and Andrzej Walicki, *The Slavophile Controversy* (1975).

On the Qing Empire of the nineteenth century, see Pamela Kyle Crossley, *Orphan Warriors: Three Manchu Generations and the End of the Qing World* (1990), and for a more detailed political history see Mary C. Wright, *The Last Stand of Chinese Conservatism: The T'ung-chih Restoration, 1862–1874* (1971). There is a very large literature on both the Opium War and the Taiping Rebellion, including reprinted editions of contemporary observers. For general histories of the Opium War, see Peter Ward Fay, *The Opium War, 1840–1842: Barbarians in the Celestial Empire in the Early Part of the Nineteenth Century and the War by Which They Forced Her Gates Ajar* (1975); Christopher Hibbert, *The Dragon Wakes: China and the West, 1793–1911* (1970); and the classic study by Chang Hsin-pao, *Commissioner Lin and the Opium War* (1964). For a recent, more monographic study on Qing political thought in the period of the Opium War, see James M. Polachek, *The Inner Opium War* (1992). On the Taiping Rebellion, enduring sources are S. Y. Têng, *The Taiping Rebellion and the Western Powers: A Comprehensive Survey* (1971), and C. A. Curwen, *Taiping Rebel: The Deposition of Li Hsiu-ch'eng* (1976); see also Caleb Carr, *The Devil Soldier: The Story of Frederick Townsend Ward* (1992). The most recent study is Jonathan D. Spence, *God's Chinese Son: The Taiping Heavenly Kingdom of Hong Xiuquan* (1996)

# State Power, the Census, and the Question of Identity

Between the American Revolution and the last decades of the nineteenth century, Europe and the Americas were transformed. The ancient power of kings and the authority of religion were eclipsed by muscular new ways of organizing political, economic, and intellectual life. The Western world was vastly different in 1870 than it had been a century earlier. One of the less heralded but enduringly significant changes was the huge expansion of government statistical services.

The rise of the nation-state was associated with the development of modern bureaucratic departments that depended on reliable statistics to measure the nation's achievements and discover its failures. The nation-state, whether democratic or not, mobilized resources on a previously unimaginable scale. Modern states were more powerful and wealthier, and they were also more ambitious and more intrusive. The growth of their power can be seen in the modernization of militaries, the commitment to internal improvements such as railroads, and the growth in state revenues. In recent years historians have begun to examine a less visible but equally important manifestation of growing state power: census taking.

Governments and religious authorities have counted people since early times. Our best estimates of the Amerindian population of the Western Hemisphere in 1500 rest almost entirely on what were little more than missionaries' guesses about the numbers of people they baptized. Spanish and Portuguese kings were eager to count native populations, since "indios" (adult male Amerindians) were subject to special labor obligations and tribute payments. So, from the mid-sixteenth century onward, imperial officials conducted regular censuses of Amerindians, adapting practices already in place in Europe.

The effort to measure and categorize populations was transformed in the last decades of the eighteenth century when the nature of European governments began to change. The Enlightenment belief that the scientific method could be applied to human society proved to be attractive both to political radicals, like the French Revolutionaries, and to reforming monarchs like Maria Theresa of Austria. Enlightenment philosophers had argued that a science of government could remove the inefficiencies and irrationalities that had long subverted the human potential for prosperity and happiness. The French intellectual Condorcet wrote in 1782:

> Those sciences, created almost in our own days, the object of which is man himself, the direct goal of which is the happiness of man, will enjoy a progress no less sure than that of the physical sciences. . . . In meditating on the nature of the moral sciences [what we now call the social sciences], one cannot help seeing that, as they are based like the physical sciences on the observation of fact, they must follow the method, acquire a language equally exact and precise, attaining the same degree of certainty.[1]

As confidence in this new "science" grew, the term previously used to describe the collection of numbers about society, *political arithmetic*, was abandoned by governments and practitioners in favor of *statistics*, a term that clearly suggests its close ties to the "state." In the nineteenth century the new objectives set out by Condorcet and others led to both the formal university training of statisticians and the creation of government statistical services.

The ambitions of governments in this new era were great. Nation-states self-consciously sought to transform society, sponsoring economic development, education, and improvements in health and welfare. They depended on statistics to measure the effectiveness of their policies and, as a result, were interested in nearly everything. They counted taverns, urban buildings, births and deaths, and arrests and convictions. They also counted their populations with a thoroughness never before seen. As statistical reporting became more uniform across Europe and the Americas, governments could measure not only their own progress but also that of their neighbors and rivals.

The revolutionary governments of France modernized the census practices of the overthrown monarchy. They spent much more money, hired many more census takers, and devoted much more energy to training the staff that designed censuses and analyzed results. Great Britain set up an official census in 1801, but established a special administrative structure only in the 1830s. In the Western Hemisphere nearly every independent nation provided for "scientific" censuses. In the United States the federal constitution required that a census be taken every ten years. Latin American nations, often torn by civil war in the nineteenth century, took censuses less regularly, but even the poorest nations took censuses when they could. It was as if the census itself confirmed the existence of the government, demonstrating its modernity and seriousness.

Until recently, historians who relied on these documents in their research on economic performance, issues of race and ethnicity, family life, and fertility and mortality asked few questions about the politics of census design. What could be more objective than rows of numbers? But the advocates of statistics who managed census taking were uninhibited in advertising the usefulness of reliable numbers to the governments that employed them. At the 1860 International Statistical Congress held in London one speaker said, "I think the true meaning to be attached to 'statistics' is not every collection of figures, but figures collected with the sole purpose of applying the principles deduced from them to questions of importance to the state."[2] The desire to be useful meant that statistics could not be fully objective.

Subjectivity was an unavoidable problem with censuses. Censuses identified citizens and foreign residents by place of residence, sex, age, and family relationships within households as well as profession and literacy. These determinations were sometimes subjective. Modern scholars have demonstrated that census takers also often undercounted the poor and those living in rural areas.

Because census takers, as agents of nation-states, were determined to be useful, they were necessarily concerned with issues of nationality and, in the Americas, with race because these characteristics commonly determined political rights and citizenship. The assessment and recording of nationality and race would prove to be among the most politically problematic objectives of the new social sciences.

Nationality had not been a central question for traditional monarchies. For the emerging nation-state, nationality was central. A nation's strength was assumed to depend in large measure on the growth of its population, a standard that, once articulated, suggested that the growth of minority populations was dangerous. Who was French? Who was Austrian or Hungarian? European statisticians relied on both *language of use* and *mother tongue* as proxies for *nationality,* the first term being flexible enough to recognize the assimilation of minorities, the second suggesting a more permanent identity based on a person's original language. Both terms forced bilingual populations to simplify their more complex identities. Ethnic minorities, once identified, were sometimes subject to discrimination such as exclusion from military careers or from universities. In parts of Spanish America language was used as a proxy for *race*. Those who spoke Spanish were citizens in the full sense, even if they were indistinguishable from Amerindians in appearance. Those who spoke indigenous languages were "indios" and therefore subject to special taxes and labor obligations and effectively denied the right to vote.

Beyond providing a justification for continuing discrimination, census categories compressed and distorted the complexity and variety of human society to fit the preconceptions of bureaucrats and politicians. Large percentages of the residents of Mexico, Peru, and Bolivia, among other parts of the Americas, were descended from both Europeans and Amerindians and, in the Caribbean region, from Europeans and Africans. Census categories never adequately captured the complexities of these biological and cultural mixtures. We now know that the poor were often identified as "indios" or "blacks" and the better-off were often called something else, "Americanos," "criollos" (creoles), or even whites. Since this process flattened and streamlined the complexities of identity, censuses on their own are not reliable guides to the distribution of ethnicity and race in a population.

In Europe the issue of nationality proved similarly perplexing for census takers and similarly dangerous to those identified as minorities. Linguistic and ethnic minorities had always lived among the politically dominant majorities: Jewish and Polish minorities in areas controlled by German speakers, German speakers among the French, and Serbo-Croatian speakers among Hungarians, for example. The frontiers between these minority populations and their neighbors were always porous. Sexual unions and marriages were common, and two or more generations of a family often lived together in the same household, with the elder members speaking one language and the younger members another. Who was what? In a very real sense, nationality, like race in the Americas, was ultimately fixed by the census process, where the nation-state forced a limited array of politically utilitarian categories onto the rich diversity of ethnicity and culture.

## Notes

1. Quoted in James C. Scott, *Seeing Like a State. How Certain Schemes to Improve the Human Condition Have Failed* (New Haven: Yale University Press, 1998), 91.
2. This discussion relies heavily on Eliza Johnson (now Ablovatski), "Counting and Categorizing: The Hungarian Gypsy Census of 1893" (M.A. Thesis, Columbia University, 1996), especially Chapter III. She quotes from the *Proceedings of the Sixth International Statistical Congress Held in London,* 1860, 379.

## PART SEVEN

# Global Diversity and Dominance, 1850–1949

CHAPTER 23
The New Power Balance, 1850–1900

CHAPTER 24
The New Imperialism, 1869–1914

CHAPTER 25
The Crisis of the Imperial Order, 1900–1929

CHAPTER 26
The Collapse of the Old Order, 1929–1949

CHAPTER 27
Striving for Independence: Africa, India, and Latin America, 1900–1949

In 1850, despite centuries of global contacts, the world still embraced a huge diversity of societies and cultures and of independent states. During the century that followed, much of the world came to be dominated by a few European nations, along with the United States and Japan.

Industrializing nations used their newfound power to dominate Africa, South and Southeast Asia, and the Pacific in a wave of conquest termed the New Imperialism. Domination went beyond military or economic measures as soldiers, administrators, missionaries, teachers, and merchants tried to promote their own cultures, business practices, and ways of life. They were partly successful, as the spread of Western religions, languages, clothing, and political ideas testifies.

By 1900, Europe had been largely at peace for almost a century. As memories of war faded, the rise of nationalism and the awesome power of modern armies and navies made national rivalries dangerously inflammable. Germany, a latecomer to national unity, found its imperial ambitions frustrated by the earlier conquests of France, Britain, and Russia. Mounting tensions between these powers led to the devastating Great War of 1914–1918. Far from settling issues, this war destabilized the victors as much as the vanquished. Russia and China erupted in revolution. The collapse of the Ottoman Empire led to the emergence of modern Turkey, while its Arab provinces were taken over by France and Britain. In the 1920s, the European powers struggled to maintain a precarious peace.

By the 1930s, the political and economic system crafted after the Great War fell apart. While the capitalist nations fell into a deep economic depression that their governments seemed helpless to stop, the Soviet Union industrialized at breakneck speed. Social disruption in Germany and Japan brought to power extremist leaders who sought to solve economic woes and political grievances by military conquest. Nationalism and industrial warfare assumed their most hideous forms in World War II, leading to the massacre of millions of innocent people and the destruction of countless cities.

World War II weakened European control of their overseas empires. Leaders of liberation movements in Asia, Latin America, and Africa adopted Western ideas of nationalism and communism as they sought to acquire the benefits of industrialization. India gained its independence in 1947. Two years later, Chinese communists led by Mao Zedong overthrew a government they viewed as subservient to the West. In Latin America, leaders turned to nationalist economic and social policies. Of all the once great powers, only the United States and the Soviet Union remained to compete for global dominance.

| | 1850 | 1870 | 1890 |
|---|---|---|---|
| **Americas** | | U.S. Civil War **1861–1865** | British build railroads in Brazil and Argentina **1880s** • | Spanish–American War **1898** • |
| **Europe** | • **1851** Majority of British population living in cities • **1856** Transformation of steel and chemical industries begins | **1870–1914** Era of the New Imperialism • **1871** Unification of Germany, Italy | **1894–1906** Dreyfus affair in France |
| **Africa** | End of transatlantic slave trade **1867** • | Berlin Africa Conference **1884–1885** • • **1880s** West Africa conquered by France and Britain Nigeria becomes British protectorate **1899** • | • **1896** Ethiopians defea Italian army at Adowa |
| **Middle East** | Suez Canal opens **1869** • | • **1882** British occupy Egypt • **1878** Ottoman Empire loses most of its European territories | • **1904** Young Turk reforms in Ottoman Empire |
| **Asia and Oceania** | Direct British rule in India **1858** • Meiji Restoration in Japan **1868** • | • **1862** French conquer Indochina First Indian National Congress **1885** • Russia conquers Central Asia **1884–1887** | Boxer Rebellion in China **1900** • Sino-Japanese War **1894** • **1904–1905** Russo-Japanese War |

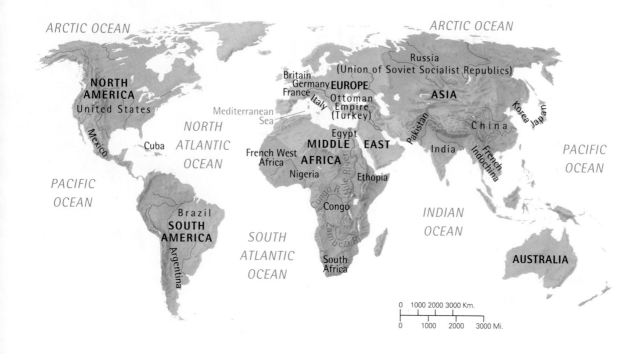

ARCTIC OCEAN

ARCTIC OCEAN

Russia
(Union of Soviet Socialist Republics)

Britain
Germany EUROPE
France Ottoman
Italy Empire
(Turkey)

ASIA

Korea
Japan

China

Pakistan

NORTH
AMERICA
United States

NORTH
ATLANTIC
OCEAN

Mediterranean
Sea

Egypt

PACIFIC
OCEAN

Cuba

MIDDLE EAST

French West
Africa

AFRICA

India

French
Indochina

Mexico

Nigeria

Ethopia

PACIFIC
OCEAN

Brazil
SOUTH
AMERICA

SOUTH
ATLANTIC
OCEAN

Congo River
Congo

INDIAN
OCEAN

Argentina

Congo River
Zambezi River

South
Africa

AUSTRALIA

0   1000 2000 3000 Km.

0      1000    2000    3000 Mi.

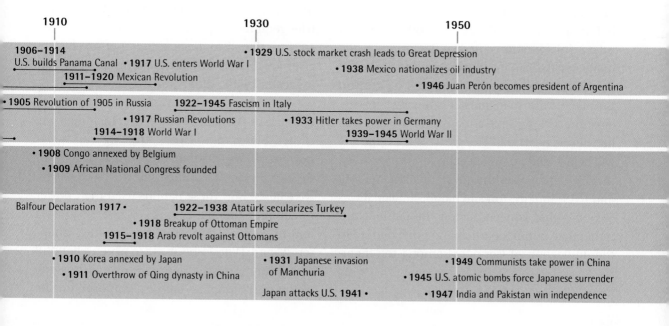

**1910**

**1930**

**1950**

**1906–1914**
U.S. builds Panama Canal • **1917** U.S. enters World War I

• **1929** U.S. stock market crash leads to Great Depression

• **1938** Mexico nationalizes oil industry

**1911–1920** Mexican Revolution

• **1946** Juan Perón becomes president of Argentina

• **1905** Revolution of 1905 in Russia   **1922–1945** Fascism in Italy

• **1917** Russian Revolutions        • **1933** Hitler takes power in Germany

**1914–1918** World War I         **1939–1945** World War II

• **1908** Congo annexed by Belgium

• **1909** African National Congress founded

Balfour Declaration **1917** •      **1922–1938** Atatürk secularizes Turkey

• **1918** Breakup of Ottoman Empire

**1915–1918** Arab revolt against Ottomans

• **1910** Korea annexed by Japan

• **1931** Japanese invasion
  of Manchuria

• **1949** Communists take power in China

• **1911** Overthrow of Qing dynasty in China

• **1945** U.S. atomic bombs force Japanese surrender

Japan attacks U.S. **1941** •

• **1947** India and Pakistan win independence

# 23 The New Power Balance, 1850–1900

CHAPTER OUTLINE

New Technologies and the World Economy
Social Transformations
Nationalism and the Unification of Germany
The Great Powers of Europe, 1871–1900
New Great Powers: The United States and Japan
DIVERSITY AND DOMINANCE: Marx and Engels on Global Trade and the Bourgeoisie

On January 18, 1871, in the Hall of Mirrors of the palace of Versailles, King Wilhelm I of Prussia was proclaimed emperor of Germany before a crowd of officers and other German rulers. This ceremony marked the unification of many small German states into one nation. Off to one side stood Prussian chancellor Otto von Bismarck°, the man most responsible for the creation of a united Germany. A few years earlier, he had declared, "The great issues of the day will be decided not by speeches and votes of the majority—that was the great mistake of 1848 and 1849—but by iron and blood." Indeed it was "blood"—that is, victories on the battlefield—rather than popular participation that had led to the unification of Germany; among the digni-

taries in the Hall of Mirrors that day, only two or three were civilians. As for "iron," it meant not only weapons but, more important, the industries required to produce weapons. Thus, after 1871, nationalism, once a dream of revolutionaries and romantics, became ever more closely associated with military force and with industry.

This chapter deals with a small group of countries—Germany, France, Britain, Russia, the United States, and Japan—that we call "great powers." In the next chapter, which deals with the era of the "New Imperialism" (1869–1914), we will see how these nations used their power to conquer colonial empires in Asia and Africa and to control Latin America. Together, Chapters 23 and 24 describe an era in which a handful of wealthy industrialized nations—all but one of them of European culture—imposed on the

---

**Otto von Bismarck** (UTT-oh fun BIS-mark)

other peoples of the world a domination more powerful than any experienced before or since.

As you read this chapter, ask yourself the following questions:

- What new technologies and industries appeared between 1850 and 1900, and how did they affect the world economy?
- How did the societies of the industrial countries change during this period?
- Why do we call certain countries "great powers" but not others?

# NEW TECHNOLOGIES AND THE WORLD ECONOMY

After 1850, industrialization took off in new directions. Germany and the United States surpassed Great Britain as the world's leading industrial powers by 1890. Small companies were overshadowed by large corporations owned by wealthy capitalists or (especially in Russia and Japan) by governments. New technologies based on advances in physics and chemistry revolutionized everyday life and transformed the world economy.

## The Steel and Chemical Industries

**Steel** is a special form of iron, both hard and elastic. A series of inventions in the 1850s made steel the cheapest and most versatile metal ever known. As a result, world steel production rose from a half-million tons in 1870 to 28 million in 1900, of which the United States produced 10 million, Germany 8, and Britain 4.9. Steel became cheap and abundant enough to make rails, bridges, ships, and even "tin" cans meant to be used once and thrown away.

The new steel mills were hungry consumers of coal, iron ore, limestone, and other raw materials. They took up as much space as whole towns, belched smoke and particulates night and day, and left behind huge hills of slag and other waste products. Environmental degradation affected steel-producing regions such as the English Midlands, the German Ruhr, and parts of Pennsylvania.

The chemical industry followed a similar pattern. In the early nineteenth century, only soda, sulfuric acid, and chlorine bleach (used in the cotton industry) were manufactured on a large scale, especially in Britain. Then in 1856, the development of the first synthetic dye, aniline purple, from coal tar launched the mass production of organic chemicals—compounds containing carbon atoms. These bright, long-lasting colors delighted consumers but hurt tropical countries, such as India, that produced indigo, a blue vegetable dye.

Chemistry also made important advances in the manufacture of explosives. In 1866, the Swedish scientist Alfred Nobel found a way to turn nitroglycerin into a stable solid—dynamite. This and other new explosives were very useful in mining and the construction of railroads and canals. They also enabled the armies and navies of the great powers to arm themselves with increasingly accurate and powerful rifles and cannon.

The growing complexity of industrial chemistry made it one of the first fields where science and technology interacted on a daily basis. This development gave a great advantage to Germany, which had the most advanced engineering schools and scientific institutes of its time. By the end of the nineteenth century, Germany was the world's leading producer of dyes, drugs, synthetic fertilizers, ammonia, and nitrates used in making explosives.

## Electricity

The third great innovation of the late nineteenth century was **electricity.** In the 1870s, inventors devised efficient generators that turned mechanical energy into electric current and opened the way to a host of new applications. Arc lamps lit up public squares, theaters, and stores. Then in 1879, **Thomas Edison** in the United States developed an incandescent lamp well suited to lighting small rooms and in 1882 created the world's first electrical distribution network, in New York City. By the turn of the century, electric lighting was rapidly replacing dim and smelly gas lamps in the cities of Europe and North America.

Other uses of electricity quickly appeared. Electric streetcars and, later, subways helped reduce the traffic jams that clogged large cities. Electric motors replaced steam engines and power belts, increasing productivity and improving workers' safety. As demand for electricity grew, engineers learned to use waterpower to produce electricity, and hydroelectric plants were built.

Electricity helped alleviate some environmental problems, since electric motors and lamps did not pollute the air. Power plants were built at a distance from cities. As electric trains and streetcars replaced horse-drawn trolleys and coal-burning locomotives, cities became noticeably cleaner and healthier. At the same time, electricity created a huge demand for copper, bringing Chile, Montana, and southern Africa into the world economy as never before.

### Shipping and Telegraph Cables

At midcentury, a series of developments radically transformed ocean shipping. Iron and steel took the place of wood. Propellers replaced paddle wheels and sails. By the turn of the century, more efficient engines could convert the heat produced by burning a single sheet of paper into the power to move 1 ton over half a mile. The average size of freighters increased from 200 tons in 1850 to 7,500 tons in 1900. The Suez Canal, constructed in 1869, shortened the distance between Europe and Asia and triggered a massive switch from sail power to steam.

The world's fleet of merchant ships grew from 9 million to 35 million tons between 1850 and 1910, as passengers, mail, and perishable freight traveled on fast and reliable scheduled liners. To control their ships around the globe, shipping companies used a new medium of communications: **submarine telegraph cables** laid on the ocean floor linking the continents. Cables were laid across the Atlantic in 1866, and by the turn of the century, cables connected every country and almost every inhabited island.

### Railroads

The fifty years after 1850 saw a tremendous expansion of the world's **railroad** networks. At the end of its Civil War in 1865, the United States already had 35,000 miles (over 56,000 kilometers) of track, three times as much as Britain, and still growing. Germany, France, Canada, Russia, and Japan also built large networks.

Railroads were not confined to industrialized nations, but were constructed around the world. The British built the fourth largest rail network in the world in India (see Chapter 21). Many old cities doubled in size to accommodate railroad stations, sidings, tracks, warehouses, and repair shops. In the countryside, railroads consumed vast amounts of land and timber for ties to hold the rails and for bridges. Throughout the world, they opened new land to agriculture, mining, and other uses.

### World Trade and Finance

Thanks to the growing speed and falling cost of transportation between 1850 and 1913, world trade expanded tenfold, transforming the economies of different parts of the world in different ways. The capitalist economics of western Europe and North America grew more prosperous and diversified, despite deep depressions in which workers lost their jobs and investors their fortunes.

Long after German and American industries surpassed the British, Britain continued to dominate the flow of trade, finance, and information. In 1900, two-thirds of the world's submarine cables were British or passed through Britain. Over half of the world's shipping was British owned. Britain invested one-fourth of its national wealth overseas, much of it in the United States and Argentina.

Nonindustrial areas were more vulnerable to changes in price and demand than were the industrialized nations, for many of them produced raw materials that could be replaced by synthetic substitutes or alternative sources of supply. Nevertheless, until World War I, the value of exports from the tropical countries generally remained high.

## SOCIAL TRANSFORMATIONS

The technological and economic changes of the late nineteenth century sparked profound social changes in the industrial nations. A fast-growing

## C H R O N O L O G Y

| | Europe | United States | East Asia |
|---|---|---|---|
| **1850** | **1851**  Majority of British population living in cities | | |
| | | | **1853**  Commodore Perry "opens" Japan |
| | **1859**  Charles Darwin, *On the Origin of Species* | | |
| | **1861**  Emancipation of serfs (Russia) | | |
| | | **1865**  Civil War ends; economic expansion begins | |
| | **1866**  Alfred Nobel develops dynamite | | |
| | **1867**  Karl Marx, *Das Kapital* | **1865–1914**  Surge of immigration from southern and eastern Europe | **1868**  Meiji Restoration begins modernization drive in Japan |
| | **1871**  Unification of Germany; unification of Italy | | |
| **1875** | | **1879**  Thomas Edison develops incandescent lamp | |
| | **1882**  Married Women's Property Act (Britain) | | |
| | | **1890s**  "Jim Crow" laws enforce segregation in southern states | |
| | | | **1894**  Sino-Japanese War |
| | | **1899**  United States acquires Puerto Rico and the Philippines | |
| **1900** | | | **1900**  Boxer uprising ended |
| | | | **1904–1905**  Russo-Japanese War |
| | **1905**  Revolution of 1905 (Russia) | | |
| | | | **1910**  Japan annexes Korea |

population swelled cities to unprecedented size, and millions of Europeans emigrated to the Americas. Workers spawned labor movements and new forms of radical policies, and women's lives were dramatically altered.

## Population and Migrations

The population of Europe grew faster from 1850 to 1914 than ever before or since, almost doubling from 265 million to 468 million, despite mass migrations of Europeans to the United States, Canada, Australia, New Zealand, and Argentina. Between 1850 and 1900, on average, 400,000 Europeans migrated overseas every year; between 1900 and 1914, the flood rose to over 1 million a year. People of European ancestry rose from one-fifth to one-third in the world's population.

Much of the increase came from a drop in the death rate, as epidemics and starvation became less common. The Irish famine of 1847–1848 was the last peacetime famine in European history. North American wheat supplemented Europe's food. Year-round supplies of meat, fruit, vegetables, and oils improved the diet of European and North American city dwellers.

## Urbanization and Social Structures

In 1851, Britain became the first nation to have a majority of its population living in towns and cities. By 1914, 80 percent of its population was urban, as were 60 percent of the German and 45 percent of the French populations. London grew from 2.7 million in 1850 to 6.6 million in 1900. New York reached 3.4 million by 1900, a fiftyfold increase in the century. In the English Midlands, in the German Ruhr, and around Tokyo Bay, towns fused into one another, filling in the fields and woods that once had separated them.

In early industrial cities, the poor crowded together in unsanitary tenements. New urban technologies transformed city life for most residents. Pipes brought in clean water and carried away sewage. First gas and then electric lighting made cities safer and more pleasant at night. By the end of the century, municipal governments provided police and fire departments, schools, parks, and other amenities unheard of a century earlier.

As sanitation improved, urban death rates fell below birthrates for the first time. Confident that their children would survive infancy, couples began to limit the number of children they had. To accommodate the growing population, planners laid out new cities, such as Chicago, on a rectangular grid, and middle-class families moved to new developments on the edges of cities. In Paris, older neighborhoods with narrow, crooked streets and rickety tenements were replaced with broad boulevards and modern apartment buildings. Brilliantly lit by gas and electricity, Paris became the "city of lights," a model for city planners from New Delhi to Buenos Aires. By 1900, electric streetcars and subways allowed working-class people to live miles from their workplaces.

In fast-growing cities such as London, New York, and Chicago, newcomers arrived so quickly that housing construction and municipal services could not keep up. Immigrants who saved their money to reunite their families could not afford costly municipal services. As a result, the poorest neighborhoods remained as overcrowded, unhealthy, and dangerous as they had been since the early decades of industrialization.

While urban environments improved in many ways, air quality worsened. Coal, burned to power steam engines and heat buildings, polluted the air, coating everything with a film of grimy dust. And the thousands of horses that pulled the carts and carriages covered the streets with their wastes, causing a terrible stench.

## Labor Movements and Socialist Politics

Industrialization combined with the revolutionary ideas of the late eighteenth century to produce two kinds of movements—socialism and labor movements—calling for further changes. **Socialism** was an ideology developed by radical thinkers who questioned the sanctity of private property and argued in support of industrial workers against their employers. **Labor unions** were organizations formed by industrial workers to defend their interests in negotiations with employers. The socialist and labor movements were never identical. Most of the time they were allies; occasionally they were rivals.

Labor unions sought not only better wages but also improved working conditions and insurance against illness, accidents, disability, and old age. They grew slowly because strikes were illegal and hard to sustain. When laws were relaxed, British, German, and American labor grew rapidly.

By far the best-known socialist was **Karl Marx** (1818–1883), a German journalist who lived most of his life in England. The ideas he expressed succinctly in the *Communist Manifesto* (1848) and in great detail in *Das Kapital°* (1867) provided an intellectual framework for the growing dissatisfaction with raw industrial capitalism (see Diversity and Dominance: Marx and Engels on Global Trade and the Bourgeoisie). He argued that the capitalists unfairly extracted the "surplus value" of workers' labor—that is, the difference between workers' wages and the value of the goods they manufactured. The concentration of wealth in a few hands convinced Marx that class struggle between workers and owners was inevitable. But the International Working Man's Association Marx helped found in 1864 attracted more intellectuals than workers. Workers found other means of redressing their grievances, such as the vote and labor unions.

The nineteenth century saw a gradual extension of the right to vote throughout Europe and North America. Universal male suffrage became law in the United States in 1870, in France and Germany in 1871, in Britain in 1885, and in the rest of Europe soon after. With universal male suffrage, socialist politicians could expect to capture many seats in their nations' parliaments, because the newly enfranchised working class was so numerous. Democratic socialist parties sought to use voting power to gain concessions from government and eventually even to win elections.

## Working-Class Women and Men

Working-class women led lives of toil and pain, considerably harder than the lives of their menfolk. Although the worst abuses of child labor had been banned in most European countries by 1850, parents expected girls as young as ten to contribute to the household. Many became domestic servants, commonly working six-

*Das Kapital* (DUSS cop-ee-TALL)

teen or more hours a day, six and a half days a week, for little more than room and board. Their living quarters, usually in the attic or basement, contrasted with the luxurious quarters of their masters. Female servants were vulnerable to sexual abuse by their masters or their masters' sons.

Young women often preferred work in a factory to domestic service. Men worked in construction, iron and steel, heavy machinery, or on railroads; women worked in textiles and the clothing trades, two extensions of traditional women's household work. Most industrial countries passed legislation limiting the hours or forbidding the employment of women in the hardest and most dangerous occupations, such as mining and foundry work. Such legislation also reinforced gender divisions in industry, keeping women in low-paid, subordinate positions.

Married women with children were expected to stay home, even if their husbands did not make enough to support the family. In addition to the work of child rearing and housework, married women of the working class contributed to the family's income by taking in boarders, sewing, or weaving baskets. The hardest and worst-paid work was washing other people's clothes. Since electric lighting and indoor plumbing cost more than most working-class families could afford, even ordinary household duties like cooking and washing remained heavy burdens.

The poorest of the poor were orphans and single women with children. Unable to find jobs or support themselves at home, many turned to prostitution. The wealth of middle-class men made it easy for them to take advantage of the poverty of working-class women.

## The Victorian Age and Women's "Separate Sphere"

In English-speaking countries, the period from about 1850 to 1914 is known as the **Victorian Age.** The expression refers not only to the reign of Queen Victoria of England (r. 1837–1901) but also to rules of behavior and to an ideology surrounding the family and the relations between men and women. The Victorians contrasted the masculine ideals of strength and courage with the feminine virtues of beauty and kindness, and they idealized

파운드폭탄 4발 투하··· 두 아들과 함께 사망

심진지 구축··· 이틀째 시가戰

령이 대중 앞에 나타나거나 애국심
을 고취하는 노래만을 내보내던 방
송마저 중단됐다.

라크 전
의에서
영국 주

# DIVERSITY AND DOMINANCE

## MARX AND ENGELS ON GLOBAL TRADE AND THE BOURGEOISIE

*In 1848 the German philosophers Karl Marx (1818–1883) and Friedrich Engels (1820–1895), who were living in England at the time, published a small book called* Manifesto of the Communist Party. *In it, they tried to explain why owners of manufactures and business—the "bourgeoisie"—had become the wealthiest and most powerful class of people in industrializing countries like Britain, and why urban and industrial workers—the "proletariat"—lived in poverty. In their view, the dominance of the European commercial and industrial bourgeoisie was in the process of destroying the diversity of human cultures, reducing all classes in Europe and all cultures to the status of proletarians selling their labor.*

*In the* Manifesto, *Marx and Engels did not limit themselves to publicizing social inequities. They also called for a social revolution in which the workers would overthrow the bourgeoisie and establish a new society without private property or government. Their* Manifesto *was soon translated into many languages and became the best-known expression of radical communist ideology.*

*Whatever one may think of their call to revolution, Marx and Engels's analysis of class relations has had a lasting impact on social historians. Their ideas are especially interesting from the perspective of global history because of the way in which they connect the rise of the bourgeois with world trade and industrial technology. The following paragraphs explain these connections.*

The history of all hitherto existing society is the history of class struggles.

Freeman and slave, patrician and plebeian, lord and serf, guild-master and journeyman, in a word, oppressor and oppressed, stood in constant opposition to one another, carried on an uninterrupted, now hidden, now open fight, a fight that each time ended, either in a revolutionary re-constitution of society at large, or in the common ruin of the contending classes.

In the earlier epochs of history, we find almost everywhere a complicated arrangement of society into various orders, a manifold gradation of social rank. In ancient Rome we have patricians, knights, plebeians, slaves; in the middle ages, feudal lords, vassals, guild-masters, journeymen, apprentices, serfs; in almost all of these classes, again, subordinate gradations.

The modern bourgeois society that has sprouted from the ruins of feudal society, has not done away with class antagonisms. It has but established new classes, new conditions of oppression, new forms of struggle in place of the old ones.

Our epoch, the epoch of the bourgeoisie, possesses, however, this distinctive feature; it has simplified the class antagonisms. Society as a whole is more and more splitting up into two great hostile camps, into two great classes directly facing each other: Bourgeoisie and Proletariat.

From the serfs of the middle ages sprang the chartered burghers of the earliest towns. From these burgesses the first elements of the bourgeoisie were developed.

The discovery of America, the rounding of the Cape, opened up fresh ground for the rising bourgeoisie. The East-Indian and Chinese markets, the colonization of America, trade with the colonies, the increase in the means of exchange and in commodities generally, gave to commerce, to navigation, to industry, an impulse never before known, and thereby, to the revolutionary element in the tottering feudal society, a rapid development.

The feudal system of industry, under which industrial production was monopolised by closed guilds, now no longer sufficed for the growing wants of the new markets. The manufacturing system took its place. The guild-masters were pushed on one side by the manufacturing middle-class; division of labour between the different corporate guilds vanished in the face of division of labour in each single workshop.

Meantime the markets kept ever growing, the demand, ever rising. Even manufacture no longer sufficed. Thereupon, steam and machinery revolutionised industrial production. The place of manufacture was taken by the giant, Modern Industry, the place of the industrial middle-class, by industrial millionaires, the leaders of whole industrial armies, the modern bourgeois.

Modern industry has established the world-market, for which the discovery of America paved the way. This market has given an immense importance to commerce, to navigation, to communication by land. This development has, in its turn, reacted on the extension of industry; and in proportion as industry, commerce, navigation, railways extended, in the same proportion the bourgeoisie developed, increased its capital, and pushed into the background every class handed down from the Middle Ages.

We see, therefore, how the modern bourgeoisie is itself the product of a long course of development, of a series of revolutions in the modes of production and of exchange. . . .

[T]he bourgeoisie has at last, since the establishment of Modern Industry and of the world-market, conquered for itself, in the modern representative State, exclusive political sway. The executive of the modern State is but a committee for managing the common affairs of the whole bourgeoisie.

The bourgeoisie, historically, has played a most revolutionary part. . . .

It has been the first to shew what man's activity can bring about. It has accomplished wonders far surpassing Egyptian pyramids, Roman aqueducts, and Gothic cathedrals; it has conducted expeditions that put in the shade all former Exoduses of nations and crusades.

The bourgeoisie cannot exist without constantly revolutionising the instruments of production, and thereby the relations of production, and with them the whole relations of society. Conservation of the old modes of production in unaltered form, was, on the contrary, the first condition of existence for all earlier industrial classes. Constant revolutionising of production, uninterrupted disturbance of all social conditions, everlasting uncertainty and agitation distinguish the bourgeois epoch from all earlier ones. All fixed, fast-frozen relations, with their train of ancient and venerable prejudices and opinions, are swept away, all new-formed ones become antiquated before they can ossify. All that is solid melts into air, all that is holy is profaned, and man is at last compelled to face with sober senses, his real conditions of life, and his relations with his kind.

The need of a constantly expanding market for its products chases the bourgeoisie over the whole surface of the globe. It must nestle everywhere, settle everywhere, establish connexions everywhere.

The bourgeoisie has through its exploitation of the world-market given a cosmopolitan character to production and consumption in every country. To the great chagrin of Re-actionists, it has drawn from under the feet of industry the national ground on which it stood. All old-fashioned national industries have been destroyed or are daily being destroyed. They are dislodged by new industries, whose introduction becomes a life or death question for all civilised nations, by industries that no longer work up indigenous raw material, but raw material drawn from the remotest zones; industries whose products are consumed, not only at home, but in every quarter of the globe. In place of the old wants, satisfied by the productions of the country, we find new wants, requiring for their satisfaction the products of distant lands and climes. In place of the old local and national seclusion and self-sufficiency, we have intercourse in every direction, universal interdependence of nations. And as in material, so also in intellectual production. The intellectual creations of individual nations become common property. National one-sidedness and narrow-mindedness become more and more impossible, and from the numerous national and local literatures there arises a world-literature.

The bourgeoisie, by the rapid improvement of all instruments of production, by the immensely facilitated means of communication, draws all, even the most barbarian, nations into civilisation. The cheap prices of its commodities are the heavy artillery with which it batters down all Chinese walls, with which it forces the barbarians' intensely obstinate hatred of foreigners to capitulate. It compels all nations, on pain of extinction, to adopt the bourgeois mode of production; it compels them to introduce what it calls civilisation into their midst, i.e., to become bourgeois themselves. In a word, it creates a world after its own image.

The bourgeoisie has subjected the country to the rule of the towns. It has created enormous cities, has greatly increased the urban population as compared with the rural, and has thus rescued a considerable part of the population from the idiocy of rural life. Just as it has made the country dependent on the towns, so it has made barbarian and semi-barbarian countries dependent on the civilised ones, nations of peasants on nations of bourgeois, the East on the West. . . .

The bourgeoisie, during its rule of scarce one hundred years, has created more massive and more colossal productive forces than have all preceding generations together. Subjection of Nature's forces to man, machinery, application of chemistry to industry and agriculture, steam-navigation, railways, electric telegraphs, clearing of whole continents for cultivation, canalization of rivers, whole populations conjured out of the ground—what earlier century had even a presentiment that such productive forces slumbered in the lap of social labour?

## QUESTIONS FOR ANALYSIS

1. How did the growth of world trade since the European discovery of America affect relations between social classes in Europe?

2. What effect did the growth of trade and industry have on products, intellectual creations, and consumer tastes around the world?

3. Why does Marx think the bourgeoisie requires constant changes in technology and social relations? How well does that description fit the world you live in?

4. Can you think of recent examples of the Western bourgeoisie's creating "a world after its own image"?

Source: Karl Marx and Frederick Engels, Manifesto of the Communist Party, Authorized English Translation: Edited and Annotated by Frederick Engels (Chicago: Charles H. Kerr & Company, 1906), 12–20.

the home as a peaceful and loving refuge from the dog-eat-dog world of competitive capitalism.

Victorian morality claimed to be universal, yet it best fit the European upper- and middle-class family. Men and women were thought to belong in **"separate spheres."** Successful businessmen spent their time at work or relaxing in men's clubs. They put their wives in charge of rearing the children, running the household, and spending the family money to enhance the family's social status.

The most important duty of middle-class women was rearing children. Unlike the rich of previous eras, who handed their children over to wet nurses and tutors, Victorian mothers nursed their own babies and showered their children with love and attention. Even those who could afford nannies and governesses remained personally involved in their children's education. While boys were being prepared for the business world or the professions, girls were taught such skills as embroidery, drawing, and music, which offered no monetary reward or professional preparation but enhanced their social graces and marriage prospects.

Young women could work until they got married, but only in genteel occupations such as retail and office work. Jobs that required higher education, especially jobs in the professions, were closed to women. Until late in the century, few universities granted degrees to women. The first profession open to women was teaching, as more and more countries passed laws calling for universal compulsory education. Women were considered well suited to teaching young children and girls—an extension of the duties of Victorian mothers. Teaching, however, was judged suitable only for single women; married women were expected to stay home and take care of their own children.

Governments enforced legal discrimination against women. Until the end of the century, most European countries considered women minors for life—that is, subject to their fathers before marriage and to their husbands after. Even Britain,

**Separate Spheres in Great Britain** In the Victorian Age, men and women of the middle and upper classes led largely separate lives. In *Aunt Emily's Visit* (1845), we see women and children at home, tended by a servant. *The Royal Exchange*, meanwhile, was a place for men to transact business. (Mary Evans Picture Library)

among the most progressive countries, did not give women the right to control their own property until 1882, with passage of the Married Women's Property Act.

Some middle-class women organized to fight prostitution, alcohol, and child labor. By the turn of the century, a few were challenging male domination of politics and the law. By 1914, women had won the right to vote in twelve states of the United States. British women did not vote until 1918.

# NATIONALISM AND THE UNIFICATION OF GERMANY

The most influential idea of the nineteenth century was **nationalism.** The French revolutionaries had defined people, previously considered the subjects of a sovereign, as the citizens of a *nation*—a concept identified with a territory, the state that ruled it, and the culture of its people. Because the most widely spoken language in nineteenth-century Europe was German, the unification of most German-speaking people into a single state in 1871 had momentous consequences for the world.

## National Identity Before 1871

The idea of redrawing the boundaries of states to accommodate linguistic, religious, or cultural differences was revolutionary. Language was usually the crucial element in creating a feeling of national unity, but language and citizenship seldom coincided. The fit between France and the French language was exceptional. The Italian- and German-speaking peoples were divided among many small states. Living in the Austrian Empire were peoples who spoke German, Czech, Slovak, Hungarian, Polish, and other languages. Even where people spoke a common language, they could be divided by religion or institutions. The Irish, though English speaking, were mostly Catholic, whereas the English were primarily Protestant.

Until the 1860s, nationalism was associated with **liberalism,** the revolutionary middle-class ideology emerging from the French Revolution (see Chapter 19) that asserted the sovereignty of the people and demanded constitutional government, a national parliament, and freedom of expression. The most famous nationalist of the early nineteenth century, Giuseppe Mazzini° (1805–1872), led

**Giuseppe Mazzini** (jew-SEP-pay mat-SEE-nee)

a failed liberal revolution of 1848 in Italy that sought to unify the Italian peninsula. Although the revolutions of 1848 failed except in France, their strength convinced conservative governments that they could not forever keep their citizens out of politics and that mass politics, if properly managed, could strengthen rather than weaken the state. A new generation of conservative political leaders learned how to preserve the social status quo through public education, universal military service, and colonial conquests, all of which built a sense of national unity.

## The Unification of Germany

Some German nationalists wanted to unite all Germans under the Catholic Austrian throne. Others wanted to exclude Austria with its many non-Germanic peoples and unite all other German-speaking areas under Lutheran Prussia. The Prussian state had two advantages: (1) the newly developed industries of the Rhineland and (2) the first European army to make use of railroads, telegraphs, breechloading rifles, steel artillery, and other products of modern industry. The king of Prussia, Wilhelm I (r. 1861–1888), had entrusted the running of his government to his chancellor, the brilliant and authoritarian aristocrat **Otto von Bismarck** (1815–1898), who was determined to use Prussian military and German nationalism to advance the interests of the Prussian state.

In 1864, after a quick victory against Denmark, Bismarck set his sights on Austria, which surrendered in 1866. To everyone's surprise, Prussia took no Austrian territory. Instead, Prussia and some smaller states formed the North German Confederation, the nucleus of a future Germany. Then in 1870, Bismarck provoked a war with France. In this "Franco-Prussian War," German armies used their superior firepower and tactics to achieve a quick victory.

The spoils of victory included a large indemnity and two provinces of Alsace and Lorraine (see Map 23.1). To the Germans, this region was German because a majority of its inhabitants spoke German. To the French, it was French because it had been so when the nation of France was forged in the Revolution and because most of its inhabitants considered themselves French. These two conflicting definitions of nationalism kept enmity between France and Germany smoldering for decades.

## Nationalism After 1871

The Franco-Prussian War changed the political climate of Europe. France became wholeheartedly liberal. The Italian peninsula became unified as the kingdom of Italy. Germany, Austria-Hungary (as the Austrian Empire had renamed itself in 1867), and Russia remained conservative.

All politicians tried to manipulate public opinion to bolster their governments. The spread of literacy allowed politicians and journalists to appeal to the emotions of the poor, diverting their anger from their employers to foreigners and their votes from socialist to nationalist parties.

In many countries, the dominant group used nationalism to justify the imposing of its language, religion, or customs on minority populations. The Russian Empire attempted to "Russify" its diverse ethnic populations. The Spanish government made the Spanish language compulsory in the schools, newspapers, and courts of its Basque- and Catalan-speaking provinces. Immigrants to the United States were expected to learn English.

Some people looked to science for support of political dominance. One of the most influential scientists of the century, and the one whose ideas were most widely cited and misinterpreted, was the English biologist **Charles Darwin** (1809–1882), who had spent years traveling through South America and the South Pacific studying plant and animal life. His famous book, *On the Origin of Species by Means of Natural Selection* (1859), argued that over hundreds of thousands of years, living beings had either evolved in the struggle for survival or become extinct. The philosopher Herbert Spencer (1820–1903) and others took up Darwin's ideas of "natural selection" and "survival of the fittest" and applied them to human society. Extreme Social Darwinists developed elaborate pseudo-scientific theories of racial differences, claiming that they were the result not of history but of biology.

**Map 23.1    The Unification of Germany, 1866–1871**    Germany was united after a series of short, successful wars by the kingdom of Prussia against Austria in 1866 and against France in 1871.

# THE GREAT POWERS OF EUROPE, 1871–1900

After 1871, politicians and journalists discovered how easily they could whip up popular frenzy against neighboring countries. Rivalries over colonial territories, ideological differences between liberal and conservative governments, and even minor border incidents or trade disagreements contributed to a growing atmosphere of international tension.

## Germany at the Center of Europe

International relations revolved around a united Germany, because Germany was located in the center of Europe and had the most powerful army on the European continent. After creating a unified Germany in 1871, Bismarck worked to maintain peace in Europe. To isolate France, he forged a loose coalition with Austria-Hungary and Russia, which he was able to keep together for twenty years.

Bismarck proved equally adept at manipulating mass politics at home. To weaken the influence of middle-class liberals, he extended the vote to all adult men. By imposing high tariffs on manufactured goods and wheat, he gained the support of both the wealthy industrialists of the Rhineland and the great landowners of eastern Germany. He stole the thunder of the socialists by introducing social legislation—medical, unemployment, and disability insurance and old-age pensions—long before other industrial countries did. Under his leadership, the German people developed a strong sense of national unity and pride in their industrial and military power.

In 1888, Wilhelm I was succeeded by his grandson Wilhelm II (r. 1888–1918), who dismissed Chancellor Bismarck. Wilhelm II talked about his "global policy" and demanded that Germany, with the mightiest army and the largest industrial economy in Europe, have a colonial empire, "a place in the sun."

## The Liberal Powers: France and Great Britain

France, once the dominant nation in Europe, had difficulty reconciling itself to being in second place. Its population and its army lagged far behind Germany's, and its industry was growing more slowly, thanks to the loss of the iron and coal mines of Lorraine. The French people were deeply divided over the very nature of the state: some were monarchists and Catholics; a growing number held republican and anticlerical views. Despite these problems, a long tradition of popular participation in politics and a strong sense of nationhood, reinforced by a fine system of universal public education, gave the French people a deeper cohesion than appeared on the surface.

Great Britain was the only other country in Europe with a democratic tradition. The British government alternated smoothly between the Liberal and Conservative Parties, and the income gap between rich and poor gradually narrowed. Nevertheless, Britain had problems that grew more apparent as time went on.

One problem was Irish resentment of English rule as a foreign occupying force. Another problem was the British economy. Once the workshop of the world, Great Britain had fallen behind the United States and Germany in such important industries as iron and steel, chemicals, electricity, and textiles. Even in shipbuilding and shipping, Britain's traditional specialties, Germany was catching up. Britain was also preoccupied with its enormous and fast-growing empire. Though a source of wealth for investors and the envy of other imperialist nations, the empire was a constant drain on Britain's finances.

After the Crimean War of 1853–1856 (see Chapter 22), Britain turned its back on Europe and pursued a policy of "splendid isolation." Britain's preoccupation with India led British statesmen to exaggerate the Russian threat to the shipping routes through the Mediterranean and Central Asia.

## The Conservative Powers: Russia and Austria-Hungary

The forces of nationalism weakened rather than strengthened Russia and Austria-Hungary. The reason for this effect was that

**The Doss House**   Late-nineteenth-century cities showed more physical than social improvements. This painting by Makovsky of a street in St. Petersburg contrasts the broad avenue and impressive new buildings with the poverty of the crowd.   (The State Museum/St. Petersburg)

their populations were far more divided, socially and ethnically, than were the German, French, or British peoples.

Nationalism was most divisive in the Austrian Empire. The decision to rename itself the Austro-Hungarian Empire in 1867 appeased its Hungarian critics but alienated its Slavic-speaking minorities. The Austro-Hungarian Empire still thought of itself as a great power and attempted to dominate the Balkans. This strategy irritated Russia, which thought of itself as the protector of Slavic peoples everywhere, and it eventually led to war.

Russia was the most misunderstood country in Europe. Its enormous size and population led many Europeans to exaggerate its military potential, but Russia was weakened by national and so-

cial divisions. All in all, only 45 percent of the peoples of the tsarist empire spoke Russian.

To strengthen the bonds between the monarchy and the Russian people and promote industrialization by enlarging the labor pool, the moderate conservative Tsar Alexander II (r. 1855–1881) emancipated the peasants from serfdom in 1861. That measure, however, did not create a modern society but only turned serfs into communal farmers with few skills and little capital. Though technically "emancipated," the great majority of Russians had little education, few legal rights, and no say in their government. After Alexander's assassination in 1881, his successors Alexander III (r. 1881–1894) and Nicholas II (r. 1894–1917) opposed all forms of social change. Industrialization consisted largely of state-sponsored projects, such as railroads, iron foundries, and armament factories, and led to social unrest among urban workers. Wealthy landowning aristocrats continued to dominate the Russian court and administration and succeeded in blocking most reforms.

The weaknesses in Russia's society and government became glaringly obvious after Russia's defeat in the Russo-Japanese War of 1904–1905 (see below). The shock of defeat caused a popular uprising, the Revolution of 1905, that forced Tsar Nicholas II to grant a constitution and an elected Duma (parliament). But as soon as he was able to rebuild the army and the police, he reverted to the traditional despotism of his forefathers. Small groups of radical intellectuals, angered by the contrast between the wealth of the elite and the poverty of the common people, began plotting the violent overthrow of the tsarist autocracy.

# NEW GREAT POWERS: THE UNITED STATES AND JAPAN

Europeans had come to regard their continent as the center of the universe and their states as the only great powers in the world. The rest of the world was either ignored or used as bargaining chips in the game of power politics. The late nineteenth century marked the high point of European power and arrogance, yet at that very moment, two nations outside Europe were becoming great powers. One of them, the United States, was inhabited mainly by people of European origin, and its rise to great-power status had been predicted early in the nineteenth century by astute observers like the French statesman Alexis de Tocqueville. The other one, Japan, seemed so distant and exotic in 1850 that no European had guessed it would join the ranks of the great powers.

## The United States, 1865–1900

After the Civil War ended in 1865, the United States entered a period of vigorous growth. Hundreds of thousands of immigrants arrived every year, mainly from Russia, Italy, and central Europe, raising the population to 63 million in 1891. Although many settled on the newly opened lands west of the Mississippi, most of the migrants moved to the towns, which mushroomed into cities in a few years. In the process, the nation became an industrial giant. By 1900, the United States had overtaken Britain and Germany as the world's leading industrial power.

This explosive growth was accomplished with few government restrictions and much government help, such as free land for railroads and protective tariffs. In this atmosphere of unfettered free enterprise, the nation got rich fast, as did its upper and middle classes.

Expansion created many victims. First among them were the American Indians. When the railroads penetrated the west after the Civil War, they brought white colonists eager to start farming, ranching, or mining. The indigenous Indians whose lands they invaded fought back with great courage but were outnumbered and outgunned. In Canada, the government tried to protect the Indians from the whites. The United States Army, however, always sided with the settlers. The U.S. government had signed numerous treaties with the Indians but tore them up when settlers demanded land. After decades of warfare, massacres, and starvation, the government confined the remaining Indians to reservations on the poorest lands.

The U.S. government also abandoned African-Americans in 1877, after the end of Reconstruction, especially in the defeated southern states. Though freed from slavery in 1865, most of them became sharecroppers who were at the mercy of their landowners. In the 1890s, the southern states instituted "Jim Crow" laws segregating blacks in public transportation, jobs, and schools. Not only did southern judges apply harsh laws in a biased manner, but black Americans were also subject to the lawless violence of mobs, which lynched an average of fifty blacks a year until well into the twentieth century.

Racism also affected Asian immigrants, many of whom had come to the United States to build railroads in the western states. In 1882, the U.S. government barred the Chinese from immigrating by enacting the first of many racial exclusion laws.

Working-class whites benefited little from the booming economy. Economic depressions in

1873 and 1893 caused more distress in the United States than in Europe, because the United States had few labor laws and no unemployment compensation to soften the hardships. Police or the army repressed strikes and unions. The courts consistently supported employers against their employees, capital against labor, and business against government.

Working-class women bore the brunt of repressive labor practices because they earned less than men, had more responsibilities, and seldom were members of labor unions. As in Britain, activist middle-class women organized to demand female suffrage and to fight against alcohol, prostitution, and other social evils.

The booming economy and the waves of immigrants radically transformed the environment. Timber companies clear-cut large areas of Michigan, Wisconsin, and the Appalachian Mountains to provide lumber for railroad ties and frame houses, pulp for paper, and fuel for locomotives and iron foundries. Farmers cleared the forests and plowed the prairies. Buffalo, the dominant animals of the western territories, were massacred by the hundreds of thousands to starve out the Indians and clear the land for cattle. In the west, the government began massive irrigation projects. In the industrial northeast, iron foundries, steel mills, and steam engines caused severe local air pollution.

In spite of all the assaults, the North American continent was so huge that large parts of it remained unspoiled. A few especially beautiful areas were declared national parks, beginning with Yellowstone in Wyoming in 1872, thereby marking a new stage in Americans' attitude toward nature. Thanks to the efforts of naturalist John Muir and President Theodore Roosevelt (1901–1909), large parts of the western states were set aside as national forests.

Most citizens showed little interest in foreign affairs. Patriots tended to celebrate American freedom and democracy, the conquest of a huge continent, and the country's remarkable technological achievements. In this period, the inventor Thomas Edison was probably the most admired man in America.

The expansionism of the United States and its businesses did not stop at the borders but exerted a strong influence on Mexico and the Caribbean.

Naval officers, bankers, and politicians urged active intervention in the Western Hemisphere. In 1899, the United States defeated Spain, annexed Puerto Rico and the Philippines, and turned Cuba into an American protectorate (see Chapter 24). Long recognized as the leading power in the Americas, the United States found itself involved in Asian affairs as well. Nevertheless, although their country was fast becoming a global power, most Americans still preferred George Washington's policy of "no European entanglements."

## The Crisis of the Tokugawa Shogunate

Japan's response to imperialist pressure differed entirely from China's. In the latter country, the **Empress Dowager Cixi**° (r. 1862–1908), who had once encouraged the construction of shipyards, arsenals, and telegraph lines, came to oppose railways and other foreign technologies that could carry foreign influences to the interior (see Chapter 22). Government officials secretly encouraged crowds to attack and destroy the intrusive devices. They were able to slow the foreign intrusion, but in doing so, they denied themselves the best means of defense against foreign pressure.

In Japan, which was very differently organized politically under the Tokugawa Shogunate (see Chapter 18), local lords called *daimyo* controlled their lands and populations with little interference from the shogunate and none at all from the emperor, whose political role was purely symbolic. Though the shoguns passed stringent laws against dealing with foreigners, many Japanese ignored them. The most flagrant violators were powerful lords in southern Japan who ran large and successful pirate or black-market operations. Though they took advantage of shogunal weakness, some lords recognized that a genuine foreign challenge, such as the one presaged by the appearance of Russian and British ships off the Japanese coast in 1792, might overwhelm them. The regional lords of Satsuma° and Choshu,° two large domains in southern Japan, responded by upgrading their armies, arsenals, and shipyards. Their remoteness from the

---

**Cixi** (TSUH-shee)    **Satsuma** (SAT-soo-mah)    **Choshu** (CHOE-shoo)

capital Edo (now Tokyo) along with their economic vigor and growing populations fostered a strong sense of local self-reliance.

In 1853 the American commodore Matthew C. Perry arrived off the coast of Japan with a fleet of steam-powered warships that the Japanese called "black ships." He demanded that Japan open its ports to trade and allow American ships to refuel and take on supplies during their voyages between China and California. He promised to return a year later to receive the Japanese answer.

Perry's demands sparked a crisis. After consultation with the provincial daimyo, the shogun's advisers advocated capitulation to Perry. They pointed to China's humiliating defeats in the Opium and Arrow Wars (see Chapter 22). The solution they proposed, the Treaty of Kanagawa,° resembled the unequal treaties between China and the Western powers. This spurred some angry provincial governors to encourage agitation against the Tokugawa regime and in favor of banning foreigners from Japan.

Political tensions between the shogunate and provincial leaders in Choshu, Satsuma, and elsewhere increased in the early 1860s. When British and French ships shelled the southwestern coasts in 1864 to protest the treatment of foreigners, provincial samurai exploded with anger against the treaty and the shogunate's inability to protect the country. Young, educated men who faced mediocre prospects under the rigid Tokugawa class system emerged as provincial leaders. In 1867 the Choshu leaders Yamagata Aritomo and Ito Hirobumi finally realized that they should stop warring with Satsuma and join forces to lead a rebellion against the shogunate.

## The Meiji Restoration and the Modernization of Japan, 1868–1894

The civil war was intense but brief. In 1868 provincial rebels overthrew the Tokugawa Shogunate and declared the young emperor Mutsuhito° (r. 1868–1912) "restored." The new leaders called their regime the **"Meiji° Restoration,"** after Mutsuhito's reign name (*Meiji* means "enlightened rule"). Dedicated

Kanagawa (KAH-nah-GAH-wah)   **Mutsuhito** (moo-tsoo-HE-toe)   **Meiji** (MAY-gee)

to protecting their country from Western imperialism, the architects of the new regime visualized Japan's transformation into "a rich country with a strong army" and world-class industries. Though imposed from above, the Meiji Restoration changed Japan as profoundly as the French Revolution changed France.

In the Charter Oath issued in 1868, the young emperor included a prophetic sentence (written by his advisers): "Knowledge shall be sought throughout the world and thus shall be strengthened the foundation of the imperial polity." With the highest literacy rate in Asia, Japan was well prepared to learn and disseminate those foreign ideas, institutions, and techniques that could strengthen the nation, including a new educational system and a conscript army. Experimentation with industrial development and financing in the provinces in the earlier 1800s taught the government how to establish heavy industries through state financing without extensive foreign debt.

The Meiji leaders copied the government structure of imperial Germany. They modeled the new Japanese navy on the British and the army on the Prussian. They introduced Western-style postal and telegraph services, railroads and harbors, banking, clocks, and calendars. To learn the secrets of Western strength, they sent hundreds of students to Britain, Germany, and the United States. They even encouraged foreign clothing styles and pastimes.

Western technology was highly prized. The government opened vocational, technical, and agricultural schools and founded four imperial universities. Foreign experts gave advice on medicine, science, and engineering. At the newly created Imperial College of Engineering, an Englishman, William Ayrton, became the first professor of electrical engineering anywhere in the world. His students later went on to found major corporations and government research institutes.

State-owned factories turned out textiles and inexpensive consumer goods for sale abroad. The first Japanese industries, some dating to the early nineteenth century, exploited their workers ruthlessly, just as the first industries in Europe and America had done. Peasant families, squeezed by rising taxes and rents, sent their daughters to work in textile mills. In 1881, to pay off its debts, the government sold these enterprises to private investors,

**Silk Factory in Japan**    Silk manufacture, Japan's best-known industry, began to be mechanized in the 1870s. In this factory, as in most textile mills, the workers were women.    (The Metropolitan Museum of Art, gift of Lincoln Kirstein, 1959 [JP 3346]. Photograph by Otto E. Nelson. Photograph © 1986 The Metropolitan Museum of Art.)

mainly large *zaibatsu*°, or conglomerates. But individual technological innovation was also encouraged. Thus the carpenter Toyoda Sakichi founded the Toyoda Loom Works (now Toyota Motor Company) in 1906; ten years later he patented the world's most advanced automatic loom.

## The Birth of Japanese Imperialism, 1894–1905

Japan's path to imperialism was laid out by **Yamagata Aritomo,** an influential Meiji leader. He believed that to be independent Japan had to define a "sphere of influence" that included Korea, Manchuria, and part of China (see Map 23.2). If other countries controlled these areas, Japan would be at risk. To protect this sphere of influence, Yamagata called for a vigorous program of military industrialization, culminating in the building of battleships.

Meanwhile, as Japan grew stronger, China weakened. In 1894 the two nations went to war over Japanese encroachments in Korea. The Sino-Japanese War, which lasted less than six months, forced China to evacuate Korea, cede Taiwan and the Liaodong° Peninsula, and pay a heavy indemnity. France, Germany, Britain, Russia, and the United States made Japan give up Liaodong in the name of the "territorial integrity" of China but in return forced China to grant them territorial and trade concessions, including ninety treaty ports.

In 1900 Chinese officials around the Empress Dowager Cixi encouraged a series of antiforeign riots known as the Boxer Uprising. European, American,

---

**zaibatsu** (zye-BOT-soo

**Liaodong** (li-AH-oh-dong)

**Map 23.2    Expansion and Modernization of Japan, 1868–1918**    As Japan acquired modern industry, it followed the example of the European powers in seeking overseas colonies. Its colonial empire grew at the expense of its neighbors: Taiwan was taken from China in 1895; Karafutu (Sakhalin) from Russia in 1905; and all of Korea became a colony in 1910.

and Japanese military forces put down the riots and occupied Beijing. Emboldened by China's obvious weakness, Japan and Russia competed for possession of the mineral-rich Chinese province of Manchuria.

In 1905 Japan stunned the world by defeating Russia in the Russo-Japanese War. By the Treaty of Portsmouth that ended the war, Japan established a protectorate over Korea. In spite of Western attempts to restrict it to the role of junior partner,

Japan continued to increase its influence. It gained control of southern Manchuria, with its industries and railroads. In 1910 it finally annexed Korea, joining the ranks of the world's colonial powers.

## CONCLUSION

A fter World War I broke out in 1914, many people, especially in Europe, looked back on the period from 1850 to 1914 as a golden age. For some, and in certain ways, it was. Industrialization was a powerful torrent changing Europe, North America, and East Asia. While other technologies like shipping and railroads increased their global reach, new ones—electricity, the steel and chemical industries, and the global telegraph network—contributed to the enrichment and empowerment of the industrial nations. Memories of the great scourges—famines, wars, and epidemics—faded. Clean water, electric lights, and railways began to improve the lives of city dwellers, even the poor. Goods from distant lands, even travel to other continents, came within the reach of millions.

European and American society seemed to be heading toward better organization and greater security. Municipal services made city life less dangerous and chaotic. Through labor unions, workers achieved some measure of recognition and security. By the turn of the century, liberal political reforms had taken hold in western Europe and the United States and seemed about to triumph in Russia as well. Morality and legislation aimed at providing security for women and families, though equality between the sexes was still beyond reach.

The framework for all these changes was the nation-state. The world economy, international politics, and even cultural and social issues revolved around a handful of countries—the great powers—that believed themselves in control of the destiny of the world. These included the most powerful European nations of the previous century, as well as two newcomers—the United States and Japan—that were to play important roles in the future. Seldom in history had there been such a concentration of wealth, power, and self-confidence.

The success of the great powers rested on their ability to extract resources from nature and from other societies, especially in Asia, Africa, and Latin America. In a global context, the counterpart of the rise of the great powers is the story of imperialism and colonialism. To complete our understanding of the period before 1914, let us turn now to the relations between the great powers and the rest of the world.

## ■ Key Terms

| | |
|---|---|
| steel | Victorian Age |
| electricity | "separate spheres" |
| Thomas Edison | nationalism |
| submarine telegraph cables | liberalism |
| railroads | Otto von Bismarck |
| socialism | Charles Darwin |
| labor union | Empress Dowager Cixi |
| Yamagata Aritomo | Meiji Restoration |
| Karl Marx | |

## ■ Suggested Reading

More has been written on the great powers in the late nineteenth century than on any previous period in their histories. The following are some interesting recent works and a few classics.

Industrialization is the subject of Peter Stearns, *The Industrial Revolution in World History* (1993), and David Landes, *The Unbound Prometheus: Technological Change and Industrial Development in Western Europe from 1750 to the Present* (1969). Two interesting works on nationalism are E. J. Hobsbawm, *Nation and Nationalism Since 1780* (1990), and Benedict Anderson, *Imagined Communities: Reflections on the Origin and Spread of Nationalism* (1991).

Barrington Moore, *The Social Origins of Dictatorship and Democracy* (1966), is a classic essay on European society. On European women, see Renate Bridenthal, Susan Mosher Stuard, and Merry E. Wiesner, eds., *Becoming Visible: Women in European History,* 3d ed. (1998); Patricia Branca, *Silent Sisterhood: Middle-Class Women in the Victorian Home* (1975); Louise Tilly and Joan Scott, *Women, Work, and Family* (1987); and Theresa McBride, *The Domestic Revolution: The Modernization of Household Service in England and France, 1820–1920* (1976). The history of family life is told in Beatrice Gottlieb, *The Family in the Western World from the Black Death to the Industrial Age* (1993). Albert Lindemann, *A History of European Socialism* (1983), covers the labor movements as well.

There are many excellent histories of individual countries. On Germany in the nineteenth century, see David

Blackbourne, *The Long Nineteenth Century: A History of Germany, 1780–1918* (1998), and Gordon A. Craig, *Germany, 1866–1945* (1980). The standard works on Bismarck and the unification of Germany are Otto Pflanze, *Bismarck and the Development of Germany* (1990), and Lothar Gall, *Bismarck, the White Revolutionary* (1986). On Britain, see Donald Read, *The Age of Urban Democracy: England, 1868–1914* (1994), and David Thomson, *England in the Nineteenth Century, 1815–1914* (1978). On France, Eugen Weber, *Peasants into Frenchmen* (1976), and Roger Price, *A Social History of Nineteenth-Century France* (1987), are especially recommended. For Austria, see Alan Sked, *The Decline and Fall of the Habsburg Empire, 1815–1918* (1989). Two good introductions to Russian history are Hans Rogger, *Russia in the Age of Modernization and Revolution, 1881–1917* (1983), and Gregory L. Freeze, ed., *Russia: A History* (1997).

There are several interesting books on Japan, in particular Peter Duus, *The Rise of Modern Japan*, 2d ed. (1998), and Tessa Morris-Suzuki, *The Technological Transformation of Japan* (1994). Two fine books that cover the history of modern China are John King Fairbank, *The Great Chinese Revolution, 1800–1985* (1987), and Jonathan D. Spence, *The Search for Modern China* (1990).

# The New Imperialism, 1869–1914

# 24

## CHAPTER OUTLINE

The New Imperialism: Motives and Methods

The Scramble for Africa

Asia and Western Dominance

Imperialism in Latin America

The World Economy and the Global Environment

DIVERSITY AND DOMINANCE: Two Africans Recall the Arrival of the Europeans

In 1869 Ismail°, the khedive° (ruler) of Egypt, invited all the Christian princes of Europe and all the Muslim princes of Asia and Africa—except the Ottoman sultan, his nominal overlord—to celebrate the inauguration of the greatest construction project of the century: the **Suez Canal.** Among the sixteen hundred dignitaries from the Middle East and Europe who assembled at Port Said° were Emperor Francis Joseph of Austria-Hungary and Empress Eugénie of France. A French journalist wrote:

> This multitude, coming from all parts of the world, presented the most varied and singular spectacle. All races were represented. . . . We saw, coming to attend this festival of civilization, men of the Orient wearing clothes of dazzling

colors, chiefs of African tribes wrapped in their great coats, Circassians in war costumes, officers of the British army of India with their shakos [hats] wrapped in muslin, Hungarian magnates wearing their national costumes.[1]

Ismail used the occasion to emphasize the harmony and cooperation between the peoples of Africa, Asia, and Europe and to show that Egypt was not only independent but was also an equal of the great powers. To bless the inauguration, Ismail had invited clergy of the Muslim, Orthodox, and Catholic faiths. A reporter noted: "The Khedive . . . wished to symbolize thereby the unity of men and their brotherhood before God, without distinction of religion; it was the first time that the Orient had seen such a meeting of faiths to celebrate and bless together a great event and a great work."[2]

---

**Ismail** (is-mah-EEL)   **khedive** (kuh-DEEV)   **Port Said** (port sah-EED)

The canal was a great success, but not in the way Ismail intended. Ships using it could travel between Europe and India in less than two weeks—much less time than the month or longer consumed by sailing around Africa and across the Indian Ocean. By lowering freight costs, the canal stimulated shipping and the construction of steamships, giving an advantage to nations that had heavy industry and a large maritime trade over land-based empires and countries with few merchant ships. Great Britain, which long opposed construction of the canal for fear that it might fall into enemy hands, benefited more than any other nation. France, which provided half the capital and most of the engineers, came in a distant second, for it had less trade with Asia than Britain did. Egypt, which contributed the other half of the money and most of the labor, was the loser. Instead of making Egypt powerful and independent, the Suez Canal provided the excuse for a British invasion and occupation of Egypt.

Far from inaugurating an era of harmony among the peoples of three continents and three faiths, the canal triggered a wave of European domination over Africa and Asia. Between 1869 and 1914 Germany, France, Britain, Russia, Japan, and the United States used industrial technology to impose their will on the nonindustrial parts of the world. Historians use the expression **New Imperialism** to describe this exercise of power.

As you read this chapter, ask yourself the following questions:

- What motivated the industrial nations to conquer new territories, and what means did they use?

- Why were some parts of the world annexed to the new empires, while others became economic dependencies of the great powers?

- How did the environment change in the lands subjected to the New Imperialism?

## THE NEW IMPERIALISM: MOTIVES AND METHODS

The New Imperialism was characterized by an explosion of territorial conquests even more rapid than the Spanish conquests of the sixteenth century. Between 1869 and 1914, in a land grab of unprecedented speed, Europeans seized territories in Africa and Central Asia, and both Europeans and Americans took territories in Southeast Asia and the Pacific. Approximately 10 million square miles (26 million square kilometers) and 150 million people fell under the rule of Europe and the United States in this period.

The New Imperialism was more than a land grab. The imperial powers used economic and technological means to reorganize dependent regions and bring them into the world economy as suppliers of foodstuffs and raw materials and as consumers of industrial products. In Africa and other parts of the world, this was done by conquest and colonial administration. In the Latin American republics the same result was achieved indirectly. Even though they remained politically independent, they became economic dependencies of the United States and Europe.

What inspired Europeans and Americans to venture overseas and impose their will on other societies? There is no simple answer to this question. Economic, cultural, and political motives were involved in all cases.

**Political Motives** The great powers of the late nineteenth century, as well as less powerful countries like Italy, Portugal, and Belgium, were competitive and hypersensitive about their status. France, humiliated by its defeat by Prussia in 1871 (see Chapter 23), sought to reestablish its prestige through territorial acquisitions overseas. Great Britain, already in possession of the world's largest and richest empire, felt the need to protect India, its "jewel in the crown,"

## CHRONOLOGY

| | The Scramble for Africa | Asia and Western Dominance | Imperialism in Latin America |
|---|---|---|---|
| | | **1862–1895** French conquer Indochina | |
| | | **1865–1876** Russian forces advance into Central Asia | |
| **1870** | **1869** Opening of the Suez Canal | | **1870–1910** Railroad building boom; British companies in Argentina and Brazil; U.S. companies in Mexico |
| | **1874** Warfare between the British and the Asante (Gold Coast) | | |
| | **1877–1879** Warfare between the British and the Xhosa and between the British and the Zulu (South Africa) | | |
| | | **1878** United States obtains Pago Pago Harbor (Samoa) | |
| | **1882** British forces occupy Egypt | | |
| | **1884–1885** Berlin Conference; Leopold II obtains Congo Free State | | |
| | | **1885** Britain completes conquest of Burma | |
| | | **1887** United States obtains Pearl Harbor (Hawaii) | |
| **1890** | | **1894–1895** China defeated in Sino-Japanese War | |
| | | **1895** France completes conquest of Indochina | **1895–1898** Cubans revolt against Spanish rule |
| | **1896** Ethiopians defeat Italian army at Adowa; warfare between the British and the Asante | | |
| | **1898** Battle of Omdurman | **1898** United States annexes Hawaii and purchases Philippines from Spain | **1898** Spanish-American War; United States annexes Puerto Rico and Guam |

*(continued)*

| C H R O N O L O G Y *(continued)* | | |
| --- | --- | --- |
| **The Scramble for Africa** | **Asia and Western Dominance** | **Imperialism in Latin America** |
| **1899–1902**  South African War between Afrikaners and the British | **1899–1902**  U.S. forces conquer and occupy Philippines | |
| | | **1901**  United States imposes Platt Amendment on Cuba |
| **1902**  First Aswan Dam completed (Egypt) | | |
| | **1903**  Russia completes Trans-Siberian Railway | **1903**  United States backs secession of Panama from Colombia |
| | **1904–1905**  Russia defeated in Russo-Japanese War | **1904–1907, 1916**  U.S. troops occupy Dominican Republic |
| | | **1904–1914**  United States builds Panama Canal |
| **1910** | **1908**  Belgium annexes Congo | |
| | | **1912**  U.S. troops occupy Nicaragua and Honduras |

by acquiring colonies in East Africa and Southeast Asia. German Chancellor Otto von Bismarck had little interest in acquiring colonies, but many Germans believed that a country as important as theirs deserved an overseas empire.

Political motives were not limited to statesmen in the capital cities. Colonial governors and political officers practiced their own diplomacy, often making a claim to a territory just to forestall some rival. Armies fighting frontier wars found it easier to defeat their neighbors than to make peace with them. In response to border skirmishes with neighboring states, colonial agents were likely to send in troops, take over their neighbors' territories, and then inform their home governments. Governments felt obligated to back up their men-on-the-spot in order not to lose face. The

great powers of Europe acquired much of West Africa, Southeast Asia, and the Pacific islands in this manner.

## Cultural Motives

The late nineteenth century saw a Christian revival in Europe and North America, as both Catholics and Protestants founded new missionary societies. Their purpose was not only religious—to convert nonbelievers, whom they regarded as "heathen"—but also cultural in a broader sense. They sought to export their own norms of "civilized" behavior: they were determined to abolish slavery in Africa and bring Western education, medicine, hygiene, monogamous marriage, and modest dress to all the world's peoples.

**Opening the Suez Canal**   When the canal opened in 1869, thousands of dignitaries and ordinary people gathered to watch the ships go by.   (Bildarchiv Preussischer Kulturbesitz/Art Resource, NY)

Many women joined missionary societies to become teachers and nurses, sometimes attaining positions of greater authority than they could hope to find at home. Their influence often helped soften the harshness of colonial rule—for example, by calling attention to issues of maternity and women's health. Mary Slessor, a British missionary who lived for forty years among the people of southeastern Nigeria, campaigned against slavery, human sacrifice, and the killing of twins and, generally, for women's rights. In India missionaries denounced the customs of child marriages and *sati* (the burning of widows on their husbands' funeral pyres). Such views often clashed with the customs of the people among whom they settled.

The sense of moral duty and cultural superiority was not limited to missionaries. Many Europeans and Americans equated technological innovations with "progress." They believed that Western technology proved the superiority of Western ideas, customs, and culture. While some concluded that non-Western peoples could achieve, through education, the same cultural level as Europeans and Americans, many others espoused racist ideas that relegated non-Europeans to a status of permanent inferiority. Racists assigned different stages of biological development to the world's various peoples based on physical appearance and ranked these races in a hierarchy that ranged from "civilized" at the highest level down through "semibarbarous," "barbarian," and finally, at the bottom, "savage." Caucasians—whites—were always at the top of this ranking. Such ideas were often presented as an excuse for permanent rule over Africans and Asians.

Imperialism first interested small groups of explorers, clergy, and businessmen but soon attracted people from other walks of life. Young men, finding few opportunities for adventure and glory at home in an era of peace, sought them overseas as the Spanish conquistadors had done over three centuries earlier. At first, European people and parliaments were indifferent or hostile to overseas adventures, but a few easy victories in the 1880s helped to overcome their reluctance. The United States was fully preoccupied with its westward expansion until the 1880s, but in the 1890s popular attention shifted to lands outside U.S. borders. Newspapers, which achieved wide readership in the second half of the nineteenth century, discovered that they could boost circulation with reports of wars and conquests. By the 1890s imperialism was a popular cause; it was the overseas extension of the nationalism propelling the power politics of the time.

## Economic Motives

The industrialization of Europe and North America stimulated the demand for minerals—copper for electrical wiring, tin for canning, chrome and manganese for the steel industry, coal for steam engines, and, most of all, gold and diamonds. The demand for such industrial crops as cotton and rubber and for stimulants such as sugar, coffee, tea, and tobacco also grew. These products were found in the tropics, but never in sufficient quantities.

An economic depression lasting from the mid-1870s to the mid-1890s caused European merchants, manufacturers, and shippers to seek protection against foreign competition (see below). They argued that their respective countries needed secure sources of tropical raw materials and protected markets for their industries. Declining business opportunities at home prompted entrepreneurs and investors to look for profits from mines, plantations, and railroads in Asia, Africa, and Latin America. Since these investments were often extremely risky, businessmen sought the backing of their governments, preferably with soldiers.

The sudden increase in the power that industrial peoples could wield over nonindustrial peoples and over the forces of nature underlay the new imperialism as much as cultural and political factors. Indeed, technological advances explain

**Pears Soap Is Best**   This advertisement appeared in the *Illustrated London News* in 1887. In identifying a brand of soap as "the formula for British conquest," it credited British manufactured products with the power to overawe spear-wielding indigenous warriors.   (*Illustrated London News* Picture Library)

both the motives and the outcome of the New Imperialism.

## The Tools of the Imperialists

To succeed, empire builders needed the means to achieve their objectives at a reasonable cost. The Industrial Revolution (see Chapter 20) provided these means. In the early part of the nineteenth century technological innovations began to tip the balance of power in favor of Europe.

Dominant at sea since about 1500, the Europeans increased their naval power still more with the introduction of steamships. The first steamer reached India in 1825; regular mail service followed in the 1830s. The long voyage around Africa was at first too costly for cargo steamers, for coal had to be shipped from England. The building of the Suez Canal and the development of increasingly efficient engines solved this problem and led to a boom in shipping to the Indian Ocean and East Asia. Whenever fighting broke out, passenger liners were requisitioned as troopships. This advantage in mobility was enhanced by the development of a global network of submarine telegraph cables connecting Europe with North America in the 1860s, with Latin America and Asia in the 1870s, with Africa in the 1880s, and finally across the Pacific in 1904.

Until the middle of the nineteenth century, western Europeans were much weaker on land than at sea. Thereafter, Europeans used gunboats with considerable success in China, Burma, Indochina, and the Congo Basin. Although gunboats opened the major river basins to European penetration, the invaders often found themselves hampered by other natural obstacles. *Falciparum* malaria, found only in Africa, was so deadly to Europeans that few explorers survived before the 1850s. In 1854 a British doctor discovered that the drug quinine, taken regularly during one's stay in Africa, could prevent the disease. This and a few sanitary precautions reduced the annual death rate among whites in West Africa from between 250 and 750 per thousand in the early nineteenth century to between 50 and 100 per thousand after 1850. This reduction was sufficient to open the continent to merchants, officials, and missionaries.

Muzzle-loading smoothbore muskets had been used in Europe, Asia, and the Americas since the late seventeenth century, and by the early nineteenth century they were also common in much of Africa. The development of new and much deadlier firearms in the 1860s and 1870s shifted the balance of power on land between Westerners and other peoples. One of these was the breechloading rifle: ten times faster to load and five or six times longer in range than a musket. By the 1870s all European and American armies had switched to these new rifles. The 1880s saw two more innovations, smokeless powder, which did not foul the gun or reveal the soldier's position, and repeating rifles, which could shoot fifteen rounds in fifteen seconds. Machine guns, which could fire eleven bullets per second, appeared a decade later.

In the course of the century Asians and Africans also acquired better firearms, mostly old weapons that European armies had discarded. As European firearms improved, however, the firepower gap widened, making colonial conquests easier than ever. By the 1880s and 1890s European-led forces of a few hundred could defeat non-European armies of thousands. Against the latest weapons, African and Asian soldiers armed with muskets or, in some cases, with spears did not stand a chance, no matter how numerous and courageous they were.

At the **Battle of Omdurman** in Sudan, on September 2, 1898, forty thousand Sudanese attacked an Anglo-Egyptian expedition that had come up the Nile on six steamers and four other boats. General Horatio Kitchener's troops had twenty machine guns and four artillery pieces; the Sudanese were equipped with muskets and spears. Within a few hours eleven thousand Sudanese and forty-eight British lay dead. Winston Churchill, the future British prime minister, witnessed the battle and called it

> the most signal triumph ever gained by the arms of science over barbarians. Within the space of five hours the strongest and best-armed savage army yet arrayed against a modern European Power had been destroyed and dispersed, with hardly any difficulty, comparatively small risk, and insignificant loss to the victors.[3]

### Colonial Agents and Administration

Once colonial agents took over a territory, their home government expected them to cover their own costs and, if possible, return some profit to the home country. The system of administering and exploiting territories for the benefit of the home country is known as **colonialism.** In some places, such as along the West African coast or in Indochina, there was already a considerable trade that could be taxed. In other places profits could come only from investments and a thorough

**The Battle of Omdurman**   In the late nineteenth century, most battles between European (or European-led) troops and African forces were one-sided encounters because of the disparity in the opponents' firearms and tactics. The Battle of Omdurman in Sudan in 1898 is a dramatic example. The forces of the Mahdi, some on horseback, were armed with spears and single-shot muskets. The British troops and their Egyptian allies, lined up in the foreground, used repeating rifles and machine guns able to shoot much farther than the Sudanese weapons. As a result, there were many Sudanese casualties but very few British or Egyptian.   (The Art Archive)

reorganization of the indigenous societies. In applying modern scientific and industrial methods to their colonies, colonialists started the transformation of Asian and African societies and landscapes that has continued to our day.

Legal experts and academics emphasized the differences between various systems of colonial government and debated whether colonies eventually should be assimilated into the ruling nation, associated in a federation, or allowed to rule themselves. Colonies that were protectorates retained

their traditional governments, even their monarchs, but had a European "resident" or "consul-general" to "advise" them. Other colonies were directly administered by a European governor. In fact, the impact of colonial rule depended much more on economic and social conditions than on narrow legal distinctions.

One important factor was the presence or absence of European settlers. In Canada, Australia, and New Zealand, whites were already in the majority by 1869, and their colonial "mother-country,"

Britain, encouraged them to elect parliaments and rule themselves. Where European settlers were numerous but still a minority of the population, as in Algeria and South Africa, settlers and the home country contested for control over the indigenous population. In colonies with few white settlers, the European governors ruled autocratically.

In the early years of the New Imperialism, colonial administrations consisted of a governor and his staff, a few troops to keep order, and a small number of tax collectors and magistrates. The cooperation of indigenous elites was essential to the maintenance of order. In most cases the colonial governors exercised power through traditional rulers willing to cooperate. Areas governed indirectly in this fashion were called "Princely States." In addition, colonial governments educated a few local youths for "modern" jobs as clerks, policemen, customs inspectors, and the like. These individuals came in time to rival the traditional rulers.

Western women seldom took part in the early stages of colonial expansion. Once peace was achieved and steamships and railroads made travel less difficult, however, colonial officials and settlers began bringing their wives to the colonies. By the 1880s the British Women's Emigration Association was recruiting single women to go out to the colonies to marry British settlers. As one of its founders, Ellen Joyce, explained, "The possibility of the settler marrying his own countrywoman is of imperial as well as family importance."

The arrival of white women in Asia and Africa increased racial segregation. Sylvia Leith-Ross, wife of a colonial officer in Nigeria, explained: "When you are alone, among thousands of unknown, unpredictable people, dazed by unaccustomed sights and sounds, bemused by strange ways of life and thought, you need to remember who you are, where you come from, what your standards are." Many colonial wives found themselves in command of numerous servants and expected to follow the complex etiquette of colonial entertainment in support of their husbands' official positions. Occasionally they found opportunities to exercise personal initiatives, usually charitable work involving indigenous women and children. However well meaning, their efforts were always subordinate to the work of men.

# THE SCRAMBLE FOR AFRICA

Until the 1870s African history was largely shaped by internal forces and local initiatives (see Chapter 21). Outside Algeria and southern Africa, only a handful of Europeans had ever visited the interior of Africa, and European countries possessed only small enclaves on the coasts. As late as 1879 Africans ruled more than 90 percent of the continent. Then, within a decade, Africa was invaded and divided among the European powers in a movement often referred to as the **"scramble" for Africa** (see Map 24.1). This invasion affected all regions of the continent.

## Egypt

Ironically, European involvement in Egypt resulted from Egypt's attempt to free itself from Ottoman Turkish rule. The khedives of Egypt, hereditary governors descended from Muhammad Ali (see Chapter 22), used profits from exporting cotton during the American Civil War to modernize their armed forces and build canals, harbors, railroads, and other public works. Their support for the Suez Canal project was part of this policy. Khedive Ismail even tried to make Egypt the center of an empire reaching south into Sudan and Ethiopia.

Once cotton prices returned to normal after 1865, the khedives supported their ambitions by borrowing from European creditors at high interest rates. By 1876 Egypt's foreign debt had risen to £100 million sterling. Interest payments alone consumed one-third of its foreign export earnings. To avoid bankruptcy the Egyptian government sold its shares in the Suez Canal to Great Britain and accepted four foreign "commissioners of the debt" to oversee its finances. French and British bankers, still not satisfied, lobbied their governments to secure the loans by stronger measures. In 1878 the two governments obliged Ismail to appoint a Frenchman as minister of public works and a Briton as minister of finance. When high taxes caused hardship and popular discontent, the French and British persuaded the Ottoman sultan to depose Ismail. This foreign intervention provoked a military uprising under Egyptian army colonel Arabi Pasha, which threatened the Suez Canal.

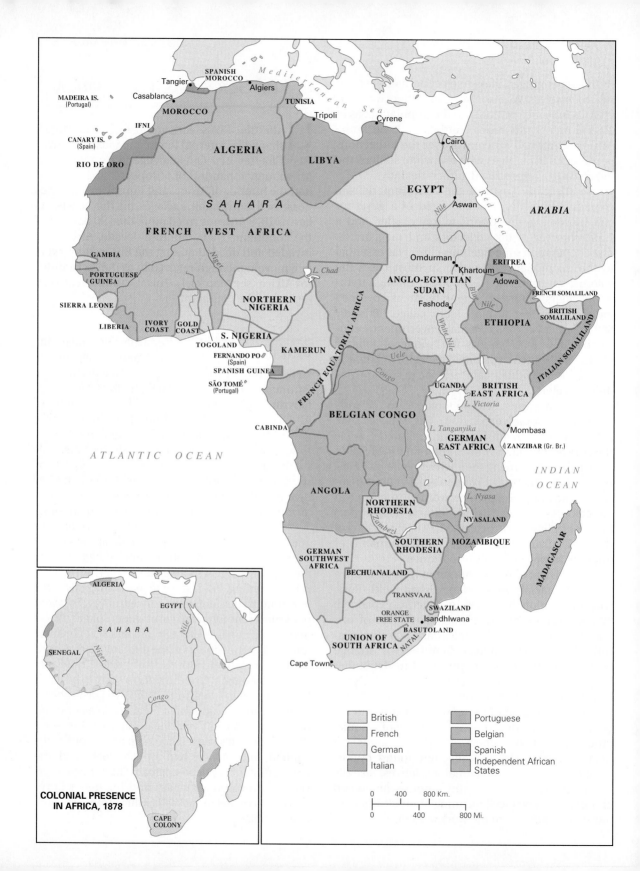

Mediterranean Sea

MADEIRA IS.
(Portugal)

SPANISH
MOROCCO
Tangier
Casablanca
Algiers
TUNISIA
Tripoli
Cyrene

MOROCCO

IFNI

CANARY IS.
(Spain)

RIO DE ORO

ALGERIA

LIBYA

EGYPT

Cairo

Aswan

Red Sea

ARABIA

Nile

SAHARA

FRENCH   WEST   AFRICA

GAMBIA

PORTUGUESE
GUINEA

SIERRA LEONE

LIBERIA

IVORY
COAST
GOLD
COAST

Niger

L. Chad

NORTHERN
NIGERIA

S. NIGERIA

TOGOLAND

FERNANDO PO
(Spain)

SPANISH GUINEA

SÃO TOMÉ
(Portugal)

KAMERUN

Omdurman
Khartoum

ERITREA

Adowa

ANGLO-EGYPTIAN
SUDAN

Fashoda

FRENCH SOMALILAND

BRITISH
SOMALILAND

White Nile

Blue Nile

ETHIOPIA

ITALIAN SOMALILAND

Uele

Congo

UGANDA

BRITISH
EAST
AFRICA

L. Victoria

Mombasa

ZANZIBAR (Gr. Br.)

FRENCH EQUATORIAL AFRICA

BELGIAN CONGO

CABINDA

L. Tanganyika

GERMAN
EAST AFRICA

ATLANTIC   OCEAN

INDIAN
OCEAN

ANGOLA

NORTHERN
RHODESIA

L. Nyasa

NYASALAND

Zambezi

MADAGASCAR

GERMAN
SOUTHWEST
AFRICA

SOUTHERN
RHODESIA

MOZAMBIQUE

BECHUANALAND

TRANSVAAL

SWAZILAND
Isandhlwana

ORANGE
FREE STATE

BASUTOLAND

NATAL

UNION OF
SOUTH AFRICA

Cape Town

ALGERIA

EGYPT

SAHARA

Nile

SENEGAL

Niger

Congo

**COLONIAL PRESENCE
IN AFRICA, 1878**

CAPE
COLONY

British

French

German

Italian

Portuguese

Belgian

Spanish

Independent African
States

| 0 | 400 | 800 Km. |
|---|-----|---------|
| 0 | 400 | 800 Mi. |

**Map 24.1   Africa in 1878 and 1914**   In 1878 the European colonial presence was limited to a few coastal enclaves, plus portions of Algeria and South Africa. By 1914, Europeans had taken over all of Africa except Ethiopia and Liberia.

Fearing for their investments, the British sent an army into Egypt in 1882. They intended to occupy Egypt for only a year or two. But theirs was a seaborne empire that depended on secure communications between Britain and India. So important was the Suez Canal to their maritime supremacy that they stayed for seventy years. During those years the British ruled Egypt "indirectly"—that is, they maintained the Egyptian government and the fiction of Egyptian sovereignty but retained real power in their own hands.

Eager to develop Egyptian agriculture, especially cotton production, the British brought in engineers and contractors to build the first dam across the Nile, at Aswan in upper Egypt. When completed in 1902, it was one of the largest dams in the world. It captured the annual Nile flood and released its waters throughout the year, allowing farmers to grow two, sometimes three, crops a year. This doubled the effective acreage compared with the basin system of irrigation practiced since the time of the pharaohs, in which the annual floodwaters of the Nile were retained by low dikes around the fields.

The economic development of Egypt by the British enriched a small elite of landowners and merchants, many of them foreigners. Egyptian peasants got little relief from the heavy taxes collected to pay for their country's crushing foreign debt and the expenses of the British army of occupation. Western ways that conflicted with the teachings of Islam—such as the drinking of alcohol and the relative freedom of women—offended Muslim religious leaders. Most Egyptians found British rule more onerous than that of the Ottomans. By the 1890s Egyptian politicians and intellectuals were demanding that the British leave, to no avail.

## Western and Equatorial Africa

While the British were taking over Egypt, the French were planning to extend their empire into the interior of West Africa. Starting from the coast of Senegal, which had been in French hands for centuries, they hoped to build a railroad from the upper Senegal River to the upper Niger in order to open the interior to French merchants. This in turn led the French military to undertake the conquest of western Sudan.

Meanwhile, the actions of three individuals, rather than a government, brought about the occupation of the Congo Basin, an enormous forested region in the heart of equatorial Africa (see Map 24.1). In 1879 the American journalist **Henry Morton Stanley,** who had explored the area, persuaded King **Leopold II** of Belgium to invest his personal fortune in "opening up" equatorial Africa. With Leopold's money, Stanley returned to Africa from 1879 to 1884 to establish trading posts along the southern bank of the Congo River. At the same time, **Savorgnan de Brazza,** an Italian officer serving in the French army, obtained from an African ruler living on the opposite bank a treaty that placed the area under the "protection" of France.

These events sparked a flurry of diplomatic activity. German chancellor Bismarck called the **Berlin Conference** on Africa of 1884 and 1885. There the major powers agreed that henceforth "effective occupation" would replace the former trading relations between Africans and Europeans. This meant that every country with colonial ambitions had to send troops into Africa and participate in the division of the spoils. As a reward for triggering the "scramble" for Africa, Leopold II acquired a personal domain under the name "Congo Free State," while France and Portugal took most of the rest of equatorial Africa. In this manner, the European powers and King Leopold managed to divide Africa among themselves, at least on paper.

"Effective occupation" required many years of effort. In the interior of West Africa, Muslim rulers resisted the French invasion for up to thirty years. The French advance encouraged the Germans to stake claims to parts of the region and the British to move north from their coastal enclaves, until the entire region was occupied by Britain, France, and Germany.

Because West Africa had long had a flourishing trade, the new rulers took advantage of existing trade networks, taxing merchants and farmers, investing the profits in railroads and harbors, and paying dividends to European stockholders. In the Gold Coast (now Ghana) British trading companies bought the cocoa grown by African farmers at low prices and resold it for large profits. The interior of French West Africa lagged behind. Although the region could produce cotton, peanuts, and other crops, the difficulties of transportation limited its development before 1914.

Compared to West Africa, equatorial Africa had few inhabitants and little trade. Rather than try to govern these vast territories directly, authorities in the Congo Free State, the French Congo, and the Portuguese colonies of Angola and Mozambique granted huge pieces of land as concessions to private companies that thereby gained monopolies on natural resources and trade and the right to employ soldiers and impose taxes.

Freed from outside supervision, the companies forced the African inhabitants at gunpoint to produce cash crops and carry them, on their heads or backs, to the nearest railroad or navigable river. The worst abuses took place in the Congo Free State, where a rubber boom lasting from 1895 to 1905 made it profitable for private companies to coerce Africans to collect latex from vines that grew in the forests. One Congolese refugee told the British consul Roger Casement who investigated the atrocities:

> We begged the white men to leave us alone, saying we could get no more rubber, but the white men and their soldiers said: "Go. You are only beasts yourselves, you are only *nyama* (meat)." We tried, always going further into the forest, and when we failed and our rubber was short, the soldiers came to our towns and killed us. Many were shot, some had their ears cut off; others were tied up with ropes around their necks and bodies and taken away.[4]

After 1906 the British press began publicizing the horrors. The public outcry that followed, coinciding with the end of the rubber boom, convinced the Belgian government to take over Leopold's private empire in 1908.

## Southern Africa

The history of southern Africa between 1869 and 1914 differs from that of the rest of the continent in attracting white settlers. **Afrikaners,** descendants of Dutch settlers on the Cape of Good Hope, moved inland throughout the nineteenth century; British prospectors and settlers arrived later in the century; and, finally, Indians were brought over by the British and stayed.

Southern Africa attracted European settlers because of its good pastures and farmland and its phenomenal deposits of diamonds, gold, and copper, as well as coal and iron ore. This was the new El Dorado that imperialists had dreamed of since the heyday of the Spanish Empire in Peru and Mexico in the sixteenth century.

The discovery of diamonds at Kimberley in 1868 lured thousands of European prospectors as well as Africans looking for work. It also attracted the interest of Great Britain, colonial ruler of the Cape Colony, which annexed the diamond area in 1871, thereby angering the Afrikaners. Once in the interior, the British defeated the Xhosa° people in 1877 and 1878. Then in 1879 they confronted the Zulu, militarily the most powerful of the African peoples in the region.

The Zulu, led by their king Cetshwayo°, resented their encirclement by Afrikaners and British. A growing sense of nationalism and their proud military tradition led them into a war with the British in 1879. At first they held their own, defeating the British at Isandhlwana°, but a few months later they were defeated. Cetshwayo was captured and sent into exile, and the Zulu lands were given to white ranchers. Yet throughout those bitter times, the Zulu's sense of nationhood remained strong.

Relations between the British and the Afrikaners, already tense as a result of British encroachment, took a turn for the worse when gold was discovered in the Afrikaner republic of Transvaal° in 1886. In the gold rush that ensued, the British soon outnumbered the Afrikaners.

Britain's invasion of southern Africa was driven in part by the ambition of **Cecil Rhodes** (1853–1902), who once declared that he would "annex the stars" if he could. Rhodes made his fortune in the Kimberley diamond fields, founding De Beers Consolidated, a company that has dominated the world's diamond trade ever since. He

**Xhosa** (KOH-sah)   **Cetshwayo** (set-SHWAH-yo)
**Isandhlwana** (ee-sawn-dull-WAH-nuh)   **Transvaal** (trans-VAHL)

then turned to politics. He encouraged a concession company, the British South Africa Company, to push north into Central Africa, where he named two new colonies after himself: Southern Rhodesia (now Zimbabwe) and Northern Rhodesia (now Zambia). The Ndebele° and Shona peoples, who inhabited the region, resisted this invasion, but the machine guns of the British finally defeated them.

British attempts to annex the two Afrikaner republics, Transvaal and Orange Free State, and the inflow of English-speaking whites into the gold- and diamond-mining areas led to the South African War (also called the Boer War), which lasted from 1899 to 1902. At first the Afrikaners had the upper hand, for they were highly motivated, possessed modern rifles, and knew the land. In 1901, however, Great Britain brought in 450,000 troops and crushed the Afrikaner armies. Ironically, the Afrikaners' defeat in 1902 led to their ultimate victory. Wary of costly commitments overseas, the British government expected European settlers in Africa to manage their own affairs, as they were doing in Canada, Australia, and New Zealand. Thus, in 1910 the European settlers created the Union of South Africa, in which the Afrikaners eventually emerged as the ruling element.

Unlike Canada, Australia, and New Zealand, South Africa had a majority of indigenous inhabitants and substantial numbers of Indians and "Cape Coloureds" (people of mixed ancestry). Yet the Europeans were both numerous enough to demand self-rule and powerful enough to deny the vote and other civil rights to the majority. In 1913 the South African parliament passed the Natives Land Act, assigning Africans to reservations and forbidding them to own land elsewhere. This and other racial policies turned South Africa into a land of segregation, oppression, and bitter divisions.

## Political and Social Consequences

Africa was home to a wide variety of indigenous societies, some of them long-established kingdoms with aristocracies or commercial towns dominated by a merchant class, others centered on agricultural villages without any outside government, and still others consisting of pastoral nomads organized along military lines. Not surprisingly, these societies responded in very different ways to the European invasion.

Some peoples welcomed the invaders as allies against local enemies. Once colonial rule was established, they sought work in government service or in European firms and sent their children to mission schools. In exchange, they were often the first to receive benefits such as clinics and roads.

Others, especially peoples with a pastoral or a warrior tradition, fought tenaciously. Examples abound, from the Zulu and Ndebele of southern Africa to the pastoral Herero° people of Southwest Africa (now Namibia), who rose up against German invaders in 1904; in repressing their uprising, the Germans exterminated two-thirds of them. In the Sahel, a belt of grasslands south of the Sahara, charismatic leaders rose up in the name of a purified Islam, gathered a following of warriors, and led them on part-religious, part empire-building campaigns called *jihads*. These leaders included Samori Toure in western Sudan (now Mali), Rabih in the Chad basin, and the Mahdi° in eastern Sudan. All of them eventually came into conflict with European-led military expeditions and were defeated.

Some commercial states with long histories of contact with Europeans also fought back. The kingdom of **Asante**° in Gold Coast rose up in 1874, 1896, and 1900 before it was finally overwhelmed. In the Niger Delta, the ancient city of Benin, rich with artistic treasures, resisted colonial control until 1897, when a British "punitive expedition" set it on fire and carted its works of art off to Europe.

One resistance movement succeeded, to the astonishment of Europeans and Africans alike. When **Menelik II** became emperor of Ethiopia in 1889 (see Chapter 21), his country was threatened by Sudanese Muslims to the west and by France and Italy, which controlled the Red Sea coast to the east. For many years, Ethiopia had been purchasing weapons. By the Treaty of Wichelle (1889), Italy agreed to sell more weapons to Ethiopia. Six years later, when Italians attempted to establish a protectorate over Ethiopia, they found the Ethiopians armed with thousands of rifles and even a few machine guns and artillery pieces. Although Italy sent

---

**Ndebele** (en-duh-BELL-ay)

**Herero** (hair-AIR-oh)   **Mahdi** (MAH-dee)   **Asante** (uh-SAWN-tay)

twenty thousand troops to attack Ethiopia, in 1896 they were defeated at Adowa° by a larger and better-trained Ethiopian army.

Most Africans neither joined nor fought the European invaders but tried to continue living as before. They found this increasingly difficult because colonial rule disrupted every traditional society. The presence of colonial officials meant that rights to land, commercial transactions, and legal disputes were handled very differently, and that traditional rulers lost all authority, except where Europeans used them as local administrators.

Changes in landholding were especially disruptive, for most Africans were farmers or herders for whom access to land was a necessity. In areas with a high population density, such as Egypt and West Africa, colonial rulers left peasants in place, encouraged them to grow cash crops, and collected taxes on the harvest. Elsewhere, the new rulers declared any land that was not farmed to be "waste" or "vacant" and gave it to private companies or to European planters and ranchers. In Kenya, Northern Rhodesia, and South Africa, Europeans found the land and climate to their liking, in contrast to other parts of Africa, where soldiers, officials, missionaries, or traders stayed only a few years. White settlers forced Africans to become squatters, sharecroppers, or ranch hands on land they had farmed for generations. In South Africa they forced many Africans off their lands and onto "reserves," much like the nomadic peoples of North America, Russia, and Australia.

The colonial rulers were even more interested in African labor than in the land. To get workers to take low-paid jobs on plantations, railroads, or other European enterprises, they imposed various taxes, such as the hut tax and the head tax. To pay the tax, Africans had little choice but to accept whatever work the Europeans offered. In the South African mines Africans were paid, on average, one-tenth as much as Europeans.

Some Africans migrated great distances to the cities and mining camps in search of a better life. Most migrant workers were men who left their wives and children behind in villages and on reserves, sometimes for years. Only occasionally did the authorities allow them to bring their families

and settle permanently. This caused great hardship for African women, who had to grow food for their families during the men's absences and care for sick and aged workers. Long separations between spouses also led to prostitution and the spread of sexually transmitted diseases.

Some African women welcomed colonial rule, for it brought an end to fighting and slave raiding, but others were led into captivity (see Diversity and Dominance: Two Africans Recall the Arrival of the Europeans). A few succeeded in becoming wealthy traders or owners of livestock. On the whole, however, African women benefited less than men from the economic changes that colonialism introduced. Whenever colonial rulers replaced communal property (traditional in most of Africa) with private property, property rights were assigned to the head of the household—that is, to the man. Almost all the jobs open to Africans, even those considered "women's work" in Europe, such as nursing and domestic service, were reserved for men.

## Cultural Responses

More Africans came into contact with missionaries than with any other Europeans. Mission schools taught reading, writing, and arithmetic to village children. Boys learned crafts like carpentry and blacksmithing, while girls were taught domestic skills.

The first generation of Africans educated in mission schools also acquired Western ideas of justice and progress. Samuel Ajayi Crowther, a Yoruba rescued from slavery as a boy and educated in mission schools in Sierra Leone, went on to become an Anglican minister and, in 1864, the first African bishop. Crowther thought that Africa needed European assistance in achieving both spiritual and economic development:

> Africa has neither knowledge nor skill . . .
> to bring out her vast resources for her own
> improvement. . . . Therefore to claim Africa for
> the Africans alone, is to claim for her the right of
> a continued ignorance. . . . For it is certain, un-
> less help [comes] from without, a nation can
> never rise above its present state.[5]

After the first generation, many mission teachers were themselves African, the products of a mis-

---

**Adowa** (AH-do-ah)

sion education. They discovered that Christian ideals clashed with the reality of colonial exploitation. One convert wrote in 1911:

> There is too much failure among all Europeans in Nyasaland. The three combined bodies— Missionaries, Government and Companies or gainers of money—do form the same rule to look upon the native with mockery eyes. . . . If we had enough power to communicate ourselves to Europe, we would advise them not to call themselves Christendom, but Europeandom. Therefore the life of the three combined bodies is altogether too cheaty, too thefty, too mockery. Instead of "Give," they say "Take away from." There is too much breakage of God's pure law.[6]

Missionaries were not the only ones to bring religious change to Africa. In southern and Central Africa indigenous preachers adapted Christianity to African values and customs and founded new denominations known as "Ethiopian" churches.

Christianity proved successful in converting followers of traditional religions but made no inroads among Muslims. Instead, Islam, long predominant in northern and eastern Africa, spread southward as Muslim teachers established Quranic schools and founded Muslim brotherhoods. European colonialism unwittingly helped the diffusion of Islam. By building cities and increasing trade, colonial rule permitted Muslims to settle in new areas. As Islam—a universal religion untainted by colonialism—became increasingly relevant to Africans, the number of Muslims in sub-Saharan Africa probably doubled between 1869 and 1914.

# ASIA AND WESTERN DOMINANCE

From 1869 to 1914 the pressure of the industrial powers was felt throughout Asia, the East Indies, and the Pacific islands (see Map 24.2). As trade with these regions grew in the late nineteenth century, so did their attractiveness to imperialists eager for economic benefits and national prestige.

By 1869 Britain already controlled most of India and Burma; Spain occupied the Philippines; and the Netherlands held large parts of the East Indies (now Indonesia). Between 1862 and 1895 France conquered Indochina (now Vietnam, Kampuchea, and Laos).

## Central Asia

Farther north, Russia continued its colonial expansion, aided by the acquisition of modern rifles and artillery. Between 1865 and 1876 Russian forces advanced into Central Asia. Nomads like the Kazakhs, who lived east of the Caspian Sea, resisted; but soon Kazakhstan became home to 200,000 Russian settlers. Although the governments of Tsar Alexander II (r. 1855–1881) and Tsar Alexander III (r. 1881–1894) claimed not to interfere in indigenous customs, they declared communally owned grazing lands "waste" or "vacant" and turned them over to farmers from Russia. By the end of the century the nomads were fenced out and reduced to starvation. An eminent Russian jurist declared: "International rights cannot be taken into account when dealing with semibarbarous peoples."

South of the Kazakh steppe the fabled cities of Tashkent, Bukhara, and Samarkand served the caravan trade between China and the Middle East. By the 1860s and 1870s the Qing Empire was losing control over Central Asia, so it was fairly easy for Russian expeditions to conquer the indigenous peoples. Russia thereby acquired land suitable for cotton, along with a large Muslim population.

The Russians abolished slavery, built railroads to link the region with Europe, and planted hundreds of thousands of acres of cotton. Unlike the British in India, however, they did not attempt to change the customs, languages, or religious beliefs of their subjects.

## Southeast Asia and Indonesia

Until the mid-nineteenth century, independent kingdoms ruled most of the Southeast Asian peninsula and the Indonesian archipelago. As in Africa, colonialism varied considerably from region to region. Burma (now Myanmar), nearest India, was gradually taken over by the British, the last piece being annexed in 1885. Indochina fell under French control bit by bit until it was finally subdued in 1895. Similarly, Malaya (now Malaysia) came under British rule in stages

# DIVERSITY AND DOMINANCE

## TWO AFRICANS RECALL THE ARRIVAL OF THE EUROPEANS

*We know a great deal about the arrival of the Europeans into the interior of Africa from the perspective of the conquerors, but very little about how the events were experienced by Africans. Here are two accounts by African women, one from northern Nigeria whose land was occupied by the British, the other from the Congo Free State, a colony of King Leopold II of Belgium. They show not only how Africans experienced European colonial dominance, but also the great diversity of their experiences.*

### Baba of Karo, a Nigerian Woman, Remembers Her Childhood

When I was a maiden the Europeans first arrived. Ever since we were quite small the *malams* had been saying that the Europeans would come with a thing called a train, they would come with a thing called a motor-car, in them you would go and come back in a trice. They would stop wars, they would repair the world, they would stop oppression and lawlessness, we should live at peace with them. We used to go and sit quietly and listen to the prophecies. They would come, fine handsome people, they would not kill anyone, they would not oppress anyone, they would bring all their strange things. . . .

I remember when a European came to Karo on a horse, and some of his foot soldiers went into the town. Everyone came out to look at them, but in Zerewa they didn't see the European. Everyone at Karo ran away—"There's a European, there's a European!" He came from Zaria with a few black men, two on horses and four on foot. We were inside the town. Later on we heard that they were there in Zaria in crowds, clearing spaces and building houses. One of my younger "sisters" was at Karo, she was pregnant, and when she saw the European she ran away and shut the door.

At that time Yusufu was the king of Kano. He did not like the Europeans, he did not wish them, he would not sign their treaty. Then he say that perforce he would have to agree, so he did. We Habe wanted them to come, it was the Fulani who did not like it. When the Europeans came the Habe saw that if you worked for them they paid you for it, they didn't say, like the Fulani, "Commoner, give me this! Commoner, bring me that!" Yes, the Habe wanted them; they saw no harm in them. From Zaria they came to Rogo, they were building their big road to Kano City. They called out the people and said they were to come and make the road, if there were trees in the way they cut them down. The Europeans paid them with goods, they collected the villagers together and each man brought his large hoe. Money was not much use to them, so the Europeans paid them with food and other things.

The Europeans said that there were to be no more slaves; if someone said "Slave!" you could complain to the *alkali* who would punish the master who said it, the judge said, "That is what the Europeans have decreed." The first order said that any slave, if he was younger than you, was your younger brother, if he was older than you was your elder brother—they were all brothers of their master's family. No one used the word "slave" any more. When slavery was stopped, nothing much happened at our *rinji* except that some slaves whom we had bought in the market ran away. Our own father went to his farm and worked, he and his son took up their large hoes; they loaned out their spare farms. Tsoho our father and Kadiri my brother with whom I live now and Babambo worked, they farmed guineacorn and millet and groundnuts and everything; before this they had supervised the slaves' work—now they did their own. When the midday food was ready, the women of the compound would give us children the food, one of us drew water, and off we went to the farm to take the men their food at the foot of a tree; I was about eight or nine at that time, I think. . . .

In the old days if the chief liked the look of your daughter he would take her and put her in his house; you could do nothing about it. Now they don't do that.

## Ilanga, a Congolese Woman, Recounts her Capture by Agents of the Congo Free State

Our village is called Waniendo, after our chief Niendo. . . . It is a large village near a small stream, and surrounded by large fields of *mohago* (cassava) and *muhindu* (maize) and other foods, for we all worked hard at our plantations, and always had plenty to eat. The men always worked in the fields clearing the ground, or went hunting. . . . We never had war in our country, and the men had not many arms except knives; but our chief Niendo had a gun, which he had bought long ago from another chief for forty-three beads, but he had no powder or caps, and only carried it when he went on a journey.

. . . we were all busy in the fields hoeing our plantations, for it was the rainy season, and the weeds sprang quickly up, when a runner came to the village saying that a large band of men was coming, that they all wore red caps and blue cloth, and carried guns and long knives, and that many white men were with them, the chief of whom was *Kibalanga* (Michaux). Niendo at once called all the chief men to his house, while the drums were beaten to summon the people to the village. A long consultation was held, and finally we were all told to go quietly to the fields and bring in groundnuts, plantains, and cassava for the warriors who were coming, and goats and fowl for the white men. The women all went with baskets and filled them, and put them in the road, which was blocked up, so many were there. Niendo then commanded everyone to go and sit quietly in the houses until he gave other orders. This we did, everyone remaining quietly seated while Niendo went up the road with the head men to meet the white chief. We did not know what to think, for most of us feared that so many armed men coming boded evil; but Niendo thought that, by giving presents of much food, he would induce the strangers to pass on without harming us. And so it proved, for the soldiers took the baskets, and were then ordered by the white men to move off through the village. Many of the soldiers looked into the houses and shouted at us words we did not understand. We were glad when they were all gone, for we were much in fear of the white

men and the strange warriors, who are known to all the people as being great fighters, bringing war wherever they go. . . .

When the white men and their warriors had gone, we went again to our work, and were hoping that they would not return; but this they did in a very short time. As before, we brought in great heaps of food; but this time *Kibalanga* did not move away directly, but camped near our village, and his soldiers came and stole all our fowl and goats and tore up our cassava; but we did not mind as long as they did not harm us. The next morning it was reported that the white men were going away; but soon after the sun rose over the hill, a large band of soldiers came into the village, and we all went into the houses and sat down. We were not long seated when the soldiers came rushing in shouting, and threatening Niendo with their guns. They rushed into the houses and dragged the people out. Three or four came to our house and caught hold of me, also my husband Oleka and my sister Katinga. We were dragged into the road, and were tied together with cords about our necks, so that we could not escape. We were all crying, for now we knew that we were to be taken away to be slaves. The soldiers beat us with the iron sticks from their guns, and compelled us to march to the camp of *Kibalanga*, who ordered the women to be tied up separately, ten to each cord, and the men in the same way. When we were all collected— and there were many from other villages whom we now saw, and many from Waniendo—the soldiers brought baskets of food for us to carry, in some of which was smoked human flesh (*niama na nitu*).

We then set off marching very quickly. My sister Katinga had her baby in her arms, and was not compelled to carry a basket; but my husband Oleka was made to carry a goat. We marched until the afternoon, when we camped near a stream, where we were glad to drink, for we were much athirst. We had nothing to eat, for the soldiers would give us nothing, so we lay upon the ground, and at night went to sleep. The next day we continued the march, and when we camped at noon were given some maize and plantains, which were gathered near a village from which the people had run away. So it continued each day until the fifth day, when the soldiers took my sister's baby and threw it in the grass, leaving it to die, and made her carry some cooking pots which they found in the deserted village. On the sixth day we became very weak from lack of food and from constant marching and sleeping in the damp grass, and my husband, who marched behind us with the goat, could not stand up longer, and so he sat down beside the path and refused to walk more. The soldiers beat him, but still he refused to move. Then one of them struck him on the head with the end of his gun, and he fell upon the ground. One of the soldiers caught the goat, while two or three others stuck the long knives they put on the ends of their guns into my husband. I saw the blood spurt out, and then saw him no more, for we passed over the brow of a hill and he was out of sight. Many of the young men were killed the same way, and many babies thrown into the grass to die. A few escaped; but we were so well guarded that it was almost impossible.

After marching ten days we came to the great water (Lualaba) and were taken in canoes across to the white men's town at Nyangwe. Here we stayed for six or seven days, and were then put in canoes and sent down the river; . . . but on the way we could get nothing to eat, and were glad to rest here, where there are good houses and plenty of food; and we hope we will not be sent away.

## QUESTIONS FOR ANALYSIS

1. How do Baba and Ilanga recall their existence before the Europeans came?
2. What did they expect when they first heard of the arrival of Europeans? Instead, what happened to them, their relatives, and their towns?
3. How do you explain the difference between these two accounts?

---

*Source:* From M. F. Smith, ed., *Baba of Karo: A Woman of the Muslim Hausa* (New York: Philosophical Library, 1955), 66–68; and Edgar Canisius, *A Campaign Amongst Cannibals* (London: R. A. Everett & Co., 1903), 250–256. Used by permission of the Philosophical Library.

during the 1870s and 1880s. By the early 1900s the Dutch had subdued northern Sumatra, the last part of the Dutch East Indies to be conquered. Only Siam (now Thailand) remained independent, although it lost several border provinces.

Despite their varied political histories, all these regions had features in common: fertile soil, constant warmth, and heavy rains along with a long tradition of intensive gardening, irrigation, and terracing. Where the population was sparse, Europeans imported landless laborers from China and India. The climate favored the transfer of commercially valuable plants from other parts of the world. Tobacco, cinchona° (an antimalarial drug), manioc (an edible root crop), maize (corn), and natural rubber came from the Americas; sugar from India; tea from China; and coffee and oil palms from Africa. By 1914 much of the world's supply of these valuable products—in the case of rubber, almost all—came from Southeast Asia and Indonesia.

Europe and North America formed the export market for most of these products. In exchange, the inhabitants of the region benefited from peace and a reliable food supply. As a result, their numbers increased at an unprecedented rate. For instance, the population of Java (an island the size of Pennsylvania) doubled from 16 million in 1870 to over 30 million in 1914.

Colonialism and population growth spurred many social changes. Agricultural and commercial peoples gradually moved into mountainous and forested areas, displacing groups that practiced hunting and gathering or shifting agriculture and had not experienced as much population growth. Javanese migrating to Borneo and Sumatra are but one example. Immigrants from China and India changed the ethnic composition and culture of every country in the region. Thus the population of the Malay Peninsula became one-third Malay, one-third Chinese, and one-third Indian.

As in Africa, European missionaries spread Christianity under the colonial umbrella. Islam, however, was much more successful in gaining new converts, for it had been established in the re-

---

cinchona (sin-CHO-nah)

**Lim Nee Soon's Plantation**   In British Malaya, pineapples and rubber trees were often cultivated together, because pineapples could be grown between the trees during the five or six years it took for the saplings to grow large enough to be tapped. Not all plantation owners were British. In this picture, Lim Nee Soon, known as the "Pineapple King," stands next to a truck that is taking pineapples to his canning factory.   (National Archives of Singapore)

gion for centuries and people did not consider it a religion imposed on them by foreigners.

Education and European ideas had an impact on the political perceptions in Southeast Asia and Indonesia, as did events in neighboring Asian countries: in India, where a nationalist movement arose in the 1880s; in China, where modernizers were undermining the authority of the Qing; and especially in Japan, whose rapid industrialization culminated in its brilliant victory over Russia in the Russo-Japanese War (1904–1905). A young Vietnamese writing soon after the Russo-Japanese War expressed the spirit of a rising generation:

I, . . . an obscure student, having had occasion to study new books and new doctrines, have discovered in a recent history of Japan how they have been able to conquer the impotent Europeans. This is the reason why we have formed an organization. . . . We have selected from young

Annamites [Vietnamese] the most energetic, with great capacities for courage, and are sending them to Japan for study. . . . Several years have passed without the French being aware of the movement. . . . Our only aim is to prepare the population for the future.[7]

### Hawaii and the Philippines, 1878–1902

By the 1890s the United States had a fast-growing population and industries that produced more manufactured goods than they could sell at home. Merchants and bankers began to look for export markets. The political mood was also expansionist, and many echoed the feelings of the naval strategist Alfred T. Mahan°: "Whether they will or

**Mahan** (mah-HAHN)

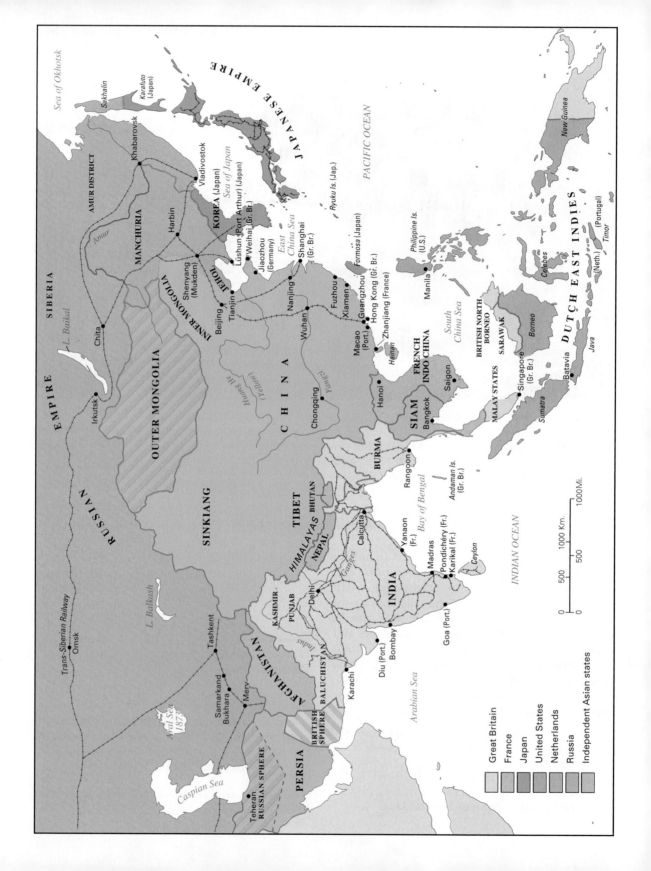

Sea of Okhotsk

*Karafuto* (Japan)

*Sakhalin*

JAPANESE EMPIRE

PACIFIC OCEAN

AMUR DISTRICT

Khabarovsk

Vladivostok

*Sea of Japan*

*Amur*

SIBERIA

MANCHURIA

Harbin

KOREA (Japan)

Lüshun (Port Arthur) (Japan)

Weihai (Gr. Br.)

*East China Sea*

JEHOL

Shenyang (Mukden)

Jiaozhou (Germany)

Shanghai (Gr. Br.)

*Ryuku Is.* (Jap.)

INNER MONGOLIA

Beijing

Tianjin

Nanjing

Fuzhou

Formosa (Japan)

*Philippine Is.* (U.S.)

EMPIRE

L. Baikal

Irkutsk

Chita

OUTER MONGOLIA

C H I N A

Wuhan

Xiamen

Guangzhou (Gr. Br.)

Hong Kong (Gr. Br.)

Zhanjiang (France)

Manila

DUTCH EAST INDIES

*New Guinea*

*Timor* (Portugal)

(Neth.)

RUSSIAN

Trans-Siberian Railway

Omsk

SINKIANG

*Hung He* (Yellow)

*Yangzi*

Chongqing

Macao (Port.)

Hainan

South China Sea

FRENCH INDO CHINA

*Celebes*

*Borneo*

*Java*

L. Balkash

TIBET

BHUTAN

HIMALAYAS

NEPAL

BURMA

Hanoi

Saigon

SIAM

Bangkok

BRITISH NORTH BORNEO

SARAWAK

*Batavia*

*Sumatra*

MALAY STATES

Singapore (Gr. Br.)

Tashkent

Samarkand

Bukhara

Merv

AFGHANISTAN

BALUCHISTAN

KASHMIR

PUNJAB

Delhi

Rangoon

Calcutta

Yanaon (Fr.)

*Andaman Is.* (Gr. Br.)

*Bay of Bengal*

INDIA

Madras

Pondichéry (Fr.)

Karikal (Fr.)

*Ceylon*

INDIAN OCEAN

*Aral Sea* 1873

*Indus*

*Ganges*

Goa (Port.)

Bombay

Diu (Port.)

Karachi

*Arabian Sea*

BRITISH SPHERE

RUSSIAN SPHERE

PERSIA

Teheran

*Caspian Sea*

1000 Mi.

1000 Km.

500

500

0

0

Great Britain
France
Japan
United States
Netherlands
Russia
Independent Asian states

**Map 24.2  Asia in 1914**  By 1914, much of Asia was claimed by colonial powers. The southern rim, from the Pacific Gulf to the Pacific, was occupied by Great Britain, France, the Netherlands, and the United States. Central Asia had been incorporated into the Russian Empire. Japan, now industrialized, had joined the Western imperialist powers in expanding its territory and influence at the expense of China.

no, Americans must now begin to look outward. The growing production of the country requires it."

Some Americans had been looking outward for quite some time, especially across the Pacific to China and Japan. In 1878 the United States obtained the harbor of Pago Pago in Samoa as a coaling and naval station, and in 1887 it secured the use of Pearl Harbor in Hawaii for the same purpose. Six years later American settlers in Hawaii deposed Queen Liliuokalani (1838–1917) and offered the Hawaiian Islands to the United States. At the time President Grover Cleveland (1893–1897) was opposed to annexation, and the settlers had to content themselves with an informal protectorate. By 1898, however, the United States under President William McKinley (1897–1901) had become openly imperialistic, and it annexed Hawaii as a steppingstone to Asia. As the United States became ever more involved in Asian affairs, Hawaii's strategic location brought an inflow of U.S. military personnel, and its fertile land caused planters to import farm laborers from Japan, China, and the Philippines. These immigrants soon outnumbered the native Hawaiians.

While large parts of Asia were falling under colonial domination, the people of the Philippines were chafing under their Spanish rulers. The movement for independence began among young Filipinos studying in Europe. José Rizal, a young doctor working in Spain, was arrested and executed in 1896 for writing anti-Spanish and anticlerical novels. Thereafter, the center of resistance shifted to the Philippines, where **Emilio Aguinaldo,** leader of a secret society, rose in revolt and proclaimed a republic in 1899. The revolutionaries had a good chance of winning independence, for Spain had its hands full with a revolution in Cuba (see below).

Unfortunately for Aguinaldo and his followers, the United States went to war against Spain in April 1898 and quickly overcame Spanish forces in the

Philippines and Cuba. President McKinley had not originally intended to acquire the Philippines; but after the Spanish defeat, he realized that a weakened Spain might lose the islands to another imperialist power. Japan, having recently defeated China in the Sino-Japanese War (1894–1895) and annexed Taiwan, was eager to expand. So was Germany, which had taken over parts of New Guinea and Samoa and several Pacific archipelagoes during the 1880s. To forestall them, McKinley purchased the Philippines from Spain for $20 million.

The Filipinos were not eager to trade one master for another. For a while, Aguinaldo cooperated with the Americans in the hope of achieving full independence. When his plan was rejected, he rose up again in 1899 and proclaimed the independence of his country. In spite of protests by antiimperialists in the United States, the U.S. government decided that its global interests outweighed the interests of the Filipino people. In rebel areas, a U.S. army of occupation tortured prisoners, burned villages and crops, and forced the inhabitants into "reconcentration camps." Many American soldiers tended to look on Filipinos with the same racial contempt with which Europeans viewed their colonial subjects. By the end of the insurrection in 1902, the war had cost the lives of 5,000 Americans and 200,000 Filipinos.

After the insurrection ended, the United States attempted to soften its rule with public works and economic development projects. New buildings went up in the city of Manila; roads, harbors, and railroads were built; and the Philippine economy was tied ever more closely to that of the United States. In 1907 Filipinos were allowed to elect representatives to a legislative assembly, but ultimate authority remained in the hands of a governor appointed by the president of the United States. An American promise of independence made in 1916 was not fulfilled until thirty years later.

## IMPERIALISM IN LATIN AMERICA

Nations in the Americas followed two divergent paths. In Canada and the United States manufacturing industries, powerful corporations, and wealthy financial institutions arose. By contrast,

Latin America and the Caribbean exported raw materials and imported manufactured goods. The poverty of their people, the preferences of their elites, and the pressures of the world economy made them increasingly dependent on the industrialized countries. Instead of suffering outright annexation by the colonial empires, they experienced manipulation by the industrial powers, including the United States, in a form of economic dependence called **free-trade imperialism.**

In the Western Hemisphere, therefore, the New Imperialism manifested itself not by a "scramble" for territories but in two other ways. In the larger republics of South America, the pressure was mostly financial and economic. In Central America and the Caribbean, it also included military intervention by the United States.

## Railroads and the Imperialism of Free Trade

Latin America's economic potential was huge, for the region could produce many agricultural and mineral products in demand in the industrial countries. What was needed was a means of opening the interior to development. Railroads seemed the perfect answer.

Foreign merchants and bankers as well as Latin American landowners and politicians embraced the new technology. Starting in the 1870s almost every country in Latin America acquired railroads, usually connecting mines or agricultural regions with the nearest port rather than linking up the different parts of the interior. Since Latin America did not have any steel or mechanical industries, railroad equipment and building materi-

**Railroads Penetrate South America**   The late nineteenth century saw the construction of several railroad networks in South America, often through rugged and dangerous terrain. This photograph shows the opening of a bridge on the Transandine Railroad in Peru. Flags were raised in honor of American construction and British ownership of the railroad.   (Tony Morrison/South American Pictures)

als came from Britain or the United States. So did the money to build the networks, the engineers who designed and maintained them, and the managers who ran them.

Argentina, a rich source of wheat, beef, and hides, gained the longest and best-developed rail network south of the United States. By 1914, British firms owned 86 percent of the railroads in Argentina; 40 percent of the employees were British; and the official railroad language was English, not Spanish. Similar situations arose elsewhere throughout Latin America. The Argentine nationalist Juan Justo saw a parallel with Ireland:

> English capital has done what English armies could not do. Today our country is tributary to England . . . the gold that the English capitalists take out of Argentina or carry off in the form of products does us no more good than the Irish get from the revenues that the English lords take out of Ireland.[8]

The Irish, however, had little say in the matter because they were under British rule. But in Latin America the political elites encouraged foreign companies with generous concessions as the most rapid way to modernize their countries and enrich the property owners. In countries where the majority of the poor were Indians (as in Mexico and Peru) or of African origin (as in Brazil), they were neither consulted nor allowed to benefit from the railroad boom.

The United States had long had interests in Cuba, the closest and richest of the Caribbean islands and a Spanish colony. American businesses had invested great sums of money in Cuba's sugar and tobacco industries, and tens of thousands of Cubans had migrated to the United States. In 1895 the Cuban nationalist José Martí started a revolution against Spanish rule. American newspapers thrilled readers with lurid stories of Spanish atrocities; businessmen worried about their investments; and politicians demanded that the U.S. government help liberate Cuba.

On February 15, 1898, the U.S. battleship *Maine* accidentally blew up in Havana harbor, killing 266 American sailors. The U.S. government immediately blamed Spain and issued an ultimatum that the Spanish evacuate Cuba. Spain agreed to the ultimatum, but the American press and Congress were eager for war, and President McKinley did not restrain them.

The Spanish-American War was over quickly. On May 1, 1898, U.S. warships destroyed the Spanish fleet at Manila in the Philippines. Two months later the United States Navy sank the Spanish Atlantic fleet off Santiago, Cuba. By mid-August Spain was suing for peace. U.S. secretary of state John Hay called it "a splendid little war." The United States purchased the Philippines from Spain but took over Puerto Rico and Guam as war booty. The two islands remain American possessions to this day. Cuba became an independent republic, subject, however, to intense interference by the United States.

## American Expansionism and the Spanish-American War, 1898

After 1865 Europeans used their financial power to penetrate Latin America. But they avoided territorial acquisitions for four reasons: (1) they were overextended in Africa and Asia; (2) there was no need, because the Latin American governments provided the political backing for their economic penetration; (3) Mexico's resistance to the French in the 1860s had shown that invasion would not be easy; and (4) the United States claimed to defend the entire Western Hemisphere against all outside intervention. This claim, made in the Monroe Doctrine (1823), did not prevent the United States itself from intervening in Latin American affairs.

## American Intervention in the Caribbean and Central America, 1907–1914

The nations of the Caribbean and Central America were small and poor, and their governments were corrupt, unstable, and often bankrupt. They seemed to offer an open invitation to foreign interference. A government would borrow money to pay for railroads, harbors, electric power, and other symbols of modernity. When it could not repay the loan, the lending banks in Europe or the United States would ask for assistance from their home governments. To ward off European intervention, the United States sent in the marines on more than one occasion.

Presidents Theodore Roosevelt (1901–1909), William Taft (1909–1913), and Woodrow Wilson (1913–1921) felt impelled to intervene in the region, though they differed sharply on the proper policy the United States should follow toward the small nations to the south. Roosevelt encouraged regimes friendly to the United States, like Porfirian Mexico; Taft sought to influence them through loans from American banks; and the moralist Wilson tried to impose clean governments through military means.

Having "liberated" Cuba from Spain, the United States forced the Cuban government to accept the Platt Amendment in 1901. This gave the United States the "right to intervene" to maintain order on the island. The United States used this excuse to occupy Cuba militarily from 1906 to 1909, in 1912, and again from 1917 to 1922. In all but name Cuba became an American protectorate. U.S. troops also occupied the Dominican Republic from 1904 to 1907 and again in 1916, Nicaragua and Honduras in 1912, and Haiti in 1915. They brought sanitation and material progress but no political improvements.

The United States was especially forceful in Panama, which was a province of Colombia. Here the issue was not corruption or debts but the construction of a canal to speed shipping between the east and west coasts of the United States. In 1878 the Frenchman Ferdinand de Lesseps, builder of the Suez Canal, had obtained a concession from Colombia to construct a canal across the isthmus of Panama, which lay in Colombian territory. Financial scandals and yellow fever, however, doomed his project.

When the United States acquired Hawaii and the Philippines, it recognized the strategic value of a canal that would allow warships to move quickly between the Atlantic and Pacific Oceans. The main obstacle was Colombia, whose senate refused to give the United States a piece of its territory. In 1903 the U.S. government supported a Panamanian rebellion against Colombia and quickly recognized the independence of Panama. In exchange, it obtained the right to build a canal and to occupy a zone 5 miles (8 kilometers) wide on either side of it. Work began in 1904, and the **Panama Canal** opened on August 15, 1914.

# THE WORLD ECONOMY AND THE GLOBAL ENVIRONMENT

The New Imperialists were not traditional conquerors or empire builders like the Spanish conquistadors. Their aim was not just to extend their power over new territories and peoples but also to control both natural resources and indigenous societies and put them efficiently to work. Both their goals and their methods were industrial. A railroad, for example, was an act of faith as well as a means of transportation. The imperialists expressed their belief in progress and their good intentions in the clichés of the time: "the conquest of nature," "the annihilation of time and space," "the taming of the wilderness," and "our civilizing mission."

### Expansion of the World Economy

The Industrial Revolution vastly expanded the traditional demand for tropical products. Imports of foods and stimulants such as tea, coffee, and cocoa increased substantially during the nineteenth century. The trade in industrial raw materials, whether agricultural (cotton, jute for bags, and palm oil for soap and lubricants) or mineral (diamonds, gold, and copper), grew even faster. Wild forest products came only later to be cultivated: timber for buildings and railroad ties, cinchona bark, rubber for rainwear and tires, and gutta-percha° to insulate electric cables.

The growing needs of the industrial world could not be met by the traditional methods of production and transportation of the nonindustrial world. When the U.S. Civil War interrupted the export of cotton to England in the 1860s, the British turned to India, only to find that Indian cotton was ruined by exposure to rain and dust while being carted from interior regions to the harbors. To prevent such technological backwardness in the colonies from stifling the expansion of industry, the imperialists made every effort to bring those territories into the mainstream of the world market.

**gutta-percha** (gut-tah-PER-cha)

Transportation was key. The Suez and Panama Canals cut travel time and lowered freight costs dramatically. Steamships became more numerous, and as their size increased, deeper harbors were needed. As for railroads, India alone had 37,000 miles (nearly 60,000 kilometers) of track by 1915, almost as much as Germany or Russia. Railroads reached into the interior of Latin America, Canada, China, and Australia. In 1903 the Russians completed the Trans-Siberian Railway from Moscow to Vladivostok on the Pacific. Visionaries even made plans for railroads from Europe to India and from Egypt to South Africa.

## Transformation of the Global Environment

The economic changes brought by Europeans and Americans altered environments around the world. The British, whose craving for tea could not be satisfied with the limited exports available from China, introduced tea into the warm, rainy hill country of Ceylon and northeastern India. In those areas and in Java thousands of square miles of tropical rain forests were felled to make way for tea plantations.

Economic botany and agricultural science were applied to every promising plant species. European botanists had long collected and classified exotic plants from around the world. In the nineteenth century they founded botanical gardens in Java, India, Mauritius°, Ceylon, Jamaica, and other tropical colonies. These gardens not only collected local plants but also exchanged plants with other gardens. They were especially active in systematically transferring commercially valuable plant species from one tropical region to another. Cinchona, tobacco, sugar, and other crops were introduced, improved, and vastly expanded in the colonies of Southeast Asia and Indonesia. Cocoa and coffee growing spread over large areas of Brazil and Africa; oil-palm plantations were established in Nigeria and the Congo Basin. Rubber originally came from the latex of *Hevea* trees growing wild in the Brazilian rain forest. Then, in the 1870s, British agents smuggled seedlings from Brazil to the Royal Botanic Gardens at Kew near London, and from

**Mauritius** (maw-REE-shuss)

there to the Botanic Garden of Singapore. These plants formed the nucleus of the enormous rubber economy of Southeast Asia.

Throughout the tropics forests and lands devoted to shifting slash-and-burn agriculture gave way to permanent farms and plantations. Even in areas not developed to export crops, growing populations put pressure on the land. In Java and India farmers felled trees to obtain arable land and firewood. They terraced hillsides, drained swamps, and dug wells.

Irrigation and water control transformed the dry parts of the tropics as well. In the 1830s British engineers in India had restored ancient canals that had fallen into disrepair. Their success led them to build new irrigation canals, turning thousands of previously barren acres into well-watered, densely populated farmland. The migration of European experts spread the newest techniques of irrigation engineering around the world. By the turn of the century irrigation projects were under way wherever rivers flowed through dry lands. In Egypt and Central Asia irrigation brought more acres under cultivation in one forty-year span than in all previous history.

Railroads had voracious appetites for land and resources. They cut into mountains, spanned rivers and canyons with trestles, and covered as much land with their freight yards as whole cities had needed in previous centuries. They also consumed vast quantities of iron, timber for ties, and coal or wood for fuel. Most important of all, railroads brought people and their cities, farms, and industries to areas previously occupied by small, scattered populations.

Prospectors looking for valuable minerals opened the earth to reveal its riches: gold in South Africa, Australia, and Canada; tin in Nigeria, Malaya, and Bolivia; copper in Chile and Central Africa; iron ore in northern India; and much else. Where mines were dug deep inside the earth, the dirt and rocks brought up with the ores formed huge mounds near mine entrances. Open mines dug to obtain ores lying close to the surface created a landscape of lunar craters, and runoff from the minerals poisoned the water for miles around. Refineries that processed the ores fouled the environment with slag heaps and more toxic runoff.

The transformation of the land by human beings, a constant throughout history, accelerated sharply. Only the changes occurring since 1914 can compare with the transformation of the global environment that took place between 1869 and 1914.

## CONCLUSION

The industrialization of the late nineteenth century increased the power of Europeans and North Americans over nature and over the peoples of other continents. They used their new-found power to conquer empires.

The opening of the Suez Canal in 1869 was the symbolic beginning of the New Imperialism. It stimulated shipping and trade between the industrial countries and the tropics, and it deepened the involvement of Europeans in the affairs of the Middle East, Africa, and Asia. From that year until 1914, not only the great powers but smaller countries too—even, in some cases, individual Europeans or Americans—had the power to decide the fate of whole countries. This was not just a matter of political will, but also of the gap that opened between European and American technologies and forms of organization and those available to Asians, Africans, and Latin Americans.

The result was in the most rapid conquest of territories in the history of the world. In less than half a century almost all of Africa and large parts of Asia and Oceania were added to the colonial empires, while Latin America, nominally independent, was turned into an economic colony of the industrial powers. In the process of developing the economic potential of their empires, the colonial powers transformed natural environments around the world.

The opening of the Panama Canal in August 1914 confirmed the new powers of the industrializing nations—but with a twist: it was the United States, a latecomer to the game of imperialism, that created the canal. In that same month, the other imperialist nations turned their weapons against one another and began a life-or-death struggle for supremacy in Europe. That conflict is the subject of the next chapter.

## ■ Key Terms

| | |
|---|---|
| Suez Canal | Berlin Conference |
| New Imperialism | Afrikaners |
| Battle of Omdurman | Cecil Rhodes |
| colonialism | Asante |
| "scramble" for Africa | Menelik II |
| Henry Morton Stanley | Emilio Aguinaldo |
| Leopold II | free-trade imperialism |
| Savorgnan de Brazza | Panama Canal |

## ■ Suggested Reading

Two good introductions to imperialism are D. K. Fieldhouse, *Colonialism, 1870–1945* (1981), and Scott B. Cook, *Colonial Encounters in the Age of High Imperialism* (1996). The debate on the theories of imperialism is presented in Roger Owen and Robert Sutcliffe, *Studies in the Theory of Imperialism* (1972), and in Winfried Baumgart, *Imperialism* (1982). The British Empire is the subject of Bernard Porter, *The Lion's Share: A Short History of British Imperialism, 1850–1970* (1976).

On Africa in this period, see Roland Oliver and Anthony Atmore, *Africa Since 1800*, new ed. (1994); Roland Oliver and G. N. Sanderson, eds., *From 1870 to 1905* (1985); A. D. Roberts, ed., *From 1905 to 1940* (1986), in *The Cambridge History of Africa;* and A. Adu Boahen, ed., *Africa Under Colonial Domination, 1880–1935* (1985), in *UNESCO General History of Africa.* The European conquest of Africa is recounted in Thomas Pakenham, *The Scramble for Africa* (1991); Bruce Vandervort, *Wars of Imperial Conquest in Africa, 1830–1914* (1998); and Ronald Robinson and John Gallagher, *Africa and the Victorians: The Climax of Imperialism* (1961). Adam Hochschild's *King Leopold's Ghost: A Story of Greed, Terror, and Heroism in Colonial Africa* (1998) is a very readable account of imperialism in the Belgian Congo. The classic novel about the impact of colonial rule on African society is Chinua Achebe's *Things Fall Apart* (1958).

Imperial rivalries in Asia are the subject of Akira Iriye, *Across the Pacific: An Inner History of American-East Asian Relations*, rev. ed. (1992); David Gillard, *The Struggle for Asia, 1828–1914: A Study in British and Russian Imperialism* (1977); and Peter Hopkirk, *The Great Game: The Struggle for Empire in Central Asia* (1994). On other aspects of imperialism in Asia, see Clifford Geertz, *Agricultural Involution: The Process of Ecological Change in Indonesia* (1963), especially chapters 4 and 5, and Stanley Karnow, *In Our Image: America's Empire in the Philippines* (1989).

On Latin America in this period, see David Bushnell and Neill Macauley, *The Emergence of Latin America in the Nineteenth Century* (1994). Free-trade imperialism is the subject of D. C. M. Platt, *Latin America and British Trade, 1806–1914* (1973). On American expansionism, see David Healy, *Drive to Hegemony: The United States in the Caribbean, 1898–1917* (1989), and Walter LaFeber, *The Panama Canal,* rev. ed. (1990).

On race relations in the colonial world, see Noel Mostert, *Frontiers: The Epic of South Africa's Creation and the Tragedy of the Xhosa People* (1992), and Robert Huttenback, *Racism and Empire: White Settlers and Colored Immigrants in the British Self-Governing Colonies, 1830–1910* (1976). Gender relations are the subject of Caroline Oliver, *Western Women in Colonial Africa* (1982), and Cheryl Walker, ed., *Women and Gender in Southern Africa to 1945* (1990). David Northrup's *Indentured Labor in the Age of Imperialism, 1834–1922* (1995) discusses migrations and labor. Franz Fanon, *The Wretched of the Earth* (1966), and Albert Memmi, *The Colonizer and the Colonized* (1967), examine colonialism from the point of view of the colonized.

The impact of technology on the New Imperialism is the subject of Daniel R. Headrick, *The Tools of Empire: Technology and European Imperialism in the Nineteenth Century* (1981) and *The Tentacles of Progress: Technology Transfer in the Age of Imperialism, 1850–1940* (1988), and Clarence B. Davis and Kenneth E. Wilburn, Jr., eds., *Railway Imperialism* (1991).

On the economic and demographic transformation of Africa and Asia, see Eric Wolf, *Europe and the People Without History* (1982), especially chapters 11 and 12. The impact on the environment is the subject of R. P. Tucker and J. F. Richards, *Deforestation and the Nineteenth-Century World Economy* (1983); Donal McCracken, *Gardens of Empire: Botanical Institutions of the Victorian British Empire* (1997); Lucile H. Brockway, *Science and Colonial Expansion: The Role of the British Royal Botanic Gardens* (1979); and David Arnold and Ramchandra Guha, eds., *Nature, Culture, Imperialism: Essays on the Environmental History of South Asia* (1995). In *Late Victorian Holocausts: El Niño Famines and the Making of the Third World* (2001), Mike Davis argues that imperialism exacerbated the social and demographic effects of famines.

# ◼ Notes

1. *Journal Officiel* (November 29, 1869), quoted in Georges Douin, *Histoire du Règne du Khédive Ismaïl* (Rome: Reale Societá di Geografia d'Egitto, 1933), 453.
2. E. Desplaces in *Journal de l'Union des Deux Mers* (December 15, 1869), quoted in ibid., 453.
3. Winston Churchill, *The River War: An Account of the Reconquest of the Soudan* (New York: Charles Scribner's Sons, 1933), 300.
4. "Correspondence and Report from His Majesty's Consul at Boma respecting the Administration of the Independent State of the Congo," *British Parliamentary Papers, Accounts and Papers,* 1904 (Cd. 1933), lxii, 357.
5. Robert W. July, *A History of the Africa People,* 3d ed. (New York: Charles Scribner's Sons, 1980), 323.
6. George Shepperson and Thomas Price, *Independent African* (Edinburgh: University Press, 1958), 163–164, quoted in Roland Oliver and Anthony Atmore, *Africa Since 1800,* 4th ed. (Cambridge: Cambridge University Press, 1994), 150.
7. Thomas Edson Ennis, *French Policy and Development in Indochina* (Chicago: University of Chicago Press, 1936), 178, quoted in K. M. Panikkar, *Asia and Western Dominance* (New York: Collier, 1969), 167.
8. Quoted in Stanley J. Stein and Barbara H. Stein, *The Colonial Heritage of Latin America* (New York: Oxford University Press, 1970), 151.

# 25 The Crisis of the Imperial Order, 1900–1929

**CHAPTER OUTLINE**

Origins of the Crisis in Europe and the Middle East

The "Great War" and the Russian Revolutions

Peace and Dislocation in Europe

China and Japan: Contrasting Destinies

The New Middle East

Science, Culture, and Technology in the Industrialized World

ENVIRONMENT AND TECHNOLOGY: Cities Old and New

On June 28, 1914, Archduke Franz Ferdinand, heir to the throne of Austria-Hungary, was riding in an open carriage through Sarajevo, capital of the province of Bosnia-Herzegovina, which Austria had annexed six years before. When the carriage stopped momentarily, Gavrilo Princip, a member of a pro-Serbian conspiracy, fired his pistol twice, killing the archduke and his wife.

Those shots ignited a war that spread throughout Europe and then turned into a global war as the Ottoman Empire fought against Britain in the Middle East and Japan attacked German positions in China. France and Britain involved their empires in the war and brought Africans, Indians, Australians, and Canadians to Europe to fight and labor on the front lines. Finally, in 1917, the United States entered the fray.

The next three chapters tell a story of violence and hope. This chapter looks at the causes of war between the great powers; the consequences of that conflict in Europe, the Middle East, and Russia; and the upheavals in China and Japan. It also reviews the accelerating rate of technological change that made the first half of the twentieth century so violent and so hopeful. Entirely new technologies made war more dangerous yet allowed far more people to live healthier, more comfortable, and more interesting lives than ever before.

As you read this chapter, ask yourself the following questions:

- How did the First World War lead to revolution in Russia and the disintegration of other empires?

- What role did the war play in eroding European dominance in the world?

- Why did China and Japan follow such divergent paths in this period?

- How did European and North American society and technology change in the aftermath of the war?

# ORIGINS OF THE CRISIS IN EUROPE AND THE MIDDLE EAST

When the twentieth century opened, the world seemed firmly under the control of the great powers (see Environment and Technology: Cities Old and New). Its first decade saw peace and economic growth in most of the world. New technologies—airplanes, automobiles, radio, and cinema—aroused much excitement. With their colonial conquests over, the great powers seemed matched and likely to maintain peace. The only international war of the period, the Russo-Japanese War (1904–1905), ended quickly with a decisive Japanese victory.

However, two major changes were undermining the apparent stability of the world. In Europe, tensions mounted as Germany challenged Britain at sea and France in Morocco. As the Ottoman Empire grew weaker, the resulting chaos in the Balkans gradually drew the European powers into its hostilities.

## The Ottoman Empire and the Balkans

By 1900, economic, technological, and military decline had made the once-great Ottoman Empire the "sick man of Europe," and it was losing its outlying provinces. Between 1902 and 1913, Macedonia rebelled, Austria-Hungary annexed Bosnia, Crete merged with Greece, Italy conquered Libya, the Ottomans' last foothold in Africa, and Albania became independent. In 1912–1913, Serbia, Bulgaria, Romania, and Greece chased the Turks out of the Balkans, except for a small enclave around Constantinople.

The European powers meddled in the internal affairs of the Ottoman Empire. Russia and Austria-Hungary competed to become the protector of the Slavic peoples of the Balkans. France and Britain, posing as protectors of Christian minorities, controlled Ottoman finances, taxes, railroads, mines, and public utilities.

In reaction, Turks began to assert themselves against rebellious minorities and meddling foreigners. In 1909, the group known as the Young Turks overthrew the sultan and replaced him with his brother. The new regime began to reform the police, the bureaucracy, and the education system and hired a German general to modernize Turkey's armed forces. At the same time, it cracked down on Greek and Armenian minorities.

## Nationalism, Alliances, and Military Strategy

Nationalism was deeply rooted in European culture. It united the citizens of France, Britain, and Germany behind their respective governments and gave them tremendous cohesion and strength of purpose. But nationalism could also be a dividing rather than a unifying force. In the large but fragile multinational Russian, Austro-Hungarian, and Ottoman Empires, ethnic and religious minorities, repressed for centuries, were stirring. The easy victories in the wars of the New Imperialism led some in power to believe that only war could heal the divisions in their societies.

What turned assassination of the Archduke Franz Ferdinand in a small town in the Balkans into a conflict involving all the great powers was the system of alliances that had grown up over the previous decades. At the center of Europe stood Germany, the most heavily industrialized country in Europe and yearning to dominate. Its army was the best trained and equipped, and its heavily armed battleships were challenging Great Britain's naval supremacy. Germany joined Austria-Hungary and Italy in the Triple Alliance in 1882. When in 1907 Britain, France, and Russia formed

# ENVIRONMENT + TECHNOLOGY

## Cities Old and New

Cities do not just grow larger; they change, sometimes radically, in response to culture and technology. The impact of cultural dominance and technological innovations on urban design is evident in these photographs of Cairo.

The European colonial presence was felt more strongly in cities than in the countryside. Cairo, the largest city in the Arab world before the British conquest, grew much larger after 1882. However, the construction of modern quarters for Europeans and wealthy Egyptians had little impact on the older quarters where most Cairenes lived. In the picture of the old quarter of Cairo in 1900 with its narrow streets and open stalls, men wear the burnoose and women cover their faces with a veil. The later picture, taken in 1904, shows Shepheard's Hotel, one of the most luxurious hotels in the world, built on a broad avenue in the city's modern quarter.

The picture at left reflects the traditional architecture of hot desert countries: narrow streets, thick whitewashed walls, small windows, and heavy doors, all designed to keep out the heat of the day and protect privacy. The picture below shows the ideas Europeans brought with them about how a city should look. The wide streets and high airy buildings with windows and balconies mimic the urban design of late-nineteenth-century Paris, London, and Rome.

**Cairo—Modern and Traditional** The luxurious Shepheard's Hotel (below) was built in the European style on a broad avenue in the new quarter of Cairo. In stark contrast is the street (left) in the old quarter of the city: the street is narrow, the walls of the buildings are thick, and the windows small to protect the interiors from the heat of the sun. (Billie Love Historical Collection)

# CHRONOLOGY

| | Europe and North America | Middle East | East Asia |
|---|---|---|---|
| **1900** | | | **1900** Boxer Rebellion in China<br>**1904–1905** Russo-Japanese War |
| | **1907** British-French-Russian Entente | | |
| **1910** | | **1909** Young Turks overthrow Sultan Abdul Hamid | **1911** Chinese revolutionaries led by Sun Yat-sen overthrow Qing dynasty |
| | **1912-1913** Balkan Wars<br>**1914** Assassination of Archduke Franz Ferdinand sparks World War I | | **1915** Japan presents Twenty-One Demands to China |
| | **1916** Battles of Verdun and the Somme<br>**1917** Russian Revolutions; United States enters the war<br>**1918** Armistice ends World War I<br>**1919** Treaty of Versailles | **1916** Arab Revolt in Arabia<br>**1917** Balfour Declaration | **1919** May Fourth Movement in China |
| **1920** | **1920** First commercial radio broadcast (United States)<br>**1921** New Economic Policy in Russia | **1922** Egypt nominally independent<br>**1923** Mustafa Kemal proclaims Turkey a republic | |
| | **1927** Charles Lindbergh flies alone across the Atlantic | | **1927** Guomindang forces occupy Shanghai and expel Communists |

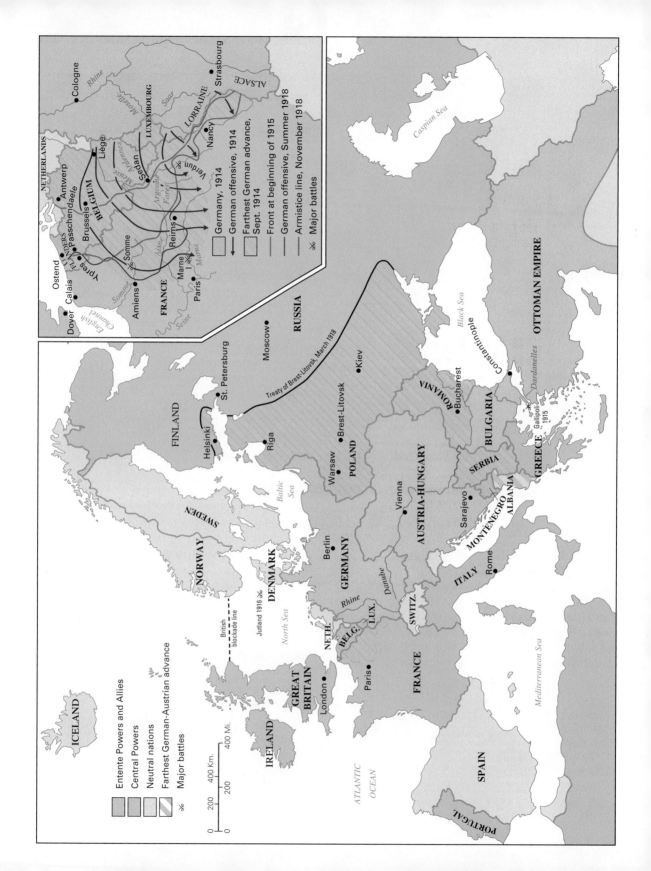

ICELAND

Entente Powers and Allies
Central Powers
Neutral nations
Farthest German-Austrian advance
Major battles

400 Mi.
400 Km.
200
200
0
0

IRELAND

GREAT BRITAIN
London

British blockade line

Jutland 1916

North Sea

NETH.
BELG.
LUX.

Paris
FRANCE

SWITZ.

ATLANTIC OCEAN

PORTUGAL

SPAIN

Mediterranean Sea

NORWAY

SWEDEN

DENMARK

Baltic Sea

Berlin
GERMANY

Rhine
Danube

AUSTRIA-HUNGARY
Vienna

ITALY
Rome

MONTENEGRO
ALBANIA
SERBIA
Sarajevo

GREECE

FINLAND

Helsinki
St. Petersburg
Riga

Warsaw
POLAND
Brest-Litovsk

Moscow

RUSSIA

Treaty of Brest-Litovsk, March 1918

Kiev

ROMANIA
Bucharest

BULGARIA

Black Sea
Constantinople

Dardanelles
Gallipoli 1915

OTTOMAN EMPIRE

Caspian Sea

Germany, 1914
German offensive, 1914
Farthest German advance, Sept. 1914
Front at beginning of 1915
German offensive, Summer 1918
Armistice line, November 1918
Major battles

Cologne
Rhine
Moselle
Saar
Strasbourg
ALSACE
LORRAINE
LUXEMBOURG
Nancy
Verdun
Meuse
Argonne Forest
Sedan
Liège
Antwerp
NETHERLANDS
BELGIUM
Brussels
Passchendaele
Ostend
Ypres
FLANDERS
Calais
Dover
English Channel
Amiens
Somme
Somme
Aisne
Reims
Marne
Marne
Paris
Seine
FRANCE

**Map 25.1    The First World War in Europe**    Most of the fighting in World War I took place on two fronts. After an initial surge through Belgium into northern France, the German offensive bogged down for four years along the Western Front. To the east, the German armies conquered a large part of Russia during 1917 and early 1918. Despite spectacular victories in the east, Germany lost the war because its armies collapsed along the strategically important Western Front.

an Entente° ("understanding"), Europe was divided into two blocs of roughly equal power (see Map 25.1).

The alliance system was cursed by inflexible military planning. In the years before World War I, military planners in France and Germany had worked out elaborate railroad timetables to mobilize their respective armies in a few days. Other countries were less well prepared. Russia, a large country with an underdeveloped rail system, needed several weeks to mobilize its forces. Britain, with only a tiny volunteer army, had no mobilization plans. German generals, believing that the British would stay out of a future European war, made war plans to defeat France in a matter of days and then to transport their entire army by train across Germany to the Russian border before Russia could fully mobilize.

On July 28, 1914, emboldened by the backing of Germany, Austria-Hungary declared war on Serbia, triggering the mobilization plans of Russia, France, and Germany. On July 29, the Russian government ordered general mobilization to force Austria to back down. On August 1, France honored its treaty obligation to Russia and ordered general mobilization. Minutes later, Germany did the same. Because of the rigid railroad timetables, war was now automatic.

The German General Staff expected France to capitulate before the British could get involved. But on August 3, when German troops entered Belgium, Britain demanded their withdrawal. When Germany refused, Britain declared war on Germany.

**Entente** (on-TONT)

# THE "GREAT WAR" AND THE RUSSIAN REVOLUTIONS

Throughout Europe, people greeted the outbreak of war with parades and hopes for a quick victory. The German sociologist Max Weber wrote: "This war, with all its ghastliness, is nevertheless grand and wonderful. It is worth experiencing." Very few imagined that their side might not win, and no one foresaw that everyone would lose. The effect of the war was especially devastating in Russia, for it destroyed the old society, introduced a radical new political system, and put professional revolutionaries in charge of Russia's industrialization.

## Stalemate, 1914–1917

In 1914, the generals' carefully drawn-up plans went awry from the start. Believing that a spirited attack would always prevail, French generals hurled their troops, dressed in bright blue-and-red uniforms, against the well-defended German border and suffered a crushing defeat. By early September, the German armies held Belgium and northern France and were fast approaching Paris.

German victory seemed assured. But when Russia attacked, German troops needed for the final push into France were shifted to the Russian front. A gap opened between two German armies along the Marne River, into which France's last reserves moved. At the Battle of the Marne, the Germans were thrown back several miles.

During the next month, both sides spread out until they formed an unbroken line extending over 300 miles (some 500 kilometers) from the North Sea to the border of Switzerland. All along this **Western Front,** machine guns provided an almost impenetrable defense against advancing infantry but were useless for the offensive because they were too heavy for one man to carry and took too much time to set up. To escape the deadly streams of bullets, soldiers dug holes for themselves in the ground, connected the holes to form shallow trenches, and then dug communications trenches to the rear. Within weeks, the battlefields

**Trench Warfare in World War I**  German and Allied soldiers on the Western Front faced each other from elaborate networks of trenches. Attacking meant jumping out of the trenches and racing across a no man's land of mud and barbed wire. Here we see Princess Patricia's Canadian Light Infantry repelling a German attack near Ypres, in northern France, in March 1915, using machine guns, rifles, and hand grenades.  (Courtesy, The Princess Patricia's Canadian Light Infantry, Regimental Museum and Archives)

were scarred with lines of trenches several feet deep, their tops protected by sandbags and their floors covered with planks.

For four years, generals on each side again and again ordered their troops to attack. In battle after battle, thousands of young men on one side climbed out of their trenches, raced across the open fields, and were mowed down by enemy machine-gun fire. Poison gas added to the horror of battle.

The year 1916 saw the bloodiest and most futile battles of the war. The Germans attacked French forts at Verdun, losing 281,000 men and causing 315,000 French casualties. In retaliation, the British attacked the Germans at the Somme River and suffered 420,000 casualties—60,000 on the first day alone—while the Germans lost 450,000 and the French 200,000.

This was not warfare as it had ever been waged before; it was mass slaughter. Neither side could win, for the armies were stalemated by trenches and machine guns. During four years of the bloodiest fighting the world had ever seen, the Western Front moved no more than a few miles one way or another.

At sea, the war was just as inconclusive. As soon as the war broke out, the British cut the German overseas telegraph cables, blockaded the coasts of Germany and Austria-Hungary, and set out to capture or sink all enemy ships still at sea. The German High Seas Fleet, built at enormous cost, seldom left port. Only once, in May 1916, did it confront the British Grand Fleet. At the Battle of Jutland, off the coast of Denmark, the two fleets lost roughly equal numbers of ships, and the Germans escaped back to their harbors.

In early 1915, in retaliation for the British naval blockade, Germany announced a blockade of Britain by submarines. German submarines attacked every vessel they could. One attack sank the British ocean liner *Lusitania,* killing 1,198 people, 139 of them Americans. When the United States protested, Germany ceased its submarine campaign, hoping to keep America neutral.

### The Home Front and the War Economy

The war economy transformed civilian life. In France and Britain, food rations were allocated according to need, improving nutrition among the poor. Unemployment vanished. Thousands of Africans, Indians, and Chinese were recruited for heavy labor in Europe. Employers hired women to fill jobs in steel mills, mines, and munitions plants vacated by men off to war. Women became streetcar drivers, mail carriers, and police or found work in government bureaucracies. Many joined auxiliary military services as doctors, nurses, mechanics, and ambulance drivers. These positions gave thousands of women a sense of participation and a taste of independence.

German civilians paid an especially high price because of the British naval blockade. The German chemical industry developed synthetic explosives and fuel, but synthetic food was not an option. Wheat flour disappeared, replaced first by rye, then by potatoes and turnips, then by acorns and chestnuts, and finally by sawdust. After the failure of the potato crop in 1916 came the "turnip winter," when people had to survive on 1,000 calories per day, half of the normal amount that an active adult needed. Women, children, and the elderly were especially hard hit.

During the war, the British and French overran all of Germany's African colonies except German

East Africa, which remained undefeated until the end of the war (see Map 24.1). The war brought hardships to many African colonies, whose inhabitants faced heavy taxes, low prices for requisitioned export crops, and forced recruitment. Many Europeans stationed in Africa left to join the war, leaving large areas with little or no European presence. Over a million Africans served in the various armies, and perhaps three times that number were drafted as porters to carry army equipment. In some places, these impositions provoked African uprisings that lasted for years.

One country grew rich during the war: the United States, which for two and a half years stayed technically neutral while businesses engaging in war production did a roaring business supplying France and Britain. After the United States entered the war in 1917, civilians were exhorted to help the war effort by investing their savings in war bonds and growing food in backyard "victory gardens." Employment created by the war opened up jobs for women and African-Americans.

### The Ottoman Empire at War

On August 2, 1914, the Turks signed a secret alliance with Germany. In November, they joined the fighting, hoping to gain land at Russia's expense. But the campaign in the Caucasus proved disastrous for both armies and for the civilian populations. Suspecting the Armenians of being pro-Russian, the Turks forced them to march from their homelands across the mountains in the winter. Hundreds of thousands of Armenians died of hunger and exposure, an omen of even ghastlier tragedies to come.

The Turks also closed the Dardanelles, the strait between the Mediterranean and Black Seas (see Map 25.1). When a British attempt to force open the Dardanelles failed, the British tried to subvert the Ottoman Empire from within by promising the emir (prince) of Mecca, Hussein ibn Ali, a kingdom of his own. In 1916, Hussein started an Arab revolt against the Turks. His son **Faisal**° led an Arab army into Palestine and Syria in support of the British advance from Egypt, thereby contributing to the Ottoman defeat.

---

**Faisal** (fie-SAHL)

The British made promises to Chaim Weizmann°, leader of the British Zionists, that a Jewish homeland in Palestine would be carved out of the Ottoman Empire and placed under British protection. In November, as British armies were advancing on Jerusalem, Foreign Secretary Sir Arthur Balfour wrote that "His Majesty's Government view with favor the establishment in Palestine of a national home for the Jewish people and will use their best endeavours to facilitate the achievement of that object, it being clearly understood that nothing shall be done which may prejudice the civil and religious rights of existing non-Jewish communities in Palestine." The British did not foresee that this statement, known as the **Balfour Declaration,** would lead to conflicts between Palestinians and Jewish settlers.

## Double Revolution in Russia, 1917

At the beginning of the war, Russia had the largest army in the world, but its generals were incompetent, supplies were lacking, and soldiers were poorly trained and equipped. In August 1914, two Russian armies invaded eastern Germany but were thrown back. Several times the Russians defeated the Austro-Hungarian army, only to be defeated by the Germans. In 1916, after a string of defeats, the Russian army ran out of ammunition and other essential supplies. Soldiers were ordered into battle unarmed and told to pick up the rifles of fallen comrades.

With so many men in the army, railroads broke down for lack of fuel and parts, and crops rotted in the fields. Civilians faced shortages and widespread hunger. In the cities, food and fuel became scarce. During the bitterly cold winter of 1916–1917, factory workers and housewives had to line up in front of grocery stores before dawn to get something to eat. The court of Tsar° Nicholas II, however, remained as extravagant and corrupt as ever.

When food ran out in Petrograd, the capital, in early March 1917, housewives and women factory workers staged mass demonstrations. Soldiers mutinied and joined striking workers to form soviets (councils) to take over factories and barracks. A few

days later, the tsar abdicated, and leaders of the parliamentary parties formed a Provisional Government. Thus began what Russians called the "February Revolution" because their calendar was two weeks behind the one in use elsewhere.

Revolutionary groups came out of hiding. Most numerous were the Social Revolutionaries, who advocated the redistribution of land to the peasants. The Social Democrats, a Marxist party, were divided. The Mensheviks, who advocated electoral politics and reform in the tradition of European Socialists, had a large following among intellectuals and factory workers. The rival **Bolsheviks** were a small but tightly disciplined group dedicated to radical revolution. **Vladimir Lenin** (1870–1924), the Bolshevik leader, became a revolutionary in his teens when his older brother was executed for plotting to kill the tsar. His goal was to create a party that would lead the revolution rather than wait for it.

In early April 1917, the German government, hoping to destabilize Russia, allowed Lenin to travel from exile in Switzerland to Russia in a sealed railway car. As soon as he arrived in Petrograd, he announced his program: immediate peace, all power to the soviets, and transfers of land to the peasants and factories to the workers. This plan proved immensely popular among the soldiers and workers exhausted by the war.

When the Provisional Government ordered another offensive against the Germans a few months later, Russian soldiers began to desert by the hundreds of thousands, throwing away their rifles and walking back to their villages. The Bolsheviks, meanwhile, were gaining support among the workers of Petrograd and the soldiers and sailors stationed there. On November 6, 1917 (October 24 in the Russian calendar), they rose up and took over the city. This "October Revolution" overthrew the Provisional Government and arrested Mensheviks, Social Revolutionaries, and other rivals.

The Bolsheviks nationalized all private land and ordered the peasants to hand over their crops without compensation. The peasants, having seized their landlords' estates, resisted. In the cities, the Bolsheviks took over the factories and drafted the workers into compulsory labor brigades. To enforce his rule, Lenin created the Cheka, a secret police force with powers to arrest and execute op-

**Chaim Weizmann** (hi-um VITES-mun)    **tsar** (zahr)

ponents. The Bolsheviks also sued for peace with Germany and Austria-Hungary. By the Treaty of Brest-Litovsk, signed on March 3, 1918, Russia lost territories containing a third of its population and wealth.

## The End of the War in Western Europe, 1917–1918

Like many other Americans, President **Woodrow Wilson** wanted to stay out of the European conflict. For nearly three years, he kept the United States neutral and tried to persuade the belligerents to compromise. But in late 1916, German leaders decided to starve the British into submission by using submarines to sink merchant ships carrying food supplies to Great Britain. The Germans knew that unrestricted submarine warfare was likely to bring the United States into the war, but they were willing to gamble that Britain and France would collapse before the United States could send enough troops to help them.

The submarine campaign resumed on February 1, 1917, but the German gamble failed. The British organized their merchant ships into convoys protected by destroyers, and on April 6, President Wilson asked the United States Congress to declare war on Germany.

On the Western Front, the two sides were so evenly matched in 1917 that the war seemed unlikely to end until one side or the other ran out of young men. Losing hope of winning, soldiers began to mutiny. In May 1917, before the arrival of U.S. forces, fifty-four of one hundred French divisions along the Western Front refused to attack. At Caporetto, Italian troops were so demoralized that 275,000 were taken prisoner.

Between March and August 1918, General Erich von Ludendorff launched a series of surprise attacks that broke through the front at several places and pushed to within 40 miles (64 kilometers) of Paris. But victory eluded him. Meanwhile, every month was bringing another 250,000 American troops to the front. In August, the Allies counterattacked, and the Germans began a retreat that could not be halted, for German soldiers, many of them sick with the flu, had lost the will to fight.

In late October, Ludendorff resigned, and sailors in the German fleet mutinied. Two weeks later, Kaiser Wilhelm fled to Holland as a new German government signed an armistice. On November 11 at 11 A.M., the guns on the Western Front went silent.

# PEACE AND DISLOCATION IN EUROPE

The Great War lasted four years. It took almost twice as long for Europe to recover. Millions of people had died or been disabled, political tensions lingered, and national economies remained depressed until the mid-1920s. The return of peace and prosperity in the late 1920s soon proved illusory.

## The Impact of the War

The war left more dead and wounded and more physical destruction than any previous conflict. It is estimated that between 8 million and 10 million people died, almost all of them young men. Perhaps twice that many returned home wounded, gassed, or shell-shocked, many of them injured for life. In addition, the war created millions of refugees.

Many refugees found shelter in France, which welcomed 1.5 million people, but the preferred destination was the United States. About 800,000 immigrants succeeded in reaching it before U.S. immigration laws passed in 1921 and 1924 closed the door to eastern and southern Europeans. Canada, Australia, and New Zealand adopted similar restrictions on immigration. The Latin American republics welcomed European refugees, but their poverty discouraged potential immigrants.

One unexpected byproduct of the war was the great influenza epidemic of 1918–1919, which started among soldiers heading for the Western Front. This was no ordinary flu but a virulent strain that infected almost everyone on earth and killed one person in every forty. It caused the largest number of deaths in so short a time in the history of the world. Half a million Americans perished in the epidemic—five times as many as died in the war. Worldwide, some 30 million people died, 20 million in India alone.

The war also caused serious damage to the environment. No place on earth was ever so completely devastated as the scar across France and Belgium known as the Western Front. The fighting ravaged forests and demolished towns. The earth was gouged by trenches, pitted with craters, and littered with ammunition, broken weapons, chunks of concrete, and the bones of countless soldiers. After the war, it took a decade to clear away the debris and create military cemeteries with neat rows of crosses stretching for miles. The war also hastened the buildup of industry, with mines, factories, and railroad tracks.

## The Peace Treaties

In early 1919, delegates of the victorious Allies met in Paris. The defeated powers were kept out until the treaties were ready for signing. Russia, in the throes of civil war, was not invited.

From the start, three men dominated the Paris Peace Conference: United States president Wilson, British prime minister David Lloyd George, and French premier Georges Clemenceau°. They ignored the Italians, who had joined the Allies in 1915, and paid even less attention to the delegates of smaller European nations. They rejected the Japanese proposal that all races be treated equally and ignored the call of the Pan-African Congress for attention to the concerns of African peoples around the world. They also ignored the ten thousand other delegates of various nationalities who did not represent sovereign states—the Arab leader Faisal, the Zionist Chaim Weizmann, and several Armenian delegations—who came to Paris to lobby for their causes.

Each man had his own agenda. Wilson wanted to apply the principle of self-determination, by which he meant creating nations that reflected European ethnic or linguistic divisions. He proposed a **League of Nations,** a world organization to safeguard the peace and foster international cooperation. His idealism clashed with the more hardheaded and self-serving nationalism of the Europeans. Lloyd George insisted that Germany pay a heavy indemnity. Clemenceau wanted Germany to give back Alsace and Lorraine, cede the industrial Saar region to France, and make the Rhineland a buffer state.

The result was a series of compromises that satisfied no one. The European powers formed a League of Nations, but the United States Congress, reflecting the isolationist feelings of the American people, refused to join. France recovered Alsace and Lorraine but was unable to detach the Rhineland and had to content itself with vague promises of British and American protection if Germany ever rebuilt its army. Britain acquired new territories in Africa and the Middle East but was greatly weakened by human losses and the disruption of its trade.

On June 28, 1919, the German delegates reluctantly signed the **Treaty of Versailles°.** Germany was forbidden to have an air force and was permitted only a token army and navy. It gave up large parts of its eastern territory to a newly reconstituted Poland. The Allies made Germany promise to pay reparations, but they did not set a figure or a period of time for payment. A "guilt clause," which was to rankle for years to come, obliged the Germans to accept "responsibility for causing all the loss and damage" of the war. The Treaty of Versailles left Germany humiliated but largely intact and potentially the most powerful nation in Europe. Establishing a peace neither of punishment nor of reconciliation, the treaty was one of the great failures in history.

In eastern Europe, the Allies created new national states in the lands lost by the old Russian, German, and Austro-Hungarian Empires. Austria and Hungary became separate states; Poland was resurrected after over a century; Czechoslovakia and Yugoslavia were created from parts of Austria-Hungary. These small nations all contained disaffected minorities and were safe only as long as Germany and Russia remained weak.

## Russian Civil War and the New Economic Policy

Fighting continued in Russia for another three years after the end of the Great War. The Bolshevik Revolution had provoked Allied intervention, and, in December 1918, civil war broke out in Russia.

---

**Georges Clemenceau** (zhorzh cluh-mon-SO)

**Versailles** (vuhr-SIGH)

The Communists, as the Bolsheviks now called themselves, held central Russia, but all the surrounding provinces rose up against them. Counter-revolutionary armies led by former tsarist officers obtained weapons and supplies from the Allies. However, by 1921, the superior discipline of the Red Army, led by Leon Trotsky, gave the Communists victory over their enemies.

Gradually, the Communists reunited most of the rebellious provinces of the old Russian Empire. In 1920, Ukrainian Communists declared the independence of a Soviet republic of Ukraine; then, in 1922, this merged with Russia to create the Union of Soviet Socialist Republics (USSR), or Soviet Union. In 1920–1921, the Red Army reconquered the oil-rich Caucasus and reestablished Soviet control of Central Asia. In 1922, the new Soviet republics of Georgia, Armenia, and Azerbaijan joined the USSR.

Years of warfare, revolution, and mismanagement had ruined the Russian economy. Factories and railroads had shut down. Farmland had been devastated and livestock killed, causing hunger in the cities. Lenin decided to release the economy from party and government control. In March 1921, he announced the **New Economic Policy** (NEP), which allowed peasants to own land and sell their crops, private merchants to trade, and private workshops to produce goods and sell them on the free market. Only the biggest businesses, such as banks, railroads, and factories, remained under government ownership.

The relaxation of controls had an immediate effect. Production began to climb, and food and other goods became available. In the cities, food remained scarce because farmers used their crops to feed their livestock rather than sell them. But the NEP reflected no change in the goal of the Communist Party to create a modern industrial economy without private property, under party guidance. It merely provided breathing space—what Lenin called "one step back to advance two steps forward." This meant investing in heavy industry and electrification, moving farmers to the new industries, and providing food for the urban workers. In other words, it meant making the peasants, the great majority of the Soviet people, pay for the industrialization of Russia.

When Lenin died in January 1924, his associates jockeyed for power. Leon Trotsky, commander of the Red Army, had the support of many "Old Bolsheviks" who had joined the party before the Revolution, but Joseph Stalin, general secretary of the Communist Party, got the support of the majority and filled the party bureaucracy with individuals loyal to himself. In January 1929, he forced Trotsky to flee the country. Then, as absolute master of the party, he prepared to industrialize the Soviet Union at breakneck speed.

## An Ephemeral Peace

The decade after the end of the war can be divided into two distinct periods: five years of painful recovery and readjustment (1919–1923), followed by six years of growing peace and prosperity (1924–1929). One of the big adjustments in many Western societies was granting political rights to women (see "Class and Gender" below). Changes in international politics and economics were more upsetting. In the first period, the German government had printed money recklessly to fund reparations payments, causing the most severe inflation the world had ever seen. As Germany teetered on the brink of civil war, radical nationalists called for revenge and tried to overthrow the government. Finally, the German government issued a new currency and promised to resume reparations payments, and the French agreed to withdraw their troops from the Ruhr.

Then in 1924, the vexed issue of reparations vanished as Germany borrowed money from New York banks to make its payments to France and Britain, which used the money to repay their wartime loans from the United States. This triangular flow of money stimulated the rapid recovery of the European economies. France began rebuilding its war-torn northern zone, Germany recovered from its hyperinflation and joined the League of Nations, and in the United States a boom began that was to last over five years.

While their economies flourished, governments grew more cautious and businesslike. Yet neither Germany nor the Soviet Union accepted its borders with the small nations that had arisen between them. In 1922, they signed a secret pact allowing the German army to conduct maneuvers in Russia (in violation of the Versailles treaty) in exchange for German help in building up Russian industry.

For a time, the League of Nations proved adept at resolving issues pertaining to health, labor relations, and postal and telegraph communications. But without U.S. participation, sanctions against states that violated League rules carried little weight.

# CHINA AND JAPAN: CONTRASTING DESTINIES

China and Japan took different directions in the early twentieth century. Still in need of deep internal reform, giant China went through a revolution but soon collapsed into chaos. Japan's re-

forms before 1900 had gained it industry and a powerful military, which it used to take advantage of China's weakness.

## Revolution in China

China's population—about 400 million in 1900—was the largest of any country in the world and growing fast, but China's society and government were falling behind. Most Chinese worked incessantly, survived on a diet of grain and vegetables, and spent their lives in fear of floods, bandits, and tax collectors. Peasant plots averaged half as large as they had been two generations earlier. Landowners lived off the rents of their tenants. Officials, chosen through an elaborate examination system, enriched themselves from taxes and the government's monopolies on salt, iron, and other products. Wealthy merchants handled China's growing import-export trade in collaboration with foreign companies. The contrast between the squalor in which most urban residents lived and the luxury of the foreigners' enclaves in the treaty ports sharpened the resentment of educated Chinese.

In 1900, China's **Empress Dowager Cixi°,** who had seized power in a palace coup two years earlier, encouraged a secret society, the Righteous Fists, or Boxers, to rise up and expel all the foreigners from China. When the Boxers threatened the foreign legation in Beijing, an international force from the Western powers and Japan captured the city and forced China to pay a huge indemnity. Shocked by these events, many Chinese students became convinced that China needed a revolution to get rid of the Qing dynasty and modernize their country.

When Cixi died in 1908, the Revolutionary Alliance led by **Sun Yat-sen°** (Sun Zhongshan, 1867–1925) prepared to take over. Sun had spent much of his life in Japan, England, and the United States, plotting the overthrow of the Qing dynasty. His ideas, a mixture of nationalism, socialism, and Confucian philosophy, and his tenacious spirit attracted a large following. A revolutionary assembly elected Sun president of China in December 1911, and the last Qing ruler, the boy-emperor Puyi, abdicated

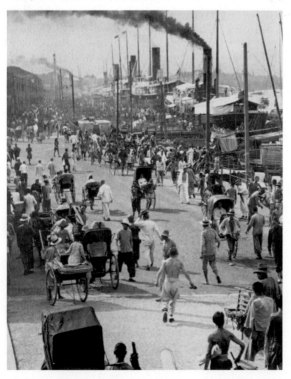

**The Bund, Shanghai**  Shanghai was the most important port and industrial city in China. This picture shows the Bund, or waterfront, where oceangoing ships docked and where Chinese and foreign merchants did business. Many of the people you see in the picture were stevedores, who loaded and unloaded ships, and drivers of rickshaws or man-powered taxis.  (Corbis)

**Cixi** (TSUH-shee)  **Sun Yat-sen** (soon yot-SEN)

the throne. But Sun had no military forces at his command. To avoid a clash with the army, he resigned after a few weeks, and a new national assembly elected **Yuan Shikai°**, the most powerful of the regional generals, president of the new Chinese republic.

Yuan was an able military leader, but he had no political program. When Sun reorganized his followers into a political party called **Guomindang°** (National People's Party), Yuan quashed every attempt at creating a Western-style government and harassed Sun's followers. Victory in the first round of the struggle to create a new China went to the military.

## Japan and World War I

Japan's population reached 60 million in 1925 and was increasing by a million a year. The crash program of industrialization begun in 1868 by the Meiji oligarchs (see Chapter 23) accelerated during the First World War, when Japan exported textiles, consumer goods, and munitions. In the war years, its economy grew four times as fast as western Europe's and eight times faster than China's. Blessed with a rainy climate and many fast-flowing rivers, Japan quickly expanded its hydroelectric capacity. By the mid-1930s, 89 percent of Japanese households had electric lights, compared with 44 percent of British households.

The main beneficiaries of prosperity were the *zaibatsu°*, four giant corporations—Mitsubishi, Sumitomo, Yasuda, and Mitsui—that controlled most of Japan's industry and commerce. Farmers, who constituted half of the population, remained poor; some, in desperation, sold their daughters to textile mills or into domestic service, where young women formed the bulk of the labor force. Labor unions were weak and repressed by the police.

The Japanese were quick to join the Allied side in World War I. They saw the war as a golden opportunity to advance their interests while the Europeans were occupied elsewhere. The war created an economic boom, as the Japanese suddenly found their products in greater demand than before.

The Japanese soon conquered the German colonies in the northern Pacific and on the coast of China, and then turned their attention to the rest of China. In 1915, Japan presented China with Twenty-One Demands, which would have turned it into a virtual protectorate. Britain and the United States persuaded Japan to soften the demands but could not prevent it from keeping the German coastal enclaves and extracting railroad and mining concessions at China's expense. Thus began a bitter struggle between the two countries that was to last for thirty years.

## China in the 1920s

To many educated Chinese, the great powers' decision at the Paris Peace Conference to go along with Japan's seizure of the German enclaves in China was a cruel insult. On May 4, 1919, students demonstrated in front of the Forbidden City of Beijing. Despite a government ban, the May Fourth Movement spread to other parts of China. A new generation was growing up to challenge the old officials, the regional generals, and the foreigners.

China's regional generals—the warlords—still supported their armies through plunder and arbitrary taxation. They frightened off trade and investment in railroads, industry, and agricultural improvement. While neglecting the dikes and canals on which the livelihood of Chinese farmers depended, they fought one another and protected the gangsters who ran the opium trade. During the warlord era, China grew poorer, and only the treaty ports prospered.

Sun Yat-sen tried to make a comeback in Canton (Guangzhou) in the early 1920s. Though not a communist, he was impressed with the efficiency of Lenin's revolutionary tactics and let a Soviet adviser reorganize the Guomindang along Leninist lines. He also welcomed members of the newly created Chinese Communist Party into the Guomindang.

When Sun died in 1925, the leadership of his party passed to Chiang Kai-shek° (1886–1975). An officer and director of the military academy, Chiang trained several hundred young officers, who remained loyal to him thereafter. In 1927, he determined to crush the regional warlords. As his

---

**Yuan Shikai** (you-AHN she-KIE)   **Guomindang** (gwo-min-dong)   *zaibatsu* (zie-BOT-soo)

**Chiang Kai-shek** (chang kie-shek)

army moved north from its base in Canton, he briefly formed an alliance with the Communists. Once his troops had occupied Shanghai, however, he allied himself with local gangsters to crush the labor unions and decimate the Communists, whom he considered a threat. He then defeated or co-opted most of the other warlords and established a dictatorship.

Chiang's government issued ambitious plans to build railroads, develop agriculture and industry, and modernize China from the top down. However, his followers were neither competent administrators like the Japanese officials of the Meiji Restoration nor ruthless modernizers like the Russian Bolsheviks. Instead, the government attracted thousands of opportunists whose goal was to "become an official and get rich" by taxing and plundering businesses. In the countryside, tax collectors and landowners squeezed the peasants ever harder. What little money reached the government went to the military. Twenty years after the fall of the Qing, China remained mired in poverty, subject to corrupt officials and the whims of nature.

# THE NEW MIDDLE EAST

At the Paris Peace Conference, France, Britain, Italy, and Japan proposed to divide the territories of the Ottoman Empire among themselves, but their ambitions clashed with President Wilson's ideal of national self-determination. Turkish nationalists made modern Turkey a new independent country. The Arab-speaking territories of the old Ottoman Empire became part of the League of Nations' new **mandate system,** run by French and British administrations that were accountable to the League of Nations for "the material and moral well-being and the social progress of the inhabitants." In the midst of these territories, Zionists were encouraging Jewish immigration (see Map 25.2).

### The Rise of Modern Turkey

At the end of the First World War, the Allied forces occupied the Ottoman Empire and made the sultan give up most of his lands. But they had to reckon with Mustafa Ke-

**Mustafa Kemal Atatürk**    After World War I, Mustafa Kemal was determined to modernize Turkey on the Western model. Here he is shown wearing a European-style suit and teaching the Latin alphabet.    (Stock Montage)

mal, a war hero who had formed a nationalist government in central Anatolia with the backing of fellow army officers. His armies reconquered Anatolia and the area around Constantinople in 1922 and expelled hundreds of thousands of Greeks. In response, the Greek government expelled all Muslims from Greece.

**Map 25.2   Territorial Changes in the Middle East After World War I**   The defeat and dismemberment of the Ottoman Empire at the end of World War I resulted in an entirely new political map of the region. The Turkish Republic inherited Anatolia and a small piece of the Balkans, while the Ottoman Empire's Arab provinces were divided between France and Great Britain as "Class A Mandates." The French acquired Syria and Lebanon, and the British got Palestine (now Israel), Transjordan (now Jordan), and Iraq. Only Iran and Egypt remained as they had been.

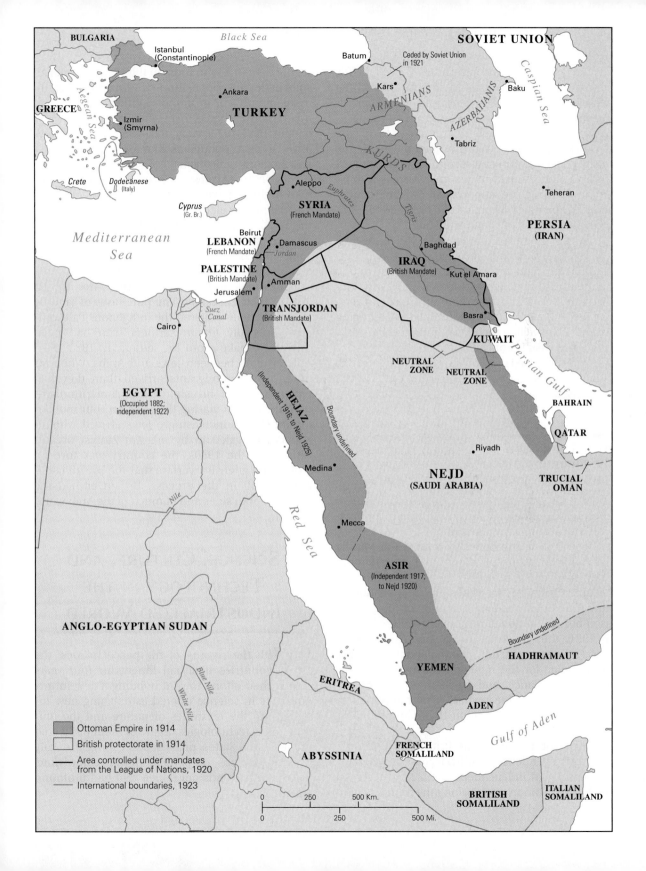

BULGARIA

*Black Sea*

Istanbul
(Constantinople)

SOVIET UNION

Batum

Ceded by Soviet Union
in 1921

Ankara

Kars

ARMENIANS

Baku

*Caspian Sea*

GREECE

*Aegean Sea*

Izmir
(Smyrna)

TURKEY

AZERBAIJANIS

Tabriz

KURDS

Teheran

Crete

Dodecanese
(Italy)

Cyprus
(Gr. Br.)

Aleppo

*Euphrates*

SYRIA
(French Mandate)

*Tigris*

Baghdad

PERSIA
(IRAN)

*Mediterranean
Sea*

Beirut

LEBANON
(French Mandate)

Damascus

*Jordan*

IRAQ
(British Mandate)

Kut el Amara

PALESTINE
(British Mandate)

Jerusalem

Amman

*Suez
Canal*

Cairo

TRANSJORDAN
(British Mandate)

Basra

KUWAIT

*Persian Gulf*

NEUTRAL
ZONE

NEUTRAL
ZONE

EGYPT
(Occupied 1882;
independent 1922)

HEJAZ

(Independent 1916; to Nejd 1925)

*Red Sea*

*Nile*

Medina

Boundary undefined

BAHRAIN

QATAR

Riyadh

NEJD
(SAUDI ARABIA)

TRUCIAL
OMAN

Mecca

ASIR
(Independent 1917;
to Nejd 1920)

ANGLO-EGYPTIAN SUDAN

Boundary undefined

HADHRAMAUT

*Blue Nile*

*White Nile*

YEMEN

ERITREA

ADEN

ABYSSINIA

*Gulf of Aden*

FRENCH
SOMALILAND

BRITISH
SOMALILAND

ITALIAN
SOMALILAND

Ottoman Empire in 1914

British protectorate in 1914

Area controlled under mandates
from the League of Nations, 1920

International boundaries, 1923

| 0 | 250 | 500 Km. |

| 0 | 250 | 500 Mi. |

As a war hero and proclaimed savior of his country, Kemal was able to impose wrenching changes on his people faster than any other reformer would have dared. An outspoken modernizer, he was eager to bring Turkey closer to Europe as quickly as possible. He abolished the sultanate, in 1923 declared Turkey a secular republic, and introduced European laws. In a radical break with Islamic tradition, he suppressed Muslim courts, schools, and religious orders and replaced the Arabic alphabet with the Latin alphabet.

Kemal attempted to Westernize the traditional Turkish family. Women received civil equality, including the right to vote and be elected to the national assembly. Kemal forbade polygamy and instituted civil marriage and divorce. He even changed people's clothing, strongly discouraging women from veiling their faces and ordering Turkish men to wear European brimmed hats instead of the fez. He ordered everyone to take a family name, choosing the name Atatürk ("father of the Turks") for himself.

## Arab Lands and the Question of Palestine

Among the Arab people, the thinly disguised colonialism of the mandate system set off protests and rebellions. Arabs viewed the European presence not as "liberation" from Ottoman "oppression" but as foreign occupation.

The British attempted to control the Middle East with a mixture of bribery and intimidation. They helped Faisal, leader of the Arab Revolt, become king of Syria. When the French ousted him, the British made him king of Iraq. They used bombers to quell rural insurrections in Iraq. In 1931, they reached an agreement with King Faisal's government: official independence for Iraq in exchange for the right to keep two air bases, a military alliance, and an assured flow of petroleum. France, meanwhile, sent thousands of troops to Syria and Lebanon to crush nationalist uprisings.

In Egypt as in Iraq, the British substituted a phony independence for official colonialism. They declared Egypt independent in 1922 but reserved the right to station troops along the Suez Canal to secure their link with India in the event of war. Despite nationalist opposition, Britain was successful in keeping Egypt in limbo—neither independent nor a colony—thanks to an alliance with King Fuad (sultan 1917–1922; king 1922–1936) and conservative Egyptian politicians who feared both secular and religious radicalism.

As soon as Palestine became a British mandate in 1920, Jewish immigrants, encouraged by the Balfour Declaration of 1917, arrived to join the small community that had immigrated in the nineteenth century. Most settled in the cities, but some purchased land to establish *kibbutzim*, communal farms. Their goals were to become self-sufficient and reestablish their ties to the land of their ancestors. The purchases of land by Jewish agencies angered the indigenous Palestinians, especially tenant farmers who had been evicted to make room for settlers. In 1920–1921, riots erupted between Jews and Arabs. When far more Jewish immigrants arrived than they had anticipated, the British tried to limit immigration, thereby alienating the Jews without mollifying the Arabs. Increasingly, Jews arrived without papers, smuggled in by militant Zionist organizations. In the 1930s, the country was torn by strikes and guerrilla warfare that the British could not control. In the process, Britain earned the hatred of both sides and of much of the Arab world as well.

# SCIENCE, CULTURE, AND TECHNOLOGY IN THE INDUSTRIALIZED WORLD

With the signing of the peace treaties, the countries that had fought for four years turned their efforts toward building a new future. Advances in science offered astonishing new insights into the mysteries of nature and the universe. New technologies, many of them pioneered in the United States, promised to change the daily lives of millions of people. At the same time, new cultural trends developed that had profound effects.

## Class and Gender

After the war, class distinctions began to fade. Many European aristocrats had died on the battlefields, and with them went their class's long domination of the army, the diplomatic corps, and other elite sectors of society. The United States and Canada had never had as rigidly defined a class structure as European societies or as elaborate a set of traditions and manners. During the war, displays of wealth and privilege seemed unpatriotic. On both sides of the Atlantic, engineers, businessmen, lawyers, and other professionals rose to prominence, increasing the relative importance of the middle class.

The activities of governments had expanded during the war and continued to grow. Governments provided housing, highways, schools, public health facilities, broadcasting, and other services. This growth of government influence created a need for thousands more bureaucrats. Department stores, banks, insurance companies, and other businesses also increased the white-collar work force.

In contrast with the middle class, the working class did not expand. The introduction of new machines and new ways of organizing work, such as the automobile assembly line that Henry Ford devised, increased workers' productivity so that greater outputs could be achieved without a larger labor force.

Women's lives changed more rapidly in the 1920s than in any previous decade. Although the end of the war marked a retreat from wartime job opportunities, some women remained in the work force as wage earners and as salaried professionals. The young and wealthy enjoyed more personal freedoms than their mothers had before the war; they drove cars, played sports, traveled alone, and smoked in public. For others the upheavals of war brought more suffering than liberation. Millions of women had lost their fathers, brothers, sons, husbands, and fiancés in the war or in the great influenza epidemic. After the war the shortage of young men caused many single women to lead lives of loneliness and destitution.

In Europe and North America advocates of women's rights had been demanding the vote for women since the 1890s. New Zealand was the only nation to grant women the vote before the twentieth century. Women in Norway were the first to obtain it in Europe, in 1915. Russian women followed in 1917, and Canadians and Germans in 1918. Britain gave women over age thirty the vote in 1918 and later extended it to younger women. The Nineteenth Amendment to the U.S. Constitution granted suffrage to American women in 1920. Women in Turkey began voting in 1934. Most other countries did not allow women to vote until after 1945.

In dictatorships voting rights for women made no difference, and in democratic countries women tended to vote like their male relatives. In the British elections of 1918—the first to include women—they overwhelmingly voted for the Conservative Party. Everywhere, their influence on politics was less radical than feminists had hoped and conservatives had feared. Even when it did not alter politics and government, however, the right to vote was a potent symbol.

Women were active in many other areas besides the suffrage movement. On both sides of the Atlantic women participated in social reform movements to prevent mistreatment of women and children and of industrial workers. In the United States such reforms were championed by Progressives such as Jane Addams (1860–1935), who founded a settlement house in a poor neighborhood and received the Nobel Peace Prize in 1931. In Europe reformers were generally aligned with Socialist or Labour Parties.

Since 1874 the Women's Christian Temperance Union had campaigned against alcohol and taverns. In the early twentieth century the American Carrie Nation (1846–1911) became famous for destroying saloons and lecturing in the United States and Europe against the evils of liquor. As a result of this campaign, the Eighteenth Amendment imposed prohibition in the United States from 1919 until it was revoked by the Twenty-First Amendment fourteen years later.

Among the most controversial, and eventually most effective, of the reformers were those who advocated contraception, such as the American **Margaret Sanger** (1883–1966). Her campaign brought her into conflict with the authorities, who equated birth control with pornography. Finally, in 1923 she was able to found a birth control clinic in New York. In France, however, the government prohibited contraception and abortion in 1920 in an effort to increase the birthrate and make up for the loss of so many young men in the war. Only the Russian communists allowed abortion, for ideological reasons (see Diversity and Dominance: Women, Family Values, and the Russian Revolution in Chapter 26).

## Revolution in the Sciences

For two hundred years, scientists, following in Isaac Newton's footsteps, had applied the same laws and equations to astronomical observations and to laboratory experiments. At the end of the nineteenth century, however, a revolution in physics undermined all the old certainties about nature. Physicists discovered that atoms, the building blocks of matter, are not indivisible but consist of far smaller subatomic particles. In 1900, the German physicist **Max Planck** (1858–1947) found that light and energy do not flow in a continuous stream but travel in small units, which he called *quanta*. These findings seemed strange enough, but what really undermined Newtonian physics was the general theory of relativity developed by **Albert Einstein** (1879–1955), another German physicist. In 1916, Einstein announced that not only is matter made of insubstantial particles, but also that time, space, and mass are not fixed but are relative to one another.

To nonscientists, it seemed as though theories expressed in arcane mathematical formulas were replacing truth and common sense. Far from being mere speculation, however, the new physics promised to unlock the secrets of matter and provide humans with plentiful—and potentially dangerous—new sources of energy.

The new social sciences were even more unsettling than the new physics, for they challenged Victorian morality, middle-class values, and notions of Western superiority. Sigmund Freud (1856–1939), a Viennese physician, developed a technique—psychoanalysis—to probe the minds of his patients. He found not only rationality but also hidden layers of emotion and desire repressed by social restraints. "The primitive, savage and evil impulses have not vanished from any individual, but continue their existence, although in a repressed state," he warned. Meanwhile, sociologists and anthropologists had begun the empirical study of societies, both Western and non-Western. Before the war, the French sociologist Emile Durkheim (1858–1917) had come to the then-shocking conclusion that "there are no religions that are false. All are true in their own fashion."

If the words *primitive* and *savage* applied to Europeans as well as to other peoples, and if religions were all equally "true," then what remained of the superiority of Western civilization? Cultural relativism, as the new approach to human societies was called, was as unnerving as relativity in physics.

Wartime experiences helped call into question the West's faith in reason and progress. Some people accepted the new ideas with enthusiasm. Others condemned and rejected them, clinging to the sense of order and faith in progress that had energized European and American culture before the war.

## The New Technologies of Modernity

Some Europeans and Americans viewed the new sciences with mixed feelings, but new technologies aroused almost universal excitement. In North America, even working-class people could afford some of the new products of scientific research, inventors' ingenuity, and industrial production. Mass consumption lagged in Europe, but science and technology were just as advanced, and public fascination with the latest inventions—the cult of the modern—was just as strong.

No other innovation attracted public interest as much as airplanes. In 1903, two young American mechanics, Wilbur and Orville Wright, built the first aircraft that was heavier than air and could be maneuvered in flight. From that moment on, wherever they appeared, airplanes fascinated people. During the war, the exploits of air aces relieved the tedium of news from the front. In the 1920s, aviation became a sport and a form of entertainment, and flying daredevils achieved extraordinary fame by pushing their planes to the very limit—and often beyond. Among the most celebrated pilots were three Americans: Amelia Earhart, the first woman to fly across the Atlantic Ocean; Richard Byrd, the first to fly over the North Pole, in 1926; and Charles Lindbergh, the first person to fly alone across the Atlantic, in 1927. The heroic age of flight lasted until the late 1930s, when aviation became a means of transportation.

Electricity's impact on home life was more sweeping. The first home use of electricity was for lighting, thanks to the economical and long-lasting tungsten bulb. Then, having persuaded people to wire their homes, electrical utilities joined manufacturers in advertising electric irons, fans, washing machines, hot plates, radios, and other electric appliances. After the war, radio moved from the battlefield into the home. The first commercial station began broadcasting in Pittsburgh in 1920. By 1930, hundreds of stations were broadcasting news, sports, soap operas, and advertising to 12 million homes in North America. In Europe, radio spread more slowly because governments reserved the airwaves for cultural and official programs and taxed radio owners to pay for the service.

Another medium that spread explosively in the 1920s was film. Motion pictures had begun in France in 1895 and flourished in Europe. In the United States, filmmaking started at almost the same time, but American filmmakers saw the medium's potential to entertain audiences rather than preserve outstanding theatrical performances. After World War I, filmmaking took root and flourished in Japan, India, Turkey, Egypt, and a suburb of Los Angeles, California, called Hollywood. American and European movie studios were both successful in exporting films, since silent movies presented no language problems. Then in 1927 the United States introduced the first "talking" motion picture, *The Jazz Singer,* which changed all the rules. The number of Americans who went to see their favorite stars in thrilling adventures and heart-breaking romances rose from 40 million in 1922 to 100 million in 1930, at a time when the population of the country was about 120 million. Europeans had the technology and the art but neither the wealth nor the huge market of the United States. Hollywood studios began the diffusion of American culture that has continued to this day.

Advances in medicine—some learned in the war—were another important and life-saving technology. Wounds were regularly disinfected, and x-ray machines helped diagnose fractures. After the war, cities built costly water supply and sewage treatment systems. By the 1920s, indoor plumbing and

flush toilets were becoming common even in working-class neighborhoods. Interest in cleanliness altered private life. Soap and appliance manufacturers filled women's magazines with advertisements for products to help housewives keep their family's homes and clothing spotless and their meals fresh and wholesome. The decline in infant mortality and the improvements in general health and life expectancy in this period owe as much to the cult of cleanliness as to advances in medicine.

## Technology and the Environment

Two new technologies— the skyscraper and the automobile—transformed the urban environment even more radically than the railroad had done in the nineteenth century. At the end of the nineteenth century, architects had begun to design ever-higher buildings using load-bearing steel frames and passenger elevators. Major corporations in Chicago and New York competed to build the most daring buildings in the world, such as New York's 55-story Woolworth Building (1912) and Chicago's 34-story Tribune Tower (1923). A building boom in the late 1920s produced dozens of skyscrapers, culminating with the 86-story, 1,239-foot (377-meter) Empire State Building in New York City, completed in 1932.

European cities restricted the height of buildings to protect their architectural heritage; Paris forbade buildings over 56 feet (17 meters) high. In innovative designs, however, European architects led the way. In the 1920s, the Swiss architect known as Le Corbusier° outlined a new approach to architecture that featured simplicity of form, absence of surface ornamentation, easy manufacture, and inexpensive materials. Among his influential designs were the main buildings of Chandigarh, the new capital of the Indian state of Punjab. Other architects—including the Finn Eero Saarinen, the Germans Ludwig Mies van der Rohe° and Walter Gropius, and the American Frank Lloyd Wright— advanced his lines of thought and added their own to create what became known as the International Style.

---

**Le Corbusier** (luh cor-booz-YEH)   **Ludwig Mies van der Rohe** (LOOD-vig MEES fon der ROW-uh)

**The Archetypal Automobile City**    As Los Angeles grew from a modest town into a sprawling metropolis, broad avenues, parking lots, and garages were built to accommodate automobiles. By 1929, most families owned a car, and streetcar lines had closed for lack of passengers. This photograph shows a street in the downtown business district.    (South Pacific Collection/Los Angeles Public Library)

While central business districts were reaching for the sky, outlying areas were spreading far out into the countryside, thanks to the automobile. The assembly line pioneered by Henry Ford mass-produced vehicles in ever-greater volume and at falling prices. By 1929, the United States had one car for every five people, five-sixths of the world's automobiles. Far from being blamed for their exhaust emissions, automobiles were praised as the solution to urban pollution. As cars replaced carts and carriages, horses disappeared from city streets, as did tons of manure.

The most important environmental effect of automobiles was suburban sprawl. Middle-class families could now live in single-family homes too spread apart to be served by public transportation. By the late 1920s, paved roads rivaled rail networks both in length and in the surface they occupied. As middle- and working-class families bought cars, cities acquired rings of automobile suburbs. Los Angeles, the first true automobile city, consisted of suburbs spread over hundreds of square miles and linked together by broad avenues. In those sections of the city where streetcar lines went out of business, the automobile, at first a plaything for the wealthy, became a necessity for commuters. Many Americans saw Los Angeles as the portent of a glorious future when everyone would have a car;

only a few foresaw the congestion and pollution that would ensue.

Farmers began buying cars and light trucks, using them to transport produce as well as passengers. Governments obliged by building new roads and paving old ones to make automobile travel smoother and safer. In 1915, Ford introduced a gasoline-powered tractor, and by the mid-1920s, these versatile machines began replacing horses. Tractors hastened the end of agriculture as a family enterprise.

## CONCLUSION

The Great War caused a major realignment among the nations of the world. France and Britain, the two leading colonial powers, emerged economically weakened despite their victory. The war brought defeat and humiliation to Germany but did not reduce its military or industrial potential. It destroyed the old regime and the aristocracy of Russia, leading to civil war and revolution from which the victorious powers sought to isolate themselves. Two other old empires—the Austro-Hungarian and the Ottoman—were divided into many smaller and weaker nations. For a while, the Middle East seemed ripe for a new wave of imperialism. But there and throughout Asia, the war unleashed revolutionary nationalist movements that challenged European influence.

Only two countries benefited from the war. Japan took advantage of the European conflict to develop its industries and press its demands on a China weakened by domestic turmoil and social unrest. The United States emerged as the most prosperous and potentially most powerful nation, restrained only by the isolationist sentiments expressed by many Americans.

Modern technology and industrial organization had long been praised in the name of "progress" for their ability to reduce toil and disease and improve living standards. The war showed that they possessed an equally awesome destructive potential. In the late 1920s, it seemed as though the victors in the Great War might restore the prewar prosperity and European dominance of the globe. But the spirit of the 1920s was an illusion—not real peace but the eye of a hurricane. The prosperity of the late 1920s in most industrial states also proved illusory.

## ■ Key Terms

| | |
|---|---|
| Western Front | Empress Dowager Cixi |
| Faisal | Sun Yat-sen |
| Balfour Declaration | Yuan Shikai |
| Bolsheviks | Guomindang |
| Vladimir Lenin | mandate system |
| Woodrow Wilson | Margaret Sanger |
| League of Nations | Max Planck |
| Treaty of Versailles | Albert Einstein |
| New Economic Policy | |

## ■ Suggested Reading

Bernadotte Schmitt and Harold C. Bedeler, *The World in the Crucible, 1914–1918* (1984), and John Keegan, *The First World War* (1999), are two engaging overviews of World War I. Imanuel Geiss, *July 1914: The Outbreak of the First World War* (1967), argues that Germany caused the conflict. Barbara Tuchman's *The Guns of August* (1962) and Alexander Solzhenitsyn's *August 1914* (1972) recount the first month of the war in detail. Keegan's *The Face of Battle* (1976) vividly describes the Battle of the Somme from the soldiers' perspective. On the technology of warfare, see William H. McNeill, *The Pursuit of Power: Technology, Armed Force, and Society* (1982), and John Ellis, *The Social History of the Machine Gun* (1975). The role of women and the home front is the subject of essays in Margaret Higonnet et al., eds., *Behind the Lines: Gender and the Two World Wars* (1987), and sections of Lynn Weiner, *From Working Girl to Working Mother* (1985). The definitive work on the flu epidemic is Alfred W. Crosby, *America's Forgotten Pandemic: The Influenza of 1918* (1989). Two famous novels about the war are Erich Maria Remarque's *All Quiet on the Western Front* (1928) and Robert Graves's *Goodbye to All That* (1929). The war in English literature is the subject of Paul Fussell, *The Great War and Modern Memory* (1975).

For the background to the Russian Revolution, read Theodore von Laue's *Why Lenin? Why Stalin?* 2d ed. (1971); but see also Richard Pipes, *The Russian Revolution* (1990), and Orlando Figes, *A People's Tragedy: The Russian Revolution, 1891–1924* (1996). The classic eyewitness account of the Revolution is John Reed's *Ten Days That Shook the World* (1919). On gender issues see Wendy Goldman, *Women, the State, and Revolution: Soviet Family Policy and Social Life, 1917–1936* (1993). The best-known novel about the Revolution and civil war is Boris Pasternak's *Doctor Zhivago* (1958).

John Maynard Keynes's *The Economic Consequences of the Peace* (1920) is a classic critique of the Paris Peace Conference. Arno Mayer's *Political Origins of the New Diplomacy, 1917–1918* (1959) analyzes the tensions and failures of great-power politics. The 1920s are discussed in Raymond Sontag's *A Broken World, 1919–1939* (1971).

The best recent book on Japan in the twentieth century is Daikichi Irokawa's *The Age of Hirohito: In Search of Modern Japan* (1995). See also Richard Storry, *A History of Modern Japan* (1982), and Tessa Morris-Suzuki, *The Technological Transformation of Japan* (1994). In the large and fast-growing literature on twentieth-century China, two general introductions are especially useful: John K. Fairbank, *The Great Chinese Revolution, 1800–1985* (1986), and Jonathan Spence, *The Search for Modern China* (1990). On the warlord and Guomindang periods, see Lucien Bianco, *Origins of the Chinese Revolution, 1915–1949* (1971).

On the war and its aftermath in the Middle East, see David Fromkin, *A Peace to End All Peace* (1989), and M. E. Yapp, *The Near East Since the First World War* (1991). Bernard Lewis, *The Emergence of Modern Turkey* (1968),

is a good introduction. On Africa in this period see A. Adu Boahen, ed., *Africa Under Colonial Domination, 1880–1935*, vol. 7 of the *UNESCO General History of Africa* (1985), and A. D. Roberts, ed., *Cambridge History of Africa*, vol. 7, *1905–1940* (1986).

The cultural transformation of Europe is captured in H. Stuart Hughes, *Consciousness and Society: The Reorientation of European Social Thought, 1890–1930* (1958). The towering intellectuals of that era are the subject of Peter Gay, *Freud: A Life for Our Time* (1988), and Abraham Pais, *Subtle Is the Lord: The Science and Life of Albert Einstein* (1982). Three books capture the enthusiastic popular response to technological innovations: David E. Nye, *Electrifying America: Social Meanings of a New Technology* (1990); Peter Fritzsche, *A Nation of Fliers: German Aviation and the Popular Imagination* (1992); and the sweeping overview by Thomas Hughes, *American Genesis: A Century of Invention and Technological Enthusiasm, 1870–1970* (1989). On the role of women in this period, see Ellen DuBois, *Woman Suffrage and Women's Rights* (1998); Sheila Rowbotham, *A Century of Women: The History of Women in Britain and the United States* (1997); and Renate Bridenthal, Claudia Koonz, and Susan Stuard, eds., *Becoming Visible: Women in European History* (1987).

# The Collapse of the Old Order, 1929–1949

# 26

## CHAPTER OUTLINE

Stalin's Revolution
The Depression
The Rise of Fascism
East Asia, 1931–1945
The Second World War
The Character of Warfare
DIVERSITY AND DOMINANCE: Women, Family Values, and the Russian Revolution

Before the First World War, the Italian futurist poets exalted violence as a noble and manly idea. Filippo Marinetti defined their creed in these words: "We want to glorify war, the world's only hygiene—militarism, deed, destroyer of anarchisms, the beautiful ideas that are death-bringing, and the subordination of women." His friend Gabriele d'Annunzio said: "If it is a crime to incite citizens to violence, I shall boast of this crime."

The war taught most survivors to abhor violence. During the 1920s, the world seemed to return to what United States president Warren Harding called "normalcy": prosperity in Europe and America, European colonialism in Asia and Africa, paternalistic U.S. domination of Latin America, and peace almost everywhere. But for a few, war and domination became a creed and a goal.

In 1929, the artificial normalcy of the 1920s began to come apart. The Great Depression caused governments to turn against one another in a desperate attempt to protect their people's livelihood. As the economic crisis spread around the world, businesses went bankrupt, prices fell, factories closed, and workers were laid off. Even wholly agricultural nations and colonies suffered as markets for their exports shriveled.

Some countries chose to solve their problems by violent means. When nations shut their doors to Japan's products, the Japanese military tried to save their country by conquering China. In Germany, the Depression reawakened resentments against the victors of the Great War; people who feared communism or blamed Jews for their troubles turned to Hitler and the Nazis, who promised to save their society by dominating others. In the Soviet Union, Stalin used energetic and murderous means to force his country into a communist version of the Industrial Revolution.

The result was war. The Second World War engulfed more lands and peoples and caused far more deaths and destruction than any previous conflict. At the end of it, much of Europe and East Asia lay in ruins, and millions of destitute refugees sought safety in other lands. The European colonial powers were either defeated or so weakened that they could no longer hold onto their empires when Asian and African peoples asserted their desire for independence.

As you read this chapter, ask yourself the following questions:

• How did the Soviet Union change under Stalin, and at what cost?

• What were the main causes of the Second World War?

• How was the war fought, and why did Japan and Germany lose?

# STALIN'S REVOLUTION

After **Joseph Stalin** (1879–1953) achieved total mastery over the USSR in early 1929 (see Chapter 25), he led it through another revolution: an economic and social transformation that turned it into a great industrial and military power and intensified both admiration for and fear of communism throughout the world.

## Five-Year Plans

Stalin's ambition to turn the USSR into an industrial nation was not intended initially to produce consumer goods for a mass market, much less enrich individuals as in Britain and the United States. Instead, his aim was to increase the power of the Communist Party domestically and the power of the Soviet Union in relation to other countries. By building up Russia's industry, Stalin was determined to prevent a repetition of the humiliating defeat Russia had suffered at the hands of Germany in 1917.

Stalin encouraged rapid industrialization through a series of **Five-Year Plans,** a system of centralized control copied from the German experience of World War I. The goal of the first five-year plan was to quintuple the output of electricity and double that of heavy industry: iron, steel, coal, and machinery. Beginning in October 1928, the Communist government created whole industries and cities from scratch, then recruited millions of peasants and trained them to work in the new factories and mines and offices. In every way except actual fighting, Stalin's Russia resembled a nation at war.

Rapid industrialization hastened environmental changes. Hydroelectric dams turned rivers into strings of reservoirs. Roads, canals, and railroad tracks cut the landscape. Forests and grassland were turned into farmland. From an environmental perspective, the outcome of the Five-Year Plans resembled the transformation that had occurred in the United States and Canada a few decades earlier.

## Collectivization of Agriculture

Since the Soviet Union was still a predominantly agrarian country, the only way to pay for these massive investments, provide the labor, and feed the millions of new industrial workers was to squeeze the peasantry. Stalin therefore proceeded with the most radical social experiment conceived up to that time: the collectivization of agriculture.

Collectivization meant consolidating small private farms into vast collectives and making the farmers work together in commonly owned fields. Each collective was expected to supply the government with a fixed amount of food and distribute what was left among its members. Collectives were to become outdoor factories through the use of machinery and techniques of mass production. Collectivization was expected to bring the peasants once and for all under government control so they never again could withhold food supplies as

| | | |
|---|---|---|
| **C H R O N O L O G Y** | | |
| | **Europe and North Africa** | **Asia and the Pacific** |
| **1930** | **1931** Great Depression reaches Europe | **1931** Japanese forces occupy Manchuria |
| | **1933** Hitler comes to power in Germany | |
| **1935** | **1936** Hitler invades the Rhineland | |
| | | **1937** Japanese troops invade China, conquer coastal provinces; Chiang Kai-shek flees to Sichuan |
| | | **1937–1938** Japanese troops take Nanjing |
| | **1939 (Sept. 1)** German forces invade Poland | |
| **1940** | **1940 (March–April)** German forces conquer Denmark, Norway, the Netherlands, and Belgium | |
| | **1940 (May–June)** German forces conquer France | |
| | **1940 (June–Sept.)** Battle of Britain | |
| | **1941 (June 21)** German forces invade USSR | **1941 (Dec. 7)** Japanese aircraft bomb Pearl Harbor |
| | **1942–1943** Allies and Germany battle for control of North Africa; Soviet victory in Battle of Stalingrad (1943) | **1942 (Jan–March)** Japanese conquer Thailand, Philippines, Malaya |
| | | **1942 (June)** United States Navy defeats Japan at Battle of Midway |
| | **1943–1944** Red Army slowly pushes Wehrmacht back to Germany | |
| | **1944 (June 6)** D-day: U.S., British, and Canadian troops land in Normandy | |
| **1945** | **1945 (May 7)** Germany surrenders | **1945 (Aug. 6)** United States drops atomic bomb on Hiroshima |
| | | **1945 (Aug. 14)** Japan surrenders |
| | | **1945–1949** Civil war in China |
| | | **1949** Communists defeat Guomindang; Mao proclaims People's Republic (Oct. 1) |

they had done during the period of Lenin's New Economic Policy (see Chapter 25).

The government mounted a massive propaganda campaign to enlist the farmers' support. At first, all seemed to go well, but soon *kulaks*° ("fists"),

the better-off peasants, began to resist giving up all their property. When soldiers came to force them into collectives at gunpoint, the kulaks burned their own crops, smashed their own equipment, and slaughtered their own livestock. Within a few months, they slaughtered half of the Soviet Union's horses and cattle and two-thirds of its sheep and

*kulaks* (COO-lox)

goats. In retaliation, Stalin ruthlessly ordered the "liquidation of kulaks as a class" and incited the poor peasants to attack their wealthier neighbors. Over 8 million kulaks were arrested. Many were executed. The rest were sent to slave labor camps, where most starved to death.

The peasants who were left had been the least successful before collectivization and proved to be the least competent after. Many were sent to work in factories. The rest were forbidden to leave their farms. With half of their draft animals gone, they could not plant or harvest enough to meet the swelling demands of the cities. Yet government agents took whatever they could find, leaving little or nothing for the farmers themselves. After bad harvests in 1933 and 1934, a famine swept through the countryside, killing some 5 million people, about one in every twenty farmers.

Stalin's second Five-Year Plan, designed to run from 1933 to 1937, was originally intended to increase the output of consumer goods. But when the Nazis took over Germany in 1933 (see below), Stalin changed the plan to emphasize heavy industries that could produce armaments. Between 1927 and 1937, the Soviet output of metals and machines increased fourteen-fold while consumer goods became scarce and food was rationed. After a decade of Stalinism, the Soviet people were more poorly clothed, fed, and housed than they had been during the years of the New Economic Policy.

## Terror and Opportunities

The 1930s brought both terror and new opportunities to the Soviet people. The forced pace of industrialization, the collectivization of agriculture, and the uprooting of millions of people could be accomplished only under duress. To prevent any possible resistance or rebellion, the NKVD, Stalin's secret police force, created a climate of suspicion and fear. The terror that pervaded the country was a reflection of Stalin's own paranoia, for he distrusted everyone and feared for his life.

First "Old Bolsheviks" and high officials were put on trial; then the terror spread steadily downward. The government regularly made demands on people that they could not meet, so everyone was guilty of breaking some regulation. People from all walks of life were arrested—sometimes on a mere suspicion or because of a false accusation by a jealous coworker or neighbor, sometimes for expressing a doubt or working too hard or not hard enough, sometimes for being related to someone previously arrested, sometimes for no reason at all. Millions of people were sentenced without a trial. At the height of the terror, some 8 million were sent to *gulags*° (labor camps), where perhaps a million died each year of exposure or malnutrition. To its victims, the terror seemed capricious and random.

Yet Stalin's regime received the support of many Soviet citizens. Suddenly, with so many people gone and new industries and cities being built everywhere, there were opportunities for those who remained, especially the poor and the young. Women entered careers and jobs previously closed to them, becoming steelworkers, physicians, and office managers; but they retained their household and child-rearing duties, receiving little help from men (see Diversity and Dominance: Women, Family Values, and the Russian Revolution). People who moved to the cities, worked enthusiastically, and asked no questions could hope to rise into the upper ranks of the Communist Party, the military, the government, or the professions, where the privileges and rewards were many.

Stalin's brutal methods helped the Soviet Union industrialize faster than any country had ever done. By the late 1930s, the USSR was the world's third largest industrial power, after the United States and Germany. To foreign observers, it seemed to be booming with construction projects, production increases, and labor shortages. Even anti-Communist observers admitted that only a planned economy subject to strict government control could avoid the Depression. To millions of Soviet citizens who took pride in the new strength of their country, and to many foreigners who contrasted conditions in the Soviet Union with the unemployment and despair in the West, Stalin's achievement seemed worth any price.

*gulag* (GOO-log)

# THE DEPRESSION

On October 24, 1929—"Black Thursday"—the New York stock market went into a dive. Within days, stocks lost half their value, and their value continued to fall for three years. Thousands of banks and businesses collapsed. Millions of workers lost their jobs. The stock market crash started the deepest and most widespread depression in history.

## Economic Crisis

As consumers reduced their purchases, businesses cut production. General Motors, for example, saw its sales drop by half between 1929 and 1931. Companies laid off thousands of workers, throwing them onto public charity. Business and government agencies replaced their women workers with men, arguing that men had to support their families, whereas women worked only for "pin money." Jobless men deserted their families. As farm prices fell, small farmers went bankrupt and lost their land. By mid-1932, the American economy had fallen by half, and 25 percent of the work force was unemployed. Government spending on welfare and public works was unable to restore prosperity. Many observers thought the free-enterprise system would be replaced by bread lines, soup kitchens, men selling apples on street corners, and hoboes riding freight trains.

Frightened by the stock market collapse, the New York banks called in their loans to Germany and Austria. Without American money, Germany and Austria stopped paying reparations to France and Britain, which then could not repay their war loans to America. By 1931, the Depression had spread to Europe. Governments canceled both reparations payments and war loans, but it was too late to save the world economy.

In 1930, the U.S. government, hoping to protect domestic industries from foreign competition, imposed the highest import duty in American history. In retaliation, other countries raised their tariffs. As a result, global industrial production declined by 36 percent between 1929 and 1932, while world trade dropped by a breathtaking 62 percent.

## Depression in Industrial Nations

This massive economic upheaval had profound political repercussions. In the United States, Franklin D. Roosevelt was elected president in 1932 on a "New Deal" platform of government programs to stimulate and revitalize the economy. British and French governments also intervened in their economies and escaped the worst of the Depression by making their colonial empires purchase their products. In the Soviet Union, the five-year plans continued to provide jobs and economic growth.

Nations that relied on exports to pay for imported food and fuel, in particular Japan and Germany, suffered much more. In Germany, unemployment reached 6 million by 1932, twice as high as in Britain. Half the German population lived in poverty. In Japan, the burden of the Depression fell on the farmers and fishermen, who saw their incomes drop sharply. Some, in desperation, revived the ancient practice of selling their daughters. As economic grievances worsened, radical politicians took over the governments in Germany and Japan, manipulated the economies, and turned their nations' military might to acquiring empires large enough to support a self-sufficient economy.

## Depression in Nonindustrial Regions

The Depression affected Asia, Africa, and Latin America in different ways. A wall of new import duties protected India's infant industries from foreign competition; living standards stagnated but did not drop. The Depression added little to China's problems, except in coastal regions.

Countries that depended on exports were hard hit by the Depression. When automobile production dropped by half in the United States and Europe, so did imports of rubber, devastating the economies of Southeast Asia. When the Depression hit, American tourists vanished from Cuba's beaches and bars, and with them went Cuba's prosperity. The industrialization of Argentina and Brazil was set back a decade or more by the loss of their export markets. In response, military officers

운드폭탄 4발 투하… 두 아들과 함께 사망

지 구축… 이틀째 시가戰

령이 대중 앞에 나타나거나 애국심
을 고취하는 노래만을 내보내던 방
송마저 중단됐다.

라크 전후
의에서는
영국 주도

# DIVERSITY AND DOMINANCE

## WOMEN, FAMILY VALUES, AND THE RUSSIAN REVOLUTION

*The Bolsheviks were of two minds on the subject of women. Following in the footsteps of Marx, Engels, and other revolutionaries, they were opposed to bourgeois morality and to the oppression of women, especially working-class women, under capitalism, with its attendant evils of prostitution, sexual abuse, and the division of labor. But what to put in its place?*

*Alexandra Kollontai was the most outspoken of the Bolsheviks on the subject of women's rights and the equality of the sexes. Before and during the Russian Revolution, she advocated the liberation of women, the replacement of housework by communal kitchens and laundries, and divorce on demand. Under socialism, love, sex, and marriage would be entirely equal, reciprocal, and free of economic obligations. Childbearing would be encouraged, but children would be raised communally, rather than individually by their fathers and mothers: "The worker mother . . . must remember that there are henceforth only our children, those of the communist state, the common possession of all workers."*

*In a lecture she gave at Sverdlov University in 1921, Kollontai declared:*

. . . it is important to preserve not only the interests of the woman but also the life of the child, and this is to be done by giving the woman the opportunity to combine labour and maternity. Soviet power tries to create a situation where a woman does not have to cling to a man she has learned to loathe only because she has nowhere else to go with her children, and where a woman alone does not have to fear her life and the life of her child. In the labour republic it is not the philanthropists with their humiliating charity but the workers and peasants, fellow-creators of the new society, who hasten to help the working woman and strive to lighten the burden of motherhood. The woman who bears the trials and tribulations of reconstructing the economy on an equal footing with the man, and who participated in the civil war, has a right to demand that in this most important hour of her life, at the moment when she presents society with a new member, the labour republic, the collective, should take upon itself the job of caring for the future of the new citizen. . . .

I would like to say a few words about a question which is closely connected with the problem of maternity—the question of abortion, and Soviet Russia's attitude toward it. On 20 November 1920 the labour republic issued a law abolishing the penalties that had been attached to abortion. What is the reason behind this new attitude? Russia after all suffers not from an overproduction of living labour but rather from a lack of it. Russia is thinly, not densely populated. Every unit of labour power is precious. Why then have we declared abortion to be no longer a criminal offence? Hypocrisy and bigotry are alien to proletarian politics. Abortion is a problem connected with the problem of maternity, and likewise derives from the insecure position of women (we are not speaking here of the bourgeois class, where abortion has other reasons—the reluctance to "divide" an inheritance, to suffer the slightest discomfort, to spoil one's figure or miss a few months of the season, etc.).

Abortion exists and flourishes everywhere, and no laws or punitive measures have succeeded in rooting it out. A way round the law is always found. But "secret help" only cripples women; they become a burden on the labour government, and the size of the labour force is reduced. Abortion, when carried out under proper medical conditions, is less harmful and dangerous, and the woman can get back to work quicker. Soviet power realizes that the need for abortion will only disappear on the one hand when Russia has a broad and developed network of institutions protecting motherhood and providing social education, and on the other hand when women understand that *childbirth is a social obligation;* Soviet power has therefore allowed abortion to be performed openly and in clinical conditions.

Besides the large-scale development of motherhood protection, the task of labour Russia is to strengthen in women the healthy instinct of motherhood, to make motherhood and labour for the collective compatible and thus do away with the need for abortion. This is the approach of the labour republic to the question of abortion, which still faces women in the bourgeois countries in all its magnitude. In these countries women are exhausted by the dual burden of hired labour for capital and motherhood. In Soviet Russia the working woman and peasant woman are helping the Communist Party to build a new society and to undermine the old way of life that has enslaved women. As soon as woman is viewed as being essentially a labour unit, the key to the solution of the complex question of maternity can be found. In bourgeois society, where housework complements the system of capitalist economy and private property creates a stable basis for the isolated form of the family, there is no way out for the working woman. The emancipation of women can only be completed when a fundamental transformation of living is effected; and life-styles will change only with the fundamental transformation of all production and the establishment of a communist economy. The revolution in everyday life is unfolding before our very eyes, and in this process the liberation of women is being introduced in practice.

*Fifteen years later Joseph Stalin reversed the Soviet policy on abortion.*

The published draft of the law prohibiting abortion and providing material assistance to mothers has provoked a lively reaction throughout the country. It is being heatedly discussed by tens of millions of people and there is no doubt that it will serve as a further strengthening of the Soviet family. Parents' responsibility for the education of their children will be increased and a blow will be dealt at the lighthearted, negligent attitude toward marriage.

When we speak of strengthening the Soviet family, we are speaking precisely of the struggle against the survivals of a bourgeois attitude towards marriage, women, and children. So-called "free love" and all disorderly sex life are bourgeois through and through, and have nothing to do with either socialist principles or the ethics and standards of conduct of the Soviet citizens. Socialist doctrine shows this, and it is proved by life itself.

The elite of our country, the best of the Soviet youth, are as a rule also excellent family men who dearly love their children. And vice versa: the man who does not take marriage seriously, and abandons his children to the whims of fate, is usually also a bad worker and a poor member of society.

Fatherhood and motherhood have long been virtues in this country. This can be seen at first glance, without searching enquiry. Go through the parks and streets of Moscow or of any other town in the Soviet Union on a holiday, and you will see not a few young men walking with pink-cheeked, well-fed babies in their arms. . . .

It is impossible even to compare the present state of the family with that which obtained before the Soviet regime—so great has been the improvement towards greater stability and, above all, greater humanity and goodness. The single fact that millions of women have become economically independent and are no longer at the mercy of men's whims, speaks volumes. Compare, for instance, the modern woman collective farmer who sometimes earns more than her husband, with the pre-revolutionary peasant women who completely depended on her husband and was a slave in the household. Has not this fundamentally changed family relations, has it not rationalized and strengthened the family? The very motives for setting up a family, for getting married, have changed for the better, have been cleansed of atavistic and barbaric elements. Marriage has ceased to be matter of sell-and-buy. Nowadays a girl from a collective farm is not given away (or should we say "sold away"?) by her father, for now she is her own mistress, and no one can give her away. She will marry the man she loves. . . .

We alone have all the conditions under which a working woman can fulfill her duties as a citizen and as a mother responsible for the birth and early upbringing of her children.

A woman without children merits our pity, for she does not know the full joy of life. Our Soviet women, full-blooded citizens of the freest country in the world, have been given the bliss of motherhood. We must safeguard the family and raise and rear healthy Soviet heroes!

1. How does Kollontai expect women to be both workers and mothers without depending on a man? How would Soviet society make this possible?

2. Why does Alexandra Kollontai advocate the legalization of abortion in Soviet Russia? Does she view abortion as a permanent right or as a temporary necessity?

3. Why does Stalin characterize a "lighthearted, negligent attitude toward marriage" and "all disorderly sex life" as "bourgeois through and through"?

4. How does Stalin's image of the Soviet family differ from Kollontai's? Are his views a variation of her views, or the opposite?

5. Do the views of Kollontai and Stalin on the role of women represent a diversity of opinions within the Communist Party, or the dominance of one view over others?

*Source:* First selection from *Selected Writings of Alexandra Kollontai,* translated by Alix Holt (Lawrence Hill Books, 1978). Reprinted with permission. Second selection from Joseph Stalin, *Law on the Abolition of Legal Abortion* (1936).

seized power in several Latin American countries, consciously imitating dictatorships emerging in Europe.

Southern and Central Africa recovered from the Depression quickly, because falling prices made their gold and other minerals more valuable. But this mining boom benefited only a small number of mine owners and investors. For Africans, it was at best a mixed blessing, for mining offered jobs and cash wages to men, while women had to manage without them in the villages.

## THE RISE OF FASCISM

The Depression sharpened the polarization of European society that had been under way for decades. Many underpaid or unemployed workers saw in the seeming collapse of the capitalist economy an opportunity as well as temporary suffering. They urged the establishment of a socialist society through the ballot box and strikes instead of the violent revolution that had torn Russia apart.

Frightened investors and factory owners, along with conservative elements in society such as the church and the military, feared the consequences of this political shift to the left. In the democracies of western Europe and North America, middle-income voters kept politics in balance.

But in some societies, the war and the Depression left people vulnerable to the appeals of ultranationalist politicians who became adept at using propaganda to appeal to people's fears. They promised to bring back full employment, stop the spread of communism, and achieve the territorial conquests that World War I had denied them.

### Mussolini's Italy

The first country to seek radical answers was Italy. World War I, which had never been popular, left thousands of veterans who found neither pride in their victory nor jobs in the postwar economy. Unemployed veterans and violent youths banded together into *fasci di combattimento* (fighting units) to demand action and intimidate politicians. When socialist unions threatened to strike, factory and property owners hired gangs of these *fascisti* to defend them.

**Benito Mussolini** (1883–1945), a spellbinding orator, quickly became the leader of the **Fascist Party,** which glorified warfare and the Italian nation. By 1921, the party had 300,000 members, many of whom used violent methods to repress strikes, intimidate voters, and seize municipal governments. A year later, when the Fascists failed to win an election, Mussolini threatened to march on Rome if he was not appointed prime minister. The government gave in.

Mussolini proceeded to install Fascist Party members in all government jobs, crush all opposition parties, and jail anyone who criticized him. The party took over the press, public education, and youth activities and gave employers control over their workers. The Fascists lowered living standards but reduced unemployment and provided social security and public services. On the whole, they proved to be neither ruthless radicals nor competent administrators.

What Mussolini and the fascist movement really excelled at was publicity: bombastic speeches, spectacular parades, news bulletins full of praise for *Il Duce*° ("the leader"), and signs everywhere proclaiming "Il Duce is always right!" Mussolini's genius was to apply the techniques of modern mass communications and advertisement to political life. Billboards, movie footage, and radio news bulletins galvanized the masses in ways never before seen in peacetime. Although his rhetoric was filled with words like *war, violence,* and *struggle,* his foreign policy was cautious. But his techniques of whipping up public enthusiasm were not lost on other radicals. By the 1930s, fascist movements had appeared in most European countries, as well as in Latin America, China, and Japan.

### Hitler's Germany

Like Mussolini, **Adolf Hitler** (1889–1945) had served in World War I and looked back fondly on the clear lines of authority and the camaraderie he had experienced in battle. After the war, he too recreated that experience in a paramilitary group, the National Socialist German Workers' Party—**Nazis** for short. Hitler used his gifts as an orator to appeal to Germans disappointed at Germany's humiliation after the war and the hyperinflation of 1923. In 1924, he too led an uprising, but the attempted seizure of Munich was a failure. Germany was not yet ready to follow Italy's path.

The Depression changed that. While serving a jail sentence for the coup attempt, Hitler wrote *Mein Kampf*° (*My Struggle*), but when it was published in 1925, no one took the book or its author's extreme nationalist, racist, and anti-Jewish ideas seriously. Hitler believed that Germany should in-

*Il Duce* (eel DOO-chay)    *Mein Kampf* (mine compf)

**Hitler the Orator**    A masterful public speaker, Adolf Hitler often captivated mass audiences at Nazi Party rallies. (Roger-Viollet/Getty Images)

corporate all German-speaking people, even those who lived in neighboring countries. He distinguished among a "master race" of Aryans (he meant Germans, Scandinavians, and Britons), a degenerate "Alpine" race of French and Italians, and an inferior race of Russian and eastern European Slavs, who, he believed, were fit only to be slaves of the master race. He reserved his most intense hatred for Jews, on whom he blamed every disaster that had befallen Germany, especially the defeat of 1918. He glorified violence, which would enable the "master race" to defeat and subjugate all others.

When the Depression hit, the Nazis gained supporters among the unemployed who believed Nazi promises of jobs for all and among property owners frightened by the growing popularity of Communists. In March 1933, as leader of the largest party in Germany, Hitler became chancellor.

Once in office, he quickly assumed dictatorial power, just as Mussolini had done. He expelled the Communist Party from the Reichstag° (parliament), intimidated it to give him dictatorial powers, and then put Nazis in charge of all government agencies, educational institutions, and professional organizations. He banned all other political parties and threw their leaders into concentration camps. The Nazis deprived Jews of their citizenship and civil rights, prohibited them from marrying "Aryans," ousted them from the professions, and confiscated their property. In August 1934, Hitler proclaimed himself *Führer°* ("leader") and called Germany the "Third Reich" (empire)—the third after the Holy Roman Empire and the German Empire of 1871 to 1918.

The Nazis' economic and social policies were spectacularly effective. The government undertook massive public works projects. Businesses got contracts to manufacture weapons for the armed forces. Women, who had entered the work force during and after World War I, were urged to return to *"Kinder, Kirche, Küche"* (children, church, kitchen), releasing jobs for men. By 1936, business was booming, unemployment was at its lowest level since the 1920s, and living standards were rising. Hitler's popularity soared because most Germans believed their economic well-being outweighed the loss of liberty.

## The Road to War, 1933–1939

Hitler sought not prosperity or popularity, but conquest. As soon as he came to office, he began to build up the armed forces with conquest in mind. Meanwhile, he tested the reactions of the other powers through a series of surprise moves followed by protestations of peaceful intent.

**Reichstag** (RIKES-tog)   *Führer* (FEW-rer)

In 1933, Hitler withdrew Germany from the League of Nations. France and Britain hesitated to retaliate by blockading or invading Germany. Two years later, he announced that Germany was going to introduce conscription, build up its army, and create an air force—in violation of the Versailles treaty. Instead of protesting, Britain signed a naval agreement with Germany. The message was clear: neither Britain nor France was willing to risk war by standing up to Germany. The United States, absorbed in its own domestic economic problems, had reverted to isolationism.

Emboldened by the weakness of the democracies, Italy in 1935 invaded Ethiopia, one of only two independent states in Africa and a member of the League of Nations. The League and the democracies protested but refused to close the Suez Canal to Italian ships or impose an oil embargo. The following year, when Hitler sent troops into the Rhineland on the borders of France and Belgium, the other powers merely protested.

By 1938, Hitler decided his rearmament plans were far enough advanced that he could escalate his demands. In March, Germany invaded and soon annexed Austria, with little protest from its German-speaking citizens. Then came the turn of Czechoslovakia. Hitler demanded autonomy for its German-speaking borderlands, then their annexation. At the Munich Conference of September 1938, the leaders of France, Britain, and Italy gave Hitler everything he wanted to keep him from starting a war. Once again, Hitler learned that aggression paid off and that the democracies always gave in.

The democracies' policy of "appeasement" ran counter to the European balance-of-power tradition for three reasons. The first was the deep-seated fear of war among all people who had lived through World War I. The second was fear of communism. The conservative politicians who ruled France and Britain were more afraid of Stalin than of Hitler, for Hitler claimed to respect Christianity and private property. Rather than revive the pre–World War I alliance of Britain, France, and Russia, they sold out the Czechs. The third cause was the very novelty of fascist tactics. Britain's prime minister, Neville Chamberlain, assumed that political leaders (other than the Bolsheviks) were honorable men and that an agreement was as valid as a business contract. Thus, when Hitler said he had "no further territorial demands," Chamberlain believed him.

After Munich, it was too late to stop Hitler, short of war. Germany and Italy were now united in an alliance called the Axis. In March 1939, Germany invaded what was left of Czechoslovakia. Belatedly realizing that Hitler could not be trusted, France and Britain sought Soviet help. Stalin, however, distrusted the "capitalists" as much as they distrusted him. Hitler, meanwhile, offered to divide Poland between Germany and the Soviet Union. On August 23, Stalin accepted. The Nazi-Soviet Pact freed Hitler from the fear of a two-front war and gave Stalin two more years of peace to build up his armies. One week later, on September 1, 1939, German forces swept into Poland across the Eastern Front. The war was on.

# East Asia, 1931–1945

When the Depression ruined Japan's export trade, ultranationalists, including young army officers, resented their country's dependence on foreign trade. If only Japan had a colonial empire, they thought, it would not be beholden to the rest of the world. But Europeans and Americans had already taken most potential colonies in Asia. Japan had only Korea, Taiwan, and a railroad in Manchuria. Japanese nationalists saw China, with its vast population and resources, as the solution to their country's problems.

### The Manchurian Incident of 1931

Meanwhile, the Guomindang° was becoming stronger in China and preparing to challenge the Japanese presence in Manchuria, a province rich in coal and iron ore. Junior officers in the Japanese army guarding the South Manchurian Railway, frustrated by the caution of their superiors, determined to take action. In September 1931, an explosion on a railroad track, probably staged, gave them an excuse to conquer the entire province. In Tokyo, weak civilian ministers acquiesced to the attack to avoid losing face

Guomindang (gwo-min-dong)

and shortly recognized the "independence" of Manchuria under the name *Manchukuo*°.

The U.S. government condemned the Japanese conquest. The League of Nations refused to recognize Manchukuo and urged the Japanese to remove their troops from China. Persuaded that the Western powers would not fight, Japan resigned from the League.

During the next few years, the Japanese built railways and heavy industries in Manchuria and northeastern China and sped up their rearmament. The government grew more authoritarian, jailing thousands of dissidents. On several occasions, superpatriotic junior officers who mutinied or assassinated leading political figures received mild punishments, and generals and admirals sympathetic to their views replaced more moderate civilian politicians.

### The Chinese Communists and the Long March

Until the Japanese seized Manchuria, the Chinese government seemed to be consolidating its power and creating the conditions for a national recovery. The main challenge to the government of **Chiang Kai-shek**° came from the Chinese Communists, who were organizing industrial workers and who worked in alliance with the Nationalists until 1927, when Chiang Kai-shek arrested and executed Communists and labor leaders alike.

The few Communists who escaped the mass arrests fled to the remote mountains of Jiangxi°, in southeastern China. Among them was **Mao Zedong**° (1893–1976), a farmer's son who had left home to study philosophy. In the early 1920s, Mao discovered the works of Karl Marx, joined the Communist Party, and soon became one of its leaders. In Jiangxi, Mao began studying conditions among the peasants, in whom Communists had previously shown no interest. He planned to redistribute land from the wealthier to the poorer peasants, thereby gaining adherents for the coming struggle with the Guomindang army.

Mao's reliance on the peasantry was a radical departure from Marxist-Leninist ideology, which

Manchukuo (man-CHEW-coo-oh)    Chiang Kai-shek (chang kie-shek)    Jiangxi (jang-she)    Mao Zedong (ma-oh zay-dong)

stressed the backwardness of the peasants and pinned its hopes on industrial workers. Mao was also an advocate of women's equality. Before 1927, the Communists had organized the women who worked in Shanghai's textile mills, the most exploited of all Chinese workers. Later, in their mountain stronghold in Jiangxi, they organized women farmers, allowed divorce, and banned arranged marriages and footbinding.

The Guomindang army pursued the Communists into the mountains, building small forts throughout the countryside. Rather than risk direct confrontations, Mao responded with guerrilla warfare. Government troops often mistreated civilians, but Mao insisted that his soldiers help the peasants, pay a fair price for food and supplies, and treat women with respect. In spite of their good relations with the peasants of Jiangxi, the Communists decided to break out of the southern mountains and trek to Shaanxi°, an even more remote province in northwestern China. The so-called **Long March** took them 6,000 miles (nearly 9,700 kilometers) in one year, 17 miles (27 kilometers) a day over desolate mountains and through swamps and deserts, pursued by the army and bombed by Chiang's aircraft. Of the 100,000 Communists who left Jiangxi in October 1934, only 4,000 reached Shaanxi a year later.

## The Sino-Japanese War, 1937–1945

On July 7, 1937, Japanese troops attacked Chinese forces near Beijing. As in 1931, the junior officers who ordered the attack quickly obtained the support of their commanders and then, reluctantly, of the government. By November, Japanese troops had seized Beijing, Tianjin, Shanghai, and other coastal cities, and the Japanese navy blockaded the entire coast of China.

Once again, the United States and the League of Nations denounced the Japanese atrocities. Yet the Western powers were too preoccupied with events in Europe and with their own economic problems to risk a military confrontation in Asia. When the Japanese sank a U.S. gunboat and shelled a British ship on the Yangzi River, the U.S. and

**Shaanxi** (SHAWN-she)

British governments responded only with righteous indignation and pious resolutions.

The large Chinese armies were poorly led and armed and lost every battle. Within a year, Japan controlled the coastal provinces of China and the lower Yangzi and Yellow River Valleys, China's richest and most populated regions, but the Chinese people continued to resist, either in the army or, increasingly, with the Communist guerrilla forces. Japan's periodic attempts to turn the tide by conquering one more piece of China only pushed Japan deeper into the quagmire.

Warfare between Chinese and Japanese was incredibly violent. In the winter of 1937–1938, Japanese troops took Nanjing, raped 20,000 women, killed 200,000 prisoners and civilians, and looted and burned the city. To slow them down, Chiang ordered the Yellow River dikes blasted open, causing a flood that destroyed 4,000 villages, killed 890,000 people, and made 12.5 million homeless. Two years later, when the Communists ordered a massive offensive, the Japanese retaliated with a "kill all, burn all, loot all" campaign, destroying hundreds of villages down to the last person, building, and farm animal.

The Chinese government, led by Chiang Kai-shek, escaped to the mountains of Sichuan in the center of the country. There he built up a huge army, both to fight Japan and to prepare for a future confrontation with the Communists. The army drafted over 3 million men, even though it had only a million rifles and could not provide food or clothing for all its soldiers. The Guomindang raised farmers' taxes, even when famine forced farmers to eat the bark of trees. Such taxes were not enough to support both a large army and the thousands of government officials and hangers-on who had fled to Sichuan. To avoid taxing its wealthy supporters, the government printed money, causing inflation, hoarding, and corruption.

From his capital of Yan'an in Shaanxi province, Mao also built up his army and formed a government. Unlike the Guomindang, the Communists listened to the grievances of the peasants, especially the poor, to whom they distributed land confiscated from wealthy landowners. Because they could present themselves as the only group in China that was serious about fighting the Japanese, the Communists obtained support and intelligence from farmers in Japanese-occupied territory.

# THE SECOND WORLD WAR

The Second World War was much bigger and deadlier than the First in every way. It was fought around the world, from Norway to New Guinea, from Hawaii to Egypt, and on every ocean. It was a total war that showed how effectively industry, science, and nationalism could be channeled into mass destruction.

## The War of Movement

Defensive maneuvers had dominated in World War I. In World War II, motorized weapons gave back the advantage to the offensive. Opposing forces moved fast, their victories hinging as much on the aggressive spirit of their commanders and the military intelligence they obtained as on numbers of troops or firepower.

The Wehrmacht°, or German armed forces, was the first to learn this lesson. It not only had tanks, trucks, and fighter planes but also had perfected their combined use in a tactic called *blitzkrieg*° (lightning war): fighter planes scattered enemy troops and disrupted communications, and tanks punctured the enemy's defenses and then, with the help of the infantry, encircled and captured enemy troops. At sea, the navies of both Japan and the United States had developed aircraft carriers that could launch planes against targets hundreds of miles away.

The very size and mobility of the opposing forces made the fighting far different from any the world had ever seen. Countries were conquered in a matter of days or weeks. The belligerents mobilized the economies of entire continents, squeezing them for every possible resource. They tried not only to defeat their enemies' armed forces but—by means of blockades, submarine attacks on shipping, and bombing raids on industrial areas—to damage the economies that supported those armed forces. They thought of civilians not as innocent bystanders but as legitimate targets and, later, as vermin to be exterminated.

## War in Europe and North Africa

It took less than a month for the Wehrmacht to conquer Poland. Britain and France declared war on Germany but took no military action. Meanwhile, the Soviet Union invaded eastern Poland and the Baltic republics of Lithuania, Latvia, and Estonia. Although the Poles fought bravely, the Polish infantry and cavalry were no match for German or Russian tanks. During the winter of 1939–1940, Germany and the Western democracies faced each other in what soldiers called a "phony war" and watched as the Soviet Union attacked Finland, which resisted for many months.

In April 1940, Hitler went on the offensive again, conquering Denmark, Norway, the Netherlands, and Belgium in less than two months. In May, he attacked France. Although the French army had as many soldiers, tanks, and aircraft as the Wehrmacht, its morale was low, and it quickly collapsed. By the end of June, Hitler was master of all of Europe between Russia and Spain.

Germany still had to face one enemy: Britain. The British had no army to speak of, but they had other assets: the English Channel, the Royal Navy and Air Force, and a tough new prime minister, Winston Churchill. The Germans knew they could invade Britain only by gaining control of the airspace over the Channel, so they launched a massive air attack—the Battle of Britain—lasting from June through September. They failed, however, because the Royal Air Force had better fighters and used radar and code breaking to detect approaching German planes.

Frustrated, Hitler turned his attention eastward against the Soviet Union. Within five months, the Wehrmacht conquered the Baltic states, Ukraine, and half of European Russia; captured a million prisoners of war; and stood at the very gates of Moscow and Leningrad (now St. Petersburg). The USSR seemed on the verge of collapse when suddenly the weather turned cold, machines froze, and the fighting came to a halt. Like Napoleon, Hitler had ignored the environment of Russia at his peril.

The next spring, the Wehrmacht renewed its offensive. It surrounded Leningrad in a siege that was to cost a million lives. Leaving Moscow aside, it turned toward the Caucasus and its oil wells. In

---

**Wehrmacht** (VAIR-mokt)  *blitzkrieg* (BLITS-creeg)

**German Dive-Bomber over Eastern Europe**   In this painting, a German ME-100 fighter plane attacks a Soviet troop convoy on the Eastern Front.   (akg-images)

August, the Germans attacked **Stalingrad** (now Volgograd), the key to the Volga River and the supply of oil. For months, German and Soviet soldiers fought over every street and every house. When winter came, the Red Army counterattacked and encircled the city. In February 1943, the remnants of the German army in Stalingrad surrendered. Hitler had lost his greatest gamble (see Map 26.1).

From Europe, the war spread to Africa. During 1941, British forces conquered Italian East Africa and invaded Libya as well. The Italian rout in North Africa brought the Germans to their rescue. During 1942, the German army and the forces of the British Empire seesawed back and forth across the deserts of Libya and Egypt. Because the British could decode German messages and had more weapons and supplies, they were finally able to expel the Germans from Africa in May 1943.

## War in Asia and the Pacific

The war presented Japan with the opportunity to take over European colonies in Southeast Asia, with their abundant oil, rubber, and other strategic materials. After Japanese forces occupied French Indochina in September 1940, the United States and Britain cut off shipments of steel, scrap iron, oil, and other products that Japan

**Map 26.1   World War II in Europe and North Africa**
In a series of quick and decisive campaigns from September 1939 to December 1941, German forces overran much of Europe and North Africa. There followed three years of bitter fighting as the Allies slowly pushed the Germans back. This map shows the maximum extent of Germany's conquests and alliances, as well as the key battles and the front lines at various times.

ATLANTIC OCEAN

North Sea

Baltic Sea

Black Sea

Mediterranean Sea

SOVIET UNION

FINLAND

NORWAY

SWEDEN

DENMARK

GREAT BRITAIN

IRELAND

NORTHERN IRELAND

NETHERLANDS

BELGIUM

GERMANY

FRANCE

SWITZERLAND

VICHY FRANCE
(occupied Nov. 1942)

SPAIN

PORTUGAL

SP. MOROCCO

FRENCH MOROCCO

ALGERIA
(Vichy France)

TUNISIA

LIBYA

EGYPT

SLOVAKIA

HUNGARY

ROMANIA

BULGARIA

YUGOSLAVIA

CROATIA

SERBIA

ALBANIA

GREECE

ITALY

Crete

DODECANESE
(Italy)

TURKEY

CYPRUS

SYRIA

PALESTINE
(Br. Mandate)

TRANS-
JORDAN
(Br. Mandate)

UKRAINE

Moscow

Tula

Smolensk

Kiev

Pinsk

Riga

Leningrad

Helsinki

Oslo

Stockholm

Copenhagen

Berlin

Posen

Warsaw

Krakow

Vienna

Budapest

Bucharest

Sofia

Bologna

Rome

Athens

Ankara

Cairo

Madrid

Lisbon

London

Paris

Dunkirk

Stalingrad

Baku

Yalta

El Alamein,
summer 1942

Casablanca,
Nov. 1942

Sicily

MALTA
(Gr. Br.)

GIBRALTAR (Gr. Br.)

Volga

Don

Dnieper

Dniester

Vistula

Danube

Danube

Po

Elbe

Rhine

Ebro

Nile

Suez Canal

Russian front, Nov. 1942

Siege of Stalingrad,
Aug. 21, 1942–Jan. 31, 1943

Russian front,
Dec. 1941

Russian front,
spring 1944

Siege of Leningrad,
Sept. 1941–Jan. 1944

Russian front, Feb. 1945

Rhine Crossing,
March 7, 1945

German surrender:
Reims, May 7, 1945
Berlin, May 8, 1945

Battle of
the Bulge,
Dec. 1944

Western front, Feb. 1945

Battle of Britain, fall 1940

Invasion of Normandy,
June 6, 1944

Axis troops occupy
Vichy France,
Nov. 10 and 11, 1942

Allies land in Provence,
Aug. 15, 1944

Italian front,
Feb. 1945

Monte Casino,
May 1944

Salerno,
Sept. 1943

Allies invade
Sicily and Italy,
July–Sept. 1943

Sicily,
July 1943

Rommel defeated
in Tunisia; Axis
troops evacuated,
May 1943

### Legend

- Hitler's Greater Germany
- Allied with Germany
- Occupied by Germany and its allies
- Grand Alliance
- Neutral nations
- ✕ Major battles

0   200   400 Km.

0   200   400 Mi.

desperately needed. This left Japan with three alternatives: accept the shame and humiliation of giving up its conquests, as the Americans insisted; face economic ruin; or widen the war. Japan chose war.

On December 7, 1941, Japanese planes bombed the U.S. naval base at **Pearl Harbor,** Hawaii, sinking or damaging scores of warships. Then, between December 1941 and March 1942, the Japanese bombed Singapore and occupied Thailand, the Philippines, and Malaya. Within a few months, they occupied all of Southeast Asia and the Dutch East Indies. The Japanese claimed to be liberating the inhabitants of these lands from European colonialism. But they soon began to confiscate food and raw materials and demand heavy labor from the inhabitants, whom they treated with contempt. Those who protested were brutally punished.

The entry of the United States into the war, in alliance with Britain and the Soviet Union, challenged Japan's dream of an East Asian empire. In April 1942, American planes bombed Tokyo. In May, the United States Navy defeated a Japanese fleet in the Coral Sea, ending Japanese plans to conquer Australia. A month later, at the **Battle of Midway,** Japan lost four of its six largest aircraft carriers. Japan did not have enough industry to replace them, for its war production was only one-tenth that of the United States. In the vastness of the Pacific Ocean, aircraft carriers held the key to victory, and without them, Japan faced a long and hopeless war (see Map 26.2).

## The End of the War

Its new American ally also helped the Soviet Union capitalize on the advantage it had won in the Battle of Stalingrad. Aided by a growing stream of supplies from factories in the United States, the Red Army began pushing the Wehrmacht back toward Germany.

The Western powers, meanwhile, staged two invasions of Europe. Beginning in July 1943, they captured Sicily and invaded Italy. Mussolini resigned, and Italy signed an armistice, but German troops held off the Allied advance for two years. Then on D-day (June 6, 1944), 156,000 British, American, and Canadian troops landed on the coast of Normandy in western France. Within a week, the

Allies had more troops in France than Germany did. To meet this growing force, Hitler had to transfer part of the Wehrmacht from the Eastern Front. Despite advancing armies on three sides, Germany held out for almost a year. On May 7, 1945, a week after Hitler committed suicide, German military leaders surrendered.

By June 1944, U.S. bombers were also attacking Japan from newly captured island bases in the Pacific, and U.S. submarines were sinking larger numbers of Japanese merchant ships, gradually cutting off Japan's oil and other raw materials. After May 1945, with the Japanese air force grounded for lack of fuel, U.S. planes began destroying Japanese shipping, industries, and cities at will.

On August 6, 1945, the United States dropped an atomic bomb on **Hiroshima,** killing some 80,000 people in a flash and leaving about 120,000 more to die agonizing deaths from burns and radiation. Three days later, another atomic bomb destroyed Nagasaki. On August 14, Japan offered to surrender, and Emperor Hirohito gave the order to lay down arms. Two weeks later, Japanese leaders signed the terms of surrender. The war was officially over.

## Chinese Civil War and Communist Victory

The Japanese surrender also meant the end of Japanese occupation of much of China, but instead of bringing peace, it marked an intensification of the contest between the Guomindang and the Communists. Guomindang forces started with many advantages: more troops and weapons, U.S. support, and control of China's cities. But their behavior eroded whatever popular support they had. They taxed the people they "liberated" more heavily than the Japanese had, looted businesses, confiscated supplies, and enriched themselves at the expense of the population. To pay its bills, Chiang's government printed money so fast that it soon lost all its value, ruining merchants and causing hoarding and shortages. In the countryside, the Guomindang's brutality alienated the peasants.

In contrast, the Communists' land reform programs had won them popular support, which was even more important than the heavy equipment brought by Guomindang soldiers, who began deserting by the thousands, and the Japanese equip-

**Hiroshima After the Atomic Bomb**    On August 6, 1945, an atomic bomb destroyed the city, killing over fifty thousand people. This photo shows the devastation of the city center, where only a few concrete buildings remained standing.    (Corbis)

ment seized by the Soviets in the last weeks of the war. By 1949, the Guomindang armies were collapsing everywhere, defeated more by their own greed and ineptness than by the Communists. As the Communists advanced, high-ranking members of the Guomindang fled to Taiwan, protected from the mainland by the United States Navy. On October 1, 1949, Mao Zedong announced the founding of the People's Republic of China.

# THE CHARACTER OF WARFARE

The war left an enormous death toll. Recent estimates place the figure at close to 60 million deaths, six to eight times more than in World War I. Over half of the dead were civilian victims of massacres, famines, or bombs. The Soviet Union lost between 20 and 25 million people, more than any other country. China suffered 15 million deaths;

Poland lost some 6 million, of whom half were Jewish; the Jewish people lost another 3 million outside Poland. Over 4 million Germans and over 2 million Japanese died. In much of the world, almost every family mourned one or more of its members. In contrast, Great Britain lost 400,000 people, the United States 300,000.

One reason for the terrible toll in human lives and suffering was a change in moral values, as belligerents identified not just soldiers but entire peoples as enemies. Another reason for the devastation was the appearance of new technologies that carried destruction deep into enemy territory far beyond the traditional battlefields.

## The War of Science

Scientists made many contributions to the technology of warfare. Chemists found ways to make synthetic rubber from coal or oil. Physicists perfected radar, which warned of

**Map 26.2  World War II in Asia and the Pacific**  After having conquered much of China between 1937 and 1941, Japanese forces launched a sudden attack on Southeast Asia, Indonesia, and the Pacific in late 1941 and early 1942. American forces slowly reconquered the Pacific islands and the Philippines until August 1945, when the atomic bombing of Hiroshima and Nagasaki forced Japan's surrender.

approaching enemy aircraft and submarines. Others broke enemy codes and developed antibiotics that saved the lives of countless wounded soldiers. Aircraft development was especially striking.

As war approached, German, British, and Japanese aircraft manufacturers developed fast, maneuverable fighter planes. U.S. industry produced aircraft of every sort but was especially noted for its heavy bombers designed to fly in huge formations and drop tons of bombs on enemy cities. The Japanese developed the Mitsubishi "Zero" fighter plane—light, fast, and agile. Unable to produce heavy planes in large numbers, Germany responded with radically new designs, including the first jet fighters, low-flying buzz bombs, and fearful V-2 missiles.

In October 1939, President Roosevelt received a letter from physicist Albert Einstein, a Jewish refugee from Nazism, warning of the dangers of nuclear power. Fearing that Germany might develop a nuclear bomb first, Roosevelt placed the vast resources of the U.S. government at the disposal of physicists and engineers, both Americans and refugees from Europe. By 1945, they had built two atomic bombs, each one powerful enough to annihilate an entire city.

## Bombing Raids

The Germans began the war from the air, but it was the British and Americans who excelled at large-scale urban bombardment. Since it was very hard to pinpoint individual buildings, especially at night, such raids were aimed at weakening the morale of the civilian population.

In May 1942, 1,000 British planes dropped incendiary bombs on Cologne, setting fire to most of the old city. Between July 24 and August 2, 1943, 3,330 British and Americans bombers set fire to Hamburg, killing 50,000 people. Later raids destroyed Berlin, Dresden, and other German cities. All in all, the bombing raids against Germany killed 600,000 people—more than half of them women and children—and injured 800,000. If the air strategists had hoped thereby to break the morale of the German people, they failed. The only effective bombing raids were those directed against oil depots and synthetic fuel plants; by early 1945, they had almost brought the German war effort to a standstill.

American bombing raids on Japanese cities were even more devastating than the fire-bombing of German cities, for Japanese cities were built of wood. In March 1945, a large raid set Tokyo ablaze, killing 80,000 people and leaving a million homeless. Five months later, single atomic bombs did something similar.

## The Holocaust

The Nazis killed defenseless civilians on an even larger scale. Their murders were not the byproducts of some military goal but a calculated policy of extermination.

Their first targets were Jews. Soon after Hitler came to power, he deprived German Jews of their citizenship and legal rights. When eastern Europe fell under Nazi rule, the Nazis herded its large Jewish population into ghettos in the major cities, where many died of starvation and disease. Then, in early 1942, the Nazis decided to carry out Hitler's "final solution to the Jewish problem" by applying

**U.S. Army Medics and Holocaust Victims**   At the end of World War II, Allied troops entered the Nazi concentration camps, where they found the bodies of thousands of victims of the Holocaust. In this picture, taken at Dachau in southern Germany, two U.S. Army medics are overseeing a truckload of corpses to be taken to a burial site.   (Hulton Deutsch Collection/Corbis)

modern industrial methods to the slaughter of human beings. German companies built huge extermination camps in eastern Europe. Every day, trainloads of cattle cars arrived at the camps and disgorged thousands of captives and the corpses of those who had died of starvation or asphyxiation along the way. The strongest survivors were put to work and fed almost nothing until they died. Women, children, the elderly, and the sick were shoved into gas chambers and asphyxiated with poison gas. **Auschwitz,** the biggest camp, was a giant industrial complex designed to kill up to twelve thousand people a day. Most horrifying of all were the tortures inflicted on prisoners selected by Nazi doctors for "medical experiments." This mass extermination, now called the **Holocaust** ("burning"), claimed some 6 million Jewish lives.

Besides the Jews, the Nazis also killed 3 million Polish Catholics—especially professionals, army officers, and the educated—in an effort to reduce the Polish people to slavery. They also exterminated homosexuals, Jehovah's Witnesses, Gypsies, the disabled, and the mentally ill—all in the interests of "racial purity." Whenever a German was killed in an occupied country, the Nazis retaliated by burning a village with all its inhabitants. After the invasion of Russia, the Wehrmacht was given orders to execute all captured communists, government employees, and officers. They also worked millions of prisoners of war to death or let them die of starvation.

## The Home Front

Rapid military movements and air power carried the war to people's homes in China, Japan, Southeast Asia, and Europe. Armies swept through the land, confiscating food, fuel, and anything else of value. Bombers and heavy artillery pounded cities into rubble, leaving only the skeletons of buildings, while survivors cowered in cellars. Air-raid sirens awakened people throughout the night. Millions fled their homes in terror. Of all the major belligerents, only Americans escaped such nightmares, and war production ended the deprivations of the Depression years.

The war demanded an enormous production effort from civilians. In the face of advancing Germans in 1941, the Soviets dismantled over fifteen hundred factories and rebuilt them in the Ural Mountains and Siberia, where workers soon turned out more tanks and artillery than the Axis. American factories produced an unending supply of ships, aircraft, trucks, tanks, and other materiel for the Allied effort. The Axis powers could not compete with this vast outpouring.

With so many men mobilized for war, women were responsible for much of this production. For example, 6 million women entered the American labor force during the war, 2.5 million of them in manufacturing jobs previously considered "men's work." Soviet women took over half of all industrial and three-quarters of all agricultural jobs. In the other belligerent countries, women also played a major role in the war effort, replacing men in fields, factories, and offices. The Nazis, in contrast, believed that German women should stay home and bear children, and they imported 7 million "guest workers"—a euphemism for war prisoners and captured foreigners.

## War and the Environment

As in World War I, battles scarred the landscape, leaving behind spent ammunition and damaged equipment. Retreating armies flooded large areas of China and the Netherlands. The bombing of cities left ruins that remained visible for a generation or more. The main cause of environmental stress, however, was not the fighting but the economic development that sustained it.

As war industries boomed—the United States increased its industrial production fourfold during the war—so did the demand for raw materials. Mining companies opened new mines and towns in Central Africa to supply strategic minerals. Brazil, Argentina, and other Latin American countries deprived of manufactured imports began building their own steel mills, factories, and shipyards. In India, China, and Europe, timber felling accelerated far beyond forest regrowth.

We must keep the environmental effects of the war in perspective. From the vantage point of the present, the environmental impact of the war seems quite modest in comparison with the damage inflicted on the earth by the long consumer boom that began in the post–World War II years.

## CONCLUSION

etween 1929 and 1949, the old global order—
conservative, colonialist, and dominated by
Great Britain and France—was shattered by the Depression, the politics of violence, and the most devastating war in history. Stalin transformed the Soviet
Union into an industrial giant at enormous human
cost. Reacting to the Depression, which weakened
the Western democracies, Hitler in Germany and
military leaders in Japan prepared for a war of conquest. Though Germany and Japan achieved stun-
ning victories at first, their forces soon faltered in the
face of the greater industrial production of the United
States and the Soviet Union.

The war was so destructive and spread to so
much of the globe because rapidly advancing technology was readily converted from civilian to military production. Machines that had made cars could
also manufacture bombers or tanks. Engineers
could design factories to kill people with maximum efficiency. The accelerating technology of
missiles and nuclear bombs made the entire planet
vulnerable to human destruction for the first time
in history.

Into the power vacuum left by the collapse of
Germany and Japan stepped the two superpowers:
the United States and the USSR. When the war
ended, U.S. soldiers were stationed in Australia,
Japan, and western Europe, and the Red Army occupied all of eastern Europe and parts of northern
China. Within months of their victory, these one-
time allies became ideological enemies.

The global impact of World War II was drastic
and almost immediate, because the war weakened
the European colonial powers and because so much
of the fighting took place in North Africa, Southeast Asia, and other colonial areas. Within fifteen
years of the end of the war, almost every European
colonial empire had disappeared. As the long era
of European domination receded, Asians and
Africans began reclaiming their independence.

## ■ Key Terms

Joseph Stalin

Five-Year Plans

Benito Mussolini

Fascist Party

Adolf Hitler

Nazis

Chiang Kai-shek

Mao Zedong

Long March

Stalingrad

Pearl Harbor

Battle of Midway

Hiroshima

Auschwitz

Holocaust

## ■ Suggested Reading

The literature on the period from 1929 to 1945 is enormous and growing fast. The following list is but a very
summary introduction.

Charles Kindelberger's *The World in Depression, 1929–39*
(1973) and Robert McElvaine's *The Great Depression:
America, 1929–1941* (1984) provide a sophisticated economic analysis of the Depression. A. J. H. Latham's *The
Depression and the Developing World, 1914–1939* (1981)
gives a global perspective.

The best recent book on Japan in the twentieth century is
Daikichi Irokawa's *The Age of Hirohito: In Search of
Modern Japan* (1995). On Japanese expansion, see W. G.
Beasley, *Japanese Imperialism, 1894–1945* (1987). The
race to war is covered in Akira Iriye, *The Origins of the
Second World War in Asia and the Pacific* (1987). Michael
Barnhart, *Japan Prepares for Total War* (1987), is short
and well written.

In the large and fast-growing literature on twentieth-
century China, two general introductions are especially
useful: John K. Fairbank, *The Great Chinese Revolution,
1800–1985* (1986), and Jonathan Spence, *The Search for
Modern China* (1990). On the warlord and Guomindang
periods, see Lucien Bianco, *Origins of the Chinese Revolution, 1915–1949* (1971). The Japanese invasion of China is
the subject of Iris Chang, *The Rape of Nanking: The Forgotten Holocaust of World War II* (1997), and of James Hsiung
and Steven Levine, eds., *China's Bitter Victory: The War
with Japan, 1937–1945* (1992). Jung Chang, *Wild Swans:
Three Daughters of China* (1991), is a fascinating account
of women's experiences during the Revolution and the
Mao era by the daughter of two Communist officials.

Among recent biographies of Stalin, see Dmitrii Volko-
gonov's *Stalin: Triumph and Tragedy* (1991) and Robert
Tucker's *Stalin as Revolutionary, 1879–1929* (1973) and
*Stalin in Power: The Revolution from Above, 1928–1941*
(1990). On the transformation of the USSR, see Roy
Medvedev's *Let History Judge: The Origins and Consequences of Stalinism* (1989) and Stephen Kotkin's *Magnetic Mountain: Stalinism as Civilization* (1995). Stalin's
collectivization of agriculture is vividly portrayed in Robert
Conquest's *Harvest of Sorrow* (1986); see also Sheila Fitz-
patrick's *Stalin's Peasants: Resistance and Survival in the
Russian Village After Collectivization* (1994). Conquest's

*The Great Terror: A Reassessment* (1990) describes the purges of the 1930s. Alexander Solzhenitsyn, a veteran of Stalin's prisons, explores them in a detailed history, *The Gulag Archipelago, 1918–1956* (3 vols., 1974–1978), and in a short, brilliant novel, *One Day in the Life of Ivan Denisovich* (1978).

Alexander De Grand provides an excellent interpretation of fascism in *Italian Fascism: Its Origins and Development,* 2d ed. (1989). William Shirer's *The Rise and Fall of the Third Reich* (1960) is a long but very dramatic eyewitness description of Nazi Germany by a journalist. The dictators are the subject of two fine biographies: Denis Mack Smith's *Mussolini* (1982) and Alan Bullock's *Hitler: A Study in Tyranny* (1965). See also A. J. P. Taylor's controversial classic, *The Origins of the Second World War* (1966) and Michael Burleigh's *Third Reich: A New History* (2000).

Two very detailed books on World War II are John Keegan, *The Second World War* (1990), and Gerhard Weinberg, *A World at Arms: A Global History of World War II* (1994). Particular aspects of the war in Europe are covered in Alexander Werth, *Russia at War, 1941–1945* (1965), and Conrad Crane, *Bombs, Cities, and Civilians* (1993). One of the most readable accounts of the war in Asia and the Pacific is Ronald Spector's *Eagle Against the Sun* (1988). Also see Akira Iriye, *Power and Culture: The Japanese-American War, 1941–1945* (1981), and James Hsiung and Steven Levine, eds., *China's Bitter Victory: The War with Japan, 1937–1945* (1992).

The terror of life under Nazi rule is the subject of two powerful memoirs: Anne Frank's *The Diary of a Young Girl* (1953) and Eli Wiesel's *Night* (1960). On the Holocaust, see Lucy Dawidowicz, *The War Against the Jews, 1933–1945,* 2d ed. (1986); Leni Yahil, *The Holocaust: The Fate of European Jewry* (1990); and a controversial book by Daniel Goldhagen, *Hitler's Willing Executioners: Ordinary Germans and the Holocaust* (1996).

Among the many books that capture the scientific side of warfare, two are especially recommended: Richard Rhodes's long but fascinating *The Making of the Atomic Bomb* (1986) and F. H. Hinsley and Alan Stripp, eds., *Code Breakers* (1993).

Among the many books on the home front in the United States, the most vivid is Studs Terkel, *"The Good War": An Oral History of World War Two* (1984). Margaret Higonnet et al., eds., *Behind the Lines: Gender and the Two World Wars* (1987), discusses the role of women in the war.

# Striving for Independence: Africa, India, and Latin America, 1900–1949

## 27

CHAPTER OUTLINE

**Sub-Saharan Africa, 1900–1945**

**The Indian Independence Movement, 1905–1947**

**The Mexican Revolution, 1910–1940**

**Argentina and Brazil, 1900–1949**

ENVIRONMENT AND TECHNOLOGY: **Gandhi and Technology**

Emiliano Zapata°, leader of a peasant rebellion in the Mexican Revolution, liked to be photographed on horseback, carrying a sword and a rifle and draped with bandoliers of bullets. Mahatma Gandhi°, who led the independence movement in India, preferred to be seen sitting at a spinning wheel, dressed in a *dhoti*°, the simple loincloth worn by Indian farmers. The images they liked to project and the methods they used could not have been more opposed. Yet their goals were similar: each wanted social justice and a better life for the poor in a country free of foreign domination.

---

Zapata (sah-PAH-tah)    Gandhi (GAHN-dee)    *dhoti* (DOE-tee)

The previous two chapters focused on a world convulsed by war and revolution. The world wars involved Europe, East Asia, the Middle East, and the United States, and they sparked violent revolutions in Russia and China. They accelerated the development of aviation, electronics, nuclear power, and other technologies. Although these momentous events dominate the history of the first half of the twentieth century, parts of the world that were little touched by war also underwent profound changes in this period, partly for internal reasons and partly because of the warfare and revolution in other parts of the world.

In this chapter we examine the changes that took place in sub-Saharan Africa, in India, and in three major countries of Latin America—Mexico, Brazil, and Argentina. These three regions represent three very distinct cultures, yet they had much in common. Africa and India were colonies of Europe, both politically and economically. Though politically independent, the Latin American republics were dependent on Europe and the United States for the sale of raw materials and commodities and for imports of manufactured goods, technology, and capital. In all three regions independence movements tried to wrest control from distant foreigners and improve the livelihood of their peoples. Their success was partial at best.

As you read this chapter, ask yourself the following questions:

- How did wars and revolutions in Europe and East Asia affect the countries of the Southern Hemisphere?

- Why did educated Indians and Africans want independence?

- What could Latin Americans do to achieve social justice and economic development? Were these two goals compatible?

# SUB-SAHARAN AFRICA, 1900–1945

Of all the continents, Africa was the last to come under European rule (see Chapter 24). The first half of the twentieth century, the time when nationalist movements threatened European rule in Asia, was Africa's period of classic colonialism. After World War I Britain, France, Belgium, and South Africa divided Germany's African colonies among themselves. In the 1930s Italy invaded Ethiopia. The colonial empires reached their peak shortly before World War II.

## Colonial Africa: Economic and Social Changes

Outside of Algeria, Kenya, and South Africa, few Europeans lived in Africa. In 1930 Nigeria, with a population of 20 million, was ruled by 386 British officials and by 8,000 policemen and military, of whom 150 were European. Yet even such a small presence stimulated deep social and economic changes.

Since the turn of the century the colonial powers had built railroads from coastal cities to mines and plantations in the interior in order to provide raw materials to the industrial world. The economic boom of the interwar years benefited few Africans. Colonial governments took lands that Africans owned communally and sold or leased them to European companies or, in eastern and southern Africa, to white settlers. Large European companies dominated wholesale commerce, while immigrants from various countries—Indians in East Africa, Greeks and Syrians in West Africa—handled much of the retail trade. Airplanes and automobiles were even more alien to the experience of Africans than railroads had been to an earlier generation.

Where land was divided into small farms, some Africans benefited from the boom. Farmers in the Gold Coast (now Ghana°) profited from the high price of cocoa, as did palm-oil producers in Nigeria and coffee growers in East Africa. In most of Africa women played a major role in the retail trades, selling pots and pans, cloth, food, and other items in the markets. Many maintained their economic independence and kept their household finances separate from those of their husbands, following a custom that predated the colonial period.

For many Africans, however, economic development meant working in European-owned mines and plantations, often under compulsion. Colonial governments were eager to develop the resources of the territories under their control but could not afford to pay high enough wages to attract workers. Instead, they used their police powers to force Africans to work under harsh conditions for little or no pay. In the 1920s, when the government of French Equatorial Africa decided to build a rail-

**Ghana** (GAH-nuh)

# C H R O N O L O G Y

| | Africa | India | Latin America |
|---|---|---|---|
| | | | **1876–1910** Porfirio Díaz, dictator of Mexico |
| **1900** | **1900s** Railroads connect ports to the interior | | |
| | **1909** African National Congress founded | **1905** Viceroy Curzon splits Bengal; mass demonstrations | |
| | | **1906** Muslims found All-India Muslim League | |
| | | **1911** British transfer capital from Calcutta to Delhi | **1911–1919** Mexican Revolution; Emiliano Zapata and Pancho Villa against the Constitutionalists |
| | | | **1917** New constitution proclaimed in Mexico |
| | | **1919** Amritsar Massacre | |
| **1920** | **1920s** J. E. Casely Hayford organizes political movement in British West Africa | | |
| | | | **1928** Plutarco Elías Calles founds Mexico's National Revolutionary Party |
| | | **1929** Gandhi leads March to the Sea | |
| | | **1930s** Gandhi calls for independence; he is repeatedly arrested | |
| | | | **1930–1945** Getulio Vargas, dictator of Brazil |
| | | | **1934–1940** Lázaro Cárdenas, president of Mexico |
| | | | **1938** Cárdenas nationalizes Mexican oil industry; Vargas proclaims Estado Novo in Brazil |
| | **1939–1945** A million Africans serve in World War II | **1939** British bring India into World War II | |
| **1940** | | **1940** Muhammad Ali Jinnah demands a separate nation for Muslims | |

*(continued)*

| C H R O N O L O G Y *(continued)* | | |
|---|---|---|
| **Africa** | **India** | **Latin America** |
| | | **1943**   Juan Perón leads military coup in Argentina |
| | | **1946**   Perón elected president of Argentina |
| | **1947**   Partition and independence of India and Pakistan | |

road from Brazzaville to the Atlantic coast, a distance of 312 miles (502 kilometers), it drafted 127,000 men to carve a roadbed across mountains and through rain forests. Because of lack of food, clothing, and medical care, 20,000 of them died, an average of 64 deaths per mile of track.

Europeans prided themselves on bringing modern health care to Africa; yet before the 1930s there was too little of it to help the majority of Africans, and other aspects of colonialism actually worsened public health. Migrants to cities, mines, and plantations and soldiers moving from post to post spread syphilis, gonorrhea, tuberculosis, and malaria. Sleeping sickness and smallpox epidemics raged throughout Central Africa. In recruiting men to work, colonial governments depleted rural areas of farmers needed to plant and harvest crops. Forced requisitions of food to feed the workers left the remaining populations undernourished and vulnerable to diseases. Not until the 1930s did colonial governments realize the negative consequences of their labor policies and begin to invest in agricultural development and health care for Africans.

In 1900 Ibadan° in Nigeria was the only city in sub-Saharan Africa with more than 100,000 inhabitants; fifty years later, dozens of cities had reached that size, including Nairobi° in Kenya, Johannesburg in South Africa, Lagos in Nigeria, Accra in Gold Coast, and Dakar in Senegal. Africans migrated to cities because they offered hope of jobs and excitement and, for a few, the chance to become wealthy.

However, migrations damaged the family life of those involved, for almost all the migrants were men leaving women in the countryside to farm and raise children. Cities built during the colonial period reflected the colonialists' attitudes with racially segregated housing, clubs, restaurants, hospitals, and other institutions. Patterns of racial discrimination were most rigid in the white-settler colonies of eastern and southern Africa.

## Religious and Political Changes

Traditional religious belief could not explain the dislocations that foreign rule, migrations, and sudden economic changes brought to the lives of Africans. Many therefore turned to one of the two universal religions, Christianity and Islam, for guidance.

Christianity was introduced into Africa by Western missionaries, except in Ethiopia, where it was indigenous. It was most successful in the coastal regions of West and South Africa, where the European influence was strongest. A major attraction of the Christian denominations was their mission schools, which taught both craft skills and basic literacy, providing access to employment as minor functionaries, teachers, and shopkeepers. These schools educated a new elite, many of whom learned not only skills and literacy but Western political ideas as well. Many Africans accepted Christianity enthusiastically, reading the suffering of their own peoples into the biblical stories of Moses

---

**Ibadan** (ee-BAH-dahn)    **Nairobi** (nie-ROE-bee)

**Diamond Mining in Southern Africa**   The discovery of diamonds in the Transvaal in 1867 attracted prospectors to the area around Kimberley. The first wave of prospectors consisted of individual "diggers," including a few Africans. By the late 1870s, surface deposits had been exhausted and further mining required complex and costly machinery. After 1889, one company, De Beers Consolidated, owned all the diamond mines. This photograph shows the entrance to a mineshaft and mine workers surrounded by heavy equipment.   (Royal Commonwealth Society. By permission of the Syndics of Cambridge University Library.)

and the parables of Jesus. The churches trained some of the brighter pupils to become catechists, teachers, and clergymen. A few rose to high positions, such as James Johnson, a Yoruba who became the Anglican bishop of the Niger Delta Pastorate. Independent Christian churches—known as "Ethiopian" churches—associated Christian beliefs with radical ideas of racial equality and participation in politics.

Islam spread inland from the East African coast and southward from the Sahel° toward the

**Sahel** (SAH-hel)

West African coast, through the influence and example of Arab and African merchants. Islam also emphasized literacy—in Arabic through Quaranic schools rather than in a European language—and was less disruptive of traditional African customs such as polygamy.

In a few places, such as Dakar in Senegal and Cape Town in South Africa, small numbers of Africans could obtain secondary education. Even smaller numbers went on to college in Europe or America. Though few in number, they became the leaders of political movements. The contrast between the liberal ideas imparted by Western education and the realities of racial discrimination under colonial rule contributed to the rise of nationalism among educated Africans. In Senegal **Blaise Diagne°** agitated for African participation in politics and fair treatment in the French army. In the 1920s J. E. Casely Hayford began organizing a movement for greater autonomy in British West Africa. In South Africa Western-educated lawyers and journalists founded the **African National Congress** in 1912 to defend the interests of Africans. These nationalist movements were inspired by the ideas of Pan-Africanists from America such as W. E. B. Du Bois and Marcus Garvey, who advocated the unity of African peoples around the world, as well as by European ideas of liberty and nationhood. Before World War II, however, they were small and had little influence.

The Second World War (1939–1945) had a profound effect on the peoples of Africa, even those far removed from the theaters of war. The war brought hardships, such as increased forced labor, inflation, and requisitions of raw materials. Yet it also brought hope. During the campaign to oust the Italians from Ethiopia, Emperor **Haile Selassie°** (r. 1930–1974) led his own troops into Addis Ababa, his capital, and reclaimed his title. A million Africans served as soldiers and carriers in Burma, North Africa, and Europe, where many became aware of Africa's role in helping the Allied war effort. They listened to Allied propaganda in favor of European liberation movements and against Nazi racism, and they returned to their countries with new and radical ideas.

The early twentieth century was a relatively peaceful period for sub-Saharan Africa. But this peace—enforced by the European occupiers—masked profound changes that were to transform African life after the Second World War. The building of cities, railroads, and other enterprises brought Africa into the global economy, often at great human cost. Colonialism also brought changes to African culture and religion, hastening the spread of Christianity and Islam. And the foreign occupation awakened political ideas that inspired the next generation of Africans to demand independence (see Chapter 28).

---

**Diagne** (dee-AHN-yuh)  **Haile Selassie** (HI-lee seh-LASS-ee)

# THE INDIAN INDEPENDENCE MOVEMENT, 1905–1947

India was a colony of Great Britain from the late eighteenth to the mid-twentieth centuries. Under British rule the subcontinent acquired many of the trappings of Western-style economic development, such as railroads, harbors, modern cities, and cotton and steel mills, as well as an active and worldly middle class. The economic transformation of the region awakened in this educated middle class a sense of national dignity that demanded political fulfillment. In response, the British gradually granted India a limited amount of political autonomy while maintaining overall control. Religious and communal tensions among the Indian peoples were carefully papered over under British rule. Violent conflicts tore India apart after the withdrawal of the British in 1947.

## The Land and the People

Much of India is fertile land, but it is vulnerable to the vagaries of nature, especially droughts caused by the periodic failure of the monsoons. When the rains failed from 1896 to 1900, 2 million people died of starvation.

Despite periodic famines the Indian population grew from 250 million in 1900 to 319 million in 1921 and 389 million in 1941. This growth created pressures in many areas. Landless young men converged on the cities, exceeding the number of jobs available in the slowly expanding industries. To produce timber for construction and railroad ties, and to clear land for tea and rubber plantations, government foresters cut down most of the tropical hardwood forests that had covered the subcontinent in the nineteenth century. In spite of deforestation and extensive irrigation, the amount of land available to peasant families shrank with each successive generation. Economic development—what the British called the "moral and material progress of India"—hardly benefited the average Indian.

Indians were divided into many classes. Peasants, always the great majority, paid rents to the landowner, interest to the village moneylender, and taxes to the government and had little left to improve their land or raise their standard of living. The government protected property owners, from village moneylenders all the way up to the maharajahs,° or ruling princes, who owned huge tracts of land. The cities were crowded with craftsmen, traders, and workers of all sorts, most very poor. Although the British had banned the burning of widows on their husbands' funeral pyres, in other respects women's lives changed little under British rule.

The peoples of India spoke many different languages: Hindi in the north, Tamil in the south, Bengali in the east, Gujerati around Bombay, Urdu in the northwest, and dozens of others. As a result of British rule and increasing trade and travel, English became, like Latin in medieval Europe, the common medium of communication of the Western-educated middle class. This new class of English-speaking government bureaucrats, professionals, and merchants was to play a leading role in the independence movement.

The majority of Indians practiced Hinduism and were subdivided into hundreds of castes, each affiliated with a particular occupation. Hinduism discouraged intermarriage and other social interactions among the castes and with people who were not Hindus. Muslims constituted one-quarter of the people of India but formed a majority in the northwest and in eastern Bengal. Muslim rulers had dominated northern and central India until they were displaced by the British in the eighteenth century. More reluctant than Hindus to learn English, Muslims felt discriminated against by both British and Hindus.

## British Rule and Indian Nationalism

Colonial India was ruled by a viceroy appointed by the British government and administered by a few thousand members of the Indian Civil Service. These men, imbued with a sense of duty toward their subjects, formed one of the more honest (if not efficient) bureaucracies of all time. Drawn mostly from the English gentry, they liked to think of India as a land of lords and peasants. They believed it was their duty to protect the Indian people from the

maharajah (mah-huh-RAH-juh)

dangers of industrialization, while defending their own positions from Indian nationalists.

As Europeans they admired modern technology but tried to control its introduction into India so as to maximize the benefits to Britain and to themselves. For example, they encouraged railroads, harbors, telegraphs, and other communications technologies, as well as irrigation and plantations, because these increased India's foreign trade and strengthened British control. At the same time, they discouraged the cotton and steel industries and limited the training of Indian engineers, ostensibly to spare India the social upheavals that had accompanied the Industrial Revolution in Europe, while protecting British industry from Indian competition.

At the turn of the century the majority of Indians—especially the peasants, landowners, and princes—accepted British rule. But the Europeans' racist attitude toward dark-skinned people increasingly offended Indians who had learned English and absorbed English ideas of freedom and representative government, only to discover that thinly disguised racial quotas excluded them from the Indian Civil Service, the officer corps, and prestigious country clubs.

In 1885 a small group of English-speaking Hindu professionals founded a political organization called the **Indian National Congress.** For twenty years its members respectfully petitioned the government for access to the higher administrative positions and for a voice in official decisions, but they had little influence outside intellectual circles. Then, in 1905, Viceroy Lord Curzon divided the province of **Bengal** in two to improve the efficiency of its administration. This decision, made without consulting anyone, angered not only educated Indians, who saw it as a way to lessen their influence, but also millions of uneducated Hindu Bengalis, who suddenly found themselves outnumbered by Muslims in East Bengal. Soon Bengal was the scene of demonstrations, boycotts of British goods, and even incidents of violence against the British.

In 1906, while the Hindus of Bengal were protesting the partition of their province, Muslims, fearful of Hindu dominance elsewhere in India, founded the **All-India Muslim League.** Caught in an awkward situation, the government responded by granting Indians a limited franchise based on wealth. Muslims, however, were on average poorer than Hindus, for many poor and low-caste Hindus had converted to Islam to escape caste discrimination. Taking advantage of these religious divisions, the British instituted separate representation and different voting qualifications for Hindus and Muslims. Then, in 1911, the British transferred the capital of India from Calcutta to Delhi°, the former capital of the Mughal° emperors. These changes disturbed Indians of all classes and religions and raised their political consciousness. Politics, once primarily the concern of Westernized intellectuals, turned into two mass movements: one by Hindus and one by Muslims.

To maintain their commercial position and prevent social upheavals, the British resisted the idea that India could, or should, industrialize. Their geologists looked for minerals, such as coal or manganese, that British industry required. However, when the only Indian member of the Indian Geological Service, Pramatha Nath Bose, wanted to prospect for iron ore, he had to resign because the government wanted no part of an Indian steel industry that could compete with that of Britain. Bose joined forces with Jamsetji Tata, a Bombay textile magnate who decided to produce steel in spite of British opposition. With the help of German and American engineers and equipment, Tata's son Dorabji opened the first steel mill in India in 1911, in a town called Jamshedpur in honor of his father. Although it produced only a fraction of the steel that India required, Jamshedpur became a powerful symbol of Indian national pride. It prompted Indian nationalists to ask why a country that could produce its own steel needed foreigners to run its government.

During World War I Indians supported Britain enthusiastically; 1.2 million men volunteered for the army, and millions more voluntarily contributed money to the government. Many expected the British to reward their loyalty with political concessions. Others organized to demand concessions and a voice in the government. In 1917, in response to the agitation, the British government announced "the gradual development of self-governing institutions with a view to the progressive realization of responsible government in India

as an integral part of the British Empire." This sounded like a promise of self-government, but the timetable was so vague that nationalists denounced it as a devious maneuver to postpone India's independence.

In late 1918 and early 1919 a violent influenza epidemic broke out among soldiers in the war zone of northern France. Within a few months it spread to every country on earth and killed approximately 30 million people. India was especially hard hit; of the millions who died, two out of three were Indian. This dreadful toll increased the mounting political tensions. Leaders of the Indian National Congress declared that the British reform proposals were too little, too late.

On April 13, 1919, in the city of Amritsar in Punjab, General Reginald Dyer ordered his troops to fire into a peaceful crowd of some 10,000 demonstrators, killing at least 379 and wounding 1,200. Waves of angry demonstrations swept over India, but the government waited six months to appoint a committee to investigate the massacre. After General Dyer retired, the British House of Lords voted to approve his actions, and a fund was raised in appreciation of his services. Indians interpreted these gestures as showing British contempt for their colonial subjects. In the charged atmosphere of the time, the period of gradual accommodation between the British and the Indians came to a close.

## Mahatma Gandhi and Militant Nonviolence

For the next twenty years India teetered on the edge of violent uprisings and harsh repression, possibly even war. That it did not succumb was due to **Mohandas K. Gandhi** (1869–1948), a man known to his followers as "Mahatma," the "great soul."

Gandhi began life with every advantage. His family was wealthy enough to send him to England for his education. After his studies he lived in South Africa and practiced law for the small Indian community there. During World War I he returned to India and was one of many Western-educated Hindu intellectuals who joined the Indian National Congress.

Gandhi had some unusual political ideas. Unlike many radical political thinkers of his time, he

**Delhi** (DEL-ee)   **Mughal** (MOO-guhl)

denounced the popular ideals of power, struggle, and combat. Instead, inspired by both Hindu and Christian concepts, he preached the saintly virtues of *ahimsa*° (nonviolence) and *satyagraha*° (the search for truth). He refused to countenance violence among his followers, and he called off several demonstrations when they turned violent.

Gandhi had an affinity for the poor that was unusual even among socialist politicians. In 1921 he gave up the Western-style suits worn by lawyers and the fine raiment of wealthy Indians and henceforth wore simple peasant garb: a length of homespun cloth below his waist and a shawl to cover his torso (see Environment and Technology: Gandhi and Technology). He spoke for the farmers and the outcasts, whom he called *harijan*°, "children of God." He attracted ever-larger numbers of followers among the poor and the illiterate, who soon began to revere him; and he transformed the cause of Indian independence from an elite movement of the educated into a mass movement with a quasi-religious aura.

Gandhi was a brilliant political tactician and a master of public relations gestures. In 1929, for instance, he led a few followers on an 80-mile (129-kilometer) walk, camped on a beach, and gathered salt from the sea in a blatant and well-publicized act of civil disregard for the government's monopoly on salt. But he discovered that unleashing the power of popular participation was one thing and controlling its direction was quite another. Within days of his "Walk to the Sea," demonstrations of support broke out all over India, in which the police killed a hundred demonstrators and arrested over sixty thousand.

Many times during the 1930s Gandhi threatened to fast "unto death," and several times he did come close to death, to protest the violence of both the police and his followers and to demand independence. He was repeatedly arrested and spent a total of six years in jail. But every arrest made him more popular. He became a cult figure not only in his own country but also in the Western media. He never won a battle or an election; instead, in the words of historian Percival Spear, he made the British "uncomfortable in their cherished field of moral rectitude," and he gave Indians the feeling that theirs was the ethically superior cause.

## India Moves Toward Independence

In the 1920s, slowly and reluctantly, the British began to give in to the pressure of the Indian National Congress and the Muslim League. They handed over control of "national" areas such as education, the economy, and public works. They also gradually admitted more Indians into the Civil Service and the officer corps.

India took its first tentative steps toward industrialization in the years before the First and then the Second World Wars. Indian politicians obtained the right to erect high tariff barriers against imports in order to protect India's infant industries from foreign, even British, competition. Behind these barriers, Indian entrepreneurs built plants to manufacture iron and steel, cement, paper, cotton and jute textiles, sugar, and other products. This early industrialization provided jobs, though not enough to improve the lives of the Indian peasants or urban poor. These manufactures, however, helped create a class of wealthy Indian businessmen. Far from being satisfied by the government's policies, they supported the Indian National Congress and its demands for independence. Though paying homage to Gandhi, they preferred his designated successor as leader of the Indian National Congress, **Jawaharlal Nehru**° (1889–1964). A highly educated nationalist and subtle thinker, Nehru, unlike Gandhi, looked forward to creating a modern industrial India.

Congress politicians won regional elections but continued to be excluded from the viceroy's cabinet, the true center of power. When World War II began in September 1939 Viceroy Lord Linlithgow declared war without consulting a single Indian. The Congress-dominated provincial governments resigned in protest and found that boycotting government office increased their popular support. When the British offered to give India its independence once the war ended, Gandhi called the offer a "postdated cheque on a failing bank" and demanded full independence immediately. His "Quit

---

*ahimsa* (uh-HIM-sah)    *satyagraha* (suh-TYAH-gruh-huh)
*harijan* (HAH-ree-jahn)

---

**Nehru** (NAY-roo)

## Gandhi and Technology

In the twentieth century all political leaders but one embraced modern industrial technology. That one exception is Gandhi.

After deciding to wear only handmade cloth, Gandhi made a bonfire of imported factory-made cloth and began spending half an hour every day spinning yarn on a simple spinning wheel, a task he called a "sacrament." The spinning wheel became the symbol of his movement. Any Indian who wished to come before him had to dress in handwoven cloth.

Gandhi had several reasons for reviving this ancient craft. One was his revulsion against "the incessant search for material comforts," an evil to which he thought Europeans were "becoming slaves." Not only had materialism corrupted the people of the West, it had also caused massive unemployment in India. In particular, he blamed the impoverishment of the Indian people on the cotton industries of England and Japan, which had ruined the traditional cotton manufacturing by which India had once supplied all her own needs.

Gandhi looked back to a time before India became a colony of Britian, when "our women spun fine yarns in their own cottages, and supplemented the earnings of their husbands." The spinning wheel, he believed, was "presented to the nation for giving occupation to the millions who had, at least four months of the year, nothing to do." Not only would a return to the spinning wheel provide employment to millions of Indians, it would also become a symbol of "national consciousness and a contribution by every individual to a definite constructive national work."

Nevertheless, Gandhi was a shrewd politician who understood the usefulness of modern devices for mobilizing the masses and organizing his followers. He wore a watch and used the telephone and the printing press to keep in touch with his followers. When he traveled by train, he rode third class—but in a third-class railroad car of his own. His goal was the independence of his country, and he pursued it with every nonviolent means he could find.

Gandhi's ideas challenge us to rethink the purpose of technology. Was he opposed on principle to all modern devices? Was he an opportunist who used those devices that served his political ends and rejected those that did not? Or did he have a higher principle that accounts for his willingness to use the telephone and the railroad but not factory-made cloth?

*Source:* Quotations from Louis Fischer, *Gandhi: His Life and Message for the World* (New York: New American Library, 1954), 82–83.

**Gandhi at the Spinning Wheel**  Mahatma Gandhi chose the spinning wheel as his symbol because it represented the traditional activity of millions of rural Indians whose livelihoods were threatened by industrialization.  (Margaret Bourke-White, *LIFE Magazine* © Time Warner Inc.)

India" campaign aroused popular demonstrations against the British and provoked a wave of arrests, including his own. Nehru remarked: "I would fight Japan sword in hand, but I can only do so as a free man."

The Second World War divided the Indian people. Most Indian soldiers felt they were fighting to defend their country rather than to support the British Empire. As in World War I, Indians contributed heavily to the Allied war effort, supplying 2 million soldiers and enormous amounts of resources, especially the timber needed for emergency construction. A small number of Indians, however, were so anti-British that they joined the Japanese side.

India's subordination to British interests was vividly demonstrated in the famine of 1943 in Bengal. Unlike previous famines, this one was caused not by drought but by the Japanese conquest of Burma, which cut off supplies of Burmese rice that normally went to Bengal. Although food was available elsewhere in India, the British army had requisitioned the railroads to transport troops and equipment in preparation for a Japanese invasion. As a result, supplies ran short in Bengal and surrounding areas, while speculators hoarded whatever they could find. Some 2 million people starved to death before the army was ordered to supply food.

| Partition and Independence | When the war ended, Britain's new Labour Party government prepared for |

**Partition and Independence**   When the war ended, Britain's new Labour Party government prepared for Indian independence, but deep suspicions between Hindus and Muslims complicated the process. The break between the two communities had started in 1937, when the Indian National Congress won provincial elections and refused to share power with the Muslim League. In 1940 the leader of the League, **Muhammad Ali Jinnah°** (1876–1948), demanded what many Muslims had been dreaming of for years: a country of their own, to be called Pakistan (from "Punjab-Afghans-Kashmir-Sind" plus the Persian suffix -*stan* meaning "kingdom").

As independence approached, talks between Jinnah and Nehru broke down and battle lines were drawn. Violent rioting between Hindus and

**Jinnah** (jee-NAH)

Muslims broke out in Bengal and Bihar. Gandhi's appeals for tolerance and cooperation fell on deaf ears. In despair, he retreated to his home near Ahmedabad. The British made frantic proposals to keep India united, but their authority was waning fast.

By early 1947 the Indian National Congress had accepted the idea of a partition of India into two states, one secular but dominated by Hindus, the other Muslim. In June Lord Mountbatten, the last viceroy, decided that independence must come immediately. On August 15 British India gave way to a new India and Pakistan. The Indian National Congress, led by Nehru, formed the first government of India; Jinnah and the Muslim League established a government for the provinces that made up Pakistan.

The rejoicing over independence was marred by violent outbreaks between Muslims and Hindus. In protest against the mounting chaos, Gandhi refused to attend the independence day celebration. Throughout the land, Muslim and Hindu neighbors turned on one another, and armed members of one faith hunted down people of the other faith. For centuries Hindus and Muslims had intermingled throughout most of India. Now, leaving most of their possessions behind, Hindus fled from predominantly Muslim areas, and Muslims fled from Hindu areas. Trainloads of desperate refugees of one faith were attacked and massacred by members of the other or were left stranded in the middle of deserts. Within a few months some 12 million people had abandoned their ancestral homes and a half-million lay dead. In January 1948 Gandhi died too, gunned down by an angry Hindu refugee.

After the sectarian massacres and flights of refugees, few Hindus remained in Pakistan, and Muslims were a minority in all but one state of India. That state was Kashmir, a strategically important region in the foothills of the Himalayas. India annexed Kashmir because the local maharajah was Hindu and because the state held the headwaters of the rivers that irrigated millions of acres of farmland in the northwestern part of the subcontinent. The majority of the inhabitants of Kashmir were Muslims, however, and would probably have joined Pakistan if they had been allowed to vote on the matter. The consequence of the partition and of Kashmir in particular was to turn India and Pakistan

**The Partition of India**   When India became independent, Muslims fled from Hindu regions, and Hindus fled from Muslims. Margaret Bourke-White photographed a long line of refugees, with their cows, carts, and belongings, trudging down a country road toward safety.   (Time Life Pictures/Getty Images)

into bitter enemies that have fought several wars in the past half-century.

# THE MEXICAN REVOLUTION, 1910–1940

In the nineteenth century Latin America achieved independence from Spain and Portugal but did not industrialize. Throughout much of the century most Latin American republics suffered from ideological divisions, unstable governments, and violent upheavals. By trading their raw materials and agricultural products for foreign manufactured goods and capital investments, they became economically dependent on the wealthier countries to the north, especially on the United States and Great Britain. Their societies, far from fulfilling the promises of their independence, remained deeply split between wealthy landowners and desperately poor peasants.

Mexico, Brazil, and Argentina contained well over half of Latin America's land, population, and wealth, and their relations with other countries and their economies were quite similar. Mexico, however, underwent a traumatic social revolution, while Argentina and Brazil evolved more peaceably.

**Mexico in 1910**   Few countries in Latin America suffered as many foreign invasions and interventions as Mexico. A Mexican saying observed wryly: "Poor Mexico: so far from God, so close to the United States." In Mexico the chasm between rich and poor was so deep that only a revolution could move the country toward prosperity and democracy.

Mexico was the Latin American country most influenced by the Spanish during three centuries of colonial rule. After independence in 1821 it suffered from a half-century of political turmoil. At the beginning of the twentieth century Mexican society was divided into rich and poor and into persons of Spanish, Indian, and mixed ancestry. A few very wealthy families of Spanish origin, less than 1 percent of the population, owned 85 percent of Mexico's land, mostly in huge *haciendas* (estates). Closely tied to this elite were the handful of American and British companies that controlled most of Mexico's railroads, silver mines, plantations, and other productive enterprises. At the other end of the social scale were Indians, many of whom did not speak Spanish. *Mestizos*°, people of mixed Indian and European ancestry, were only slightly better off; most of them were peasants who worked on the haciendas or farmed small communal plots near their ancestral villages.

The urban middle class was small and had little political influence. Few professional and government positions were open to them, and foreigners owned most businesses. Industrial workers also were few in number; the only significant groups were textile workers in the port of Veracruz on the Gulf of Mexico and railroad workers spread throughout the country.

During the colonial period, the Spanish government had made halfhearted efforts to defend Indians and mestizos from the land-grabbing tactics of the haciendas. After independence in 1821 wealthy Mexican families and American companies used bribery and force to acquire millions of acres of good agricultural land from villages in southern Mexico. Peasants lost not only their fields but also their access to firewood and pasture for their animals. Sugar, cotton, and other commercial crops replaced corn and beans, and peasants had little choice but to work on haciendas. To survive, they had to buy food and other necessities on credit from the landowner's store; eventually, they fell permanently into debt. Sometimes whole communities were forced to relocate.

In the 1880s American investors purchased from the Mexican government dubious claims to more than 2.5 million acres (1 million hectares) traditionally held by the Yaqui people of Sonora, in northern Mexico. When the Yaqui resisted the expropriation of their lands, they were brutally repressed by the Mexican army.

Northern Mexicans had no peasant tradition of communal ownership, for the northern half of

the country was too dry for farming, unlike the tropical and densely populated south. The north was a region of silver mines and cattle ranches, some of them enormous. It was thinly populated by cowboys and miners. The harshness of their lives and the vast inequities in the distribution of income made northern Mexicans as resentful as people in the south.

Despite many upheavals in Mexico in the nineteenth century, in 1910 the government seemed in control. For thirty-four years General Porfirio Díaz° (1830–1915) had ruled Mexico under the motto "Liberty, Order, Progress." To Díaz "liberty" meant freedom for rich hacienda owners and foreign investors to acquire more land. The government imposed "order" through rigged elections and a policy of *pan o palo* (bread or the stick)—that is, bribes for Díaz's supporters and summary justice for those who opposed him. "Progress" meant mainly the importing of foreign capital, machinery, and technicians to take advantage of Mexico's labor, soil, and natural resources.

During the Díaz years (1876–1910) Mexico City—with paved streets, streetcar lines, electric street lighting, and public parks—became a showplace, and new telegraph and railroad lines connected cities and towns throughout Mexico. But this material progress benefited only a handful of well-connected businessmen. The boom in railroads, agriculture, and mining at the turn of the century actually caused a decline in the average Mexican's standard of living.

Though a mestizo himself, Díaz discriminated against the nonwhite majority of Mexicans. He and his supporters tried to eradicate what they saw as Mexico's embarrassingly rustic traditions. On many middle- and upper-class tables French cuisine replaced traditional Mexican dishes. The wealthy replaced sombreros and ponchos with European garments. Though bullfighting and cockfighting remained popular, the well-to-do preferred horse racing and soccer. To the educated middle class—the only group with a strong sense of Mexican nationhood—this devaluation of Mexican culture became a symbol of the Díaz regime's failure to defend national interests against foreign influences.

*mestizo* (mess-TEE-zoh)

**Díaz** (DEE-as)

## Revolution and Civil War, 1911–1920

Many Mexicans feared or anticipated a popular uprising after Díaz. Unlike the independence movement in India, the Mexican Revolution was not the work of one party with a well-defined ideology. Instead, it developed haphazardly, led by a series of ambitious but limited leaders, each representing a different segment of Mexican society.

The first was Francisco I. Madero (1873–1913), the son of a wealthy landowning and mining family, educated in the United States. When minor uprisings broke out in 1911, the government collapsed and Díaz fled into exile. The Madero presidency was welcomed by some, but it aroused opposition from peasant leaders like **Emiliano Zapata** (1879–1919). In 1913, after two years as president, Madero was overthrown and murdered by one of his former supporters, General Victoriano Huerta. Woodrow Wilson (1856–1924), president of the United States, showed his displeasure by sending the United States Marines to occupy Veracruz.

The inequities of Mexican society and foreign intervention in Mexico's affairs angered Mexico's middle class and industrial workers. They found leaders in Venustiano Carranza, a landowner, and in Alvaro Obregón°, a schoolteacher. Calling themselves Constitutionalists, Carranza and Obregón organized private armies and succeeded in overthrowing Huerta in 1914. By then, the revolution had spread to the countryside.

As early as 1911 Zapata, an Indian farmer, had led a revolt against the haciendas in the mountains of Morelos, south of Mexico City (see Map 27.1). His soldiers were peasants, some of them women, mounted on horseback and armed with pistols and rifles. For several years they periodically came down from the mountains, burned hacienda buildings, and returned land to the Indian villages to which it had once belonged.

Another leader appeared in Chihuahua, a northern state where seventeen individuals owned two-fifths of the land and 95 percent of the people had no land at all. Starting in 1913 **Francisco "Pancho" Villa** (ca. 1877–1923), a former ranch hand, mule driver, and bandit, organized an army of three thousand men, most of them cowboys. They

too seized land from the large haciendas, not to rebuild traditional communities as in southern Mexico but to create family ranches.

Zapata and Villa were part agrarian rebels, part social revolutionaries. They enjoyed tremendous popular support but could never rise above their regional and peasant origins and lead a national revolution. The Constitutionalists had fewer soldiers than Zapata and Villa; but they held the major cities, controlled the country's exports of oil, and used the proceeds of oil sales to buy modern weapons. Fighting continued for years, and gradually the Constitutionalists took over most of Mexico. In 1919 they defeated and killed Zapata; Villa was assassinated four years later. An estimated 2 million people lost their lives in the civil war, and much of Mexico lay in ruins.

During their struggle to win support against Zapata and Villa, the Constitutionalists adopted many of their rivals' agrarian reforms, such as restoring communal lands to the Indians of Morelos. The Constitutionalists also proposed social programs designed to appeal to workers and the middle class. The Constitution of 1917 promised universal suffrage and a one-term presidency; state-run education to free the poor from the hold of the Catholic Church; the end of debt peonage; restrictions on foreign ownership of property; and laws specifying minimum wages and maximum hours to protect laborers. Although these reforms were too costly to implement right away, they had important symbolic significance, for they enshrined the dignity of Mexicans and the equality of Indians, mestizos, and whites, as well as of peasants and city people.

## The Revolution Institutionalized, 1920–1940

In the early 1920s, after a decade of violence that exhausted all classes, the Mexican Revolution lost momentum. Only in Morelos did peasants receive land, and President Obregón and his closest associates made all the important decisions. Nevertheless, the Revolution changed the social makeup of the governing class. For the first time in Mexico's history, representatives of rural communities, unionized workers, and public employees were admitted to the inner circle.

**Obregón** (oh-bray-GAWN)

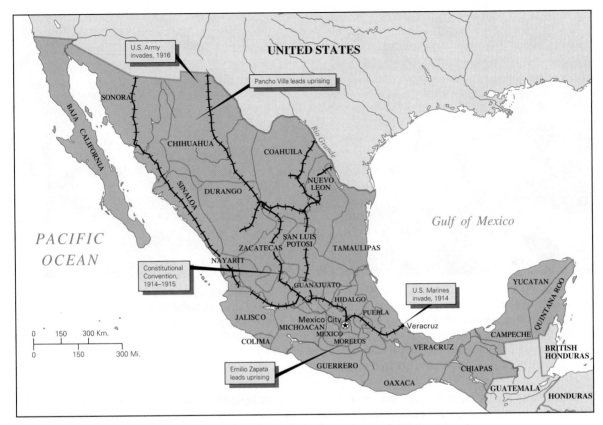

**Map 27.1   The Mexican Revolution**   The Mexican Revolution began in two distinct regions of the country. One was the mountainous and densely populated area south of Mexico City, particularly Morelos, homeland of Emiliano Zapata. The other was the dry and thinly populated ranch country of the north, such as Chihuahua, home of Pancho Villa. The fighting that ensued crisscrossed the country along the main railroad lines, shown on the map.

In the arts the Mexican Revolution sparked a surge of creativity. The political murals of José Clemente Orozco and Diego Rivera and the paintings of Frida Kahlo focused on social themes, showing peasants, workers, and soldiers in scenes from the Revolution.

In 1928 Obregón was assassinated. His successor, Plutarco Elías Calles°, founded the National Revolutionary Party, or PNR (the abbreviation of its name in Spanish). The PNR was a forum where all the pressure groups and vested interests—labor, peasants, businessmen, landowners, the military, and others—worked out compromises. The estab-

lishment of the PNR gave the Mexican Revolution a second wind.

**Lázaro Cárdenas°,** chosen by Calles to be president in 1934, brought peasants' and workers' organizations into the party, renamed it the Mexican Revolutionary Party (PRM), and removed the generals from government positions. Then he set to work implementing the reforms promised in the Constitution of 1917. Cárdenas redistributed 44 million acres (17.6 million hectares) to peasant communes. He closed church-run schools, replacing them with government schools. He nationalized the railroads and numerous other businesses.

**Calles** (KAH-yace)

**Lázaro Cárdenas** (LAH-sah-roe KAHR-dih-nahs)

***The Agitator*, a Mural by Diegas Rivera**   Diego Rivera (1886–1957) was politically committed to the Mexican Revolution and widely admired as an artist. This mural, painted at the National Agricultural School at Chapingo near Mexico City, shows a political agitator addressing peasants and workers. With one hand, the speaker points to miners laboring in a silver mine; with the other, to a hammer and sickle.   (Universidad Autonoma de Chapingo/ CENIDIAP-INBA)

Cárdenas's most dramatic move was the expropriation of foreign-owned oil companies. In the early 1920s Mexico was the world's leading producer of oil, but a handful of American and British companies exported almost all of it. In 1938 Cárdenas seized the foreign-owned oil industry, more as a matter of national pride than of economics. The oil companies expected the governments of the United States and Great Britain to come to their rescue, perhaps with military force. But Mexico and the United States chose to resolve the issue through negotiation, and Mexico retained control of its oil industry.

When Cárdenas's term ended in 1940, Mexico, like India, was still a land of poor farmers with a small industrial base. The Revolution had brought great changes, however. The political system was free of both chaos and dictatorships. A small group of wealthy people no longer monopolized land and other resources. The military was tamed; the Catholic Church no longer controlled education; and the nationalization of oil had demonstrated Mexico's independence from foreign corporations and military intervention.

The Mexican Revolution did not fulfill the democratic promise of Madero's campaign, for it brought to power a party that monopolized the government for eighty years. However, it allowed far more sectors of the population to participate in politics and made sure no president stayed in office more than six years. The Revolution also promised far-reaching social reforms, such as free education, higher wages and more security for workers, and the redistribution of land to the peasants. These long-delayed reforms began to be implemented during the Cárdenas administration. They fell short of the ideals expressed by the revolutionaries, but they laid the foundation for the later industrialization of Mexico.

# ARGENTINA AND BRAZIL, 1900–1949

On the surface, Argentina and Brazil seem very different. Argentina is Spanish-speaking, temperate in climate, and populated almost exclusively by people of European origin. Brazil is tropical and Portuguese-speaking, and its inhabitants are of mixed European and African origin, with a substantial Indian minority. Yet in the twentieth century their economic, political, and technological experiences were remarkably similar.

## The Transformation of Argentina

Most of Argentina consists of *pampas*°, flat, fertile land that is easy to till, much like the prairies of the midwestern United States and Canada. Throughout the nineteenth century Argentina's economy was based on two exports: the hides of longhorn creole cattle and the wool of merino sheep, which roamed the pampas in huge herds. Centuries earlier, Europeans had haphazardly introduced the animals and the grasses they ate. Natural selection had made the animals tough and hardy.

At the end of the nineteenth century railroads and refrigerator ships, which allowed the safe transportation of meat, changed not only the composition of Argentina's exports but also the way they were produced—in other words, the land itself. European consumers preferred the soft flesh of Lincoln sheep and Hereford cattle to the tough, sinewy meat of creole cattle and merino sheep. However, the valuable Lincolns and Herefords could not be allowed to roam and graze on the pampas; they were carefully bred and received a diet of alfalfa and oats. To safeguard them, the pampas had to be divided, plowed, cultivated, and fenced with barbed wire to keep out predators and other unwelcome animals. Once fenced, the land could be used to produce wheat as well as beef and mutton. Within a few years grasslands that had stretched to the horizon were transformed into farmland. Like the North American Midwest, the pampas became one of the world's great producers of wheat and meat.

Argentina's government represented the interests of the *oligarquía*°, a very small group of wealthy landowners. Members of this elite controlled enormous haciendas where they raised cattle and sheep and grew wheat for export. They also owned fine homes in Buenos Aires°, a city that was built to look like Paris. They traveled frequently to Europe and spent so lavishly that the French coined the superlative "rich as an Argentine." They showed little interest in any business other than farming, however, and were content to let foreign companies, mainly British, build Argentina's railroads, processing plants, and public utilities. In exchange for its agricultural exports Argentina imported almost all its manufactured goods from Europe and the United States. So important were British interests in the Argentinean economy that English, not Spanish, was used on the railroads, and the biggest department store in Buenos Aires was a branch of Harrods of London.

## Brazil and Argentina, to 1929

Before the First World War Brazil produced most of the world's coffee and cacao, grown on vast estates, and natural rubber, gathered by Indians from rubber trees growing wild in the Amazon rain forest. Brazil's elite was made up of coffee and cacao planters and rubber exporters. Like their Argentinean counterparts, they spent their money lavishly, building palaces in Rio de Janeiro° and one of the world's most beautiful opera houses in Manaus°, deep in the Amazon. They had little interest in other forms of development; let British companies build railroads, harbors, and other infrastructure; and imported most manufactured goods. At the time this seemed to allow each country to do what it did best. If the British did not grow coffee, why should Brazil build locomotives?

Both Argentina and Brazil had small but outspoken middle classes that demanded a share in government and looked to Europe as a model. Beneath each middle class were the poor. In Argentina these were mainly Spanish and Italian immigrants who had ended up as landless farm laborers or workers in urban packing plants. In Brazil there was a large class of sharecroppers and plantation workers, many of them descendants of slaves.

Rubber exports collapsed after 1912, replaced by cheaper plantation rubber from Southeast Asia. The outbreak of war in 1914 put an end to imports from Europe as Britain and France focused all their

---

*pampas* (POM-pus)     *oligarquía* (oh-lee-gar-KEE-ah)
**Buenos Aires** (BWAY-nihs AIR-eze)

**Rio de Janeiro** (REE-oh day zhuh-NAIR-oh)
**Manaus** (meh-NOWSE)

industries on war production and Germany was cut off entirely. The disruption of the old trade patterns weakened the landowning class. In Argentina the urban middle class obtained the secret ballot and universal male suffrage in 1916 and elected a liberal politician, **Hipólito Irigoyen°**, as president. To a certain extent, the United States replaced the European countries as suppliers of machinery and consumers of coffee. European immigrants built factories to manufacture textiles and household goods. Desperate for money to pay for the war, Great Britain sold many of its railroad, streetcar, and other companies to the governments of Argentina and Brazil.

In contrast to Mexico, the postwar years were a period of prosperity in South America. Trade with Europe resumed; prices for agricultural exports remained high; and both Argentina and Brazil used profits accumulated during the war to industrialize and improve their transportation systems and public utilities. Yet it was also a time of social turmoil, as workers and middle-class professionals demanded social reforms and a larger voice in politics. In Argentina students' and workers' demonstrations were brutally crushed. In Brazil junior officers rose up several times against the government, calling for universal suffrage, social reforms, and freedom for labor unions. Though they accomplished little, they laid the groundwork for later reformist movements. In neither country did the urban middle class take power away from the wealthy landowners. Instead, the two classes shared power at the expense of both the landless peasants and the urban workers.

Yet as Argentina and Brazil were moving forward, new technologies again left them dependent on the advanced industrial countries. Brazilians are justly proud that the first person to fly an airplane outside the United States was Alberto Santos-Dumont, a Brazilian. He did so in 1906 in France, where he lived most of his life and had access to engine manufacturers and technical assistance. Aviation reached Latin America after World War I, when European and American companies such as Aéropostale and Pan American Airways introduced airmail service between cities and linked Latin America with the United States and Europe.

Before and during World War I radio, then called "wireless telegraphy," was used not for broadcasting but for point-to-point communications. Transmitters powerful enough to send messages across oceans or continents were extraordinarily complex and expensive: their antennas covered many acres; they used as much electricity as a small town; and they cost tens of thousands of pounds sterling (millions of dollars in today's money).

Right after the war, the major powers scrambled to build powerful transmitters on every continent to compete with the telegraph cable companies and to take advantage of the boom in international business and news reporting. At the time, no Latin American country possessed the knowledge or funds to build its own transmitters. In 1919, therefore, President Irigoyen of Argentina granted a radio concession to a German firm. France and Britain protested this decision, and eventually four powerful radio companies—one British, one French, one German, and one American—formed a cartel to control all radio communications in Latin America. This cartel set up a national radio company in each Latin American republic, installing a prominent local politician as its president, but the cartel held all the stock and therefore received all the profits. Thus, even as Brazil and Argentina were taking over their railroads and older industries, the major industrial countries controlled the diffusion of the newer aviation and radio technologies.

## The Depression and the Vargas Regime in Brazil

The Depression hit Latin America as hard as it hit Europe and the United States; in many ways, it marks a more important turning point for the region than either of the world wars. As long-term customers cut back their orders, the value of agricultural and mineral exports fell by two-thirds between 1929 and 1932. Argentina and Brazil could no longer afford to import manufactured goods. An imploding economy also undermined their shaky political systems. Like European countries, Argentina and Brazil veered toward authoritarian regimes that promised to solve their economic problems.

In 1930 **Getulio Vargas°** (1883–1954), a state governor, staged a coup and proclaimed himself president of Brazil. He proved to be a masterful

---

**Hipólito Irigoyen** (ee-POH-lee-toe ee-ree-GO-yen)

**Getulio Vargas** (jay-TOO-lee-oh VAR-gus)

politician. He wrote a new constitution that broadened the franchise and limited the president to one term. He raised import duties and promoted national firms and state-owned enterprises, culminating in the construction of the Volta Redonda steel mill in the 1930s. By 1936 industrial production had doubled, especially in textiles and small manufactures. Under his guidance, Brazil was on its way to becoming an industrial country. Vargas's policy, called **import-substitution industrialization,** became a model for other Latin American countries as they attempted to break away from neocolonial dependency.

The industrialization of Brazil brought all the familiar environmental consequences. Powerful new machines allowed the reopening of old mines and the digging of new ones. Cities grew as poor peasants looking for work arrived from the countryside. Around the older neighborhoods of Rio de Janeiro and São Paulo°, the poor turned steep hillsides and vacant lands into immense *favelas°* (slums) of makeshift shacks.

The countryside also was transformed. Scrubland was turned into pasture, and new acreage was planted in wheat, corn, and sugar cane. Even the Amazon rain forest—half of the land area of Brazil—was affected. In 1930 American industrialist Henry Ford invested $8 million to clear land along the Tapajós River and prepare it to become the site of the world's largest rubber plantation. Ford encountered opposition from Brazilian workers and politicians; the rubber trees proved vulnerable to diseases; and he had to abandon the project—but not before leaving 3 million acres (1.2 million hectares) denuded of trees. The ecological changes of the Vargas era, however, were but a tiny forerunner of the degradation of the Brazilian environment that was to take place later in the century.

Vargas instituted many reforms favorable to urban workers, such as labor unions, pension plans, and disability insurance, but he refused to take any measures that might help the millions of landless peasants or harm the interests of the great landowners. Although the Brazilian economy recovered from the Depression, the benefits of recovery were so unequally distributed that communist and fascist movements demanded even more radical changes.

In 1938, prohibited by his own constitution from being reelected, Vargas staged another coup, abolished the constitution, and instituted the Estado Novo°, or "New State," with himself as supreme leader. He abolished political parties, jailed opposition leaders, and turned Brazil into a fascist state. When the Second World War broke out, however, Vargas aligned Brazil with the United States and contributed troops and ships to the Allied war effort.

Despite his economic achievements, Vargas harmed Brazil. By running roughshod over laws, constitutions, and rights, he infected not only Brazil but all of South America with the temptations of political violence. It is ironic, but not surprising, that Vargas was overthrown in 1945 by a military coup.

## Argentina After 1930

Economically, the Depression hurt Argentina almost as badly as it hurt Brazil. Politically, however, the consequences were delayed for many years. In 1930 General José Uriburu° overthrew the popularly elected President Irigoyen. The Uriburu government represented the large landowners and big business interests. For thirteen years the generals and the oligarquía ruled, doing nothing to lessen the poverty of the workers or the frustrations of the middle class. When World War II broke out, Argentina sympathized with the Axis but remained officially neutral.

In 1943 another military revolt flared, this one among junior officers angry at conservative politicians. It was led by Colonel **Juan Perón°** (1895–1974). The intentions of the rebels were clear:

> Civilians will never understand the greatness of our ideal; we shall therefore have to eliminate them from the government and give them the only mission which corresponds to them: work and obedience.[1]

Once in power the officers took over the highest positions in government and business and began to lavish money on military equipment and their own salaries. Their goal, inspired by Nazi victories, was nothing less than the conquest of South America.

As the war turned against the Nazis, the officers

---

**São Paulo** (sow PAL-oh)    *favela* (feh-VEL-luh)

**Estado Novo** (esh-TAH-doe NO-vo)    **José Uriburu** (hoe-SAY oo-ree-BOO-roo)    **Juan Perón** (hoo-AHN pair-OWN) saw their popularity collapse. Perón, however, had other plans. Inspired by his charismatic wife **Eva Duarte Perón°** (1919–1952), he appealed to the urban workers. Eva Perón became the champion of the *descamisados°*, or "shirtless ones," and campaigned tirelessly for social benefits and for the cause of women and children. With his wife's help, Perón won the presidency in 1946 and created a populist dictatorship in imitation of the Vargas regime in Brazil.

Like Brazil, Argentina industrialized rapidly under state sponsorship. Perón spent lavishly on social welfare projects as well as on the military, depleting the capital that Argentina had earned during the war. Though a skillful demagogue who played off the army against the navy and both against the labor unions, Perón could not create a stable government out of the chaos of coups and conspiracies. He had to back down from a plan to make Eva his vice president. When she died in 1952, he lost his political skills (or perhaps they were hers), and soon thereafter he was overthrown in yet another military coup.

### Mexico, Argentina, and Brazil: A Comparison

Until 1910 Mexico, Argentina, and Brazil shared a common history and similar cultures. In the first half of the twentieth century their economies followed parallel trajectories, based on unequal relations with the industrialized countries of Europe and North America. All three countries—indeed, all of Latin America—struggled with the failure of neocolonial economics to improve the lives of the middle class, let alone the peasants. And when the Depression hit, all three turned to state intervention and import-substitution industrialization. Like all industrializing countries, they did so by mining, farming, ranching, cutting down forests, and irrigating land, all at the expense of the natural environment.

Yet their political histories diverged radically. Mexico underwent a traumatic and profound social revolution. Argentina and Brazil, meanwhile, languished under conservative regimes devoted to the interests of wealthy landowners, sporadically interrupted by military coups and populist dema-

gogues. Mexicans, thanks to their experience of revolution, developed an acute sense of their national identity and civic pride in their history—pride largely missing in South America. Despite shortcomings, Mexico seriously committed itself to education, land reform, social justice, and political stability as national goals, not merely as the campaign platform of a populist dictator.

## CONCLUSION

Sub-Saharan Africa, India, and Latin America lay outside the theaters of war that engulfed most of the Northern Hemisphere, but they were deeply affected by global events and by the demands of the industrial powers. Sub-Saharan Africa and India were still under colonial rule, and their political life revolved around the yearnings of their elites for political independence and their masses for social justice. Mexico, Argentina, and Brazil were politically independent, but their economies, like those of Africa and India, were closely tied to the economies of the industrial nations with which they traded. Their deeply polarized societies and the stresses caused by their dependence on the industrial countries clashed with the expectations of ever-larger numbers of their peoples.

In Mexico these stresses brought about a long and violent revolution, out of which Mexicans forged a lasting sense of national identity. Argentina and Brazil moved toward greater economic independence, but the price was social unrest, militarism, and dictatorship. In India the conflict between growing expectations and the reality of colonial rule produced both a movement for independence and an ethnic split that tore the nation apart. In sub-Saharan Africa demands for national self-determination and economic development were only beginning to be voiced by 1949 and did not come to fruition until the second half of the century.

Nationalism and the yearning for social justice were the two most powerful forces for change in the early twentieth century. These ideas originated in the industrialized countries but resonated in the independent countries of Latin America as well as in colonial regions such as the Indian subcontinent and sub-Saharan Africa. However, they did

**Eva Duarte Perón** (AY-vuy doo-AR-tay pair-OWN)
*descamisados* (des-cah-mee-SAH-dohs)

not always unite people against their colonial rulers or foreign oppressors; instead, they often divided them along social, ethnic, or religious lines. Western-educated elites looked to industrialization as a means of modernizing their country and ensuring their position in it, while peasants and urban workers supported nationalist and revolutionary movements in the hope of improving their lives. Often these goals were not compatible.

## ■ Key Terms

Blaise Diagne
African National Congress
Haile Selassie
Indian National Congress
Bengal
All-India Muslim League
Mohandas K. (Mahatma) Gandhi
Jawaharlal Nehru
Muhammad Ali Jinnah
Emiliano Zapata
Francisco "Pancho" Villa
Lázaro Cárdenas
Hipólito Irigoyen
Getulio Vargas
import-substitution industrialization
Juan Perón
Eva Duarte Perón

## ■ Suggested Reading

On Africa under colonial rule the classic overview is Melville Herskovits, *The Human Factor in Changing Africa* (1958). Two excellent general introductions are Roland Oliver and Anthony Atmore, *Africa Since 1800*, 4th ed. (1994), and A. E. Afigbo et al., *The Making of Modern Africa*, vol. 2, *The Twentieth Century* (1986). More detailed and challenging are *UNESCO General History of Africa*, vols. 7 and 8; *The Cambridge History of Africa*, vols. 7 and 8; and Adu Boahen, *African Perspectives on Colonialism* (1987). Outstanding novels about Africa in the colonial era include Chinua Achebe, *Arrow of God* (1964); Buchi Emecheta, *The Joys of Motherhood* (1980); and Peter Abraham, *Mine Boy* (1946).

For a general introduction to Indian history, see Sumit Sarkar, *Modern India, 1885–1947* (1983), and Percival Spear, *India: A Modern History*, rev. ed. (1972). On the in-

fluenza epidemic of 1918–1919 see Alfred W. Crosby, *America's Forgotten Pandemic: The Influenza of 1918* (1989). The Indian independence movement has received a great deal of attention. Judith M. Brown's most recent book on Gandhi is *Gandhi: Prisoner of Hope* (1989). *Gandhi's Truth: On the Origin of Militant Nonviolence* (1969) by noted psychoanalyst Erik Erikson is also recommended. Two collections of memoirs of the last decades of British rule are worth looking at: Charles Allen, ed., *Plain Tales of the Raj: Image of British India in the Twentieth Century* (1975), and Zareer Masani, ed., *Indian Tales of the Raj* (1988). The transition from colonialism to partition and independence is the subject of the very readable *Freedom at Midnight* (1975) by Larry Collins and Dominique Lapierre. The environment is discussed in M. Gadgil and R. Guha, *This Fissured Land: An Ecological History of India* (1993).

Thomas Skidmore and Peter Smith, *Modern Latin America*, 3d ed. (1992), offers the best brief introduction. Two fine general overviews of modern Mexican history are Enrique Krauze, *Mexico: Biography of Power: A History of Modern Mexico, 1810–1996* (1997), and Colin MacLachlan and William Beezley, *El Gran Pueblo: A History of Greater Mexico* (1994). On the Mexican Revolution, two recent books are essential: Alan Knight, *The Mexican Revolution*, 2 vols. (1986), and John M. Hart, *Revolutionary Mexico: The Coming and Process of the Mexican Revolution* (1987). But see also two classics by sympathetic Americans: Frank Tannenbaum, *Peace by Revolution: Mexico After 1910* (1933), and Robert E. Quirk, *The Mexican Revolution, 1914–1915* (1960). Mexico's most celebrated revolutionary is the subject of Manuel Machado, *Centaur of the North: Francisco Villa, the Mexican Revolution, and Northern Mexico* (1988). Mariano Azuela, *The Underdogs* (1988), is an interesting fictional account of this period. The standard work on Brazil is E. Bradford Burns, *A History of Brazil*, 3d ed. (1993). On the environmental history of Brazil, see Warren Dean, *Brazil and the Struggle for Rubber: A Study in Environmental History* (1987). The history of modern Argentina is ably treated in David Rock, *Argentina, 1517–1987: From Spanish Colonization to Alfonsín* (1987). Mark Jefferson, *Peopling the Argentine Pampas* (1971), and Jeremy Adelman, *Frontier Development: Land, Labour and Capital on the Wheatlands of Argentina and Canada, 1890–1914* (1994), describe the transformation of the Argentinean environment.

## ■ Notes

1. George Blanksten, *Perón's Argentina* (Chicago: University of Chicago Press, 1953), 37.

# Famines and Politics

Nature is never reliable, and all living things periodically suffer from a catastrophic drop in food supplies. Human history is filled with tales of famines—times when crops failed, food supplies ran out, and people starved.

**Natural famines** India, dependent on the monsoon rains, has been particularly prone to such calamities, with famines striking two to four times a century, whenever the rains failed for several years in succession. Three times in the eighteenth century (1702–1704, 1769–1770, and 1790–1792) famines killed several million people in different parts of the subcontinent. The nineteenth century was worse, with famines in 1803–1804, 1837–1838, 1868–1870, and 1876–1878. The latter also afflicted northern China, causing between 9 and 13 million deaths from hunger and from the diseases of malnutrition. There were even incidents of cannibalism, as starving adults killed and ate starving children.

When a drought hit a region, it decimated not only the human population but also the animals they relied on to transport goods and plow the land. Likewise, droughts lowered the water levels in rivers and canals, so food could not be moved from one place to another.

**Commercial famines** That all changed in the nineteenth century. Railroads and steamships could transport foodstuffs across great distances in a matter of days or weeks, regardless of drought or heavy rains. Great Britain became dependent on imports of wheat from Russia and the American Midwest, and later of beef from Argentina. Yet famines were worse than ever, and the global death toll from starvation has been far higher since the mid-nineteenth century than it ever was in earlier times. Why?

Consider the Irish famine of 1845–1848. By the early nineteenth century the potato had become the main source of nutrition for the Irish people. Potatoes grew abundantly in the cool, moist climate of Ireland and produced more calories per acre than any other crop. Most of the Irish were poor tenant farmers, and potatoes had allowed their population to increase far more than wheat or rye could have.

In fall 1845 the blight turned the potatoes in the fields black, mushy, and inedible. The harvest was ruined the following year as well. It recovered slightly in 1847, but was bad again in 1848. Tens of thousands died of starvation, while hundreds of thousands died from the diseases that strike malnourished people, especially dysentery, typhus, and cholera. Travelers saw corpses rotting in their hovels or on the sides of roads. Altogether, a million or more people died, while another million managed to emigrate, reducing the population of Ireland by half.

Throughout those years, wheat grew in Ireland, but much of it was exported to England, where customers had money to pay for it. Like any other commodity, food cost money. The Irish farmers, poor even before the famines, were destitute and could not afford to buy the wheat. The British government, wedded to the ideology of laissez-faire, was convinced that interfering with the free market would only make things worse. Relief efforts were half-hearted at best; the official responsible for Irish affairs preferred to leave the situation to "the operation of natural causes."

The same held true in India, like Ireland a colony of Great Britain. The drought of 1876–1878 killed over 5 million Indians in the Deccan region, while British officials were helpless or indifferent. Part of the problem was transportation. In the 1870s only a few railway lines connected major cities. Most goods were still transported in bullock carts, but the bullocks also starved during the drought. Another obstacle was political. The idea that a government should be responsible for feeding the population was unthinkable at the time. And so, while millions were starving in the Deccan, the Punjab region was exporting wheat to Britain.

Over the next twenty years so-called famine railways were built in the regions historically most affected by the failures of the monsoon. When drought struck again at the end of the century, the railways were ready to transport food to areas that had previously been accessible only by bullock carts. However, the inhabitants of the affected regions had no money with which to buy what little food there was, and the government was still reluctant to interfere with free enterprise. Grain merchants bought all the stocks, hoarded them until the price rose, then used the railways to transport them out of the famine regions to regions where the harvests were better and people had more money.

In the twentieth century commercial famines have become rare, as governments have come to realize that they have a responsibility for food supplies not only for their own people, but for people in other countries as well. Yet commercial famines have not entirely disappeared. In 1974, when a catastrophic flood covered half of Bangladesh, the government was too disorganized to distribute its stocks of rice, while merchants bought what they could and exported it to India. Thousands died, and thousands more survived only because of belated shipments of food from donor countries.

**Political famines**   To say that governments are responsible for food supplies does not mean that they exercise that responsibility for the good of the people. Some do, but in many instances food is used as a weapon. In the twentieth century global food supplies were always adequate for the population of the world, and transportation was seldom a problem. Yet the century witnessed the most murderous famines ever recorded.

War-induced famines were not new. In 1812, as the Russian army retreated, it practiced a "scorched-earth" policy of burning food stocks to prevent them from falling into the hands of Napoleon's army. In doing so, it also caused a famine among Russian peasants. Similar famines resulted from the destruction or requisitioning of crops in the Russian civil war of 1921–1922, the Japanese occupation of Indochina in 1942–1945, and the Biafran war in Nigeria in 1967–1969.

The Bengal famine of 1943 was also war-related. In 1942 the Japanese army had conquered Burma, a rich rice-producing colony. Food supplies in Bengal, which imported rice from Burma, dropped by 5 percent. As prices began to rise, merchants bought stocks of rice and held them in the hope that prices would continue to increase. Sharecroppers sold their stocks to pay off their debts to landlords and village moneylenders. Meanwhile,

the railroads that in peacetime would have carried food from other parts of India were fully occupied with military traffic. In October 1943, when a new viceroy, Lord Wavell, arrived in India and ordered the army to transport food to Bengal, food prices dropped to a level that the poor could afford. By then, however, between 1.5 and 2 million Bengalis had starved to death.

Worst of all were the famines that happened in peacetime as a result of the deliberate decisions of governments. The most famous of these political famines was caused by Stalin's collectivization of agriculture in 1932–1934. The Communist Party tried to force the peasants to give up their land and livestock and join collectives, where they could be made to work harder and provide food for the growing cities and industries. When they resisted, their crops were seized. Millions were sent to prison camps and millions of others died of starvation. Stalin chided the overly enthusiastic party members who had caused the famine for being "dizzy with success."

An even worse famine took place in China from 1958 to 1961 during the "Great Leap Forward" (see Chapter 28). Communist Party Chairman Mao Zedong decided to hasten the transformation of China into a communist state and industrial power by relying not on the expertise of economists and technocrats but on the enthusiasm of the masses. All farms were consolidated into huge communes. Peasants were mobilized to work on giant construction projects or to make steel out of household utensils and tools in backyard furnaces. The harvest of 1959 was poor, and later ones were even worse. The amount of grain per person declined from 452 pounds (205 kilograms) in 1957 to 340 pounds (154 kilograms) in 1961. Since the Central Statistical Bureau had been shut down, the central government was unaware of the shortages and demanded ever higher requisitions of food to feed the army and urban and industrial workers and to export to the Soviet Union to pay off China's debts. The amount of food left to the farmers was between one-fifth and one-half of their usual subsistence diet. From 1958 to 1961 20 to 30 million Chinese are estimated to have starved or died of the diseases of malnutrition in the most catastrophic famine in the history of the world. The leaders of the Communist Party either were unaware of its extent or, if they knew, did not dare mention it for fear of displeasing Mao, who denied its existence.

Nothing quite as horrible has happened since the Great Leap Forward. During the droughts in Africa in the 1970s and 1980s, most people in the affected regions received international food aid, but the governments of Ethiopia and Sudan either denied that their people were hungry or prevented food shipments from reaching drought victims in order to crush rebellions.

In the world today, natural disasters are as frequent as ever, and many countries are vulnerable to food shortages. No one now claims, as many did in the nineteenth century, that governments have no business providing free food to the starving. Though food is not equitably distributed, there is enough for all human beings now, and there will be enough for the foreseeable future. However, humanitarian feelings compete with other political agendas, and the specter of politically motivated famines still stalks the world.

## PART EIGHT

# Perils and Promises of a Global Community, 1945 to the Present

CHAPTER 28
The Cold War and Decolonization, 1945–1975

CHAPTER 29
Crisis, Realignment, and the Dawn of the
Post–Cold War World, 1975–1991

CHAPTER 30
Globalization at the Turn of the Millennium

The post–World War II decades brought promising changes to an increasingly interconnected world. Through the United Nations efforts were made to promote peace and international cooperation, and most countries agreed to human rights standards. Colonized peoples in Asia and Africa gained their independence, and expanding global trade offered the hope of economic growth.

However, these decades also saw major threats to peace, prosperity, and the environment. A Cold War between communist and anticommunist states disrupted dreams of a new era of peace and cooperation. The Iron Curtain divided Soviet-dominated eastern Europe from American-supported western Europe. Regional wars in Korea and Vietnam pitted the United States and its allies against communist regimes. Cold War rivalries sometimes provided a windfall of aid for new states but also intensified civil conflicts in Latin America, Africa, and elsewhere.

With the signing of nuclear arms limitation agreements in the 1970s tensions between the United States and the Soviet Union eased. In 1991 the Cold War finally ended with the collapse of the Soviet Union. As the sole remaining superpower, the United States had a unique capacity to act globally and a unique burden of suspicion of its motives.

Economic promises and perils also abounded in the post-war world. The wartime victors experienced rapid economic recovery, as did Germany and Japan, but in less developed lands prosperity came slowly or not at all. Global markets favored the industrialized nations. After 1975 a number of countries, including China, South Korea, Brazil, and Argentina, made dramatic strides in industrialization. But in less developed nations rapid population growth often offset economic gains. The divide between rich and poor nations widened.

Economic development meant new possibilities and perils for the environment. In the 1960s, the Green Revolution in agriculture greatly increased world food supplies, and in the 1990s genetic engineering produced plants that yielded more and resisted disease, drought, and insect damage better. But industrial growth accelerated the pollution of water and land. Atmospheric pollution increased exposure to harmful ultraviolet rays and led to increased global temperatures. Over-fishing and over-hunting imperiled many animal species, while thousands of acres of tropical forests were cut or burned for timber and farmland.

Finally, growing global interconnectedness held its own promises and perils. Many welcomed the emergence of English as the global language and the rapid spread of news, money, and ideas via the Internet. Others feared that Western material values and political and economic dominance posed a severe threat to cultural diversity around the world. A dangerous few reacted with violence.

|  | 1950 | 1960 | 1970 |
|---|---|---|---|
| **Americas** | •1945 United Nations charter signed in San Francisco | •1962 Cuban missile crisis | |
|  | •1946 International Monetary Fund and World Bank founded    Cuban Revolution 1959• | •1964 Military takes power in Brazil | |
|  | •1952 U.S. tests first hydrogen bomb | Neil Armstrong walks on moon 1969• | |
| **Europe** | 1948–1952 Marshall Plan helps rebuild western Europe | •1961 Berlin Wall built | |
|  | •1949 NATO founded    •1955 Warsaw Pact formed | Student uprising in France 1968• | |
|  | Soviet troops crush revolt in Hungary 1956•    •1957 Common Market founded | | |
| **Africa** | •1948 Apartheid becomes official in South Africa | •1960 Nigeria, Congo, Somalia, Togo win independence | |
|  | Ghana first British colony in Africa to win independence 1957• | •1963 Kenya independent | |
|  | •1958 Guinea wins independence from France | | |
| **Middle East** | •1948 State of Israel founded; first Arab-Israeli War    •1956 Suez crisis | •1967 Six Day Arab-Israeli War | |
|  | 1954–1962 Algerian war for Independence | | |
| **Asia and Oceania** | 1951–1953 Korean War    1954–1975 Vietnam War | Cultural Revolution in China 1966–1969 | |
|  | •1949 Indonesia wins independence from Netherlands | Japan becomes world economic power 1970s• | |

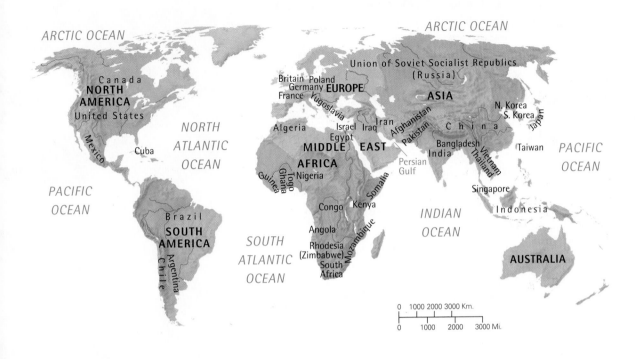

ARCTIC OCEAN

ARCTIC OCEAN

Canada
**NORTH AMERICA**
United States

Mexico

Cuba

NORTH ATLANTIC OCEAN

PACIFIC OCEAN

Brazil
**SOUTH AMERICA**

Argentina
Chile

SOUTH ATLANTIC OCEAN

Britain Poland
Germany **EUROPE**
France
Yugoslavia

Algeria

Israel Iraq
Egypt
**MIDDLE EAST**
**AFRICA**

Iran
Afghanistan
Pakistan

Persian Gulf

Guinea
Togo
Ghana
Nigeria

Congo Kenya

Angola

Rhodesia (Zimbabwe)
South Africa

Somalia

Mozambique

INDIAN OCEAN

Union of Soviet Socialist Republics
(Russia)

**ASIA**

China

N. Korea
S. Korea

Japan

Bangladesh
India
Thailand
Vietnam

Taiwan

Singapore

Indonesia

PACIFIC OCEAN

**AUSTRALIA**

0  1000 2000 3000 Km.

0    1000    2000    3000 Mi.

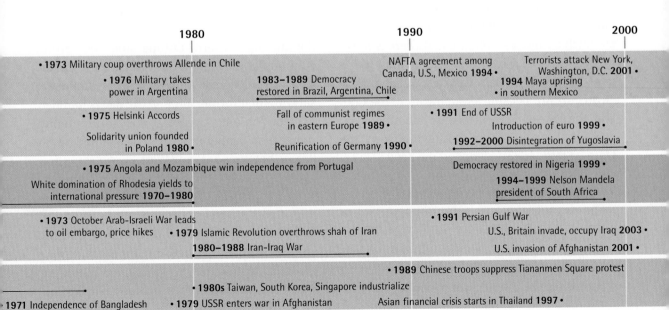

**1980**    **1990**    **2000**

• **1973** Military coup overthrows Allende in Chile

• **1976** Military takes power in Argentina

**1983–1989** Democracy restored in Brazil, Argentina, Chile

NAFTA agreement among Canada, U.S., Mexico **1994** •

Terrorists attack New York, Washington, D.C. **2001** •

**1994** Maya uprising • in southern Mexico

• **1975** Helsinki Accords

Solidarity union founded in Poland **1980** •

Fall of communist regimes in eastern Europe **1989** •

Reunification of Germany **1990** •

• **1991** End of USSR

Introduction of euro **1999** •

**1992–2000** Disintegration of Yugoslavia

• **1975** Angola and Mozambique win independence from Portugal

White domination of Rhodesia yields to international pressure **1970–1980**

Democracy restored in Nigeria **1999** •

**1994–1999** Nelson Mandela president of South Africa

• **1973** October Arab-Israeli War leads to oil embargo, price hikes

• **1979** Islamic Revolution overthrows shah of Iran

**1980–1988** Iran-Iraq War

• **1991** Persian Gulf War

U.S., Britain invade, occupy Iraq **2003** •

U.S. invasion of Afghanistan **2001** •

• **1989** Chinese troops suppress Tiananmen Square protest

• **1980s** Taiwan, South Korea, Singapore industrialize

• **1971** Independence of Bangladesh

• **1979** USSR enters war in Afghanistan

Asian financial crisis starts in Thailand **1997** •

# 28 The Cold War and Decolonization, 1945–1975

CHAPTER OUTLINE

**The Cold War**

**Decolonization and Nation Building**

**Beyond a Bipolar World**

DIVERSITY AND DOMINANCE: **Race and the Struggle for Justice in South Africa**

In 1946, in a speech at Fulton, Missouri, Great Britain's wartime leader Winston Churchill declared that "an iron curtain has descended across the Continent [of Europe]. . . . I am convinced there is nothing they [the communists] so much admire as strength, and there is nothing for which they have less respect than weakness, especially military weakness." The phrase **"iron curtain"** became a watchword of the **Cold War,** the state of political tension and military rivalry that was then beginning between the United States and its allies and the Soviet Union and its allies.

In the early years of World War II, Churchill and President Franklin Roosevelt had looked forward to a postwar world of economic cooperation and restoration of sovereignty to peoples suffering Axis occupation and, above all, to a world where war and territorial conquest would not be tolerated. By the time Churchill delivered his "iron curtain" speech, however, Britain's electorate had voted him out of power, Harry S Truman had succeeded to the presidency after Roosevelt's death, and the Soviet Union was dominating eastern Europe and supporting communist movements in China, Iran, Turkey, Greece, and Korea. Although Soviet diplomats sat with their former allies in the newly founded United Nations Organization, confrontation rather than cooperation was the hallmark of relations between East and West.

The intensity of the Cold War sometimes obscured a postwar phenomenon of even greater importance. Western domination of Asia, Africa, and Latin America was largely ended, and the colonial empires of the New Imperialism were gradually dismantled. A new generation of national leaders sometimes skillfully played Cold

War antagonism to their own advantage. Their real business, however, was the difficult task of nation building.

Each land freeing itself from imperialism had its own specific history and conditions. After independence, some new nations sided openly with the United States and some with the Soviet Union. Others banded together in a posture of neutrality and spoke with one voice about their need for economic and technical assistance and the obligation of the wealthy nations to satisfy those needs.

The Cold War military rivalry stimulated extraordinary advances in weaponry and associated technologies, but many new nations struggled to educate their citizens, nurture industry, and escape the economic constraints imposed by their former imperialist masters. The environment suffered severe pressures, whether from oil exploration and transport to feed the growing economies of the wealthy nations or from deforestation in poor regions challenged by the need for cropland. Neither rich nor poor realized the costs associated with environmental change.

As you read this chapter, ask yourself the following questions:

- What impact did economic philosophy have on both the Cold War and the decolonization movement?

- How was a third world war averted?

- Was world domination by the superpowers good or bad for the rest of the world?

## THE COLD WAR

The wartime alliance between the United States, Great Britain, and the Soviet Union had been an uneasy one. Fear of working-class revolution, which the Nazis had played on in their rise to power, was not confined to Germany. For more than a century political and economic leaders committed to free markets and untrammeled capital investment had loathed socialism in its several forms. After World War II, the iron curtain in Europe and communist insurgencies in China and elsewhere seemed to confirm the threat of worldwide revolution.

To protect themselves from the Soviet Union, which they perceived as the nerve center of world revolution and as a military power capable of launching a terrible new war, the United States and the countries of western Europe established the **North Atlantic Treaty Organization (NATO)** military alliance in 1949. Soviet leaders felt themselves surrounded by hostile forces just when they were trying to recover from the terrible losses sustained in the war. The distrust and suspicion between the two sides played out on a worldwide stage. The United Nations provided the venue for face-to-face debate.

## The United Nations

In 1944, representatives from the United States, Great Britain, the Soviet Union, and China met and drafted specific charter proposals that finally bore fruit in the United Nations Charter, a treaty ratified on October 24, 1945. Like the League of Nations, the **United Nations** had two main bodies: the General Assembly, with representatives from all member states; and the Security Council, with five permanent members—China, France, Great Britain, the United States, and the Soviet Union—and seven rotating members. Various United Nations agencies focused on specialized international problems—for example, UNICEF (United Nations Children's Emergency Fund), FAO (Food and Agriculture Organization), and UNESCO (United Nations Educational, Scientific and Cultural Organization). The United Nations operated by majority vote, except that the five permanent members of the Security Council had veto power in that chamber.

All signatories to the United Nations Charter renounced war and territorial conquest. Nevertheless, peacekeeping, the sole preserve of the Security Council, became a vexing problem. The permanent members often exercised their veto to protect their friends and interests, though from time to time they authorized the United Nations to send observers or peacekeeping forces to monitor truces or agreements.

The decolonization of Africa and Asia greatly swelled the size of the General Assembly but not the Security Council. Many of the new nations looked to the United Nations for material assistance and access to a wider political world. While the vetoes of the Security Council's permanent members often stymied actions touching even indirectly on Cold War concerns, the General Assembly became an arena for expressing opinions on many issues involving decolonization, a movement that the Soviet Union strongly encouraged but the Western colonial powers resisted.

In the early years of the United Nations, General Assembly resolutions carried great weight. An example is a 1947 resolution that sought to divide Palestine into sovereign Jewish and Arab states. Gradually, though, the flood of new members produced a voting majority concerned more with poverty, racial discrimination, and the struggle against imperialism than with the Cold War. As a result, the Western powers increasingly disregarded the General Assembly, allowing the new nations of the world to have their say but not to act collectively.

## Capitalism and Communism

In July 1944, with Allied victory a forgone conclusion, economic specialists representing over forty countries met at Bretton Woods, a New Hampshire resort, to devise a new international monetary system. The signatories eventually agreed to fix exchange rates. They also created the International Monetary Fund (IMF) to use currency reserves from member nations to finance temporary trade deficits and the **World Bank** to provide funds for reconstructing Europe and helping needy countries.

The Soviet Union attended the Bretton Woods Conference and signed the agreements, but by 1946, suspicion between the Soviet Union and the United States and Britain had deepened. While the rest of the world moved to a monetary system that relied for stability on most countries holding reserves of dollars and the United States holding reserves of gold, the Soviet Union established a closed monetary system for itself and the new communist regimes in eastern Europe. In the Western countries, supply and demand determined prices; in the Soviet command economy, government priorities and agencies allocated goods and set prices, irrespective of market forces.

Many leaders from the newly independent states preferred the Soviet Union's socialist example to the capitalism of their former colonizers. Thus, the relative success of economies patterned on Eastern or Western models became an element in the Cold War rivalry. Each side trumpeted economic successes measured by such things as industrial output, changes in per capita income, and productivity gains as evidence of its superiority.

During World War II, increased military spending and the draft brought full employment and high wages to the United States. With peace, the United States enjoyed prosperity and an international competitive advantage, while European economies were still heavily damaged from the war. To support European reconstruction, the U.S. **Marshall Plan** provided $12.5 billion to friendly countries between 1948 and 1952. By 1963, a resurgent European economy had doubled 1940 output.

Western European governments generally increased their role in economic management during this period. In Great Britain, the Labour Party government of the 1950s nationalized coal, steel, railroads, and health care. The French government nationalized public utilities; the auto, banking, and insurance industries; and parts of the mining industry.

In 1948, European governments also promoted economic cooperation and integration with the creation of the Organization of European Economic Cooperation (OEEC). After cooperative policies on coal and steel proved successful, some OEEC countries were ready to begin lowering tariffs to encourage the movement of goods and capital. In 1957, France, West Germany, Italy, the Netherlands, Belgium, and Luxembourg signed a treaty creating the European Economic Community, also known as the Common Market. The word "economic" was dropped from the group's title in 1967, making it simply the **European Community (EC).** By the 1970s, the EC nations had nearly over-

| C H R O N O L O G Y | |
| --- | --- |
| **Cold War** | **Decolonization** |

**1945**

| Cold War | Decolonization |
| --- | --- |
| | **1947**  Partition of India |
| **1948–1949**  Berlin airlift | |
| **1949**  NATO formed | **1949**  Dutch withdraw from Indonesia |
| **1950–1953**  Korean War | |
| **1952**  United States detonates first hydrogen bomb | |
| | **1954**  CIA intervention in Guatemala; defeat at Dienbienphu ends French hold on Vietnam |
| **1955**  Warsaw Pact concluded | **1955**  Bandung Conference |
| **1956**  Soviet Union suppresses Hungarian revolt | |
| **1957**  Soviet Union launches first artificial satellite into earth orbit | **1957**  Ghana becomes first British colony in Africa to gain independence |
| | **1959**  Fidel Castro leads revolution in Cuba |
| | **1960**  Shootings in Sharpeville intensify South African sturggle against apartheid; Nigeria becomes independent |
| **1961**  East Germany builds Berlin Wall | |
| **1962**  Cuban missile crisis | **1962**  Algeria wins independence |
| | **1971**  Bangladesh secedes from Pakistan |
| **1975**  Helsinki Accords; end of Vietnam War | |

**1955**

**1965**

**1975**

taken the United States in industrial production. The economic alliance expanded after 1970, as Great Britain, Denmark, Greece, Ireland, Spain, Portugal, Finland, Sweden, and Austria joined.

Prosperity brought dramatic changes to European society. Average wages increased, unemployment fell, and social welfare benefits were expanded. Governments increased spending on health care, unemployment benefits, old-age pensions, public housing, and grants to poor families with children. The combination of economic growth and income redistribution raised living standards and fueled demand for consumer goods.

The Soviet experience provided a dramatic contrast. The economy of the Soviet Union was just as devastated at the end of the Second World War as those of western Europe. However, with enormous natural resources, a large population, and abundant energy at its disposal, Soviet recovery was rapid at first. Moreover, Soviet planners had made large investments in technical and scientific education, and the Soviet state had developed heavy industry in the 1930s and during the war years. But as the postwar period progressed, bureaucratic control of the economy grew less efficient. In the 1970s, the gap with the West widened. The Soviet economy failed to meet domestic demand for clothing, housing, food, automobiles, and consumer electronics. Agricultural inefficiency forced the Soviet Union to rely on food imports.

The socialist nations of eastern Europe were compelled to follow the Soviet economic model, although some national differences appeared. Poland and Hungary, for example, implemented agricultural collectivization more slowly than did Czechoslovakia. Significant growth occurred among the socialist economies, but the inefficiencies and failures that plagued the Soviet economy troubled them as well.

The United States and the Soviet Union competed in providing loans and grants and in supplying arms (at bargain prices) to countries willing to align with them politically. Thus, the relative success or failure of capitalism and communism in Europe and the United States was not necessarily the strongest consideration in other parts of the world when the time came to construct new national economies.

## West Versus East in Europe and Korea

For Germany, Austria, and Japan, peace brought foreign military occupation and new governments that were initially controlled by the occupiers. When relations with the Western powers cooled at the end of the war, the Soviet Union sought to prevent the reappearance of hostile regimes on its borders. Initially, the Soviet Union seemed willing to accept governments in neighboring states that included a mix of parties as long as they were not hostile to local communist groups or to the Soviets. The nations of central and eastern Europe were deeply split by the legacies of the war, and many were willing to embrace the communists as a hedge against those who had supported fascism or cooperated with the Germans. As relations between the Soviets and the West worsened in the late 1940s, local communists, their strength augmented by Soviet military occupation, gained victories across eastern Europe. Western leaders saw the rapid emergence of communist regimes in Poland, Czechoslovakia, Hungary, Bulgaria, Romania, Yugoslavia, and Albania as a threat.

For the United States, the shift from viewing the Soviet Union as an ally against Germany to seeing it as a worldwide enemy took two years. In the waning days of World War II, the United States had seemed amenable to the Soviet desire for freer access to the Mediterranean through Turkish straits. But in July 1947, the **Truman Doctrine** offered military aid to help both Turkey and Greece resist Soviet military pressure and subversion. In 1951, Greece and Turkey were admitted to NATO. NATO's Soviet counterpart, the **Warsaw Pact,** emerged in 1955 in response to the Western powers' decision to allow West Germany to rearm within limits set by NATO.

The Soviet Union tested Western resolve in 1948–1949 by blockading the areas of Berlin occupied by British, French, and American forces, which were surrounded by Soviet-controlled East Germany. Airlifts of food and fuel defeated the blockade. In 1961, the East German government accentuated Germany's political division by building the Berlin Wall, as much to prevent its citizens from fleeing to the noncommunist western part of that city as to keep Westerners from entering East German territory. The West tested the East, in turn, by encouraging a rift between the Soviet Union and Yugoslavia. Western aid and encouragement resulted in Yugoslavia's signing a defensive treaty with Greece and Turkey (but not with NATO) and deciding against joining the Warsaw Pact.

Soviet power set clear limits on how far any eastern European country might stray from Soviet domination. In 1956, Soviet troops crushed an anti-Soviet revolt in Hungary. Czechoslovakia suffered Hungary's fate in 1968. The West, a passive onlooker, had no recourse but to acknowledge that the Soviet Union had the right to intervene in the domestic affairs of any Soviet-bloc nation whenever it wished.

A more explosive crisis erupted in Korea, where the Second World War had left Soviet troops in control north of the thirty-eighth parallel and American troops in control to the south. When no agreement could be reached on holding countrywide elections, communist North Korea and noncommunist South Korea became independent states in 1948. Two years later, North Korea invaded South Korea. The United Nations Security Council, in the absence of the Soviet delegation, voted to condemn the invasion and called on members of the United Nations to come to the defense of South Korea. The United States was the primary ally of South Korea. The People's Republic of China supported North Korea. The **Korean War** lasted until 1953, when the two sides eventually agreed to a truce along the thirty-eighth parallel, but no peace treaty was concluded.

Japan benefited from the Korean War in an unexpected way. Massive purchases of supplies by the United States and spending by American servicemen on leave provided a financial stimulus to the Japanese economy similar to the stimulus that Europe received from the Marshall Plan.

## U.S. Defeat in Vietnam

A shooting war also developed in Vietnam. In 1954, United States president Dwight D. Eisenhower (1953–1961) and his foreign policy advisers decided not to aid France in its effort to sustain colonial rule in Vietnam, perceiving that the days of the European colonial empires were numbered. After winning independence, however, communist North Vietnam supported a guerrilla movement—the Viet Cong—against the noncommunist government of South Vietnam.

When John F. Kennedy became president (1961–1963), he and his advisers decided to support the South Vietnamese government of President Ngo Dinh Diem°. They realized that the Diem government was corrupt and unpopular, but they feared that a communist victory would encourage communist movements throughout Southeast Asia and alter the Cold War balance of power. Kennedy steadily increased the number of American military advisers from 685 to almost 16,000 while secretly encouraging the overthrow and execution of Diem in hopes of seeing a more popular and honest government come to power.

Lyndon Johnson, who became president (1963–1969) after Kennedy was assassinated, gained support from Congress for unlimited expansion of U.S. military deployment. By the end of 1966, 365,000 U.S. troops were engaged in the **Vietnam War.** Nothing the Americans tried, however, succeeded in stopping the Viet Cong guerrillas and their North Vietnamese allies. Diem's successors turned out to be just as corrupt and unpopular as he was, and the heroic nationalist image of North Vietnam's leader, Ho Chi Minh, evoked strong sympathies among many South Vietnamese.

In 1973, a treaty between North Vietnam and the United States ended U.S. involvement in the war and promised future elections. Two years later,

in violation of the treaty, Viet Cong and North Vietnamese troops overran the South Vietnamese army and captured the southern capital of Saigon, renaming it Ho Chi Minh City. The two parts of Vietnam were reunited in a single state ruled from the north. The war was bloody and traumatic. The Vietnamese had over a million casualties. The deaths of fifty-eight thousand Americans overseas and the vigorous antiwar movement at home ensured that the United States would not easily be drawn into another shooting war.

**The Vietnamese People at War**  American and South Vietnamese troops burned many villages to deprive the enemy of civilian refuges. This policy undermined support for the South Vietnamese government in the countryside. (Dana Stone/stockphoto.com)

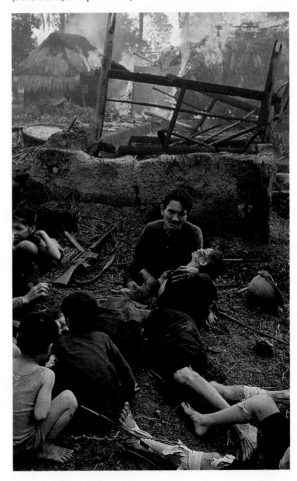

**Diem** (dee-EM)

## The Race for Nuclear Supremacy

Fear of nuclear warfare affected strategic decisions in the Korean and Vietnam Wars. It also affected all other aspects of Cold War confrontation. The devastation of Hiroshima and Nagasaki by atomic weapons (see Chapter 26) had ushered in a new era. Nuclear weapons fed into a logic of total war that was already reaching a peak in Nazi genocide and terror bombing and in massive Allied air raids on large cities. After the Soviet Union exploded its first nuclear device in 1949, fears of a worldwide holocaust grew. Fears increased when the United States exploded a far more powerful weapon, the hydrogen bomb, in 1952 and the Soviet Union followed suit less than a year later. The possibility of the theft of nuclear secrets by Soviet spies fostered paranoia in the United States, and the conviction that the nuclear superpowers were willing to use their terrible weapons if their vital interests were threatened spread despair around the world.

In 1954, President Eisenhower warned Soviet leaders against attacking western Europe. In response to such an attack, he said, the United States would reduce the Soviet Union to "a smoking, radiating ruin at the end of two hours." A few years later, the Soviet leader Nikita Khrushchev° offered an equally stark promise: "We will bury you." His reference was to economic competition, but the image produced in Americans was of literal burial.

Everyone's worst fears seemed about to be realized in the **Cuban missile crisis** of 1962. When the Soviet Union deployed nuclear-tipped missiles in Cuba in response to the U.S. installation of similar missiles in Turkey, the world held its breath. Confronted by unyielding diplomatic pressure and military threats from President Kennedy, Khrushchev backed down and pulled the missiles from Cuba. Subsequently, the United States removed its missiles from Turkey.

Arms limitation also saw progress. In 1963, Great Britain, the United States, and the Soviet Union agreed to ban the testing of nuclear weapons in the atmosphere, in space, and under water, thus reducing the environmental danger of radioactive fallout. In 1968, the United States and the Soviet Union together proposed a world treaty against further proliferation of nuclear weapons. It was signed by 137 countries. Not until 1972, however, did the two superpowers truly recognize the futility of squandering their wealth on ever-larger missile forces.

In Europe, the Soviet-American arms race outran the economic ability of atomic powers France and Britain to keep pace. Instead, the European states sought to relax tensions. Between 1972 and 1975, the Conference on Security and Cooperation in Europe (CSCE) brought delegates from thirty-seven European states, the United States, and Canada to Helsinki. The goal of the Soviet Union was to gain European acceptance of the political boundaries of the Warsaw Pact nations. The **Helsinki Accords** affirmed that no boundaries should be changed by military force. It also contained formal (but nonbinding) declarations calling for economic, social, and governmental contacts across the iron curtain, and for cooperation in humanitarian fields, a provision that paved the way for dialogue about human rights.

Space exploration was another offshoot of the nuclear arms race. The contest to build larger and more accurate missiles for delivery of warheads prompted the superpowers to prove their skills in rocketry by launching space satellites. The Soviet Union placed a small *Sputnik* satellite into orbit around the earth in October 1957. The United States responded with its own satellite three months later. The space race was on, a contest in which accomplishments in space were understood to signify equivalent achievements in the military sphere. *Sputnik* administered a deep shock to American pride and confidence, but in 1969 two Americans, Neil A. Armstrong and Edwin E. "Buzz" Aldrin, became the first humans to walk on the moon.

Despite rhetorical Cold War saber-rattling by Soviet and American leaders, the threat of nuclear war forced a measure of restraint on the superpower adversaries. Because fighting each other directly would have risked escalation to the level of nuclear exchange, they carefully avoided crises that might provoke such confrontations.

---

**Khrushchev** (KROOSH-chef)

# DECOLONIZATION AND NATION BUILDING

///

Whereas the losing countries in World War I were stripped of colonies, it was primarily countries on the winning side in World War II that ended up losing their colonies (see Map 28.1).

Circumstances differed profoundly from place to place. In some Asian countries, where colonial rule was of long standing, newly independent states found themselves in possession of viable industries, communications networks, and education systems. In other countries, notably in Africa, decolonization gave birth to nations facing dire economic problems and internal disunity. In Latin America, where political independence already had been achieved, the quest was for freedom from foreign economic domination, particularly by the United States.

## New Nations in Southern Asia

Newly independent India and Pakistan were strikingly dissimilar. Muslim Pakistan defined itself according to religion and quickly fell under the control of military leaders. Though 90 percent Hindu, the much larger republic of India, led by Prime Minister Jawaharlal Nehru, was secular. It inherited most of the considerable industrial and educational resources the British had developed, along with the larger share of trained civil servants and military officers.

The decision of the Hindu ruler of the northwestern state of Jammu and Kashmir to join India without consulting his overwhelmingly Muslim subjects led to a war between India and Pakistan in 1947 that ended with an uneasy truce, only to resume briefly in 1965. Though Kashmir remains a flashpoint of patriotic feeling, the two countries managed to avoid further warfare.

Despite recurrent predictions that multilingual India might break up into a number of linguistically homogeneous states, most Indians recognized that unity benefited everyone; and the country pursued a generally democratic and socialist line of development. Pakistan, in contrast, did break up. In 1971, its Bengali-speaking eastern section seceded to become the independent country of Bangladesh.

Elsewhere in the region, nationalist movements won independence as well. Britain granted independence to Burma (now Myanmar°) in 1948 and established the Malay Federation that same year. (Singapore, once a member of the federation, became an independent city-state itself in 1965.) In 1946, the United States kept its promise of postwar independence for the Philippine Islands but retained close economic ties and leases on military bases. In the Dutch East Indies, Sukarno (1901–1970) had cooperated with the Japanese occupation in hopes that the Dutch would never return. After a military confrontation, Dutch withdrawal was finally negotiated in 1949, and Sukarno went on to become the dictator of his resource-rich but underdeveloped nation of Indonesia.

In all these cases, communist insurgents plagued the departing colonial powers and the newly formed governments. The most important postwar communist movement arose in the part of Southeast Asia known as French Indochina. There, Ho Chi Minh° (1890–1969), who had spent several years in France during World War I, played the pivotal role. After training in Moscow, he returned to Vietnam to found the Indochina Communist Party in 1930.

Ho Chi Minh's nationalist coalition, then called the Viet Minh, fought the French with help from the People's Republic of China. After a brutal struggle, the French stronghold of Dienbienphu° fell in 1954, marking the doom of France's colonial enterprise. Ho's Viet Minh government took over in the north, and a noncommunist nationalist government ruled in the south. As already described, fighting between North and South Vietnam eventually became a major Cold War conflict (see "U.S. Defeat in Vietnam" above).

## The Struggle for Independence in Africa

In the quarter-century between 1955 and 1980, African nationalists succeeded in ending European colonial rule. Mostly they gained their

---

**Myanmar** (myahn-MAH)  **Ho Chi Minh** (hoe chee min)
**Dienbienphu** (dyen-byen-phu)

Date is year independence was achieved.
Shading indicates former ruler.

Great Britain
France
Netherlands
Italy
Belgium
Portugal
United States
Other

PACIFIC OCEAN

JAPAN

NORTH KOREA 1948
SOUTH KOREA 1948
From Japan

PHILIPPINES 1946

PAPUA NEW GUINEA 1975

NORTH VIETNAM 1954
Unified 1974
SOUTH VIETNAM 1954

BRUNEI 1984
From Great Britain

INDONESIA 1949

EAST TIMOR 1999
From Indonesia

CAMBODIA 1954

MALAYSIA 1963

SINGAPORE 1965

LAOS 1949

MYANMAR (BURMA) 1947

PAKISTAN 1947
BANGLADESH 1973

SRI LANKA (CEYLON) 1948

INDIA 1947

PAKISTAN 1947

INDIAN OCEAN

KUWAIT 1961

BAHRAIN 1971
QATAR 1971
UNITED ARAB EMIRATES 1971

DJIBOUTI 1977

YEMEN P.D.R. OF YEMEN 1967

MAURITIUS 1968
From Great Britain

IRAQ 1932

JORDAN 1946

SOMALIA 1960

SYRIA 1944

CYPRUS 1960
LEBANON 1944
ISRAEL 1948

ETHIOPIA 1941

KENYA 1963

MALAWI 1964

MADAGASCAR 1960

EGYPT 1922

ERITREA 1993
From Ethiopia

SUDAN 1956

UGANDA 1962

TANZANIA 1964

MOZAMBIQUE 1974

SWAZILAND 1968

TUNISIA 1956
MALTA 1964
From Great Britain

LIBYA 1951

CHAD 1960

DEM. REP OF CONGO 1960

RWANDA 1962
BURUNDI 1962

ZAMBIA 1964

ZIMBABWE 1980

LESOTHO 1966

GREAT BRITAIN

NETHERLANDS
BELGIUM
FRANCE

ITALY

SPAIN

PORTUGAL

NIGER 1960

NIGERIA 1960

CENTRAL AFRICAN REPUBLIC 1960

CAMEROON 1960

GABON 1960

ANGOLA 1975

NAMIBIA 1985
From South Africa

BOTSWANA 1966

SOUTH AFRICA (Republic 1961)

ALGERIA 1962

MALI 1960

BENIN 1960

TOGO 1960

EQUATORIAL GUINEA 1968 From Spain

REPUBLIC OF CONGO 1960

MOROCCO 1956

BURKINA FASO 1960

CÔTE D'IVOIRE 1960

GHANA 1957

WESTERN SAHARA (Morocco) 1975
From Spain

MAURITANIA 1960

SENEGAL 1960
GAMBIA 1965
GUINEA-BISSAU 1974
GUINEA 1958
SIERRA LEONE 1961
LIBERIA 1820s

ATLANTIC OCEAN

0   500   1000   1500 Km.
0   500   1000   1500 Mi.

**Map 28.1  Decolonization, 1947–1999**  Notice that independence came a decade or so earlier in South and Southeast Asia than in Africa. Numerous countries that gained independence after World War II in the Caribbean, in South and Central America, and in the Pacific are not shown.

independence peacefully, but where European settlers were numerous, violence became the norm.

Algeria rebelled in 1954. The French government was as determined to hold on to Algeria as it had been to keep Vietnam. Ten percent of the Algerian population was European, and Algeria's economy was strongly oriented toward France. Both sides pursued the revolt with great brutality. When the Algerians finally won independence in 1962, the flood of angry colonists returning to France undermined the Algerian economy because very few Arabs had received technical training or acquired management experience.

None of the independence movements in sub-Saharan Africa matched the Algerian struggle in scale. Some of the politicians who led the nationalist movements had devoted their lives to ridding their homelands of foreign occupation. An example is Kwame Nkrumah° (1909–1972), who in 1957 became prime minister of Ghana (formerly the Gold Coast), the first British colony in Africa to achieve independence. Only a few hundred Ghanaian children of Nkrumah's generation had graduated each year from the seven-year elementary schools, and he was one of only a handful who made it through teacher training college. After graduation, he spent a decade reading philosophy and theology in the United States and absorbing ideas about black pride and independence then being propounded by black leaders W. E. B. Du Bois and Marcus Garvey.

After a brief stay in Britain, Nkrumah returned in 1947 to the Gold Coast to work for independence. The time was right. Great Britain had already freed its Asian colonies, and Nkrumah quickly united the people of Ghana behind him. Independence thus came without war or protracted bloodshed. Nkrumah turned out to be more effective internationally as a spokesman for colonized peoples than

he was at home as an administrator. In 1966, a group of army officers ousted him.

Jomo Kenyatta (ca. 1894–1978) traveled a more difficult road in Kenya, where a substantial number of European coffee planters strengthened Britain's desire to retain control. A movement the settlers called Mau Mau, formed mostly by the Kikuyu° people, became active in 1952. As violence between settlers and movement fighters escalated, British troops hunted down the leaders and resettled the Kikuyu. The British charged Kenyatta with being a Mau Mau leader and held him in prison and then in internal exile for eight years during a declared state of emergency. They released him in 1961, and negotiations with the British to write a constitution for an independent Kenya followed. In 1964, Kenyatta was elected the first president of the Republic of Kenya. He proved to be an effective, though autocratic, ruler.

In contrast, African leaders in the French colonies of sub-Saharan Africa were slow to call for independence. They visualized change in terms of promises of greater political and civil rights made in 1944 by the Free French movement of General Charles de Gaulle at a conference in Brazzaville. This Brazzaville Conference also had promised to expand French education at the village level, to improve health services, and to open more lower-level administrative positions to Africans, but the word *independence* was never mentioned.

African politicians also realized that some French colonies—such as Ivory Coast with its coffee and cacao exports, fishing, and hardwood forests—had good economic prospects and others, such as land-locked, desert Niger, did not. As a Malagasy politician said in 1958, "When I let my heart talk, I am a partisan of total and immediate independence [for Madagascar]; when I make my reason speak, I realize that it is impossible." Ultimately, however, the heart prevailed everywhere. Guinea, under the dynamic leadership of Sékou Touré°, led the way in 1958. By the time Nigeria, the most populous West African state, achieved independence from Great Britain in 1960, the leaders of many former French colonies in West Africa could attend the celebrations as independent heads of state.

**Kwame Nkrumah** (KWAH-mee nn-KROO-muh)

**Kikuyu** (kih-KOO-you)    **Sékou Touré** (SAY-koo too-RAY)

European settlers fought hard to hold on in southern Africa. The African struggle against Portuguese rule in Angola and Mozambique dragged on until frustrated Portuguese military commanders overthrew the government of Portugal in 1974 and granted the African colonies independence the following year. After a ten-year fight, European settlers in the British colony of Southern Rhodesia ceded power in 1980 to the African majority, who renamed the country Zimbabwe. The change had been swift; a century after the "scramble" for Africa began, European colonial rule in Africa had ended.

Only South Africa and neighboring Southwest Africa remained in the hands of European minorities. After World War II, the white minority government had reconstructed South Africa along extreme racial separation, or *apartheid*°. The cities, the best jobs, and most of the land were reserved for Europeans. Africans and others classified as "nonwhites" were subjected to strict limitations on place of residence, right to travel, and access to jobs and public facilities.

The African National Congress (ANC), formed in 1912, led the fight against apartheid and in favor of a nonracial society. After police fired on demonstrators in the African town of Sharpeville in 1960, an African lawyer named Nelson Mandela (b. 1918) organized guerrilla resistance by the ANC. Mandela was sentenced to life in prison in 1964, and the government outlawed the ANC and other opposition organizations. For a time, things were quiet, but in 1976 young students reignited the bloody and prolonged struggle that would force an end to apartheid (see Diversity and Dominance: Race and the Struggle for Justice in South Africa).

## The Quest for Economic Freedom in Latin America

In Latin America, the postwar decades saw continuing struggles over foreign ownership and social inequality. American and European companies dominated Chile's copper, Cuba's sugar and resort hotels, Colombia's coffee, Guatemala's bananas, and the communications networks of several countries. Even in a country like Mexico, where the ruling Institutional Revolutionary Party, or PRI, was officially committed to revolutionary independence and economic development, a yawning gulf between rich and poor, urban and rural, persisted. According to one estimate from the mid-1960s, not more than 300 foreign and 800 Mexican companies dominated the country, and some 2,000 families made up the industrial-financial elite. At the other end of the economic scale were peasants and the 14 percent of the population classified as Indian.

Jacobo Arbenz Guzmán, elected president of Guatemala in 1951, was typical of Latin American leaders who tried to confront the power of foreign interests. His expropriation of large estates angered the United Fruit Company, a U.S. corporation that dominated banana exports and held vast tracts of land in reserve. Reacting to reports that Arbenz was becoming friendly toward communism, the United States Central Intelligence Agency (CIA) prompted a takeover by the Guatemalan military in 1954. CIA intervention removed Arbenz from the scene; it also condemned Guatemala to decades of governmental instability and growing violence between leftist and rightist elements in society.

In Cuba, U.S. companies owned 40 percent of raw sugar production, 23 percent of nonsugar industry, 90 percent of telephone and electrical services, and 50 percent of public service railways. The needs of the U.S. economy largely determined Cuban foreign trade and held back development. Profits went north to the United States or to a small class of wealthy Cubans, many of foreign origin. Cuba's ruler during that period, Fulgencio Batista, became a symbol of corruption, repression, and foreign economic domination.

In 1959, a popular rebellion forced Batista to flee the country. Fidel Castro, the lawyer leader of the rebels, his brother Raoul Castro, and Ernesto "Che" Guevara°, who was the main theorist of communist revolution in Latin America, created a new regime. Within a year, Fidel Castro's government had redistributed land, lowered urban rents, and raised wages, effectively transferring 15 percent of the national income from rich to poor. Within twenty-two months, the Castro government seized almost all U.S. property in Cuba and most Cuban corporations. This action resulted in a

---

**apartheid** (uh-PART-hate)

**Che Guevara** (chay guh-VAHR-uh)

blockade by the United States, the flight of middle-class and technically trained Cubans, a drop in foreign investment, and the beginning of chronic food shortages.

Little evidence supports the view that Castro undertook his revolution to install a communist government. But at that time, the East-West rivalry of the Cold War was increasingly influencing international politics, and Castro soon turned to the Soviet Union for economic aid. In doing so, he unwittingly committed his nation to economic stagnation and dependence on a foreign power as damaging as the previous relationship with the United States had been.

In April 1961, some fifteen hundred Cuban exiles, whom the CIA had trained for a year in Guatemala, landed at the Bay of Pigs in an effort to overthrow Castro. The Cuban army defeated the attempted invasion in a matter of days, partly because the new U.S. president, John F. Kennedy, decided not to provide all the air support that the plan originally called for. The failure of the Bay of Pigs invasion tarnished the reputation of the United States and the CIA and provoked Castro into declaring that he and his revolution were and always had been Marxist-Leninist.

### Challenges of Nation Building

Decolonization occurred on a vast scale. Fifty-one nations signed the United Nations Charter in the closing months of 1945. During the United Nations' first decade twenty-five new members joined, a third of them upon gaining independence. During the next decade forty-six more new members were admitted, nearly all of them former colonial territories.

Each of these nations had to organize and institute some form of government. Comparatively few were able to do so without experiencing coups, rewritten constitutions, or regional rebellions. Leaders did not always agree on the form independence should take. In the absence of established constitutional traditions, leaders frequently tried to impose their own visions by force. Most of the new nations, while trying to establish political stability, also faced severe economic challenges, including foreign ownership and operation of key resources and the need to build infrastructure.

Overdependence on world demand for raw materials and on imported manufactured goods persisted in many places long after independence.

Because the achievement of political and economic goals called for educated and skilled personnel, education was another common concern in newly emerging nations. Addressing that concern required more than building and staffing schools. In some countries, leaders had to decide which language to teach and how to inculcate a sense of national unity in students from different—and sometimes historically antagonistic—ethnic, religious, and linguistic groups. Another problem was how to provide satisfying jobs for new graduates, many of whom had high expectations because of their education.

Only rarely were the new nations able to surmount these hurdles. Even the most economically and educationally successful, such as South Korea, suffered from tendencies toward authoritarian rule. Costa Rica, a country with a remarkably stable parliamentary regime from 1949 onward and a literacy rate of 90 percent, remained heavily dependent on world prices for agricultural commodities and on importation of manufactured goods.

## BEYOND A BIPOLAR WORLD

Although the East-West superpower rivalry dominated world affairs, newly independent states had concerns that were primarily domestic and regional. The challenge they faced was to find a way to pursue their ends within the bipolar structure of the Cold War—and possibly to take advantage of the East-West rivalry. In short, the superpowers dominated the world but did not control it. And as time progressed, they dominated it less and less.

### The Third World

As one of the most successful leaders of the decolonization movement, Indonesia's President Sukarno was an appropriate figure to host a meeting in 1955 of twenty-nine African and Asian countries at Bandung, Indonesia. The conferees proclaimed solidarity among all peoples fighting

운드폭탄 4발 투하… 두 아들과 함께 사망

진지 구축… 이틀째 시가戰

령이 대중 앞에 나타나거나 애국심
을 고취하는 노래만을 내보내던 방
송마저 중단됐다.

라크 전후
의에서는
영국 주도

# DIVERSITY AND DOMINANCE

## RACE AND THE STRUGGLE FOR JUSTICE IN SOUTH AFRICA

*One of South Africa's martyrs in the struggle against apartheid was Steve Biko (1946–1977), a thinker and activist especially concerned with building pride among Africans and asserting the importance of African cultures. Biko was one of the founders of the Black Consciousness Movement, focusing on the ways in which white settlers had stripped Africans of their freedom. As a result of his activism, he was restricted to his hometown in 1973. Between 1975 and 1977 he was arrested and interrogated four times by the police. After his arrest in August 1977 he was severely beaten while in custody. He died days later without having received medical care. His death caused worldwide outrage. The following is an excerpt from a 1970 essay by Biko.*

But these are not the people we are concerned with [those who support apartheid]. We are concerned with that curious bunch of nonconformists who explain their participation in negative terms: that bunch of do-gooders that goes under all sorts of names—liberals, leftists etc. These are the people who argue that they are not responsible for white racism and the country's "inhumanity to the black man." These are the people who claim that they too feel the oppression just as acutely as the blacks and therefore should be jointly involved in the black man's struggle for a place under the sun. In short, these are the people who say that they have black souls wrapped up in white skins.

The role of the white liberal in the black man's history in South Africa is a curious one. Very few black organisations were not under white direction. True to their image, the white liberals always knew what was good for the blacks and told them so. The wonder of it all is that the black people have believed in them for so long. It was only at the end of the 50s

that the blacks started demanding to be their own guardians.

Nowhere is the arrogance of the liberal ideology demonstrated so well as in their insistence that the problems of the country can only be solved by a bilateral approach involving both black and white. This has, by and large, come to be taken in all seriousness as the modus operandi in South Africa by all those who claim they would like a change in the status quo. Hence the multiracial political organisations and parties and the "nonracial" student organisations, all of which insist on integration not only as an end goal but also as a means.

The integration they talk about is first of all artificial in that it is a response to conscious manoeuvre rather than to the dictates of the inner soul. In other words the people forming the integrated complex have been extracted from various segregated societies with their inbuilt complexes of superiority and inferiority and these continue to manifest themselves even in the "nonracial" setup of the integrated complex. As a result the integration so achieved is a one-way course, with the whites doing all the talking and the blacks the listening. Let me hasten to say that I am not claiming that segregation is necessarily the natural order; however, given the facts of the situation where a group experiences privilege at the expense of others, then it becomes obvious that a hastily arranged integration cannot be the solution to the problem. It is rather like expecting the slave to work together with the slave-master's son to remove all the conditions leading to the former's enslavement.

Secondly, this type of integration as a means is almost always unproductive. The participants waste lots of time in an internal sort of mudslinging designed to prove that A is more of a liberal than B. In other words the lack of common ground for solid identification is all the time manifested in internal strifes [sic] inside the group.

It will not sound anachronistic to anybody genuinely interested in real integration to learn that blacks are asserting themselves in a society where they are being treated as perpetual under-16s. One does not need to plan for or actively encourage real integration. Once the various groups within a given community have asserted themselves to the point that mutual respect has to be shown then you have the ingredients for a true and meaningful integration. At the heart of true integration is the provision for each man, each group to rise and attain the envisioned self. Each group must be able to attain its style of existence without encroaching on or being thwarted by another. Out of this mutual respect for each other and complete freedom of self-determination there will obviously arise a genuine fusion of the life-styles of the various groups. This is true integration.

From this it becomes clear that as long as blacks are suffering from [an] inferiority complex—a result of 300 years of deliberate oppression, denigration and derision—they will be useless as co-architects of a normal society where man is nothing else but man for his own sake. Hence what is necessary as a prelude to anything else that may come is a very strong grass-roots build-up of black consciousness such that blacks can learn to assert themselves and stake their rightful claim.

Thus in adopting the line of a nonracial approach, the liberals are playing their old game. They are claiming a "monopoly on intelligence and moral judgement" and setting the pattern and pace for the realisation of the black man's aspirations. They want to remain in good books with both the black and white worlds. They want to shy away from all forms of "extremisms," condemning "white supremacy" as being just as bad as "Black Power!" They vacillate between the two worlds, verbalising all the complaints of the blacks beautifully while skilfully extracting what suits them from the exclusive pool of white privileges. But ask them for a moment to give a concrete meaningful programme that they intend adopting, then you will see on whose side they really are. Their protests are directed at and appeal to white conscience, everything they do is directed at finally convincing the white electorate that the black man is also a man and that at some future date he should be given a place at the white man's table.

*In the following selection Anglican bishop Desmond Tutu (b. 1931) expressed his personal anguish at the death of Steve Biko. He summarized Biko's contributions to the struggle for justice in South Africa. Tutu won the Noble Peace Prize in 1984 and was named archbishop in 1988. From 1995 to 1998 he chaired the Truth and Reconciliation Commission, which investigated atrocities in South Africa during the years of apartheid. He stated that his objective was to create "a democratic and just society without racial divisions."*

When we heard the news "Steve Biko is dead" we were struck numb with disbelief. No, it can't be true! No, it must be a horrible nightmare, and we will awake and find that really it is different—that Steve is alive even if it be in detention. But no, dear friends, he is dead and we are still numb with grief, and groan with anguish "Oh God, where are you? Oh God, do you really care—how can you let this happen to us?"

It all seems such a senseless waste of a wonderfully gifted person, struck down in the bloom of youth, a youthful bloom that some wanted to see blighted. What can be the purpose of such wanton destruction? God, do you really love us? What must we do which we have not done, what must we say which we have not said a thousand times over, oh, for so many years—that all we want is what belongs to all God's children, what belongs as an inalienable right—a place in the sun in our own beloved mother country. Oh God, how long can we go on? How long can we go on appealing for a more just ordering of society where we all, black and white together, count not because of some accident of birth or a biological irrelevance—where all of us black and white count because we are human persons, human persons created in your own image.

God called Steve Biko to be his servant in South Africa—to speak up on behalf of God, declaring what the will of this God must be in a situation such as ours, a situation of evil, injustice, oppression and exploitation. God called him to be the founder father of the Black Consciousness Movement against which we have had tirades and fulminations. It is a movement by which God, through Steve, sought to awaken in the Black person a sense of his intrinsic value and worth as a child of God, not needing to apologise for his existential condition as a black person, calling on blacks to glorify and praise God that he had created them black. Steve, with his brilliant mind that always saw to the

681

heart of things, realised that until blacks asserted their humanity and their personhood, there was not the remotest chance for reconciliation in South Africa. For true reconciliation is a deeply personal matter. It can happen only between persons who assert their own personhood, and who acknowledge and respect that of others. You don't get reconciled to your dog, do you? Steve knew and believed fervently that being pro-black was not the same thing as being anti-white. The Black Consciousness Movement is not a "hate white movement," despite all you may have heard to the contrary. He had a far too profound respect for persons as persons, to want to deal with them under ready-made, shopsoiled [sic] categories.

All who met him had this tremendous sense of a warm-hearted man, and as a notable acquaintance of his told me, a man who was utterly indestructible, of massive intellect and yet reticent; quite unshakeable in his commitment to principle and to radical change in South Africa by peaceful means; a man of real reconciliation, truly an instrument of God's peace, unshakeable in his commitment to the liberation of all South Africans, black and white, striving for a more just and more open South Africa.

## QUESTIONS FOR ANALYSIS

1. What are Steve Biko's charges against white liberals in South Africa?

2. What was the proper role for whites in the anti-apartheid movement according to Biko?

3. How does Bishop Tutu's eulogy differ from the political spirit and point of view expressed in Biko's 1970 essay?

4. According to Bishop Tutu, what were Biko's strongest characteristics? Were these characteristics demonstrated in Biko's essay?

*Source:* First selection from Steve Biko, *I Write What I Like,* ed. by Aelred Stubbs (Harper & Row, 1972). Reprinted with the permission of Bowerdean Publishing Co., Ltd.; second selection from *Crying in the Wilderness: The Struggle for Justice in South Africa,* ed. John Webster (William B. Eerdmans Publishing Co., 1982). Reprinted by permission of the Continuum International Publishing Group.

against colonial rule. The Bandung Conference marked the beginning of an effort by the many new, poor, mostly non-European nations emerging from colonialism to gain more weight in world affairs by banding together. The terms **nonaligned nations** and **Third World,** which became commonplace in the following years, signaled these countries' collective stance toward the rival sides in the Cold War. If the West, led by the United States, and the East, led by the Soviet Union, represented two worlds locked in mortal struggle, the Third World consisted of everyone else.

Leaders of the so-called Third World countries preferred the label *nonaligned,* which signified freedom from membership on either side. However, because the Soviet Union supported national liberation movements and the nonaligned movement included communist countries such as China and Yugoslavia, many Western leaders did not take the term *nonaligned* seriously. They saw Sukarno, Nehru, Nkrumah, and Egypt's Gamal Abd al-Nasir° as stalking horses for a communist takeover of the world. This may also have been the hope of some Soviet leaders, who were quick to offer some of these countries military and financial aid.

For the movement's leaders, however, non-alignment was a means to extract money and support from one or both superpowers. By flirting with the Soviet Union, the United States, or the People's Republic of China, a country could get military and economic aid.

Some skillful nonaligned leaders were able to gain from both sides. Nasir, who ruled Egypt from 1952 to 1970, and his successor, Anwar al-Sadat°, played the game well. The United States offered to build a dam at Aswan°, on the Nile River, to increase Egypt's electrical generating and irrigation capacity. When Egypt turned to the Soviet Union for arms, the United States reneged on the dam project in 1956. The Soviet Union then picked it up and in the 1960s brought it to conclusion. In 1956, Israel, Great Britain, and France conspired to invade Egypt. Their objective was to overthrow Nasir, regain the Suez Canal (he had recently nationalized it), and secure Israel from any Egyptian threat. The invasion succeeded militarily,

**Gamal Abd al-Nasir** (gah-MAHL AHB-d al-NAH-suhr)

**al-Sadat** (al-seh-DAT)   **Aswan** (AS-wahn)

**Bandung Conference, 1955** India's Jawaharlal Nehru (in white hat) was a central figure at the conference held in Indonesia to promote solidarity among nonaligned developing nations. The nonalignment movement failed to achieve the influence that Nehru, Egypt's Nasir, and Indonesia's Sukarno sought.   (Wide World Photos)

but both the United States and the Soviet Union pressured the invaders to withdraw, thus saving Nasir's government. In 1972, Sadat evicted his Soviet military advisers but a year later used his Soviet weapons to attack Israel. After he lost that war, he announced his faith in the power of the United States to solve Egypt's political and economic problems.

Numerous other countries adopted similar balancing strategies. In each case, local leaders were trying to develop their nation's economy and assert or preserve their nation's interests. Manipulating the superpowers was simply a means toward those ends and implied very little about true ideological orientation.

## Japan and China

No other countries took better advantage of the opportunities presented by the superpowers' preoccupation than did Japan and China. Japan signed a peace treaty with most of its former enemies in 1951 and regained independence from American occupation the following year. Renouncing militarism and its imperialist past, Japan remained on the sidelines throughout the Korean War. Its new constitution, written under American supervision in 1946, allowed only a limited self-defense force, banned the deployment of Japanese troops abroad, and gave the vote to women.

The Japanese turned their talents and energies to rebuilding their industries and engaging in world commerce. By isolating Japan from most world political issues, the Cold War provided an exceptionally favorable environment for Japan to develop its economic strength.

Three industries that took advantage of government aid and the newest technologies paved the way for Japan's emergence as an economic superpower after 1975. Projects producing 60 million kilowatts of electricity were completed between 1951 and 1970, almost a third through dams on Japan's many rivers. Between 1960 and 1970, steel production more than quadrupled, reaching 15.7 percent of the total capacity of countries outside the Soviet bloc. The shipbuilding industry produced six times as much tonnage in 1970 as in 1960, almost half of the new tonnage produced outside the Soviet bloc.

While Japan benefited from being outside the Cold War, China was deeply involved in Cold War politics. When Mao Zedong° and the communists

**Mao Zedong** (maow dzuh-dong)

defeated the nationalists in 1949 and established the People's Republic of China (PRC), their main ally and source of arms was the Soviet Union. By 1956, however, the PRC and the Soviet Union were beginning to diverge politically, partly in reaction to the Soviet rejection of Stalinism and partly because of China's reluctance to be cast forever in the role of student. Mao had his own notions of communism, focusing strongly on the peasantry, whom the Soviets ignored in favor of the industrial working class.

Mao's Great Leap Forward in 1958 was supposed to vault China into the ranks of world industrial powers by maximizing the use of labor in small-scale, village-level industries. The policy failed but demonstrated Mao's willingness to carry out massive economic and social projects of his own devising.

In 1966, Mao instituted another radical nation-wide program, the **Cultural Revolution.** He ordered the mass mobilization of Chinese youth into Red Guard units. His goal was to kindle revolutionary fervor in a new generation and to ward off the stagnation and bureaucratization he saw in the Soviet Union. Red Guard units criticized and purged teachers, party officials, and intellectuals for "bourgeois values." Internal party conflict continued until 1971, when Mao admitted that attacks on individuals had gotten out of hand. Meanwhile, small-scale industrialization resulted in record levels of agricultural and industrial production. The last years of the Cultural Revolution were dominated by radicals led by Mao's wife, Jiang Qing°, who focused on restrictions on artistic and intellectual activity.

In the meantime, the rift between the PRC and the Soviet Union had opened so wide that United States President Richard Nixon (1969–1974), by reputation a staunch anticommunist, dropped objections to the PRC's joining the United Nations. In 1971, the PRC occupied China's permanent seat on the Security Council, displacing the Chinese nationalist government on Taiwan. The following year, Nixon visited Beijing, making dramatically clear the new cooperation between the People's Republic of China and the United States.

---

**Jiang Qing** (jyahn ching)

## The Middle East

Independence had come gradually to the Arab countries of the Middle East. Britain granted Syria and Lebanon independence after World War II. Other Arab countries—Iraq, Egypt, Jordan—enjoyed nominal independence during the interwar period but remained under indirect British control until the 1950s.

Overshadowing all Arab politics, however, was the struggle with the new state of Israel. British policy on Palestine between the wars oscillated between favoring Zionist Jewish immigrants and the indigenous Palestinian Arabs. After the war, under intense pressure to resettle European Jewish refugees, Britain turned the Palestine problem over to the United Nations. In November 1947, the General Assembly voted in favor of partitioning Palestine into two states, one Jewish and one Arab. The Jewish community made plans to declare independence while the Palestinians, who felt the proposed land division was unfair, reacted in horror and took up arms. When Israel declared its independence in May 1948, neighboring Arab countries sent armies to help the Palestinians crush the newborn state.

Israel, however, prevailed on all fronts. Some 700,000 Palestinians became refugees. They found shelter in United Nations refugee camps in Jordan, Syria, Lebanon, and the Gaza Strip (a bit of coastal land on the Egyptian-Israeli border). The right of these refugees to return home remains a focal point of Arab politics. In 1967, Israel responded to threatening military moves by Egypt's Nasir by preemptively attacking Egyptian and Syrian air bases. In six days, Israel won a smashing victory. Israel won control of Jerusalem, previously split with Jordan, the West Bank, the Gaza Strip, the strategic Golan Heights in southern Syria, and the entire Sinai Peninsula (see Map 28.2). Acquiring all of Jerusalem satisfied Jews' deep longing to return to their holiest city, but Palestinians continued to

**Map 28.2   Middle East Oil and the Arab-Israeli Conflict, 1947–1973**   Oil resources were long controlled by private European and American companies. In the 1960s most countries, guided by OPEC, negotiated agreements for sharing control, eventually leading to national ownership. This set the stage for the use of oil as a weapon in the 1973 Arab-Israeli war and for subsequent price increases.

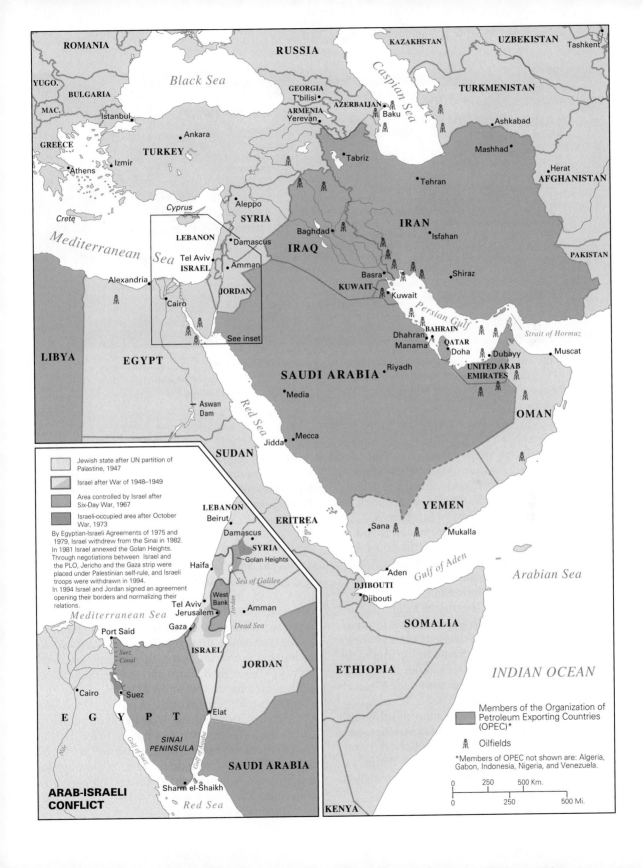

ROMANIA

RUSSIA

KAZAKHSTAN

UZBEKISTAN

Tashkent

YUGO.

*Black Sea*

GEORGIA
T'bilisi

BULGARIA

MAC.

Istanbul

Ankara

AZERBAIJAN
Baku

*Caspian Sea*

TURKMENISTAN

Ashkabad

ARMENIA
Yerevan

GREECE

Izmir

TURKEY

Tabriz

Mashhad

Athens

Crete

Cyprus

Aleppo

SYRIA

Tehran

IRAN

Herat

AFGHANISTAN

*Mediterranean*

LEBANON

Damascus

Baghdad

Isfahan

*Sea*

Tel Aviv

ISRAEL

Amman

IRAQ

PAKISTAN

Alexandria

JORDAN

Basra

Shiraz

Cairo

KUWAIT

Kuwait

*Persian Gulf*

BAHRAIN

See inset

Dhahran

QATAR

Manama

Doha

Dubayy

Muscat

*Strait of Hormuz*

LIBYA

EGYPT

SAUDI ARABIA

Riyadh

UNITED ARAB
EMIRATES

Aswan
Dam

*Red Sea*

Media

OMAN

Mecca

Jidda

SUDAN

YEMEN

Sana

Mukalla

*Gulf of Aden*

*Arabian Sea*

Aden

DJIBOUTI

Djibouti

SOMALIA

ETHIOPIA

*INDIAN OCEAN*

KENYA

**Legend (inset):**

Jewish state after UN partition of Palastine, 1947

Israel after War of 1948–1949

Area controlled by Israel after Six-Day War, 1967

Israeli-occupied area after October War, 1973

By Egyptian-Israeli Agreements of 1975 and 1979, Israel withdrew from the Sinai in 1982. In 1981 Israel annexed the Golan Heights. Through negotiations between Israel and the PLO, Jericho and the Gaza strip were placed under Palestinian self-rule, and Israeli troops were withdrawn in 1994.
In 1994 Israel and Jordan signed an agreement opening their borders and normalizing their relations.

LEBANON
Beirut

ERITREA

Damascus

SYRIA

Haifa

Golan Heights

*Sea of Galilee*

*Mediterranean Sea*

West
Bank

Amman

Tel Aviv

Jerusalem

Gaza

*Dead Sea*

Port Said

ISRAEL

JORDAN

*Suez
Canal*

Cairo

Suez

Elat

*Gulf of Suez*

*SINAI
PENINSULA*

SAUDI ARABIA

*Nile*

E G Y P T

*Gulf of Aqaba*

Sharm el-Shaikh

*Red Sea*

**ARAB-ISRAELI
CONFLICT**

Members of the Organization of Petroleum Exporting Countries (OPEC)*

Oilfields

*Members of OPEC not shown are: Algeria, Gabon, Indonesia, Nigeria, and Venezuela.

0      250      500 Km.

0      250      500 Mi.

**Oil Crisis at the Gas Station**    Dislocations in the oil industry caused by OPEC price increases that began in 1974 produced long lines at gas pumps and local shortages. The crisis brought Middle East politics home to consumers and created a negative stereotype of "oil sheikhs."    (Keza/Gamma)

regard Jerusalem as their destined capital, and Muslims in many countries protested Israeli control of the Dome of the Rock, a revered Islamic shrine located in the city. These acquisitions resulted in a new wave of Palestinian refugees.

The rival claims to Palestine continued to plague Middle Eastern politics. The Palestine Liberation Organization (PLO), headed by Yasir Arafat°, waged guerrilla war against Israel, frequently engaging in acts of terrorism. The militarized Israelis were able to blunt or absorb these attacks and launch counterstrikes that likewise involved assassinations and bombings. Though the United States proved a firm friend of Israel and the Soviet Union armed the Arab states, neither superpower saw the struggle between Zionism and Palestinian nationalism as a vital concern—until oil became a political issue.

The phenomenal concentration of oil wealth in the Persian Gulf states—Iran, Iraq, Kuwait, Saudi Arabia, Qatar, Bahrain, and the United Arab Emirates—was not fully realized until after World War II when demand for oil rose sharply as civilian

economies recovered. As a world oversupply diminished in the face of rising demand, oil-producing states in 1960 formed the **Organization of Petroleum Exporting Countries (OPEC)** to promote their collective interest in higher revenues.

Oil politics and the Arab-Israeli conflict intersected in October 1973. A surprise Egyptian attack across the Suez Canal threw the Israelis into temporary disarray. Within days, the war turned in Israel's favor, and an Egyptian army was trapped at the canal's southern end. The United States then arranged a cease-fire and the disengagement of forces. But before that could happen, the Arab oil-producing countries voted to embargo oil shipments to the United States and the Netherlands as punishment for their support of Israel.

The implications of oil as an economic weapon profoundly disturbed the worldwide oil industry. Prices rose—along with feelings of insecurity. In 1974, OPEC responded to the turmoil in the oil market by quadrupling prices, setting the stage for massive transfers of wealth to the producing countries and provoking a feeling of crisis throughout the consuming countries.

---

**Arafat** (AR-uh-fat)

## The Emergence of Environmental Concerns

Skyrocketing oil prices focused new attention on natural resource issues. Before the mid-1960s, only a few people noticed that untested technologies and all-out drives for industrial productivity were rapidly degrading the environment. The superpowers were particularly negligent of the environmental impact of pesticide and herbicide use, automobile exhaust, industrial waste disposal, and radiation hazards.

New youth activism focused awareness on environmental problems. In 1968, a wave of student unrest swept many parts of the world. Earth Day was first celebrated in 1970, the year in which the United States established its Environmental Protection Agency.

After 1974, making gasoline engines and home heating systems more efficient and lowering highway speed limits to conserve fuel became matters of national debate in the United States while poorer countries struggled to find the money to import oil. A widely read 1972 study, *The Limits of Growth,* forecast a need to cut back on consumption of natural resources in the twenty-first century. Thus, as the most dangerous moments of the Cold War seemed to be passing, ecological and environmental problems of worldwide impact vied with the superpower rivalry and Third World nation building for public attention.

## CONCLUSION

The Cold War and the decolonization movement seemed to arise as logical extensions of World War II. The question of who would control the parts of Europe and Asia liberated from Axis occupation led to Churchill's notion of an iron curtain dividing East and West. The war exhaustion of the European imperialist powers encouraged Asian and African peoples to seek independence and embark on building their own nations.

Intellectuals often framed their understanding of the period in terms of a philosophical struggle between capitalism and socialism dating back to the nineteenth century. But for leaders facing the challenge of governing new nations and creating viable economies, ideology became intertwined with questions of how to profit from the Cold War rivalry between the United States and the Soviet Union.

Historians do not all agree on the year 1975 as the end of the postwar era. The end of the Vietnam War, the beginning of the world oil crisis, and the signing of the Helsinki Accords that brought a measure of agreement among Europeans on both sides of the iron curtain were pivotal events for some countries. But the number of independent countries in the world had grown enormously, and each was in the process of working out its own particular problems. What marks the mid-1970s as the end of an era, therefore, is not a single event so much as the emergence of new concerns. Young people with no memories of World War II were less concerned with the Cold War and the specter of nuclear annihilation than with newly recognized threats to the world environment and with making their own way in the world. In the wealthier nations, this meant taking advantage of economic growth and increasing technological sophistication. In the developing world, it meant seeking the education and employment needed for playing active roles in the drama of nation building.

## ■ Key Terms

**iron curtain**

**Cold War**

**North Atlantic Treaty Organization (NATO)**

**United Nations**

**World Bank**

**Marshall Plan**

**European Community (EC)**

**Truman Doctrine**

**Warsaw Pact**

**Korean War**

**Vietnam War**

**Cuban missile crisis**

**Helsinki Accords**

**nonaligned nations**

**Third World**

**Cultural Revolution (China)**

**Organization of Petroleum Exporting Countries (OPEC)**

# ■ Suggested Reading

The period since 1945 has been particularly rich in memoirs by government leaders. Some that are particularly relevant to the Cold War and decolonization are Dean Acheson (U.S. secretary of state under Truman), *Present at the Creation* (1969); Nikita Khrushchev, *Khrushchev Remembers* (1970); and Anthony Eden (British prime minister), *Full Circle* (1960).

Geoffrey Barraclough, *An Introduction to Contemporary History* (1964), is a remarkable early effort at understanding the broad sweep of history during this period. See also David Reynolds, *One World Divisible: A Global History Since 1945* (2000).

Scholarship on the origins of the Cold War is extensive and includes Akira Iriye, *The Cold War in Asia: A Historical Introduction* (1974); Bruce Kuniholm, *The Origins of the Cold War in the Middle East* (1980); Madelaine Kalb, *The Congo Cables: The Cold War in Africa—From Eisenhower to Kennedy* (1982); and Michael J. Hogan, *A Cross of Iron: Harry S Truman and the Origins of the National Security State* (1998). For a recent reconsideration of earlier historical viewpoints, see Melvyn P. Leffler and David S. Painter, eds., *Origins of the Cold War: An International History* (1994).

Good general histories of the Cold War include Martin Walker, *The Cold War: A History* (1993), and Walter Lafeber, *America, Russia, and the Cold War, 1945–1992* (1993). The latter emphasizes how the Cold War eroded American democratic values. For a look at the Cold War from the Soviet perspective, see William Taubman, *Stalin's America Policy* (1981); for the American perspective, see John Lewis Gaddis, *Strategies of Containment: A Critical Appraisal of Postwar American National Security Policy* (1982). The Cuban missile crisis is well covered in Graham Allison, *Essence of Decision: Explaining the Cuban Missile Crisis* (1971), and Michael Beschloss, *The Crisis Years: Kennedy and Khrushchev, 1960–1963* (1991). Also see Aleksandr Fursenko and Timothy Naftali, *"One Hell of a Gamble": Khrushchev, Castro, and Kennedy, 1958–1964: The Secret History of the Cuban Missile Crisis* (1997); and the more recent John L. Gaddis, *We Now Know: Rethinking Cold War History* (1997); Mark Mazower, *Dark Continent* (1999); and William Hitchcock, *The Struggle for Europe: The Turbulent History of a Divided Continent 1945–2002* (2003).

The nuclear arms race and the associated Soviet–U.S. competition in space are well covered by McGeorge Bundy, *Danger and Survival: Choices About the Bomb in the First Fifty Years* (1988), and Walter MacDougall, *The Heavens and the Earth: A Political History of the Space Age* (1985). Among the many novels illustrating the alarming impact of the arms race on the general public are Philip Wylie, *Tomorrow!* (1954), and Nevil Shute, *On the Beach* (1970). At a technical and philosophical level, Herman Kahn's *On Thermonuclear War* (1961) had a similar effect.

The end of the European empires is broadly treated by D. K. Fieldhouse, *The Colonial Empires* (1982); a broad view is provided by D. A. Low, *The Egalitarian Moment: Asia and Africa, 1950–1980* (1996); for the British Empire in particular, see Brian Lapping, *End of Empire* (1985). For a critical view of American policies toward the decolonized world, see Gabriel Kolko, *Confronting the Third World: United States Foreign Policy, 1945–1980* (1988).

Books on some of the specific episodes of decolonization treated in this chapter include the following: on Algeria, Alistaire Horne, *A Savage War of Peace: Algeria, 1954–1962* (1987); on Africa, H. S. Wilson, *African Decolonization* (1994), and Frederick Cooper, *Decolonization and African Society: The Labor Question in French and British Africa* (1996); on Cuba, Hugh Thomas, *Cuba: The Pursuit of Freedom* (1971); on the Suez crisis of 1956, Keith Kyle, *Suez 1956* (1991); on Britain's role in the Middle East over the period of the birth of Israel, William Roger Louis, *The British Empire in the Middle East, 1945–1951* (1984); on Vietnam, George Herring, *America's Longest War: The United States and Vietnam, 1950–1975* (1986), and Stanley Karnow, *Vietnam: A History* (1991); and on Latin America, Thomas E. Skidmore and Peter H. Smith, *Modern Latin America*, 5th ed. (2001).

The special cases of Japan and China in this period are covered by Takafusa Nakamura, *A History of Showa Japan, 1926–1989* (1998); John Dower, *Embracing Defeat: Japan in the Wake of World War II* (1999); Marius B. Jansen, *Japan and China: From War to Peace, 1894–1972* (1975); and Maurice Meisner, *Mao's China and After: A History of the People's Republic* (1986). On the consequences of the Great Leap Forward, see Jasper Becker, *Hungry Ghosts* (1998); and on the Cultural Revolution, see Lynn T. White, *Policies of Chaos: The Organizational Causes of Violence in China's Cultural Revolution* (1989). John Merrill, *Korea: The Peninsular Origins of the War* (1989), presents the Korean War as a civil and revolutionary conflict as well as an episode of the Cold War. Among the hundreds of books on the Arab-Israeli conflict, Charles D. Smith, *Palestine and the Arab-Israel Conflict* (1992), and Trevor N. Dupuy, *Elusive Victory: The Arab-Israeli Wars, 1947–1974* (1978), stand out.

# Crisis, Realignment, and the Dawn of the Post–Cold War World, 1975–1991

# 29

## CHAPTER OUTLINE

Postcolonial Crises and Asian Economic Expansion, 1975–1991

The End of the Bipolar World, 1989–1991

The Challenge of Population Growth

Unequal Development and the Movement of Peoples

Technological and Environmental Change

DIVERSITY AND DOMINANCE: The Struggle for Women's Rights in an Era of Global Political and Economic Change

On Thursday, July 22, 1993, police officers in Rio de Janeiro's banking district attempted to arrest a young boy caught sniffing glue. In the resulting scuffle, one police officer was injured by stones thrown by a group of homeless children who lived in nearby streets and parks. Late the following night, hooded vigilantes in two cars fired hundreds of shots at a group of these children sleeping on the steps of a church. The attackers, later identified as off-duty police officers, killed five children there and two more in a park.

At that time, more than 350,000 abandoned children lived in Rio's streets and parks and resorted to begging, selling drugs, stealing, and prostitution to survive. In 1993 alone, death squads and drug dealers killed more than four hundred of them. Few people sympathized with the victims. One person living near the scene of the July shootings said, "Those street kids are bandits, and bandits have to die. They are a rotten branch that has to be pruned."[1]

At the end of the twentieth century, the brutality of those children's lives was an increasingly common feature of life in the developing world, where rapid population growth was outstripping economic resources. Similar problems of violence, poverty, and social breakdown could be found in most developing nations.

In wealthy industrialized nations as well, politicians and social reformers worried about the effects of unemployment, family breakdown, substance abuse, and homelessness. As had been true during the eighteenth-century Industrial Revolution (see Chapter 20), dramatic economic growth, increased global economic integration, and rapid technological progress in the post–World War II period coincided with growing social dislocation and inequality. Among the most important events of the period were the emergence of new industrial powers in Asia and the precipitous demise of the Soviet Union and its socialist allies.

New challenges also appeared in the form of world population growth and large-scale migrations. Population grew most rapidly in the world's poorest nations, worsening social and economic problems and undermining fragile political institutions. In the industrialized nations, the arrival of large numbers of culturally and linguistically distinct immigrants fueled economic growth but also led to the appearance of anti-immigrant political movements and, in some cases, violent ethnic conflict.

As you read this chapter, ask yourself the following questions:

- How did the Cold War affect politics in Latin America and the Middle East in the 1970s and 1980s?

- What forces led to the collapse of the Soviet Union?

- What is the relationship between the rate of population growth and the wealth of nations?

- How has technological change affected the global environment in the recent past?

# POSTCOLONIAL CRISES AND ASIAN ECONOMIC EXPANSION, 1975–1991

//

Between 1975 and 1991, wars and revolutions provoked by a potent mix of ideology, nationalism, ethnic hatred, and religious fervor spread death and destruction through many of the world's least developed regions. Although often tied to earlier colonialism and foreign intervention, each conflict reflected a specific set of historical experiences. In many cases, conflicts provoked by local and regional causes tended to become more deadly and long lasting because the United States and the Soviet Union intervened. Conflicts in which the rival superpowers financed and armed competing factions or parties were called **proxy wars.**

Local and regional conflicts and proxy wars were not universal. During this same period, Japan gained a position among the world's leading industrial powers, while a small number of other Asian economies quickly entered the ranks of industrial and commercial powers. By the early 1990s, the collapse of the Soviet system in eastern Europe had ended the Cold War. As former socialist nations opened their markets to foreign investment and competition, economic transformation was often accompanied by wrenching social change. Other challenges facing the late twentieth century included growing inequalities among nations and within nations, rapid population expansion, and degradation of the environment.

## Revolutions, Repression, and Democratic Reform in Latin America

After the Cuban Revolution, Fidel Castro sought to end the domination of the United States and uplift the Cuban masses by changing the economy in fundamental ways. Both objectives led to confrontation with the United States. The Cuban Revolution was the first revolution in the Western Hemisphere to nationalize foreign investment, redistribute the wealth of the elite, and forge an alliance with the

| | The Americas | Middle East | Asia | Eastern Europe |
|---|---|---|---|---|
| **1970** | **1964**  Military takeover in Brazil<br><br>**1970**  Salvador Allende elected president of Chile<br><br>**1973**  Allende overthrown<br><br>**1976**  Military takeover in Argentina | | **1975**  Vietnam war ends<br><br>**1978**  China opens its economy | |
| **1980** | **1979**  Sandinistas overthrow Anastasio Somoza in Nicaragua<br><br>**1983–1990** Democracy returns in Argentina, Brazil, and Chile | **1979**  Islamic Revolution over-throws shah of Iran<br><br>**1980–1988**  Iran-Iraq War | | **1979**  USSR sends troops to Afghanistan<br><br>**1985**  Mikhail Gorbachev becomes Soviet head of state |
| | | | **1986**  Average Japanese income overtakes income in United States<br><br>**1989**  Tiananmen Square confrontation | **1989**  USSR with-draws troops from Afghanistan; Berlin Wall falls<br><br>**1989–1991**  End of communism in eastern Europe |
| **1990** | **1990**  Sandinistas defeated in elections in Nicaragua | **1990**  Iraq invades Kuwait<br><br>**1991**  Persian Gulf War | | **1990**  Reunifica-tion of Germany |

**C H R O N O L O G Y**

Soviet Union. The fact that a communist government could come to power and thwart efforts by the United States to overthrow it energized the revolutionary left throughout Latin America (see Chapter 28). Unable to overthrow Castro and fearful that revolution would spread across Latin America, the United States mobilized its political and military allies in Latin America to defeat communism at all costs.

Brazil was the first to experience the full effects of the conservative reaction to the Cuban Revolution. Claiming that Brazil's civilian political leaders could not protect the nation from communist subversion, the army overthrew the democratically elected government in 1964. The military suspended the constitution, outlawed all existing political parties, and exiled former presidents and opposition leaders. Death squads—illegal paramilitary organizations sanctioned by the government—detained, tortured, and executed thousands of citizens. The dictatorship also undertook an ambitious economic program that promoted industrialization through import substitution, using tax and tariff policies to compel foreign-owned companies to increase investment in manufacturing.

Elements of this "Brazilian Solution" were imposed across much of Latin America in the 1970s and early 1980s. In 1970, Chile's new president, **Salvador Allende°,** undertook an ambitious program of socialist reforms to redistribute wealth from the elite and middle classes to the poor. He also nationalized most of Chile's heavy industry and mines, including the American-owned copper companies that dominated the Chilean economy. From the beginning of Allende's presidency, the administration of United States President Richard Nixon (1969–1973) worked in Chile to organize opposition to Allende's reforms. After Chile's economy weakened, Allende was overthrown in 1973 by a military uprising led by General Augusto Pinochet° and supported by the United States. President Allende and thousands of Chileans died in this uprising, and thousands of others were illegally seized, tortured, and imprisoned without trial. Once in power, Pinochet rolled back Allende's reforms, reduced state participation in the economy, and en-

couraged foreign investment. In 1976, Argentina followed Brazil and Chile into military dictatorship. During the next seven years, the military fought what it called the **Dirty War** against terrorism. More than nine thousand Argentines lost their lives, and thousands of others endured arrest, terrible tortures, and the loss of property.

The flow of U.S. arms to regimes with the worst human rights records stopped during the four-year term of United States president Jimmy Carter (1977–1980). Carter championed human rights in the hemisphere and sought to placate Latin American resentment for past U.S. interventions by renegotiating the Panama Canal treaty and agreeing to the reestablishment of Panamanian sovereignty in the Canal Zone at the end of 1999. He also tried, but failed, to find some common ground with the **Sandinistas°,** a revolutionary movement in Nicaragua that overthrew the corrupt dictatorship of Anastasio Somoza in 1979. The Sandinistas received significant political and financial support from Cuba and, once in power, sought to imitate the command economies of Cuba and the Soviet Union. The Nicaraguan Revolution nationalized properties owned by members of the Nicaraguan elite and U.S. citizens.

In 1981, Ronald Reagan became president and replaced Carter's policy of conciliation with efforts at reversing the results of the Nicaraguan Revolution and defeating a revolutionary movement in neighboring El Salvador. His options, however, were limited by the U.S. Congress, which feared that Central America might become another Vietnam. The Reagan administration sought to roll back the Nicaraguan Revolution through punitive economic measures and support for the anti-Sandinista Contras (counterrevolutionaries), using both legal and illegal funds.

The Contras were unable to defeat the Sandinistas, but they did gain a bloody stalemate by the end of the 1980s. Confident that they were supported by the majority of Nicaraguans and assured that the U.S. Congress was close to cutting off aid to the Contras, the Sandinistas called for free elections in 1990. But they had miscalculated and lost the election. Exhausted by more than a decade of violence, a majority of Nicaraguan voters rejected

---

**Salvador Allende** (sal-vah-DOR ah-YEHN-day)    **Augusto Pinochet** (ah-GOOS-toh pin-oh-CHET)

**Sandinistas** (sahn-din-EES-tahs)

the Sandinistas and elected a middle-of-the-road coalition led by Violeta Chamorro°.

The military dictatorships established in Brazil, Chile, and Argentina all came to an end between 1983 and 1990. In each case, reports of kidnappings, tortures, and corruption by military governments undermined public support. In Argentina, the military junta foolishly decided in 1982 to seize the Falkland Islands—the Argentines called them the "Malvinas." The Argentine junta had helped President Reagan support the Contras in Nicaragua and believed he would keep Britain's prime minister, Margaret Thatcher, from taking military action. When the Argentine garrison in the Falklands surrendered, military rule in Argentina itself collapsed.

In Chile and Brazil, the military dictatorships ended without the drama of foreign war. Despite significant economic growth under Pinochet, Chileans resented the violence and corruption of the military. In 1988, Pinochet called a plebiscite to extend his authority, but the majority vote went against him. Brazil's military initiated a gradual transition to civilian rule in 1985. By 1991, nearly 95 percent of Latin America's population lived under civilian rule.

In 1991 most Latin American countries were also dominated by the United States and were reducing the economic role of the state. However, after 1994 new political movements have been demanding more government participation in the economy (see Diversity and Dominance: The Struggle for Women's Rights in an Era of Global Political and Economic Change).

## Islamic Revolutions in Iran and Afghanistan

The Middle East was another region where the superpowers were involved in local revolutions. The United States was motivated to act in support of Israel and to protect access to petroleum from the region. The Soviet Union wished to prevent the spread of radical Islamic movements across the border into its own Muslim regions.

The Iranian Revolution of 1979 proved enormously frustrating to the United States. In 1953, covert intervention by the United States Central Intelligence Agency (CIA) helped Shah Muhammad Reza Pahlavi° retain his throne in the face of a movement to usurp royal power. Even when he finally nationalized the foreign-owned oil industry, the shah continued to enjoy special American support. As oil revenues increased following the price increases of the 1970s, the United States encouraged the shah to spend his nation's growing wealth on equipping the Iranian army with advanced American weaponry. By the 1970s, there was mounting popular resentment against the shah's dependence on the United States, the ballooning wealth of the elite families that supported him, and the inefficiency, malfeasance, and corruption of his government, which led to mass opposition.

**Ayatollah Ruhollah Khomeini°,** a Shi'ite° philosopher-cleric who had spent most of his eighty-plus years in religious and academic pursuits, became the voice and symbolic leader of the opposition. Massive street demonstrations and crippling strikes forced the shah to flee Iran and ended the monarchy in 1979. In the Islamic Republic of Iran, which replaced the monarchy, Ayatollah Khomeini was supreme arbiter of disputes and guarantor of religious legitimacy. Elections were held, but monarchists, communists, and other groups opposed to the idea of an Islamic Republic were barred from running for office. Shi'ite clerics with little training for government service emerged in many of the highest posts, and stringent measures were taken to replace Western styles and culture with Islamic norms. Universities were temporarily closed, and their faculties were purged of secularists and monarchists. Women were compelled to wear modest Islamic garments outside the house, and semi-official vigilante committees policed public morals.

The United States under President Carter had criticized the shah's repressive regime, but the overthrow of a long-standing ally and the creation of the Islamic Republic were blows to American prestige. Khomeini saw the United States as a "Great Satan" opposed to Islam, and he helped to foster Islamic revolutionary movements elsewhere, which threatened the interests of both the United

---

Violeta Chamorro (vee-oh-LET-ah cha-MOR-roe)

Reza Pahlavi (REH-zah PAH-lah-vee)   **Ayatollah Ruhollah Khomeini** (eye-uh-TOLL-uh ROOH-ol-LAH ko-MAY-nee) **Shi'ite** (SHE-ite)

# DIVERSITY AND DOMINANCE

## THE STRUGGLE FOR WOMEN'S RIGHTS IN AN ERA OF GLOBAL POLITICAL AND ECONOMIC CHANGE

*The struggle for women's rights is one of the most important social movements of the twentieth century. Although fundamental similarities in objectives can be identified across cultural and political boundaries, women in less-developed nations are forced to recognize that their objectives and strategies must take into account international inequalities in power and wealth. In this section Gladys Acosta, a militant Peruvian feminist, discusses the appropriate agenda for this struggle in the era after the fall of the Soviet Union and the rise of **neo-liberalism.***

*Neo-liberalism is the term used in Latin America to identify the free-market economic policies advocated by the United States. Among its chief characteristics are an end to the protection of local industries, a reduction in government social welfare policies, a reduction in public-sector employment, a commitment to paying debts to international creditors, and the removal of impediments to foreign investment. Many Latin Americans believe neo-liberalism is a new form of imperialism.*

No one can abstain from the debate about the great historical systems of our time. Not even those of us who are trying to change the complex web of human relationships from a feminist perspective. Everywhere people are talking about the end of ideologies. But before we can grasp the significance of current events and their consequences, we need to pinpoint our various doubts and blank spots. Capitalism is the main pivot of our lives because we were born under its influence. It [has] hegemony. . . .

Gender, the main distinction between all people, is ignored in most philosophical, political or economic discussions. The reason for this lies partly in the low level of women's participation, but not entirely, because women are not always aware of the system of submission and repression to which we are subjected against our will. We need to find something which unites women in a gender-specific manner. That doesn't mean sweeping under the carpet all the differences between us, like social position, culture or age. . . .

### Neo-Liberalism in Action

For those of us who live under the influence of the capitalist system, the situation is different. When I talk of neo-liberalism, I mean austerity measures, foreign debts, and increased liberties for all those who have the power of money at their disposal and the power of repression over those who make demands. We have now reached a new form of capitalist accumulation. The world's economic system is in a state of change and capital has become more concentrated and centralised. I would not go as far as to say countries don't exist anymore but national identities do certainly play a different role now. It is important to understand the dynamics because otherwise historical responsibilities are obscured and we no longer know whom we're fighting against. If we look at the bare face of neo-liberalism from a woman's point of view, we cannot fail to notice its murderous consequences. To create a more humane society we must continue to reject neo-liberalism here and now in the hope of being able to change the dead present into a living future. Under neo-liberalism there is a breathtaking circulation of commodities, but also an exchange of ideas, illusions and dreams. At the moment we're experiencing capitalism's greatest ideological offensive. It's all business: everything is bought and sold and everything has its price.

### The Consequences of Neo-Liberal Politics

We women play an important role in this ever-more internationalized economy because we represent, as ever, a particularly exploitable workforce. A number of studies have revealed the existence of subcontractor chains who work for transnational companies "informally" and mainly employ women. Basically we are dealing with a kind of integration into the world market which often uses our own homes as its outlet. Obviously, this work is badly paid and completely unprotected and has to be done without any of those social rights which were formerly achieved by trade union struggles. The most important thing for us is to keep hold of just one thread of the enterprise so we can show how the commodities make their way to their final destination. As it advances worldwide, this capitalism also encourages the expansion of certain kinds of tourism. A visible increase in prostitution is part of this, whereby women from poor countries are smuggled into large, internationally-operated rings which exploit them. The reports of Filipina women traded on the West German market send shivers down our spines. . . . What kind of freedom are you talking about there?

## How the Adoption of Austerity Measures Affects Women's Lives

It is obvious that foreign debt is one of the most inhuman forms of exploitation in our countries when one considers the ratio between work necessary for workers' needs and work producing profit for employers. The experts have already explained how the prevailing exchange and investment structures have created international finance systems which keep whole populations in inhuman conditions. Although many people might think it crazy, the development model of the global economy has a marked relation to gender. As long as prices were slapped on some luxury consumer items there weren't any serious problems; but now the snares have been set around basic commodities. Women in every household are suffering every day as a result of impoverished economies and those who are most exposed to the effects of foreign debt are women.

When it comes to shopping, caring for sick children or the impossibility of meeting their schooling costs, the illusion of "leaving poverty behind" evaporates. Yet the problem is not only of an economic nature because under such circumstances the constant tension leads to grave, often lasting exhaustion. The psychosocial damage is alarming. The situation is ready to explode, so to speak. . . . The adoption of austerity measures means a curtailment of the state's commitment to social services with a direct effect on women. Daily life becomes hell for them. The lack of even minimal state welfare presents women (and obviously children too) with crushing working days. There is a constant expenditure of human energy without any hope of rest! No relaxation, no breaks. . . . And if we consider what happens within the family, we notice that women keep the smallest portion of the meagre family income. They give everything to their children or those adults who bring home a pay packet. As a result malnutrition among women is increasing at an alarming rate and their frequent pregnancies represent a superhuman physical achievement.

Women's valiant achievements in defending life and survival are not acknowledged by society. The efforts of women's organisations, whether it be communal kitchens, the glass-of-milk committees [milk distribution among the poor] or health services don't get the appropriate social esteem. The social value of women cannot be calculated. Perhaps in years to come the fate of millions of women who sacrifice everything to support the children and youth of Peru and other countries in Latin America will be acknowledged. We should not ignore the fact that violence of every form . . . goes hand-in-hand with the difficult situation I have described.[1] It's nothing new for women because the open wounds of sexual violence, abuse at home and the contempt of this *machista* culture, have always featured in our lives and our mothers' lives. The challenge is to prevent these from also affecting our future generations.

## And the Future?

The neo-liberal offensive is international and demands international opposition strategies combined with political proposals by new social forces which address women's problems. We want to change estimations of our worth and achieve society's acknowledgement of what has been belittled until now as "women's affairs." Such important decisions as the right to the termination of unwanted pregnancies can no longer be ignored on the political stage. We want our place in the political decision-making process; we want to have a say in all problems which concern the Peruvian people and the

---

[1] In the last Report of the Comisaria de mujeres in Lima (the only one in the country at present) 4,800 rapes were filed for 1990, of which 4,200 went to trial. The police commissioner, in reading the document, personally acknowledged the alarming social problem which is posed by the violence of men who are connected to their victims in some way and which, indeed, persists throughout all levels of society.

whole world. We want to be informed so as not to be deceived by those who are used to practising politics for a flock of sheep. This road will be difficult but at least we shall regain the strengths of socialism and create social alternatives which are aimed at changing the destructive technological order as well as eliminating the international division of labour and the sexual hierarchy inherent within it. In so doing we shall try to create democratic structures which include the people in the decision-making process. The barriers thrown up by formal representative structures must be overcome urgently. A new democracy should be founded as the basic prerequisite for the society of the future.

## QUESTIONS FOR ANALYSIS

1. What is neo-liberalism?
2. According to Acosta, how does global economic integration fostered by neo-liberalism affect the lives of women as workers?
3. Acosta claims that indebtedness to foreign lenders leads to austerity measures. How does this impact families in poor countries?
4. What does Acosta advocate?

*Source:* Gaby Küppers, ed., *Compañeras. Voices from the Latin American Women's Movement* (London: Latin American Bureau, 1994), 167–172.

States and Israel. In November 1979, Iranian radicals seized the U.S. embassy in Tehran and then held fifty-two diplomats hostage for 444 days. Americans felt humiliated by their inability to do anything, particularly after the failure of a military rescue attempt. In the fall of 1980, shortly after negotiations for the release of the hostages began, **Saddam Husayn°,** the ruler of neighboring Iraq, invaded Iran to topple the Islamic Republic. His own dictatorial rule rested on a secular Arab nationalist philosophy and long-standing friendship with the Soviet Union, which had provided him with advanced weaponry. He feared that the fervor of Iran's revolutionary Shi'ite leaders would infect his own country's Shi'ite majority and threaten his power. The war pitted American weapons in the hands of the Iranians against Soviet weapons in the hands of the Iraqis, but the superpowers avoided overt involvement during eight years of bloodshed. Covertly, however, the Reagan administration sent arms via Israel to Iran, hoping to gain the release of other American hostages held by radical Islamic groups in Lebanon and to help finance the Contra war against the Sandinista government of Nicaragua. When this deal came to the light in 1986, the resulting political scandal intensified American hostility toward Iran. Openly tilting toward Iraq, President Reagan sent the United States Navy to the Persian Gulf, ostensibly to protect nonbelligerent shipping. The move helped persuade Iran to accept a cease-fire in 1988.

**Saddam Husayn** (sah-DAHM who-SANE)

While the United States faced anguish and frustration in Iran, the Soviet Union found itself facing even more serious problems in neighboring Afghanistan. Since World War II, the Soviet Union had succeeded in staying out of shooting wars by using proxies to challenge the United States. But in 1979, the Soviet Union sent its army to Afghanistan to bolster communist rule against a hodgepodge of local, religiously inspired guerrilla bands that had taken control of much of the countryside.

With the United States, Saudi Arabia, and Pakistan paying, equipping, and training the Afghan rebels, the Soviet Union found itself in the same kind of unwinnable war the United States had stumbled into in Vietnam. Unable to justify the continuing drain on manpower, morale, and economic resources and facing widespread domestic discontent over the war, Soviet leaders finally withdrew their troops in 1989. The Afghan communists held on for another three years. But once rebel groups took control of the entire country, they began to fight among themselves over who should rule.

## Asian Transformation

Japan has few mineral resources and is dependent on oil imports, but the Japanese economy weathered the oil price shocks of the 1970s better than did the economies of Europe and the United States. In fact, Japan experienced a faster rate of economic growth in the 1970s and 1980s than did any other major developed economy, growing at about 10 percent a year. Average income also increased rapidly, overtaking that of the United States in 1986.

There are some major differences between the Japanese industrial model and that of the United States. During the American occupation, Japanese industrial conglomerates, *zaibatsu* (see Chapter 25), were broken up. Although ownership of major industries became less concentrated as a result, new industrial alliances appeared. There are now six major **keiretsu**° that each include firms in industry, commerce, construction, and a major bank tied together in an interlocking ownership structure. There are also minor keiretsu dominated by a major corporation, like Toyota, and including its major suppliers. These combinations of companies have close relationships with government. Government assistance in the form of tariffs and import regulations inhibiting foreign competition was crucial in the early stages of the development of Japan's automobile and semiconductor industries, among others.

Through the 1970s and 1980s, Japanese success at exporting manufactured goods produced huge trade surpluses with other nations, prompting the United States and the European Community to try to pry open the Japanese market through tough negotiating. These efforts had only limited success. In 1990, Japan enjoyed a trade surplus with the rest of the world that was twice as large as in 1985. Many experts assumed that the competitive advantages that Japan enjoyed in the 1980s would propel Japan past the United States as the world's preeminent industrial economy. But the Japanese economy began to stall at the end of the decade.

The Japanese model of close cooperation between government and industry was imitated by a small number of other Asian states. The most important of them was South Korea, which overcame the devastation of the Korean War in little more than a decade through a combination of inexpensive labor, strong technical education, and substantial domestic capital reserves. Despite large defense expenditures, South Korea developed heavy industries such as steel and shipbuilding, as well as consumer industries such as automobiles and consumer electronics. Japanese investment and

*keiretsu* (kay-REHT-soo)

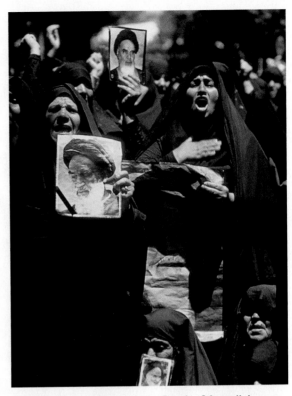

**Muslim Women Mourning the Death of Ayatollah Khomeini in 1989**    An Islamic revolution overthrew the shah of Iran in 1979. Ayatollah Khomeini sought to lead Iran away from the influences of Western culture and challenged the power of the United States in the Persian Gulf. (Alexandra Avakian/Woodfin Camp & Associates)

technology transfers accelerated this process. Hyundai was typical of the four giant corporations that accounted for nearly half of South Korea's gross domestic product (GDP) in manufacturing products ranging from supertankers and cars to electronics and housing.

Taiwan, Hong Kong, and Singapore also developed modern industrial and commercial economies so rapidly that these three nations and South Korea were often referred to as the **Asian Tigers.** All shared many characteristics that helped explain their rapid industrialization. All had disciplined and hard-working labor forces, and all invested heavily in education. For example, as early as 1980, Korea had as many engineering graduates as Germany, Britain, and Sweden combined. All had high

**Dry Docks Owned by Korea's Hyundai Corporation**    Korea's rapid industrialization symbolizes Pacific Rim economic growth.    (Paul Chesley/Getty Images)

rates of personal saving that allowed them to fund investment in new technology generously. In 1987, the saving rates in Taiwan and South Korea were three times higher than in the United States. All emphasized outward-looking export strategies. And, like Japan, all of these dynamic Pacific Rim economies benefited from government sponsorship and protection. All were beneficiaries of the extraordinary expansion in world trade and international communication that permitted technology to be disseminated more rapidly than at any other time in the past. As a result, newly industrializing nations began with current technologies.

In China after Mao Zedong's death in 1976, the communist leadership introduced a comprehensive economic reform that allowed more individual initiative and permitted individuals to accumulate wealth. Beginning in 1978, the Communist Party in

Sichuan province freed more than six thousand firms to compete for business outside the state planning process. The results were remarkable. Under China's leader, **Deng Xiaoping°**, these reforms were expanded across the nation. China also began to permit foreign investment for the first time since the communists came to power in 1949. Between 1978 and the end of the 1990s, foreign investors committed more than $180 billion to the Chinese economy, and McDonald's, Coca-Cola, Airbus, and other foreign companies opened for business. But more than 100 million workers were still employed in state-owned enterprises, and most foreign-owned companies were segregated in special economic zones. The result was a dual industrial sector—one modern and efficient and

---

**Deng Xiaoping** (dung show-ping)

connected to international markets, the other dominated by government and directed by political decisions.

In the countryside, Deng Xiaoping permitted the contracting of land to individuals and families, who were free to consume or sell whatever they produced. By 1984, 93 percent of China's agricultural land was in effect in private hands and producing for the market, tripling agricultural output.

Perhaps the best measure of the success of Deng's reforms is that between 1980 and 1993, China's per capita output more than doubled, averaging more than 8 percent growth per year in comparison with the world average of slightly more than 1 percent and Japan's average of 3.3 percent. This growth was overwhelmingly the result of exports to the developed nations of the West, especially the United States. Nevertheless, per capita measures of wealth indicated that China remained a poor nation. China's per capita GDP was roughly the same as Mexico's—about $3,600 per year. By comparison, Taiwan had a per capita GDP of $14,700.

Deng Xiaoping's strategy of balancing change and continuity helped China avoid some of the social costs and political consequences experienced by Russia and other European socialist countries that abruptly plunged into capitalism and democracy. As Chinese officials put it, China was "changing a big earthquake into a thousand tremors." The nation's leadership faced a major challenge in 1989. Responding to mass movements in favor of democracy across the globe and to inflation, Chinese students and intellectuals, many of whom had studied outside China, led a series of protests demanding more democracy and an end to inflation and corruption. This movement culminated in a massive occupation of **Tiananmen Square**° by protestors, in the heart of Beijing. After weeks of standoff, tanks pushed into the square, killing hundreds, perhaps thousands. Many more were arrested. Although the Communist Party survived this challenge, it was not clear whether rapid economic growth, increasing inequality, high levels of unemployment, and massive migration from the countryside to the cities could occur without triggering a political transformation.

# THE END OF THE BIPOLAR WORLD, 1989–1991

F ew in 1980 predicted the startling collapse of the Soviet Union and the socialist nations of the Warsaw Pact. The once-independent nations and ethnic groups that had been brought within the Soviet Union and the eastern European nations seemed securely transformed by the experiences and institutions of communism. By 1990, however, nationalism was resurgent, and communism was nearly finished.

## Crisis in the Soviet Union

Under United States president Ronald Reagan and the Soviet Union's general secretary, Leonid Brezhnev°, the rhetoric of the Cold War remained intense. Massive new U.S. investments in armaments, including a space-based missile protection system that never became operational, placed heavy burdens on the Soviet economy, which was unable to absorb the cost of developing similar weapons. Soviet economic problems were systemic. Obsolete industrial plants and centralized planning stifled initiative and responsiveness to market demand. Government bureaucrats and Communist Party favorites received special privileges, including permission to shop in stores that stocked Western goods, but the average citizen faced long lines and waiting lists for goods. Soviet citizens contrasted their lot with the free and prosperous life of the West depicted in the increasingly accessible Western media. The arbitrariness of the bureaucracy, the cynical manipulation of information, and deprivations created a generalized crisis in morale.

Despite the unpopularity of the war in Afghanistan and growing discontent, Brezhnev refused to modify his rigid and unsuccessful policies. But he was unable to contain an underground current of protest. Self-published underground writings by critics of the regime circulated widely despite government efforts to suppress them. The physicist Andrei Sakharov and his wife, Yelena

Tiananmen (tee-yehn-ahn-men)

Leonid Brezhnev (leh-oh-NEED BREZ-nef)

Bonner, protested the nuclear arms race and human rights violations and were condemned to banishment within the country. Some Jewish dissidents spoke out against anti-Semitism, but many more left for Israel or the United States.

By the time **Mikhail Gorbachev°** took up the reins of the Soviet government in 1985, war weariness, economic decay, and vocal protest had reached critical levels. Casting aside Brezhnev's hard line, Gorbachev authorized major reforms in an attempt to stave off total collapse. His policy of political openness (*glasnost*) permitted criticism of the government and the Communist Party. His policy of **_perestroika_°** ("restructuring") was an attempt to address long-suppressed economic problems by moving away from central state planning and toward a more open economic system. In 1989, he ended the war in Afghanistan, which had cost many lives and much money.

## The Collapse of the Socialist Bloc

Events in eastern Europe were very important in forcing change on the Soviet Union. In 1980, protests by Polish shipyard workers in the city of Gdansk led to the formation of **Solidarity,** a labor union that soon enrolled 9 million members. The Roman Catholic Church in Poland, strengthened by the elevation of a Pole, Karol Wojtyla°, to the papacy as John Paul II in 1978, gave strong moral support to the protest movement. As Gorbachev loosened political controls in the Soviet Union after 1985, communist leaders elsewhere lost confidence in Soviet resolve, and critics and reformers in Poland and throughout the rest of eastern Europe were emboldened (see Map 29.1).

Beleaguered Warsaw Pact governments vacillated between relaxation of control and the suppression of dissent. As the Catholic clergy in Poland had supported Solidarity, Protestant and Orthodox religious leaders aided the rise of opposition groups elsewhere. This combination of nationalism and religion provided a powerful base for opponents of the communist regimes. Threatened by these forces, communist governments sought to

Gorbachev (GORE-beh-CHOF)   *perestroika* (per-ih-STROY-kuh)   **Karol Wojtyla** (KAH-rol voy-TIL-ah)

**The Fall of the Berlin Wall**   The Berlin Wall was the most important symbol of the Cold War. Constructed to keep residents of East Germany from fleeing to the West and defended by armed guards and barbed wire, for many in the West it was the public face of communism. As the Soviet system fell apart, the residents of East and West Berlin broke down sections of the wall. Here young people straddle the wall, signaling the end of an era.   (Bossu Regis/Corbis Sygma)

quiet the opposition by seeking solutions to their severe economic problems. They turned to the West for trade and financial assistance and opened their nations to travelers, ideas, styles, and money from Western countries, all of which accelerated the demand for change.

By the end of 1989, communist governments across eastern Europe had fallen. The dismantling of the Berlin Wall, the symbol of a divided Europe and the bipolar world, vividly represented this transformation. In Poland, Hungary, Czechoslovakia, and

**Map 29.1    The End of Soviet Domination in Eastern Europe**    The creation of new countries out of Yugoslavia and Czechoslovakia and the reunification of Germany marked the most complicated changes of national borders since World War I. The Czech Republic and Slovakia separated peacefully, but Slovenia, Croatia, Macedonia, and Bosnia and Herzegovina achieved independence only after bitter fighting.

Bulgaria, communist leaders decided that change was inevitable and initiated political reforms. When Romanian dictator Nicolae Ceausescu° refused to surrender power, he provoked a rebellion that ended with his arrest and execution. The comprehensiveness of these changes became clear in 1990, when Solidarity leader Lech Walesa° was elected president of Poland and dissident playwright Vaclav Havel°

---

**Nicolae Ceausescu** (neh-koh-LIE chow-SHES-koo)    **Lech Walesa** (leck wah-LEN-suh)    **Vaclav Havel** (vah-SLAV hah-VEL)

was elected president of Czechoslovakia. That same year, East and West Germany were reunited, and the eastern Baltic states of Lithuania, Estonia, and Latvia declared their independence from the Soviet Union.

The end of the Soviet Union came suddenly in 1991 (see Map 29.2). Gorbachev's efforts to transform the Soviet system could not keep up with the tide of change sweeping through the region. After communist hardliners botched a poorly conceived coup against Gorbachev, disgust with communism boiled over. Boris Yeltsin, the president of the Russian Republic and long-time member of the

**Map 29.2    The End of the Soviet Union**    When Communist hardliners failed to overthrow Gorbachev in 1991, popular anti-Communist sentiment swept the Soviet Union. Following Boris Yeltsin's lead in Russia, the republics that constituted the Soviet Union declared their independence.

Communist Party, led popular resistance to the coup in Moscow and emerged as the most powerful leader in the country. Russia, the largest republic in the Soviet Union, was effectively taking the place of the disintegrating USSR. In September 1991, the Congress of People's Deputies voted to dissolve the union. Mikhail Gorbachev went into retirement.

The ethnic and religious passions that fueled the breakup of the Soviet Union soon challenged the survival of Yugoslavia and Czechoslovakia. The dismemberment of Yugoslavia began with declarations of independence in Slovenia and Croatia in 1991. A year later, Czechoslovakia peacefully divided into the Czech Republic and Slovakia.

## The Persian Gulf War, 1990–1991

The breakup of the Soviet Union and the end of the Cold War did not bring an end to international conflict. The Persian Gulf War began when Iraq's ruler, Saddam Husayn, invaded Kuwait in August 1990. Husayn had failed to get Kuwait's royal family to reduce the size of Iraq's debt to the oil-rich nation. He was also eager to gain control of Kuwait's oil fields. Husayn believed that the smaller and militarily weaker nation could be quickly defeated and suspected, as a result of a conversation with an American diplomat, that the United States would not react.

Saudi Arabia, a key regional ally of the United States and a major oil producer, felt threatened by Iraq's action and helped draw the United States into the conflict. Soon the United States and its allies had concentrated an imposing military force of 500,000 in the region. With his intention to use force endorsed by the United Nations and with many Islamic nations supporting military action, President George Bush ordered an attack in early 1991. Iraq proved incapable of countering the sophisticated weaponry of the coalition. The missiles and bombs of the United States destroyed not only military targets but also "relegated [Iraq] to a pre-industrial age," reported the United Nations after the war. Although Iraq's military defeat was comprehensive, Husain remained in power, and the country was not occupied. Husain, in fact, crushed an uprising in the months following this defeat. In the wake of this event, the United States and its key allies imposed "no fly" zones that denied Iraq's military aircraft access to the northern and southern regions of the country.

In the United States, the results of the war were interpreted to mean that the U.S. military defeat in the Vietnam War could be forgotten and that U.S. military capability was unrivaled. Unable to deter military action by the U.S.-led coalition or to meaningfully influence the diplomacy that surrounded the war, Russia had been of little use to its former ally Iraq, and its impotence was clear.

# THE CHALLENGE OF POPULATION GROWTH

For most of human history, population growth was viewed as beneficial, and human beings were seen as a source of wealth. Since the late eighteenth century, however, population growth has been viewed with increasing alarm. Some feared that food supplies could not keep up with population growth. Others foresaw class and ethnic struggle as numbers overwhelmed resources. By the second half of the twentieth century, population growth was increasingly seen as a threat to the environment.

## Demographic Transition

World population exploded in the twentieth century (see Table 29.1). Unlike population growth in the eighteenth and nineteenth centuries, when much of the increase occurred in the wealthiest nations, population growth at the end of the twentieth century was overwhelmingly in the poorest nations. Fertility rates had dropped in most developing nations but remained much higher than rates in the industrialized nations. At the same time, improvements in hygiene and medical treatment caused mortality rates to fall. The result was rapid population growth. At current rates of growth, the world population still increases by a number equal to the total population of the United States every three years.

Educated Europeans of the nineteenth century had been ambivalent about the rapid increase in human population. Some saw it as a blessing that would promote economic well-being. Others warned that the seemingly relentless increase would bring disaster. Best known of these pessimists was the English cleric **Thomas Malthus,** who in 1798 argued convincingly that unchecked population growth would outstrip food production. When Malthus looked at Europe's future, he used a prejudiced image of China's huge population to terrify his European readers.

The generation that came of age in the years immediately following World War II inherited a world in which the views of Malthus were casually dismissed. Industrial and agricultural productivity had multiplied supplies of food and other necessities. Cultural changes associated with expanded female employment, older age at marriage, and more effective family planning had combined to slow the rate of population increase. And by the late 1960s, Europe and other industrial societies had made what was called the **demographic transition** to lower fertility rates (average number of births per woman) and reduce mortality. The number of births in the developed nations was just adequate for the maintenance of current population levels. Thus, many experts argued that the population growth then occurring in developing nations was a short-term phenomenon that would be ended by the combination of economic and social changes that had altered European patterns.

**Table 29.1**   **Population for World and Major Areas, 1750–2050**

Population Size (Millions)

| Major Area | 1750 | 1800 | 1850 | 1900 | 1950 | 1995 | (estimated) 2050 |
|---|---|---|---|---|---|---|---|
| World | 791 | 978 | 1,262 | 1,650 | 2,521 | 5,666 | 8,909 |
| Africa | 106 | 107 | 111 | 133 | 221 | 697 | 1,766 |
| Asia | 502 | 635 | 809 | 947 | 1,402 | 3,437 | 5,268 |
| Europe | 163 | 203 | 276 | 408 | 547 | 728 | 628 |
| Latin America and the Caribbean | 16 | 24 | 38 | 74 | 167 | 480 | 809 |
| North America | 2 | 7 | 26 | 82 | 172 | 297 | 392 |
| Oceania | 2 | 2 | 2 | 6 | 13 | 28 | 46 |

Percentage Distribution

| Major Area | 1750 | 1800 | 1850 | 1900 | 1950 | 1995 | (estimated) 2050 |
|---|---|---|---|---|---|---|---|
| World | 100 | 100 | 100 | 100 | 100 | 100 | 100 |
| Africa | 13.4 | 10.9 | 8.8 | 8.1 | 8.8 | 12 | 19.8 |
| Asia | 63.5 | 64.9 | 64.1 | 57.4 | 55.6 | 61 | 59.1 |
| Europe | 20.6 | 20.8 | 21.9 | 24.7 | 21.7 | 13 | 7.0 |
| Latin America and the Caribbean | 2.0 | 2.5 | 3.0 | 4.5 | 6.6 | 8 | 9.1 |
| North America | 0.3 | 0.7 | 2.1 | 5.0 | 6.8 | 5 | 4.4 |
| Oceania | 0.3 | 0.2 | 0.2 | 0.4 | 0.5 | 1 | 0.5 |

*Source:* J. D. Durand, "Historical Estimates of World Population: An Evaluation" (Philadelphia: University of Pennsylvania, Population Studies Center, 1974, mimeographed); United Nations, *The Determinants and Conse-quences of Population Trends,* vol. 1 (New York: United Nations, 1973); United Nations, *World Population Prospects as Assessed in 1963* (New York: United Nations, 1966); United Nations, *World Population Prospects: The 1998 Revision* (New York: United Nations, forthcoming); United Nations Population Division, Department of Economic and Social Affairs, http://www.popin.org/pop1998/4.htm.

When the demographic transition failed to occur in the Third World by the late 1970s, the issue of population growth had become politicized. The leaders of some developing nations actively promoted large families, arguing that larger populations would increase national power. Industrialized, mostly white, nations raised concerns about rapid population growth in Asia, Africa, and Latin America. Populist political leaders in those regions asked whether these concerns were not fundamentally racist.

However, once the economic shocks of the 1970s and 1980s revealed the vulnerability of developing economies, governments in the developing world jettisoned pronatalist policies. In the 1970s, Mexico's government had encouraged high fertility, and population growth in Mexico rose to 3 percent per year. By the 1980s, Mexico started to promote birth control, and the annual population growth rate fell to 2.3 percent.

## The Industrialized Nations

In much of Europe and Japan at the beginning of the twenty-first century, fertility levels are so low that population will fall unless immigration increases. In Japan, women have an average of 1.39 children; in Italy, the number is 1.2. Sweden provides cash payments, tax incentives, and job leaves to families with children, but the average number of births there fell to 1.4 in recent years. The low fertility found in mature industrial nations is tied to higher levels of female education and employment, the material values of consumer culture, and access to contraception and abortion. Educated women now defer marriage and child rearing until they are established in careers.

As fertility has declined in the industrialized nations of western Europe, life expectancy has improved because of more abundant food, improved hygiene, and better medical care. Italy, for example, soon will have more than twenty adults fifty years old or over for each five-year-old child. Japan faces an even more drastic aging of its population. This demographic transformation presents a challenge very different from the one foreseen by Malthus. These nations generally offer a broad array of social services, including retirement income, medical services, and housing supplements for the elderly. As the number of retirees increases relative to the number of people who are employed, the costs of these services may become unsustainable.

In contrast, in Russia and some former socialist nations, life expectancy and birthrates have both fallen. Life expectancy for Russian men is now only fifty-seven years, down almost ten years since 1980. In the Czech Republic, Hungary, and Poland, life expectancy is improving in response to improved economic conditions, but most of the rest of eastern Europe follows the Russian pattern of declining life expectancy. High unemployment, low incomes, food shortages, and the dismantling of the social welfare system of the communist era have all contributed to this decline.

## The Developing Nations

Population pyramids generated by demographers clearly illustrate the profound transformation in human reproductive patterns and life expectancy in the years since World War II. Figure 29.1 shows the 2001 age distributions in Pakistan, South Korea, and Sweden—nations at three different stages of economic development. Sweden is a mature industrial nation. South Korea is a rapidly industrializing nation that has surpassed many European nations in both industrial output and per capita wealth. Pakistan is a poor, traditional Muslim nation with rudimentary industrialization, low educational levels, and little effective family planning.

These demographic changes are transforming the global balance of population. At current rates, 95 percent of all future population growth will be in developing nations (see Table 29.1). A comparison between Europe and Africa illustrates these changes. In 1950, Europe had twice the population of Africa. By 1985, Africa had drawn even. According to projections, by 2025 Africa's population will be three times larger than Europe's.

As the 1990s ended, the populations of Latin America and Asia also were expanding dramatically, but at rates slower than those in sub-Saharan Africa and the Muslim world. In Asia, the populations of India and China continued to grow despite government efforts to reduce family size. In China, efforts

**Figure 29.1    Age Structure Comparison:**  Islamic Nation (Pakistan), Non-Islamic Developing Nation (South Korea), and Developed Nation (Sweden), 2001.   *Source:* U.S. Bureau of the Census, *International Database,* 2001.

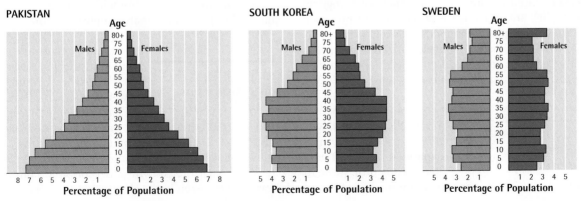

to enforce a limit of one child per family led to large-scale female infanticide as rural families sought to produce male heirs. India's policies of forced sterilization created widespread outrage and led to the electoral defeat of the ruling Congress Party. Yet both countries achieved some successes. Between 1960 and 1982, India's birthrate fell from 48 to 34 per thousand, while China's rate declined even more sharply—from 39 to 19. Still, by 2025, China and India will each have some 1.5 billion people.

# UNEQUAL DEVELOPMENT AND THE MOVEMENT OF PEOPLES

Two characteristics of the postwar world should now be clear. First, despite decades of experimentation with state-directed economic development, most nations that were poor in 1960 were as poor or poorer at the end of the 1990s. The only exceptions were a few rapidly developing Asian industrial nations and an equally small number of oil-exporting nations. Second, world population increased to startlingly high levels, and most of the increase was in the poorest nations.

The combination of intractable poverty and growing population generated a surge in international immigration, both legal and illegal. Few other issues stirred more controversy. Even moderate voices sometimes framed the discussion of immigration as a competition among peoples. One commentator summarized his analysis this way: "As the better-off families of the northern hemisphere individually decide that having only one or at the most two children is sufficient, they may not recognize that they are in a small way vacating future space (that is, jobs, parts of inner cities, shares of population, shares of market preferences) to faster-growing ethnic groups both inside and outside their boundaries. But that, in fact, is what they are doing."[2]

**The Problem of Growing Inequality**

Since 1945, global economic productivity has expanded more rapidly than at any other time in the past. Faster, cheaper communications and

transportation have combined with improvements in industrial and agricultural technologies to create levels of material abundance that would have amazed those who experienced the first Industrial Revolution (see Chapter 20). Despite this remarkable economic expansion and growing market integration, the majority of the world's population remains in poverty. The industrialized nations of the Northern Hemisphere now enjoy a larger share of the world's wealth than they did a century ago. As a result, the gap between rich and poor nations has grown much wider. The thousands of homeless street children who live among the gleaming glass and steel towers of Rio's banking district can be seen as a metaphor for the social consequences of postwar economic development.

Wealth inequality within nations also grew. In the United States, for example, the South and Southwest grew richer in the past three decades relative to the older industrial regions of the Midwest. Regional inequalities also appeared in developing nations. Generally, capital cities such as Buenos Aires, in Argentina, and Lagos, in Nigeria, attracted large numbers of migrants from rural areas because they offered more opportunities, even if those opportunities could not compare to the ones available in developed nations.

Even in the industrialized world, people were divided into haves and have-nots. During the presidency of Ronald Reagan (1981–1989), wealth inequality in the United States reached its highest level since the 1929 stock market crash. Some scholars estimated that the wealthiest 1 percent of households in the United States controlled more than 30 percent of the nation's total wealth. Even in Europe, where tax and inheritance laws redistributed wealth, unemployment, homelessness, and substandard housing were increasingly common.

**Internal Migration: The Growth of Cities**

Migration from rural areas to urban centers in developing nations increased threefold from 1925 to 1950. After that, the pace accelerated (see Table 29.2). Shantytowns sprawling around major cities in developing nations are commonly seen as signs of social breakdown and economic failure. Nevertheless, even in the shantytowns city life was

**Table 29.2    The World's Largest Metropolitan Areas (Population of 10 Million or More)**

| City | 1950 | City | 1975 | City | 2000 | City | 2015 |
|---|---|---|---|---|---|---|---|
| 1 New York | 12.3 | 1 Tokyo | 19.8 | 1 Tokyo | 26.4 | 1 Tokyo | 26.4 |
| | | 1 New York | 15.9 | 2 Mexico City | 18.1 | 2 Bombay | 26.1 |
| | | 3 Shanghai | 11.4 | 3 Bombay | 18.1 | 3 Lagos | 23.2 |
| | | 4 Mexico City | 11.2 | 4 Sao Paulo | 17.8 | 4 Dhaka | 21.1 |
| | | 5 Sao Paulo | 10.0 | 5 New York | 16.6 | 5 Sao Paulo | 20.4 |
| | | | | 6 Lagos | 13.4 | 6 Karachi | 19.2 |
| | | | | 7 Los Angeles | 13.1 | 7 Mexico City | 19.2 |
| | | | | 8 Calcutta | 12.9 | 8 New York | 17.4 |
| | | | | 9 Shanghai | 12.9 | 9 Jakarta | 17.3 |
| | | | | 10 Buenos Aires | 12.6 | 10 Calcutta | 17.3 |
| | | | | 11 Dhaka | 12.3 | 11 Delhi | 16.8 |
| | | | | 12 Karachi | 11.8 | 12 Metro Manila | 14.8 |
| | | | | 13 Delhi | 11.7 | 13 Shanghai | 14.6 |
| | | | | 14 Jakarta | 11.0 | 14 Los Angeles | 14.1 |
| | | | | 15 Osaka | 11.0 | 15 Buenos Aires | 14.1 |
| | | | | 16 Metro Manila | 10.9 | 16 Cairo | 13.8 |
| | | | | 17 Beijing | 10.8 | 17 Istanbul | 12.5 |
| | | | | 18 Rio de Janeiro | 10.6 | 18 Beijing | 12.3 |
| | | | | 19 Cairo | 10.6 | 19 Rio de Janeiro | 11.9 |
| | | | | | | 20 Osaka | 11.0 |
| | | | | | | 21 Tianjin | 10.7 |
| | | | | | | 22 Hyderabad | 10.5 |
| | | | | | | 23 Bangkok | 10.1 |

*Source:* International Migration Report 2002, United Nations, Department of Economic and Social Affairs, Population Division, "World Urbanization Prospects: The 1999 Revision," p. 6. Reprinted by permission of United States Publications.

generally better than life in the countryside. A World Bank study estimated that three out of four migrants to cities made economic gains. Residents of cities in sub-Saharan Africa, for example, were six times more likely than rural residents to have safe water. An unskilled migrant from the depressed northeast of Brazil could triple his or her income by moving to Rio de Janeiro.

As the scale of rural-to-urban migration grew, these benefits proved more elusive, however. In many West African cities, basic services were crumbling under the pressure of rapid population growth. In 1990 in Mexico City, one of the world's largest cities, more than thirty thousand people lived in garbage dumps, where they scavenged for food and clothing. Worsening conditions and the threat of crime and political instability led many governments to try to slow migration to cities and, in some cases, to return people to the countryside. Indonesia, for example, has relocated more than half a million urban residents since 1969. Despite some successes with slowing the rate of internal migration, nearly every poor nation still faces the challenge of rapidly growing cities.

## Global Migration

Each year, hundreds of thousands of men and women leave the developing world to emigrate to industrialized nations. After 1960, this movement increased in scale, and ethnic and racial tensions in the host nations worsened. By the 1990s, levels of immigration posed daunting social and cultural challenges for both host nations and immigrants.

When an expanding European economy first confronted labor shortages in the 1960s, many European nations actively promoted guest worker programs and other inducements to immigration. However, attitudes toward immigrants changed as the size of the immigrant population grew and as European economies slowed in the 1980s. Facing higher levels of unemployment, native-born workers saw immigrants as competitors willing to work for lower wages and less likely to support unions.

Because immigrants generally are young adults and commonly retain the positive attitudes toward early marriage and large families dominant in their native cultures, immigrant communities in Europe and the United States tended to have fertility rates higher than the rates of the host populations. In Germany in 1975, for example, immigrants made up about 7 percent of the population but accounted for nearly 15 percent of all births. Although the fertility of the Hispanic population in the United States is lower than the rates in Mexico and other Latin American nations, Hispanic groups will contribute well over 20 percent of all population growth in the United States during the next twenty-five years.

As the Muslim population in Europe and the Asian and Latin American populations in the United States expand in the twenty-first century, cultural conflicts will test definitions of citizenship and nationality. The United States will have some advantages in meeting these challenges because of long experience with immigration and relatively open access to citizenship. Yet in the 1990s, the United States was moving slowly in the direction of European efforts to restrict immigration and defend a culturally conservative definition of nationality.

# TECHNOLOGICAL AND ENVIRONMENTAL CHANGE

Technological innovation powered the economic expansion that began after World War II by increasing productivity and disseminating human creativity. Because most of the economic benefits were concentrated in the advanced industrialized nations, technology increased the power of those nations relative to the developing world. Even within developed nations, postwar technological innovations did not benefit all classes, industries, and regions equally.

The multiplication of farms and factories intensified environmental threats. Loss of rain forest, soil erosion, global warming, pollution of air and water, and extinction of species imperiled human societies. Environmental protection measures, like the acquisition of new technology, progressed furthest in societies with the most economic resources.

## New Technologies and the World Economy

Nuclear energy, jet engines, radar, and tape recording were among the many World War II developments that later had an impact on consumers' lives. When applied to industry, new technology increased productivity, reduced labor requirements, and improved the flow of information. As the Western economies recovered from the war and incomes rose, consumers purchased new products that reduced their workloads or provided entertainment.

Improvements in existing technologies accounted for much of the developed world's productivity increases during the 1950s and 1960s. Larger and faster trucks, trains, and airplanes cut transportation costs. Both capitalist and socialist governments expanded highway systems, improved railroad track, and constructed airports and nuclear power plants.

No other technology had greater significance in this period than the computer. Only large corporations, governments, and universities could afford the first computers. But by the mid-1980s, desktop computers had replaced typewriters in most of the developed world's offices, and technological advances continued. Each new generation of computers was faster and more powerful than the one before.

Computers also altered manufacturing. Small dedicated computers were used to control and monitor machinery in some industries. European and Japanese companies were the first to introduce such robots into the factory. The United States introduced robots more slowly because it enjoys lower labor costs.

The transnational corporation became the primary agent of these technological changes. In the post–World War II years, many companies with multinational ownership and management invested in and marketed products throughout the world. International trade agreements and open markets furthered the process.

As transnational manufacturers, agricultural conglomerates, and financial giants became wealthier and more powerful, they increasingly escaped the controls imposed by national governments. If labor costs were too high in Japan, antipollution measures too intrusive in the United States, or taxes too high in Great Britain, transnational companies relocated—or threatened to do so. Governments in the developing world were often hard-pressed to control the actions of these powerful enterprises. As a result, the worst abuses of labor or of the environment usually occurred in poor nations.

## Conserving and Sharing Resources

In the 1960s, environmental activists and political leaders began warning about the devastating environmental consequences of population growth, industrialization, and the expansion of agriculture onto marginal lands. Assaults on rain forests and redwoods, the disappearance of species, and the poisoning of streams and rivers raised public consciousness. Environmental damage occurred in the advanced industrial economies and in the poorest of the developing nations. Perhaps the worst environmental record was achieved in the former Soviet Union, where industrial and nuclear wastes were often dumped with little concern for environmental consequences. The accumulated effect of scientific studies and public debate led to national and international efforts to slow, if not undo, damage to the environment.

The expanding global population required increasing quantities of food, housing, energy, and other resources as the twentieth century ended. In the developed world, the consumer-driven economic expansion of the post–World War II years became an obstacle to addressing environmental problems. How could the United States, Germany, or Japan change consumption patterns to protect the environment without endangering corporate profits, wages, and employment levels?

Many developing countries saw exploitation of their environmental resources and industrialization as the solution to their rapidly growing populations. The results were predictable: erosion and pollution.

## Responding to Environmental Threats

Despite the gravity of environmental threats, there were many successful efforts to preserve and protect the environment. The Clean Air Act, the Clean Water Act, and the Endangered Species Act were passed in the United States in the 1970s as part of an environmental effort that included the nations of the European Community and Japan. Environmental awareness spread by means of the media and grassroots political movements, and most nations in the developed world enforced strict antipollution laws and sponsored massive recycling efforts. Many also encouraged resource conservation by rewarding energy-efficient factories and the manufacturers of fuel-efficient cars and by promoting the use of alternative energy sources such as solar and wind power.

These efforts produced significant results. In western Europe and the United States, air quality improved dramatically. In the United States, smog levels were down nearly a third from 1970 to 2000 even though the number of automobiles increased more than 80 percent. Emissions of lead and sulfur dioxide were down as well. The Great Lakes, Long Island Sound, and Chesapeake Bay were all much cleaner at the end of the century than they had been in 1970. The rivers of North America and Europe also improved. Still, more than thirty thousand deaths each year in the United States are attributed to exposure to pesticides and other chemicals.

New technologies made much of this improvement possible. Pollution controls on automobiles, planes, and factory smokestacks reduced harmful emissions. Similar progress was made in the chemical industry. Scientists identified the chemicals that threaten the ozone layer, and the phase-out of their use in new appliances and cars began.

Clearly the desire to preserve the natural environment was growing around the world. In the developed nations, continued political organization and enhanced awareness of environmental issues seemed likely to lead to step-by-step improvements in environmental policy. In the developing world and most of the former Soviet bloc, however, population pressures and weak governments were major obstacles to effective environmental policies. In China, for example, respiratory disease caused by pollution was the leading cause of death. Thus, it was likely that the industrialized nations would have to fund global improvements, and the cost was likely to be high.

# CONCLUSION

The world was profoundly altered between 1975 and 1991. The Cold War dominated international relations to the end of the 1980s. Every conflict threatened to provoke a confrontation between the nuclear-armed superpowers, for both the United States and the Soviet Union feared that every conflict and every regime change represented a potential threat to their strategic interests. As a result, the superpowers were drawn into a succession of civil wars and revolutions. The costs in lives and property were terrible, the gains small. As defense costs escalated, the Soviet system crumbled. By 1991, the Soviet Union and the socialist Warsaw Pact had disappeared, transforming the international stage.

Latin America was pulled into the violence of the late Cold War period and paid a terrible price. The 1970s and 1980s witnessed a frontal assault on democratic institutions, a denial of human rights, and economic decline. This was the period of death squads and Dirty War. With the end of the Cold War, peace returned there, and democracy began to replace dictatorship.

In the Persian Gulf, the end of the Cold War did not lead to peace. Iran and Iraq have experienced deep cycles of political turmoil, war, and foreign threats since the late 1970s.

The world also was altered by economic growth and integration, by population growth and movement, and by technological and environmental change. Led by the postwar recovery of the industrial powers and the remarkable economic expansion of Japan and the Asian Tigers, the world economy grew dramatically. The development and application of new technology contributed significantly to this process. International markets were more open and integrated than at any other time. The new wealth and exciting technologies of the postwar era were not shared equally, however.

Population growth in the developing world was one reason for this divided experience. Unable to find adequate employment or, in many cases, bare subsistence, people in developing nations migrated across borders hoping to improve their lives. These movements often provided valuable labor in the factories and farms of the developed world, but they also provoked cultural, racial, and ethnic tension. Problems of inequality, population growth, and international migration would continue to challenge the global community in the coming decades.

Technology seemed to offer some hope for meeting these challenges. Engineering, financial services, education, and other professions developed an international character thanks to the communications revolution. Ambitious and talented people in the developing world could now fully participate in global intellectual and economic life. However, most people working in the developing world remained disconnected from this liberating technology by poverty. Technology also bolstered efforts to protect the environment, providing the means to clean auto and factory emissions, even while it helped produce much of the world's pollution. Technology has been intertwined with human culture since the beginning of human history. Our ability to control and direct its use will determine the future.

## ■ Key Terms

| | |
|---|---|
| proxy wars | Asian Tigers |
| Salvador Allende | Deng Xiaoping |
| Dirty War | Tiananmen Square |
| Sandinistas | Mikhail Gorbachev |
| Ayatollah Ruhollah Khomeini | *perestroika* |
| neo-liberalism | Solidarity |
| Saddam Husayn | Thomas Malthus |
| *keiretsu* | demographic transition |

## ■ Suggested Reading

Among the works devoted to postwar economic performance are W. L. M. Adriaasen and J. G. Waardensburg, eds., *A Dual World Economy: Forty Years of Development Experience* (1989); P. Krugman, *The Age of Diminished Expectations: U.S. Economic Policy in the 1990s* (1990); B. J. McCormick, *The World Economy: Patterns of Growth and Change* (1988); and H. van der Wee, *Prosperity and Upheaval: The World Economy, 1945–1980* (1986).

For Latin America, Thomas E. Skidmore and Peter H. Smith, *Modern Latin America,* 4th ed. (1996), provides an excellent general introduction to the period 1975 to 1991.

For the Pacific Rim, see Jonathan Spence, *The Search for Modern China* (1990); Edwin O. Reischauer, *The Japanese* (1988); H. Patrick and H. Rosovsky, *Asia's New Giant: How the Japanese Economy Works* (1976); and Staffan B. Linder, *Pacific Century: Economic and Political Consequences of Asian-Pacific Dynamism* (1986).

Focused examinations of the Soviet bloc are provided in K. Dawisha, *Eastern Europe, Gorbachev and Reform: The Great Challenge* (1988); Barbara Engel and Christine Worobec, eds., *Russia's Women: Accommodation, Resistance, Transformation* (1990); David Remnick, *Lenin's Tomb: The Last Days of the Soviet Empire* (1993); and Charles Maier, *Dissolution: The Crisis of Communism and the End of East Germany* (1997).

The story of the Iranian Revolution and the early days of the Islamic Republic of Iran is well told by Shaul Bakhash, *The Reign of the Ayatollahs: Iran and the Iranian Revolution* (1990). Barnet Rubin, *The Fragmentation of Afghanistan* (1995), provides excellent coverage of the struggle between Soviet forces and the Muslim resistance in that country.

A number of studies examine the special problems faced by women in the postwar period. See, for example, Elisabeth Croll, *Feminism and Socialism in China* (1978); J. Ginat, *Women in Muslim Rural Society: Status and Role in Family and Community* (1982); June Hahner, *Women in Latin America* (1976); P. Hudson, *Third World Women Speak Out* (1979); A. de Souza, *Women in Contemporary India and South Asia* (1980); and M. Wolf, *Revolution Postponed: Women in Contemporary China* (1985).

For general discussions of economic, demographic, and environmental problems facing the world, see R. N. Gwynne, *New Horizons? Third World Industrialization in an International Framework* (1990); P. R. Ehrlich and A. E. Ehrlich, *The Population Explosion* (1990); Paul M. Kennedy, *Preparing for the Twenty-First Century* (1993); and J. L. Simon, *Population Matters: People, Resources, Environment and Immigration* (1990).

For issues associated with technological and environmental change, see M. Feshbach and A. Friendly, *Ecocide in the U.S.S.R.* (1992); John Bellamy Foster, *Economic History of the Environment* (1994); S. Hecht and A. Cockburn, *The Fate of the Forest: Developers, Destroyers, and Defenders of the Amazon* (1989); K. Marton, *Multinationals, Technology, and Industrialization: Implications and Impact in Third World Countries* (1986); S. P. Huntington, *The Third Wave: Demoralization in the Late Twentieth Century* (1993); L. Solomon, *Multinational Corporations and the Emerging World Order* (1978); and B. L. Turner II et al., eds., *The Earth as Transformed by Human Action: Global and Regional Changes in the Biosphere over the Past 300 Years* (1990).

## ■ Notes

1. *New York Times,* July 24, 1993, 1.
2. Paul Kennedy, *Preparing for the Twenty-First Century* (New York: Random House, 1993), 45.

# 30 Globalization at the Turn of the Millennium

## CHAPTER OUTLINE

Global Political Economies

Trends and Visions

Global Culture

ENVIRONMENT AND TECHNOLOGY: Global Warming

The workday began normally at the World Trade Center in lower Manhattan on the morning of September 11, 2001. The 50,000 people who work there were making their way to the two 110-story towers, as were some 140,000 others who visit on a typical day. Suddenly, at 8:46 A.M., an American Airlines Boeing 767 with 92 people on board, traveling at a speed of 470 miles per hour (756 kilometers per hour), crashed into floors 94 to 98 of the north tower, igniting the 10,000 gallons (38,000 liters) of fuel in its tanks. Just before 9:03 A.M. a United Airlines flight with 65 people on board and a similar fuel load hit floors 78 to 84 of the south tower.

As the burning jet fuel engulfed the collision areas, the buildings' surviving occupants struggled through smoke-filled corridors and down dozens of flights of stairs. Many of those trapped above the crash sites used cell phones to say good-bye to loved ones. Rather than endure the flames and fumes, a few jumped to their deaths.

Just before 10 o'clock, temperatures that had risen to 2,300° Fahrenheit (1,260° Celsius) caused the steel girders in the impacted area of the south tower to give way. The collapsing upper floors crushed the floors underneath one by one, engulfing lower Manhattan in a dense cloud of dust. Twenty-eight minutes later the north tower pancaked in a similar manner. Miraculously, most of the buildings' occupants had escaped before the towers collapsed. Besides the people on the planes, nearly 2,600 lost their lives, including some 200 police officers and firefighters helping in the evacuation.

That same morning another American Airlines jet crashed into the Pentagon, killing all 64 people on board and 125 others inside the military complex near Washington, D.C. Passengers

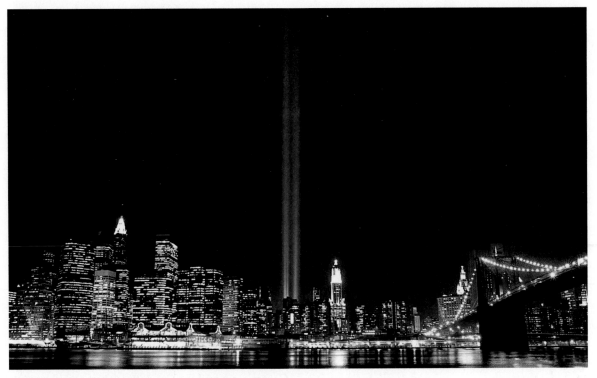

**Lower Manhattan, March 11, 2002**   Six months after the terrorist attacks, beams of light commemorated the destroyed twin towers of the World Trade Center and those who perished in them.

on a fourth plane managed to overpower their hijackers, and the plane crashed in rural Pennsylvania, killing all 45 on board.

The four planes had been hijacked by teams of Middle Eastern men who slit the throats of service and flight personnel and seized control. Of the nineteen hijackers, fifteen were from Saudi Arabia. All had links to an extremist Islamic organization, al Qaeda° (the base or foundation), supported by a rich Saudi named Usama bin Laden°, who was incensed with American political, military, and cultural influence in the Middle East. The men were educated and well traveled, had lived in the United States, and

spoke English. Some had trained as pilots so that they could fly the hijacked aircraft.

The hijackers left few records of their personal motives, but the acts spoke for themselves. The Pentagon was the headquarters of the American military, the most technologically sophisticated and powerful fighting force the world had even seen. The fourth plane was probably meant to hit the Capitol or the White House, the legislative and executive centers of the world's only superpower. The Twin Towers may have been targeted because they were the tallest buildings in New York, but they were not just American targets. The World Trade Center housed 430 companies involved in international commerce and finance. Among the dead were people from more than half the countries in the world. New York was the site

---

**al Qaeda** (el KAW eh duh)    **Usama bin Laden** (oo-SAH-mah bin LAH-din) of the attack, but the World Trade Center was a powerful symbol of the international economy.

The events of September 11 (9/11) can be understood on many levels. The hijackers and their supporters saw themselves as engaged in a holy struggle against economic, political, and military institutions they believed to be evil. They believed so deeply in their mission that they were willing to give their lives for it and to take as many other lives as they could. People directly affected and political leaders around the world tended to describe the attacks as evil acts against innocent victims.

To understand why the nineteen attackers were heroes to some and terrorists to others, one needs to explore the historical context of global changes at the turn of the millennium and the ideological tensions they have generated. While domestic and localized issues in Muslim countries provide part of the explanation, another part is unique prominence of the United States in every major aspect of global integration, which elicits sharply divergent views in the rest of the world's peoples.

As you read this chapter, ask yourself the following questions:

- What are the main benefits and dangers of growing political, economic, and cultural integration?

- What roles do religious beliefs and secular ideologies play in the contemporary world?

- How has technology contributed to the process of global interaction?

# GLOBAL POLITICAL ECONOMIES

At the turn of the millennium growing trade and travel and new technologies were bringing all parts of the world into closer economic, political, and cultural contact. The collapse of the Soviet Union had ended the colonial era, and au-

tonomous national states (numbering about two hundred) had become an almost universal norm. Yet many world leaders had become convinced of the need to balance national autonomy with international agreements and associations in areas of trade and markets.

## The Spread of Democracy

Democratic institutions spread widely in the last decades of the twentieth century. In 2003, 140 countries regularly held elections and people in 125 had access to free (or partly free) presses.[1] The appeal of democracy has been that elections provide a peaceful way of settling differences among a country's social classes, cultural groups, and regions. Democracies also tend to encourage political moderation.

In eastern Europe, the Czech Republic, Poland, Romania, and most other formerly communist-ruled states adopted democratic institutions. In the Russian Federation and neighboring Ukraine and Belarus, democratic institutions experienced a shakier start, while the former Soviet republics of Central Asia and the Caucasus mostly continued to experience authoritarian rule and rigged elections.

Since 1991 democracy, sometimes accompanied by significant shifts in the political balance, has become almost universal in South and Central America. In 2000 Mexican voters elected a reformist president with a centrist agenda, Vincente Fox, ending the half-century rule of the corrupt Institutional Revolutionary Party (PRI). In 2002 leftist Workers' Party candidate Luiz Inácio Lula da Silva° won the presidency of Brazil by appealing to nationalism and popular discontent with the economy.

In Asia, the death of long-time Chinese Communist leader Deng Xiaoping in 1997 ushered in a period of somewhat greater freedom of expression, but democracy seemed a long way off despite a booming economy. India saw a major political shift in 1998 when the Bharatiya Janata Party (BJP) ended four decades of Congress Party rule. The BJP success came through blatant appeals to Hindu nationalism, the condoning of violence against India's

---

**Luiz Inácio Lula da Silva** (loo-EES ee-NAH-see-oh LOO-lah dah SEAL-vah)

# C H R O N O L O G Y

| | Politics | Economics and Society |
|---|---|---|
| **1991** | | **1991**  Mercosur free trade association formed |
| | **1992**  Yugoslavia disintegrates—Croatia and Slovenia become independent states | |
| | **1992–1995**  Bosnia crisis | |
| | **1994**  Nelson Mandela elected president of South Africa; Tutsi massacred in Rwanda | **1994**  North Atlantic Free Trade Agreement adopted |
| **1995** | | **1995**  World Trade Organization founded; United Nations women's conference in China |
| | **1997**  Hong Kong reunited with China | **1997**  Asian financial crisis begins |
| | **1998**  Terrorists bomb U.S. embassies in Kenya and Tanzania; India and Pakistan test atomic bombs | |
| | **1999**  East Timor secedes from Indonesia (officially independent 2002) | **1999**  Nobel Peace Prize to Doctors Without Borders |
| **2000** | **2001**  Terrorists destroy the World Trade Center and damage the Pentagon on September 11; The United States invades Afghanistan and overthrows Taliban regime | **2001**  Start of global recession |
| | | **2002**  Euro the only currency in twelve European countries |
| | **2003**  United States and Britain invade and occupy Iraq | |
| | **2004**  Presidential election in Afghanistan | |

Muslims, and opposition to the social and economic progress of the Untouchables (those traditionally confined to the dirtiest jobs). In 2004, the Congress Party regained control of the government.

In sub-Saharan Africa, democracy had mixed results. Many elected leaders used their offices to enrich themselves and limit their opponents, while other countries experienced military coups and conflicts over resources such as diamonds. Southern Africa, however, has seen democratic progress and a decline in armed conflicts since 1991. A key change came in South Africa in 1994, when longtime political prisoner Nelson Mandela and his African National Congress (ANC) won the first national elections in which the African majority

could participate equally. Also hopeful has been the return to democracy in Nigeria, Africa's most populous state. In 1999, after a succession of military governments, Nigerians elected President Olusegun Obasanjo° (a former coup leader), and a 2003 vote renewed his term, despite serious voting irregularities.

Democracy is as exceptional in the Middle East as it is in much of Africa. Some once-democratic states such as Algeria have manipulated elections because those in power fear the rising power of Islamic militants. On the other hand, in Turkey, the most democratic Muslim-majority state in the

**Olusegun Obasanjo** (oh-LOO-say-goon oh-bah-SAHN-joh)

region, a once-strident Islamist party won a parliamentary majority in 2002 by moderating its tone and politics. A presidential election in Afghanistan in 2004 and plans for elections in Iraq may mark a move toward more democratic rule in these countries.

As examples later in the chapter will indicate, the growth (or decline) of democracy has only partly been due to internal changes in individual countries. Two international factors have also played important roles: the changed politics of the post–Cold War era and the demands of global economic forces.

## Global Politics

Modern nation-states have considerable autonomy under international law. Other nations may intervene in a state's affairs only when seriously threatened or when the state is engaging in extreme human rights abuses. Although necessary to protect smaller, weaker countries from the imperial bullying that was once common, this autonomy greatly complicates international policing and peacekeeping efforts.

After the Cold War ended, the United Nations struggled to reclaim its roles as defender of human rights and peacekeeper. This was especially noticeable under the leadership of Kofi Annan, who became United Nations secretary general in 1997. The members of the United Nations Security Council often had difficulty agreeing on a course of action. Individual countries often acted alone or with their neighbors to resolve conflicts in nearby countries, whether through peaceful negotiation or military intervention. As the lone superpower, the United States was in a unique position to use its economic power and military might to defend its national interests and promote the general good. However, interventions also brought charges of American imperialism.

There were some notable peacemaking successes. The United Nations, South Africa, and other countries helped end the long civil war in Mozambique in 1992 and struggled to do the same in Angola, where peace shakily returned in 2002. Nigeria, the major military power in West Africa, helped end fighting in Sierra Leone in 1998, and again in 2003 in Liberia, which had become the

world's poorest country as the result of warlords and embezzlement.

However, the international community sometimes had great difficulty in agreeing on when and how to stop civil conflicts and human rights abuses. In 1991 Yugoslavia, which had existed since 1920, dissolved into a morass of warring ethnic and religious groups. Slovenia and Croatia, the heavily Roman Catholic western provinces, became independent states in 1992 after brief struggles with federal Yugoslav forces. Reflecting centuries of Muslim, Catholic, and Orthodox competition in the Balkans, the people of the province of Bosnia and Herzegovina were religiously mixed—40 percent Muslim, 30 percent Serbian Orthodox, and 18 percent Catholic. The murderous three-sided fighting that broke out with the declaration of Bosnian national independence in 1992 gave rise to **ethnic cleansing,** an effort by one racial, ethnic, or religious group to eliminate the people and culture of a different group. In this case, the Orthodox Serbs attempted to rid the state of Muslims.

At first, no European power acted to stop the growing tragedy in the Balkans. Finally, after much indecision—and extensive television coverage of atrocities and wanton destruction—the United States made a cautious intervention and eventually brokered a tentative settlement in 1995. In 1999 vicious new fighting and ethnic cleansing broke out in the southernmost Yugoslavian province of Kosovo, the ancient homeland of the Serbs, which had become predominantly Muslim and Albanian. When NATO's warnings went unheeded in Kosovo, the United States, with aid from Britain and France, launched an aerial war against Serbia. Suffering few casualties themselves, the NATO allies damaged military and infrastructure targets in Serbia and forced the withdrawal of Serbian forces from Kosovo. A trial of former Serbian president Slobodan Milosevic° at a special tribunal in the Hague on charges of crimes against humanity began in 2002 but was often delayed by his ill health.

Another tragedy unfolded in 1994, when political leaders in the Central African nation of Rwanda incited Hutu people to massacre their Tutsi neighbors. The major powers avoided characterizing the

---

**Slobodan Milosevic** (SLOH-boh-duhn mee-LOH-seh-vitch)

slaughter as genocide because an international agreement mandated intervention to stop genocide. Only after some 750,000 people were dead and millions of refugees had fled into neighboring states did the United States and other powers intervene. Belatedly, the United Nations set up a tribunal to try those responsible for the genocide. In 1998 violence spread from Rwanda to neighboring Congo, where growing opposition and ill health had forced President Joseph Mobutu from office after over three decades of dictatorial misrule. Various peacemaking attempts failed to restore order. By mid-2003 more than 3 million Congolese had died from disease, malnutrition, and injuries related to the fighting.

Fear that intervention could result in long and costly commitments was one reason the major powers were reluctant to intervene. Nor was it easy to distinguish conflicts that would benefit from forceful intervention from those that might better be resolved by diplomatic pressure. Many conflicts reflected deep-seated differences that were difficult to resolve. Tamil-speaking Hindus in Sri Lanka have waged a merciless guerrilla struggle against the dominant Sinhalese-speaking Buddhists for decades. Militant Hindus and Muslims in South Asia continue a violent struggle over the territories of the state of Kashmir, which was divided between India and Pakistan at their independence in 1947. Sometimes it took decades of international pressure to bring a conflict to an end, as was the case in East Timor (a mostly Catholic former Portuguese colony that Indonesia had annexed in 1975), whose people voted to separate from Muslim Indonesia in 1999 and gained full independence in 2002.

### Arms Control and Terrorism

In addition to agreements on collective action against genocide and other crimes against humanity (see below), international treaties govern **weapons of mass destruction.** Nuclear, biological, and chemical devices pose especially serious dangers to global security because they can kill large numbers of people quickly.

For a time after international agreements were signed in the 1960s and 1970s (see Chapter 28), considerable progress was made in restricting the testing and spread of nuclear weapons and reducing their numbers. When the Soviet Union broke up, Russia alone retained a nuclear arsenal, but disposing of raw materials for nuclear weapons remained a problem in several successor states. Meanwhile, China resumed nuclear weapons tests in 1992.

Anxiety over nuclear proliferation increased in 1998 when India and Pakistan openly tested nuclear bombs and missile delivery systems, acts that raised the stakes in any future conflict between them. Although North Korea was a signatory of the nuclear nonproliferation treaty, it secretly continued nuclear weapons programs. Iran too pursued nuclear research while denying any intention of producing weapons, a practice that Israel had engaged in in the 1970s when it was developing its undeclared nuclear arsenal.

Chemical and biological weapons are difficult to detect and can easily be produced in seemingly ordinary chemical and pharmaceutical plants. As part of the settlement of the 1991 Persian Gulf War, United Nations inspectors in Iraq uncovered and destroyed extensive stocks of chemical munitions and plants for producing nerve gas and lethal germs. In 1997, however, the government of Saddam Husain, while pursuing an effective disarmament program, refused to allow United Nations weapons inspectors access to suspected weapons sites.

Weapons of mass destruction in the hands of terrorists constituted a growing fear. Terrorists believe that horrendous acts of violence can provoke harsh reprisals that will win them sympathy or cause the regimes they oppose to lose legitimacy. **Terrorism** has a long history, but much recent concern has focused on the network of terrorist organizations created by **Usama bin Laden,** a wealthy Saudi. Though his own family disowned him and Saudi Arabia stripped him of his citizenship, his anti-American stance and patronage attracted followers throughout the Islamic world. In 1992 bin Laden established himself in Sudan, where he invested in many projects. Suspecting that a pharmaceutical plant near the Sudanese capital Khartoum was being used for making chemical weapons, President Clinton had it destroyed by rockets in 1998, but no evidence of weapons production was found.

After being expelled from Sudan in 1996, bin Laden went to Afghanistan, where he had close ties with the Taliban, a fundamentalist Islamic organization that had taken control of most of that country in 1995. Bin Laden's agents bombed the American embassies in Kenya and Tanzania in 1998 as well as the destroyer USS *Cole,* which was making a port call in Yemen in 2000, before turning to targets in the United States itself. In response to the terrorist attacks of September 2001 and the subsequent panic caused by an unknown terrorist mailing spores of anthrax, a lethal disease, the U.S. government adopted a more aggressive policy against terrorism and weapons of mass destruction. In December 2001, American and other NATO forces joined with Afghan opposition groups to overthrow the Taliban-supported regime in Afghanistan, an act that President Bush declared to be the first step in a much larger "war on terrorism."

The issue of when military intervention is justified became the focus of international debate after President Bush pushed for extension of the war on terrorism against the brutal regime of Saddam Husayn in Iraq. Strong opposition to unilateral action came from America's NATO allies France and Germany, as well as from Russia and China. German chancellor Gerhard Schröder won a close election in September 2002 by campaigning against American imperialism. Faced with this opposition, the Bush administration changed tactics. In November 2002 it persuaded the United Nations Security Council to order the return of United Nations weapons inspectors to Iraq and require the Iraqi government to specify what weapons of mass destruction it still possessed.

When the new United Nations inspectors in Iraq failed to find any evidence of banned weapons, which the Iraqis had already destroyed, the split widened between those nations wanting to continue inspections and those, led by the United States and Britain, wanting to intervene militarily. Abandoning efforts to gain Security Council authorization, an American-led "coalition of the willing" invaded Iraq in March 2003.

By the time the new Persian Gulf war began, the overwhelming international sympathy the United States had received after September 11 had evaporated. Public disapproval ran well over 80 percent in Russia and in NATO allies France, Germany, and Turkey (whose parliament voted not to allow American troops to attack Iraq from Turkish soil). Public opinion in most of the Muslim world was almost unanimously against the intervention. Even in Britain and Poland, which sent troops to Iraq, most people disapproved of the war.

Driving Saddam's regime from power took only six weeks. But postwar Iraqi looters and saboteurs did immense damage to utility plants, oil well equipment, and government offices. Moreover, the arsenals of banned weapons that the Bush administration had used to justify the war were never found.

In May the Security Council authorized the American and British occupation of Iraq and lifted the sanctions on petroleum exports that had been imposed on the old regime. But American efforts to secure a larger United Nations role in rebuilding Iraq faced resistance from other world powers, who insisted on curbing American control. Meanwhile, a growing insurgency featuring daily ambushes, kidnappings, and car bombings prevented the establishment of security.

Most Iraqis welcomed the end of Saddam's rule and applauded his capture, but they were also eager for American occupiers to leave. They criticized the slow pace of restoring electricity and water to the cities and the lack of law and order. They had scant faith in the American-nominated Iraqi Governing Council, and only slightly more in the provisional government led by Ayad Allawi that took power at the end of June 2003. As in Afghanistan, reestablishing political and civil order in Iraq would be a long and costly process.

## The Global Economy

From 1991 to 2000 the world experienced a rapid expansion in manufacturing and trade that tied the world ever more tightly together. Manufactured products were increasingly likely to be the product of materials and labor from many countries. Overall, the already developed economies increased their wealth the most, but the fastest rates of growth were in developing countries and in economies making a transition from communism. Net private capital flows to developing nations rose almost sevenfold between 1990 and 2000. This was not foreign aid. Investors

# The New York Times

**New England Edition**
Boston: Windy, some clearing late. High 37. Mainly clear, brisk. Low 28. Tomorrow, partly sunny and not as cold, much lighter winds. High 42. Weather map appears on Page D12.

VOL. CLIII .... No. 52,698    Copyright © 2003 The New York Times    MONDAY, DECEMBER 15, 2003    ONE DOLLAR

# HUSSEIN CAUGHT IN MAKESHIFT HIDE-OUT; BUSH SAYS 'DARK ERA' FOR IRAQIS IS OVER

## BETRAYED BY CLAN

Breakthrough Capped a Renewed Effort to Ferret Out Leads

By ERIC SCHMITT

BAGHDAD, Iraq, Dec. 14 — The hunt for Saddam Hussein ended late Saturday with information from a member of his tribal clan.

Seizing Mr. Hussein, a man who one senior general said had 20 to 30 hide-outs and moved as often as every three to four hours, had become a maddening challenge. Eleven previous times in the last several months, a brigade combat team from the Army's Fourth Infantry Division thought it had a bead on Mr. Hussein and began raids to kill or capture him, only to come up empty, sometimes missing its man by only a matter of hours, military officials here said.

But at 8:26 p.m. Saturday, less than 11 hours after receiving the decisive tip, 600 American soldiers and Special Operations forces backed by tanks, artillery and Apache helicopter gunships surrounded two farmhouses, and near one of them found Mr. Hussein hiding alone at the bottom of an eight-foot hole.

He surrendered without a shot.

"He was just caught like a rat," Maj. Gen. Raymond T. Odierno, the commander of the Fourth Infantry Division, told reporters at his headquarters in Tikrit on Sunday. "He could have been hiding in a hundred different places, a thousand different places like this all around Iraq. It just takes finding the right person who will give you a good idea where he might be."

In recent weeks, American officials had started a new effort to draw up a list of people likely to be hiding Mr. Hussein, including bodyguards, former palace functionaries, tribal

## Arrest by U.S. Soldiers — President Still Cautious

By SUSAN SACHS

BAGHDAD, Iraq, Dec. 14 — Saddam Hussein, once the all-powerful leader of Iraq, was arrested without a fight on Saturday night by American soldiers who found him crouching in an eight-foot hole at an isolated farm near Tikrit, haggard, dirty and disoriented after eluding capture for nearly nine months.

News of Mr. Hussein's arrest, announced Sunday after being kept secret for 18 hours, electrified Iraq and much of the world, sending joyous Iraqis into the streets with the first real catharsis of liberation since the invasion toppled him in April.

For the Bush administration, which has been struggling to stabilize Iraq, the capture of Mr. Hussein was the most triumphal moment since American forces ousted him.

"In the history of Iraq, a dark and painful era is over," President Bush said in a televised noontime address from Washington. "A hopeful day has arrived. All Iraqis can now come together and reject violence and build a new Iraq." But Mr. Bush was careful to couch his message with caution that Iraq remains violent and dangerous.

American officials said Mr. Hussein was being held in Iraq, but they would not disclose the exact location. They said he had been unresistant in medical tests and other procedures but was not cooperating with interrogators on substantive matters.

American-appointed Iraqi leaders said he would eventually face a war crimes trial, but it was unclear when.

President Bush, in a brief televised speech yesterday. Page A16.

Maj. Gen. Raymond T. Odierno, commander of the Fourth Infantry Division, which captured Mr. Hussein with a force of 600 soldiers, said he was armed with only a pistol and had surrendered without firing a shot. Two AK-47 rifles and $750,000 in American cash were found nearby.

It was an ignominious ending for Mr. Hussein, 66, who survived American attempts to kill him during the invasion and had eluded capture apparently by moving from one dingy hide-out to another.

Whether his arrest will undermine the insurgency against the American-led forces in Iraq is unclear. Hours after his capture but before it was announced publicly, a car bomb killed at least 17 people in a town west of Baghdad. [Page A12.]

Even in hiding, Mr. Hussein had

Continued on Page A12

## In the Streets, a Shadow Lifts

By JOHN F. BURNS

**Capture of Saddam in Iraq**    Acting on a tip from Iraqi sources, American troops captured Saddam Husayn in December 2003. The bearded former dictator of Iraq was discovered in a small underground "spider hole" about ten miles southeast of the city of Tikrit.    (©New York Times. Reprinted with permission.)

---

put their funds in countries whose political stability, legal systems, level of education, and labor costs promised the most profitable returns.

The greatest single beneficiary was China. While officially espousing communism, the Chinese government took major steps to open its economy to freer trade and investment. Newly opened markets in eastern Europe and the former Soviet Union also received significant private investment. Stimulated by foreign investment, the Latin American nations of Brazil, Argentina, and Mexico experienced great economic growth. Investors put much less money into the shaky economies and political systems of sub-Saharan Africa, except for countries with significant petroleum resources.

Electronic transfers via the Internet made it possible to invest capital quickly; but when conditions became unfavorable, funds could be withdrawn just as fast. When investors lost faith in Thailand in 1997 and shifted their funds out, the country's currency and stock values plummeted. Political corruption and unrest in Indonesia brought on a similar capital flight the next year, and the widening Asian collapse eventually triggered a serious recession in Japan, business failures in South Korea, and a slowing of economic growth in China.

Government intervention sometimes helped. When Mexico's economy stumbled badly in 1995, U.S. loan guarantees helped it recover rapidly, and by 2001 Mexico had the largest economy in Latin America. However, when Argentina had to abandon its attempt to link its currency to the U.S. dollar in 2001, the value of the Argentine peso plummeted.

Although the largest economies were better able to weather tough times, they were not immune to economic downturns. The extraordinary economic and stock market boom of the 1990s cooled in 2000 and plunged deeper into recession in the wake of the September 11 attacks. The rate of growth in world trade fell from 13 percent in 2000 to only 1 percent in 2001.

The economic boom of the 1990s did little to change historic disparities in regional economic size and in per capita income. The gigantic U.S. economy continued to be larger than the economies of the next five countries combined— Japan, Germany, Great Britain, China (including Hong Kong), and France. In 2002 one person in six lived in a country whose per capita income was over $20,000, while four of every six lived in countries with per capita incomes of under $2,000. Some sixty countries grew poorer in the 1990s, but there were some remarkable overall improvements in the length and quality of life. The average lifespan grew by ten years in three decades. Infant mortality fell by 40 percent and adult illiteracy by 50 percent.

## Managing the Global Economy

To promote economic growth and reduce their vulnerabilities, many countries joined with their neighbors in free-trade zones and regional trade associations (see Map 30.1). The granddaddy of these is the European Union (EU), most of whose members replaced their coins and bills with a new common currency (the Euro) in 2002. Ten new members from eastern Europe and the Mediterranean were admitted in May 2004. Turkey, Bulgaria, and Romania were hoping to join. Despite the EU's expansion, the North American Free Trade Agreement (NAFTA), which eliminated tariffs among the United States, Canada, and Mexico in 1994, governed the world's largest free-trade zone. A South American free-trade zone, Mer-

**Map 30.1   Regional Trade Associations, 2004** International trade and development are major concerns of governments in developed and developing countries. NAFTA, Mercosur, and the EU are free-trade areas. The other associations promote trade and development.

cosur, created by Argentina, Brazil, Paraguay, and Uruguay in 1991, is the world's third largest trading group. In 2002 Mercosur decided to allow the free movement of people within its area and gave equal employment rights to the citizens of all member states. President Bush promoted a Free Trade Area of the Americas, which would include all the democracies of the Western Hemisphere. Chile was the first to sign on. Other free-trade associations operate in West Africa, southern Africa, Southeast Asia, Central America, the Pacific Basin, and the Caribbean.

Because of the inequalities and downturns that are intrinsic to capitalism, the global economic bodies that try to manage world trade and finance find it hard to convince poorer nations that they are not concerned only with the welfare of richer countries. In 1995 the world's major trading powers established the **World Trade Organization (WTO)** to replace earlier collective efforts to negotiate tariffs and trading rules. The WTO encourages reduced trading barriers and enforces international trade agreements. Despite the membership of some 150 nations, the WTO has many critics, as became evident in Seattle in 1999, when street demonstrations, partly organized by American labor unions fearful of foreign competition, forced the organization to suspend a meeting. Moreover, the seven richest nations plus Russia form the Group of Eight (G-8), whose annual meetings have an enormous impact on international trade and politics and also attract a variety of protestors.

Countries in economic trouble have little choice but to turn to the international financial agencies for funds to keep things from getting worse. The International Monetary Fund (IMF) and World Bank make their assistance conditional on internal economic reforms that are often politically unpopular, such as terminating government subsidies for basic foodstuffs, cutting social programs, and liberalizing investment. Although the bitter pill of economic reform may be good in the

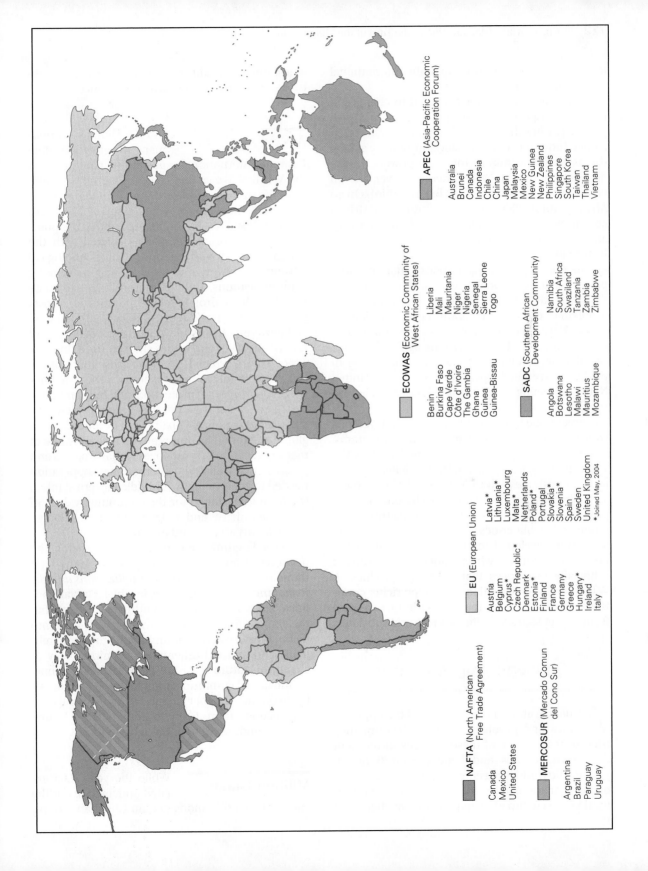

long run, it also fuels criticism of the international economic system.

The emphasis on free trade led to changes in the term of government-to-government aid programs. During the Cold War countries had often gained funds for economic development by allying themselves with one of the superpowers. In the decade after the Cold War ended, however, foreign economic aid to poor nations fell by a third. On an African tour in 2000 President Clinton told African countries that the days of large handouts were over and that they would have to rely on their own efforts to expand their economies.

In the face of rising criticism at home and protests at international meetings, world leaders in the 2000s have pledged to increase attention to the problem of economic backwardness, especially in Africa. At a Millennium Summit in September 2000 the states of the United Nations agreed to make sustainable development and the elimination of world poverty their highest priorities. A 2002 United Nations meeting in Monterrey, Mexico, called for special commitments to Africa.

Freer trade has also put pressure on developed countries to change domestic aid programs. Though agriculture occupies a small part of the work force in Europe and the United States, agricultural interests are politically powerful. Government subsidies have led to vast overproduction of some products. Some of this surplus food is distributed as famine relief, but critics point out that subsidies to farmers in developed countries actually hurt farmers in poor countries, who cannot compete with the artificially low prices that subsidies produce. A WTO meeting collapsed in 2003 when richer countries refused to meet the demands of delegates from poorer states to reduce agricultural subsidies.

# TRENDS AND VISIONS

As people around the world faced the opportunities and problems of **globalization,** they tried to make sense of these changes in terms of their own cultures and beliefs. With 6 billion people, the world is big enough to include a variety of different approaches, from intensely religious or local visions to broad secular views that champion a new universal value system. In some cases, however, conflicting visions have fed violence.

### A New Age?

In 1999 Thomas L. Friedman, a veteran Middle East and international reporter and columnist for the *New York Times*, published a penetrating analysis of the state of the planet. "The world is ten years old," proclaimed the opening essay of *The Lexus and the Olive Tree*. Friedman argued that the political and economic changes associated with the collapse of the Soviet Empire and the technological advances (computers, satellite and fiber-optic communications, and the Internet) that had made possible a huge drop in telecommunications costs had ushered in a new age of political and economic globalization. In his view, global capitalism and American power and values characterized this new era of history, which held the promise (but not the certainty) of increased prosperity, peace, democracy, environmental protection, and human rights.

In Friedman's analysis, the Lexus, a splendidly engineered Japanese luxury car produced for a global market on a computer-run assembly line of mechanical robots, symbolizes global progress and prosperity, as well as the international cooperation needed to achieve them. A Middle Eastern symbol, the olive tree, stands for the communal values of family, ethnicity, and religion that give people's lives stability, depth, and meaning.

Was Friedman too optimistic in seeing the dawning of an age of great promise? Many who thought so cited *The Clash of Civilizations and the Remaking of the World Order,* in which Harvard political scientist Samuel P. Huntington argues that the end of the Cold War left the world divided into distinct regional civilizations. For Huntington, religious and cultural differences are more likely to shape the future than are globalizing economic, political, and communication forces. It is impossible to predict whether global clashes or global convergence are more likely to dominate the future. Recent trends seem to point in both directions.

### Militant Islam

While the year 2000 excited anticipations of the end of the world among certain Christian groups, some people in other faiths also interpreted contemporary events from deeply religious perspectives. In the Jewish calendar a millennial change (the year 6000) will not arrive until 2240 C.E., but many on the religious right in Israel interpret the struggle of modern Israel to survive and prosper in terms of the biblical accounts of the Israelites' conquests more than four thousand years ago. Some Christian believers have gone to Israel to support Jewish settlers' efforts to reclaim the lands of the ancient Jewish kingdoms. For Muslims the year 1400 coincided with the Iranian Revolution of 1979. Since that time publications dealing with the end of the world have become common among certain groups, just as they have in some Christian circles. But the issues that concern most Muslims arise from the real circumstances in which they find themselves. While moderate views on how to cope with economic stagnation and autocratic rule predominate, extreme and intolerant groups have been able to recruit supporters among those who feel politically frustrated or distressed by what they see as foreign cultural practices eroding their tradition. Since becoming independent in the 1950s, some Middle Eastern states have earned great wealth from petroleum exports, but per capita income in Muslim-majority countries in 2002 averaged half as much as in the world as a whole. No Muslim state is a major industrial or geopolitical power. The spread of mass media has also fed discontent by making ordinary Muslims more aware of the political difficulties and violence facing fellow Muslims in places like Chechnya, Iraq, Kashmir, and the occupied territories of the West Bank and Gaza.

Because American aid and support have helped Israel acquire the most powerful military force in the Middle East, much Islamic hatred and opposition has been directed against the United States. Many Muslims also denounce American support for unpopular and undemocratic governments in Muslim-majority countries like Egypt and Saudi Arabia. Although most Muslims admire American technological and cultural achievements, a 2002 poll by the Pew Research Center for the People and the Press found that the majority of Egyptians, Jordanians, and Pakistanis held a "very unfavorable" opinion of the United States, a negative appraisal that has only deepened with the prolongation of the American occupation of Iraq.

This view of the world order has many roots, but it reflects an ideological vision of Muslims under attack that is widely published in the media in Muslim states and promoted by a few Muslim leaders who use religious ideas to justify violent actions. From this perspective the Palestinian suicide bombers in Israel appear as martyrs and heroes rather than terrorists. Such a vision explains why some Muslims celebrated when the Twin Towers collapsed in New York.

## Universal Rights and Values

At the same time that religiously based visions of society and government have gained support in various faith communities, efforts to promote adherence to universal standards of human rights have also gained wider acceptance. The modern human rights movement grew out of the secular statements of the French Declaration of the Rights of Man (1789) and the U.S. Constitution (1788) and Bill of Rights (1791). Over the next century, the logic of universal rights moved Westerners to undertake international campaigns to end slave trading and slavery throughout the world and to secure equal legal rights (and eventually voting rights) for women. (As the millennium began, the cause of animal rights was gaining increasing support in Europe and North America.)

International organizations in the twentieth century secured agreement on labor standards, the rules of war, and the rights of refugees. The pinnacle of these efforts was the **Universal Declaration of Human Rights,** passed by the United Nations General Assembly in 1948, which proclaimed itself "a common standard of achievement for all peoples and nations." Its thirty articles condemned slavery, torture, cruel and inhuman punishment, and arbitrary arrest, detention, and exile. The Declaration called for freedom of movement, assembly, and thought. It asserted rights to life, liberty, and security of person; to impartial public trials; and to education, employment, and leisure. The principle of equality was most fully articulated in Article 2:

> Everyone is entitled to all the rights and freedoms set forth in this Declaration, without distinction of any kind, such as race, color, sex, language, religion, or political or other opinion,

national or social origin, property, birth or other status.[2]

This passage reflected an international consensus against racism and imperialism and a growing acceptance of the importance of social and economic equality. Most newly independent countries joining the United Nations willingly signed the Declaration because it implicitly condemned European colonial regimes.

The idea of universal human rights has not gone unchallenged. Some have asked whether a set of principles whose origins were so clearly Western could be called universal. Others have been uneasy with the idea of subordinating the traditional values of their culture or religion to a broader philosophical standard. Despite these objections, important gains have been made in implementing these standards.

Besides the official actions of the United Nations and individual states, individual human rights activists, often working through international philanthropic bodies known as **nongovernmental organizations (NGOs),** have been important forces for promoting human rights. Amnesty International, founded in 1961 and numbering a million members in 162 countries by the 1990s, concentrates on gaining the freedom of people who have been tortured or imprisoned without trial and campaigns against summary execution by government death squads or other gross violations of rights. Arguing that no right is more fundamental than the right to life, other NGOs have devoted themselves to famine relief, refugee assistance, and health care around the world. Médecins Sans Frontières (Doctors Without Borders), founded in 1971, was awarded the Nobel Peace Prize for 1999 for the medical assistance it offered in scores of crisis situations.

The rising tendency to see health care as a human right has made a new disease, acquired immune deficiency syndrome (AIDS), the focus of particular attention because its incidence and high mortality rate are closely associated with poverty, and treatments are very expensive. Over 40 million people worldwide are infected with the HIV retrovirus that causes AIDS. Of them, 70 percent live in sub-Saharan Africa (see Figure 30.1). The number of sick and dying is already large enough in some parts of Africa to pose a significant risk to the pro-

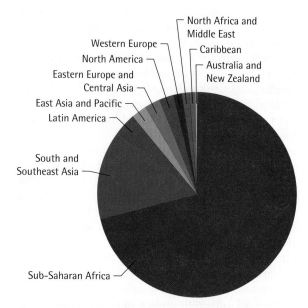

**Figure 30.1    World Distribution of HIV/AIDS Cases (2001 estimates)**    *Source:* United Nations AIDS and World Health Organization, *Report on the Global HIV/AIDS Epidemic* (June 2000).

duction of food, the care of the young and elderly, and the staffing of schools. Because sexual promiscuity among young men serving in the armed forces has made them especially likely to be infected, death and incapacitation from AIDS have significantly imperiled military preparedness in parts of Africa. Great international efforts are being made to provide drugs at a lower cost so that more Africans can be treated. Because the disease is not contagious except by very intimate contact, education is a more cost-effective way of stemming the spread of AIDS. In Uganda, South Africa, and Ethiopia, for example, education campaigns have reduced the incidence of new HIV infections in targeted groups. An inexpensive drug has also been successful in cutting the transmission of the infection from mother to infant during childbirth.

Other international agreements have made genocide a crime and have promoted environmental protection of the seas, of Antarctica, and of the atmosphere. The United States and a few other nations were greatly concerned that such treaties would unduly limit their sovereignty or threaten their national interests. For this reason the U.S. Congress delayed ratifying the 1949 convention on genocide until 1986. More recently the United States drew widespread international criticism for demanding exemption for Americans from the jurisdiction of the International Criminal Court, created in 2002 to try international criminals, and for withdrawing in 2001 from the 1997 Kyoto Protocol requiring industrial nations to sharply reduce emissions of pollutants that damage the atmosphere (see Environment and Technology: Global Warming). To many nations it seemed as if Americans, with the world's greatest industrial economy, were trying to exempt themselves from standards that they wanted to impose on other nations.

## Women's Rights

The women's rights movement, which began on both sides of the North Atlantic in the nineteenth century, became an important human rights issue in the twentieth century. Rights for women became accepted in Western countries and were enshrined in the constitutions of many nations newly freed from colonial rule. A series of international conferences on the status of women sponsored by the Division for the Advancement of Women of the United Nations have shown the international importance of women's rights at the end of the twentieth century. The first meeting, held in Nairobi, Kenya, in 1985, attracted seventeen thousand women from all over the world. The delegates focused on equal access to education and jobs and on quality-of-life matters such as ending sexual exploitation and gaining control of reproduction. A second conference in Beijing in 1995 also examined a variety of women's issues and perspectives, in some cases to the discomfort of the Chinese government. The Beijing conference recognized the advances that had been made in the status of women and called for efforts to remove remaining obstacles to equality, including those caused by poverty.

Besides highlighting the similarity of the problems women faced around the world, the conferences also revealed great variety in the views and concerns of women. Feminists from the West, who had been accustomed to dictating the agenda and who had pushed for the liberation of women in other parts of the world, sometimes found themselves accused of having narrow concerns and condescending attitudes. Some non-Western women complained about Western feminists' endorsement of sexual liberation and about the deterioration of family life in the West. They found Western feminists' concern with matters such as comfortable clothing misplaced and trivial compared to the issues of poverty and disease.

Other cultures came in for their share of criticism. Western women and many secular leaders in Muslim countries protested Islam's requirement that a woman cover her head and wear loose-fitting garments to conceal the shape of her body, practices enforced by law in countries such as Iran and Saudi Arabia. Nevertheless, many outspoken Muslim women voluntarily donned concealing garments as expressions of personal belief, statements of resistance to secular dictatorship, or defense against coarse male behavior. Much Western criticism focused on the African custom of circumcising girls, a form of genital mutilation that can cause chronic infections or permanently impair sexual enjoyment. While not denying the problems this practice can lead to, many African women saw deteriorating economic conditions, rape, and AIDS as more important issues.

The conferences were more important for the attention they focused on women's issues than for the solutions they generated. The search for a universally accepted women's rights agenda proved elusive because of local concerns and strong disagreement on abortion and other issues. Nevertheless, increases in women's education, access to employment, political participation, and control of fertility augured well for the eventual achievement of gender equality.

Such efforts raised the prominence of human rights as a global concern and put pressure on governments to consider human rights when making foreign policy decisions. Skeptics observed, however, that a Western country could successfully prod a non-Western country to improve its human rights performance—for example, by granting women

# ENVIRONMENT + TECHNOLOGY

## Global Warming

Until the 1980s environmental alarms focused mainly on localized episodes of air and water pollution, exposure to toxic substances, waste management, and the disappearance of wilderness. The development of increasingly powerful computers and complex models of ecological interactions in the 1990s, however, made people aware of the global scope of certain environmental problems.

Many scientists and policymakers came to perceive global warming, the slow increase of the temperature of the earth's lower atmosphere, as an environmental threat requiring preventive action on an international scale. The warming is caused by a layer of atmospheric gases (carbon dioxide, methane, nitrous oxide, and ozone) that allow solar radiation to reach earth and warm it, but keep infrared energy (heat) from radiating from earth's surface into space. Called the *greenhouse effect*, this process normally keeps the earth's temperature at a level suitable for life. However, increases in greenhouse-gas emissions—particularly from the burning of fossil fuels in industry and transportation—have added to this insulating atmospheric layer.

Recent events have confirmed predictions of global temperature increases and melting glaciers and icecaps. Globally, the five warmest years on record were 1995,

1997, 1998, 2001, and 2002. Record heat hit northern Europe in the summer of 2003. Greenland glaciers and Arctic Ocean sea ice melted at record rates during 2002, and a huge section of the Antarctic ice shelf broke up and floated away. Andean glaciers are shrinking so fast they could disappear in a decade, imperiling water supplies for drinking, irrigation, and hydroelectric production. Drought has affected much of the United States in recent years, and in 2002 Australia experienced the "Big Dry," its worst drought in a century.

Despite this evidence, governments of the industrialized countries that produce the most greenhouse gasses have been slow to adopt measures stringent enough to reduce emissions because of the negative effects they believe this could have on their economies. There is also fear that it may be already too late to reverse global warming. The pledges that representatives from 178 countries made at the first Earth Summit in Rio de Janeiro in 1992 to limit their *increase* in greenhouse-gas production have so far been ineffective. Fearing limits on gas emissions could cripple their plans for industrial and economic expansion, many nations hesitated to sign the 1997 Kyoto Protocol, the first international agreement to impose penalties on countries that failed to cut greenhouse-gas

---

more equal access to education and careers—but that reverse criticism of a Western country often fell on deaf ears—for example, condemnation of the death penalty in the United States. For such critics the human rights movement was not an effort to make the world more humane but another form of Western cultural imperialism, a club with which to beat former colonial societies into submission. Still, support for universal rights has grown, especially because increasing globalization has made common standards of behavior more important.

## GLOBAL CULTURE

Along with the human rights movement, other kinds of cultural globalization were also proceeding rapidly at the turn of the millennium. A global language, a global educational system, and global forms of artistic expression have all come into being. Trade, travel, and migration have made a common culture necessary. Electronic communications that were once confined to members of a jet-setting elite have enabled global cultural emissions. It was a major environmental victory when Japan added its signature in March 2001, but to the consternation of many world leaders President George W. Bush has rejected the agreement. The war on terrorism also appears to have made the environment a lower American priority. Until the destructive effects of global warming, such as the inundation of coastal regions and large cities by rising sea levels, match the destruction of terrorists, the political focus is unlikely to shift.

**Flooding in Bangladesh**   Typhoon-driven floods submerge the low-lying farmlands of Bangladesh with tragic regularity. Any significant rise in the sea level will make parts of the country nearly uninhabitable.   (D. Aubert/Sygma)

influences to move deeper into many societies, and a sort of global popular culture has also emerged. These changes have angered some and delighted others.

## The Media and the Message

Although cultural influences from every continent travel around the world, the fact that the most pervasive elements of global culture have their origins in the West raises concerns in many quarters about **cultural imperialism.** Critics complain that entertainment con-glomerates are flooding the world's movie theaters and television screens with Western tastes and styles and that manufacturers are flooding world markets with Western goods—both relying on sophisticated advertising techniques that promote consumption and cultural conformity. In this view, global marketing is an especially insidious effort not only to overwhelm the world with a single Western outlook shaped by capitalist ideology, but also to suppress or devalue traditional cultures and alternative ideologies. As the leader of the capitalist world, the United States is seen as the primary culprit.

But in truth, technology plays a more central role than ideology in spreading Western culture. Moreover, even though imperialist forces old and new shape choices, strongly democratic forces are also at work as people around the world make their selections in the cultural marketplace. Thus, a diversity of voices is more characteristic of cultural globalization than the cultural imperialism thesis maintains.

The pace of cultural globalization began to quicken during the economic recovery after World War II. The Hollywood films and American jazz recordings that had become popular in Europe and parts of Asia continued to spread. But the birth of electronic technology opened contacts with large numbers of people who could never have afforded to go to a movie or buy a record.

The first step was the development of cheap transistor radios that could run for months on a couple of small batteries. Perfected by American scientists at Bell Telephone Laboratories in 1948, solid-state electronic transistors replaced power-hungry and less reliable electron tubes in radios and a wide array of other devices. Just as tube radios had spread in Europe and America in the decades before the war, small portable transistor radios, most made in Japan and elsewhere in Asia, spread rapidly in parts of the world where homes lacked electricity.

Because the transistor radios sold in Asia and Africa were designed to receive shortwave broadcasts, they brought people in remote villages the news, views, and music that American, European, Soviet, and Chinese transmitters beamed to the world. For the first time in history, the whole world could learn of major political and cultural events simultaneously. Although such broadcasts came in local and regional languages, many were in English. Electronic audiotape and CD players added to the diversity of music available to individuals everywhere. Television, made possible by the invention of an electron scanning gun in 1928, became widely available to consumers in Western countries in the 1950s. In poorer parts of the world TVs were not common until the 1980s and 1990s, after mass production and cheap transistors made sets more affordable and reliable.

Outside the United States, television broadcasting was usually a government monopoly at first, following the pattern of telegraph and postal service and radio broadcasting. Governments expected news reports and other programming to disseminate a unified national viewpoint. These government monopolies eroded as the high cost of television production opened up global markets for rebroadcasts of American soap operas, adventure series, and situation comedies. By the 1990s a global network of satellites brought privately owned television broadcasting to even remote areas of the world, and the VCR (videocassette recorder) brought an even greater variety of programs to people everywhere. British programs found a secondary market in the United States, Canada, Australia, and other countries. As a result of wider circulation of programming, people often became familiar with different dialects of English and other languages. People in Portugal, for example, who in the 1960s had found it difficult to understand Brazilian Portuguese, have become avid fans of Brazilian soap operas. Immigrants from Albania and North Africa often arrive in Italy with a command of Italian learned from Italian stations whose signals they could pick up at home.

Further internationalization of culture resulted from satellite transmission of TV signals. Specializing in rock music videos aimed at a youth audience, MTV (Music Television) became an international enterprise offering special editions in different parts of the world. Music videos shown in Uzbekistan°, for example, often featured Russian bands, and Chinese groups appeared in MTV programs shown in Singapore. CNN (Cable News Network) expanded its international market after becoming the most-viewed and informative news source during the 1991 Persian Gulf War, when it broadcast live from Baghdad. Despite CNN's fundamentally American view of the news, its round-the-clock coverage and global resources began to supplant other commercial and government news programming as the best source of information about rapidly developing events. By the new millennium global satellite networks (Fox, Sky) assembled by Rupert Murdock and new regional networks competed for viewers.

The Internet, a linkage of academic, government, and business computer networks developed

---

**Uzbekistan** (ooz-BEK-ih-STAN)

in the 1960s, became a major cultural phenomenon. Personal computers proliferated in the 1980s, and with the establishment of the easy-to-use graphic interface of the World Wide Web in 1994, the number of Internet users skyrocketed. Myriad new companies formed to exploit "e-commerce," the commercial dimension of the Internet. In the new century many college students spent less time studying conventional books and scholarly resources than they spent exploring the Web for information and entertainment.

As has happened so often throughout history, technological developments have had unanticipated consequences. Although the new telecommunications and entertainment technologies derived disproportionately from American invention, industry, and cultural creativity, Japan and other East Asian nations came to dominate the manufacture and refinement of computer devices. In the 1990s Japan introduced digital television broadcasting at about the time that disks containing digitized movies and computer programs with movie-like action became increasingly available. In the early 2000s digital cameras, DVD players, and new generations of cell phones became popular, providing opportunities for companies in a variety of developing countries to capture a corner of the market. In contrast to these rapid changes in technology, Western, especially American, cultural domination of the content of the Web has changed more slowly, but people around the world can adapt the medium to their own purposes.

## The Spread of Pop Culture

New technologies changed perceptions of culture as well as its distribution around the world and among different social classes. For most of history, popular culture was folk culture, highly localized ways of dress, food, music, and expression. Only the educated and urban few had access to the riches of a broader "great tradition," such as Confucianism in East Asia or Western culture in Europe and the Americas. The schools of modern nation-states promoted national values and beliefs, as well as tastes in painting, literature, and art. Governments also promoted a common language or dialect and fre-

quently suppressed local traditions and languages. In a more democratic way, the transistor helped break down barriers and create a global popular culture that transcended regional great traditions and national cultures.

Initially, the content of **global pop culture** was heavily American. Singer Michael Jackson was almost as well known to the youth of Dar-es-Salaam (Tanzania) and Bangkok (Thailand) as to American fans. Basketball star Michael Jordan became a worldwide celebrity, heavily promoted by Nike, McDonald's, and television. American television programs such as *Wheel of Fortune* and *Friends* acquired immense followings and inspired local imitations. In the late twentieth century American movies, which had long had great popular appeal, substantially increased their share of world markets. In the 1990s the vast majority of the most popular films in Europe were American made. Many Europeans complained loudly about this American cultural imperialism—and then bought tickets to see the latest Hollywood spectacular.

As with music and fast food, companies spent heavily to promote profitable overseas markets, but the United States did not have a lock on global pop culture. Latin American soap operas, *telenovelas,* have a vast following in the Americas, eastern Europe, and elsewhere. Bombay, India, long the largest producer of films in the world, is now making more films for an international audience, rather than just for the home market. Bruce Lee popularized kung fu (Chinese martial arts) movies. A sophisticated kung fu film, *Crouching Tiger, Hidden Dragon* by Hong Kong–born director Ang Lee, was very popular in the United States and won four Academy Awards for 2000, including one for the best foreign-language film.

In the post–World War II decades American, European, and Japanese companies sought international markets for their products. In the 1970s and 1980s American brand names like Levi's, Coca-Cola, Marlboro, Gillette, McDonald's, and Kentucky Fried Chicken were global phenomena. But in time Asian names—Hitachi, Sony, Sanyo, and Mitsubishi—were blazoned in neon and on giant video screens on the sides of skyscrapers, along with European brands such as Nestlé, Mercedes, Pirelli, and Benetton. The location of manufacturing plants overseas and the acquisition of corporate operations by foreign buyers rendered such global firms as transnational as the products they sell.

The content of international pop culture does not have to remain any more monolithic than the typical McDonald's lunch, which consists of a meat patty named for a German city, potatoes prepared in a French manner, and a soft drink named after the South American coca leaves and West African kola that were its original ingredients. Popular music also became increasingly international. Latin American styles extended their appeal beyond the Americas. The hybrid rhythms known as Afropop spread around Africa and found fans in Europe and the Americas.

## The Emerging Global Elite Culture

While the globalization of popular culture has been criticized, cultural links across national and ethnic boundaries at a more elite level have generated little controversy. The end of the Cold War reopened intellectual and cultural contacts between former adversaries, making possible such things as Russian-American collaboration on space missions and extensive business contacts among former rivals. The English language, modern science, and higher education became the key elements of this **global elite culture.**

The emergence of English as the first global language depended on developments that had been building for centuries. The British Empire introduced the language to far-flung colonies. When the last parts of the empire gained independence after World War II, most former colonies chose to continue using English as an official language because it provided national unity and a link to the outside world that the dozens or hundreds of local languages could not. After independence, representatives of former British colonies formed the Commonwealth on the basis of their shared language and commercial ties. Newly independent countries that made a local language official for nationalist reasons often found the decision counterproductive. Indian nationalists had pushed for Hindi to be India's official language, but they found that students taught in Hindi were unable to compete internationally because of poor knowledge of English. Sri Lanka, which had made Sinhala its official language in 1956, reversed itself after local reporters revealed in 1989 that prominent officials were sending their children to English-medium private schools.

The use of English as a second language was greatly stimulated by the importance of the United States in postwar world affairs. Individuals recognized the importance of mastering English for successful business, diplomatic, and military careers. After the collapse of Soviet domination, students in eastern Europe flocked to study English instead of Russian. Ninety percent of students in Cambodia (a former French colony) choose to study English, even though a Canadian agency offers a sizeable cash bonus if they will study French. In the 1990s China made the study of English as a second language nearly universal from junior high school onwards, but it also forced an English-medium school in Hong Kong to teach most subjects in Chinese.

English has become the language of choice for most international academic conferences, business meetings, and diplomatic gatherings. International organizations that provide equal status to many languages, such as the United Nations and the European Union, tend to conduct all informal committee meetings in English. English has even replaced Latin as the working language for international consultations in the Catholic Church. In cities throughout the world, signs and notices are now posted in the local language and English.

The utility of English as a global language is also evident in the emergence of an international literature in English. The trend has been evident for decades in former British colonies in Africa, where most writers use English to reach both a national audience and an international one. Wole Soyinka, the first sub-Saharan African to win the Nobel Prize in literature for 1986, wrote in English, the national language of Nigeria, rather than his native Yoruba. When Arundhati Roy won the prestigious Booker Prize in 1997 for *The God of Small Things*, a novel set in her native state of Kerala in southwest India, she was part of an English-language literary tradition that has been growing in India for a century. V. S. Naipaul of Trinidad, winner of the Nobel Prize in literature for 2001, is a good example of the way global migration has fostered the use of English. Naipaul's ancestors had emigrated from India in the nineteenth century.

World literature remains highly diverse in form and language, but science and technology have become standardized components of global culture. Though imperialism helped spread the Western disciplines of biology, chemistry, and physics around the world, their popularity continued to expand even after imperial systems ended because they worked so much better than other approaches to the natural world. Their truth was universal even if plants and animals continue to be classified in Latin and the less common elements are called by names originally derived from Latin and Greek. Global manufacturing could not function without a common system of applied science. Because of their scientific basis, Western medicine and drugs are increasingly accepted as the best treatments, even though many cultures also use traditional remedies.

The third pillar of global elite culture is the university. The structure and curricula of modern universities are nearly indistinguishable around the world, permitting students today to cross national boundaries as freely as students in the medieval Latin West or the Muslim world. Instruction in the pure sciences varies little from place to place, and standardization is nearly as common in social science and in applied sciences such as engineering and medicine. There may be more diversity in the humanities, but professors and students around the world pay attention to the latest literary theories and topics of historical interest.

While university subjects are taught in many languages, instruction in English is spreading rapidly. Because discoveries are often first published in English, advanced students in science, business, and international relations need to know that language to keep up with the latest developments. The global mobility of professors and students also promotes classroom instruction in the most global language. Many courses in the Netherlands and in Scandinavian countries have long been offered in English, and elsewhere in Europe offering more courses in English was the obvious way to facilitate the EU's efforts to encourage students to study outside their countries of origin. When South Africa ended the apartheid educational systems that had required people to study in their own languages, most students chose to study in English.

Because global elite culture is so deeply rooted in years of training, complex institutions, and practical utility, it is less subject to fads and commercial promotion than is global pop culture. Because such elite culture is confined to a distinct minority in most places, it poses little threat to national and folk cultures and, therefore, is much less controversial.

## Enduring Cultural Diversity

Although protestors regularly denounce the "Americanization" of the world, a closer look suggests that cultural globalization is more complex and multifaceted. Just as English has largely spread as a second language, so global culture is primarily a second culture that dominates some contexts but does not displace other traditions. From this perspective, American music, fast food, and fashions are more likely to add to a society's options than to displace local culture.

Japan first demonstrated that a country with a non-Western culture could perform at a high industrial level. Individuality was less valued in Japan than the ability of each person to fit into a group, whether as an employee, a member of an athletic team, or a student in a class. Moreover, the Japanese considered it unmannerly to directly contradict, correct, or refuse the request of another person. From a Western point of view, these Japanese customs seemed to discourage individual initiative and personality development and to preserve traditional hierarchies. Japanese women, for example, even though they often worked outside the home, responded only slowly to the American and European feminist advocacy of equality in economic and social relations. However, the Japanese approach to social relations was well suited to an industrial economy. The efficiency, pride in workmanship, and group solidarity of Japanese workers, supported by closely coordinated government and corporate policies, played a major role in transforming Japan from a defeated nation with a demolished industrial base in 1945 to an economic power by the 1980s.

Japan's success in the modern industrial world called into question the older assumption that successful industrialization required the adoption of Western culture. As awareness of the economic impact of Japanese culture and society began to spread, it became apparent that Taiwan and South Korea, along with Singapore and Hong Kong (a British colony before being reunited with China in 1997), were developing dynamic industrial economies of their own. Other countries seem likely to follow this model.

This does not mean that the world's culture diversity is secure. Every decade a number of languages cease to be spoken, usually as the result of the spread of national languages. Many religious practices are also disappearing in the face of the successful expansion of Islam, Christianity, and other religions, although secular values also play a role. Televised national ceremonies or performances for tourists may prevent folk customs and costumes from dying out, but they also tend to standardize rituals that once had many local variations. Whereas it was possible to recognize the nationality of people from their clothing and grooming a century ago, today most urban men dress the same the world over, although women's clothing shows much greater variety.

## CONCLUSION

Have we entered a golden age, or is the world descending into a fiery abyss? The future is unknowable, but the study of history suggests that neither extreme is likely. Golden ages and dark ages are rare, and our understanding of our own time is easily swayed by hopes, fears, and other emotions. If the exuberant optimism of the 1990s now seems excessive, the pessimism of the early 2000s may in time seem equally far off the mark.

What is undeniable is that the turn of the millennium has been a time of important global changes. The iron curtain that had divided Europe since the end of the Second World War fell, taking with it the tensions and risks of the Cold War. The great Soviet Empire broke up, while dozens of countries joined new economic coalitions. The bastions of communism embraced capitalism with

varying degrees of enthusiasm. As trading barriers tumbled, world trade surged, creating new wealth and new inequalities in its distribution.

Aided by new electronic marvels, individuals communicate around the planet and interact across cultural barriers in ways never before imagined. News of disasters and human rights violations bring more rapid responses than ever before. Culturally, the English language, higher education, and science form a viable global culture for the elite.

History teaches that change is always uneven. The rate of change in global telecommunications and international economic institutions is notably faster than in international political institutions. The nation-state remains supreme. The structure of the United Nations has changed little since its founding six decades earlier. States resist limits on their autonomy, and the more powerful ones take unilateral actions, whether supported or opposed by international public opinion. Never before has one state, the United States, stood so far above the rest.

Rather than giving ground to globalization, many older ideas and values continue to be strong. The less powerful adapt slowly, dig in their heals to resist change, or raise voices and fists against it. Protests have forced new attention on global poverty, disease, exploitation, and environmental damage that globalization causes or fails to relieve. Adjustments have been made, but on the whole change on these fronts has come slowly.

In many places religious fundamentalism, ethnic nationalism, and social conservatism have seemed to reach new levels of intensity. In some quarters globalization has fomented and fostered violent responses, contributing to some degree to the "war on terrorism" led by the United States. The resulting clashes have raised concerns and inspired apocalyptic visions. Adjusting to the new age of globalization will be neither quick nor easy.

## ■ Key Terms

ethnic cleansing
weapons of mass destruction
terrorism
Usama bin Laden
World Trade Organization (WTO)

globalization
**Universal Declaration of Human Rights**
**nongovernmental organizations (NGOs)**
**cultural imperialism**
**global pop culture**
**global elite culture**

## ■ Suggested Reading

Among those attempting to describe the world at the turn of the millennium are Benjamin R. Barber, *Jihad vs. McWorld: How Globalism and Tribalism are Reshaping the World* (1995); Thomas L. Friedman, *The Lexus and the Olive Tree* (1999); Samuel P. Huntington, *The Clash of Civilizations and the Remaking of the World Order* (1996); and Paul Kennedy, *Preparing for the Twenty-First Century* (1993).

Recent studies of American military policies and the widening split with Europe include Dana Priest, *The Mission: Waging War and Keeping Peace with America's Military* (2003); Robert Kaplan, *Of Paradise and Power: America and Europe in the New World Order* (2002); Charles A. Kulpchan, *The End of the American Era: U.S. Foreign Policy and the Geopolitics of the Twenty-First Century* (2002); and Joseph S. Nye, Jr., *The Paradox of American Power: Why the World's Only Superpower Can't Go It Alone* (2002).

Mike Moore, a former director-general of the WTO, provides an insider's view of the global economy in *A World Without Walls: Freedom, Development, Free Trade and Global Governance* (2003). Amy Chua, *World on Fire: How Exporting Free Market Democracy Breeds Ethnic Hatred and Global Instability* (2003), offers a quite different perspective.

Gilles Kepel, *The Revenge of God: The Resurgence of Islam, Christianity and Judaism in the Modern World* (1994), Philip Jenkins, *The Next Christendom: The Coming of Global Christianity* (2002), and Bernard Lewis, *What Went Wrong? The Clash Between Islam and Modernity in the Middle East* (2003), deal with recent religious-political movements. Eugen Weber, *Apocalypses: Prophesies, Cults, and Millennial Beliefs Through the Ages* (1999), provides a deeper historical perspective. The Bosnian crisis is well covered in Susan L. Woodward, *Balkan Tragedy: Chaos and Dissolution After the Cold War* (1995). Other world crises involving international intervention are treated in William J. Durch, ed., *UN Peacekeeping, American Policy, and the Uncivil Wars of the 1990s* (1996). Terrorism is well covered by Bruce Hoffman, *Inside Terrorism* (1998).

Standard reviews of human rights include Thomas Buergenthal et al., *International Human Rights in a Nutshell*, 3d ed. (2002); Carol Devine and Carol Rae Hansen, *Human Rights: The Essential Reference* (1999); and Jack Donnelly, *International Human Rights*, 2d ed. (1998). Ronald Inglehart and Pippa Norris, *Rising Tide: Gender Equality and Cultural Change Around the World* (2003), surveys the condition of women.

The interrelationships between high culture and popular culture during the twentieth century are treated from different perspectives in Arjun Appadurai, *Modernity at Large: Cultural Dimensions of Globalization* (1996); Peter L. Berger and Samuel Huntington, eds., *Many Globalizations: Cultural Diversity in the Contemporary World* (2002); Tyler Cowen, *Creative Destruction: How Globalization Is Changing the World's Cultures* (2002); and Diana Crane, Nobuko Kawashima, and Kenichi Kawasaka, eds., *Global Culture: Media, Arts, Policy, and Globalization* (2002). Two very readable books by James B. Twitchell detail the rise of popular culture in the United States and present various reactions to this phenomenon: *Carnival Culture: The Trashing of Taste in America* (1992) and *Adcult USA: The Triumph of Advertising in American Culture* (1996). Walter LaFeber, *Michael Jordan and the New Global Capitalism* (1999), explores the relationship between a sports star and global marketing.

Some personal accounts of cultural change are Philippe Wamba, *Kinship: A Family's Journey in Africa and America* (1999); William Dalrymple, *The Age of Kali: Indian Travels and Encounters* (1998); V. S. Naipaul, *Beyond Belief: Islamic Excursions among the Converted Peoples* (1997); Fergal Keane, *A Season of Blood: A Rwandan Journey* (1995); Nelson Mandela, *Long Walk to Freedom* (1994); and Mark Mathabane, *African Women: Three Generations* (1994).

On global English see David Crystal, *English as a Global Language* (1997); Alistaire Pennycock, *The Cultural Politics of English as an International Language* (1994); and Robert Phillipson, *Linguistic Imperialism* (1992).

## ■ Notes

**1.** "Liberty's Great Advance," *The Economist*, June 28–July 4, 2003, pp. 5–6.
**2.** "Universal Declaration of Human Rights," in *Twenty-five Human Rights Documents* (New York: Center for the Study of Human Rights, Columbia University, 1994), 6.

# Glossary

The glossary for *The Earth and Its Peoples*, 3/e Brief is for the complete text, Chapters 1 through 30.

**Abbasid Caliphate** Descendants of the Prophet Muhammad's uncle, al-Abbas, the Abbasids overthrew the **Umayyad Caliphate** and ruled an Islamic empire from their capital in Baghdad (founded 762) from 750 to 1258. (*p. 187*)

**abolitionists** Men and women who agitated for a complete end to slavery. Abolitionist pressure ended the British transatlantic slave trade in 1808 and slavery in British colonies in 1834. In the United States the activities of abolitionists were one factor leading to the Civil War (1861–1865). (*p. 475*)

**Acheh Sultanate** Muslim kingdom in northern Sumatra. Main center of Islamic expansion in Southeast Asia in the early seventeenth century, it declined after the Dutch seized **Malacca** from Portugal in 1641. (*p. 427*)

**Aden** Port city in the modern south Arabian country of Yemen. It has been a major trading center in the Indian Ocean since ancient times. (*p. 309*)

**African National Congress** An organization dedicated to obtaining equal voting and civil rights for black inhabitants of South Africa. Founded in 1912 as the South African Native National Congress, it changed its name in 1923. Though it was banned and its leaders were jailed for many years, it eventually helped bring majority rule to South Africa. (*p. 646*)

**Afrikaners** South Africans descended from Dutch and French settlers of the seventeenth century. Their Great Trek founded new settler colonies in the nineteenth century. Though a minority among South Africans, they held political power after 1910, imposing a system of racial segregation called apartheid after 1949. (*p. 580*)

**Agricultural Revolution(s) (ancient)** The change from food gathering to food production that occurred between ca. 8000 and 2000 B.C.E. Also known as the Neolithic Revolution. (*p. 8*)

**agricultural revolution (eighteenth century)** The transformation of farming that resulted in the eighteenth century from the spread of new crops, improvements in cultivation techniques and livestock breeding, and the consolidation of small holdings into large farms from which tenants and sharecroppers were forcibly expelled. (*p. 481*)

**Aguinaldo, Emilio (1869–1964)** Leader of the Filipino independence movement against Spain (1895–1898). He proclaimed the independence of the Philippines in 1899, but his movement was crushed and he was captured by the United States Army in 1901. (*p. 589*)

**Akbar (1542–1605)** Most illustrious sultan of the Mughal Empire in India (r. 1556–1605). He expanded the empire and pursued a policy of conciliation with Hindus. (*p. 425*)

**Akhenaten** Egyptian pharaoh (r. 1353–1335 B.C.E.). He built a new capital at Amarna, fostered a new style of naturalistic art, and created a religious revolution by imposing worship of the sun-disk. The Amarna letters, largely from his reign, preserve official correspondence with subjects and neighbors. (*p. 66*)

**Alexander (356–323 B.C.E.)** King of Macedonia in northern Greece. Between 334 and 323 B.C.E. he conquered the Persian Empire, reached the Indus Valley, founded many Greek-style cities, and spread Greek culture across the Middle East. Later known as Alexander the Great. (*p. 113*)

**Alexandria** City on the Mediterranean coast of Egypt founded by Alexander. It became the capital of the Hellenistic kingdom of the **Ptolemies.** It contained the famous Library and the Museum—a center for leading scientific and literary figures. Its merchants engaged in trade with areas bordering the Mediterranean and the Indian Ocean. (*p. 114*)

**Allende, Salvador (1908–1973)** Socialist politician elected president of Chile in 1970 and overthrown by the military in 1973. He died during the military attack. (*p. 692*)

**All-India Muslim League** Political organization founded in India in 1906 to defend the interests of India's Muslim minority. Led by Muhammad Ali Jinnah, it attempted to negotiate with the **Indian National Congress.** In 1940, the League began demanding a separate state for Muslims, to be called Pakistan. (See also **Jinnah, Muhammad Ali.**) (*p. 647*)

**amulet** Small charm meant to protect the bearer from evil. Found frequently in archaeological excavations in Mesopotamia and Egypt, amulets reflect the religious practices of the common people. (*p. 19*)

**Amur River** This river valley was a contested frontier between northern China and eastern Russia until the settlement arranged in Treaty of Nerchinsk (1689). (*p. 442*)

**Anasazi** Important culture of what is now the Southwest United States (700–1200 C.E.). Centered on Chaco Canyon in New Mexico and Mesa Verde in Colorado, the Anasazi culture built multistory residences and worshiped in subterranean buildings called kivas. (*p. 254*)

**aqueduct**    A conduit, either elevated or underground, using gravity to carry water from a source to a location—usually a city—that needed it. The Romans built many aqueducts in a period of substantial urbanization.    (*p. 139*)

**Arawak**    Amerindian peoples who inhabited the Greater Antilles of the Caribbean at the time of Columbus.    (*p. 342*)

**Armenia**    One of the earliest Christian kingdoms, situated in eastern Anatolia and the western Caucasus and occupied by speakers of the Armenian language.    (*p. 172*)

**Asante**    African kingdom on the **Gold Coast** that expanded rapidly after 1680. Asante participated in the Atlantic economy, trading gold, slaves, and ivory. It resisted British imperial ambitions for a quarter century before being absorbed into Britain's Gold Coast colony in 1902.    (*p. 581*)

**Ashikaga Shogunate (1338–1573)**    The second of Japan's military governments headed by a shogun (a military ruler). Sometimes called the Muromachi Shogunate.    (*p. 293*)

**Ashoka**    Third ruler of the **Mauryan Empire** in India (r. 270–232 B.C.E.). He converted to Buddhism and broadcast his precepts on inscribed stones and pillars, the earliest surviving Indian writing.    (*p. 124*)

**Ashurbanipal**    The sixth century B.C.E. Assyrian ruler who assembled a large collection of writings drawn from the ancient literary, religious, and scientific traditions of Mesopotamia. The many tablets unearthed by archaeologists constitute one of the most important sources of present-day knowledge of the long literary tradition of Mesopotamia.    (*p. 75*)

**Asian Tigers**    Collective name for South Korea, Taiwan, Hong Kong, and Singapore—nations that became economic powers in the 1970s and 1980s.    (*p. 697*)

**Atahualpa (1502?–1533)**    Last ruling Inca emperor of Peru. He was executed by the Spanish.    (*p. 356*)

**Atlantic system**    The network of trading links after 1500 that moved goods, wealth, people, and cultures around the Atlantic Ocean Basin.    (*p. 388*)

**Augustus (63 B.C.E.–14 C.E.)**    Honorific name of Octavian, founder of the **Roman Principate,** the military dictatorship that replaced the failing rule of the **Roman Senate.** After defeating all rivals, between 31 B.C.E. and 14 C.E. he laid the groundwork for several centuries of stability and prosperity in the Roman Empire.    (*p. 136*)

**Auschwitz**    Nazi extermination camp in Poland, the largest center of mass murder during the **Holocaust.** Close to a million Jews, Gypsies, Communists, and others were killed there.    (*p. 638*)

**ayllu**    Andean lineage group or kin-based community.    (*p. 256*)

**Aztecs**    Also known as Mexica, the Aztecs created a powerful empire in central Mexico (1325–1521 C.E.). They forced defeated peoples to provide goods and labor as a tax.    (*p. 251*)

**Babylon**    The largest and most important city in Mesopotamia. It achieved particular eminence as the capital of the Amorite king **Hammurabi** in the eighteenth century B.C.E. and the Neo-Babylonian king Nebuchadnezzar in the sixth century B.C.E.    (*p. 13*)

**balance of power**    The policy in international relations by which, beginning in the eighteenth century, the major European states acted together to prevent any one of them from becoming too powerful.    (*p. 382*)

**Balfour Declaration**    Statement issued by Britain's Foreign Secretary Arthur Balfour in 1917 favoring the establishment of a Jewish national homeland in Palestine.    (*p. 604*)

**Bannermen**    Hereditary military servants of the **Qing Empire,** in large part descendants of peoples of various origins who had fought for the founders of the empire.    (*p. 534*)

**Bantu**    Collective name of a large group of sub-Saharan African languages and of the peoples speaking these languages.    (*p. 169*)

**Batavia**    Fort established ca. 1619 as headquarters of Dutch East India Company operations in Indonesia; today the city of Jakarta.    (*p. 430*)

**Battle of Midway**    U.S. naval victory over the Japanese fleet in June 1942, in which the Japanese lost four of their best aircraft carriers. It marked a turning point in World War II.    (*p. 634*)

**Battle of Omdurman**    British victory over the Mahdi in the Sudan in 1898. General Kitchener led a mixed force of British and Egyptian troops armed with rapid-firing rifles and machine guns.    (*p. 575*)

**Beijing**    China's northern capital, first used as an imperial capital in 906 and now the capital of the People's Republic of China.    (*p. 282*)

**Bengal**    Region of northeastern India. It was the first part of India to be conquered by the British in the eighteenth century and remained the political and economic center of British India throughout the nineteenth century. The 1905 split of the province into predominantly Hindu West Bengal and predominantly Muslim East Bengal (now Bangladesh) sparked anti-British riots.    (*p. 647*)

**Berlin Conference (1884–1885)**    Conference that German chancellor Otto von Bismarck called to set rules for the partition of Africa. It led to the creation of the Congo Free State under King **Leopold II** of Belgium. (See also **Bismarck, Otto von.**)    (*p. 579*)

**Bhagavad-Gita**    The most important work of Indian sacred literature, a dialogue between the great warrior Arjuna and the god Krishna on duty and the fate of the spirit.    (*p. 125*)

**bin Laden, Usama**    Saudi-born Muslim extremist who funded the al Qaeda organization that was responsible for several terrorist attacks, including those on the World Trade Center and the Pentagon in 2001. (*p. 717*)

**Bismarck, Otto von (1815–1898)** Chancellor (prime minister) of Prussia from 1862 until 1871, when he became chancellor of Germany. A conservative nationalist, he led Prussia to victory against Austria (1866) and France (1870) and was responsible for the creation of the German Empire in 1871. (*p. 558*)

**Black Death** An outbreak of **bubonic plague** that spread across Asia, North Africa, and Europe in the mid-fourteenth century, carrying off vast numbers of persons. (*p. 318*)

**Bolívar, Simón (1783–1830)** The most important military leader in the struggle for independence in South America. Born in Venezuela, he led military forces there and in Colombia, Ecuador, Peru, and Bolivia. (*p. 471*)

**Bolsheviks** Radical Marxist political party founded by Vladimir Lenin in 1903. Under Lenin's leadership, the Bolsheviks seized power in November 1917 during the Russian Revolution. (See also **Lenin, Vladimir.**) (*p. 604*)

**Bonaparte, Napoleon.** See **Napoleon I.**

**bourgeoisie** In early modern Europe, the class of well-off town dwellers whose wealth came from manufacturing, finance, commerce, and allied professions. (*p. 373*)

**Brazza, Savorgnan de (1852–1905)** Franco-Italian explorer sent by the French government to claim part of equatorial Africa for France. Founded Brazzaville, capital of the French Congo, in 1880. (*p. 579*)

**British raj** The rule over much of South Asia between 1765 and 1947 by the East India Company and then by a British government. (*p. 506*)

**bubonic plague** A bacterial disease of fleas that can be transmitted by flea bites to rodents and humans; humans in late stages of the illness can spread the bacteria by coughing. Because of its very high mortality rate and the difficulty of preventing its spread, major outbreaks have created crises in many parts of the world. (See also **Black Death.**) (*pp. 228, 275*)

**Buddha (563–483 B.C.E.)** An Indian prince named Siddhartha Gautama, who renounced his wealth and social position. After becoming "enlightened" (the meaning of *Buddha*) he enunciated the principles of Buddhism. This doctrine evolved and spread throughout India and to Southeast, East, and Central Asia. (See also **Mahayana Buddhism, Theravada Buddhism.**) (*p. 120*)

**Byzantine Empire** Historians' name for the eastern portion of the Roman Empire from the fourth century onward, taken from "Byzantion," an early name for Constantinople, the Byzantine capital city. The empire fell to the Ottomans in 1453. (See also **Ottoman Empire.**) (*p. 203*)

**caliphate** Office established in succession to the Prophet Muhammad, to rule the Islamic empire; also the name of that empire. (See also **Abbasid Caliphate; Sokoto Caliphate; Umayyad Caliphate.**) (*p. 185*)

**capitalism** The economic system of large financial institutions—banks, stock exchanges, investment companies—that first developed in early modern Europe. *Commercial capitalism,* the trading system of the early modern economy, is often distinguished from *industrial capitalism,* the system based on machine production. (*p. 403*)

**caravel** A small, highly maneuverable three-masted ship used by the Portuguese and Spanish in the exploration of the Atlantic. (*p. 343*)

**Cárdenas, Lázaro (1895–1970)** President of Mexico (1934–1940). He brought major changes to Mexican life by distributing millions of acres of land to the peasants, bringing representatives of workers and farmers into the inner circles of politics, and nationalizing the oil industry. (*p. 655*)

**Carthage** City located in present-day Tunisia, founded by **Phoenicians** ca. 800 B.C.E. It became a major commercial center and naval power in the western Mediterranean until defeated by Rome in the third century B.C.E. (*p. 82*)

**Catholic Reformation** Religious reform movement within the Latin Christian Church, begun in response to the **Protestant Reformation.** It clarified Catholic theology and reformed clerical training and discipline. (*p. 369*)

**Celts** Peoples sharing a common language and culture that originated in central Europe in the first half of the first millennium B.C.E.. After 500 B.C.E. they spread as far as Anatolia in the east, Spain and the British Isles in the west, and later were overtaken by Roman conquest and Germanic invasions. Their descendants survive on the western fringe of Europe (Brittany, Wales, Scotland, Ireland). (*p. 50*)

**Champa rice** Quick-maturing rice that can allow two harvests in one growing season. Originally introduced into Champa from India, it was later sent to China as a tribute gift by the Champa state. (See also **tributary system.**) (*p. 242*)

**Chang'an** City in the Wei Valley in eastern China. It became the capital of the Qin and early Han Empires. Its main features were imitated in the cities and towns that sprang up throughout the Han Empire. (*p. 147*)

**Charlemagne (742–814)** King of the Franks (r. 768–814); emperor (r. 800–814). Through a series of military conquests he established the Carolingian Empire, which encompassed all of Gaul and parts of Germany and Italy. Though illiterate himself, he sponsored a brief intellectual revival. (*p. 202*)

**chartered companies** Groups of private investors who paid an annual fee to France and England in exchange for a monopoly over trade to the West Indies colonies.    (*p. 403*)

**Chavín**    The first major urban civilization in South America (900–250 B.C.E.). Its capital, Chavín de Huántar, was located high in the Andes Mountains of Peru. Chavín became politically and economically dominant in a densely populated region that included two distinct ecological zones, the Peruvian coastal plain and the Andean foothills.    (*p. 56*)

**Chiang Kai-shek**    (1886–1975) Chinese military and political leader. Succeeded Sun Yat-sen as head of the **Guomindang** in 1925; headed the Chinese government from 1928 to 1948; fought against the Chinese Communists and Japanese invaders. After 1949 he headed the Chinese Nationalist government in Taiwan.    (*p. 629*)

**chiefdom**    Form of political organization with rule by a hereditary leader who held power over a collection of villages and towns. Less powerful than kingdoms and empires, chiefdoms were based on gift giving and commercial links.    (*p. 255*)

**Chimú**    Powerful Peruvian civilization based on conquest. Located in the region earlier dominated by **Moche**. Conquered by **Inca** in 1465.    (*p. 258*)

**chinampas**    Raised fields constructed along lake shores in Mesoamerica to increase agricultural yields.    (*p. 246*)

**city-state**    A small independent state consisting of an urban center and the surrounding agricultural territory. A characteristic political form in early Mesopotamia, Archaic and Classical Greece, Phoenicia, and early Italy. (See also **polis**.)    (*p. 15*)

**civilization**    An ambiguous term often used to denote more complex societies but sometimes used by anthropologists to describe any group of people sharing a set of cultural traits.    (*p. 5*)

**Cixi, Empress Dowager (1835–1908)**    Empress of China and mother of Emperor Guangxi. She put her son under house arrest, supported antiforeign movements, and resisted reforms of the Chinese government and armed forces.    (*p. 608*)

**clipper ship**    Large, fast, streamlined sailing vessel, often American built, of the mid-to-late nineteenth century rigged with vast canvas sails hung from tall masts.    (*p. 512*)

**Cold War (1945–1991)**    The ideological struggle between communism (Soviet Union) and capitalism (United States) for world influence. The Soviet Union and the United States came to the brink of actual war during the **Cuban missile crisis** but never attacked one another. The Cold War came to an end when the Soviet Union dissolved in 1991. (See also **North Atlantic Treaty Organization; Warsaw Pact.**)    (*p. 668*)

**colonialism**    Policy by which a nation administers a foreign territory and develops its resources for the benefit of the colonial power.    (*p. 575*)

**Columbian Exchange**    The exchange of plants, animals, diseases, and technologies between the Americas and the rest of the world following Columbus's voyages.    (*p. 407*)

**Columbus, Christopher (1451–1506)**    Genoese mariner who in the service of Spain led expeditions across the Atlantic, reestablishing contact between the peoples of the Americas and the Old World and opening the way to Spanish conquest and colonization.    (*p. 345*)

**Confucius**    Western name for the Chinese philosopher Kongzi (551–479 B.C.E.). His doctrine of duty and public service had a great influence on subsequent Chinese thought and served as a code of conduct for government officials.    (*p. 44*)

**Congress of Vienna (1814–1815)**    Meeting of representatives of European monarchs called to reestablish the old order after the defeat of **Napoleon I**.    (*p. 469*)

**conquistadors**    Early-sixteenth-century Spanish adventurers who conquered Mexico, Central America, and Peru. (See **Cortés, Hernán; Pizarro, Francisco**.)    (*p. 354*)

**Constantine (285–337 C.E.)**    Roman emperor (r. 312–337). After reuniting the Roman Empire, he moved the capital to Constantinople and made Christianity a favored religion.    (*p. 141*)

**Constitutional Convention**    Meeting in 1787 of the elected representatives of the thirteen original states to write the Constitution of the United States.    (*p. 465*)

**contract of indenture**    A voluntary agreement binding a person to work for a specified period of years in return for free passage to an overseas destination. Before 1800 most **indentured servants** were Europeans; after 1800 most indentured laborers were Asians.    (*p. 515*)

**Cortés, Hernán (1485–1547)**    Spanish explorer and conquistador who led the conquest of Aztec Mexico in 1519–1521 for Spain.    (*p. 354*)

**Cossacks**    Peoples of the Russian Empire who lived outside the farming villages, often as herders, mercenaries, or outlaws. Cossacks led the conquest of Siberia in the sixteenth and seventeenth centuries.    (*p. 442*)

**Council of the Indies**    The institution responsible for supervising Spain's colonies in the Americas from 1524 to the early eighteenth century, when it lost all but judicial responsibilities.    (*p. 388*)

**creole**    In colonial Spanish America, term used to describe someone of European descent born in the New World. Elsewhere in the Americas, the term is used to describe all nonnative peoples.    (*p. 392*)

**Crimean War (1853–1856)**    Conflict between the Russian and Ottoman Empires fought primarily in the Crimean Peninsula. To prevent Russian expansion, Britain and France sent troops to support the Ottomans.    (*p. 527*)

**Crusades (1096–1291)** Armed pilgrimages to the Holy Land by Christians determined to recover Jerusalem from Muslim rule. The Crusades brought an end to western Europe's centuries of intellectual and cultural isolation. (*p. 220*)

**Crystal Palace** Building erected in Hyde Park, London, for the Great Exhibition of 1851. Made of iron and glass, like a gigantic greenhouse, it was a symbol of the industrial age. (*p. 487*)

**Cuban missile crisis (1962)** Brink-of-war confrontation between the United States and the Soviet Union over the latter's placement of nuclear-armed missiles in Cuba. (*p. 674*)

**cultural imperialism** Domination of one culture over another by a deliberate policy or by economic or technological superiority. (*p. 727*)

**Cultural Revolution (China) (1966–1969)** Campaign in China ordered by **Mao Zedong** to purge the Communist Party of his opponents and instill revolutionary values in the younger generation. (*p. 684*)

**culture** Socially transmitted patterns of action and expression. *Material culture* refers to physical objects, such as dwellings, clothing, tools, and crafts. Culture also includes arts, beliefs, knowledge, and technology. (*p. 5*)

**cuneiform** A system of writing in which wedge-shaped symbols represented words or syllables. It originated in Mesopotamia and was used initially for Sumerian and Akkadian but later was adapted to represent other languages of western Asia. Because so many symbols had to be learned, literacy was confined to a relatively small group of administrators and **scribes.** (*p. 19*)

**Cyrus (600–530 B.C.E.)** Founder of the Achaemenid Persian Empire. Between 550 and 530 B.C.E. he conquered Media, Lydia, and Babylon. Revered in the traditions of both Iran and the subject peoples, he employed Persians and Medes in his administration and respected the institutions and beliefs of subject peoples. (*p. 96*)

**czar** See **tsar.**

**daimyo** Literally, great name(s). Japanese warlords and great landowners, whose armed **samurai** gave them control of the Japanese islands from the eighth to the later nineteenth century. Under the **Tokugawa Shogunate** they were subordinated to the imperial government. (*p. 433*)

**Daoism** Chinese school of thought, originating in the Warring States Period with Laozi (604–531 B.C.E.). Daoism offered an alternative to the Confucian emphasis on hierarchy and duty. Daoists believe that the world is always changing and is devoid of absolute morality or meaning. They accept the world as they find it, avoid futile struggles, and deviate as little as possible from the *Dao,* or "path" of nature. (See also **Confucius.**) (*p. 44*)

**Darius I (ca. 558–486 B.C.E.)** Third ruler of the Persian Empire (r. 521–486 B.C.E.). He crushed the widespread initial resistance to his rule and gave all major government posts to Persians rather than to Medes. He established a system of provinces and tribute, began construction of Persepolis, and expanded Persian control in the east (Pakistan) and west (northern Greece). (*p. 96*)

**Darwin, Charles (1809–1882)** With Alfred Russell Wallace (1823–1913) he developed the theory of evolution through natural selection. Their work was first made known simultaneously in 1858. (*p. 558*)

**Decembrist revolt** Abortive attempt by army officers to take control of the Russian government upon the death of Tsar Alexander I in 1825. (*p. 532*)

**Declaration of the Rights of Man (1789)** Statement of fundamental political rights adopted by the French **National Assembly** at the beginning of the French Revolution. (*p. 466*)

**deforestation** The removal of trees faster than forests can replace themselves. (*p. 375*)

**Delhi Sultanate (1206–1526)** Centralized Indian empire of varying extent, created by Muslim invaders. (*p. 299*)

**democracy** A system of government in which all "citizens" (however defined) have equal political and legal rights, privileges, and protections, as in the Greek city-state of Athens in the fifth and fourth centuries B.C.E. (*p. 106*)

**demographic transition** A change in the rates of population growth. Before the transition, both birthrates and death rates are high, resulting in a slowly growing population; then the death rate drops but the birthrate remains high, causing a population explosion; finally the birthrate drops and the population growth slows down. This transition took place in Europe in the late nineteenth and early twentieth centuries, in North America and East Asia in the mid-twentieth, and, most recently, in Latin America and South Asia. (*p. 703*)

**Deng Xiaoping (1904–1997)** Communist Party leader who forced Chinese economic reforms after the death of **Mao Zedong.** (*p. 698*)

**dhow** Ship of small to moderate size used in the western Indian Ocean, traditionally with a triangular sail and a sewn timber hull. (*p. 307*)

**Diagne, Blaise (1872–1934)** Senegalese political leader. He was the first African elected to the French National Assembly. During World War I, in exchange for promises to give French citizenship to Senegalese, he helped recruit Africans to serve in the French army. After the war, he led a movement to abolish forced labor in Africa. (*p. 646*)

**Dias, Bartolomeu (1450?–1500)** Portuguese explorer who in 1488 led the first expedition to sail around the southern tip of Africa from the Atlantic and sight the Indian Ocean. (*p. 345*)

**Diaspora**    A Greek word meaning "dispersal," used to describe the communities of a given ethnic group living outside their homeland. Jews, for example, spread from Israel to western Asia and Mediterranean lands in antiquity and today can be found throughout the world.    (*p. 79*)

**Dirty War**    War waged by the Argentine military (1976–1983) against leftist groups. Characterized by the use of illegal imprisonment, torture, and executions by the military.    (*p. 692*)

**divination**    Techniques for ascertaining the future or the will of the gods by interpreting natural phenomena such as, in early China, the cracks on oracle bones or, in ancient Greece, the flight of birds through sectors of the sky.    (*p. 42*)

**division of labor**    A manufacturing technique that breaks down a craft into many simple and repetitive tasks that can be performed by unskilled workers. Pioneered in the pottery works of Josiah Wedgwood and in other eighteenth-century factories, it greatly increased the productivity of labor and lowered the cost of manufactured goods. (See also **Wedgwood, Josiah.**)    (*p. 485*)

**driver**    A privileged male slave whose job was to ensure that a slave gang did its work on a plantation.    (*p. 402*)

**Druids**    The class of religious experts who conducted rituals and preserved sacred lore among some ancient Celtic peoples. They provided education, mediated disputes between kinship groups, and were suppressed by the Romans as a potential focus of opposition to Roman rule. (See also **Celts.**)    (*p. 51*)

**Dutch West India Company (1621–1794)**    Trading company chartered by the Dutch government to conduct its merchants' trade in the Americas and Africa.    (*p. 403*)

**Edison, Thomas (1847–1931)**    American inventor best known for inventing the electric light bulb, acoustic recording on wax cylinders, and motion pictures.    (*p. 549*)

**Einstein, Albert (1879–1955)**    German physicist who developed the theory of relativity, which states that time, space, and mass are relative to each other and not fixed.    (*p. 614*)

**electricity**    A form of energy used in telegraphy from the 1840s on and for lighting, industrial motors, and railroads beginning in the 1880s.    (*p. 549*)

**electric telegraph**    A device for rapid, long-distance transmission of information over an electric wire. It was introduced in England and North America in the 1830s and 1840s and replaced telegraph systems that utilized visual signals such as semaphores. (See also **submarine telegraph cables.**)    (*p. 489*)

**encomienda**    A grant of authority over a population of Amerindians in the Spanish colonies. It provided the grant holder with a supply of cheap labor and periodic payments of goods by the Amerindians. It obliged the grant holder to Christianize the Amerindians.    (*p. 392*)

**English Civil War (1642–1648)**    A conflict over royal versus parliamentary rights, caused by King Charles I's arrest of his parliamentary critics and ending with his execution. Its outcome checked the growth of royal absolutism and, with the Glorious Revolution of 1688 and the English Bill of Rights of 1689, ensured that England would be a constitutional monarchy.    (*p. 381*)

**Enlightenment**    A philosophical movement in eighteenth-century Europe that fostered the belief that one could reform society by discovering rational laws that governed social behavior and were just as scientific as the laws of physics.    (*pp. 372, 461*)

*equites*    In ancient Italy, prosperous landowners second in wealth and status to the senatorial aristocracy. The Roman emperors allied with this group to counterbalance the influence of the old aristocracy and used the *equites* to staff the imperial civil service.    (*p. 136*)

**Estates General**    France's traditional national assembly with representatives of the three estates, or classes, in French society: the clergy, nobility, and commoners. The calling of the Estates General in 1789 led to the French Revolution.    (*p. 466*)

**Ethiopia**    East African highland nation lying east of the Nile River. (See also **Menelik II; Selassie, Haile.**)    (*p. 172*)

**ethnic cleansing**    Effort to eradicate a people and its culture by means of mass killing and the destruction of historical buildings and cultural materials. Ethnic cleansing was used by both sides in the conflicts that accompanied the disintegration of Yugoslavia in the 1990s.    (*p. 716*)

**European Community (EC)**    An organization promoting economic unity in Europe formed in 1967 by consolidation of earlier, more limited, agreements. Replaced by the European Union (EU) in 1993.    (*p. 670*)

**extraterritoriality**    The right of foreign residents in a country to live under the laws of their native country and disregard the laws of the host country. In the nineteenth and early twentieth centuries, European and American nationals living in certain areas of Chinese and Ottoman cities were granted this right.    (*p. 529*)

**Faisal I (1885–1933)**    Arab prince, leader of the Arab Revolt in World War I. The British made him king of Iraq in 1921, and he reigned under British protection until 1933.    (*p. 603*)

**Fascist Party**    Italian political party created by Benito Mussolini during World War I. It emphasized aggressive nationalism and was Mussolini's instrument for the creation of a dictatorship in Italy from 1922 to 1943. (See also **Mussolini, Benito.**)    (*p. 626*)

**fief** In medieval Europe, land granted in return for a sworn oath to provide specified military service. (*p. 210*)

**First Temple** A monumental sanctuary built in Jerusalem by King Solomon in the tenth century B.C.E. to be the religious center for the Israelite god Yahweh. The Temple priesthood conducted sacrifices, received a tithe or percentage of agricultural revenues, and became economically and politically powerful. The First Temple was destroyed by the Babylonians in 587 B.C.E., rebuilt on a modest scale in the late sixth century B.C.E., and replaced by King Herod's Second Temple in the late first century B.C.E. (destroyed by the Romans in 70 C.E.) (*p. 78*)

**Five-Year Plans** Plans that Joseph Stalin introduced to industrialize the Soviet Union rapidly, beginning in 1928. They set goals for the output of steel, electricity, machinery, and most other products and were enforced by the police powers of the state. They succeeded in making the Soviet Union a major industrial power before World War II. (See also **Stalin, Joseph.**) (*p. 620*)

**foragers** People who support themselves by hunting wild animals and gathering wild edible plants and insects. (*p. 6*)

**free-trade imperialism** Economic dominance of a weaker country by a more powerful one, while maintaining the legal independence of the weaker state. In the late nineteenth century, free-trade imperialism characterized the relations between the Latin American republics, on the one hand, and Great Britain and the United States, on the other. (*p. 590*)

**Gama, Vasco da (1460?–1524)** Portuguese explorer. In 1497–1498 he led the first naval expedition from Europe to sail to India, opening an important commercial sea route. (*p. 345*)

**Gandhi, Mohandas K. (Mahatma) (1869–1948)** Leader of the Indian independence movement and advocate of nonviolent resistance. After being educated as a lawyer in England, he returned to India and became leader of the **Indian National Congress** in 1920. He appealed to the poor, led nonviolent demonstrations against British colonial rule, and was jailed many times. Soon after independence he was assassinated for attempting to stop Hindu-Muslim rioting. (*p. 648*)

**Genghis Khan (ca. 1167–1227)** The title of Temüjin when he ruled the Mongols (1206–1227). It means the "oceanic" or "universal" leader. Genghis Khan was the founder of the Mongol Empire. (*p. 270*)

*gens de couleur* Free men and women of color in Haiti. They sought greater political rights and later supported the Haitian Revolution. (See also **L'Ouverture, Toussaint.**) (*p. 469*)

**gentry** In China, the class of prosperous families, next in wealth below the rural aristocrats, from which the emperors drew their administrative personnel. Respected for their education and expertise, these officials became a privileged group and made the government more efficient and responsive than in the past. The term *gentry* also denotes the class of landholding families in England and France below the aristocracy. (*pp. 148, 374*)

**Ghana** First known kingdom in sub-Saharan West Africa between the sixth and thirteenth centuries C.E. Also the modern West African country once known as the Gold Coast. (*p. 189*)

**global elite culture** At the beginning of the twenty-first century, the attitudes and outlook of well-educated, prosperous, Western-oriented people around the world, largely expressed in European languages, especially English. (*p. 730*)

**global pop culture** Popular cultural practices and institutions that have been adopted internationally, such as music, the Internet, television, food, and fashion. (*p. 729*)

**globalization** The economic, political, and cultural integration and interaction of all parts of the world brought about by increasing trade, travel, and technology. (*p. 722*)

**Gold Coast (Africa)** Region of the Atlantic coast of West Africa occupied by modern Ghana; named for its gold exports to Europe from the 1470s onward. (*p. 345*)

**Golden Horde** Mongol khanate founded by Genghis Khan's grandson Batu. It was based in southern Russia and quickly adopted both the Turkic language and Islam. Also known as the Kipchak Horde. (*p. 276*)

**Gorbachev, Mikhail (b. 1931)** Head of the Soviet Union from 1985 to 1991. His liberalization effort improved relations with the West, but he lost power after his reforms led to the collapse of communist governments in eastern Europe. (*p. 700*)

**Gothic cathedrals** Large churches originating in twelfth-century France; built in an architectural style featuring pointed arches, tall vaults and spires, flying buttresses, and large stained-glass windows. (*p. 325*)

**Grand Canal** The 1,100-mile (1,700-kilometer) waterway linking the Yellow and the Yangzi Rivers. It was begun in the **Han** period and completed during the Sui Empire. (*p. 225*)

**Great Circuit** The network of Atlantic Ocean trade routes between Europe, Africa, and the Americas that underlay the Atlantic system (*p. 404*)

**"great traditions"** Historians' term for a literate, well-institutionalized complex of religious and social beliefs and practices adhered to by diverse societies over a broad geographical area. (See also **"small traditions."**) (*p. 168*)

**Great Western Schism** A division in the Latin (Western) Christian Church between 1378 and 1415, when rival claimants to the papacy existed in Rome and Avignon.    (*p. 333*)

**Great Zimbabwe**    City, now in ruins (in the modern African country of Zimbabwe), whose many stone structures were built between about 1250 and 1450, when it was a trading center and the capital of a large state.    (*p. 307*)

**guild**    In medieval Europe, an association of men (rarely women), such as merchants, artisans, or professors, who worked in a particular trade and banded together to promote their economic and political interests. Guilds were also important in other societies, such as the Ottoman and Safavid Empires.    (*p. 324*)

**Gujarat**    Region of western India famous for trade and manufacturing; the inhabitants are called Gujarati.    (*p. 305*)

**gunpowder**    A mixture of saltpeter, sulfur, and charcoal, in various proportions. The formula, brought to China in the 400s or 500s, was first used to make fumigators to keep away insect pests and evil spirits. In later centuries it was used to make explosives and grenades and to propel cannonballs, shot, and bullets.    (*p. 235*)

**Guomindang**    Nationalist political party founded on democratic principles by **Sun Yat-sen** in 1912. After 1925, the party was headed by **Chiang Kai-shek,** who turned it into an increasingly authoritarian movement.    (*p. 609*)

**Gupta Empire (320–550 C.E.)**    A powerful Indian state based, like its Mauryan predecessor, on a capital at Pataliputra in the Ganges Valley. It controlled most of the Indian subcontinent through a combination of military force and its prestige as a center of sophisticated culture. (See also **theater-state.**)    (*p. 125*)

**Habsburg**    A powerful European family that provided many Holy Roman Emperors, founded the Austrian (later Austro-Hungarian) Empire, and ruled sixteenth- and seventeenth-century Spain.    (*p. 379*)

**hadith**    A tradition relating the words or deeds of the Prophet Muhammad; next to the **Quran,** the most important basis for Islamic law.    (*p. 194*)

**Hammurabi**    Amorite ruler of **Babylon** (r. 1792–1750 B.C.E.). He conquered many city-states in southern and northern Mesopotamia and is best known for a code of laws, inscribed on a black stone pillar, illustrating the principles to be used in legal cases.    (*p. 16*)

**Han**    A term used to designate (1) the ethnic Chinese people who originated in the Yellow River Valley and spread throughout regions of China suitable for agriculture and (2) the dynasty of emperors who ruled from 206 B.C.E. to 220 C.E.    (*p. 146*)

**Hanseatic League**    An economic and defensive alliance of the free towns in northern Germany, founded

about 1241 and most powerful in the fourteenth century.    (*p. 322*)

**Harappa**    Site of one of the great cities of the Indus Valley civilization of the third millennium B.C.E. It was located on the northwest frontier of the zone of cultivation (in modern Pakistan), and may have been a center for the acquisition of raw materials, such as metals and precious stones, from Afghanistan and Iran.    (*p. 31*)

**Hatshepsut**    Queen of Egypt (r. 1473–1458 B.C.E.). She dispatched a naval expedition down the Red Sea to Punt (possibly northeast Sudan or Eretria), the faraway source of myrrh. There is evidence of opposition to a woman as ruler, and after her death her name and image were frequently defaced.    (*p. 66*)

**Hebrew Bible**    A collection of sacred books containing diverse materials concerning the origins, experiences, beliefs, and practices of the Israelites. Most of the extant text was compiled by members of the priestly class in the fifth century B.C.E. and reflects the concerns and views of this group.    (*p. 76*)

**Hellenistic Age**    Historians' term for the era, usually dated 323–30 B.C.E., in which Greek culture spread across western Asia and northeastern Africa after the conquests of **Alexander** the Great. The period ended with the fall of the last major Hellenistic kingdom to Rome, but Greek cultural influence persisted until the spread of Islam in the seventh century C.E.    (*p. 114*)

**Helsinki Accords (1975)**    Political and human rights agreement signed in Helsinki, Finland, by the Soviet Union and western European countries.    (*p. 674*)

**Henry the Navigator (1394–1460)**    Portuguese prince who promoted the study of navigation and directed voyages of exploration down the western coast of Africa.    (*p. 343*)

**Herodotus (ca. 485–425 B.C.E.)**    Heir to the technique of *historia*—"investigation"—developed by Greeks in the late Archaic period. He came from a Greek community in Anatolia and traveled extensively, collecting information in western Asia and the Mediterranean lands. He traced the antecedents of and chronicled the **Persian Wars** between the Greek city-states and the Persian Empire, thus originating the Western tradition of historical writing.    (*p. 107*)

**Hidalgo y Costilla, Miguel (1753–1811)**    Mexican priest who led the first stage of the Mexican independence war in 1810. He was captured and executed in 1811.    (*p. 473*)

**Hidden Imam**    Last in a series of twelve descendants of Muhammad's son-in-law Ali, whom **Shi'ites** consider divinely appointed leaders of the Muslim community. In occlusion since ca. 873, he is expected to return as a messiah at the end of time.    (*p. 421*)

**hieroglyphics**    A system of writing in which pictorial symbols represented sounds, syllables, or concepts. It was used for official and monumental inscriptions in ancient Egypt. Because of the long period of study required to master this system, literacy in hieroglyphics was confined to a relatively small group of **scribes** and administrators. Cursive symbol-forms were developed for rapid composition on other media, such as **papyrus.**  (*p. 27*)

**Hinduism**  A general term for a wide variety of beliefs and ritual practices that have developed in the Indian subcontinent since antiquity. Hinduism has roots in ancient Vedic, Buddhist, and south Indian religious concepts and practices. It spread along the trade routes to Southeast Asia.  (*p. 121*)

**Hiroshima**  City in Japan, the first to be destroyed by an atomic bomb, on August 6, 1945. The bombing hastened the end of World War II.  (*p. 634*)

**history**  The study of past events and changes in the development, transmission, and transformation of cultural practices.  (*p. 6*)

**Hitler, Adolf (1889–1945)**  Born in Austria, Hitler became a radical German nationalist during World War I. He led the National Socialist German Workers' Party—the **Nazis**—in the 1920s and became dictator of Germany in 1933. He led Europe into World War II.  (*p. 627*)

**Hittites**  A people from central Anatolia who established an empire in Anatolia and Syria in the Late Bronze Age. With wealth from the trade in metals and military power based on chariot forces, the Hittites vied with New Kingdom Egypt for control of Syria-Palestine before falling to unidentified attackers ca. 1200 B.C.E. (See also **Ramesses II.**)  (*p. 64*)

**Holocaust**  Nazis' program during World War II to kill people they considered undesirable. Some 6 million Jews perished during the Holocaust, along with millions of Poles, Gypsies, Communists, Socialists, and others.  (*p. 638*)

**Holocene**  The geological era since the end of the Great Ice Age about 11,000 years ago.  (*p. 10*)

**Holy Roman Empire**  Loose federation of mostly German states and principalities, headed by an emperor elected by the princes. It lasted from 962 to 1806.  (*pp. 212, 379*)

**hoplite**  A heavily armored Greek infantryman of the Archaic and Classical periods who fought in the close-packed phalanx formation. Hoplite armies—militias composed of middle- and upper-class citizens supplying their own equipment—were for centuries superior to all other military forces.  (*p. 105*)

**horse collar**  Harnessing method that increased the efficiency of horses by shifting the point of traction from the animal's neck to the shoulders; its adoption favors the spread of horse-drawn plows and vehicles.  (*p. 218*)

**House of Burgesses**  Elected assembly in colonial Virginia, created in 1618.  (*p. 397*)

**humanists (Renaissance)**  European scholars, writers, and teachers associated with the study of the humanities (grammar, rhetoric, poetry, history, languages, and moral philosophy), influential in the fifteenth century and later.  (*p. 329*)

**Hundred Years War (1337–1453)**  Series of campaigns over control of the throne of France, involving English and French royal families and French noble families.  (*p. 333*)

**Husayn, Saddam (b. 1937)**  President of Iraq from 1979 until overthrown by an American-led invasion in 2003. Waged war on Iran from 1980 to 1988. His invasion of Kuwait in 1990 was repulsed in the Persian Gulf War in 1991.  (*p. 696*)

**Ibn Battuta (1304–1369)**  Moroccan Muslim scholar, the most widely traveled individual of his time. He wrote a detailed account of his visits to Islamic lands from China to Spain and the western Sudan.  (*p. 296*)

**Il-khan**  A "secondary" or "peripheral" khan based in Persia. The Il-khans' khanate was founded by Hülegü, a grandson of **Genghis Khan,** and was based at Tabriz in modern Azerbaijan. It controlled much of Iran and Iraq.  (*p. 276*)

**import-substitution industrialization**  An economic system aimed at building a country's industry by restricting foreign trade. It was especially popular in Latin American countries such as Mexico, Argentina, and Brazil in the mid-twentieth century. It proved successful for a time but could not keep up with technological advances in Europe and North America.  (*p. 659*)

**Inca**  Largest and most powerful Andean empire. Controlled the Pacific coast of South America from Ecuador to Chile from its capital of Cuzco.  (*p. 259*)

**indentured servant**  A migrant to British colonies in the Americas who paid for passage by agreeing to work for a set term ranging from four to seven years.  (*p. 397*)

**Indian Civil Service**  The elite professional class of officials who administered the government of British India. Originally composed exclusively of well-educated British men, it gradually added qualified Indians.  (*p. 507*)

**Indian National Congress**  A movement and political party founded in 1885 to demand greater Indian participation in government. Its membership was middle class, and its demands were modest until World War I. Led after 1920 by Mohandas K. Gandhi, it appealed increasingly to the poor, and it organized mass protests demanding self-government and independence. (See also **Gandhi, Mohandas K.**)  (*pp. 510, 647*)

**Indian Ocean Maritime System**  In premodern times, a network of seaports, trade routes, and maritime culture linking countries on the rim of the Indian Ocean from Africa to Indonesia.  (*p. 159*)

**indulgence**   The forgiveness of the punishment due for past sins, granted by the Catholic Church authorities as a reward for a pious act. Martin Luther's protest against the sale of indulgences is often seen as touching off the **Protestant Reformation.**   (*p. 366*)

**Industrial Revolution**   The transformation of the economy, the environment, and living conditions, occurring first in England in the eighteenth century, that resulted from the use of steam engines, the mechanization of manufacturing in factories, and innovations in transportation and communication.   (*p. 480*)

**investiture controversy**   Dispute between the popes and the Holy Roman Emperors over who held ultimate authority over bishops in imperial lands.   (*p. 212*)

**Irigoyen, Hipólito (1850–1933)**   Argentine politician, president of Argentina from 1916 to 1922 and 1928 to 1930. The first president elected by universal male suffrage, he began his presidency as a reformer, but later became conservative.   (*p. 658*)

**Iron Age**   Historians' term for the period during which iron was the primary metal for tools and weapons. The advent of iron technology began at different times in different parts of the world.   (*p. 62*)

**iron curtain**   Winston Churchill's term for the Cold War division between the Soviet-dominated East and the U.S.-dominated West.   (*p. 668*)

**Iroquois Confederacy**   An alliance of five northeastern Amerindian peoples (six after 1722) that made decisions on military and diplomatic issues through a council of representatives. Allied first with the Dutch and later with the English, the Confederacy dominated the area from western New England to the Great Lakes.   (*p. 398*)

**Islam**   Religion expounded by the Prophet Muhammad (570–632 C.E.) on the basis of his reception of divine revelations, which were collected after his death into the **Quran.** In the tradition of Judaism and Christianity, and sharing much of their lore, Islam calls on all people to recognize one creator god—Allah—who rewards or punishes believers after death according to how they led their lives. (See also **hadith.**)   (*p. 184*)

**Israel**   In antiquity, the land between the eastern shore of the Mediterranean and the Jordan River, occupied by the Israelites from the early second millennium B.C.E. The modern state of Israel was founded in 1948.   (*p. 76*)

**Janissaries**   Infantry, originally of slave origin, armed with firearms and constituting the elite of the Ottoman army from the fifteenth century until the corps was abolished in 1826.   (*pp. 415, 520*)

*jati.*   See *varna.*

**Jesus (ca. 5 B.C.E.–34 C.E.)**   A Jew from Galilee in northern Israel who sought to reform Jewish beliefs and practices. He was executed as a revolutionary by the Romans. Hailed as the Messiah and son of God by his followers, he became the central figure in Christianity, a belief system that developed in the centuries after his death.   (*p. 138*)

**Jinnah, Muhammad Ali (1876–1948)**   Indian Muslim politician who founded the state of Pakistan. A lawyer by training, he joined the **All-India Muslim League** in 1913. As leader of the League from the 1920s on, he negotiated with the British and the **Indian National Congress** for Muslim participation in Indian politics. From 1940 on, he led the movement for the independence of India's Muslims in a separate state of Pakistan, founded in 1947.   (*p. 651*)

**joint-stock company**   A business, often backed by a government charter, that sold shares to individuals to raise money for its trading enterprises and to spread the risks (and profits) among many investors.   (*p. 374*)

**junk**   A very large flatbottom sailing ship produced in the **Tang, Ming,** and **Song Empires,** specially designed for long-distance commercial travel.   (*p. 234*)

**Kamakura Shogunate**   The first of Japan's decentralized military governments. (1185–1333).   (*p. 241*)

*kamikaze*   The "divine wind," which the Japanese credited with blowing Mongol invaders away from their shores in 1281.   (*p. 292*)

**Kangxi (1654–1722)**   Qing emperor (r. 1662–1722). He oversaw the greatest expansion of the **Qing Empire.**   (*p. 440*)

**karma**   In Indian tradition, the residue of deeds performed in past and present lives that adheres to a "spirit" and determines what form it will assume in its next life cycle. The doctrines of karma and reincarnation were used by the elite in ancient India to encourage people to accept their social position and do their duty.   (*p. 119*)

*keiretsu*   Alliances of corporations and banks that dominate the Japanese economy.   (*p. 697*)

**khipu**   System of knotted colored cords used by preliterate Andean peoples to transmit information.   (*p. 256*)

**Khomeini, Ayatollah Ruhollah (1900?–1989)**   Shi'ite philosopher and cleric who led the overthrow of the shah of Iran in 1979 and created an Islamic republic.   (*p. 693*)

**Khubilai Khan (1215–1294)**   Last of the Mongol Great Khans (r. 1260–1294) and founder of the **Yuan Empire.** Original architect of the Forbidden City.   (*p. 282*)

**Kievan Russia**   State established at Kiev in Ukraine ca. 879 by Scandinavian adventurers asserting authority over a mostly Slavic farming population.   (*p. 203*)

**Korean War (1950–1953)**   Conflict that began with North Korea's invasion of South Korea and came to involve the United Nations (primarily the United States) allying with South Korea and the People's Republic of China allying with North Korea.   (*p. 672*)

**Koryo**  Korean kingdom founded in 918 and destroyed by a Mongol invasion in 1259.  (*p. 239*)

**Kush**  An Egyptian name for Nubia, the region alongside the Nile River south of Egypt, where an indigenous kingdom with its own distinctive institutions and cultural traditions arose beginning in the early second millennium B.C.E. It was deeply influenced by Egyptian culture and at times under the control of Egypt, which coveted its rich deposits of gold and luxury products from sub-Saharan Africa carried up the Nile corridor.  (*p. 49*)

**labor union**  An organization of workers in a particular industry or trade, created to defend the interests of members through strikes or negotiations with employers.  (*p. 552*)

**laissez faire**  The idea that government should refrain from interfering in economic affairs. The classic exposition of laissez-faire principles is Adam Smith's *Wealth of Nations* (1776).  (*p. 493*)

**lama**  In Tibetan Buddhism, a teacher.  (*p. 282*)

**Las Casas, Bartolomé de (1474–1566)**  First bishop of Chiapas, in southern Mexico. He devoted most of his life to protecting Amerindian peoples from exploitation. His major achievement was the New Laws of 1542, which limited the ability of Spanish settlers to compel Amerindians to labor for them. (See also **encomienda**.)  (*p. 391*)

**Latin West**  Historians' name for the territories of Europe that adhered to the Latin rite of Christianity and used the Latin language for intellectual exchange in the period ca. 1000–1500.  (*p. 317*)

**League of Nations**  International organization founded in 1919 to promote world peace and cooperation but greatly weakened by the refusal of the United States to join. It proved ineffectual in stopping aggression by Italy, Japan, and Germany in the 1930s, and it was superseded by the **United Nations** in 1945.  (*p. 606*)

**Legalism**  In China, a political philosophy that emphasized the unruliness of human nature and justified state coercion and control. The **Qin** ruling class invoked it to validate the authoritarian nature of their regime and its profligate expenditure of subjects' lives and labor. It was superseded in the **Han** era by a more benevolent Confucian doctrine of governmental moderation.  (*p. 44*)

**"legitimate" trade**  Exports from Africa in the nineteenth century that did not include the newly outlawed slave trade.  (*p. 503*)

**Lenin, Vladimir (1870–1924)**  Leader of the Bolshevik (later Communist) Party. He lived in exile in Switzerland until 1917, then returned to Russia to lead the Bolsheviks to victory during the Russian Revolution and the civil war that followed.  (*p. 604*)

**Leopold II (1835–1909)**  King of Belgium (r. 1865–1909). He was active in encouraging the exploration of Central Africa and became the ruler of the Congo Free State (to 1908).  (*p. 579*)

**liberalism**  A political ideology that emphasizes the civil rights of citizens, representative government, and the protection of private property. This ideology, derived from the **Enlightenment**, was especially popular among the property-owning middle classes of Europe and North America.  (*p. 559*)

**Linear B**  A set of syllabic symbols, derived from the writing system of **Minoan** Crete, used in the Mycenaean palaces of the Late Bronze Age to write an early form of Greek. It was used primarily for palace records, and the surviving Linear B tablets provide substantial information about the economic organization of Mycenaean society and tantalizing clues about political, social, and religious institutions.  (*p. 70*)

**Li Shimin (599–649)**  One of the founders of the **Tang Empire** and its second emperor (r. 626–649). He led the expansion of the empire into Central Asia.  (*p. 225*)

**Little Ice Age**  A century-long period of cool climate that began in the 1590s. Its ill effects on agriculture in northern Europe were notable.  (*p. 375*)

**llama**  A hoofed animal indigenous to the Andes Mountains in South America. It was the only domesticated beast of burden in the Americas before the arrival of Europeans. It provided meat and wool. The use of llamas to transport goods made possible specialized production and trade among people living in different ecological zones and fostered the integration of these zones by **Chavín** and later Andean states.  (*p. 57*)

**loess**  A fine, light silt deposited by wind and water. It constitutes the fertile soil of the Yellow River Valley in northern China. Because loess soil is not compacted, it can be worked with a simple digging stick, but it leaves the region vulnerable to devastating earthquakes.  (*p. 40*)

**Long March (1934–1935)**  The 6,000-mile (9,600-kilometer) flight of Chinese Communists from southeastern to northwestern China. The Communists, led by **Mao Zedong**, were pursued by the Chinese army under orders from **Chiang Kai-shek**. The four thousand survivors of the march formed the nucleus of a revived Communist movement that defeated the **Guomindang** after World War II.  (*p. 630*)

**L'Ouverture, Toussaint (1743–1803)**  Leader of the Haitian Revolution. He freed the slaves and gained effective independence for Haiti despite military interventions by the British and French.  (*p. 471*)

**ma'at**  Egyptian term for the concept of divinely created and maintained order in the universe. Reflecting the ancient Egyptians' belief in an essentially beneficent world, the divine ruler was the earthly guarantor of this order. (See also **pyramid**.)  (*p. 26*)

**Macartney mission (1792–1793)**  The unsuccessful attempt by the British Empire to establish diplomatic relations with the **Qing Empire.** *(p. 444)*

**Magellan, Ferdinand (1480?–1521)**  Portuguese navigator who led the Spanish expedition of 1519–1522 that was the first to sail around the world. *(p. 348)*

**Mahabharata**  A vast epic chronicling the events leading up to a cataclysmic battle between related kinship groups in early India. It includes the Bhagavad-Gita, the most important work of Indian sacred literature. *(p. 125)*

**Mahayana Buddhism**  "Great Vehicle" branch of Buddhism followed in China, Japan, and Central Asia. The focus is on reverence for **Buddha** and for bodhisattvas, enlightened persons who have postponed nirvana to help others attain enlightenment. *(p. 121)*

**Malacca**  Port city in the modern Southeast Asian country of Malaysia, founded about 1400 as a trading center on the Strait of Malacca. Also spelled Melaka. *(p. 311)*

**Mali**  Empire created by indigenous Muslims in western Sudan of West Africa from the thirteenth to fifteenth century. It was famous for its role in the trans-Saharan gold trade. (See also **Mansa Kankan Musa** and **Timbuktu.**) *(p. 300)*

**Malthus, Thomas (1766–1834)**  Eighteenth-century English intellectual who warned that population growth threatened future generations because, in his view, population growth would always outstrip increases in agricultural production. *(p. 703)*

**mamluks**  Under the Islamic system of military slavery, Turkic military slaves who formed an important part of the armed forces of the **Abbasid Caliphate** of the ninth and tenth centuries. Mamluks eventually founded their own state, ruling Egypt and Syria (1250–1517). *(p. 188)*

**Manchu**  Federation of Northeast Asian peoples who founded the **Qing Empire.** *(p. 432)*

**Mandate of Heaven**  Chinese religious and political ideology developed by the **Zhou,** according to which it was the prerogative of Heaven, the chief deity, to grant power to the ruler of China and to take away that power if the ruler failed to conduct himself justly and in the best interests of his subjects. *(p. 43)*

**mandate system**  Allocation of former German colonies and Ottoman possessions to the victorious powers after World War I, to be administered under League of Nations supervision. *(p. 610)*

**manor**  In medieval Europe, a large, self-sufficient landholding consisting of the lord's residence (manor house), outbuildings, peasant village, and surrounding land. *(p. 209)*

*mansabs*  In India, grants of land given in return for service by rulers of the **Mughal Empire.** *(p. 425)*

**Mansa Kankan Musa**  Ruler of Mali (r. 1312–1337). His pilgrimage through Egypt to **Mecca** in 1324–1325 established the empire's reputation for wealth in the Mediterranean world. *(p. 301)*

**Mao Zedong (1893–1976)**  Leader of the Chinese Communist Party (1927–1976). He led the Communists on the **Long March** (1934–1935) and rebuilt the Communist Party and Red Army during the Japanese occupation of China (1937–1945). After World War II, he led the Communists to victory over the **Guomindang.** He ordered the **Cultural Revolution** in 1966. *(p. 629)*

**maroon**  A slave who ran away from his or her master. Often a member of a community of runaway slaves in the West Indies and South America. *(p. 402)*

**Marshall Plan**  U. S. program to support the reconstruction of western Europe after World War II. By 1961 more than $20 billion in economic aid had been dispersed. *(p. 670)*

**Marx, Karl (1818–1883)**  German journalist and philosopher, founder of the Marxist branch of **socialism.** He is known for two books: *The Communist Manifesto* (1848) and *Das Kapital* (Vols. I–III, 1867–1894). *(p. 553)*

**mass deportation**  The forcible removal and relocation of large numbers of people or entire populations. The mass deportations practiced by the Assyrian and Persian Empires were meant as a terrifying warning of the consequences of rebellion. They also brought skilled and unskilled labor to the imperial center. *(p. 74)*

**mass production**  The manufacture of many identical products by the division of labor into many small repetitive tasks. This method was introduced into the manufacture of pottery by Josiah Wedgwood and into the spinning of cotton thread by Richard Arkwright. (See also **Industrial Revolution; Wedgwood, Josiah.**) *(p. 484)*

**Mauryan Empire**  The first state to unify most of the Indian subcontinent. It was founded by Chandragupta Maurya in 324 B.C.E. and survived until 184 B.C.E. From its capital at Pataliputra in the Ganges Valley it grew wealthy from taxes on agriculture, iron mining, and control of trade routes. (See also **Ashoka.**) *(p. 123)*

**Maya**  Mesoamerican civilization concentrated in Mexico's Yucatán Peninsula and in Guatemala and Honduras but never unified into a single empire. Major contributions were in mathematics, astronomy, and development of the calendar. *(p. 246)*

**Mecca**  City in western Arabia; birthplace of the Prophet **Muhammad,** and ritual center of the Islamic religion. *(p. 182)*

**mechanization**  The application of machinery to manufacturing and other activities. Among the first processes to be mechanized were the spinning of cotton thread and the weaving of cloth in late-eighteenth- and early-nineteenth-century England. *(p. 486)*

**medieval** Literally "middle age," a term that historians of Europe use for the period ca. 500 to ca. 1500, signifying its intermediate point between Greco-Roman antiquity and the Renaissance. (*p. 203*)

**Medina** City in western Arabia to which the Prophet Muhammad and his followers emigrated in 622 to escape persecution in Mecca. (*p. 184*)

**megaliths** Structures and complexes of very large stones constructed for ceremonial and religious purposes in **Neolithic** times. (*p. 11*)

**Meiji Restoration** The political program that followed the destruction of the **Tokugawa Shogunate** in 1868, in which a collection of young leaders set Japan on the path of centralization, industrialization, and imperialism. (See also **Yamagata Aritomo.**) (*p. 564*)

**Memphis** The capital of Old Kingdom Egypt, near the head of the Nile Delta. Early rulers were interred in the nearby **pyramids.** (*p. 27*)

**Menelik II (1844–1911)** Emperor of Ethiopia (r. 1889–1911). He enlarged Ethiopia to its present dimensions and defeated an Italian invasion at Adowa (1896). (*p. 581*)

**mercantilism** European government policies of the sixteenth, seventeenth, and eighteenth centuries designed to promote overseas trade between a country and its colonies and accumulate precious metals by requiring colonies to trade only with their motherland country. The British system was defined by the Navigation Acts, the French system by laws known as the *Exclusif.* (*p. 403*)

**Meroë** Capital of a flourishing kingdom in southern Nubia from the fourth century B.C.E. to the fourth century C.E. In this period Nubian culture shows more independence from Egypt and the influence of sub-Saharan Africa. (*p. 49*)

**Middle Passage** The part of the **Great Circuit** involving the transportation of enslaved Africans across the Atlantic to the Americas. (*p. 404*)

**Ming Empire (1368–1644)** Empire based in China that Zhu Yuanzhang established after the overthrow of the **Yuan Empire.** The Ming emperor **Yongle** sponsored additions to the Forbidden City and the voyages of **Zheng He.** The later years of the Ming saw a slowdown in technological development and economic decline. (*pp. 285, 438*)

**Minoan** Prosperous civilization on the Aegean island of Crete in the second millennium B.C.E. The Minoans engaged in far-flung commerce around the Mediterranean and exerted powerful cultural influences on the early Greeks. (*p. 69*)

**mit'a** Andean labor system based on shared obligations to help kinsmen and work on behalf of the ruler and religious organizations. (*p. 257*)

**Moche** Civilization of north coast of Peru (200–700 C.E.). An important Andean civilization that built extensive irrigation networks as well as impressive urban centers dominated by brick temples. (*p. 257*)

**Moctezuma II (1466?–1520)** Last Aztec emperor, overthrown by the Spanish conquistador Hernán Cortés. (*p. 355*)

**modernization** The process of reforming political, military, economic, social, and cultural traditions in imitation of the early success of Western societies, often with regard for accommodating local traditions in non-Western societies. (*p. 500*)

**Mohenjo-Daro** Largest of the cities of the Indus Valley civilization. It was centrally located in the extensive floodplain of the Indus River in contemporary Pakistan. Little is known about the political institutions of Indus Valley communities, but the large-scale of construction at Mohenjo-Daro, the orderly grid of streets, and the standardization of building materials are evidence of central planning. (*p. 32*)

*moksha* The Hindu concept of the spirit's "liberation" from the endless cycle of rebirths. There are various avenues—such as physical discipline, meditation, and acts of devotion to the gods—by which the spirit can distance itself from desire for the things of this world and be merged with the divine force that animates the universe. (*p. 120*)

**monasticism** Living in a religious community apart from secular society and adhering to a rule stipulating chastity, obedience, and poverty. It was a prominent element of medieval Christianity and Buddhism. Monasteries were the primary centers of learning and literacy in medieval Europe. (*p. 213*)

**Mongols** A people of this name is mentioned as early as the records of the **Tang Empire,** living as nomads in northern Eurasia. After 1206 they established an enormous empire under **Genghis Khan,** linking western and eastern Eurasia. (*p. 270*)

**monotheism** Belief in the existence of a single divine entity. Some scholars cite the devotion of the Egyptian pharaoh **Akhenaten** to Aten (sun-disk) and his suppression of traditional gods as the earliest instance. The Israelite worship of Yahweh developed into an exclusive belief in one god, and this concept passed into Christianity and Islam. (*p. 79*)

**monsoon** Seasonal winds in the Indian Ocean caused by the differences in temperature between the rapidly heating and cooling landmasses of Africa and Asia and the slowly changing ocean waters. These strong and predictable winds have long been ridden across the open sea by sailors, and the large amounts of rainfall that they deposit on parts of India, Southeast Asia, and China allow for the cultivation of several crops a year. (*pp. 117, 297*)

**most-favored-nation status** A clause in a commercial treaty that awards to any later signatories all the privileges previously granted to the original signatories. (*p. 534*)

**movable type**    Type in which each individual character is cast on a separate piece of metal. It replaced woodblock printing, allowing for the arrangement of individual letters and other characters on a page, rather than requiring the carving of entire pages at a time. It may have been invented in Korea in the thirteenth century. (See also **printing press.**)    (*p. 239*)

**Mughal Empire**    Muslim state (1526–1857) exercising dominion over most of India in the sixteenth and seventeenth centuries.    (*p. 425*)

**Muhammad (570–632 C.E.)**    Arab prophet; founder of religion of Islam.    (*p. 182*)

**Muhammad Ali (1769–1849)**    Leader of Egyptian modernization in the early nineteenth century. He ruled Egypt as an Ottoman governor, but had imperial ambitions. His descendants ruled Egypt until overthrown in 1952.    (*pp. 500, 520*)

**mummy**    A body preserved by chemical processes or special natural circumstances, often in the belief that the deceased will need it again in the afterlife. In ancient Egypt the bodies of people who could afford mummification underwent a complex process of removing organs, filling body cavities, dehydrating the corpse with natron, and then wrapping the body with linen bandages and enclosing it in a wooden sarcophagus.    (*p. 30*)

**Muscovy**    Russian principality that emerged gradually during the era of Mongol domination. The Muscovite dynasty ruled without interruption from 1276 to 1598.    (*p. 446*)

**Muslim**    An adherent of the Islamic religion; a person who "submits" (in Arabic, *Islam* means "submission") to the will of God.    (*p. 184*)

**Mussolini, Benito (1883–1945)**    Fascist dictator of Italy (1922–1943). He led Italy to conquer Ethiopia (1935), joined Germany in the Axis pact (1936), and allied Italy with Germany in World War II. He was overthrown in 1943 when the Allies invaded Italy.    (*p. 626*)

**Mycenae**    Site of a fortified palace complex in southern Greece that controlled a Late Bronze Age kingdom. In Homer's epic poems Mycenae was the base of King Agamemnon, who commanded the Greeks besieging Troy. Contemporary archaeologists call the complex Greek society of the second millennium B.C.E. "Mycenaean."    (*p. 70*)

**Napoleon I (1769–1832)**    Overthrew French Directory in 1799 and became emperor of the French in 1804. Failed to defeat Great Britain and abdicated in 1814. Returned to power briefly in 1815 but was defeated and died in exile.    (*p. 468*)

**Nasir al-Din Tusi (1201–1274)**    Persian mathematician and cosmologist whose academy near Tabriz provided the model for the movement of the planets that helped to inspire the Copernican model of the solar system.    (*p. 278*)

**National Assembly**    French Revolutionary assembly (1789–1791). Called first as the Estates General, the three estates came together and demanded radical change. It passed the **Declaration of the Rights of Man** in 1789.    (*p. 466*)

**nationalism**    A political ideology that stresses people's membership in a nation—a community defined by a common culture and history as well as by territory. In the late eighteenth and early nineteenth centuries, nationalism was a force for unity in western Europe. In the late nineteenth century it hastened the disintegration of the Austro-Hungarian and Ottoman Empires. In the twentieth century it provided the ideological foundation for scores of independent countries emerging from **colonialism.**    (*p. 557*)

**nawab**    A Muslim prince allied to British India; technically, a semi-autonomous deputy of the Mughal emperor.    (*p. 504*)

**Nazis**    German political party joined by Adolf Hitler, emphasizing nationalism, racism, and war. When Hitler became chancellor of Germany in 1933, the Nazis became the only legal party and an instrument of Hitler's absolute rule. The party's formal name was National Socialist German Workers' Party. (See also **Hitler, Adolf.**)    (*p. 627*)

**Nehru, Jawaharlal (1889–1964)**    Indian statesman. He succeeded Mohandas K. Gandhi as leader of the **Indian National Congress.** He negotiated the end of British colonial rule in India and became India's first prime minister (1947–1964).    (*p. 649*)

**Neo-Assyrian Empire**    An empire extending from western Iran to Syria-Palestine, conquered by the Assyrians of northern Mesopotamia between the tenth and seventh centuries B.C.E. They used force and terror and exploited the wealth and labor of their subjects. They also preserved and continued the cultural and scientific developments of Mesopotamian civilization.    (*p. 72*)

**Neo-Babylonian kingdom**    Under the Chaldaeans (nomadic kinship groups that settled in southern Mesopotamia in the early first millennium B.C.E.), **Babylon** again became a major political and cultural center in the seventh and sixth centuries B.C.E. After participating in the destruction of Assyrian power, the monarchs Nabopolassar and Nebuchadnezzar took over the southern portion of the Assyrian domains. By destroying the **First Temple** in Jerusalem and deporting part of the population, they initiated the **Diaspora** of the Jews.    (*p. 86*)

**neo-liberalism**    The term used in Latin America and other developing regions to describe free-market policies that include reducing tariff protection for local industries; the sale of public-sector industries, like national airlines and public utilities, to private investors or foreign corporations; and the reduction of social welfare policies and public-sector employment. (*p. 714*)

**Neolithic** The period of the Stone Age associated with the ancient **Agricultural Revolution(s).** It follows the **Paleolithic** period. *(p. 6)*

**Nevskii, Alexander (1220–1263)** Prince of Novgorod (r. 1236–1263). He submitted to the invading Mongols in 1240 and received recognition as the leader of the Russian princes under the **Golden Horde.** *(p. 280)*

**New Economic Policy** Policy proclaimed by Vladimir Lenin in 1921 to encourage the revival of the Soviet economy by allowing small private enterprises. Joseph Stalin ended the N.E.P. in 1928 and replaced it with a series of **Five-Year Plans.** (See also **Lenin, Vladimir.**) *(p. 607)*

**New France** French colony in North America, with a capital in Quebec, founded 1608. New France fell to the British in 1763. *(p. 398)*

**New Imperialism** Historians' term for the late-nineteenth- and early-twentieth-century wave of conquests by European powers, the United States, and Japan, which were followed by the development and exploitation of the newly conquered territories for the benefit of the colonial powers. *(p. 570)*

**new monarchies** Historians' term for the monarchies in France, England, and Spain from 1450 to 1600. The centralization of royal power was increasing within more or less fixed territorial limits. *(p. 334)*

**nomadism** A way of life, forced by a scarcity of resources, in which groups of people continually migrate to find pastures and water. *(p. 271)*

**nonaligned nations** Developing countries that announced their neutrality in the **Cold War.** *(p. 682)*

**nongovernmental organizations (NGOs)** Nonprofit international organizations devoted to investigating human rights abuses and providing humanitarian relief. Two NGOs won the Nobel Peace Prize in the 1990s: International Campaign to Ban Landmines (1997) and Doctors Without Borders (1999). *(p. 724)*

**North Atlantic Treaty Organization (NATO)** Organization formed in 1949 as a military alliance of western European and North American states against the Soviet Union and its east European allies. (See also **Warsaw Pact.**) *(p. 669)*

**Olmec** The first Mesoamerican civilization. Between ca. 1200 and 400 B.C.E., the Olmec people of central Mexico created a vibrant civilization that included intensive agriculture, wide-ranging trade, ceremonial centers, and monumental construction. The Olmec had great cultural influence on later Mesoamerican societies, passing on artistic styles, religious imagery, sophisticated astronomical observation for the construction of calendars, and a ritual ball game. *(p. 54)*

**Oman** Arab state based in Musqat, the main port in the southwest region of the Arabian peninsula. Oman succeeded Portugal as a power in the western Indian Ocean in the eighteenth century. *(p. 429)*

**Opium War (1839–1842)** War between Britain and the **Qing Empire** that was, in the British view, occasioned by the Qing government's refusal to permit the importation of opium into its territories. The victorious British imposed the one-sided **Treaty of Nanking** on China. *(p. 534)*

**Organization of Petroleum Exporting Countries (OPEC)** Organization formed in 1960 by oil-producing states to promote their collective interest in generating revenue from oil. *(p. 686)*

**Ottoman Empire** Islamic state founded by Osman in northwestern Anatolia ca. 1300. After the fall of the **Byzantine Empire,** the Ottoman Empire was based at Istanbul (formerly Constantinople) from 1453 to 1922. It encompassed lands in the Middle East, North Africa, the Caucasus, and eastern Europe. *(pp. 282, 412)*

**Paleolithic** The period of the Stone Age associated with the **evolution** of humans. It predates the **Neolithic** period. *(p. 6)*

**Pan-Slavism** Movement among Russian intellectuals in the second half of the nineteenth century to identify culturally and politically with the Slavic peoples of eastern Europe. *(p. 531)*

**Panama Canal** Ship canal cut across the isthmus of Panama by United States Army engineers; it opened in 1914. It greatly shortened the sea voyage between the east and west coasts of North America. The United States turned the canal over to Panama on January 1, 2000. *(p. 592)*

**papacy** The central administration of the Roman Catholic Church, of which the pope is the head. *(pp. 211, 365)*

**papyrus** A reed that grows along the banks of the Nile River in Egypt. From it was produced a coarse, paper-like writing medium used by the Egyptians and many other peoples in the ancient Mediterranean and Middle East. *(p. 27)*

**Parthians** Iranian ruling dynasty between ca. 250 B.C.E. and 226 C.E. *(p. 155)*

**patron/client relationship** In ancient Rome, a fundamental social relationship in which the patron—a wealthy and powerful individual—provided legal and economic protection and assistance to clients, men of lesser status and means, and in return the clients supported the political careers and economic interests of their patron. *(p. 133)*

**Paul (ca. 5–65 C.E.)** A Jew from the Greek city of Tarsus in Anatolia, he initially persecuted the followers of Jesus but, after receiving a revelation on the road to Syrian Damascus, became a Christian. Taking advantage of his Hellenized background and Roman citizenship, he traveled throughout Syria-Palestine, Anatolia, and Greece, preaching the new religion and establishing churches. Finding his greatest success among pagans ("gentiles"), he began the process by which Christianity separated from Judaism.    (*p. 138*)

***pax romana***    Literally, "Roman peace," it connoted the stability and prosperity that Roman rule brought to the lands of the Roman Empire in the first two centuries C.E. The movement of people and trade goods along Roman roads and safe seas allowed for the spread of cultural practices, technologies, and religious ideas.    (*p. 137*)

**Pearl Harbor**    Naval base in Hawaii attacked by Japanese aircraft on December 7, 1941. The sinking of much of the U.S. Pacific Fleet brought the United States into World War II.    (*p. 634*)

**Peloponnesian War**    A protracted (431–404 B.C.E.) and costly conflict between the Athenian and Spartan alliance systems that convulsed most of the Greek world. The war was largely a consequence of Athenian imperialism. Possession of a naval empire allowed Athens to fight a war of attrition. Ultimately, Sparta prevailed because of Athenian errors and Persian financial support.    (*p. 113*)

***perestroika***    Policy of "openness" that was the centerpiece of Mikhail Gorbachev's efforts to liberalize communism in the Soviet Union. (See also **Gorbachev, Mikhail.**)    (*p. 700*)

**Pericles (ca. 495–429 B.C.E.)**    Aristocratic leader who guided the Athenian state through the transformation to full participatory democracy for all male citizens, supervised construction of the Acropolis, and pursued a policy of imperial expansion that led to the **Peloponnesian War.** He formulated a strategy of attrition but died from the plague early in the war.    (*p. 109*)

**Perón, Eva Duarte (1919–1952)**    Wife of **Juan Perón** and champion of the poor in Argentina. She was a gifted speaker and popular political leader who campaigned to improve the life of the urban poor by founding schools and hospitals and providing other social benefits.    (*p. 660*)

**Perón, Juan (1895–1974)**    President of Argentina (1946–1955, 1973–1974). As a military officer, he championed the rights of labor. Aided by his wife **Eva Duarte Perón,** he was elected president in 1946. He built up Argentinean industry, became very popular among the urban poor, but harmed the economy.    (*p. 659*)

**Persepolis**    A complex of palaces, reception halls, and treasury buildings erected by the Persian kings **Darius I** and Xerxes in the Persian homeland. It is believed that the New Year's festival was celebrated here, as well as the coronations, weddings, and funerals of the Persian kings, who were buried in cliff-tombs nearby.    (*p. 99*)

**Persian Wars**    Conflicts between Greek city-states and the Persian Empire, ranging from the Ionian Revolt (499–494 B.C.E.) through Darius's punitive expedition that failed at Marathon (490 B.C.E.) and the defeat of Xerxes' massive invasion of Greece by the Spartan-led Hellenic League (480–479 B.C.E.). This first major setback for Persian arms launched the Greeks into their period of greatest cultural productivity. **Herodotus** chronicled these events in the first "history" in the Western tradition.    (*p. 109*)

**Peter the Great (1672–1725)**    Russian tsar (r. 1689–1725). He enthusiastically introduced Western languages and technologies to the Russian elite, moving the capital from Moscow to the new city of St. Petersburg.    (*p. 449*)

**pharaoh**    The central figure in the ancient Egyptian state. Believed to be an earthly manifestation of the gods, he used his absolute power to maintain the safety and prosperity of Egypt.    (*p. 26*)

**Phoenicians**    Semitic-speaking Canaanites living on the coast of modern Lebanon and Syria in the first millennium B.C.E. From major cities such as Tyre and Sidon, Phoenician merchants and sailors explored the Mediterranean, engaged in widespread commerce, and founded **Carthage** and other colonies in the western Mediterranean.    (*p. 80*)

**pilgrimage**    Journey to a sacred shrine by Christians seeking to show their piety, fulfill vows, or gain absolution for sins. Other religions also have pilgrimage traditions, such as the Muslim pilgrimage to **Mecca** and the pilgrimages made by early Chinese Buddhists to India in search of sacred Buddhist writings.    (*p. 220*)

**Pilgrims**    Group of English Protestant dissenters who established Plymouth Colony in Massachusetts in 1620 to seek religious freedom after having lived briefly in the Netherlands.    (*p. 397*)

**Pizarro, Francisco (1478?–1541)**    Spanish explorer who led the conquest of the **Inca** Empire of Peru in 1531–1533.    (*p. 355*)

**Planck, Max (1858–1947)**    German physicist who developed quantum theory and was awarded the Nobel Prize for physics in 1918.    (*p. 614*)

**polis**    The Greek term for a **city-state,** an urban center and the agricultural territory under its control. It was the characteristic form of political organization in southern and central Greece in the Archaic and Classical periods. Of the hundreds of city-states in the Mediterranean and Black Sea regions settled by Greeks, some were oligarchic, others democratic, depending on the powers delegated to the Council and the Assembly.    (*p. 105*)

**positivism**    A philosophy developed by the French count of Saint-Simon. Positivists believed that social and economic problems could be solved by the application of the scientific method, leading to continuous progress. Their ideas became popular in France and Latin America in the nineteenth century.    (*p. 493*)

**Potosí**  Located in Bolivia, one of the richest silver mining centers and most populous cities in colonial Spanish America.  (*p. 391*)

**printing press**  A mechanical device for transferring text or graphics from a woodblock or type to paper using ink. Presses using movable type first appeared in Europe in about 1450. See also **movable type.**  (*p. 330*)

**Protestant Reformation**  Religious reform movement within the Latin Christian Church beginning in 1519. It resulted in the "protesters" forming several new Christian denominations, including the Lutheran and Reformed Churches and the Church of England.  (*p. 366*)

**proxy wars**  During the **Cold War,** local or regional wars in which the superpowers armed, trained, and financed the combatants.  (*p. 690*)

**Ptolemies**  The Macedonian dynasty, descended from one of Alexander the Great's officers, that ruled Egypt for three centuries (323–30 B.C.E.). From their magnificent capital at Alexandria on the Mediterranean coast, the Ptolemies largely took over the system created by Egyptian pharaohs to extract the wealth of the land, rewarding Greeks and Hellenized non-Greeks serving in the military and administration.  (*p. 114*)

**Puritans**  English Protestant dissenters who believed that God predestined souls to heaven or hell before birth. They founded Massachusetts Bay Colony in 1629.  (*p. 397*)

**pyramid**  A large, triangular stone monument, used in Egypt and Nubia as a burial place for the king. The largest pyramids, erected during the Old Kingdom near **Memphis** with stone tools and compulsory labor, reflect the Egyptian belief that the proper and spectacular burial of the divine ruler would guarantee the continued prosperity of the land. (See also **ma'at.**)  (*p. 27*)

**Qin**  A people and state in the Wei Valley of eastern China that conquered rival states and created the first Chinese empire (221–206 B.C.E.). The Qin ruler, Shi Huangdi, standardized many features of Chinese society and ruthlessly marshaled subjects for military and construction projects, engendering hostility that led to the fall of his dynasty shortly after his death. The Qin framework was largely taken over by the succeeding **Han** Empire.  (*p. 144*)

**Qing Empire**  Empire established in China by Manchus who overthrew the **Ming Empire** in 1644. At various times the Qing also controlled Manchuria, Mongolia, Turkestan, and Tibet. The last Qing emperor was overthrown in 1911.  (*p. 440*)

**Quran**  Book composed of divine revelations made to the Prophet Muhammad between ca. 610 and his death in 632; the sacred text of the religion of **Islam.**  (*p. 185*)

**railroads**  Networks of iron (later steel) rails on which steam (later electric or diesel) locomotives pulled long trains at high speeds. The first railroads were built in England in the 1830s. Their success caused a railroad-building boom throughout the world that lasted well into the twentieth century.  (*p. 550*)

**Rajputs**  Members of a mainly Hindu warrior caste from northwest India. The Mughal emperors drew most of their Hindu officials from this caste, and **Akbar** married a Rajput princess.  (*p. 425*)

**Ramesses II**  A long-lived ruler of New Kingdom Egypt (r. 1290–1224 B.C.E.). He reached an accommodation with the **Hittites** of Anatolia after a standoff in battle at Kadesh in Syria. He built on a grand scale throughout Egypt.  (*p. 68*)

**Rashid al-Din (d.1318)**  Adviser to the **Il-khan** ruler Ghazan, who converted to Islam on Rashid's advice.  (*p. 278*)

**recaptives**  Africans rescued by Britain's Royal Navy from the illegal slave trade of the nineteenth century and restored to free status.  (*p. 503*)

**reconquest of Iberia**  Beginning in the eleventh century, military campaigns by various Iberian Christian states to recapture territory taken by Muslims. In 1492 the last Muslim ruler was defeated, and Spain and Portugal emerged as united kingdoms.  (*p. 334*)

**Renaissance (European)**  A period of intense artistic and intellectual activity, said to be a "rebirth" of Greco-Roman culture. Usually divided into an Italian Renaissance, from roughly the mid-fourteenth to mid-fifteenth century, and a Northern (trans-Alpine) Renaissance, from roughly the early fifteenth to early seventeenth century.  (*pp. 325, 364*)

**Revolutions of 1848**  Democratic and nationalist revolutions that swept across Europe. The monarchy in France was overthrown. In Germany, Austria, Italy, and Hungary the revolutions failed.  (*p. 469*)

**Rhodes, Cecil (1853–1902)**  British entrepreneur and politician involved in the expansion of the British Empire from South Africa into Central Africa. The colonies of Southern Rhodesia (now Zimbabwe) and Northern Rhodesia (now Zambia) were named after him.  (*p. 580*)

**Romanization**  The process by which the Latin language and Roman culture became dominant in the western provinces of the Roman Empire. The Roman government did not actively seek to Romanize the subject peoples, but indigenous peoples in the provinces often chose to Romanize because of the political and economic advantages that it brought, as well as the allure of Roman success.  (*p. 137*)

**Roman Principate**  A term used to characterize Roman government in the first three centuries C.E., based on the ambiguous title *princeps* ("first citizen") adopted by Augustus to conceal his military dictatorship.  (*p. 136*)

**Roman Republic**   The period from 507 to 31 B.C.E., during which Rome was largely governed by the aristocratic **Roman Senate.**   *(p. 131)*

**Roman Senate**   A council whose members were the heads of wealthy, landowning families. Originally an advisory body to the early kings, in the era of the **Roman Republic** the Senate effectively governed the Roman state and the growing empire. Under Senate leadership, Rome conquered an empire of unprecedented extent in the lands surrounding the Mediterranean Sea. In the first century B.C.E. quarrels among powerful and ambitious senators and failure to address social and economic problems led to civil wars and the emergence of the rule of the emperors.   *(p. 131)*

**sacrifice**   A gift given to a deity, often with the aim of creating a relationship, gaining favor, and obligating the god to provide some benefit to the sacrificer, sometimes in order to sustain the deity and thereby guarantee the continuing vitality of the natural world. The object devoted to the deity could be as simple as a cup of wine poured on the ground, a live animal slain on the altar, or, in the most extreme case, the ritual killing of a human being.   *(p. 106)*

**Safavid Empire**   Iranian kingdom (1502–1722) established by Ismail Safavi, who declared Iran a Shi'ite state.   *(p. 420)*

**Sahel**   Belt south of the Sahara; literally "coastland" in Arabic.   *(p. 167)*

*samurai*   Literally "those who serve," the hereditary military elite of the **Tokugawa Shogunate.**   *(p. 433)*

**Sandinistas**   Members of a leftist coalition that overthrew the Nicaraguan dictatorship of Anastasia Somoza in 1979 and attempted to install a socialist economy. The United States financed armed opposition by the Contras. The Sandinistas lost national elections in 1990.   *(p. 692)*

**Sanger, Margaret (1883–1966)**   American nurse and author; pioneer in the movement for family planning; organized conferences and established birth control clinics.   *(p. 613)*

**Sasanid Empire**   Iranian empire, established ca. 226, with a capital in Ctesiphon, Mesopotamia. The Sasanid emperors established **Zoroastrianism** as the state religion. Islamic Arab armies overthrew the empire ca. 640.   *(p. 156)*

**satrap**   The governor of a province in the Achaemenid Persian Empire, often a relative of the king. He was responsible for protection of the province and for forwarding tribute to the central administration. Satraps in outlying provinces enjoyed considerable autonomy.   *(p. 99)*

**savanna**   Tropical or subtropical grassland, either treeless or with occasional clumps of trees. Most extensive in **sub-Saharan Africa** but also present in South America.   *(p. 167)*

**schism**   A formal split within a religious community. See **Great Western Schism.**   *(p. 204)*

**scholasticism**   A philosophical and theological system, associated with Thomas Aquinas, devised to reconcile Aristotelian philosophy and Roman Catholic theology in the thirteenth century.   *(p. 329)*

**Scientific Revolution**   The intellectual movement in Europe, initially associated with planetary motion and other aspects of physics, that by the seventeenth century had laid the groundwork for modern science.   *(p. 370)*

**"scramble" for Africa**   Sudden wave of conquests in Africa by European powers in the 1880s and 1890s. Britain obtained most of eastern Africa, France most of northwestern Africa. Other countries (Germany, Belgium, Portugal, Italy, and Spain) acquired lesser amounts.   *(p. 577)*

**scribe**   In the governments of many ancient societies, a professional position reserved for men who had undergone the lengthy training required to be able to read and write using **cuneiforms, hieroglyphics,** or other early, cumbersome writing systems.   *(p. 18)*

**seasoning**   An often difficult period of adjustment to new climates, disease environments, and work routines, such as that experienced by slaves newly arrived in the Americas.   *(p. 402)*

**Selassie, Haile (1892–1975)**   Emperor of Ethiopia (r. 1930–1974) and symbol of African independence. He fought the Italian invasion of his country in 1935 and regained his throne during World War II, when British forces expelled the Italians. He ruled **Ethiopia** as a traditional autocracy until he was overthrown in 1974.   *(p. 646)*

**Semitic**   Family of related languages long spoken across parts of western Asia and northern Africa. In antiquity these languages included Hebrew, Aramaic, and Phoenician. The most widespread modern member of the Semitic family is Arabic.   *(p. 14)*

**"separate spheres"**   Nineteenth-century idea in Western societies that men and women, especially of the middle class, should have clearly differentiated roles in society: women as wives, mothers, and homemakers; men as breadwinners and participants in business and politics.   *(p. 556)*

**sepoy**   A soldier in South Asia, especially in the service of the British.   *(p. 504)*

**Sepoy Rebellion**   The revolt of Indian soldiers in 1857 against certain practices that violated religious customs; also known as the Sepoy Mutiny.   *(p. 507)*

**Serbia**   The Ottoman province in the Balkans that rose up against **Janissary** control in the early 1800s. After World War II the central province of Yugoslavia. Serb leaders struggled to maintain dominance as the Yugoslav federation dissolved in the 1990s.   *(p. 520)*

**serf** In medieval Europe, an agricultural laborer legally bound to a lord's property and obligated to perform set services for the lord. In Russia some serfs worked as artisans and in factories; serfdom was not abolished there until 1861. *(pp. 209, 447)*

**shaft graves** A term used for the burial sites of elite members of Mycenaean Greek society in the mid-second millennium B.C.E. At the bottom of deep shafts lined with stone slabs, the bodies were laid out along with gold and bronze jewelry, implements, weapons, and masks. *(p. 70)*

**Shah Abbas I** (r. 1587–1629) The fifth and most renowned ruler of the **Safavid** dynasty in Iran. Abbas moved the royal capital to Isfahan in 1598. *(p. 421)*

**shamanism** The practice of identifying special individuals (shamans) who will interact with spirits for the benefit of the community. Characteristic of the Korean kingdoms of the early medieval period and of early societies of Central Asia. *(p. 239)*

**Shang** The dominant people in the earliest Chinese dynasty for which we have written records (ca. 1750–1027 B.C.E.). Ancestor worship, divination by means of oracle bones, and the use of bronze vessels for ritual purposes were major elements of Shang culture. *(p. 41)*

**Shi Huangdi** Founder of the short-lived **Qin** dynasty and creator of the Chinese Empire (r. 221–210 B.C.E.). He is remembered for his ruthless conquests of rival states, standardization of practices, and forcible organization of labor for military and engineering tasks. His tomb, with its army of life-size terracotta soldiers, has been partially excavated. *(p. 144)*

**Shi'ites** Muslims belonging to the branch of Islam believing that God vests leadership of the community in a descendant of Muhammad's son-in-law Ali. Shi'ism is the state religion of Iran. (See also **Sunnis.**) *(pp. 180, 421)*

**Siberia** The extreme northeastern sector of Asia, including the Kamchatka Peninsula and the present Russian coast of the Arctic Ocean, the Bering Strait, and the Sea of Okhotsk. *(p. 446)*

**Silk Road** Caravan routes connecting China and the Middle East across Central Asia and Iran. *(p. 155)*

**Slavophiles** Russian intellectuals in the early nineteenth century who favored resisting western European influences and taking pride in the traditional peasant values and institutions of the Slavic people. *(p. 531)*

**"small traditions"** Historians' term for a localized, usually nonliterate, set of customs and beliefs adhered to by a single society, often in conjunction with a **"great tradition."** *(p. 168)*

**socialism** A political ideology that originated in Europe in the 1830s. Socialists advocated government protection of workers from exploitation by property owners and government ownership of industries. This ideology led to the founding of socialist or labor parties throughout Europe in the second half of the nineteenth century. (See also **Marx, Karl.**) *(p. 552)*

**Socrates** Athenian philosopher (ca. 470–399 B.C.E.) who shifted the emphasis of philosophical investigation from questions of natural science to ethics and human behavior. He attracted young disciples from elite families but made enemies by revealing the ignorance and pretensions of others, culminating in his trial and execution by the Athenian state. *(p. 111)*

**Sokoto Caliphate** A large Muslim state founded in 1809 in what is now northern Nigeria. *(p. 500)*

**Solidarity** Polish trade union created in 1980 to protest working conditions and political repression. It began the nationalist opposition to communist rule that led in 1989 to the fall of communism in eastern Europe. *(p. 700)*

**Song Empire** Empire in central and southern China (960–1126) while the Liao people controlled the north. Empire in southern China (1127–1279; the "Southern Song") while the Jin people controlled the north. Distinguished for its advances in technology, medicine, astronomy, and mathematics. *(p. 232)*

**Stalin, Joseph** (1879–1953) Bolshevik revolutionary, head of the Soviet Communist Party after 1924, and dictator of the Soviet Union from 1929 to 1953. He led the Soviet Union with an iron fist, using **Five-Year Plans** to increase industrial production and terror to crush all opposition. *(p. 620)*

**Stalingrad** City in Russia, site of a Red Army victory over the German army in 1942–1943. The Battle of Stalingrad was the turning point in the war between Germany and the Soviet Union. Today Volgograd. *(p. 632)*

**Stanley, Henry Morton** (1841–1904) British-American explorer of Africa, famous for his expeditions in search of Dr. David Livingstone. Stanley helped King **Leopold II** establish the Congo Free State. *(p. 579)*

**steam engine** A machine that turns the energy released by burning fuel into motion. Thomas Newcomen built the first crude but workable steam engine in 1712. **James Watt** vastly improved his device in the 1760s and 1770s. Steam power was later applied to moving machinery in factories and to powering ships and locomotives. *(p. 487)*

**steel** A form of iron that is both durable and flexible. It was first mass-produced in the 1860s and quickly became the most widely used metal in construction, machinery, and railroad equipment. *(p. 549)*

**steppes** Treeless plains, especially the high, flat expanses of northern Eurasia, which usually have little rain and are covered with coarse grass. They are good lands for nomads and their herds. Living on the steppes promoted the breeding of horses and the development of military skills that were essential to the rise of the Mongol Empire. *(p. 167)*

**stirrup**   Device for securing a horseman's feet, enabling him to wield weapons more effectively. First evidence of the use of stirrups was among the Kushan people of northern Afghanistan in approximately the first century C.E.   (*p. 159*)

**stock exchange**   A place where shares in a company or business enterprise are bought and sold.   (*p. 374*)

**Stone Age**   The historical period characterized by the production of tools from stone and other nonmetallic substances. It was followed in some places by the Bronze Age and more generally by the Iron Age.   (*p. 6*)

**submarine telegraph cables**   Insulated copper cables laid along the bottom of a sea or ocean for telegraphic communication. The first short cable was laid across the English Channel in 1851; the first successful transatlantic cable was laid in 1866. (See also **electric telegraph.**)   (*p. 550*)

**sub-Saharan Africa**   Portion of the African continent lying south of the Sahara.   (*p. 167*)

**Suez Canal**   Ship canal dug across the isthmus of Suez in Egypt, designed by Ferdinand de Lesseps. It opened to shipping in 1869 and shortened the sea voyage between Europe and Asia. Its strategic importance led to the British conquest of Egypt in 1882.   (*p. 569*)

**Suleiman the Magnificent (1494–1566)**   The most illustrious sultan of the **Ottoman Empire** (r. 1520–1566); also known as Suleiman Kanuni, "The Lawgiver." He significantly expanded the empire in the Balkans and eastern Mediterranean.   (*p. 415*)

**Sumerians**   The people who dominated southern Mesopotamia through the end of the third millennium B.C.E. They were responsible for the creation of many fundamental elements of Mesopotamian culture—such as irrigation technology, **cuneiform,** and religious conceptions—taken over by their **Semitic** successors.   (*p. 14*)

**Sunnis**   Muslims belonging to branch of Islam believing that the community should select its own leadership. The majority religion in most Islamic countries. (See also **Shi'ites.**)   (*p. 180*)

**Sun Yat-sen (1867–1925)**   Chinese nationalist revolutionary, founder and leader of the **Guomindang** until his death. He attempted to create a liberal democratic political movement in China but was thwarted by military leaders.   (*p. 608*)

**Swahili**   Bantu language with Arabic loanwords spoken in coastal regions of East Africa.   (*p. 430*)

**Swahili Coast**   East African shores of the Indian Ocean between the Horn of Africa and the Zambezi River; from the Arabic *sawahil,* meaning "shores."   (*p. 307*)

**Taiping Rebellion (1850–1864)**   The most destructive civil war before the twentieth century. A Christian-inspired rural rebellion threatened to topple the **Qing Empire.**   (*p. 536*)

**Tamil kingdoms**   The kingdoms of southern India, inhabited primarily by speakers of Dravidian languages, which developed in partial isolation, and somewhat differently, from the Aryan north. They produced epics, poetry, and performance arts. Elements of Tamil religious beliefs were merged into the Hindu synthesis.   (*p. 125*)

**Tang Empire**   Empire unifying China and part of Central Asia, founded 618 and ended 907. The Tang emperors presided over a magnificent court at their capital, Chang'an.   (*p. 225*)

**Tanzimat**   "Restructuring" reforms by the nineteenth-century Ottoman rulers, intended to move civil law away from the control of religious elites and make the military and the bureaucracy more efficient.   (*p. 524*)

**Tenochtitlan**   Capital of the Aztec Empire, located on an island in Lake Texcoco. Its population was about 150,000 on the eve of Spanish conquest. Mexico City was constructed on its ruins.   (*p. 252*)

**Teotihuacan**   A powerful **city-state** in central Mexico (100 B.C.E.–750 C.E.). Its population was about 150,000 at its peak in 600.   (*p. 245*)

**terrorism**   Political belief that extreme and seemingly random violence will destabilize a government and permit the terrorists to gain political advantage. Though an old technique, terrorism gained prominence in the late twentieth century with the growth of worldwide mass media that, through their coverage, amplified public fears of terrorist acts.   (*p. 717*)

**theater-state**   Historians' term for a state that acquires prestige and power by developing attractive cultural forms and staging elaborate public ceremonies (as well as redistributing valuable resources) to attract and bind subjects to the center. Examples include the **Gupta Empire** in India and **Srivijaya** in Southeast Asia.   (*p. 125*)

**Thebes**   Capital city of Egypt and home of the ruling dynasties during the Middle and New Kingdoms. Amon, patron deity of Thebes, became one of the chief gods of Egypt. Monarchs were buried across the river in the Valley of the Kings.   (*p. 27*)

**Theravada Buddhism**   "Way of the Elders" branch of Buddhism followed in Sri Lanka and much of Southeast Asia. Theravada remains close to the original principles set forth by the **Buddha;** it downplays the importance of gods and emphasizes austerity and the individual's search for enlightenment.   (*p. 121*)

**third-century crisis**   Historians' term for the political, military, and economic turmoil that beset the Roman Empire during much of the third century C.E.: frequent changes of ruler, civil wars, barbarian invasions, decline of urban centers, and near-destruction of long-distance commerce and the monetary economy. After 284 C.E. Diocletian restored order by making fundamental changes.   (*p. 139*)

**Third World**   Term applied to a group of developing countries who professed nonalignment during the **Cold War.**   (*p. 682*)

**three-field system**   A rotational system for agriculture in which one field grows grain, one grows legumes, and one lies fallow. It gradually replaced two-field system in medieval Europe.   (*p. 317*)

**Tiananmen Square**   Site in Beijing where Chinese students and workers gathered to demand greater political openness in 1989. The demonstration was crushed by Chinese military with great loss of life.   (*p. 699*)

**Timbuktu**   City on the Niger River in the modern country of Mali. It was founded by the Tuareg as a seasonal camp sometime after 1000. As part of the **Mali** empire, Timbuktu became a major terminus of the trans-Saharan trade and a center of Islamic learning.   (*p. 312*)

**Timur (1336–1405)**   Member of a prominent family of the Mongols' Jagadai Khanate, Timur through conquest gained control over much of Central Asia and Iran. He consolidated the status of Sunni Islam as orthodox, and his descendants, the Timurids, maintained his empire for nearly a century and founded the **Mughal Empire** in India.   (*p. 277*)

**Tiwanaku**   Name of capital city and empire centered on the region near Lake Titicaca in modern Bolivia (375–1000 C.E.).   (*p. 258*)

**Tokugawa Shogunate (1603–1868)**   The last of the three shogunates of Japan.   (*p. 434*)

**Toltecs**   Powerful postclassic empire in central Mexico (900–1156 C.E.). It influenced much of Mesoamerica. Aztecs claimed ties to this earlier civilization.   (*p. 251*)

**trans-Saharan caravan routes**   Trading network linking North Africa with **sub-Saharan Africa** across the Sahara.   (*p. 165*)

**Treaty of Nanking (1842)**   The treaty that concluded the **Opium War.** It awarded Britain a large indemnity from the **Qing Empire,** denied the Qing government tariff control over some of its own borders, opened additional ports of residence to Britons, and ceded the island of Hong Kong to Britain.   (*p. 534*)

**Treaty of Versailles (1919)**   The treaty imposed on Germany by France, Great Britain, the United States, and other Allied Powers after World War I. It demanded that Germany dismantle its military and give up some lands to Poland. It was resented by many Germans.   (*p. 606*)

**treaty ports**   Cities opened to foreign residents as a result of the forced treaties between the **Qing Empire** and foreign signatories. In the treaty ports, foreigners enjoyed **extraterritoriality.**   (*p. 534*)

**tributary system**   A system in which, from the time of the **Han** Empire, countries in East and Southeast Asia not under the direct control of empires based in China nevertheless enrolled as tributary states, acknowledging the superiority of the emperors in China in exchange for trading rights or strategic alliances.   (*p. 228*)

**tribute system**   A system in which defeated peoples were forced to pay a tax in the form of goods and labor. This forced transfer of food, cloth, and other goods subsidized the development of large cities. An important component of the Aztec and Inca economies.   (*p. 253*)

**trireme**   Greek and Phoenician warship of the fifth and fourth centuries B.C.E. It was sleek and light, powered by 170 oars arranged in three vertical tiers. Manned by skilled sailors, it was capable of short bursts of speed and complex maneuvers.   (*p. 110*)

**tropical rain forest**   High-precipitation forest zones of the Americas, Africa, and Asia lying between the Tropic of Cancer and the Tropic of Capricorn.   (*p. 167*)

**tropics**   Equatorial region between the Tropic of Cancer and the Tropic of Capricorn. It is characterized by generally warm or hot temperatures year-round, though much variation exists due to altitude and other factors. Temperate zones north and south of the tropics generally have a winter season.   (*p. 297*)

**Truman Doctrine**   Foreign policy initiated by U.S. president Harry Truman in 1947. It offered military aid to help Turkey and Greece resist Soviet military pressure and subversion.   (*p. 672*)

**tsar (czar)**   From Latin *caesar,* this Russian title for a monarch was first used in reference to a Russian ruler by Ivan III (r. 1462–1505).   (*pp. 381, 446*)

**tyrant**   The term the Greeks used to describe someone who seized and held power in violation of the normal procedures and traditions of the community. Tyrants appeared in many Greek **city-states** in the seventh and sixth centuries B.C.E., often taking advantage of the disaffection of the emerging middle class and, by weakening the old elite, unwittingly contributing to the evolution of **democracy.**   (*p. 106*)

**Uighurs**   A group of Turkic-speakers who controlled their own centralized empire from 744 to 840 in Mongolia and Central Asia.   (*p. 232*)

**ulama**   Muslim religious scholars. From the ninth century onward, the primary interpreters of Islamic law and the social core of Muslim urban societies.   (*p. 191*)

**Umayyad Caliphate**   First hereditary dynasty of Muslim caliphs (661 to 750). From their capital at Damascus, the Umayyads ruled an empire that extended from Spain to India. Overthrown by the **Abbasid Caliphate.**   (*p. 186*)

**umma**   The community of all Muslims. A major innovation against the background of seventh-century Arabia, where traditionally kinship rather than faith had determined membership in a community.   (*p. 184*)

**United Nations** International organization founded in 1945 to promote world peace and cooperation. It replaced the **League of Nations.** *(p. 669)*

**Universal Declaration of Human Rights** A 1948 United Nations covenant binding signatory nations to the observance of specified rights. *(p. 723)*

**universities** Degree-granting institutions of higher learning. Those that appeared in Latin West from about 1200 onward became the model of all modern universities. *(p. 528)*

**Ural Mountains** This north-south range separates Siberia from the rest of Russia. It is commonly considered the boundary between the continents of Europe and Asia. *(p. 446)*

**Urdu** A Persian-influenced literary form of Hindi written in Arabic characters and used as a literary language since the 1300s. *(p. 312)*

**utopian socialism** A philosophy introduced by the Frenchman Charles Fourier in the early nineteenth century. Utopian socialists hoped to create humane alternatives to industrial capitalism by building self-sustaining communities whose inhabitants would work cooperatively. (See also **socialism.**) *(p. 493)*

**Vargas, Getulio (1883–1954)** Dictator of Brazil from 1930 to 1945 and from 1951 to 1954. Defeated in the presidential election of 1930, he overthrew the government and created a dictatorship that emphasized industrialization and helped the urban poor but did little to alleviate the problems of the peasants. *(p. 658)*

**varna/jati** Two categories of social identity of great importance in Indian history. *Varna* are the four major social divisions: the *Brahmin* priest class, the *Kshatriya* warrior/administrator class, the *Vaishya* merchant/farmer class, and the *Shudra* laborer class. Within the system of *varna* are many *jati*, regional groups of people who have a common occupational sphere, and who marry, eat, and generally interact with other members of their group. *(p. 119)*

**vassal** In medieval Europe, a sworn supporter of a king or lord committed to rendering specified military service to that king or lord. *(p. 210)*

**Vedas** Early Indian sacred "knowledge"—the literal meaning of the term—long preserved and communicated orally by Brahmin priests and eventually written down. These religious texts, including the thousand poetic hymns to various deities contained in the Rig Veda, are our main source of information about the Vedic period (ca. 1500–500 B.C.E.). *(p. 119)*

**Versailles** The huge palace built for French King Louis XIV south of Paris in the town of the same name. The palace symbolized the preeminence of French power and architecture in Europe and the triumph of royal authority over the French nobility. *(p. 382)*

**Victorian Age** The reign of Queen Victoria of Great Britain (r. 1837–1901). The term is also used to describe late-nineteenth-century society, with its rigid moral standards and sharply differentiated roles for men and women and for middle-class and working-class people. (See also **"separate spheres."**) *(p. 553)*

**Vietnam War** (1954–1975) Conflict pitting North Vietnam and South Vietnamese communist guerrillas against the South Vietnamese government, aided after 1961 by the United States. *(p. 673)*

**Villa, Francisco "Pancho" (1877–1923)** A popular leader during the Mexican Revolution. An outlaw in his youth, when the revolution started, he formed a cavalry army in the north of Mexico and fought for the rights of the landless in collaboration with **Emiliano Zapata.** He was assassinated in 1923. *(p. 654)*

**Wari** Andean civilization culturally linked to **Tiwanaku,** perhaps beginning as a colony of Tiwanaku. *(p. 258)*

**Warsaw Pact** The 1955 treaty binding the Soviet Union and countries of eastern Europe in an alliance against the **North Atlantic Treaty Organization.** *(p. 672)*

**Washington, George (1732–1799)** Military commander of the American Revolution. He was the first elected president of the United States (1789–1799). *(p. 464)*

**water wheel** A mechanism that harnesses the energy in flowing water to grind grain or to power machinery. It was used in many parts of the world but was especially common in Europe from 1200 to 1900. *(p. 321)*

**Watt, James (1736–1819)** Scot who invented the condenser and other improvements that made the **steam engine** a practical source of power for industry and transportation. The watt, an electrical measurement, is named after him. *(p. 487)*

**weapons of mass destruction** Nuclear, chemical, and biological devices that are capable of injuring and killing large numbers of people. *(p. 727)*

**Wedgwood, Josiah (1730–1795)** English industrialist whose pottery works were the first to produce fine-quality pottery by industrial methods. *(p. 484)*

**Western Front** A line of trenches and fortifications in World War I that stretched without a break from Switzerland to the North Sea. Scene of most of the fighting between Germany, on the one hand, and France and Britain, on the other. *(p. 601)*

**Wilson, Woodrow (1856–1924)** President of the United States (1913–1921) and the leading figure at the Paris Peace Conference of 1919. He was unable to persuade the U.S. Congress to ratify the **Treaty of Versailles** or join the **League of Nations.** *(p. 605)*

**witch-hunt** The pursuit of people suspected of witchcraft, especially in northern Europe in the late sixteenth and seventeenth centuries. *(p. 369)*

**Women's Rights Convention**   An 1848 gathering of women angered by their exclusion from an international antislavery meeting. They met at Seneca Falls, New York, to discuss women's rights.   *(p. 477)*

**World Bank**   A specialized agency of the United Nations that makes loans to countries for economic development, trade promotion, and debt consolidation. Its formal name is the International Bank for Reconstruction and Development.   *(p. 670)*

**World Trade Organization (WTO)**   An international body established in 1995 to foster and bring order to international trade.   *(p. 720)*

**Xiongnu**   A confederation of nomadic peoples living beyond the northwest frontier of ancient China. Chinese rulers tried a variety of defenses and stratagems to ward off these "barbarians," as they called them, and finally succeeded in dispersing the Xiongnu in the first century C.E.   *(p. 150)*

**Yamagata Aritomo (1838–1922)**   One of the leaders of the **Meiji Restoration.**   *(p. 565)*

**Yi (1392–1910)**   The Yi dynasty ruled Korea from the fall of the **Koryo** kingdom to the colonization of Korea by Japan.   *(p. 290)*

**yin/yang**   In Chinese belief, complementary factors that help to maintain the equilibrium of the world. Yin is associated with feminine, dark, and passive qualities; yang with masculine, light, and active qualities.   *(p. 45)*

**Yongle**   Reign of Zhu Di (1360–1424), the third emperor of the **Ming Empire** (r. 1403–1424). He sponsored further work on the Forbidden City, a huge encyclopedia project, the expeditions of **Zheng He,** and the reopening of China's borders to trade and travel.   *(p. 285)*

**Young Ottomans**   Movement of young intellectuals to institute liberal reforms and build a feeling of national identity in the Ottoman Empire in the second half of the nineteenth century.   *(p. 529)*

**Yuan Empire (1271–1368)**   Empire created in China and Siberia by **Khubilai Khan.**   *(p. 272)*

**Yuan Shikai (1859–1916)**   Chinese general and first president of the Chinese Republic (1912–1916). He stood in the way of the democratic movement led by **Sun Yat-sen.**   *(p. 609)*

**Zapata, Emiliano (1879–1919)**   Revolutionary and leader of peasants in the Mexican Revolution. He mobilized landless peasants in south-central Mexico in an attempt to seize and divide the lands of the wealthy landowners. Though successful for a time, he was ultimately defeated and assassinated.   *(p. 654)*

**Zen**   The Japanese word for a branch of **Mahayana Buddhism** based on highly disciplined meditation. It is known in Sanskrit as *dhyana*, in Chinese as *chan*, and in Korean as *son*.   *(p. 236)*

**Zheng He (1371–1433)**   An imperial eunuch and Muslim, entrusted by the Ming emperor **Yongle** with a series of state voyages that took his gigantic ships through the Indian Ocean, from Southeast Asia to Africa.   *(pp. 285, 340)*

**Zhou**   The people and dynasty that took over the dominant position in north China from the **Shang** and created the concept of the **Mandate of Heaven** to justify their rule. The Zhou era, particularly the vigorous early period (1027–771 B.C.E.), was remembered in Chinese tradition as a time of prosperity and benevolent rule. In the later Zhou period (771–221 B.C.E.), centralized control broke down, and warfare among many small states became frequent.   *(p. 43)*

**ziggurat**   A massive pyramidal stepped tower made of mudbricks. It is associated with religious complexes in ancient Mesopotamian cities, but its function is unknown.   *(p. 19)*

**Zoroastrianism**   A religion originating in ancient Iran with the prophet Zoroaster. It centered on a single benevolent deity—Ahuramazda—who engaged in a twelve-thousand-year struggle with demonic forces before prevailing and restoring a pristine world. Emphasizing truth-telling, purity, and reverence for nature, the religion demanded that humans choose sides in the struggle between good and evil. Those whose good conduct indicated their support for Ahuramazda would be rewarded in the afterlife. Others would be punished. The religion of the Achaemenid and Sasanid Persians, Zoroastrianism may have spread within their realms and influenced Judaism, Christianity, and other faiths.   *(p. 101)*

**Zulu**   A people of modern South Africa whom King Shaka united in 1818.   *(p. 499)*

# Index

Abbas I, Shah, 421, 422, 424
Abdul Hamid II, Sultan, 529, 532
Abdul Mejid, Sultan, 524–525
Abolition (abolitionist movement), 572. *See also* Slave trade, African, end of; in Americas, 475–477; in Cuba, 475, 476–477, 514; in Dutch colonies, 514; in French colonies, 460, 471, 514; Great Britain and, 476, 503; in Venezuela, 471
Abortion, 613–614; in Soviet Union, 624–626
Acheh Sultanate, 427, 429, 430
Acosta, Gladys, 694–696
Addams, Jane, 613
Aden, Portuguese threat to, 353, 354, 415
Administration: *See also* Bureaucracy; Ottoman, 417; colonial Americas, 462, 471; and empire, 451, 575–577, 582
Adowa, Battle of (1896), 582
Advertising, 574 *(illus.)*, 615, 727
Afghanistan (Afghans), 424, 426, 441, 531, 716; Soviet war in, 693, 696, 699, 700; Taliban regime in, 717–718
Afonso I (Kongo), 349–352
Africa (Africans). *See also* East Africa; North Africa; South Africa; Sub-Saharan Africa; West Africa; *and specific countries and peoples;* Portuguese exploration of, 344, 345, 346 *(map);* 349–350, 351–352, 429; Atlantic system and, 405–407; New World foods in, 409; Christianity in, 349, 500, 503; chronology (1795–1889), 501; in nineteenth century, 502 *(map);* "legitimate" trade in, 503; new states in, 499–500, 502 *(map);* European imperialism in, 500, 502 *(map);* 503, 570, 577–583, 603; in British colonies, 513, 514; Christian missionaries in, 582–583; chronology (1869–1908), 571–572; World War I and, 603; World War II and, 632, 646; mining boom in, 626, 638; decolonization of, 670; population growth in, 704 *(illus.),* 705; development aid to, 722; HIV/AIDS in, 724 *and illus.;* women's issues in, 725; Afropop music, 730
African-Americans: *See also* Slaves (slavery), African; as abolitionists, 475; after Civil War, 478, 562; World War I and, 603
African languages, 393, 402, 430, 431
African National Congress, 646, 678, 715
African slaves. *See* Slaves (slavery), African
African slave trade. *See* Slave trade, African
Afrikaners, 510–511 *and illus.,* 580, 581
*Agitator, The* (Rivera), 656 *(illus.)*
Agriculture: *See also* Cotton; Farmers; Landowners; Peasants; Sugar plantations, *and specific crops;* climate change and, 375; Russian, 447; Columbian exchange, 407, 408–409; Ottoman, 417; Chinese, 439, 445, 533, 538, 699; Industrial Revolution

and, 481–482; British India, 506, 507; irrigation for, 500, 507, 508, 579, 586, 593, 646; tropical, 593; global environment and, 592; mechanization of, 617; Soviet collectivization of, 620–622, 663, 672; Green Revolution in, 666; government subsidies to, 722
Aguinaldo, Emilio, 589
Ahmed III, Sultan, 420
AIDS (Acquired Immune Deficiency Syndrome), 724 *and illus.*
Aircraft (aviation): invention of, 614–615; World War II, 631, 632 *(illus.),* 634, 636–637; in Latin America, 658; September 11 (2001) attacks, 702–703
Aircraft carriers, 631, 634
Air pollution, 490, 616, 617, 709–710
Akbar (India), 354, 425, 426
Alaska, Russians in, 446, 450
Albania (Albanians), 597, 672, 716
Aldrin, Edwin E. "Buzz," 674
Alexander III (Russia), 561, 583
Alexander II (Russia), 527, 583; freeing of the serfs by, 531, 532, 562
Alexander I (Russia), 529, 530 *(illus.),* 532
Alexandria, patriarch of, 352
Algeria, 457, 500, 715; independence of, 677
Ali (Muhammad's son-in-law), 421
Ali-Quli Jubbadar, 422 *(illus.)*
Al-Jabarti, Abd al-Rahman, 522–524
Allawi, Ayad, 718
Allende, Salvador, 692
Alliances: early modern Europe, 382–383, 468; Allies in World War II, 633 *(map),* 634, 636 *(map),* 659, 669, 670; Axis in World War II, 629, 633 *(map);* World War I, 597, 600 *(map),* 601, 605, 606–607
Al Qaeda (Islamic organization), 713
Alsace and Lorraine, 558, 560, 606
Al-Umari, 342
American Revolution, 462–465; 513; France and, 464, 466, 478; frontiers and taxes, 462; military course of, 464; republican institutions in, 464–465
American system of manufactures, 487. *See also* United States, Industrial Revolution in
Americas, colonial. *See* Brazil, colonial; British North America; Latin America, colonial
Americas, the (New World; Western Hemisphere). *See also* Caribbean region; Central America; Latin America; North America; *and specific countries;* small pox in, 355 *and illus.,* 356; new foods from, 408–409; abolition of slavery in, 475–477; chronology (1754–1804), 463; Enlightenment ideas in, 462; European immigrants in, 393, 409, 487, 494–495, 562; women's

rights and social justice in, 477–478; race and nationality in, 543
Amerindians (native peoples), 372, 562. *See also specific peoples;* Pacific voyages of, 338; disease and death among, 354, 355 *and illus.,* 356, 361, 387; in Caribbean, 354, 356; traveling in France, 376–377; Christianity and, 399; fur trade and, 398–399 *and illus.;* in colonial Latin America, 387, 388, 391, 392, 393; *mestizos* (mixed race), 393 *(illus.),* 394–395, 653; horses of, 408; in colonial North America, 397, 398–399; labor of, 391, 542, 543; American Revolution and, 462; hunting by, 399, 408, 563; census of, 542, 543; in Mexico, 473, 591, 653, 678
Amnesty International, 724
Amritsar (India) Massacre (1919), 648
Amsterdam, 373, 374 *and illus.*
Amur River, 442, 447, 534
Anatolia (modern Turkey), 417, 520, 610
Ancestor worship, 443. *See also* Confucianism
Anglicanism (Church of England), 368 *(map),* 380, 381, 503; in Africa, 582, 645
Anglo-Dutch Wars (1653–1658), 383, 403
Angola, 406–407, 409, 580, 678, 716
Annan, Kofi, 716
Apartheid, in South Africa, 678, 680, 731
Appeasement of Nazi Germany, 628–629
Arabia (Arabian Peninsula), 429, 519, 603
Arabic script, 421
Arab-Jewish hostilities, 612, 684–686 *and map*
Arab Rebellion (1916), 612
Arab traders, 427, 504
Arafat, Yasir, 686
Arawak people, 342, 354
Architecture: Russian, under Peter the Great, 449, 450; of old and new Cairo, 598 *and illus.;* International style, 615
Argentina, 665; British investment in, 476–477 *and illus.,* 550, 591, 657; immigration to, 476, 552, 656, 658; livestock industry in, 408, 591, 657; manufacturing in, 638; railroads in, 591, 657; Depression of 1930s in, 623, 659; after 1930, 659–660; and Brazil compared, 656–657, 658, 660; military rule in (1976–1992), 693; economic growth in, 719; trade agreement and, 720, 721 *(map)*
Arimoto, Yamagata, 565
Aristocracy (nobility). *See also* Elite class; Landowners; European bourgeoisie and, 374–375; European monarchy and, 379; taxation of, in Europe, 383, 385; French Revolution and, 465, 466, 467, 469; Qing China, 441, 444, 539; Russian (boyars), 447, 450, 529, 562

Aristotle, 370, 371

Aritomo, Yamagata, 564

Armed forces. *See also* Cavalry; Infantry; Military; Navy; Warrior class, *and specific wars;* early modern Europe, 382, 383; Ottoman, 415 (*See also* Janissaries; Safavid, 424; China, 432, 534, 537–538; French Revolution, 467, 468; American Revolution, 464; Russian modernization, 450, 451, 530; Blacks in U.S. Civil War, 475–476; Latin American independence and, 472; Egypt, 520; Ethiopia, 500; British India, 504, 506–507; Crimean War and, 528, 530; Japan, 564, 630; New Imperialism and, 572, 575, 581, 585–586; World War I, 597, 600; World War I, 601–602 *and illus.*, 604, 605; Guomindang (China), 609–610, 630; Mexican civil war, 654; Nazi Wehrmacht, 628, 629, 631–632, 634, 638; Soviet Red Army, 607, 632; Vietnam, 673

Armenia (Armenians), 374, 606, 607; in Safavid Iran, 422, 424; Ottomans and, 531, 597, 603

Armstrong, Neil A., 674

Arrow War (1856–1860), 535 *(map)*, 538

Art and artists: *See also* Paintings; London tenements, 491 *(illus.);* Mexican Revolution and, 655, 656, *(illus.)*

Articles of Confederation (United States), 465

Artillery, 530, 534, 581. *See also* Cannon

Artisans (craftspeople), 492; apprenticeship and, 378; slaves as, 402; in Safavid Iran, 422; Ottoman glassmakers, 416 *(illus.);* East Asian, 434, 436 *and illus.;* and cotton industry, 486

Asante (Gold Coast), 406, 581

Asia (Asians): *See also* Central Asia; East Asia; East Indies; Southeast Asia; immigrant labor from, 494, 513–516, 562, 708; chronology (1862–1905), 571–572; New Imperialism in, 571–572, 583, 586–587, 589 *(map);* chronology (1931–1949), 621; World War II in, 632, 634, 636 *(map);* decolonization of, 669; chronology (1975–1989), 691; economic expansion in (1970s–1990s), 690, 696–699; population in (1730–2050), 704 *(illus.);* financial collapse in (1998), 719; trade agreement in (APEC), 721 *(map);* global pop culture and, 729

Assam, 511. *See also* Vietnam (Vietnamese)

Assembly-line manufacture, 439, 613, 616

Assembly of Notables (France), 460, 466

Astronomy, 440; Copernicus, 370–371

Aswan Dam (Egypt), 579, 682

Atahualpa (Inca), 356

Atlantic Ocean, exploration of (before 1500), 339, 341–342

Atlantic trading system, 348, 388, 403–409. *See also* Slave trade, African; Africa and, 405–407; capitalism and mercantilism, 403–404; Columbian exchange, 407–409; Great Circuit and Middle Passage, 404–405

Atomic bombing of Japan, 634, 635 *(illus.)*, 636 *(map)*, 637, 674

Aurangzeb, 426

Auschwitz death camp, 638

Australia, 430, 457, 581; aboriginal peoples of, 512, 513; immigration to, 513, 516, 552, 576, 605; drought in, 726

Austria-Hungary (1867–1918), 596; language and nationalism in, 557, 561; as conservative power, 558, 560–561; World War I and, 597, 601, 604, 605; end of, 606, 617

Austria (to 1867 and 1918 to present), 382, 671; Habsburgs of, 379; French Revolution and, 467; Napoleonic France and, 468, 469; after World War I, 606; World War I debts of, 623; German annexation of (1938), 628

Authoritarian regimes (dictatorship). *See also specific regimes;* populist in France, 468; in Japan, 629; in Latin America, 623, 626, 658–660, 692–693; in South Korea, 679; in former Soviet bloc, 714

Automobiles, 613, 616–617 *and illus.*, 623, 697; air pollution and, 616, 617, 709

Ayrton, William, 564

Azerbaijan, 531, 607

Azores, 342, 343, 344, 392

Aztec (Aztec Empire), 354–355, 388, 393

Baba of Karo, 584–585

Babur (India), 425

Baghdad, 728; Ottomans and, 420, 421, 520

Bahamas, 342, 354

Balance of power: in early modern Europe, 362, 382–383, 385; Congress of Vienna and, 469; industrialization and, 574–575; before World War II, 628; Cold War era, 673

Balboa, Vasco Núñez de, 348, 356

Balfour, Sir Arthur, 604

Balfour Declaration (1917), 604, 612

Balkans: *See also specific states;* Ottoman Empire and, 412–413, 415, 416, 417, 529; Austria-Hungary and, 561; crisis in (1912–1913), 597; breakup of Yugoslavia, 701 *(map)*, 702; ethnic cleansing in, 716

Baltic states. *See also* Estonia; Latvia; Lithuania; Soviet invasion of, 631; independence of, 701

Bandung Conference (1955), 679, 682–683

Bangladesh, 675; flooding in, 663, 727 *(illus.)*

Banks, 483, 493, 607, 623; Dutch, 373, 385; Ottoman, 527, 528 *and illus.*, 529

Bannerman (China), 534, 538

Bantu language, 430

Bastille, storming of, 466, 467 *(illus.)*

Batista, Fulgencio, 678

Bay of Pigs invasion (1961, Cuba), 679

Beer, 373, 375

Beijing, 538, 684; Manchus and, 432–433, 434, 440; Jesuits in, 440, 443 *(illus.);* Boxer Uprising (1900), 566, 608; Forbidden City of, 609; Japanese seizure of (1937), 630; Tiananmen massacre (1989), 699

Beijing Women's Conference in (1995), 725

Belgium, 631, 670; industrialization in, 482; cities in, 490; railroads in, 488; colonies of, 570, 578 *(map)*, 579, 584, 676 *(map);* World War I and, 601, 606

Bell Telephone Laboratories, 728

Bengal, 426, 504–505, 507, 647; famine in, 651, 663

Benin, 349 *and illus.*, 581

Bentham, Jeremy, 493

Bering, Vitus, 450

Berlin: bombing of, 637; airlift to, 672

Berlin Conference (1884–1885), 579

Berlin Wall, 672; dismantling of, 700 *and illus.*

Bharatiya Janata Party (India, BJP), 714

Biafra, 406, 663

Bible, 371; Luther and, 366; in vernacular, 369

Biko, Steve, 680–682

Bill of Rights (England, 1668), 381

Bill of Rights (United States,1791), 464, 723

Bin, Laden, Usama, 713, 717–718

Biological weapons, 717, 718

Birmingham Lunar Society, 480, 486

Birth control (family planning), 703, 704, 705–706; abortion, 613–614, 624–626

Birthrates (fertility rates), 552; (1970s–1990s), 703, 704–705, 708

Bishops, 379–380; African, 503, 582, 645

Bismarck, Otto von, 560; German unification and, 548, 558; imperialism and, 572, 579

Black Consciousness Movement, 681

Black Death (bubonic plague), 359, 538

"Black Hole of Calcutta," 504

Black Sea region: Russia and, 449, 525 *(map);* Crimean War (1853–1856), 527

Boer war (1899–1902), 581

Bolívar, Simón, 471–472

Bolivia, 392; independence of, 471, 472

Bolshevik Revolution (October Revolution; Russia), 604–605, 606

Bolsheviks, 606–607, 622, 624. *See also* Communist Party, Soviet Union

Bombay, film industry in, 729

Bombay Presidency, 506

Bombs and bombing (explosives): *See also* Nuclear weapons; Weapons and military technology; Taiping Rebellion, 537; dynamite, 549; hand grenades, 602 *(illus.);* World War II, 631, 632 *(illus.)*, 634, 637, 674; Persian Gulf War, 703; terrorist, 718

Bonaparte, Joseph, 471

Bonner, Yelena, 699–700

Borneo, 427, 586

Bose, Pramatha Nath, 648

Bosnia, 520, 597

Bosnia-Herzegovina, 596, 716

Boston, colonial, 397, 462, 464 *(illus.)*

Boulton, Matthew, 485, 487

Bourbon dynasty, 380 *and illus.*, 381, 382

Bourgeoisie, 373–375, 378, 379; French Revolution and, 465; Marx on, 554–556

Bourke-White, Margaret, 650 *(photo)*, 652

Bows and arrows, 415; crossbows, 340

Boxer Uprising (1900, China), 565–566, 608

Boyle, Robert, 371

Brahe, Tycho, 371

Brahmo Samaj (Divine Society), 509

Brazil, 408, 471, 638, 665. *See also* Brazil, colonial; independence of, 472–473;

abolition of slavery in, 475, 476, 478; coffee in, 492, 593, 657; rubber in, 593, 657, 659; Vargas regime in, 658–659; Argentina compared to, 656–657, 658, 660; Depression (1930s), 623, 658–659; military rule in, 692, 693; economic growth in, 719; populist leadership in, 714; Portugal and, 728; trade agreement and, 720, 721 *(map)*

Brazil, colonial, 348, 390 *(map)*, 403, 472; chronology (1540–1777), 389; sugar plantations in, 391, 392, 409, 514, *and illus.;* slaves and slave trade in, 388, 392, 400 *and illus.* 404, 406, 503, 514, 657

Brazza, Savorgnan de, 579

Brazzaville Conference (1944), 677

Brest-Litovsk, Treaty of (1918), 605

Bretton Woods Conference (1946), 670–671

Brezhnev, Leonid, 699, 700

Britain, Battle of (1940), 631

British East India Company (EIC), 444, 462, 511; in India, 496, 498, 504–506, 507

British Empire, 510–516, 560, 583. *See also* British North America; Great Britain; India, under British rule; *and specific colonies;* Caribbean colonies, 399–400, 401–402, 514, 515; African colonies, 510–511, 578 *(map)*, 579–581; trade and, 482, 495, 511–512; Australia and New Zealand, 457, 512–513, 514, 516; chronology (1763–1877), 501; in Asia, 588 *(map)*; policies and shipping, 511–512; labor migrations to, 513–516; New Imperialism and, 570, 574 *(illus.)*, 575, 576 *(illus.)*, 577, 583; decolonization of, 676 *(map)*, 677, 678; English language and, 730

British Navy, 462, 468, 482, 498; and end of slave trade, 476, 503; Japan and, 564; Ottoman Empire and, 519, 524; Qing China and, 534, 535 *(map)*; in World War I, 602–603; in World War II, 631

British North America, 387, 396–398, 401. *See also* American Revolution; Canada; chronology (1607–1763), 389; Middle Atlantic, 398; New England, 397; South, 396–397; immigrants to, 409

British South Africa Company, 581

British Women's Emigration Association, 577

Brunei Sultanate, 427

Buddha (Siddhartha Gautama), 533

Buddhism, 717; in Japan, 437; Tibetan, 439–440

Buenos Aires, 472, 476–477, 657, 706

Buffalo hunters, Amerindian, 408, 563

Bulgaria, 597, 672, 701, 720

Bureaucracy: *See also* Administration; Civil service; colonial Latin America, 391; Qing China, 518; Ottoman, 416, 524–526, 528 *(illus.)*, 529; British India, 507, 647; Russian, 532; census and, 542–543; expansion of, after World War I, 613; Soviet, 607, 671, 699

Burma (Myanmar), 511, 583, 646, 675; Japanese occupation of, 651, 663

Bush, George H. W., 703

Bush, George W., 718, 720, 727

Business (companies). *See also* Capitalism; Corporations; Industries; Monopoly; Trade; government and, 383; joint-stock, 374 *and illus.*, 429, 431, 483, 532; slave trade and, 403, 405, 406; chartered, 403, 493; Great Depression and, 623; Japanese *(zaibatsu)*, 434, 565, 609, 697

Byrd, Richard, 614

Byron, Lord (George Gordon Noel), 524

Byzantine Empire, 413

Cabral, Pedro Alvares, 345, 348

Cairo, 500; modernization of, 529, 598 *(illus.)*

Cakchiquel of Guatemala, 387

Calcutta, under British rule, 504, 505, 506, 648

Calendars: Gregorian, 371; China, 440, 442

Calicut, 341, 353, 354

Calles, Plutarco Elías, 655

Calvin, John, 366

Calvinism, 366, 368 *(map)*, 379, 380

Cambodia, 730

Canada, 674; French in, 398–399, 409; fur trade in, 387, 389, 398–399 *and illus.*, 409; Amerindians in, 398–399 *and illus.*, 562; British (Dominion of), 513; railroads in, 550; development in, 589; immigration to, 552, 576, 605; independence of, 581; women's rights in, 477, 613; in World Wars, 602 *(illus.)*, 634; and NAFTA, 720, 721 *(map)*

Canals, 412. *See also* Suez Canal; in China, 445, 533; in Europe, 374; in Russia, 450; in Britain, 482, 485, 490; Industrial Revolution and, 482, 485, 487, 490; in United States, 487; in Panama, 592, 593, 594, 692; irrigation, 500, 507, 508, 579, 586, 593

Canary Islands, 344, 347

Cannon, 364, 382, 424, 431, 549; on warships, 340; Conquistador, 356; Ottoman, 412, 413; artillery, 530, 534, 581

Canoes, Polynesian, 338, 341 *(illus.)*

Canton (Guangzhou), 535, 536, 609

Canton trading system, 444–445, 533, 534

Cape Colony, 510–511, 580–581

Cape Verde, 344, 345, 392

Capitalism, 407, 556. *See also* Free trade; and mercantilism, 403–404; laissez faire, 493, 494, 497, 662; global, 550; Marx's view of, 553; Communism and, 669, 671–672, 673

Cárdenas, Lázaro, 655–656

Caribbean region (West Indies), 390 *(map).* *See also* Cuba, Haiti; *and specific island;* Amerindian exploration of, 342; Columbus in, 354; disease in, 354, 355, 356, 387; chronology (1500–1680), 389; French colonies in, 399, 400, 404, 462, 514; sugar plantations in, 399–402, 409, 492; slavery in, 399–402, 404, 492; end of slavery in, 514; Indian immigrants in, 494, 514, 515; U.S. intervention in (1904–1914), 563, 591–592; population in (1730–2050), 704 *(illus.)*

Carib people, 342

Carpet manufacture, in Iran, 424

Carrió de la Vandera, Alonso, 394

Carter, Jimmy, 692, 693

Casement, Roger, 580

Cassava, 354, 409

Caste *(jati)* system, in India, 506, 509, 647

Castro, Fidel, 678–679, 690, 692

Catherine of Aragon, 379

Catherine the Great (Russia), 450–451, 453

Catholic Church (Catholicism), 365–366, 369. *See also* Jesuits; Papacy; Protestant Reformation and, 365–366, 368 *(map)*, 369; European monarchies and, 379–380, 381; Inquisition of, 371, 379; in colonial Latin America, 391, 393; in China, 452; French Revolution and, 465, 467, 468; in Africa, 503; in Mexico, 654, 656; in Poland, 452, 638, 700; in former Yugoslavia, 716; English language in, 730

Caucasus region, 527, 529, 531; Soviet Union and, 607, 631, 714

Cavalry: *See also* Knights; Chinese, 340; Conquistador, 354, 355, 356; Ottoman Turk, 415, 416; Safavid Iran, 420; Crimean War and, 528; Polish, 631

Ceausescu, Nicolae, 701

Census, 542–544. *See also* Population

Central America, 720. *See also specific country;* United States' interventions in, 591–592, 692–693

Central Asia, 570, 593. *See also specific country and people;* Turkic peoples of, 412, 424, 447; Qing China and, 440, 441 *(map)*; Russia and, 446, 531, 583, 588 *(map)*; Soviet Union and, 607, 714

Central Intelligence Agency (CIA), 678; Bay of Pigs invasion (1961) and, 679; Iran and, 693

Centralization: *See* Authoritarian regimes; Communist Party; European Community; Fascism; Monarchy

Cetshwayo (Zulu), 580

Ceylon (Sri Lanka), 506, 510, 593, 717, 730

Chamberlain, Neville, 628–629

Chamorro, Violeta, 693

Champlain, Samuel de, 398

Charcoal, and ironmaking, 375, 486

Charles I (England), 380–381

Charleston, colonial, 397

Charles V (Holy Roman Emperor), 379, 383

Charles X (France), 469

Chartered companies, 403, 493

Charter Oath (Japan,1868), 564

Chartist movement (England), 494

Chechnya, 531, 723

Cheka (Soviet secret police), 604

Chemical industry, 549, 603, 635, 709

Chemical weapons (poison gas), 602, 638, 717

Chiang Kai-shek (Jiang Jieshi), 609–610, 629, 630; Chinese civil war and, 634–635

Chicago, 488, 552, 615

Child labor, 481, 489, 492, 494, 553

Children: *See also* Education; Family; Schools; education of, 378; Industrial Revolution and, 481, 489, 492, 494; decline in mortality of, 552; Victorian Age, 556; and Soviet system, 624; Rio de Janeiro homeless, 689, 706

Chile, 720; colonial, 390 (map); independence of, 472; women's rights in, 477–478; copper mining in, 550; military rule in, 692, 693

China, imperial: See also Ming Empire; Qing Empire; Portuguese in (See Macao); chronology (1517–1796), 435; climate changes in, 455; population in, 359, 360 (illus.), 445, 451, 533, 703; agriculture in, 439, 445, 533; Dutch trade with, 436; footbinding of women in, 536, 630; Jesuit missionaries in, 376, 440, 442–443 and illus.; Korea and, 565; porcelain production by, 436, 439; opium trade in, 506, 507, 529, 533–534, 609; Zeng Guofan and, 539; France and, 534, 535 and map, 538, 539, 565; Heavenly Kingdom of Great Peace, 536–537, 538; revolution and war in (1900–1918), 608–609; warlords in, 609–610; Guomindang in, 609

China, Japan and: Japanese invasion of Korea (1582) and, 433–434, 440; Boxer Uprising (1900), 565–566, 608; war between (1894–1895), 565, 589; Twenty-One Demands (1915), 609; Japanese seizure of Manchuria, 629; war between (1937–1945), 630

China, People's Republic of, 665. See also Communist Party (China); Mao Zedong; civil war in (1945–1949), 634–635; famine in (1958–1961), 663–664; Great Leap Forward in, 663–664; Cold War and, 669, 672, 682, 683–684; United Nations and, 669; Taiwan and, 684; economic reform in, 698–699; foreign investment in, 698–699, 719; economic boom in, 714; family-planning in, 705–706; nuclear weapons testing in, 717; pollution and health in, 710; and U.S. invasion of Iraq (2003), 718; English language in, 730; Hong Kong and, 730, 732

Chinese immigrants, 515, 516, 603; in Southeast Asia, 440; in sugar plantations, 513, 514; to United States, 494, 538, 562; to Hawaii, 589

Chinese script, 433

Chocolate, 404, 407, 409, 444

Cholera, 490, 508–509, 515

Christianity (Christians): See also Orthodox Christianity; in colonial Americas, 347; Portuguese promotion of, in Africa, 343, 344, 349–352; Reformation and, 365–366, 369; in China, 443, 451; in Japan, 452; militancy of, 343; Ethiopian, 352, 500, 583, 644, 645; in Ottoman Empire, 525; and Islam, in Africa, 523, 583; in Israel, 722–723

Christian missionaries. See also Jesuits (Society of Jesus); in Latin America, 391, 393; in North America, 399; in Africa, 349–350, 500, 503; in China, 440, 443; Orthodox in Siberia, 447, 452; in Japan, 436–437; in Africa, 500, 503; in Ottoman Empire, 526; in China, 534, 536, 538; in East Indies, 586; in India, 506; New Imperialism and, 572–573; in colonial Africa, 582–583, 644–645, 646

Churchill, Winston, 575, 631, 668, 687

Church of England. See Anglicanism

Cities and towns (urban areas). See also City-states; Urbanization; and specific cities; European bourgeoisie and, 373; colonial Latin America, 394–396; Ming China, 439; Ottoman and Iranian compared, 421–424; industrialization and, 488, 490, 491 (illus.); Ottoman Empire, 528; Chinese treaty ports, 534, 535–536, 565, 608, 609; railroads and, 550; automobile and suburban sprawl, 616–617 and illus.; modern architecture in, 615; World War II bombing of, 634, 635 (illus.), 637, 638; in colonial Africa, 644; global growth of, 706–707

Citizenship: denied to German Jews, 628, 637; and nationality, 543, 557, 708

City-states: northern Italy, 342–343 (See also Florence; Genoa; Venice); Malacca, 353, 415, 431, 511; Hausa in Africa, 500

Civil Code of 1804 (France), 468

Civil service. See also Administration; Bureaucracy; Ottoman, 526; Indian (ICS), 507, 647, 649, 675

Civil wars: Japan (late 1500s), 433; English (1642), 380–381; United States (1861–1865), 475–476, 500, 529, 592; Russian (1918–1921), 606–607; Mexican (1910–1920), 654; Argentine (1976–1983), 692; Chinese (1945–1949), 634–635, 683–684; African, 716

Cixi (China), 539, 540 (illus.), 563, 565, 608

Clash of Civilizations and the Remaking of the World Order, The (Huntington), 722

Cleanliness, cult of, 615. See also Sanitation

Clemenceau, Georges, 606

Clergy (priests): See also Papacy; Religion; Japanese Christian, 437; colonial Latin America, 391, 473 (illus.); French Revolution and, 465, 467; fall of Communism and, 700

Cleveland, Grover, 589

Climate and weather. See also Monsoons; Rainfall; Little Ice Age, 375, 439, 455; global warming, 359, 666, 726–727

Clinton, William, 717, 722

Clothing: Russian westernization, 450; Ottoman reforms, 526, 528 (illus.); Turkish westernization, 610 (illus.), 612; for Islamic women, 725; global culture and, 732

CNN (Cable News Network), 728

Coal (coal mining), 375, 488 (illus.); and iron industry, 482 (map), 486; pollution from, 552

Cocoa (cacao), 512, 580, 582, 593, 657

Coffee, 404, 407, 417, 419, 430, 444, 512; in Brazil, 492, 593, 657; in East Africa, 642; New Imperialism and, 586, 592

Coins (coinage): copper, 439; gold, 528

Colbert, Jean Baptiste, 374, 375, 385

Cold War (Bipolar world; 1946–1991), 668–674. See also Superpowers; capitalism versus communism and, 670–672, 679; China and, 669, 672, 682, 683–684;

chronology (1945–1975), 671; decolonization and (1947–1990), 668–669; eastern Europe and, 671, 672, 699, 700–701; environment and, 669, 687; Japan and, 673, 683; Korean War and, 672–673; nonaligned nations and, 679, 682–683; nuclear arms race and, 674; United Nations and, 668, 669–670; Vietnam War and, 673–674; Middle East and, 684–686 and map; Soviet Union crisis, 699–700; end of (1989–1991), 665, 690, 699–703; Persian Gulf War and, 702–703; collapse of Soviet bloc and, 700–702 and map

Collectivized agriculture, in Soviet bloc, 620–622, 663, 672

Colleges. See Universities and colleges

Colombia, 592; independence of, 472

Colonies (colonization). See also British Empire; British North America; Decolonization; Dutch colonies; Expansion; French colonies; Imperialism; Latin America, colonial; New Imperialism and specific colonies and colonial powers; European, in Indian Ocean states, 428 (map); European, in Asia, 588 (map)

Columbian exchange, 407–409

Columbus, Christopher, 345, 346 and illus., 354

Comanche people, 399, 408

Commercial and Political Atlas, The, 485

Communication, 706. See also Telegraph; overland China, 441; radio, 615, 627, 658, 728, 729; technological revolution in, 710; telecommunication, 722; digital, 729; global culture and, 726–729; Internet, 719, 728–729; television, 727, 728, 729

Communism: and appeasement of Nazi Germany and, 628; in Vietnam, 673, 675; Cold War rivalry with capitalism, 669, 671–672, 673; in Cuba, 674, 690–691; in Afghanistan, 696; and collapse of Soviet-bloc, 700–701 (map)

Communist Manifesto (Marx and Engels), 553, 554

Communist Party (China), 609–610. See also China, People's Republic of; Mao Zedong; Long March (1934–1935) and, 629–630; civil war (1945–1949) and victory of, 634–635, 683–684; famine and, 663; Deng Xiaoping's reform of, 698–699

Communist Party (Soviet Union), 607, 622, 699. See also Soviet Union; famine and, 663; Gorbachev's perestroika and, 700, 701; fall of (1990), 700–702 and map

Companies. See Business (companies)

Company Men (India), 504–506

Compass, 343, 364

Computers, 708; Internet and, 719, 728–729

Concentration camps, 637–638 and illus.

Concordat of 1801 (France), 468

Condorcet, Marie-Jean-Antoine, 542

Conference on Security and Cooperation in Europe (CSCE), 674

Confucianism: in East Asia (other than China), 433, 437; Qing China, 442 (illus.), 443, 452, 536, 539

Congo, 717. *See also* Kongo

Congo Free State, 579; Europeans in, 580, 584, 585–586

Congo River, 503, 593

Congress of Vienna (1814–1815), 469

Congress Party (India), 714–715

Congress (United States), 475, 605, 692, 725

Conquistadors, 354–356, 392

Conservatism: and Congress of Vienna, 469; European (1871–1900), 558, 560–562; and fascism, 626

Conservative Party (Great Britain), 560, 613

Constantinople: *See also* Istanbul; Ottoman siege of, 413, 446; Russia and, 446, 449

Constitutionalists (Mexico), 654

Constitutions, 679; French, 467, 469, 557; Haitian, 460; Mexican, 654, 655; Ottoman Empire, 529; Russian, 562; United States, 464–465, 476, 543, 613, 723; Brazilian, 659; Japanese, 683

Construction and building techniques. *See also* Architecture; Housing, *and specific buildings;* British in Argentina, 476–477 *and illus.;* Industrial Revolution and, 487

Consumer electronics, 697

Continental Congress, 464

Contract of indenture, 515. *See also* Indentured labor

Contra War (Nicaragua), 692, 696

Cook, James, 512

Cooke, William, 489

Copernicus, Nicholas, 370–371

Copper, 550, 580, 692; coinage, 439

Córdoba (Argentina), 395

Corn. *See* Maize (corn)

Cornwallis, Charles, 464

Corporations, 549. *See also* Business; foreign, in Mexico, 653, 656, 678; Japanese *zaibatsu*, 565, 609, 697; South Korean, 697, 698 *(illus.);* transnational, 695, 709, 730

Cort, Henry, 486

Cortés, Hernán, 354–355

Cosmopolitanism: in Malacca, 353; Ottoman, 416, 424

Cossacks, 412, 447

Costa Rica, 679

Cotton (cotton industry). *See also* Spinning; Textiles; slavery and, 492; Caribbean, 354; Egyptian, 495, 500, 529, 577, 579; in Britain, 482 *(map)*, 484, 486, 494, 512; Indian, 404, 425, 486, 496, 506, 507–508, 592, 650; in United States, 475, 486, 490, 492, 529, 592; mechanization of, 486, 496, 508; Russian, 583; women in, 492

Council of the Indies, 388

Credit, in Japan, 437. *See also* Banks

*Creoles* (mixed race), 471, 473, 543; in colonial Latin America, 392, 393

Crete, 597

Crime, in early modern Europe, 376, 378

Crimean War (1853–1856), 527–529, 530, 531, 532, 540

Croatia, 702

Cromwell, Oliver, 381

Crowther, Samuel Adjai, 503, 582

Crystal Palace (London), 487

Cuba, 503, 623. *See also* Castro, Fidel; abolition of slavery in, 475, 476–477, 514; sugar production in, 514, 591; United States and, 563, 589, 591, 592, 674; communism in, 674, 690–691; missile crisis in (1962), 674

Cuban Revolution (1959), 678–679

Cultural imperialism, 726, 727–728, 729. *See also* Westernization (western culture)

Cultural relativism, 614

Cultural Revolution (China, 1966), 684

Culture: *See also* Art and artists; Folk culture; Literature; Society; Westernization; *and specific cultures;* Russian, 531–532; New Imperialism and, 572–574; global, 726–732; Hollywood films and, 615, 727; popular, 729–730, 731; English language and, 730–731, 732; Japanese, 731–732

Currency: coinage, 439, 528; Ottoman crisis and reform, 416, 528; paper, 439, 467; launch of Euro, 720; crisis in, 719–720

Curzon, Lord (George Nathaniel), 647

Cyrillic alphabet, 531

Czechoslovakia, 606, 700; Nazi Germany and, 628, 629; Soviet domination of, 672; division of (1992), 701 *(map)*, 702

Czech Republic, 701 *(map)*, 702, 705, 714

Da Gama, Christopher, 352

Da Gama, Vasco, 344 *(illus.)*, 345, 352, 353

Dagur peoples, 442

Daimyo (warlords), 433, 434, 437, 451, 563

Dakar (Senegal), 644, 645

Dalai Lama, 439–440

Dams: Aswan (Egypt), 579, 682; hydroelectric, 550, 620, 682; in Japan, 609, 683

D'Annunzio, Gabriele, 619

Darby, Abraham, 486

Darby, Abraham, III, 487

Dardanelles Strait, 603

Darwin, Charles, 558

Darwin, Erasmus, 480

Date Masamune, 437

Davar, Cowasjee Nanabhoy, 496

D-Day (World War II, 1944), 634

Death squads, 724; in Latin America, 692, 710

De Beers Consolidated, 580, 645 *(illus.)*

Debt. *See also* Foreign debt: Spain (sixteenth century), 383; Japanese samurai, 437; to Western powers, 519

Decembrist revolt (Russia), 532

Declaration of Independence (1776, United States), 464, 466, 471, 475

Declaration of the Rights of Man (1789, France), 466, 471, 723

Decolonization, 668, 675–683. *See also* Independence; Nationalism; in Africa, 675–678 *and map*, 680–682; chronology (1947–1971), 671; in Latin America, 678–679; in Middle East, 684; in Southern Asia, 675; of Third World, 679, 682–683 *(illus.)*

Deforestation, 362, 401, 669; in Europe, 375, 490; in Americas, 490; in China, 445; in

World War II, 638; tropical, 593, 646, 659, 666

De Gaulle, Charles, 677

De Lesseps, Ferdinand, 592

Delhi, 507, 648

Democracy (democratic reforms): colonial Virginia, 397; Revolutions of 1848 and, 469; Latin America, 471; Great Britain and France, 560; China, 699; India, 714–715; globalization and, 714–716

Deng Xiaoping, 698–699, 714

Denmark, 558, 631, 671

Depression (economic): *See also* Great Depression; Ming China, 439; French Revolution and, 466; (1870s–1890s), 550, 562–563, 574

Developing nations (Third World), 709, 729. *See also* Nonindustrial world; deforestation in, 669; in Cold War, 679, 682–683; social problems in, 690; environmental damage in, 709; foreign investment in, 718–719; immigrants from, 690, 707–708, 710; population growth in, 690, 703, 704, 705–706, 710; rural-to-urban migration in, 706–707

Diagne, Blaise, 646

Diamond mining, in Africa, 580, 645 *(illus.)*, 715

Dias, Bartholomeu, 345

Díaz, Porfirio, 653

Dictatorship. *See* Authoritarian regimes

Diem, Ngo Dinh, 673

Directory (France), 468

Dirty War (Argentina, 1976–1983), 692

Disease: *See also* Malaria; Medicine (physicians); Black Death (bubonic plague), 539, 538; Amerindians and, 354, 355 *and illus.*, 356, 387; dysentery, 405, 490, 662; measles, 387; smallpox, 355 *and illus.*, 356, 387, 405, 490, 644; influenza, 387, 605, 613, 648; slaves and, 402, 405; yellow fever, 387, 471, 472 *(illus.)*, 592; industrialization and, 490; cholera, 490, 508–509, 515, 662; native peoples and, 512; in colonial Africa, 582, 644; famine and, 662; and war, 538, 605; HIV/AIDS, 724 *and illus.*

Diu, 353, 354

Division of labor, 485, 555

Divorce, 379, 526, 612, 630. *See also* Marriage

Doctors without Borders, 724

Domestic servants, 378, 492, 497, 553

Dominican order, 443

Dominican Republic, 592. *See also* Hispaniola

Doré, Gustav, 491 *(illus.)*

*Doss House, The* (Makovsky), 561 *(illus.)*

Douglass, Frederick, 475

Drought, 726; in Africa, 407, 429, 664; famine and, 662, 664; in India, 646

Du Bois, W. E. B., 646, 677

Duma (Russian parliament), 562

Dupleix, Joseph François, 426–427

Durbars (pageants) in India, 508 *(illus.)*

Durkheim, Emile, 614

Dutch, the. *See* Netherlands (the Dutch)

Dutch colonies, 588 (map), 636 (map), 676 (map). See also Dutch East Indies; Dutch Guiana, 403, 510; Cape Colony (South Africa), 510–511, 580–581; abolition of slavery in, 514
Dutch East India Company (VOC), 374 and illus., 403, 430, 436; in China, 440, 444
Dutch East Indies, 430, 583, 588 (map). See also Indonesia; World War II and, 634, 636 (map); nationalist movement in, 675
Dutch studies (Japan), 437
Dutch West India Company, 374, 400, 403, 405
Dyer, Reginald, 648
Dysentery, 405, 490, 662

Earhart, Amelia, 614
Earthquake, in Lisbon (1755), 369
Earth Summit (Rio de Janeiro, 1992), 726
East Asia: See also Southeast Asia and specific countries; European trade with, 440; chronology (1853–1910), 551; Indian Ocean trade and, 575; chronology (1900–1927), 599; events in (1931–1945), 629–631; Chinese Communists in, 629–630; Sino-Japanese War (1937–1945), 630; Pacific Rim economies, 696–699
Eastern Africa. See also specific countries; Swahili Coast, 341, 353, 429, 504; ivory trade in, 429, 504, 512; Portuguese in, 429–430; secondary empires in, 504; Muslims in, 427, 429–430; coffee in, 642
Eastern Europe, 605, 705, 719. See also Europe and specific countries; World War II bombing in, 632 (illus.); Holocaust in, 637–638; chronology in (1979–1990), 691; Cold War and, 648, 665, 672, 674; fall of communism in, 699, 700–701 and map; democracy in, 714; English in, 730
East Germany, 672. See also Germany
East India Company, British (EIC), 444, 462, 511; in India, 496, 498, 504–506, 507
East India Company, Dutch (VOC), 374 and illus., 403, 430, 436; in China, 440, 444
East Indies (maritime Southeast Asia), 338, 583. See also Indian Ocean states; Southeast Asia; and specific islands; Muslim traders in, 427; Chinese immigration to, 440; Dutch colonies, 430, 583, 588 (map), 634, 636 (map), 675 (See also Indonesia)
East Timor, independence of, 717
Ebu's-Su'ud, 418
Economic crisis: See also Depression; Great Depression; Inflation; Recession; Safavid Iran, 424; Ming China, 439; French Revolution, 465–466; German, 607; Soviet Union, 699
Economic growth: European industrialization and, 374, 550; Japan, 434, 437; revolutionary era, 461; statistics and, 542; British India, 496, 506, 507, 646; United States, 607, 670; World War II, 638; Africa, 643; Europe, 671; Japan, 603, 609, 673, 683, 690, 696–697, 731; Asia, 696–699; China (1980s–1990s), 714; Hong Kong, 697, 732; Singapore, 697, 732; South Korea,

697–698 and illus., 732; Taiwan, 697, 698, 699, 732
Economics (economic theories). See also Capitalism; Free trade; graphmaking and, 484–485 (illus.); laissez faire, 493, 494; Lenin's N.E.P., 607; Marx's, 553, 554–556; Cold War ideology and, 670–672; neoliberalism and women's rights, 694–696; chronology (1994–2002), 715
Economy (economic factors). See also Business; Global economy; Industrialization; Taxation; Trade; government role in, 383, 385; Spanish decline, 383; Ottoman, 417; British, 495; British India, 506; Qing China, 518; New Imperialism and, 574, 590; World War I, 603; Soviet Union, 607; Cuban, 623, 679; German, 628; World War II, 638; Brazilian, 719
Ecuador, independence of, 472
Edict of Nantes (1598), 379
Edison, Thomas, 549, 563
Education (educational institutions). See also Literacy; Schools; Universities and colleges; early modern Europe, 378; Ottoman, 415, 526; British India, 510; Egyptian military, 520; Russia, 532; Qing China, 539; Victorian Age, 556; France, 560; New Imperialism and, 572–573, 577, 582–583, 587; nationalism and, 648, 679; of African leaders, 644–646; of women, 378, 477–478, 539, 704, 725–726; secular, in Mexico, 654, 656; South Korea, 697; disease and, 724; English culture and, 731
Egypt, 354, 540, 575, 684. See also Suez Canal; irrigation in, 593; industrialization in, 481, 495; Mamluks in, 412, 420, 519, 520; Ottoman rule in, 412, 415, 420, 495; under Muhammad Ali, 495, 498, 520, 527, 529; Napoleon's invasion of, 498, 500, 519–520, 522–524; Cairo, 500, 529, 598 and illus.; cotton production in, 495, 500, 529, 577, 579; British and, 577, 579, 598, 612; Aswan Dam in, 579, 682; in World War II, 632; under Nasir, 682–683 and illus.; Israeli-Arab wars and, 686
Einstein, Albert, 614, 637
Eisenhower, Dwight D., 673, 674
Electricity, 549–550; telegraph and, 489; hydroelectric dams for, 550, 609, 620, 682, 683; for lighting, 549, 552, 615
Elephants, 425 (illus.), 508 (illus.)
Elite class: See also Aristocracy; in colonial Latin America, 388, 391, 393; Russian, 450; urban, in China, 439, 440; Haitian, 460, 469, 471; Japanese, 437–438; Latin American, 476; Ottoman, 524; indigenous colonial, 577; British India, 506–507; Argentine, 657; domination of, 613; Iranian, 693; global culture and, 730–731
Elmina (St. George of the Mine), 349, 403
El Salvador, 692
Emancipation Proclamation (United States), 476
Empire State Building (New York City), 615
Enclosure movement (England), 481
Endangered Species Act (United States), 709

Engels, Friedrich, 553, 554–556, 624
Engineering: See also Construction materials and techniques; Industrial Revolution, 490–491; in Japan, 564; in British India, 647, 648
England. See also British Empire; Great Britain; dynasties in, 380 (illus.); Civil War in (1642), 381; iron industry in, 375, 382; education of women in, 378; merchant fleet of, 383; religion and state in, 379–381; society in, 372–373, 374; Atlantic trade and, 403, 404, 405, 406; Dutch wars with (1653–1658), 383, 403; Mughal India and, 426; slave trade and, 403, 405, 406; trade with Iran, 411; graph-making in, 484–485 and illus.; Irish immigration to, 494
English language, 557, 558, 591, 647, 657; as global second language, 666, 728, 730–731
Enlightenment, the, 372, 451, 484, 542; revolutionary era and, 461–462, 471, 475
Entente (France, Great Britain, and Russia), 597
Environment, the (environmental stress). See also Climate and weather; Deforestation; mining, 391–392; sugar plantation, 401; Qing China, 445; slave trade and, 407; soil erosion, 401, 490; industrialization, 490–491; steel mills, 549; global threats, 593–594; World Wars and, 606, 638; Soviet industrialization, 620; Cold War, 669, 674; population growth and, 709; Brazil, 659; preservation of, 687, 708, 709; technology and, 708, 709–710; global warming and, 726–727
Environmental Protection Agency, 687
Epidemics: See also Disease; slave trade and, 405; in China, 439; industrialization and, 490; influenza (1918–1919), 605, 613, 648; HIV/AIDS, 724 and illus.
Ericsson, Leif, 342
Estado Novo (New State, Brazil), 659
Estates General (France), 381, 466, 469
Estonia, 701; Soviet invasion of, 631
Ethiopia, 431, 502 (map), 646, 724; modernization in, 500; famine and drought in, 664; Italian invasions of, 581–582, 628, 642
Ethiopian Christianity, 352, 500, 583, 644, 645
Ethnic cleansing, 716–717. See also Genocide
Ethnicity: and race, 393 (illus.), 394–396, 543–544; and nationalism, 558, 597
Euro (currency), 720
Europe (1500–1730), 364–385; in 1720, 384 (map); bourgeoisie in, 373–375, 378; chronology, 367; culture and ideas in, 372; debt and taxes in, 383, 385; Holy Roman Empire in, 379, 382; Little Ice Age in (1590s), 455; mapmaking in, 376–377 and illus.; peasants and laborers, 375–377; political innovation in, 378–385; religious reformation, 365–366, 368 (map); scientific revolution in, 370–372; social and economic life, 372–378; religious policies, 379–380; state development in, 379; war and diplomacy in, 382–383; witch hunts

and tradition in, 369–370 *and illus.;* women and family in, 377–378

Europe, great powers of: *See also specific great power;* (1720), 384 *(map);* (1871–1900), 548, 560–562, 565, 567; (1900–1913), 596–597

European Community (EC), 670–671, 697, 709

European immigrants: to Americas, 393, 409, 487, 494, 562; in Argentina, 476, 658; colonialism and, 515–516, 570, 576–577; as indentured servants, 397, 399, 400–401; in Ottoman Empire, 525, 526, 529; in South Africa, 510–511, 582; in Africa, 584–586, 642, 677; post–World War I, 613

European Union (EU), 720, 721 *(map);* English language in, 730, 731

Europe (Europeans). *See also* Eastern Europe; European immigrants; Industrial nations; Western Europe; *and specific countries, and empires;* climate and population in, 359–360; and Atlantic economy, 404, 406, 407; China trade of, 438–439, 440, 443–445, 533; Indian Ocean trade of, 431; Japan and, 434, 436–437; Revolutionary Era, 463; Napoleonic, 470 *(map);* industrialization in, 481, 483–484 *(See also* Industrial Revolution); trading companies of, 504; Greek independence and, 524; India and, 504; nationality and census in, 543–544; Ottoman reforms and, 525, 526, 529; Russia and, 529–531; Qing China and, 519, 533, 541; domination of, 548–549; nationalism in, 557–558; population of, 552; possessions in Asia and Pacific, 570, 588 *(map);* chronology (1851–1905), 551; gunboat diplomacy of, 575; chronology (1904–1927), 599; radio in, 615; World War I in, 600 *(map);* fascism in, 626, 627; Great Depression in, 623; World War II in, 631–632, 633 *(map);* chronology (1930–1945), 621; Bretton Woods Conference (1944), 670–671; Cold War and, 674; demographic transition in, 703; guest workers in, 708; inequality in, 706; population of, 704 *(illus.),* 705; heat waves in, 726; global pop culture and, 729

Evenk peoples, 442

*Exclusif* (France), 403–404

Expansion (expansionism): *See also* Colonies; Globalization; Imperialism; Maritime Expansion; New Imperialism; *and specific empires and emperors;* Ottoman, 342, 361, 412–413, 415; Qing China, 440, 441 *(map),* 451, 533; Russia (1500–1800), 445–446, 448 *(map),* 451, 525 *(map),* 531; British India, 511; United States, 562, 563, 587, 589, 591; Western Europe, 457–458; Japan (1868–1918), 565–567; Nazi Germany, 631–632 *and map*

Exploration (expeditions): *See also* Portuguese exploration; *and specific explorers;* Chinese (Zheng He), 340–341, 344 *(illus.);* Spanish maritime, 342, 343, 345–348; Europeans in Africa, 500, 503; in outer space, 674

Extraterritoriality, 529, 534. *See also* Treaty ports

Factory Act of 1833 (Britain), 494

Fagan, Brian, 455

Faisal (Iraq), 603, 606, 612

Falkland Islands (Malvinas) war, 693

Family. *See also* Children; Marriage; Women; in Europe, 377–378; Ottoman, 527; Victorian Age, 553, 556; Stalin on, 625; Turkish westernization and, 612; African colonial, 644; global economy and, 715

Family planning. *See* Birth control

Famine, 662–664, 722; in Europe (1315–1319), 359, 455; in China, 439, 630, 662, 663–664; in Ireland (1847–1848), 494, 552, 662; warfare and, 603, 663; in Russia and Soviet Union, 622, 663; in India, 646, 651, 662, 663

Farmers (farming): *See also* Agriculture; Peasants; Ottoman, 417; Chinese, 439, 445, 609, 663; *kibbutzim,* in Palestine, 612; tractors and, 617; Great Depression and, 623; in Ghana, 642

Fascism, 626–629, 659. *See also* Nazi Germany

*Fatwas* (Islamic decrees), 418–420

Faud (Egypt), 612

Ferdinand (Spain), 345

Ferdinand VI (Spain), 471

Fertility rates (1970s–90s), 703, 704–705, 708

Festivals: Indian durbars, 508 *(illus.);* Zulu, 500

Fiji, 338, 515

Film (motion pictures), 615, 727, 728, 729

Finance. *See* Coinage; Currency; Economic factors; Economy; Fiscal crisis; Foreign debt; Inflation; Taxation

Financial institutions: *See also* Banks; British, 482; Ottoman reform, 528 *(illus.);* world trade and, 550

Financial markets (stock exchanges), 374, 493, 720; crash of (1929), 623

Finland (Finns), 631, 671; famine in, 455

Finney, Ben, 338

Firearms (guns): *See also* Rifles; Gunpowder; Weapons and military technology; Amerindians and, 399; muskets, 417, 507, 528, 534, 575; British colonies, 511; Ottoman, 415, 416, 417; Safavid Iran, 424; Japanese, 434; African trade in, 406, 499, 504; interchangeable parts for, 487; machine guns, 575, 576 *(illus.),* 581, 601, 602

Fiscal crises: *See also* Depression; Economic crisis; French Revolution and, 465–466

Five-Year Plans (Soviet Union), 620, 622, 623

Floods (flooding), 539; in Bangladesh, 663, 727 *(illus.);* in China, 445, 630, 638

Folk cultures (traditional customs): witchcraft and, 369–370 *and illus.;* Mexican, 653; global culture and, 727, 731–732

Food crops: *See also* Agriculture; *specific food crops;* Columbian exchange, 407–409; from Africa to New World, 408; from Americas to Old World, 362, 375, 408–409, 445, 552; production, and population growth, 703

Food (diet; nutrition): *See also* Famine; *and specific foods;* and climate change, 359, 376; shortages in colonial Africa, 644; World War I shortages, 603, 604; prison camp shortages, 622, 638; scarcity in Soviet Union, 607, 620–621, 622

Footbinding, of Chinese women, 536, 630

Ford, Henry, 613, 616, 617, 659

Foreign debt (international loans): British war, 462, 484 *(illus.);* French war, 466; Eurasian, 519; Ottoman, 529; Chinese, 539, 663; Egyptian, 577–578; Central American, 591, 592; German, after World War I, 607, 623; Latin American, 694; neoliberalism and, 695

Foreign investment: in Argentina, 476–477 *and illus.;* in China, 698–699, 719; in Cuba, 690; in developing countries, 718–719; in Latin America, 678, 692

Forests. *See also* Deforestation; Russian, 375; North American, 563; products of, 592; tropical, 512, 593, 646, 659, 666

"Forty-Seven Ronin" incident (Japan), 438 *(illus.)*

Fourier, Charles, 493–494

Fox, Vincente, 714

France, 493, 510. *See also* French colonies; French Revolution; canals, 374, 490; dynasties, 379, 380 *(illus.);* aristocracy, 374–375; peasant revolts, 377; religion and state, 381–382; tax reforms, 385; Mughal India and, 426–427, 504, 505–506; trading companies, 403–404; war with Britain (1756–1763), 399, 461; American Revolution and, 464; Haitian Revolution and, 471, 472 *(illus.);* Revolution of 1848, 469; graph-making, 484; industrialization, 482; railroads, 489, 550; steamships, 487; Mexico and, 473 *(illus.);* slavery and, 460, 469, 471, 514; invasion of Egypt by, 498, 519–520, 522–524; in Crimean War, 527–528, 530; Russia and, 530–531; Qing China and, 534, 535 *and map,* 538, 539, 565; census, 542; language and nation, 557; war with Prussia (1870–1871), 558; as great power, 560; British rivalry with, 564, 658; Ottoman Empire and, 597; in World War I, 597, 600–602 *and illus.,* 603, 605; birth control in, 613–614; World War I peace and, 606, 607, 617; Depression of 1930s, 623; appeasement of Germany by, 628; in World War II, 631, 633 *(map),* 634; Middle East and, 612; Suez Canal and, 577, 682–683; nationalization, 670; United Nations and, 669; Serbia and, 716; Iraq invasion and, 718

Franciscan order, 443

Francis I (France), 379

Franco-Prussian War (1870–1871), 558

Franz Ferdinand, assassination of, 596, 597

Franz Josef (Austria), 569

Free Trade Area of the Americas, 720

Free trade (free market), 562, 623, 663; as British policy, 495, 511–512; imperialism and, 590–591; women and, 694–696; China and, 719; zones, 720, 721 *(map)*

French and Indian War (1756–1763), 399, 461

French colonies, 623. *See also* French Indochina, 570, 676 *(map);* in North America, 387, 389, 398–399, 409; abolition of slavery in, 469, 471; Algeria, 457, 500, 677; in Africa, 578 *(map),* 579, 580, 581, 642, 644; in West Indies, 399, 400, 404, 462, 514 (*See also* Haiti)

French Indochina, 583, 588 *(map),* 632; independence of, 673, 675, 676 *(map);* Vietnam, 535, 673, 675

French language, 526, 557

French Revolution, 460, 465–469, 503, 510, 542; protest leading to, 466; radical reforms of, 467–468, 557–558; reaction to, and dictatorship, 468; retrenchment and reform, 469; society and fiscal crisis, 465–466

French West Indies, 399, 400, 404. *See also* Haiti (St. Domingue); migration to, 462, 514

Freud, Sigmund, 614

Friedman, Thomas L., 722

Fulani people, 584

Fulton, Robert, 487

Fur trade (furs): colonial North America, 387, 398–399 *and illus.,* 409; Russian, 446, 450

Galdan (Mongolia), 440, 442, 446

Galilei, Marie Celeste, 378

Galileo Galilei, 371

Gandhi, Mohandas K. (Mahatma), 641; assassination of, 651; nonviolence and, 648–649; technology and, 650 *and illus.*

Garvey, Marcus, 646, 677

Gender differences. *See also* Women; in late medieval Europe, 377–378; Victorian separate spheres, 553, 556–557 *and illus.;* after World War I, 613–614

Genoa, 342, 354

Genocide, 716–717, 724–725; Nazi Holocaust, 637–638 *and illus.*

George III (England), 444–445

Georgia (Caucasus), 527, 529, 531, 607

Germany (Germans), 613. *See also* Nazi Germany; Prussia; in colonial North America, 398; Lutheranism and, 366; nationalism in, 379; ethnic minorities in, 543; railroads in, 489, 550; as great power, 560; industry in, 549, 603; male suffrage in, 553; Ruhr district, 490, 549; unification of (1866–1871), 548, 557–560; African colonies of, 578 *(map),* 579, 581, 603, 642; colonies of, 570, 589, 609; before World War I, 597; World War I and, 545, 600 *(map),* 601–603, 604–605; Ottoman modernization and, 597; World War I peace and, 605, 606, 617; economic crisis in (1923), 607; Great Depression in, 619–620, 623, 627–628; radio cartel and, 658; in World War II, 631–632, 633 *(map),* 634, 635, 637, 639; Cold War division of, 670, 672; reunification of (1990), 701 *and map;* environmental awareness in, 709;

immigration to, 708; invasion of Iraq and, 718

Ghana (Gold Coast), 345, 642, 644; Asante kingdom in, 406, 581; European imperialism in, 579–580; independence of, 677

Glassmakers, 416 *(illus.)*

Global culture, 722, 726–732; and American cultural imperialism, 726, 727–728, 729; diversity in, 731–732; English language and, 730–731, 732; media and, 727–729; popular culture and, 729–730

Global economy (world economy), 718–722. *See also* Globalization; technology and (1850–1900), 549–550; Marx on, 553, 554–556; expansion of, 570, 592–593, 706; free market and, 590, 694–696; Great Depression and, 623; raw materials for, 570, 574, 592; Africa and, 646; China and, 439, 719; current problems of, 718–720; new technologies and, 708–709; management of, 720, 722

Global environment, 593–594

Global inequality, 690, 706

Globalization, 722–732. *See also* Global economy; arms control and terrorism, 717–718; culture and, 726–732; democracy and, 714–716; global warming, 726–727; Islam and, 722–723; New Age of, 722; politics of, 716–717; trade associations, 709, 714, 720, 721 *(illus.);* universal rights and, 723–725; women's rights, 725–726

Global warming, 359, 666, 726–727

Glorious Revolution of 1668 (England), 381

Goa, 353, 415, 430

*God of Small Things, The* (Roy), 730

Gold Coast. *See* Ghana (Gold Coast)

Golden Horde (Kipchak khanate), 445–446

Gold (gold trade): African, 343, 404, 406, 429; coinage, 528; from colonial Americas, 354, 356, 383, 391, 392; in Australia, 513; in South Africa, 580, 581, 626

Gomes, Fernão, 345

Gorbachev, Mikhail, 700, 701–702

Government: *See also* Administration; Constitutions; Monarchy; Political systems; Political thought; colonial Americas, 388, 391, 397; economic management by, 374, 383, 385, 439, 493; Qing China, 441, 539–540; Ottoman, 417; in United States, 464–465; British industrialization and, 482; laissez faire economics and, 493; British colonial, 506, 513; Egyptian, under French occupation, 523; and census, 542–543; Ottoman reforms, 529; Russian reform of, 532; Central American, 591; Bolshevik Revolutionary, 604–605; Great Depression and, 622, 623; in industrialized world, 613; and industry, in East Asia, 697, 698; and rural-to-urban migration, 707; economic intervention by, 720; transnational corporations and, 709; communications monopolies, 728; global pop culture and, 729

Granada, 343, 345, 356

Grand National Consolidated Trade Union, 494

Graphmaking, 484–485 *and illus.*

Great Britain, 671. *See also* British Empire; British Navy; Qing Empire (China), Britain and; England; India, British rule in; war with French (1756–1763), 399, 461; American Revolution and, 462, 464 *and illus.;* and Greek independence, 469; Napoleonic France and, 468, 470 *(map);* free trade in, 495; abolition of slavery in, 476; Ireland and, 382, 557, 560, 591, 662; Argentina and, 476–477 *and illus.,* 550, 591, 657, 658; Canada and, 513, 581; Crimean War and, 527, 528, 530; Russia and, 530–531; census in, 543; steel production in, 549; urbanization in, 552; women's rights in, 556–557, 613; as great power, 560; financial power of, 550; male suffrage in, 553; Suez Canal and, 577, 579, 682–683; Egypt and, 577–578, 579, 598, 603, 612; African independence and, 677, 678; Middle East and, 604, 612; Ottomans and, 597, 603–604; Russia and, 530; Latin America and, 672; World War I and, 597, 601, 602–603, 605; World War I peace and, 606, 617; Great Depression in, 623; Nazi Germany and, 628–629; World War II and, 631, 632, 633 *(map),* 634, 635, 637, 669; Brazil and, 658; Mexico and, 656; Cold War and, 670, 674; Falklands War and, 693; Serbia and, 716; Iraq invasion (2003) and, 718, 723

Great Britain, Industrial Revolution in (1760–1851): child labor in, 481, 494; enclosure movement in, 481; graphmaking, 484–485 *and illus.;* iron industry in, 484 *(illus.),* 486–487; laissez faire, 493; population and cities, 481, 482, 490; pottery industry, 484–486; protests and reforms, 494; railroads in, 482, 488, 494, 550 *(map);* social changes, 492; socialism in, 494; steam engines, 485, 487, 488 *(illus.);* telegraph in, 489; tenements, 490, 492 *(illus.);* textile industry, 482 *(map),* 484, 486, 494

Great Depression (1930s): in Argentina and Brazil, 623, 626, 658; in Germany, 619–620, 623, 627–628; in industrial nations, 545, 623; in Japan, 623, 629; in nonindustrial regions, 623, 626; in Soviet Union, 622

Great Lakes (North America), 399, 487, 709

Great Leap Forward (China), 663–664, 684

Great Northern War (1680–1701), 382, 450

Great powers: *See also* New Imperialism; of Europe (1720), 384 *(map);* of Europe (1871–1900), 548, 560–562, 565, 567; Japan as (1868–1900), 563–567; United States as (1865–1900), 562–563, 565, 567; Asian colonial possessions of (1914), 588 *(map);* of Europe (1900–1913), 596–597

Great Trek, 502 *(map),* 510, 511 *(illus.)*

*Great Western* (steamship), 488, 489 *(illus.)*

Greco-Roman traditions, 365, 370, 524

Greece (Greeks), 597, 671, 672; Ottoman Turks and, 412; independence of, 469, 520, 524, 540; Muslims expelled from, 610

Greek language, 731

Greenhouse effect, 726–727
Green Revolution, 666
Gregory XIII, Pope, 371
Gropius, Walter, 615
Guangzhou. *See* Canton (Guangzhou)
Guatemala, 387, 678
Guerrilla warfare: in Middle East, 612; in China, 630; in Vietnam, 673; in South Africa, 678; in Afghanistan, 696; of Palestinians, 686; in Sri Lanka, 717
Guevara, Ernest "Che," 678
Guianas, 402–403, 415, 515
Gujarat, 353, 354, 415, 427
*Gulags* (Russian/Soviet prison camps), 446, 633
Gunpowder, 412, 451, 534, 575
Guns. *See* Firearms (guns)
Guomindang (China), 609; civil war and defeat of, 634–635; Communists and, 629, 630
Guzmán, Jacobo, 678

Habsburg dynasty, 379, 380 *(illus.)*
Haiti (St. Domingue), 401, 592; slave rebellion in, 460–461, 471, 472 *(illus.);* revolution in (1789–1804), 469, 471, 503
Hakka people, 536
Hanoverian dynasty, 380 *(illus.)*
Harding, Warren, 619
Hart, Robert, 539
Hausa city-states, 500
Havel, Vaclav, 701
Hawaiian Islands, 338, 514, 587, 592; Pearl Harbor, 589, 634
Hay, John, 591
Hayford, J. E. Casely, 646
Heavenly Kingdom of Great Peace (China), 536–537, 538
Helena (Ethiopia), 352
Helsinki Accords, 674, 687
Henry IV (France), 379
Henry of Navarre (France), 379
Henry the Navigator, 343, 344
Henry VIII (England), 379–380, 382
Herero people, 581
Heresy, 379
Heshen, 518
Heyerdahl, Thor, 338
Hidalgo y Costilla, Miguel, 473, 475
Hidden Imam, 421
Hideyoshi, 433
Hindi language, 426
Hindu-Muslim relations, 507, 714–715, 717; in Mughal India, 424, 425–426; Indian independence and, 647–648, 649, 651, 652 *(illus.)*
Hirobumi, Ito, 564
Hirohito (Japan), 634
Hiroshima, atomic bombing of, 634, 635 *(illus.),* 636 *(map),* 674
Hispanic population, in U.S., 708
Hispaniola, 354, 355, 402. *See also* Dominican Republic; Haiti (St. Domingue)
Hitler, Adolf, 627–629, 631, 632, 634, 639; Jews and, 620, 627, 628, 637–638
Ho Chi Minh, 673, 675

Holocaust (World War II), 637–638 *and illus.*
Holy Roman Empire, 379, 382
Honduras, 592
Hong Kong, 534, 697, 730, 732
Hong Xiuquan, 536, 538
Hormuz, 353, 415
Horses. *See also* Cavalry; Conquistador, 354, 355, 356; in Americas, 399, 408; Afghan, 441; urban pollution and, 552, 616
Horton, James Africanus, 503
House of Burgesses (Virginia), 397
Housing (dwellings). *See also* Architecture; Industrial Revolution, 481, 490, 491 *(illus.);* tenements, 552; for Brazilian poor, 659
Huerta, Victoriano, 654
Human rights, 674, 700, 716, 723–725; and death penalty, 726; in Latin America, 692, 710; United Nations Declaration of, 665, 723–724
Hungary, 529, 543, 606, 672, 700, 705
Hunting: *See also* Fur trade; by Amerindians, 399, 408, 563; of seals and whales, 513, 514–515 *and illus.*
Huntington, Samuel P., 722
Husayn, Imam, 421
Husayn, Saddam, 696, 702–703; and invasion of Iraq (2003), 717, 718, 719 *(photo)*
Hussein ibn Ali, 603
Hutu-Tutsi rivalry, in Rwanda, 716–717
Hydroelectricity, 550, 609, 620, 682, 683
Hyundai corporation, 697, 698 *(illus.)*

Iberian expansion, 342–348. *See also* Portuguese exploration; Spanish exploration
Ibn Abd al-Wahhab, Muhammad, 519
Ibrahim (Egypt), 520, 524
Ice Age, Little (1590s), 375, 439, 455
Iceland, 342
Ignatius of Loyola, 369
Immigrants (immigration): *See also* Chinese immigrants; European immigrants; Indian immigrants; Migration; Irish, 492, 494, 662; to Americas, 397, 476, 494, 552; acculturation and, 494–495; Asian, 494, 513, 562, 708; in Hawaii, 589; to Australia and New Zealand, 513, 516, 552, 576, 605; to Caribbean, 494, 514; to United States, 494, 538, 552, 558, 562, 605; Jews to Palestine, 604, 610, 612; World War I refugees, 605; to industrialized nations, 706, 710; English language and, 730–731
Imperialism: *See also* Colonies; Expansion; New Imperialism; *and specific empires;* in Africa, 500, 502 *(map),* 503; Japanese, 565–567; in Latin America, 589–592; cultural, 726, 727–728, 729; science and, 731
Import duties, 495, 623, 697. *See also* Tariffs
Import-substitution industrialization, 659, 660, 692
Inca, 355–356, 388, 393
Indentured labor, 514–516
Indentured servants, 397, 399, 400–401
Independence (independence movements). *See also* Decolonization (1947–1990);

Dutch, 383; Haitian, 460, 469, 471; American Revolution and, 464; Latin American, 471–475 *and map,* 642; Greek, 469, 520, 524, 540; Serbian, 520, 527, 540; Philippine, 589; in sub-Saharan Africa, 642–646, 677; Vietnamese, 674; Indian, 646–652; in Soviet bloc, 700–702; in East Timor, 717
India: *See also* India, under British rule; Indian immigrants; Mughal Empire; Chinese in, 341; Portuguese in, 353–354; cotton textiles, 427, 486; British trade, 498; deforestation, 593; independence movement, 646–652; ivory trade, 504; Pakistan and, 651–652, 717; democracy in, 675; Hindu-Muslim strife, 651, 652 *(illus.);* Kashmir and, 651, 675, 717; war with Pakistan, 675; birth control, 704, 705; English language, 730
India, independence movement in (1905–1945), 646–652; chronology, 643; Gandhi and, 648–649, 650 *and illus.,* 651; Muslim League and, 647, 649, 651; Nehru and, 649, 651; partition (1947), 644, 651–652 *and illus.,* (map); World War II and famine in, 646, 651, 662, 663
India, under British rule, 504–510, 516, 570, 583; (1687–1805), 505 *(map);* bureaucracy in, 507, 510; ceremonials, 508 *(illus.);* cholera, 490, 508–509; chronology (1756–1885), 501; company men, 504–506; cotton textiles, 496, 506, 507–508, 592; expansion, 511; industrialization, 481, 496, 507–508, 648, 649; tea production, 506, 507; irrigation, 507, 593; nationalism (1828–1900), 507, 509–510, 587, 647–648; opium trade, 506, 507, 529, 533; political reform, 507; traditions, 507, 509; railroads, 496, 508, 509 *(illus.),* 550, 588 *(map),* 593, 651; raj and rebellion, 506–507; Russian threat, 531, 560; trade, 506, 507–508, 512; famine in, 646, 651; influenza epidemic in (1918–1919), 605, 648; women in, 508, 509, 573
Indian Civil Service (ICS), 507, 647, 649
Indian immigrants, 513–515, 516, 586, 603; in Caribbean, 494, 514, 515, 730–731
Indian National Congress, 510, 647, 648, 649, 651
Indian Ocean states. *See also* East Indies; *and specific states;* exploration of (before 1500), 339, 340–341; Portuguese in, 345, 353–354; European colonies in, 588 *(map)*
Indian Ocean trade: Portuguese and, 348, 361, 415, 430; Dutch in, 373, 374, 403, 430; Muslims and, 340, 427, 429–430; Europeans and, 417, 431; European colonization and, 428 *(map);* Chinese and, 440; Suez Canal and, 575
Indigo, 397, 512
Individual (individual rights). *See also* Human rights; Rights; Voting rights; Enlightenment view of, 461; Declaration of Independence (United States) and, 464; in France, 466, 468, 469; citizenship and, 543, 628, 637

Indochina. *See also* Burma; Cambodia; Southeast Asia; Thailand; Vietnam; French in, 583, 588 *(map)*, 632, 673, 675; Japanese occupation of, 632, 663; independence of, 673, 675, 676 *(map)*

Indonesia (Indonesians), 415, 707, 719. *See also* Dutch East Indies; Java; New Imperialism in, 583, 586–587; independence of, 675; East Timor independence and, 717

Industrialization. *See also* Industrial nations; Industrial Revolution; in British India, 481, 496, 507–508, 648, 649; in Egypt, 495, 520; in Europe, 481; in Japan, 564–565, 587; nationalism and, 548, 558; nonindustrial world and, 495–496, 550; in Russia, 529, 530, 561–562; in Brazil and Argentina, 658, 665; in Soviet Union, 545, 607, 620, 622; working women and, 553; import-substitution, 659, 660, 692; in Japan, 683, 731–732; in Asia, 697–699 *and illus.*, 732; environmental effects of, 709; Western culture and, 731–732

Industrial nations (developed world), 612–617. *See also* Industrialization; Industrial Revolution; domination of, 548–549, 660; New Imperialism of, 545, 570, 574, 583, 590, 592; overseas trade of, 495, 512, 519, 660; social transformations (1850–1900), 550, 552–557; women's separate sphere in, 553, 556–557 *and illus.*; technology in (1850–1900), 549–550; labor movements, 552–553; urbanization in, 552; scientific revolution in, 614; technology in, 614–617, 708; class and gender in, 613–614; Depression (1930s), 623; environment in, 615–617, 709; immigration to, 552, 690, 707–708, 710; population in, 552, 703, 704–705; Chinese trade with, 699; farm subsidies in, 722; global warming and, 726; pollution agreements by, 725; Group of Eight (G-8), 720

Industrial Revolution (1760–1851), 457, 480–497. *See also* Great Britain, Industrial Revolution in; United States, Industrial Revolution in; agriculture and, 481–482; causes of, 481–484; changes in society, 482, 492–493; chronology, 483; cities in, 490, 491 *(illus.)*; continental Europe, 482–484; cotton industry, 486; division of labor, 485; impact of, 489–493; iron industry, 484–487; mass production, 484–486; migrations, 482, 490, 494–495; new economic and political ideas, 493–495; nonindustrial world, 495–496; population growth, 490; railroads, 488–489; rural areas, 490–491; steam engines, 487–488; technology of, 484–489, 574; telegraph, 489; trade and inventiveness in, 480; women in, 492; working conditions in, 491–492

Industrial robots, 708, 722

Industries. *See also* Industrialization; Iron industry; Manufactured goods; Porcelain; Textile industry; chemical, 549, 603, 635, 709; silk trade, 424, 439, 565 *(illus.)*; steel, 434, 549, 648, 659, 683; tobacco in colonial

Mexico, 408 *(illus.)*; wool, 408, 484; World War II boom, 638; robots for, 708, 722

Infantry. *See also* Armed forces; Chinese, 340; Ottoman Empire, 413; Crimean War and, 528; in World War I, 601, 602 *(illus.)*

Inflation: sixteenth century Europe, 383; in Ottoman Empire, 416; in Safavid Iran, 424; in Ming China, 439; German crisis (1923), 607; in Guomindang China, 630, 634

Influenza, 387, 605, 613, 648

Inquisition, 371, 379

*Institutes of the Christian Religion* (Calvin), 366

Institutional Revolutionary Party (PRI), 678, 714

Intellectual life (intellectuals): Enlightenment, 372, 461–462; Russian Slavophiles, 531, 532, 562; and socialism, 553

Interchangeable-parts manufacturing, 487

International Criminal Court (the Hague), 725

International Monetary Fund (IMF), 670, 720

International Statistical Congress (1860), 543

International Style in architecture, 615

International Working Man's Association, 553

Internet, the (World Wide Web), 719, 728–729

Iran: *See also* Safavid Empire (Iran); European merchants in, 411, 412; Mughal India and, 426; Qajar dynasty in, 531; oil wealth of, 685 *(map)*, 686; Islamic Revolution (1979), 693, 697 *(illus.)*, 723; nuclear weapons research by, 717; women's rights in, 725

Iraq, 684, 696; after World War I, 611 *(map)*, 612; oil wealth of, 612, 685 *(map)*, 686, 718; Persian Gulf War (1990–1991) and, 702–703; invasion of (2003), 718, 723

Ireland (Irish), 375, 492, 671; Great Britain and, 382, 494, 557, 560, 591, 662; famine in (1847–1848), 494, 552, 662

Irigoyen, Hipólito, 658, 659

Iron curtain, 665, 668, 669, 674, 687. *See also* Cold War; Warsaw Pact

Iron industry. *See also* Steel industry; British, 375, 382, 482 *(map)*, 486–487; deforestation and, 375, 486; Industrial Revolution and, 482 *(illus.)*, 486–487

Iroquois Confederacy, 398, 399

Irrigation, 500, 507, 508, 579, 586, 593, 646

Isabella (Spain), 345

Isfahan, 421–424

Islamic law (Shar'ia), 423, 429; in Mughal India, 426; in Ottoman Empire, 416, 418–420, 526

Islamic Revolution (Iran, 1979), 693, 697 *(illus.)*

Islam (Islamic civilization): *See also* Muslims; Ottoman Empire; Islamic law; Indian Ocean trade and, 340; printing technology and, 365; *fatwas* (decrees), 418–420; pilgrims, 425, 519; Shi'ite, 415, 419, 421, 693; Sunni, 421; African trade and, 430; in

Russia, 447; in West Africa, 500, 516; *jihad* (holy war), 500, 581; slaves in, 504; Egypt and, 522–524; in East Indies, 586–587; ulama (scholars), 522–524, 526; Wahhabism, 519; spread of, in Africa, 583, 644, 645, 646; women in, 579, 612, 613, 693, 697 *(illus.)*, 725; in Iran, 693; Persian Gulf War and, 703; September 11 (2001) attacks and, 713–714; in Afghanistan, 717–718; militancy of, 715–716, 722–723

Ismail, Shah, 421

Ismail (Egypt), 500, 569–570, 577

Israel, 717, 723; Suez Canal crisis (1956), 682–683; Arab conflict, 684–686 *and map*

Istanbul (Constantinople), 413, 420, 519; and Isfahan compared, 421–424; Russia and, 446, 449; mosque in, 423 *(illus.)*; Janissary power in, 520; Ottoman reforms and, 526; French press in, 527–528

Italy (Italian peninsula), 570, 670; maize in, 375; stock exchanges in, 374; city-states of, 342–343; immigrants from, 562, 657; unification of, 557–558; in World War I, 597, 605; invasion of Ethiopia by, 581–582, 628, 642; Mussolini's fascism in, 626–627; World War II and, 632, 633 *(map)*, 634; decolonization of, 676 *(map)*; aging demographic in, 704, 705; immigration to, 728

Iturbide, Agustín de, 475

Ivan IV (Ivan the Terrible; Russia), 412

Ivory Coast (Côte d'Ivoire), 677

Ivory trade, 349 *(illus.)*, 429, 504, 512

Izmir (Smyrna), 417

Jamaica, sugar plantations on, 401–402

James I (England), 380

James II (England), 381

Jamestown, Virginia, 396

Janissaries, 415–416, 417, 519; Mahmud II's defeat of, 524; uprisings by, 420, 520, 524

Japan (Japanese), 362. *See also* China, Japan and; chronology (1543–1792), 435; climate changes in, 455; civil war in, 433; reunification of, 433–438; Korea and, 433–434, 440, 452; elite decline and social crisis in, 437–438, 563–564; foreigners and, 452, 563–564; Tokugawa shogunate, 434–438, 451, 452, 563–564; chronology (1853–1910), 551; immigrants from, 516, 589; Meiji Restoration and modernization of, 564–565; birth of imperialism in (1894–1905), 565–567, 570; Korea and, 565, 566–567, 629; railroads in, 566 *(map)*; silk industry in, 565 *(illus.)*; expansion of, 588 *(map)*, 629; war with Russia (1904–1905), 562, 566, 587, 597; as great power (1868–1900), 563–567; industrialization in, 564–565, 587, 609; World War I and, 609, 617; Great Depression in, 623, 629; ultra-nationalism in, 628; World War II and, 632, 634, 635 *(illus.)*, 636–637 *and map*; occupation of Burma by, 651, 663; Korean War and, 673, 683; booming economy and trade of, 673, 683, 690, 696–697, 731; low fertility in, 704; aging population in, 705;

environmental awareness in, 709; industrial robots in, 708; recession in, 719; development model of, 731–732

Java, 430, 510, 511; population in, 586, 593

*Jazz Singer, The* (film), 615

Jenkinson, Anthony, 411

Jerusalem, 527, 604; Israeli control of, 684, 686

Jesuits (Society of Jesus), 427. *See also* Ricci, Matteo; in North America, 399; Reformation and, 369; in Japan, 437; in China, 440, 442–443 *and illus.*, 452, 533

Jesus (Christ), 366

Jews. *See also* Israel; mapmaking by, 343; Egyptian, 523; expelled from Spain, 373, 383; in Germany, 373, 543; Ottoman, 525, 526; anti-Semitism and, 627; in Palestine (1930s), 604, 610, 612; Nazi Germany and, 620, 627, 628; Holocaust and, 635, 637–638; Soviet, 700

Jiang Jieshi. *See* Chiang Kaishek

Jiang Qing, 684

Jiangxi region (China), 629, 630

*Jihad* (Muslim holy war), 500, 581

Jim Crow laws (United States), 562

Jingdezhen, 436, 439

Jinnah, Muhammad Ali, 651

João III (Portugal), 350

John Paul II, Pope, 700

Johnson, James, 645

Johnson, Lyndon, 673

John VI (Portugal), 472

Joint-stock companies, 374 *and illus.*, 429, 431, 532; industrialization and, 483

Jordan, 684, 723

Joyce, Ellen, 577

Juan, Jorge, 394

Juarez, Benito, 473 *(illus.)*

Junta Central (Spain), 471

Justo, Juan, 591

Jutland, Battle of (1916), 603

Kahlo, Frida, 655

Kanagawa, Treaty of (1854), 564

Kangxi (China), 440–443 *and illus.*, 452

*Kapital* (Marx), 553

Kashmir, 651, 675, 717, 723

Kazakhs (Kazakhstan), 531, 535, 583

*Keiretsu* (Japanese corporate alliances), 697

Kemal Atatürk, Mustafa, 610 *and illus.*, 612

Kennedy, John F., 673; Cuba and, 674, 679

Kenya, 429, 644, 718; independence of, 677

Kenyatta, Jomo, 677

Kepler, Johannes, 371

Khomeini, Ayatollah Ruhollah, 693, 697 *(illus.)*

Khrushchev, Nikita, 674

Kikuyu people, 677

Kimberley diamond fields, 580, 645 *(illus.)*

Kitchener, Lord Horatio, 575

Knights, 343. *See also* Conquistadors

Knights of the Hospital of St. John, 415

Knights Templar, 344

Kollantai, Alexandra, 624–625

Kongo, slave trade in, 349–352. *See also* Congo

Korea (Koreans): *See also* South Korea; climate change in, 455; China and, 565; Japan and, 433–434, 440, 452, 565, 566–567, 629; North, 672, 717

Korean War (1950–1958), 665, 672–673, 674, 683, 697

Kosovo, Battle of (1389), 412–413

Kosovo crisis (1999), 716

Kremer, Gerhard (Mercator), 376–377 *(map)*

Kuwait, 686, 702

Kyoto Protocol (1997), 725, 726–727

Labor (labor force): *See also* Labor unions; Slaves; Workers; Spanish colonial *(encomienda)*, 354, 391, 392; Andean mit'a, 392; child labor, 481, 489, 492, 494, 553; division of, 485, 555; indentured, 397, 399, 400–401, 514–516; African colonial, 582, 642, 644, 645 *(illus.)*; Asian immigrant, 494, 513–516, 562, 708; Japanese occupation and, 634; robot technology and, 708, 722

Labor unions (trade unions), 695, 708, 720; in Australia, 513; in late nineteenth century, 494, 495, 552–553; in United States, 563; Polish Solidarity, 700, 701

Labour Party (Great Britain), 651, 670

Laissez faire economics, 493, 494, 497. *See also* Free trade; famine and, 662

Landowners (landownership): European gentry, 374–375; indentured Europeans, 401; Amerindians, 462, 473; imperial China, 419; Ottoman, 416, 419, 527; Russian serfs, 447, 449; Safavid Iran, 420; colonial Latin America, 471; English enclosure movement, 481; French Revolution, 466; Indian *mansabs*, 425, 426; British India, 506, 646, 647; colonial Africa, 582, 678; Russia, 583, 604; Jewish *kibbutzim*, 612; Argentine *oligarquía*, 657, 659; Brazil, 658, 659; Mexico, 653, 654

Land reform: in China, 629, 630, 634, 699; in Latin America, 655, 656, 678

Languages: *See also* English language; of Africa, 393, 402, 430, 431; in India, 426, 647; Malayo-Polynesian, 340; Osmanli, 416; Russian, 452, 531, 561; Safavid Iran, 421; and immigrants to Americas, 495; French, 526, 557; in India, 647; nationalism and, 543–544, 557, 558, 679

Las Casas, Bartolomé de, 391

Latin alphabet, 610 (illus.), 612, 731

Latin America. *See also* Americas, the; Central America; Latin America, colonial; *and specific countries;* independence, 471–475, 474 *(map)*, 642; immigration to, 494; women's rights in, 477; chronology (1870–1912), 571–572; imperialism in, 589–592, 594; European immigrants in, 605; military coups in, 623, 626, 659, 660; Depression of 1930s in, 623, 626; development in, 638; economic dependence of, 652, 659; radio cartel in, 658; chronology (1876–1946), 643–644; revolutionary movements in (1950s–1960s), 678–679, 690; chronology (1964–1990), 691; communists in, 678–679, 692; foreign investment in, 678, 692; United States and, 678–679, 690, 692–693, 696; military coups and dictatorships in (1960s–1970s), 692–693, 710; population growth in, 708; population in (1730–2050), 704 *(illus.)*; music from, 730; soap operas from, 729

Latin America, colonial, 388–396, 390 *(map)*. *See also* Brazil, colonial; *and specific colony;* in Caribbean, 354; chronology (1518–1620), 389; economy in, 391–392; gold and silver from, 356, 383, 391–392, 404, 439; livestock in, 408; Mexico, 388, 391, 408 *(illus.)*, 473, 475; North America compared to, 396; Peru, 390 *(map)*, 391, 392; race/ethnicity in, 393 *(illus.)*, 394–396; society in, 388, 392–393; state and church in, 388, 391, 393

Latvia, 701; Soviet invasion of, 631

Laws (legal codes): *See also* Islamic law (Shar'ia); Spanish colonial, 391; mercantilist, 403–404; Enlightenment and, 461; Napoleonic Code (France), 468; British factory, 494; Ottoman reforms, 525–527; gender and, in industry, 553; German social, 560; Jim Crow (United States), 562; environmental protection, 709

League of Nations, 606, 607, 608, 669; German departure from, 628; Japanese departure from, 629; mandate system and, 610; Sino-Japanese War (1937–1945) and, 630

Lebanon, 611 *(map)*, 612, 684, 696

Le Corbusier (Charles-Edouard Jeanneret), 615

Lee, Ang, 729

Lee, Bruce, 729. *See also* under Li

Legislative Assembly (France), 467, 468

Leith-Ross, Sylvia, 577

Lenin, Vladimir I., 604, 607

Leningrad, siege of, 631. *See also* St. Petersburg

Leopold II (Belgium), 579, 580, 584

Leo X, Pope, 366–367

Lepanto, Battle of (1571), 416

Le Roy, Loys, 364–365

*Lexus and the Olive Tree, The* (Friedman), 722

Liberalism, 557–558. *See also* Neo-liberalism

Liberia, 503, 716

Library, Jesuit in Beijing, 443 *(illus.)*

Libya, 597, 632

Lighting, electric, 549, 552, 615

Liliuokalani (Hawaii), 569

*Limits of Growth, The,* 687

Lim Nee Soon, 587 *(illus.)*

Lincoln, Abraham, 476

Lindbergh, Charles, 614–615

Linlithgow, Lord, 649

Lisbon, earthquake in (1755), 369

Literacy: *See also* Education; Schools; of European women, 378; nationalism and, 558; in Japan, 564; in Africa, 644, 645

Literature: Safavid (Iran) poetry, 421; Jesuits and, 443 *(illus.)*; in English, 730–731

Lithuania: Poland-Lithuania, 446, 447; Soviet invasion of, 631; independence of, 701

Livestock: in colonial Americas, 391, 408; in Argentina, 408, 591, 657; in Britain, 481; and Soviet collectivization, 621–622
Livingstone, David, 500, 503
Li Zicheng, 432–433, 440
Lloyd George, David, 606
Locke, John, 382, 461, 464
London, 543; growth of (1680), 373; Crystal Palace, 487; growth of (1850–1914), 490, 552; tenements in, 491 (illus.)
Long March (China), 629–630
Looms, power, 486, 492, 565
Lorraine. See Alsace and Lorraine
Los Angeles, automobiles in, 616 and illus.
Louisiana, 399, 486
Louis Napoleon (France), 469
Louis Philippe (France), 469
Louis XIII (France), 379
Louis XIV (France), 379, 381 (illus.), 382, 465
Louis XVI (France), 460, 466, 468
Lowell, Francis Cabot, 492
Ludendorff, Erich von, 605
Lula da Silva, Luiz Inácio, 714
Lusitania (ocean liner), 603
Luther, Martin, 366, 371, 379
Lutheranism, 366, 368 (map), 378–379

Macao, 353, 430, 440, 533
Macartney, George, 444–445
McDonald's restaurants, 729, 730
Macedonia, 597
Machine guns, 575, 576 (illus.), 581, 601, 602
McKinley, William, 589, 591
Madagascar, 340, 677
Madero, Francisco I., 654, 656
Madras, 426, 504, 506, 508
Magellan, Ferdinand, 337, 348
Mahan, Alfred T., 587
Mahdi, 576 (illus.), 581
Mahmud II, Sultan, 520, 524, 526
Maine (battleship), 591
Maize (corn), 586; in Africa, 409; in Caribbean, 354; in Europe, 408, 481; in Italy, 375
Makovsky, 561 (illus.)
Malabar Coast, 353, 354
Malacca, 353, 415, 431, 511
Malaria, 387, 644; quinine and, 442, 557; slaves and, 402, 405
Malawi (Nyasaland), 583
Malaya (Malay Peninsula), 338, 415, 431, 511, 634; British in, 583, 587 (illus.); Chinese immigrants in, 586
Malay Federation, 675
Malayo-Polynesian languages, 340
Malaysia, 583. See also Malaya
Malcomb, John, 464 (illus.)
Mali (western Sudan), 581
Malthus, Thomas, 703, 705
Malvinas (Falkland Islands), 693
Mamluk Sultanate (Egypt), 522, 523–524; Ottoman Empire and, 412, 420, 519
Manchuria, 432, 434, 452; Japan and, 565, 566, 567, 629
Manchurian Incident (1931), 629

Manchus, 434, 452, 536. See also Qing Empire; and end of Ming Empire, 432–432, 439–440
Mandate system, 610, 611 (map), 612
Mandela, Nelson, 678, 715
Mansa Kankan Musa, 342
Mansa Muhammad, 342
Manuel (Portugal), 353
Manufactured goods (manufacturing). See also Industrialization; Industrial Revolution; Mass production and specific manufactures; Atlantic trade, 404; Carpet making, in Iran, 424; Chinese wallpaper, 444; interchangeable parts for, 487; American foreign markets, 587, 652, 657; British foreign markets, 508, 512, 516, 574 (illus.), 652; import of, in Latin America, 590, 652, 657; in India, 649; by women in wartime, 638; dependence on imported, 679; foreign investment in, 692; consumer goods, 708; computers and, 708; global expansion in, 718; science and, 731
Maori people, 512, 513
Mao Zedong, 546, 629–630, 635, 683–684; death of, 698; and Great Leap Forward, 663–664, 684
Mapmaking, 343; Jesuit in China, 336, 442; Mercator and, 376–377 (illus.)
Maria Theresa (Austria), 542
Marie Antoinette (France), 467
Marinetti, Filippo, 619
Maritime expansion (to 1550): before 1450, 338–342; Americas and, 354–356; Atlantic Ocean, 341–342; chronology, 339; East Africa, 352; Iberian (1400–1550), 342–348; Indian Ocean, 340–341, 353–354; Pacific Ocean, 338; Portuguese voyages, 343–344; Spanish voyages, 337, 345–348; West Africa and, 348–352
Markets: See also Merchants; Trade; in colonial Brazil, 400 (illus.); African slave, 406; and African women, 642; global culture, 729–730
Maroons (runaway slaves), 402–403
Marriage: in early modern Europe, 377–378, 379; Hindu-Muslim, 426; Ottoman, 417, 526, 527; and class in Britain, 482; and nationality, 544; Victorian Age, 556–557; and divorce, 379, 526, 612, 630; working-class women and, 556; and abortion, in Soviet Union, 625; in China, 630; delayed, and family planning, 703
Married Women's Property Act (Britain), 557
Marshall Plan for Europe, 670, 673
Martí, José, 591
Martin, P.-D., 381 (illus.)
Marx, Karl, 553, 554–556, 624, 629
Mary, mother of Jesus, 391
Massachusetts, colonial, 397, 462
Mass media, 699, 723. See also Motion pictures; Newspapers; Radio; Television
Mass production. See also Industrial Revolution; assembly-line, 439, 613, 616; of British pottery, 484–486; division of labor in, 485; interchangeable parts for, 487; Japanese porcelain, 434, 436 and illus.;

Soviet agriculture and, 620; of transistor radios, 728
Mathematics: European revolution in, 370–371; and graphmaking, 484–485 and illus.; and new physics, 614
Mauritius, 510, 514, 515
Maximilian (Mexico), 473 (illus.)
Maya, religious practice of, 391
May Fourth Movement (China), 609
Mazzini, Guiseppe, 557–558
Mecca, 603; pilgrimage to, 425, 519
Mechanization, of cotton industry, 486, 496, 508
Medici family, 365
Medicine (physicians): See also Disease; European, in Africa, 351; Jesuit in China, 442, 443; women and, 477–478; Ottoman reforms, 526; cult of cleanliness and, 615; antibiotics, World War II, 636; health care in Africa, 644, 724; Doctors without Borders, 724; western vs. traditional, 731
Mediterranean Sea trade, 342, 415, 417
Mehmed II, Sultan, 413
Meiji Restoration (Japan), 564–565
Mein Kampf (Hitler), 627
Melanesia (Melanesians), 338, 512
Melville, Herman, 514
Menelik (Ethiopia), 500, 581
Mensheviks, 604. See also Bolsheviks
Mercantilism, 403–404. See also Capitalism
Mercator (Gerhard Kremer), 376–377 (map)
Merchants: See also Trade; European, 353–354, 372, 373–374, 407; Muslim traders, 340, 342, 353, 422; North American, 397, 462; African, 406, 407; Arab, in East Indies, 427; foreign, in Moscow, 449; in British India, 496; Japanese, 434, 437–438; European in China, 439, 440, 444, 608 and illus.
Mercosur (Mercado Comun del Cono Sur), 721
Metternich, Klemens von, 469
Mexican Revolution (1910–1940), 641, 652–656; civil war (1911–1920), 654; institutionalized (1920–1940), 654–656; social conditions for, 652–653
Mexican Revolutionary Party (PRM), 655
Mexico City, 653, 707; colonial, 388, 408 (illus.)
Mexico (Mexicans), 471; Aztecs in, 355, 388, 408 (illus.); colonial, 391, 473, 475; Amerindians in, 473, 591, 653, 678; Catholic Church in, 473 (illus.), 654, 656; independence of, 473, 475; Maximillian as emperor of, 473 (illus.); United States and, 563, 592; civil war in, 654–655; constitutionalism in, 654, 655; railroads in, 653, 655 (map); Brazil and Argentina compared to, 652, 660; nationalism in, 653; population growth in, 704, 708; under Institutional Revolutionary Party, 678, 714; and NAFTA, 720, 721 (map); democratic reform in, 714; economic swings in, 719, 720
Miao peoples, 518
Middle class, 613. See also Bourgeoisie; Chinese goods and, 443; Revolutions of

1848 and, 469; French Revolution, 557; women and domesticity, 493, 497, 556; liberalism and, 557; urbanization and, 552, 616; Victorian Age, 556–557 *and illus.;* Indian nationalism, 646, 647; in Brazil and Argentina, 657, 658, 659; in Mexico, 653

Middle East. *See also* Islam; *and specific countries and empires;* chronology (1909–1923), 599; after World War I, 610–612; Arab-Israel conflict in, 684–686 *and map;* chronology (1979–1991), 691; Islamic militants in, 715–716

Middle Passage, 404–405

Midway, Battle of (1942), 634, 636 *(map)*

Mies van der Rohe, Ludwig, 615

Migrations (population movements). *See also* Immigrants; Industrial Revolution and, 482, 490, 494–495; rural-to-urban, in Africa, 582, 644, 707; and India-Pakistan partition, 651, 652 *(illus.);* rural-to-urban, 376, 528, 706–707; unequal development and, 706; to industrialized countries, 690, 707–708

Militant nonviolence, Gandhi and, 648–649

Military. *See also* Armed forces; Navy; Warfare; Weapons and military technology; Zulu, 499 *and illus.;* Eurasian expansion, 519; Ottoman, 520, 524, 526; Egypt, 520; Qing China, 534, 536–538 *and illus.,* 609; Russian, 531; Japan, 619, 629; China (Red Guard), 684; rule of, in Latin America, 623, 659, 660, 692–693; in Africa, 715

Military slaves, 424. *See also* Janissaries

Millennium Summit (2000), 722

Milosevic, Slobodan, 716

Mines Act of 1842 (Britain), 494

Ming Empire (China), 438–440; Zheng He's exploration in, 340–341, 344 *(illus.);* end of, 432, 439–440, 452

Mining (minerals). *See also* Coal (coal mining); *and specific metals;* environmental impact of, 391–392, 593; in colonial Latin America, 391–392; Industrial Revolution and, 487; New Imperialism and, 574, 592; in Africa, 626, 638; in Mexico, 656 *(illus.);* British India, 648; in Africa, 580, 582, 626, 645 *(illus.),* 715

Missionaries. *See* Christian missionaries; Jesuits

Mitsui companies, 434

Mobutu, Joseph, 717

*Moby Dick* (Melville), 514

Moctezuma II (Aztec), 355

Modernization (modernity): *See also* Industrialization; Westernization; British in Argentina, 476–477 *and illus.;* in Egypt and Ethiopia, 500; of warfare, 528; of Turkey, 610 *(illus.),* 612; cult of, 614

Mombasa, 429, 431

Monarchy (kingship): *See also specific monarchs and emperors;* Kongo, 349–352; European, 374, 379–380 *(illus.);* nationalism and, 379; royal absolutism, 382; French Revolution and, 466–467, 468, 469; in Russia, 449–450 *and illus.,* 453, 561; Congress of Vienna and, 469; Enlighten-

ment and, 461–462; in Brazil, 472–473; overthrow of, in Iran, 693

Monasteries and convents, 378, 380

Monetary system. *See also* Banks; Coins (coinage); Currency; capitalist *vs.* communist, 670–672

Mongols (Mongolia), 359, 421; China and, 439, 533; Galdan in, 440, 442, 446

Monopolies, government, 728

Monopoly, trading: royal, 345, 349, 403; in colonial Americas, 392; Indian Ocean, 353, 354, 430; chartered companies for, 403; Portuguese, 345, 349, 403, 580; Alaskan fur, 450; African colonial, 579–580

Monroe Doctrine (1823), 591

Morelos, José, 475

Morocco, Portuguese invasion of, 343

Moro wars (Philippines), 427

Morse, Samuel, 489

Moscow, 445–446, 449, 532, 631

Mosques: in Istanbul, 423 *(illus.);* in Iran, 421

Most-favored nation status, 534

Motion pictures (film), 615, 727, 728, 729

Mountbatten, Lord, 651

Mount Huanyaputina, 455

Mozambique, 429, 430, 580, 678, 716

MTV (Music Television), 728

Mughal Empire (India), 414 *(map),* 424–427; chronology (1526–1739), 413; foundations of, 425; Hindu-Muslim coexistence in, 424, 425–426; Portuguese and, 353–354, 425; regional challenges to, 426–427; British challenge to, 504, 505 *(map)*

Muhammad Ali (Egypt), 498, 529; modernization and reforms of, 495, 500, 520

Muhammad (prophet), 427

Muir, John, 563

Munich Conference (1938), 628–629

Murdock, Rupert, 728

Muscovy, 411, 446. *See also* Moscow

Music, global culture and, 728, 730

Muslim Empires, (1520–1656), 414 *(map).* *See also* Ottoman Empire; Mughal Empire (India); Safavid Empire (Iran)

Muslim League, All-India, 647, 649, 651

Muslims (Muslim countries). *See also* Arabs; Islam; Hindu-Muslim relations; traders, 340, 342, 353, 422; astronomy of, 370; expelled from Spain, 343, 345, 383; in Africa, 352, 429, 579, 581; in East Indies, 427; and Russia, 531, 583; expelled from Greece, 610; in Pakistan, 675; in former Yugoslavia, 716; women in, 612, 613, 725; Iranian Revolution and, 723

Mussolini, Benito, 626–627, 628, 634

Mutsuhito (Japan), 564

Myanmar. *See* Burma (Myanmar)

Mysore, 498, 506

Nadir Shah, 426

Nagasaki, 437, 634, 674

Naipaul, V.S., 730–731

Nairobi (Kenya), 644, 725

Namibia (Southwest Africa), 581

Nanjing (Nanking), 537 *and illus.,* 538, 630

Nanking, Treaty of (1842), 534, 538

Napoleon Bonaparte, 468–469, 472 *(illus.);* defeat of, 468, 510; Europe of (1810), 470 *(map);* invasion of Egypt by, 498, 500, 519–520, 522–524; invasion of Portugal and Spain by, 471, 478; invasion of Russia by, 468, 529, 530 *(illus.),* 541, 663

Napoleonic Civil Code, 468

Napoleonic Wars, 470 *(map)*

Napoleon III (Louis Napoleon), 469

Nasir, Gamil Abd al-, 682–683 *and illus.*

Natal, 510, 514

Nation, Carrie, 613

National Assembly (France), 466, 467

National Convention (France), 468, 471

Nationalism (self-determination), 513, 606, 660. *See also* Decolonization; Independence; Revolutionary era (1775–1848), 457, 469; census and, 542–544; European, 557–558; Indian, 507, 509–510, 587, 647–648; Austria-Hungary, 557, 560–561; German, 379, 548, 557, 558–560, 607; language and, 543–544, 557, 558, 679; Italian, 557–558; and imperialism, 574; mandate system and, 610, 611 *(map),* 612; Zulu, 580; Arab, 610, 612, 696; World War I, 545, 597, 606, 617; fascism and, 546, 626; Japanese ultranationalism, 629; Mexican, 653; African, 675; Brazilian, 714; Eastern Europe, 700; Hindu, 714

Nationality: census and, 543–544; citizenship and, 543, 557, 708

Nationalization (expropriation): in France and Great Britain, 670; in Cuba, 690; in Iran, 693; in Latin America, 655–656, 678, 692; in Russia, 604

National liberation, 546, 682. *See also* Decolonization; Independence

National parks (North America), 563

National Revolutionary Party (Mexico), 655

National Socialist German Workers' Party (Nazis), 627. *See also* Nazi Germany

Natives Land Act (South Africa, 1913), 581

Navajo people, 408

Navigation Acts (Great Britain), 403

Navigation (navigational instruments): astrolabe, 343; compass, 343, 364; Polynesian, 338; Viking, 341; British manufacture of, 482

Navy (warships). *See also* British Navy; Pirates; English, 382; timber for, 375; Japanese, 451, 565, 630; Korean, 433; Ottoman, 413, 415, 416, 524; Panama Canal and, 592; Russian, 449, 450, 451, 525, 527; Spanish-American War (1898), 591; steam-powered (gunboats), 495, 534, 564, 575; submarine warfare, 603, 605, 631, 634; World War I, 602–603, 605; United States, 564, 634, 635, 696, 718; World War II, 631, 634; aircraft carriers, 631, 634

Nawab, 504, 505

Nazi Germany, 620, 627–629, 669. *See also* Germany, in World War II; Argentina and, 659; economic and social policies, 628, 638; Jews and, 620, 627, 628, 637–638; pact with Soviets (1939), 629

Ndebele people, 581

Nehru, Jawaharlal, 649, 651, 675; at Bandung conference, 682, 683 *(illus.)*

*Nemesis* (gunboat), 495

Neoliberalism, women's rights and, 694–696

Nerchinsk, Treaty of (1669), 442, 446

Netherlands, the (the Dutch; Holland), 670, 686. *See also* Dutch colonies; East India Company (Dutch, VOC); bourgeoisie in, 373, 374; independence of, 383; mapmaking by, 377 *and illus.*; poverty in, 376; wars with England (1653–1658), 383, 403; in North America, 398, 399; slave trade and, 401, 405; West India Company, 374, 400, 403, 405; China trade and, 444; Atlantic trade and, 403, 404; Japan and, 436 *and illus.* 437; Mughal India and, 504; German invasion of, 631; English in, 731

Newcomen, Thomas, 487, 488 *(illus.)*

New Deal (United States), 623

New England, 397, 462; industry in, 486, 492

New Guinea, 338, 589

New Imperialism (1869–1914), 545, 548, 569–595; in Africa, 571–572, 577–583, 584–586; in Asia, 571–572, 583, 588 *(map)*; chronology, 571–572; colonial administration, 575–577; cultural motives, 572–574; economic motives, 574; global environment and, 593–595; in Hawaii and Philippines, 587, 589; in Latin America, 571–572, 589–592; political motives, 570, 572; possessions of great powers, 588 *(map)*; in Southeast Asia, 583, 586–587; weapons and technology, 576 *(illus.)*; world economy and, 592–593

New Lanark, 494

New Laws of 1542 (Spain), 391

Newspapers, 520, 526; Crimean War and, 527; imperialism and, 574, 591

Newton, Isaac, 371, 614

New York (city), 488, 549, 707; colonial, 398; growth of, 552; skyscrapers in, 615; terrorist attacks in (2001), 712–714

New Zealand, 338, 430, 457, 581, 613; immigration to, 513, 516, 552, 576, 605; Maori in, 512, 513; whaling in, 513, 514

Nicaragua, 592; Sandinistas in, 692–693, 696

Nicholas I, Tsar, 527, 529, 530 *and illus.*, 532

Niger Delta, 503, 581

Nigeria, 573, 593, 644, 730; women in, 584–585; British in, 642; independence of, 677; civil war in, 663; democracy in, 715

*Niña* (ship), 345, 347

Nixon, Richard, 684, 692

Nizam al-Mulk, 426

Nkrumah, Kwame, 677, 682

Nobel, Alfred, 549

Nongovernmental organizations (NGOs), 724

Nonindustrial world: *See also* Developing nations; domination of, 570, 574; Great Depression and, 623, 626; industrialization and, 550

North Africa. *See also specific country*; Portuguese in, 343; World War II in, 621, 632, 633 *(map)*, 646

North America, 550. *See also* British North America; Canada; Mexico; United States; Viking explorers in, 342; French and Indian War, 399, 461; domination of, 495; modern technology in, 614–615; population (1730–2050), 704 *(illus.)*; environment in, 709

North American Free Trade Agreement (NAFTA), 720, 722 *(map)*

North Atlantic Treaty Organization (NATO), 669, 672, 716, 718

Northern Rhodesia (Zambia), 581

North Korea, 672, 717. *See also* Korea

*North River* (steamboat), 487

North Vietnam, 673, 675. *See also* Vietnam

Norway, 613, 631

Nuclear power, 637, 708; waste from, 709, 717

Nuclear weapons: atomic bombing of Japan, 634, 635 *(illus.)*, 636 *(map)*, 637, 674; treaties limiting, 665, 674, 717

Obregón, Alvaro, 654, 655

Ohio River Valley, 399, 487

Oil crisis (1974), 686 *and illus.*

Oil (oil industry), 719, 723; Arab-Israel conflict and, 685 *(map)*, 686; in Iran, 685 *(map)*, 686, 693; in Iraq, 612, 685 *(map)*, 686, 718; in Kuwait, 702; in Mexico, 656; World War II and, 631–632, 634, 637

Oligarchy: Argentina, 657, 659; Japan, 437–438

Olusegun Obasanjo, 715

Oman, Sultanate of, 504

Omdurman, Battle of (1898), 575, 576 *(illus.)*

*On the Origin of Species* (Darwin), 558

Opium trade, 506, 507, 529, 533–534, 609

Opium War (1839–1842), 533–536, 540

Orange Free State, 510, 581

Order of Christ, 344

Organization of European Economic Cooperation (OEEC), 670

Organization of Petroleum Exporting Countries (OPEC), 685 *(map)*, 686 *and illus.*

Orozco, José Clemente, 473 *(illus.)*, 655

Orthodox Christianity: Russian, 446, 449, 450, 452, 531, 532; Serbian, 520, 527, 716

Osman, 412, 429

Osmanli language, 416

Ottoman Empire, 412–420, 451, 519–529. *See also* Istanbul; Janissaries; Turkey; Portuguese rivalry with, 352, 353; central institutions, 415–416; chronology (1500–1710), 413; crisis in (1585–1650), 416–417; economic change in (1650–1730), 417, 420; Egypt and, 412, 415, 420, 495, 498, 519–520; expansion of, 342, 361, 412–413, 415; Greek independence and, 469, 520, 524; Holy Roman Empire and, 379; trade, 411; Islam and, 416, 418–420, 524, 525–526, 529; legal codes in, 525–527; navy of, 413, 415, 416, 524; chronology

(1805–1876), 521; Russia and, 412, 449, 469, 520, 524, 529, 531; (1829–1914), 525 *(map)*; European reform model for, 457–458, 520, 524–527, 528 *(illus.)*, 597; Tanzimat reforms, 524–526, 527, 532; Crimean War and (1853–1856), 527–529, 540; Balkan crisis and, 597; World War I and, 603–604; division of, after World War I, 545, 610, 611 *(map)*, 617

Owen, Robert, 494

Pacific Ocean (Pacific Ocean states), 337, 583. *See also specific island*; exploration of, before 1500, 338, 348; chronology, 339; immigrants from, 514, 515; colonial possessions in, 589; exploration of, before 1450, 338; World War II in, 632, 634, 636 *(map)*; whaling in, 513, 514–515 *and illus.*; population (1730–2050), 704 *(illus.)*

Pacific Rim economies, 696–699. *See also* East Asia; *specific countries*

Pahlavi, Muhammad Reza, Shah, 693

Paintings. *See also* Art and artists; of Versailles, 381 *(illus.)*; colonial Spanish, 393 *(illus.)*; Safavid Iran, 422 *(illus.)* 423; Mughal India, 425 *(illus.)*, 426; of St. Petersburg, 561 *(illus.)*; Mexican, 473 *(illus.)*, 655, 656 *(illus.)*

Pakistan, 696, 717, 723; Bangladesh and, 675; partion of 1947 and, 651–652 *(illus.)*; age distribution in, 705 *(illus)*

Palestine Liberation Organization (PLO), 686

Palestine (Palestinians), 603; Jewish homeland in, 604, 612; partitioning of (1947), 670; Israeli-Arab conflict, 684–686; terrorism and, 686, 723

Palm oil, 499, 503, 512, 516, 586, 593, 642

Pan-African Congress, 606, 646

Panama, 356; United States and, 592, 692

Panama Canal, 592, 593, 594, 692

*Pan o palo* policy (Mexico), 653

Papacy (popes): *See also individual popes*; treaty negotiation by, 347–348; and Protestant Reformation, 365–366, 369; Henry VIII's challenge to, 379–380

Paper currency, 439, 467

Paraguay, 720, 721 *(map)*

Paris, 373, 375, 615; French Revolution and, 467, 468; Parlement of, 465; Revolution of 1848 and, 469; as "City of Lights," 552

Paris Peace Conference (1919), 606, 610

Parliament (Britain), 380–381, 486; American Revolution and, 462; Chartism and, 494

Peace of Augsburg (1555), 379

Pearl Harbor, 589; Japanese attack on, 634

Peasants (peasantry): *See also* Farmers; Rural societies; Serfs; European, 375–377; rebellions by, 377, 417; French Revolution and, 465, 466; and industrialization, 481; Egyptian, 495; Indian, 496, 506, 646; Japanese, 564; Serbian, 520; African colonial, 582; Mexican, 653, 654, 655, 656; Soviet Russian, 604, 607, 620–622, 663; Brazilian, 659; Chinese Communists and, 610, 629, 630, 663; Latin American, 652

Pedro I (Brazil), 472
Penn, William, 398
Pennsylvania, 487, 549; colonial, 398
Pentagon, attack on (2001), 702–703
*Perestroika* (Soviet reform), 700, 701
Perón, Eva Duarte, 660
Perón, Juan, 659–660
Perry, Matthew C., 564
Persia, 525. *See also* Iran; languages of, 421
Persian Gulf (Persian Gulf states), 353, 686, 696. *See also specific countries*
Persian Gulf War (1990–1991), 702–703, 717, 728
Peru: colonial, 390 *(map)*, 391, 392; independence of, 472; railroad in, 590 *(illus.)*
Peter the Great (Russia), 449–450 *and illus.*, 527; westernization of: 449–450, 453, 532
Petroleum industry. *See* Oil (oil industry)
Philadelphia, 488; colonial, 398, 464
Philip II (Spain), 379, 383
Philippines, 337, 348, 675; Spanish and, 427, 429, 440, 583; United States and, 563, 587, 589, 592; World War II in, 634, 636 *(map)*
Physics, 371, 614, 637
Pilgrims (pilgrimages), Islamic, 425, 519
Pilgrims (Protestant sect), 397
Pinochet, Augusto, 692, 693
Pirates, in East Asia, 437, 440, 451, 452, 563
Pizarro, Francisco, 355–356
Planck, Max, 614
Plantations: *See also* Sugar plantations; clove, 504; indigo, 397, 512; pineapple, 587 *(illus.)*; slavery and, 475
Plantocracy *(gens de couleur)*, 460, 469, 471
Platt Amendment (United States), 592
Playfair, William, 484–485 *and illus.*
Poets and poetry: Persian, 421; Italian, 619
Poison gas (chemical weapons), 602, 638, 717
Poland, 528, 543, 705, 718; Russia and, 450, 452; independence of, 606; Nazi invasion of, 629, 631; World War II casualties, 635, 638; Catholicism of, 452, 638; Soviet model and, 672; fall of communism in, 700, 701; democracy in, 714
Poland-Lithuania, 446, 447
Political thought (ideology): Chinese, 444; Locke and, 382, 461, 464; Enlightenment and, 461–462; Industrial Revolution and, 493–495; socialism, 493–494, 553; Darwinism and, 558; Western, in Africa, 644, 646; Gandhi's nonviolence, 648–649
Politics. *See also specific political parties and movements;* European innovation in, 378–385; colonial, 397; Japanese, 434; revolutionary era, 462; in British India, 648; New Imperialism and, 570–572; of famine, 662–664; women's rights and, 613, 694–696; and population growth, 704; chronology (1992–2004), 715; environmental protection and, 709; global, 716–717
Pollution, 490, 549, 552, 563, 709–710, 725; automobiles and, 616, 617, 709
Polynesian peoples, 338, 512
Ponce de León, Juan, 354

Pope, Alexander, 371
Popular culture, 729–730
Population (population growth): and climate (to 1500), 359; Great Britain, 481; imperial China, 359, 445, 451, 533, 538, 539; industrialized Europe, 493; Russia, 452, 529; census and, 542–544; United States, 587, 708; East Indies, 586; British India, 646; environment and, 709; demographic transition and, 703–704; developing nations, 690, 705–706, 710; industrialized nations, 704–705; world (1730–2050), 704 *(illus.)*
Porcelain: Chinese, 436, 439; mass-produced, 434, 436 *(illus.)*, 484–485
Portsmouth, Treaty of (1905), 566
Portugal (Portuguese), 570, 671; African slave trade and, 344, 345, 350, 351–352, 405, 406; in China, 436, 440; Hormuz and, 353, 415; Indian Ocean trade and, 348, 361, 415, 429–430; monopoly trade of, 345, 349, 403, 580; Napoleon's invasion of, 471, 478; Brazil and, 728 *(See also* Brazil, colonial*)*
Portuguese colonies: China, 353, 354 *(See also* Macao*)*; in Africa, 578 *(map)*, 579, 580; and decolonization, 676 *(map)*, 678
Portuguese exploration, 337, 348; in Africa, 344, 346 *(map)*, 349–350, 351–352, 429; in Atlantic, before 1500, 343–345, 346 *(map)*
Positivism, 493
Potatoes, 362, 375, 408, 481, 603
Potato famine (Ireland,1845–1848), 494, 552, 662
Potosí, silver mines in, 391
Pottery, mass production of, 434, 436 *and illus.*, 484–486. *See also* Porcelain
Poverty (the poor): American foods and, 375; in Europe, 376–377; French Revolution and, 465; factory work and, 492; disease and, 490; housing for, 490; laissez faire theory and, 493; nationalism and, 558; in Tsarist Russia, 561 *(illus.)*, 562; of women, 553, 725; Amerindian, 591; in China, 610; in Great Depression, 623; in India, 508, 510, 641, 647, 649; in Mexico, 641, 678; in Brazil, 659; women and, 695; global trends in, 706; in developing nations, 710
Price controls, in Japan, 437
Price war: Chinese opium trade, 533; Arab oil embargo (1974), 686 *and illus.*
Priestley, Joseph, 480
Princip, Gavrilo, 596
Printing, 364, 365; Dutch, 373; Korean, 433; Luther and, 366; woodblock, 438 *(illus.)*
Proclamation of 1763 (Great Britain), 462
Progress, 372; technology and, 614, 617, 653
Prohibition (United States), 613
Prostitution, 376, 378, 508, 536, 553, 582, 695
Protest. *See* Student protest
Protestant Reformation, 365–366, 368 *(map)*, 372, 379; Luther and, 366, 371, 379
Proxy wars, by superpowers, 682–683, 686, 690, 696. *See also* Cold War era
Prussia, 382, 450, 489, 548, 558, 564; French Revolution and, 467, 468, 469

Psychoanalysis, 614
Puerto Madero, 476–477 *and illus.*
Puerto Rico, 354, 476, 563, 591
Puritans (Protestant sect), 380, 381, 397
Puyi, boy-emperor (China), 608
Pythagoras, 370

Qianlong (China), 440, 444, 450, 453
Qing Empire (China), 441 *(map)*, 457–458, 462, 532–540, 587. *See also* Qing Empire, Britain and; chronology (1644–1796), 435; Confucianism in, 442 *(illus.)*, 443, 452, 536; Emperor Kangxi, 440–443 *and illus.*, 452; rise of, 438, 439–440; tea and diplomacy, 444–445; European trade and, 438–439, 440, 444, 519, 533, 541; Russia and, 442, 446, 451–452, 531, 534–535, 583; missionaries in, 440, 442–443 *and illus.*, 452, 533, 534, 536, 538; chronology (1794–1860), 521; economic and social disorder in, 518, 533; decentralization at end of, 458, 539–540, 608–609; Taiping Rebellion, 535 *(map)*, 536–539
Qing Empire (China), Britain and: gunboat diplomacy, 495, 534; McCartney mission, 444–445, 533; Opium War (1839–1842), 533–536, 540; Arrow War (1856–1860), 535 *(map)*, 538; Treaty of Nanking (1842), 534
Quebec, colonial, 398, 399
Quebec Act of 1774 (Britain), 462
Quetzalcoatl, 355
Quinine and malaria, 442, 575
"Quit India" campaign, 649, 651
Quito, colonial, 394–395

Racism (racial discrimination): in colonial Americas, 393 *(illus.)*, 394–396; and slavery, 400, 471; in Americas, 478, 562; census and, 543–544; in Philippines, 589; New Imperialism and, 573, 577; in Nazi Germany, 627; in colonial Africa, 581, 644, 646; in British India, 647; in South Africa, 678–682, 731
Radio, 615, 627, 658, 728, 729
Raffles, Thomas Stamford, 511
Railroads: in Asia (1914), 588 *(map)*; in Britain, 482 *(map)*, 488, 491 *(illus.)*, 550; canal systems and, 490–491; in United States, 488, 562; in Egypt, 500; electric streetcars and subways, 550, 552; in Europe, 488–489; in India, 496, 508, 509 *(illus.)*, 550, 588 *(map)*, 593, 651, 663; in Japan, 566 *(map)*, 588 *(map)*; in Mexico, 653, 655 *and map*; in Russia, 530, 532, 550, 562, 588 *(map)*, 593; environmental impact of, 490–491; in Latin America, 590–591 *and photo;* Manchurian, 629; World War I mobilization and, 601; in Africa, 642–643, 644; in Argentina, 591, 657; famine and, 662, 663
Rainfall: *See also* Drought; in Africa, 455–456
Raw materials (resources), 549, 550, 652. *See also* Mining, *and specific materials;* world economy and, 570, 574, 592, 679; World War II and, 634, 638; of colonial Africa, 642, 646; conservation of, 709

Reagan, Ronald, 692, 696, 699, 706
Rebellions (revolts): See also under Revolution; peasant, 377, 417; slave, 402, 460–461, 471, 472 (illus.); Arab (1916), 612; in Ottoman Empire, 417, 420, 520, 524; in China, 432, 518, 533, 566, 608; in Philippines, 589; Russia, 532; Sepoy (India), 507; Taiping (1850–1864), 535 (map), 536–539; in Romania, 701
Red Army (Soviet Union), 607, 632, 634, 672
Red Guard (China), 684
Red Sea trade, 353, 415
Reforms: See also Land reform; religious, in Europe, 365–366, 369, 372; Enlightenment, 372, 461–462; French Revolution, 467; industrialization and, 494; modernization in Egypt, 500; Brazil, 659; democratic, in Europe, 469, 560; Islamic, in West Africa, 500, 516; British India, 506; Russia, 449–450, 529, 532; Ottoman, 416, 457–458, 520, 524–527, 528 (illus.), 529, 597; economic, in China, 539, 540 (illus.); New Deal (U.S.), 623; Guatemalan, 678; Mexican Revolution, 654, 655, 656; socialist, in Chile, 692; economic, in China, 698–699; Soviet perestroika, 700, 701
Reign of Terror (1793–1794, France), 468
Religion, 614. See also Christianity; Islam; Hindu-Muslim relations; scientific challenge to, 371–372; Maya, 391; in Mughal court, 426; in Russia, 452; on Caribbean plantations, 402; and nationality, 557; Heavenly Kingdom of Great Peace (China), 536–537, 538; in colonial Africa, 644–645; Eastern European nationalism and, 700; secular values and, 732
Religious orders, 344. See also Jesuits
Renaissance, in Europe, 342, 364
Revolutionary era (1730–1850), 460–478; abolition of slavery in, 457, 475–476; economic and social liberation in, 475–478; Enlightenment and old order, 461–462; equal rights for women and blacks, 477–478; in France, 465–468; Haitian Revolution (1789–1804), 460, 469, 471, 472 (illus.); in Latin America, 471–475; Napoleonic France, 468, 470 (map); nationalism in, 457, 469; in North America, 462–465; Conservative retrenchment in, 469
Revolution in Iran (1979), 693
Revolution of 1857 (India), 506–507
Revolution of 1905 (Russia), 562
Revolutions of 1848 (Europe), 469
Rhineland, 558, 606, 628
Rhodes, Cecil, 580–581
Ricci, Matteo, 372, 376, 440, 443 (illus.)
Rice and rice cultivation: in North America, 397; in India, 663; in Japan, 434, 437
Rifles, 446, 549, 576 (illus.), 581, 602 (illus.). See also Firearms; breech-loading, 528, 575; Enfield, 507; percussion-cap, 528, 534
Rights: See also Human rights; Individual; Voting rights; Women's rights; and British colonialism, 507, 510; Napoleonic France, 507; and Ottoman reforms, 525

Rio de Janeiro, 657, 707; colonial, 400 (illus.); slums of, 659; Earth Summit in (1992), 726; homeless children in, 689, 706
Rivera, Diego, 655, 656 (illus.)
Rizal, José, 589
Roads: Aztec, 355; Industrial Revolution and, 485, 490; Japanese, 434; Chinese, 533; Russian, 530; automobile and, 616–617
Robot technology, 708, 722
Romania, 527, 597, 672, 720; democracy in, 714; overthrow of Ceausescu in, 701
Romanov, Mikhail, 447
Romanov dynasty (Russia), 447, 541
Roosevelt, Franklin D., 623, 637, 668
Roosevelt, Theodore, 563, 592
Rousseau, Jean-Jacques, 461, 464
Roy, Arundhati, 730
Roy, Rammohun, 509
Royal African Company (RAC), 403, 405, 406
Royal Botanic Gardens (Kew), 593
Royal trade monopoly, 345, 349, 403
Rubber, 586, 587 (illus.), 593, 623, 657, 659; synthetic, 635
Ruhr district (Germany), 490, 549, 552, 607
Rural areas: See also Farmers; Peasants; poverty of, in Europe, 376; Ottoman, 417; industrialization and, 490–491
Russian Federation (former Soviet Union), 714, 717, 719, 720; life expectancy in, 705; and Soviet collapse (1991), 701–702 and map; and U.S. invasion of Iraq (2003), 718
Russian language, 452, 531, 561
Russian Orthodox Christianity, 449, 450, 531, 532; Siberian missions of, 447, 452
Russian Revolutions (1914–1918), 604–605; women and family values in, 624–626
Russia (Russian Empire), 445–453, 458, 540, 570, 613. See also Russian Federation; Serfs, Russian; Soviet Union (USSR); British India and, 531, 560; society and politics, 446–447, 449; war with Sweden (1680–1701), 382, 447, 450; chronology (1547–1799), 435; Crimean War and, 527–529, 531; cultural trends, 531–532; emigration from, 562, 583; Europe and, 411, 519, 529–531, 541; expansion of, 445–446, 448 (map), 525 (map); forest resources of, 375; as great power, 558, 560–562; industrialization in, 529, 530, 561–562; Napoleon's invasion of, 468, 529, 530 (illus.), 541, 663; Ottoman Empire and, 412, 449, 469, 520, 524, 529, 531; chronology (1801–1861), 521; Peter the Great and westernization of, 449–450 and illus., 453, 527, 532; Qing China and, 442, 446, 451–452, 531, 534–535, 583; railroads in, 530, 532, 550, 562, 588 (map); 593; Central Asia and, 531, 583, 588 (map); war with Japan (1904–1905), 562, 566, 587, 597; Balkans and, 529, 561, 597; double Revolution in, 604–605; civil war in, 606–607, 663; World War I and, 597, 600, 601, 604, 617
Russo-Japanese War (1904–1905), 562, 566, 587, 597
Rwanda, genocide in, 716–717

Saarinen, Eero, 615
Sadat, Anwar, 683
Safavid Empire (Iran), 415 (map), 420–424, 446; chronology (1502–1747), 413; economic crisis and collapse of, 424; Isfahan and Istanbul compared, 421–424; Ottomans and, 416, 417; Shi'ite Islam in, 419, 421
St. Domingue. See Haiti (St. Domingue)
St. Peter's Basilica (Rome), 365
St. Petersburg, 450, 530, 561 (illus.)
Saint-Simon, Claude Henri de Rouvray, 382, 493
Sakharov, Andrei, 699–700
Samori Toure, 581
Samurai warriors, 433, 437, 438, 564
Sandinistas (Nicaragua), 692–693, 696
Sanger, Margaret, 613
Sanitation: and disease, 575; and sewerage, 490, 508–509, 552, 615
Santos-Dumont, Alberto, 658
São Tomé, 345, 349, 350, 392
Sardinia-Piedmont, 527
Satellites, 674, 728
Sati (widow burning), 509, 573, 647
Saudi Arabia, 696, 702–703, 717, 723; oil wealth of, 685 (map), 686; women in, 725
Savannah (steamship), 488
Scandanavia, 366, 375, 731. See also Denmark; Finland; Norway; Sweden
Schools: See also Education; Literacy; in European cities, 378; women and, 378; in Egypt, 520; Ottoman military, 526; Islamic (Quranic), 526, 583, 645; German engineering, 549; English in, 731; in Africa, 582–583, 644–645; national culture in, 729
Schröder, Gerhard, 718
Science: See also Mathematics; Technology; physics, 371, 614, 637; revolution in, 370–372, 461, 614; of graphs, 484–485 and illus.; statistical, 542–543; and political dominance, 558; World War II, 635–637; global culture and, 731
Scotland, 380, 382
Second Treatise on Civil Government (Locke), 382
Security Council, United Nations, 669–670, 672, 684, 718; peacekeeping and, 669, 716
Sékou Touré, 677
Selassie, Haile, 646
Selim I, Sultan, 415
Selim II, Sultan, 418
Selim III, Sultan, 519, 520
Senegal, 579, 644, 645, 646
Sepoys (India), 504; rebellion of, 506–507
September 11 (2001) terrorist attacks, 712–714 and photo, 718
Serbia, 412–413, 597, 601; independence of, 520, 527, 540, 596; Orthodox Christianity in, 520, 527, 716; NATO bombing of, 716
Serfs (serfdom) in Russia, 446, 447, 449, 452; freeing of, 458, 531, 532, 562
Seven Years War (1756–1763), 399, 461, 505
Sexuality: See also Prostitution; homosexuality in Islam, 423; rape and sexual abuse, 553, 696; and AIDS crisis, 724 and illus.; women's liberation and, 725

Shaka Zulu, 499–500

Shandong (China), 539

Shanghai, 535, 538, 608 *(photo)*, 630

Shi'ite Islam, 415 *(map)*, 419, 421, 693

Ships and shipping (merchant marine): *See also* Navy; Steamships; lateen sails, 343, 347; Chinese, 340, 344 *(illus.)*; Polynesian canoes, 338, 341 *(illus.);* Portuguese, 343, 344 *(illus.)*, 353; Dutch, 373; European, 422; slave trade, 404–405, 503; Argentine, 476–477 *and illus.*, 657; British, 510, 511, 512, 560; Japanese, 634, 683; whaling, 514–515 *and illus.;* Korean, 697, 698 *(illus.)*

Shoguns, in Japan, 434, 563

Shona people, 581

Siberia, 446, 447, 452; railroad, 588 *(map)*, 593

Sierra Leone, 345, 503, 514, 582

Sikhs, 507

Silk (silk industry and trade): Chinese, 439; Japanese, 565 *(illus.);* Safavid Iran, 424

Silver: British in China, 444, 533; from colonial Americas, 356, 383, 391–392, 404, 416, 424, 527; and inflation, 383, 416, 424, 439; from Latin America, 439, 656 *(illus.)*

Singapore, 511, 533, 593; independence of, 675; Japanese in, 634; economic growth in, 697, 732

Sino-Japanese War (1894–1895), 565, 589

Sino-Japanese War (1937–1945), 630

Sioux people, 399, 408

*Sirius* (steamship), 488, 489 *(illus.)*

Skyscrapers, 615

Slave rebellions, 402, 460–461, 471, 472 *(illus.)*

Slaves, African: in Brazil, 392, 400 *and illus.*, 657; freedom for, 402, 503, 584; in Haiti, 469, 471, 472 *(illus.);* in Latin America, 388, 395; in North America, 397, 398; punishment for, 402, 405; runaway, 393, 402–403; on sugar plantations, 392, 399–402; US Constitution and, 465, 476

Slave soldiery, 424. *See also* Janissaries

Slaves (slavery): freedom for, 510 *(See also* Abolition); in Mughal India; and serfdom compared, 447, 449; on sugar plantations, 392, 399–402, 492, 514

Slave trade, African, 502 *(map)*; Portuguese and, 344, 350, 351–352, 405; Europe and, 375; sugar plantations and, 392, 400; in colonial Americas, 375, 393; disease and death in, 402, 405; Dutch and, 401, 405; Atlantic system, 403, 404–407; Middle Passage, 404–405; prisoners of war, 400, 406, 407; Eastern Africa, 429; Islam and, 500, 504; Great Britain and, 476, 503, 504; Sokoto Caliphate and, 500; trans-Saharan, 502 *(map)*; end of, 475, 476, 492, 503, 504, 584

Slavic peoples, 412, 531, 561, 597, 627. *See also specific countries*

Slavophiles, 531, 532, 562

Slessor, Mary, 573

Slovakia, 701 *(map)*, 702

Slovenia, 702

Small pox, 355 *and illus.*, 356, 387, 405, 644

Smith, Adam, 493

Social classes (social stratification). *See also specific class;* Europe (1500–1730), 372–378; colonial Americas, 388, 392–393, 397; slave plantation, 401–402; pre-revolutionary France, 465–466; Industrial Revolution and, 482, 492–493; Indian *(jati)*, 506, 509, 646–647, 648; and gender, in industrialized world, 553, 613–614; Mexican, 652–653

*Social Contract, The* (Rousseau), 461

Social Darwinism, 558

Socialism, 552–553, 560, 604, 669; in Chile, 692; utopian, 493–494

Society (societal conditions): global inequality, 690; in industrialized nations, 550, 552–557; labor movements, 552–553; Nazi Germany, 628; socialism and, 553; population and migrations, 552, 586; in colonial Africa, 642, 644; in Argentina, 660; Victorian women, 553, 556–557; working class, 553

Soil depletion, 401, 490

Sokoto Caliphate, 500

Solidarity (Polish labor union), 700, 701

Somme, Battle of (1916), 602

Somoza, Anastasio, 692

South Africa, 550, 577, 724; Zulu in, 499–500, 510, 511, 580; Afrikaners in (Cape Colony), 510–511 *and illus.*, 580, 581; diamond mining in, 580, 645 *(illus.)*, 715; landownership in, 581; gold in, 580, 581, 626; schools in, 644, 645, 731; African National Congress in, 646, 678, 715; democracy in, 715; racial justice in, 678, 680–682, 731; trade zone in, 720, 721 *(map)*

South America. *See* Latin America *and specific countries*

South Asia, decolonization of, 675. *See also specific countries*

South Carolina, colonial, 397

Southeast Asia, 720. *See also* East Asia; East Indies; Indochina *and specific country;* British colonies in, 511; Islam in, 427, 429; Chinese immigration to, 440; New Imperialism in, 583, 586–587; Japanese conquest of, 632, 634, 636 *(map)*; rubber in, 586, 587 *(illus.)*, 593, 623, 657; communist threat in, 673

South Korea, 665, 672, 679, 705 *(illus.)*, 719. *See also* Korea; economic growth in, 697–698 *(illus.)*, 732

South Vietnam, 673, 675. *See also* Vietnam

Soviet Union (Union of Soviet Socialist Republics, USSR). *See also* Russia; collectivization of agriculture in, 620–622; Communist Party in, 607, 620; European distrust of, 628; famine in, 622, 663; five-year plans in, 620, 622, 623; industry in, 545, 607, 620, 638; New Economic Policy in, 607, 622; pact with Germany (1922), 607; pact with Germany (1939), 629; in World War II, 631–632, 633 *(map)*, 634, 635, 638; United Nations and, 669, 670

Soviet Union, Cold War era, 668–674. *See also* Cold War; China and, 669; Cuba and,

692; Eastern Europe and, 648, 672, 699, 700–701 *and map;* economy of, 670, 671–672; environmental damage in, 709, 710; Korean War, 672; *perestroika* in, 700–702; rivalry with United States in, 668, 669, 674, 679, 682–683, 690; war in Afghanistan, 693, 696, 699; break up of, 690, 702, 710, 714, 722

Soylinka, Wole, 730

Space exploration, 674

Spain, 670; maritime exploration by, 342, 343, 345–348; Inquisition in, 371, 379; dynasties in, 380 *(illus.)*; economic decline in, 373; Netherlands and, 373, 383; Asian trade, 436, 440; Louisiana and, 399; Napoleon's invasion of, 471, 478; end of slave trade, 476

Spanish-American War (1898–1899), 563, 589, 591

Spanish colonies, 354–356, 462, 578 *(map)*. *See also* Latin America, colonial; Philippines, 427, 429, 440, 583

Spanish language, 558

Spear, Percival, 649

Spencer, Herbert, 558

Spice (pepper) trade, 353, 354, 427, 430

Spinning devices, 486, 650 *and illus.. See also* Textile industry

*Sputnik* (satellite), 674

Sri Lanka (Ceylon), 506, 510, 593, 717, 730

Stalin, Joseph, 607, 620, 622, 639, 684; on abortion, 625–626; Germany and, 628, 629

Stalingrad, Battle of (1942–1943), 632, 634

Stamp Act of 1765, 462

Stanley, Henry Morton, 503, 579

*Starry Messenger, The* (Galileo), 371

Statistics: census and, 542–543; graphmaking and, 484–485 *and illus.*

Steam engines, 485, 486, 487–488 *and illus.*, 496 *and illus.*

Steamships, 487–488, 489 *(illus.)*, 490, 508, 530, 550; freight costs and, 593; gunboats, 495, 534, 564, 575

Steel industry (steel weapons and tools): Conquistador, 355, 356; Japan, 434, 683; United States, 549; Brazil, 659; India, 648

Stock exchanges, 374, 493, 720

Stock market crash (1929), 623

Strikes: in Ming China, 439; legalization of, 553; Russian Revolution, 604; fascist response to, 626; and Islamic Revolution in Iran, 693

Strogonov family, 446, 447

Stuart dynasty, 380 *and illus.*, 381

Student protests: and apartheid in South Africa, 678; in China, 608, 609, 699; Earth Day, 687

Submarine telegraph cable, 489, 550, 575

Submarine warfare, 603, 605, 631, 634

Sub-Saharan Africa, 719. *See also* Africa, tropical; European expeditions in, 500, 503; rainfall in, 455–456; European trade and, 407, 579, 580; new states in, 499–500; Islam (Muslims) in, 579, 581, 583; economic and social changes, 642, 644; independence movements in, 642–646,

Sub-Saharan Africa (*cont.*)
677; religious and political changes in, 644–646; cities in, 707; democracy in, 715; AIDS in, 724 *and illus.*.

Sudan, 430, 579, 581, 717; Battle of Ondurman in, 575, 576 *(illus.)*; famine in, 664

Suez Canal, 529, 550, 612, 628; New Imperialism and, 577, 579, 592, 593; opening of (1869), 569–570, 573 *(illus.)*, 594; Arab-Israeli tensions and, 682

Sufism, 426, 429

Sugar plantations: in Africa (São Tomé), 345, 349, 350, 392; in Barbados, 399–400; in colonial Brazil, 391, 392, 400; slave labor for, 392, 399–402; technology and environment for, 401–403; in West Indies, 399–402, 409, 462; in Cuba, 514, 591, 678; Asian laborers on, 513–516

Sugar trade, 373, 404, 407, 482

Sukarno, 675, 682, 683 *(illus.)*

Suleiman the Magnificent, Sultan, 415

Sulu Empire (Philippines), 427

Sumatra, 415, 427, 430, 583, 586

Sunni Islam, 415 *(map)*, 421

Sun Yat-sen (Sun Zhongshan), 608–609

Superpowers, 665, 674, 679, 687, 722. See *also* Soviet Union, Cold War era; United States, Cold War era; proxy wars of, 682–683, 686, 690, 696

Surinam (Dutch Guiana), 402–403

Swahili Coast, 341, 353, 429, 504

Swahili language, 431

Sweden (Swedes), 398, 446, 671; war with Russia (1680–1701), 382, 447, 450; declining population in, 704, 705 *(illus.)*

Syria, 519; independence of, 684; Ottomans and, 412, 415, 603; Egypt and, 520, 524, 527; after World War I, 611 *(map)*, 612

Tacky (slave), 402

Taft, William, 592

Taiping Rebellion (1850–1864), 535 *(map)*, 536–539

Taiwan, 440, 635; Japan and, 565, 577, 589, 629, *(map)*; Chinese nationalists on, 684; economic growth in, 697, 698, 699, 732

Taliban (Afghanistan), 717–718

Tamil-speakers, in Sri Lanka, 717

Tanzania, 718

Tanzimat reforms (Ottoman Empire), 524–526, 528 *(illus.)*, 529, 532

Tariffs, 495, 649; lowering of, 526, 529, 534; by United States, 562, 623; European Community and, 670; Japanese, 697

Tasman, Abel, 430

Tasmania, 430

Tata, Jamsetji and Dorabji, 648

Taxation (taxes): Portuguese, 353, 354; peasant revolts against, 377; in France, 382, 385; in England, 380; Safavid Iran, 424; Ottoman Empire, 416, 417, 525, 526; American Revolution and, 462; French Revolution and, 465, 466; and colonial trade, 575, 580; in British India, 506; in colonial Africa, 579, 582, 603; in China, 609, 610, 630, 634

Tax farming, 385, 417, 431, 525

Tea and tea trade, 404, 407, 444, 462, 482, 492, 512; in British India, 506, 507, 593; in Ceylon, 506, 593; New Imperialism and, 586, 592

Teachers, women as, 478, 556, 573

Technology. See *also* Construction and building techniques; Engineering; Manufacturing; Science; Ships and shipping; Technology, Industrial Revolution and; Weapons and military technology; of early modern Europe, 364; colonial sugar plantation, 401; Jesuit, in China, 440, 443 *and illus.*; whaling, 514; global economy and (1850–1900), 549–550; British India, 647; early twentieth century, 596, 597, 614–617; New Imperialism and, 574–575; Japan, 564, 565; progress and, 614, 617, 653; Gandhi's rejection of, 650 *and illus.*; computers, 708, 728–729; environmental change and, 708, 709–710; industrial robots, 708, 722; globalization and, 708–709, 722

Technology, Industrial Revolution and, 482, 496. See *also* Railroads; chronology (1759–1851), 483; division of labor, 485; graph-making, 484–485 *and illus.*; iron industry, 486–487; mass production and, 484–486; mechanization in cotton industry, 486, 496, 508; steam engine, 487–488; tele-graph, 489

Telegraph, 508, 603, 653, 658; submarine, 489, 550, 575

Television, 727, 728, 729

Tenochtitlan, 355

Terrorism: in Stalinist Russia, 622; Palestinian Arab, 686, 723; in Latin America, 692; September 11 (2001) attacks, 712–714; Bin Laden and, 713, 717–718

Terrorism, War on (2001–), 718, 727, 732

Téwodros II (Ethiopia), 500

Texas, 408, 486

Textile industry: See *also* Cotton; Dutch, 373; Indian, 404; power looms, 486, 492, 565; African trade and, 404, 406, 499, 512; women in, 376, 477, 492, 564, 565 *(illus.)*, 630; British, 483, 530; Russian, 530; Japanese, 564, 609

Thailand (Siam), 511, 634; fiscal crisis in, 719

Thatcher, Margaret, 693

Theology, 366. See *also* Religion

Third Estate (France), 465, 466

Third Reich, 628. See *also* Nazi Germany

Third World. See Developing nations; Nonindustrial world; *and specific countries*

Thirty Years War (1618–1648), 382

Tiananmen Square massacre (1989), 699

Tibet (Tibetans), 535; Buddhism in, 439–440

Tipu, Sultan, 498, 505, 510

Tobacco, 354, 373, 406, 586, 591; in Caribbean, 399, 400; in colonial Americas, 397, 408 *(illus.)*; in Middle East, 417, 422 *(illus.)*

Tokugawa Ieyasu, 434

Tokugawa shogunate (Japan), 434–438, 451, 452, 564; porcelain in, 434, 436 *and illus.*.

Tokyo (Edo), 434, 437; population growth in, 552, 564, 707; bombing of (World War II), 634, 637

Tordesillas, Treaty of (1494), 346 *(map)*, 347–348, 429

Toussaint L'Ouverture, François, 460, 471

Toyota Motor Company, 565, 697

Trade: See *also* Free trade; Merchants; Monopoly, trading; Tariffs; Trade, with Africa *and specific commodities*; Dutch, 373–374; Anglo-Dutch rivalry in, 383; colonial Americas, 388; North American colonies and, 397, 398–399, 462; English with Iran, 411; Ottoman, 417; Europe with Japan, 434, 436, 437; Russian, 450; Mughal India, 425; Industrial Revolution and, 481, 483; laissez faire and, 493; British Empire, 482, 495, 511–512; colonial, 575; British India, 506, 507–508; industrialized nations, 495, 512, 519, 660; Opium War and, 533–536; in tropical products, 550, 592; Great Depression and, 623; European with Latin America, 658; Japan, 697; global, 623, 718; e-commerce, 729

Trade, with Africa. See *also* Gold (gold trade); Palm oil; Slave trade, African: ivory trade, 349 *(illus.)*, 429, 504, 512; West African, 348–349; Sub-Saharan with Europe, 407, 579, 580; legitimate trade, 503; nineteenth century, 502 *(map)*

Trade associations, 709, 714, 720, 721 *(illus.)*

Trade (trading) networks. See Atlantic trading system; Indian Ocean trade

Trading companies: See *also specific companies*; British, in Africa, 579; European, in China, 440, 444; European, in India, 504

Trading monopolies. See Monopoly, trading

Traditions. See *also* Folk traditions; in British India, 506, 507, 509; Mexican, 653

Transnational corporations, 695, 709, 729–730

Transportation: See *also* Canals; Railroads; Roads; Ships and shipping; Industrial Revolution and, 482, 487–489, 490–491; in Russia, 530; streetcars and subways, 550, 552; global economy and, 593; and famine, 662; twentieth century, 706, 708

Transvaal, 581, 645 *(illus.)*

Treaty ports, in China, 534, 535–536, 565, 608, 609. See *also* Hong Kong; Macao; Shanghai

Trench warfare, World War I, 602 *(illus.)*

Trent, Council of (1545), 366, 369

Tributary systems: Aztec, 355; Chinese, 433

Trinidad, 510, 515, 730–731

Tropical countries: See *also* Africa, tropical, *and specific countries and regions*; botany of, 593; exports of, 550, 592; forests of, 512, 593, 646, 659, 666

Trotsky, Leon, 607

Truman, Harry S, 668

Truman Doctrine (1947), 672

Tsars, 446. See *also specific tsar*

Tudor dynasty, 380 *(illus.)*

Turkey, 672, 715–716, 718. *See also* Anatolia; Ottoman Empire; rise of, 610–612 *and map;* women's rights in, 612, 613; European Union and, 720

Turkic (Turkish) peoples: *See also* Mamluk Sultanate; Uzbeks; Central Asian, 412, 424, 447; Crimean, 446

Tutu, Desmond, 681–682

Twenty-One Demands (Japan), 609

Ukraine, 447, 607, 631, 714

Ulloa, Antonio de, 394

Union of South Africa, 581. *See also* South Africa

Union of Soviet Socialist Republics (USSR). *See* Soviet Union

United Fruit Company, 678

United Nations (UN), 731, 732; Arab-Israeli conflict and, 684; Charter of, 669, 679; Cold War and, 668, 669–670; General Assembly, 669, 670, 723; human rights declarations of, 665, 723, 725; Millennium Summit (2000), 722; Persian Gulf War and, 703; Security Council, 669–670, 672, 684, 716, 718; peacekeeping efforts of, 669–670, 672, 716, 717; weapons inspection in Iraq, 717, 718

United Provinces of the Río de la Plata, 472

*USS Cole* (destroyer), 718

United States. *See also* American Revolution; United States, Cold War era; United States, Industrial Revolution in; slavery debate in, 475, 503; civil war (1861–1865) in, 475–476, 500, 529; abolition of slavery in, 476; racism in, 478, 538; Qing China and, 538, 539; technology and development in, 550, 560; male suffrage in, 553; chronology (1865–1899), 551; women's rights in, 477, 557, 613; steel production in, 549; census in, 543; as great power, 562–563, 565, 567; immigrants and English in, 558; national parks in, 563; Mexico and, 563, 592; imperialism of, 570, 574, 588 *(map),* 594; Hawaii and Philippines, 587, 589; war with Spain (1898–1899), 563, 589, 591; Central America and Caribbean and, 590, 591–592, 692; World War I and, 603, 605, 606, 607; technology in, 612; automobiles in, 613, 616–617 *and illus.;* filmmaking in, 615; isolationism in, after World War I, 617, 628; Great Depression in, 623; Japanese and, 629, 630, 632, 634; in World War II, 634, 635, 636–637 *and illus.;* World War II, 638; Latin America and, 659, 672; Mexico and, 655 *(map)* 656; manufactured goods of, 657; Philippine independence and, 675, 676 *(map); savings* rate in, 698; and NAFTA, 720, 721 *(map);* Persian Gulf War (1990–1991), 702–703, 717; wealth inequality in, 706; environmental awareness in, 709; Hispanics in, 708; industrial robots in, 708; invasion of Iraq by, 717–718; economic growth in, 720; Serbia and, 716; Muslim militancy and, 723; English language in, 730; cultural imperialism of, 726, 727–728, 729; war on terrorism of, 718, 727, 732

United States, Cold War era (1946–1991), 668–674; economic growth in, 670; Japan and, 673, 697; Korean War and, 672–673, 674; monetary policy, 670; nuclear arms race, 674; rivalry with Soviet Union, 668, 669, 674, 679, 690, 710; United Nations and, 669, 672; Vietnam War and, 673–674; oil crisis (1974), 686; China and, 684, 698–699; interventions in Latin America, 678–679, 690, 692–693, 696; Iranian hostage crisis and, 693, 696

United States, Industrial Revolution in (1760–1851): cotton industry in, 486, 490, 492; steamships in, 487; telegraph in, 489; railroads in, 488, 550, 562; rural areas in, 490; manufacturing innovation, 487

Universal Declaration of Human Rights, 723–724

Universities and colleges: in British India, 510; in Japan, 564; in Russia, 532; statistical science and, 542; women in, 556; Islamic Revolution (Iran) and, 693; English in, 731

*Upanishads,* 509

Urbanization: *See also* Cities and towns; Migration, rural-to-urban; industrialization and, 481, 552, 556; Ottoman, 528–529

Urdu language, 426

Uriburu, José, 659

Uruguay, 408, 477, 720, 721 *(map)*

Usuman dan Fodio, 500

Utilitarianism, 493

Utopian socialism, 493–494

Uzbeks (Uzbekistan), 424, 531, 728

Valois dynasty, 379, 380 *(illus.)*

Vargas, Getulio, 658–659

Venezuela, independence of, 471–472

Venice, 342, 354, 415

Verdun, Battle of (1916), 602

Versailles, Treaty of (1919), 606, 628

Versailles Palace, 381 *(illus.),* 382, 466, 548

Vespucci, Amerigo, 347

Victoria (England), 507, 553

Victorian Age, 553, 556–557, 614

Vienna, 379, 415

Vienna, Congress of (1814–1815), 469

Vietnam, 535, 538, 587, 673, 675

Vietnam War, 665, 673–674, 703

Vikings, 341–342, 359

Villa, Francisco "Pancho," 654, 655 *(map)*

Virginia, colonial, 396–397, 399

Vivaldo brothers, 342

Volta, Alessandro, 489

Voltaire, 372, 444, 461–462

Voting rights (suffrage), 494; Europe, 469, 553; for Blacks, 478; Amerindian, 543; British colonies, 513, 647–648; Germany, 553, 560; Mexico, 654; for women, 513, 573, 607, 612, 613, 683; Argentina, 658

Walesa, Lech, 701

Warfare: *See also* Civil wars; Cold War; Guerrilla wars; World Wars; in late medieval Europe, 382, 383, 403, 450; prisoners of, as slaves, 400, 406, 407; Napoleonic,

470 *(map);* disease and, 538, 605; Islamic *jihad,* 500, 581; modernization of, 528; Russo-Japanese, 562, 566, 587, 597; in South Africa, 581; Spanish-American (1898), 563, 589, 591; trench, World War I, 601–602 *and illus.;* Nazi *Blitzkrieg,* 631; famine and, 603, 663; French-Algerian, 677; India-Pakistan, 675; superpower proxy wars, 682–683, 686, 690, 696; Falkland Islands, 693; in Middle East, 684–686, 696, 702–703, 717; Nicaraguan, 692, 696; Soviet, in Afghanistan, 693, 696, 699, 700

War of the Spanish Succession (1681–1694), 382

War on terrorism (2001–), 718, 727, 732

Warrior elite: *See also* Janissaries; Indian rajputs, 425; Japanese, 433, 434, 437, 438, 451, 563–564; Russian Cossacks, 412, 447

Warsaw Pact, 672, 674; collapse of, 699, 700–701 *and map,* 710

Wars of Religion (1562–1598), 379, 381

Washington, George, 464

Watt, James, 480, 485, 487, 488

Wavell, Lord (Archibald Percival), 663

Wealth: Industrial Revolution, 481; concentration of, 553; global inequality in, 690, 706; redistribution of, 678, 690, 692

*Wealth of Nations, The* (Smith), 493

Weapons and military technology: *See also* Bombs and bombing; Cannon; Firearms; Nuclear weapons; Rifles; Conquistador, 355, 356; early modern Europe, 382; gunpowder, 412, 451, 534, 575; Ottoman Empire, 413, 415, 416, 526; Zulu, 499 *(illus.);* industry and, 548; Russian, 449, 450, 530; transition to modern warfare, 528; for whale hunting, 514; New Imperialism and, 575, 576 *(illus.);* Qing China, 534, 537 *(illus.),* 538; Ethiopian, 500, 581; machine guns, 575, 576 *(illus.),* 581, 601, 602 *and illus.;* hand grenades, 602 *(illus.);* poison gas, 602, 638, 717; Soviet industry, 622; machine guns, *(illus.);* poison gas, 602, 638; World War I, 602, 638; World War II, 628, 631, 635–637, 639; Cold War, 669, 674, 699; military aid, 682; United States arms trade, 682, 692, 693; Persian Gulf War, 703

Weapons of mass destruction, 717–718. *See also* Nuclear weapons

Weather. *See* Climate and weather; Rainfall

Weaving. *See also* Spinning; Textiles; Navajo, 408; industrialization and, 486, 496, 508, 527

Webb, James L. A., Jr., 455

Weber, Max, 601

Wedgwood, Josiah, 480, 484–486

Wehrmacht (Nazi German army), 628, 629, 631–632, 634, 638

Weizmann, Chaim, 604, 606

West Africa. *See also specific countries;* Europe and, 349–352; Islamic reform in, 500, 516; slave trade and, 406, 503; new states in, 500, 502 *(map);* sanitation and disease in, 575; New Imperialism and, 579–580; vegetable oil trade in, 503, 512,

West Africa (*cont.*)

516; independence of, 677; mission schools in, 644; urban growth in, 707; trade agreement in (ECOWAS), 720, 721 (*map*)

Western Europe, 451. *See also* Europe; *and specific countries;* telegraph in, 489; deforestation in, 490; domination of, 495, 519; economic growth in, 550, 670–671; Marshall Plan for, 670; NATO and, 669; arms race and, 674; aging population in, 705

Westernization (Western culture): *See also* Industrialization; Modernization; in Russia, 449–451, 453, 532; in West Africa, 503; in British India, 506, 510; in Turkey, 610 (*illus.*), 612; industrialization and, 731–732

West Germany, 670, 672. *See also* Germany; reunification and, 701 (*map*)

West India Company, Dutch, 374, 400, 403, 405

West Indies. *See* Caribbean region (West Indies)

Whaling, 513, 514–515 *and illus.*

Wheat, 375, 407, 495, 552, 657, 662

Wheatstone, Charles, 489

Whistler, James McNeill, 530

White Lotus Rebellion (1794–1804), 533

Whitney, Eli, 486

Wichelle, Treaty of (1889), 581

Wilhelm I (Germany), 548, 558, 560

Wilhelm II (Germany), 560, 605

Williams, Eric, 400

Wilson, Woodrow, 592, 605; League of Nations and, 606, 610; Mexico and, 654

Witch-hunts, 365, 369–370 *and illus.*, 372

Women. *See also* Family; Gender differences; Marriage; Women's rights; colonial Latin America, 393 (*illus.*), 400 (*illus.*); European families and, 377–378; prostitutes, 376, 378; slave, 402; as Acheh rulers, 429; witches, 369–370 *and illus.*; Ottoman and Iranian compared, 422–423; Revolutionary era, 466, 468, 471; abolitionist, 475, 478; domesticity of, 493, 497; factory work, 492, 494, 497; colonial Australia, 513; education of, 378, 477–478, 539; teachers, 478, 556, 573; textile manufacture by, 376, 477, 492; British India (widow burning), 508, 509, 573, 647; Ottoman, 526–527; Taiping Rebellion and, 536–537; in Japanese silk industry,

564–565 *and illus.;* prostitutes, 508, 536, 553; separate sphere of, 553, 556–557 *and illus.;* working-class, 492, 553, 556, 564, 565 (*illus.*); colonialism and, 513, 573, 577, 582, 642; textile manufacture by, 564, 565 (*illus.*), 609, 630; African, and Europeans, 584–586; in World Wars, 603, 613, 638; Islamic, 579, 612, 613; missionary, 573; and abortion, 613–614, 624–626; poverty of, 553, 725; Great Depression, 623; Russian Revolution, 622, 624–626; Nazi German, 638; Chinese Communism, 630; Islamic, 693, 697 (*illus.*), 725; birth control and, 704–705, 725–726; European fertility rates and, 703, 704–705; education of, 704, 725–726; feminism and, 725, 731

Women's Christian Temperance Movement, 613

Women's Convention (Beijing, 1995), 725

Women's rights, 573, 607, 723, 725–726; in Americas, 477–478; property and inheritance, 377, 527, 557, 582; in Britain, 556–557, 613; voting rights, 477, 513, 557, 612, 613, 683; in United States, 477, 557, 613; neo-liberalism and, 694–696; United Nations declaration on, 725

Women's Rights Convention (1848), 477

Woodblock printing, 438 (*illus.*)

Wool industry: British, 484; Navajo, 408

Worker's Party (Brazil), 714

Workers (working class): *See also* Labor; Labor unions; China, 439; French Revolution, 466, 468, 469; Industrial Revolution, 481, 491–492; women's rights and, 478; housing for, 490, 491 (*illus.*); socialism and unions, 493–494, 552–553; women, 492, 553, 556, 564, 565 (*illus.*); depressions and, 550, 562–563; Russian Revolution, 604; automobile and, 616; industrialized world, 613, 614, 615; Argentine, 659, 660; Mexican, 653

World Bank, 720

World economy. *See* Global economy

World Trade Center attack (2001), 712–714 *and photo*

World Trade Organization (WTO), 720, 722

World War I (1914–1918), 545, 596–608. *See also specific combatant and battle;* alliances in, 597, 600 (*map*), 601, 605, 606–607; origins of, 596–597; stalemate (1914–1917), 601–603; in Europe, 600 (*map*); homefront and economy, 603;

impact of, 605–606, 619; Indian soldiers in, 648, 651; military strategy in, 597, 601; aircraft in, 614; casualties in, 602, 603, 605, 606; Ottoman Empire and, 603–604; peace treaties after, 606; Russian Revolutions and, 604–605; Western (battle) front, 601–602 *and illus.*, 605, 606

World War II (1939–1945), 620, 631–639. *See also specific combatant and battle;* Africa and, 632, 646; aircraft in, 631, 632 (*illus.*), 634, 636–637; alliances in, 629, 633 (*map*), 634, 636 (*map*), 659, 669, 670; in Asia and the Pacific, 632, 634, 636 (*map*); bombing in, 632 (*illus.*), 634, 635 (*illus.*), 637; China and, 634–635; deaths in, 546, 635, 637–638; environment and homefront in, 638; in Europe and North Africa, 631–632, 633 (*map*); Japan in, 632, 634, 635 (*illus.*), 636–637 *and map;* science of, 635–637, 708; as war of movement, 631

World Wide Web (Internet), 719, 728–729

Wright, Frank Lloyd, 615

Wright, Orville and Wilbur, 614

Wu Sangui, 432

Xavier, Francis, 436–437

Xhosa people, 580

Yangzi (Yellow) River, 534, 539, 630

Yaqui people, 653

Yellow fever, 387, 471, 472 (*illus.*), 592

Yellowstone national park, 563

Yeltsin, Boris, 701–702

Yemen, 417, 718

Yi dynasty (Korea), 433–434

Yohannes IV (Ethiopia), 500

Young Ottomans (Young Turks), 529, 532, 597

Ypres, France, 602 (*illus.*)

Yuan Shikai, 609

Yugoslavia, 606, 672, 682; breakup of, 701 (*map*), 702; ethnic cleansing in, 716

*Zaibatsu* (conglomerates), 565, 609, 697

Zambia (Northern Rhodesia), 581

Zanzibar, 504

Zapata, Emiliano, 641, 654, 655 (*map*)

Zeng Guofan, 539

Zheng He, voyages of, 340–341, 344 (*illus.*)

Zimbabwe (Southern Rhodesia), 581, 678

Zionism, 606, 610, 612, 684. *See also* Israel

Zulu, 499–500 *and illus.*, 510, 511, 516, 580, 581